AF573971

Commentary on First Corinthians

Commentary on First Corinthians

by

Frederic Louis Godet

KREGEL PUBLICATIONS
Grand Rapids, Michigan 49501

COMMENTARY ON FIRST CORINTHIANS
Published in 1977 by Kregel Publications, a division of Kregel, Inc.

Printed in the United States of America

Library of Congress Cataloging in Publication Data

Godet, Frédéric, 1812-1900.
Commentary on I Corinthians.

(Kregel Reprint Library series)
Translation of Commentaire sur la première épitre aux Corinthiens.
Reprint of the 1889 ed. published by T. & T. Clark, Edinburgh, under title: Commentary on St. Paul's First Epistle to the Corinthians, which was issued as v. 27 and 30, new ser., of Clark's foreign theological library.
1. Bible. N.T. 1 Corinthians — Commentaries.
I. Title.
BS2675.G6913 227' .2'07 77-79190
ISBN 0-8254-2716-9

First Kregel Publications Edition 1977

Second Printing 1979

CONTENTS

CONCLUSION OF THE EPISTLE (16:1-24)

CONCLUSIONS

PREFACE

In publishing this new Commentary, I do not feel altogether free from anxiety. The welcome given to its elder brothers encourages me, it is true; but the apostolic book explained in these pages is so practical in its nature, and consequently touches on so many existing religious phenomena, that it is difficult to avoid drawing certain parallels which may injure the objectivity of the work. Then the commentator's responsibility increases the more the results which he obtains are fitted to exercise a direct influence on the solution of questions which are now occupying the Church. And so I am specially constrained to ask God to avert every hurtful consequence that might flow from errors I may have committed in interpreting this important book, and to say to my readers, like the apostle himself, but in a sense slightly different from his: "Judge yourselves what I say."

I shall only add a word of explanation in regard to the fixing of the text. I have been charged more than once in England with my *defective criticism* on this point, which, if I am not mistaken, means at bottom that I am wrong in not fully adhering to the critical theory and practice of Westcott and Hort. I respect and admire as much as any one the immense labour of these two critics; but it is impossible for me to accept without reserve the result at which they have arrived. Exegesis has too often convinced me of the mistakes of the *Sinaïticus* and *Vaticanus*, taken separately or even together, to allow me to give myself up with eyes bandaged to these manuscripts, as the esteemed authors whom I have just named think themselves bound to do. I shall call the attention of my readers to three passages only in our Epistle, where the faultiness of the text of the documents, which are called neuter or Alexandrine or both, seems to me manifest; they are: iv. 1, ix. 10, and xiii. 3. In these cases, as in many others, it seems to me that healthy criticism dares not sacrifice exegetical sound sense to the transcription of two copyists of the fourth century, who are so often found in the wrong. Besides, I cannot possibly believe that a man like Chrysostom could, by adopting in full and without scruple the Syrian or Byzantine text, blindly give the preference to a work of quite recent compilation, and the authority of which found no support in earlier documents.

May this work contribute somewhat to the glory of the Lord and to the good of His Church!

F. GODET

INTRODUCTION

A QUITE peculiar interest attaches to the correspondence of St. Paul with the Church of Corinth. Having founded the Church himself and lived in the heart of it for nearly two years, he had not to expound *his gospel* to it in writing, as to the Church of Rome. But he was called by particular circumstances to complete his teaching on various points, and especially to combat certain corruptions which had arisen or which threatened to force their way into the life of the Church. Our two Epistles to the Corinthians were thus the product of special circumstances, local and temporary. This is the reason why an eminent critic, Weizsäcker, has called them : " A fragment of ecclesiastical history like no other."

It might be concluded from the purely occasional character of these two Epistles that they belong to a past which no more concerns us, and consequently have no longer for us a present religious value. Even if it were so, would it not be something to be transported by them into the full ecclesiastical life of the earliest times, and to stand by, as it were, and witness the crises through which the new converts of eighteen centuries ago had to pass ? But the interest excited by these Epistles goes much further and deeper. The heart of man remains the same throughout all ages. The experiences of the apostolic Christians do not differ essentially from those through which we pass ourselves. This observation is especially true in regard to the Church of Corinth. For it is not here, as in Galatia, against Jewish prejudices that the apostle has mainly to contend, at least in the First Epistle. In Achaia we witness the first contact of the gospel with Hellenic life, so richly endowed and brilliant, but, on the other hand, so frivolous and fickle, and in so many respects resembling our modern life. In particular, the tendency to make religious truths the subjects of intellectual study rather than a work of conscience and of heart-acceptance, the disposition resulting therefrom, not always to place the moral conduct under the influence of religious conviction, and to give scope to the latter rather in oratorical discourse than in vigour of holiness,—these are defects which more than one modern nation shares in common with the Greek people. And the question is whether the apostle, after having drawn from the gospel, as the Lord had revealed it to him (Gal. i. 11, 12), the word of emancipation fitted to free the conscience from the Mosaic yoke, will find in it also the power necessary to check Gentile licence and lead the will captive to the law of holiness, without relapsing into the use of legal forms.

But what gives the liveliest interest to the questions raised by the state of the Church of Corinth, is the manner in which the apostle discusses and resolves them. In treating each particular matter submitted to his judgment, the apostle does not stop at the surface; he endeavours to penetrate to the very root of those various manifestations. Instead of summarily settling the questions as by the article of a code, he searches the depths of the gospel for the permanent principle which applies to the passing phenomenon, so that to judge of the analogous manifestations and tendencies of our day, we have only ourselves to fall back from the practical rule with which he closes each of those discussions on the evangelical principle from which he drew it, that in our turn we may apply this principle to the contemporary phenomenon with which we have to do. There is no exercise at once more stimulating to the understanding and more fitted to form the Christian conscience than this. By the Epistle to the Romans, we know St. Paul as a teacher; in that to the Galatians he appears as the consummate polemic and dialectician; we learn to know him in the First Epistle to the Corinthians in his character of apostolical pastor and casuist, taking the latter word in its best sense.

Finally, another kind of interest is awakened in us by the study of this letter. M. Renan says of St. Paul: "He had not the patience needed for writing; he was incapable of method." These summary judgments are law with many, and are eagerly repeated by superficial writers. We shall have occasion very particularly, in the study of this Epistle, to put this judgment to the proof. The question of method presented itself in this case in a more difficult way than in any other. When the apostle had to develop a side of Christian truth, his course was marked out for him by the subject itself and by the logical form of his thought. Here there is nothing of the kind. St. Paul finds himself face to face with a certain number of particular practical questions, without any direct relation to one another. The matters in question include divisions, scandals, trials at law, marriage and celibacy, meats offered in sacrifice, the behaviour of women in public worship, love feasts, the resurrection, and we ask, not without curiosity, whether his mind will succeed in commanding this multiplicity of subjects and arranging them rationally, so that here, as well as elsewhere, he will leave the impression of order and unity.

In the introduction to the Epistle to the Romans, I have treated of the life of St. Paul in general; I shall not return to it here. Four subjects will occupy us:

1. The founding of the Church of Corinth.

2. The external circumstances in which our first canonical Epistle was addressed to it.

3. The events which had supervened since the founding of the Church and which gave occasion to this letter

4. The arrangement adopted by the apostle in the order and grouping of the subjects to be treated.

CHAPTER 1

THE FOUNDING OF THE CHURCH

It was, if we are not mistaken, about the autumn of the year 52, shortly after the assembly called the Council of Jerusalem, that Paul set out from Antioch with Silas to make a second missionary journey. They first visited the Churches of Lycaonia and Pisidia, founded by Paul and Barnabas, in the course of their first journey. Then, according to all probability, they proclaimed the gospel in the province of Galatia, situated more to the north, and, crossing Asia Minor from east to west without being permitted by the Spirit to preach in it, they reached the shore of the Egean Sea, at Troas, and there, with the young Timothy, whom they had associated with them in Lycaonia, and the physician Luke, already no doubt a Christian, whom they met in this city, they embarked for Macedonia. After founding the Church in the two principal cities of that province, Philippi and Thessalonica, Paul set out alone for southern Greece, and repaired first to Athens, then to Corinth, the capital of the province of Achaia. He was soon afterwards rejoined in the latter city by his two fellow-labourers, Silas and Timothy, and he remained there with them for about two years.

Destroyed by the Romans in 146 B.C., it was nearly a century since Corinth had risen from its ruins. In the year 44 Julius Cæsar had rebuilt it and peopled it with numerous colonists, mostly Roman freedmen; these had been joined by a certain population of Greeks, and shortly afterwards by a Jewish colony. At the time when the apostle arrived in it, the city counted from six to seven hundred thousand inhabitants, of whom two hundred thousand were freemen and four hundred thousand slaves. It had a circuit of a league and a half. This immense and rapid growth, which compares with that of certain cities in the United States of America, was due above all to its situation on the isthmus which bears its name, and which, connecting the Peloponnesus with the continent, separated the Egean and Ionian seas. Corinth possessed two principal ports, that of Cenchrea, opening to the east, and that of Lechæum, to the west. It had quickly become the great emporium of commerce between Asia and the west. So speedily had this city, which was formerly called "the light and ornament of Greece," recovered its ancient splendour. On the summit of its Acropolis shone the temple of Venus, of incomparable magnificence. Corinth possessed all the means of culture then enjoyed by the capitals of the civilized world, workshops and studios, halls of rhetoric and schools of philosophy. An ancient historian says that one could not take a step in the streets of Corinth without meeting a sage.

But here, as elsewhere and still more, corruption of morals had proceeded step by step with the development of culture and riches. The mixture of heterogeneous elements composing the population of new Corinth had no doubt contributed to produce this state of things. One word tells all. By the term κορινθιάζειν, *to live as a Corinthian*, men designated a kind of life which was absolutely dissolute. The phrases *Corinthian banquet, Corinthian drinker*, were proverbial.

It was in the midst of this society, in a state of full outward prosperity, but also of complete moral dissolution, that the quickening salt of the gospel was now to fall with the arrival of St. Paul, twenty-four years after the Ascension of the Lord Jesus.

If Paul, at the time of his conversion, about the year 37, was thirty years old at least, he must have been approaching the fifties on the day when he entered Corinth. Let us imagine the apostle, making his solitary entry as a simple workman, into the great city. His profession was that either of a tent-weaver or tent-carpenter; the term tent-maker (Acts xviii. 3) admits of both significations. The second, however, seems the more probable. The apostle was not long in discovering a Jewish family who followed the same trade as himself; they had just arrived from Rome, in consequence of an edict of the Emperor Claudius banishing the Jews from the capital. He joined them, and while sharing their work, gained them for his faith. Some have held that Aquila and Priscilla were already believers on their arrival. This supposition is contrary to the terms of the narrative ("a certain *Jew* named Aquila"); it has no other object than to furnish support to the idea of the existence of a Judeo-Christian Church at that period among the Jews of Rome.

The narrative of the Acts shows us the apostle beginning his work at Corinth in the midst of the Jewish colony. This narrative has been recently relegated to the domain of fable.[1] For what reasons? Paul, says Heinrici, would never have been so imprudent, as by his preaching of the gospel, needlessly to brave the anger of the synagogue, whose insurmountable prejudices he knew. But, though Paul certainly did not flatter himself that he would convert all the members of the synagogue, he could hope to gain at least some of the better disposed, and

[1] Heinrici, *Erklärung der Corintherbriefe*, 1880, i. p. 7 seq.; Holsten, *das Evangelium des Paulus*, 1881, i. p. 186.

to find in them the solid nucleus of the society of believers which he desired to form at Corinth. He knew well it was not in vain that God had paved the way for the preaching of the gospel in the Gentile world by the dispersion of the people of Israel, and that this was the door providentially opened for the proclamation of the good news in the midst of heathendom. The manner in which the foundation of the Church in general had taken place by the preaching of the apostles among the Jewish people, prior to any mission to the Gentiles, was a guide to him as to the method to be followed in founding the Church in every heathen city in particular. It was on this principle that Paul had proceeded with Barnabas on his first mission in Asia Minor (Acts xiii. 14 seq., xiv. 1 seq.); it was thus he had continued with Silas in his second, at Philippi (Acts xvi. 13 seq.), at Thessalonica (xvii. 1 seq.), at Berea (v. 10 seq.). He himself positively declares (Rom. i. 16: "to the Jews *first*, then to the Greeks") that this procedure was not accidental, but rested on a deliberate conviction. Why should he not have remained faithful to it at Corinth? The narrative of the Acts is therefore not in the least open to suspicion on this point, and if this initial preaching in the synagogue were not expressly recorded, we should have to suppose it. Holsten raises another objection. If Paul had begun among the Jews of the synagogue, why should he have been intimidated even to trembling, according to his own description, ii. 1–5? Was he not accustomed to this kind of hearers? But when the apostle arrived at Corinth, he knew well that if he came there with the intention of addressing the

Jews first, he did not come solely or even mainly for them. He had before him the spectacle of that great Greek capital, and felt himself charged alone, at least in those first days, with the responsibility of the Divine message which he carried. He was not unaware that even in the synagogue he would meet a select body of proselytes belonging to every class of Corinthian society, and that the time was not far off when it would be among these latter especially, and the entire Greek population, that he would have to deliver his message. It was the first time he found himself in such a situation, if we except the case of his preaching at Athens, the result of which was not fitted to encourage him. Face to face with such audiences, he had no longer the support which was afforded him before Jews by the law and the prophets; and, on the other hand, he was resolved not to have recourse to the modes of action generally used in public conferences, brilliance of oratorical art, dialectic skill, profound speculation. There remained to him only one force—and his grandest act of faith was to wish no other—the simple testimony rendered to Christ and His Cross; the Divine fact itself expounded without art, and, if one may so speak, in its nakedness. If we put ourselves in the apostle's place at this point of his career, we can understand the feeling of powerlessness and anxiety which overwhelmed him at the outset of his ministry in this city. Far from our finding therein anything fitted to raise a doubt of the circumspection with which he proceeded in addressing himself first to the Jews, it may be said that this prudent step was imposed on him by the very anxiety which he felt.

Paul then preached for some weeks in the synagogue. But soon, seeing the exasperation of his Jewish adversaries increase to such a degree that it was no longer possible to labour usefully in this sphere, he established himself with the believers, Jews and proselytes, in a neighbouring house belonging to one of his Jewish converts, and from that time he preached especially to Gentiles, not clothing the salvation of Christ either with the charms of eloquence, or with the attraction of human wisdom, so that if his preaching exercised a powerful influence, it was solely through the Divine working which accompanied it, and, as the apostle says, by the demonstration of Spirit and of power. Hearts seriously disposed were laid hold of in their depths, really gained. A church formed of a certain number of Jews, and "of a great multitude of Gentiles," rose in the midst of this city of business and debauchery. The majority of its members did not belong to the upper, rich, cultivated classes (1 Cor. i. 26–28); they were for the most part poor, slaves, people despised for their ignorance and their low social condition. But the work was only the more solid; it was not mingled with human alloy. There were only so many wounded consciences which the power of God had healed and restored.

For nearly two years (Acts xviii. 11, 18), Paul continued to sow this fruitful soil, living by the labour of his hands, sometimes also on the help which was sent him by the churches recently founded in Macedonia (2 Cor. xi. 7–9, xii. 13–15). The proconsul of Achaia resided at Corinth; at that time Gallio, the brother of the philosopher Seneca. He is known by his correspondence with his brother; he was an equitable man, and full of urbanity. He showed himself such toward St. Paul, when the latter was dragged by the Jews before his tribunal. Thus this first sojourn of Paul at Corinth closed in peace. Paul left this city about Pentecost of the year 54 to go to Jerusalem, and thence to Antioch, where he thought of making only a short stay. His plans for the future were formed. Between the two domains where he had broken ground in his two first journeys lay the western portion of Asia Minor, the rich and interesting country of ancient Ionia, then called the province of Asia, with Ephesus for its capital; there it was that he now felt himself called to labour. On his departure from Corinth, he was accompanied by Aquila and Priscilla, who were to await him at Ephesus, and to prepare the way for him in this new field of labour.

CHAPTER 2

THE EXTERNAL CIRCUMSTANCES IN WHICH THE EPISTLE WAS COMPOSED

We have not to discuss at length the authenticity of the First Epistle to the Corinthians, against which no serious objection has ever been raised. Its composition by St. Paul appears with great evidence from the letter itself; and first from the testimony of its author (i. 1), as well as from the manner in which he speaks of himself as founder of the Church (iv. 15 *et al.*). In confirmation of this testimony, Schleiermacher has brought out the relation between the historical details of our Epistle and those contained in the book of Acts. "When we compare," says this theologian,[1] "many passages of the Acts (chaps. xviii.–xx.) with the personal details which begin and close the two Epistles to the Corinthians, everything fits in, all is perfectly complete, and that nevertheless in such a way that each of the documents follows its own course, and the facts contained in the one cannot be borrowed from those of the other." But these coincidences of detail are a still less striking proof than is the picture, so living and real, which the letters give us of the state of a primitive Christian Church. The following is Baur's[2] impression on this point: Our First Epistle carries the seal of its authenticity in itself; for, "more than any other writing of the New Testament, it transports us into the living centre of a Christian Church in formation, and procures for us a view of the circumstances through which the development of the new life evoked by Christianity had to pass." Beet (*Commentary*) also brings out forcibly the proof of authenticity contained in the very severe and humiliating rebukes addressed to the Church of Corinth in these two letters. No Church would so easily and without a rigorous investigation have accepted and preserved "the monument of its degradation."

These internal evidences are confirmed by the testimony of *tradition*. So early as about the end of the first century, Clement of Rome, in his letter to the Corinthians, quotes our Epistle several times. The

[1] *Einleitung in das N. T.*, p. 148.
[2] Baur, *Der Apostel Paulus*, 1st edit. p. 260.

passage of chap. xlvii. is particularly remarkable: "Take up again the Epistle of the blessed Apostle Paul: what did he write to you in the outset, at the beginning of the preaching of the gospel? Verily, he gave you spiritual directions as well about himself as about Cephas and Apollos, because even then ye were giving yourselves up to preferences." It does not seem to us to admit of question that when Ignatius, in his Epistle to the Ephesians, chap. xviii., calls the cross "a stumbling-block to unbelievers," and exclaims, "Where is the wise, where is the disputer?" he is reproducing the terms of our Epistle. The same is the case with Polycarp, in his Epistle to the Philippians, chap. v., the enumeration which he makes of the vicious is exactly parallel to that of 1 Cor. vi. 9, 10, and he closes it also by declaring that such believers "shall not inherit the kingdom of God." In the homily commonly called *the Second Epistle of Clement*, and which must have been written in Greece between 120 and 140, we find these words taken from the first chapter of our Epistle: "It pleased Him to make us to be of that which is not." It would be useless to pursue this list of testimonies in detail. We should have to mention, probably, Justin Martyr, *Dialogue*, chap. xiv. ("the old leaven" and "the unleavened bread"; comp. 1 Cor. v. 8) and chap. iii. ("Christ our Passover"); more certainly the *Epistle to Diognetus*, filled with thoughts drawn from our Epistle; probably also the *Doctrine of the Twelve Apostles* (between 120 and 160), where there are thought to be some allusions to 1 Cor. (Gebhardt, Edwards); very certainly the *Fragment of Muratori*; Athenagoras, Theophilus; finally, Irenæus,

Clement of Alexandria, and Tertullian. I refer readers who desire to be more exactly informed on this point to Charteris, *Canonicity*, 222–229.

What really concerns us is to fix the time and place in the apostle's life at which he composed this letter; and the task is not difficult.

The *place* of composition can be no other than Ephesus. "I will tarry," says the apostle, "at Ephesus till Pentecost; for a great door is opened unto me" (xvi. 8, 9). It is not clear at the first glance how, in view of so positive a text, the subscription of the Epistle in a certain number of manuscripts, as well as in many of our translations, can be thus stated: "The First Epistle to the Corinthians was written from Philippi." It is probable that this account arises from the ignorant or superficial reading of xvi. 5: "For I do pass through Macedonia." It was not understood that the present *I do pass* referred, not to a present fact, but to the journey as planned by the apostle. It was obvious, however, that if Paul was already in Macedonia, he must have sent salutations from the Churches of this province, and not from those of Asia, as he does in ver. 19. In this same verse there is likewise found the salutation of Aquila and Priscilla, who, as we have seen, had gone with Paul to settle at Ephesus. The subscription in the *Vaticanus* is accurate: "*was written from Ephesus.*"

The entire stay of Paul at Ephesus lasted about three years (Acts xx. 31). Our concern is to know at what time of this sojourn we must place the composition of our letter. On this point we have several clear enough indications:

1st. The words we have just quoted prove that Paul's stay in Asia was drawing to a close.

2nd. At the time when Paul was composing this letter, he had Apollos beside him, who had returned from Corinth (xvi. 12). Now, this Alexandrine teacher, converted at Ephesus by Aquila and Priscilla shortly after their arrival in that city, and before that of Paul (Acts xviii. 24, 26), had gone thence to Achaia with a recommendation from Aquila to continue the work of Paul there, and had exercised a very influential ministry, after which he had returned to Ephesus. This all supposes a considerable time to have elapsed since Paul's arrival at Ephesus, and so brings us to an advanced period of his sojourn in that city.

3rd. We read Acts xix. 21, that after labouring two years and three months at Ephesus (vers. 8, 10), Paul formed in his mind vast designs. He meditated bidding a final adieu to the East and consecrating the remainder of his life to the West. But before proceeding to Rome he felt bound to visit Jerusalem once more, and to offer the Church of that city a solemn testimony of love and spiritual fellowship from all the Churches founded by him among the Gentiles. He therefore determined, according to Acts xix. 22, to send Timothy and Erastus from Ephesus to make preparation in Macedonia and Achaia for the execution of his project. Now this sending of Timothy to Corinth coincides perfectly with that which is twice mentioned in our First Epistle (iv. 17; xvi. 10). It took place at the time when the apostle was composing it, and shortly before his setting out, for in it Paul announces the sending of his young fellow-labourer as an already accomplished fact.

4th. This great collection for which Timothy was to prepare, and which is expressly mentioned, xvi. 1, and 2 Cor. viii. and ix., can only be that with which the apostle closed his ministry in the East, and of which he speaks in the two passages, Rom. xv. 24, 33, and Acts xxiv. 17. Here is a new indication which again brings us to the same date.

As it is impossible for all these reasons to suppose a date previous to the circumstances mentioned, it is no less so to suppose a later one. In fact, at the time when the apostle writes, he is yet freely disposing of his person. But it is well known that shortly after, when he had delivered the sum collected into the hands of the leaders of the flock at Jerusalem, he was thrown into prison, and from that time remained a prisoner for a long course of years.

If the sojourn of Paul in Asia, by the time when our letter was written, had lasted about two years and three months (Acts xix. 8, 10), dating from the end of the year 54 when Paul arrived at Ephesus, it was composed in the spring of the year 57, before the Pentecost of that year, probably at the time of the feast of Passover to which there seems to be an allusion in the passage v. 7, 8. We shall afterwards see how the indication of Acts xx. 31 is to be explained, according to which the stay at Ephesus lasted three entire years.

CHAPTER 3

THE EVENTS WHICH TOOK PLACE AT CORINTH IN THE INTERVAL BETWEEN THE FOUNDING OF THE CHURCH AND THE COMPOSITION OF THE EPISTLE

WE have here to enumerate a series of facts which it is indispensable to know if we are to understand our Epistle, but in regard to which we have almost no information except from the Epistle itself. It is one of the most striking examples of the legitimate influence which exegesis and criticism have to exercise on one another.

1. The first fact known to us which modified the state of the Church of Corinth after the departure of its founder, was the ministry of the Alexandrine teacher Apollos. We possess two testimonies of the influence exercised at Corinth by this eloquent preacher,—the one, the first four chapters of our Epistle, the other, the end of chap. xviii. of Acts. "He helped much through grace," it is said in the latter passage, "them which had believed: for he disputed powerfully with the Jews, and that publicly, showing by the Scriptures that Jesus was the Christ." From this passage it follows that the ministry of Apollos must have brought about a double change in the state of the Church. Powerful in the interpretation of the Scriptures, Apollos gained to the gospel a very large number of Jews, evidently of those who had withstood the ministry of St. Paul. The proportion between the two elements of which the young Church was composed was thus modified to the

advantage of the Jewish element. It is probable, moreover, that while the Jewish minority was increased through the labours of Apollos, a certain number of Gentiles belonging to the lettered class were attracted by the oratorical talent and brilliant gifts of the young teacher. Only it is natural to suppose that the conversion of these newcomers did not proceed from such profound conscience-work as that which had led the most of the former converts to baptism. The wants of the understanding and imagination had, in many cases, more to do with their adherence than those of the heart and conscience.

2. Besides the visit of Apollos, must we hold the arrival at Corinth of a still more important personage, the Apostle Peter? In the passage chap. i. 12 mention is made of a party of Cephas, which is placed after that of Apollos. Are we to regard this as an indication of a stay made by this apostle in Achaia at this period? Such a fact seems far from probable. In the year 54 we find Peter at Antioch (Gal. ii.). No doubt, in the course of the three years which followed down to the spring of the year 57, he might have gone from Syria to Achaia. But there is no reason to suppose that Peter turned so early toward the west; and it would be difficult to understand how our Epistle, which bears such evident traces of Apollos' sojourn at Corinth, did not present some still more marked traces of Peter's visit. Still, while abstracting wholly from a personal visit of Peter to Corinth, we cannot mistake in the phrase to which we have just pointed, the evidence of a serious fact in the development of the young Church, a sensible influence from Palestinian Christianity must

certainly have been exercised at that period in the Church of Corinth. In what direction? This is a point we shall consider afterwards.

3. We are forced to hold at the same time a vexatious recrudescence of the old pagan habits, with which the new converts had at first completely broken. The powerful earnestness of St. Paul's preaching had at first ruled the Church and repressed the vicious tendencies under the dominion of which the most of the new Christians had formerly lived (1 Cor. vi. 11). But in proportion as the first impressions grew weak, and the community received new members less profoundly stirred and transformed, Greek lightness revived again and threatened the Divine work. We have proofs even of the abuse made by many of the principle of spiritual liberty which St. Paul proclaimed (vi. 12, x. 23). The truly sanctified members of the Church were obliged then to ask what they had to do respecting those who thus fell back into their old way of living. The question was put to the apostle. He replied in a letter anterior to our two canonical Epistles (comp. 1 Cor. v. 9). He asked "that they should not mingle with such men," that is to say, that by breaking off every private relation with the vicious members, the Church should protest against that false profession of the Christian faith, and should show conspicuously that they did not recognise it as earnest.

4. This letter from Paul was followed by a reply from the Corinthians to the apostle. They objected that if they were to break thus with all the vicious, there was nothing left them but to go out of the world (v. 10). They questioned him also on some new

subjects, such as the preference to be given to celibacy over marriage, and the free use of meats which had figured on the altars of idols. As to the former of those subjects, Paul introduces it expressly with the words: "Concerning the things *whereof ye wrote unto me*" (vii. 1). And it is probable that when he introduces the latter by saying (viii. 1): "Concerning meats offered to idols," he passes to another point also treated in their letter. As we again find the same form (xii. 1) when the apostle comes to deal with the questions relating to the use of spiritual gifts, it is equally probable that here again he takes up a subject about which they had consulted him. There had therefore been since the founding of the Church a somewhat active correspondence between it and the apostle.[1]

5. Besides this reply of the Corinthians to Paul, three delegates from the Church had reached the apostle. They are designated by their names and characterized in the most honourable way (xvi. 15–18). Were they the bearers of the Church's letter? or did they arrive later under the stress of new and more delicate circumstances? We cannot tell. But such a step proves in any case the gravity of the situation, even then. We do not think that, as the subscription of our Epistle has it, and as is frequently repeated, it

[1] The two letters found in the Armenian Church, and the authenticity of which has been defended by Rinck, could not, even if they were Paul's, be those the loss of which we are here asserting. Rinck acknowledges this himself, for they treat of quite different subjects from those which are supposed by our Epistle. And in those letters it is the Corinthians who write first and Paul who replies. But their authenticity is moreover wholly untenable. They are simple collections of Pauline sayings, without logical connection; and their citation by Gregory the Illuminator, in the fourth century, cannot evidently guarantee their apostolic composition.

was those deputies who, on their return, were the bearers of the First Epistle to the Corinthians. The passage xvi. 11: "I expect him (Timothy) with the brethren," seems to me to prove that they were yet at Ephesus with the apostle, when this letter, which was to arrive in time to recommend Timothy to a cordial welcome from the Corinthians, was sent off.

6. In fact Timothy was then on his way first to Macedonia, then to Corinth, charged with an important mission from Paul. He was to support by his personal influence the effect which Paul desired to produce by our First Epistle (iv. 17), and then no doubt to prepare for the carrying out of the projected collection in favour of the Church of Jerusalem (1 Cor. xvi. 1). Though Timothy had set out before the letter, it was to arrive before him, because it was sent directly by sea, while Timothy made the tour through Macedonia.

7. To these various circumstances there must be added another, purely accidental, but which had perhaps the most considerable influence on the letter we are to study. A lady, named Chloe, arrived at Ephesus from Corinth, where she had lived (i. 12). We do not know whether, being herself of Corinth, she had made a journey to Ephesus, or whether, being an Ephesian by birth, she was returning from a visit to Corinth. Those of her household, either her children or slaves, informed Paul of a circumstance which must have touched him deeply. The Church was divided into parties which came into conflict in the general gatherings. Cries such as these were raised: "*As for me, I am of Paul;*"—thus no doubt spake the oldest converts, those who had felt most deeply the holy efficacy

of the gospel;—or, "*But as for me, I am of Apollos;*" —this was the watchword of those who had been gained by the eloquent and able demonstrations of this teacher; —then again, "*But as for me, I am of Cephas;*"— these were no doubt chiefly Christians of Jewish origin who had heard tell of Peter, or who had met him in their journeys to Jerusalem at the feasts. They naturally enough concluded that the first place in the Church belonged to the head of the apostolic college chosen by Jesus, and that if there was any difference between Paul and him, it was the latter who should be followed. Lastly, others, daringly casting off all apostolic authority,—Peter's, as it seems, no less than Paul's,—replied to all the others: "*But as for me, I am of Christ,*" as if to say: "I recognise no one intermediate between the Lord and me; I claim to depend directly on Him and on Him alone."

It is asked, Who could these last be, and how could such a party have arisen at Corinth? Were they Christians of Gentile origin, who, admiring Christ's teachings, thought that these should be disentangled from the Jewish forms in which the apostles, and even to a certain extent Paul himself, clothed them? Or were they Christians of Jewish origin and tendency, who, rejecting Paul's gospel, condemned the concessions which the Twelve thought it right to make to this apostle, and that by alleging against them the example and sayings of Christ? This is a question which we cannot examine here, and which we shall treat in the commentary in connection with i. 12. St. Paul has said somewhere, "Is any offended, and I burn not?" If it was so when the offence of a simple believer was in question, what must he have felt on learning that one of the most flourishing Churches which it had been given him to found, was almost threatened with dissolution?

We have now before us the whole of the circumstances which had filled the time since St. Paul had left Corinth, and we can form an idea of the manifold concerns which filled his heart as he set himself to dictate our First, or strictly speaking, his Second Epistle to this Church.

It remains to examine here in few words a question much discussed of late, and on which the most recent investigations are not at one. From several passages of the Second Epistle to the Corinthians, it seems to follow that the apostle had been twice at Corinth before the time when he wrote this letter. These passages are mainly the four following: ii. 1, xii. 14, xii. 21, xiii. 1 and 2. Indeed, in the last three Paul seems to say that his next visit to Corinth will be the third, and from the first it seems to follow that the second had been so painful to him that he had shrunk from exposing himself till now from visiting them anew in similar circumstances. Now, nothing in all we have seen can lead us to suppose that Paul had returned to Corinth after his first sojourn, during which he had founded the Church.

There are three ways of treating these passages. Either they may be regarded, as is done by Baur, Hilgenfeld, Renan,[1] and others, not as indicating real visits so much as *projects* which the apostle had formed, but had not been able to execute. But it is impossible

[1] *Saint Paul*, p. 451, note; comp. also Farrar, *Life and Work of St Paul*, ii. p. 101, note 2; Edwards, p. xiv.

on this view to account for the two passages xii. 14 and ii. 1. The former is thus translated: "Lo, this is the third time I am ready to come to you," instead of: "Lo, I am ready to come to you for the third time." But it is forgotten that the apostle is here declaring his firm resolution not to allow himself to be supported by the Church during his next sojourn, for he adds: "and I shall not be chargeable to you." Now it follows that the "*for the third time*" implies two previous sojourns, not only announced, but *real*. For a projected sojourn costs nothing. The passage ii. 1 confirms this conclusion. The words: "I determined that I would not come again to you with sorrow," are explained in this sense: "I have determined that my second sojourn, which I am about to make among you, shall not be a painful and sorrowful one." This meaning is compatible with the form of the received text; but the latter has against it the authority of all the Majuscules. According to the true position of the words "*with sorrow*," this regimen refers not only to the idea of *coming*, but to the whole phrase, "*coming again to you.*" It follows, therefore, from these words, that Paul had already made a *sorrowful* sojourn among them, which cannot refer to the sojourn during which he had founded the Church, and consequently implies a second visit which had taken place since then.[1]

If, then, the apostle had certainly stayed twice at Corinth before writing our Second Epistle to this

[1] Farrar thinks with Chrysostom that the phrase thus understood might also refer to a purely hypothetical sojourn, a sojourn which, if it had taken place, *would have had* a sorrowful character (ii. p. 101, note 3). But the authority of Chrysostom does not suffice to render so forced an interpretation possible.

Church, the question is, Whether this stay ought to be placed before or after our First Epistle to the Corinthians? Following Bleek, who first treated this question thoroughly,[1] a large number of writers have placed the second journey before our First Epistle. Some, like Anger, have taken it to be simply the second part of the sojourn occupied in founding the Church, which was divided into two by an excursion to the north of Greece. Others, like Reuss, suppose that during his long stay at Ephesus, Paul made a rapid visit to Greece, and specially to Corinth. But the former of these explanations does not correspond with the expression *come,* which indicates an arrival strictly so called, and not a return after a simple excursion. As to the latter, Hilgenfeld rightly asks, How could Paul's adversaries at Corinth have said that he was always putting off his arrival because he dared not return to this Church (1 Cor. iv. 18), if he had visited it quite recently? Reuss rests on 1 Cor. xvi. 7: "I will not see you now by the way;" words which, according to him, imply that he had recently made a short stay with them. But this conclusion, drawn from the word *now,* is unfounded. Paul simply means: "The circumstances are such at this moment that I do not wish to see you simply by the way," which does not at all suppose that a short visit had preceded. By this observation Paul would explain a change in the plan of his journey which he had previously announced, according to which he had proposed to make a rapid visit to Corinth, on his way to Macedonia, and then to return for a longer time from

[1] *Studien und Kritiken,* 1830.

Macedonia to Corinth. He now gives up the thought of doing so; he first visits Macedonia, and thence he will proceed to them to stay. — There is one fact above all which prevents our placing Paul's second visit to Corinth before the First Epistle to the Corinthians. In this letter Paul does not make a single allusion to a second stay in the midst of this Church, while he frequently refers to the circumstances of his stay at its founding (i. 14–17, 26 seq., ii. 1 seq., iii. 1 seq., 10, 11, iv. 15, xv. 1, 2). That would be impossible, if he had visited the Corinthians again in the time which preceded this Epistle. On the other hand, it is in the Second Epistle that all the allusions occur to the stay of which we are speaking. It must therefore be placed, as has been thought by Ewald and Eylau, in a remarkable programme,[1] between the composition of our two canonical Epistles. In general, I think with the latter, that the interval between the First and Second Epistles to the Corinthians must have been much more considerable and more full of incidents than is generally held. Bleek has proved, in the article quoted above, that many passages of the Second Epistle suppose not only a second stay of Paul at Corinth, but even an Epistle now lost which should be placed between our First and Second Epistles to the Corinthians. If this second fact is admitted,—as I think it ought to be,—the history of the relations between Paul and the Church at this period necessarily becomes complicated, and must have been completed by important and numerous facts, into the exposition

[1] *Programm des Gymnasiums zu Landsberg*, a. d. W. 1873; *Zur Chronologie der Corintherbriefe*, v. Dr. Gustav Otto Eylau.

of which we cannot enter here, and which explain the strange expression *three years,* which the apostle uses (Acts xx. 31) to denote the duration of his stay at Ephesus.

We hold, then, a second visit of Paul to Corinth, oefore the stay which he made in this city during the three months of winter, in the years 58–59. But we must not rank this stay among the factors which told on the composition of the First Epistle, because in our view it is posterior to this letter, and should be placed between our two Epistles.

CHAPTER 4

PLAN OF THE EPISTLE

Ten subjects, more or less extended and very heterogeneous, were present to the apostle's mind, when he set himself to compose this letter; and the question which arises is this: Will he confine himself to passing from the one to the other by way of juxtaposition, or will he find the means of binding them to one another by a logical or moral gradation, so as to leave an impression of order and unity on the mind of the reader. In other words, will the First Epistle to the Corinthians be a heap or a building? In this very letter St. Paul compares himself to an architect who has wisely laid the foundation of the Church. We shall immediately see that, whatever Renan may think, he has shown himself such also in the composition of the letter which he has addressed to it.

What must have concerned him above all, was to put an end to the divisions which reigned in the Church. To be listened to by all on the different subjects which he had to treat, he must first have reconquered his position of authority with the entire congregation. Hence the subject to which he assigns the first place is that of the parties which have been formed at Corinth. He begins by examining the real nature of the gospel; then he expounds that of the ministry; finally, he states the true relation between the Church and its teachers, and thus saps the evil at the root.

This question belongs to the ecclesiastical domain; thence he passes to the subjects which enter into the moral domain, and that by beginning with a question which belongs still in a way to the organization of the Church, that of the action which the community should exercise on those of its members who, by scandalous conduct, dishonour the Christian profession. There follow four questions of a purely moral order: first, these two which are easily settled by the very spirit of the gospel, that of lawsuits between Christians, carried before heathen tribunals, and that of the vice of impurity; then two others, the treatment of which is more difficult, because it is complicated by the part which the fact of Christian liberty plays in such matters: they are that of the preference to be given to celibacy over marriage, and that of the use of meats which have been offered to idols. Accordingly the solution of these two last questions gives rise to long discussions and very delicate distinctions.

After these matters of a moral nature, the apostle places those which refer to the religious life and to the celebration of worship. Here he meets with three subjects,—the first, in which the element of Christian liberty still plays a certain part, is the behaviour of women in the assemblies. The apostle afterwards deals with the way in which believers ought to conduct themselves at the love-feast preceding the observance of the Supper. Finally, he treats with particular care the most difficult and delicate of all the subjects : the best way of using spiritual gifts, gifts bestowed at Corinth with remarkable abundance, especially the gifts of tongues and of prophecy.

Thus far we observe in the course followed by the letter a tendency to go from the external to the internal : Paul in closing reaches what is most profound, most decisive, and most vital for the Church, the domain of doctrine. For, as the plant is only the embodied sap, the Church and the Christian are only evangelical doctrine realized. The apostle here treats of the resurrection of the body, which some at Corinth denied, and he shows the relation of this point of doctrine, apparently so secondary, to the Christian salvation viewed as a whole, and to the victory gained by Christ over evil in the midst of humanity.

The subjects treated are thus classified, notwithstanding their profound diversity, in four natural groups, and these groups show a rational gradation :

I. An *ecclesiastical* question : chaps. i. 10–iv. end.

II. Five *moral* questions ; foremost that of discipline, which still touches the ecclesiastical side : chaps. v.–x.

III. Three questions which are *liturgical* or relative to public worship : chaps. xi.–xiv.

IV. A *doctrinal* question : chap. xv.

The passage i. 1-9 forms the preface ; as usual it comprehends the address and a thanksgiving. Chap. xvi. is a conclusion like that with which Paul closes each of his Epistles, containing commissions, news, and greetings.

Are we to think with Renan that St. Paul "was incapable of method," and "that he did not possess the patience necessary to make a book"? Never, as it seems to us, was an intellectual edifice more admirably conceived and carried out than the First Epistle to the Corinthians, though with the most varied materials.

It has been asked whence the apostle drew the means of resolving all those doctrinal and practical problems which were put to him at that time by the state of the Church, and the answer has been given : "From the conception which forms the pivot of his whole theology, the *mystical union* between Christ and the believer" (Edwards, p. xxii.). We think this answer would rather satisfy certain of Paul's modern commentators than Paul himself. The apostle's clear and positive mind is averse to all that is vague and cloudy. As the basis of every judgment of his, there is always a precise idea, and this idea is always the inner representation of a positive fact. The Christ crucified, whom the apostle makes the foundation of our Epistle (chap. i.), and the risen Christ, whom he makes the consummation of his letter (chap. xv.), these are the twofold treasure from which he draws the solutions he needs throughout the whole course of his work. It is by analyzing the historical Christ that he resolves the question of the ministry (i. 13, iii. 23); it is to the power of the glorified Christ that he appeals to resolve that of discipline (v. 4); and so successively on to that magnificent chapter in which the study of the risen Christ furnishes him with the solution of all eschatological problems.

It is therefore not the mystical union, that cloud-land whence every one brings whatever pleases him, it is the historical, ever-living Christ, who is the foundation on which Paul rests the edifice raised in his letter.

APPENDIX

It remains to say a few words regarding the most important *documents* of the text, and also on the most recent *works* on our Epistle.

Of the nineteen manuscripts or fragments of manuscripts written in uncial letters, in which the Epistles of St. Paul have been preserved, there are fifteen which contain the First Epistle to the Corinthians in whole or in part.

These are,

א (*Sinaïticus*) and B (*Vaticanus*), of the 4th century.

A (*Alexandrinus*) and C (*C. of Ephrem*), of the 5th century.

D (*Claromontanus*), H (*Coislinianus*), I (fragment, at St. Petersburg), of the 6th century.

F^a (two verses quoted as marginal notes in H), of the 7th century.

E (*Sangermanensis*), F (*Augiensis*), G (*Börnerianus*), K (*Mosquensis*), L (*Angelicus*), M (fragment, in London), P (*Porfirianus*), of the 9th century.

We do not speak here either of minuscules, or versions, or quotations of the Fathers, referring for such apparatus of criticism to the works of general introduction to the New Testament.

As to commentaries, it is needless to speak of the most ancient and of those among the moderns which are universally known, the more so as we can refer on this head to the truly masterly exposition of the history of interpretation from its beginning to our day in Edwards' introduction to his commentary (pp. 25–35). Of the most recent works, we shall mention only the following as in our estimation the most important:

Hofmann (1874): sagacious, exact, profound, but often fanciful in the extreme.

Reuss (*Les épîtres pauliniennes*, 1878): the spirit and manner of this author are well known.

Lang (in the 2nd vol. of the *Protestanten-Bibel*): short notes interpreting our Epistle according to the views of Baur's school.

Heinrici (1880). Two features distinguish this commentary: the great abundance of interesting parallels taken from classical writers, and the attempt to deduce the forms of Church organization, established in Greece by St. Paul, from the constitution of the religious associations which then flourished in the country with a view to protect the individual against the sufferings of isolation and indigence (θίασοι, θιασῶται); comp. in the commentary, pp. 20–29, and moreover the author's profound treatise: *Die christliche Gemeinde und die religiösen Gemeinschaften der Griechen* (*Zeitschr. für wissensch. Theol.*, 1876, iv.). Nevertheless this latter opinion has not hitherto found a very favourable reception among the critics who have discussed it (Weizsäcker, Hilgenfeld, Holsten, Schürer). The formation of the Christian ecclesiastical constitution might rather be explained by the importation of synagogal forms. But it is evidently the product of the Christian mind itself, and in its development it has followed its own course. In any case, as Holsten observes, the apostle would not have been the man to borrow the forms of the Church of God from religious brotherhoods celebrating a worship which he regarded as that of demons. It is at Jerusalem we see the first elements of organization appear: elders and deacons. It is in the Churches of Asia Minor, founded long before Paul's arrival in Greece, that we meet with the first election of elders under his direction (Acts xiv. 23). Baptism, the love feast, the Holy Supper go back much further than the first contact of the gospel with the Greek world, even to our Lord Himself. That the Greek consciousness made a close relationship between the Church and those Hellenic brotherhoods is possible, even probable; and this seems to follow from the term θιασῶται, which Celsus applies to Christ's disciples (Orig. *Cont. Cels.* iii. 22), and from the title θιασάρχης (Christian), which Lucian gives to his *Peregrinus.* Comp. Neumann: θιασῶται Ἰησοῦ, in *Jahrbücher für protestantische Theologie*, 1885, i. But this close relationship, which the Pagans naturally made, has nothing in common with the influence which Heinrici attributes to the forms of the Hellenic associations on the constitution of the Christian Church.

Holsten (*Das Evangelium des Paulus*, Theil. i., 1880) : penetrating, brief, original, bold, but swayed by the premisses of the Tübingen school. In imitation of the Dutch theologian Straatmann, who has recently discovered a whole series of interpolations, more or less grave, in chaps. xi.–xv. of our Epistle, but with more moderation and less fancifulness, Holsten thinks he can eliminate from the text a host of alleged glosses : as if the apostolic documents had not been preserved in the Churches with the greatest care, but had been abandoned to the mercy of the first comer !

Beet (1883). This English commentator is known by his work on the Epistle to the Romans. He seems to me to possess in a high degree the gift of expounding the course of the apostle's ideas in a simple, clear, and judicious way.

Edwards (1885). The author of this, the most recent commentary, is Principal of a University College in Wales ; he possesses high philological culture. The spirit and value of his exegesis will appear from the quotations which we shall not fail to make from his important work.

THE TITLE

THE title comes to us in its simplest form in the documents dating from the 4th, 5th and 6th cents. (ℵ B A C D) : πρὸς Κορινθίους ἡ πρώτη, *the First to the Corinthians*. Later it is gradually amplified till it takes the form found in L (9th cent.): *the First Epistle to the Corinthians of the holy and illustrious Apostle Paul.*

The original title must have been quite simply πρὸς Κορινθίους; for this letter was not *the first* which the apostle addressed to this Church (Introduction, p. 26), and had it been, he could not have foreseen that he would afterwards write a second. The title, as we find it in the oldest MSS., has been edited by those who formed the collection of St. Paul's letters.

This letter presents the same general framework as all the others of the same apostle:

1. The *preface*, comprehending the address and a thanksgiving: i. 1–9.

2. The *body of the letter*, where the subjects are treated which gave rise to its composition: i. 10–xv. end.

3. The *conclusion*, containing commissions, news, and greetings: chap. xvi.

COMMENTARY

PREFACE (1:1-9)

VER. 1. "Paul, an apostle of Christ Jesus[1] by call,[2] through the will of God, and Sosthenes the brother."—The addresses of Paul's letters are generally drawn on the type of the ancient address: N. to N., greeting! Comp. Acts xxiii. 26. Paul does not confine himself to translating this received form into Christian language; he modifies it each time according to the interests which occupy his heart, and with a view to the state of the Church to which he writes. To his name he adds the title in virtue of which he is now addressing his readers; it is as an *apostle* that he writes them. The special mark of this office is the call directly received from Christ Himself. Paul puts this mark in relief by the epithet κλητός, *called;* a qualifying adjective, and not a participle (κληθείς), as if the apostle had meant, called *to be* an apostle. The meaning is, "an apostle in virtue of a call." He means that he has not taken this office at his own

[1] B D E F G It. place Χριστου (*Christ*) after Ιησου.
[2] A D E omit κλητος (*called*).

hand, but that he has received it by a Divine act. I do not think that there is here a polemical intention against parties who might deny his apostleship : what would this assertion prove ? He means rather to place the whole contents of the letter which is to follow under the warrant of Him who confided to him his mission. We must read, according to several ancient Mjj. : *of Christ Jesus*, that is to say, " of the Messiah who is Jesus ;" and not *of Jesus Christ* (Jesus who is the Messiah), according to the received text. The technical form has been mechanically substituted for the less ordinary by the copyists. By this complement, Paul may designate Christ as the *Author* of the call, or perhaps as the Master whose *property* he became by that call. As the regimen following ascribes the call to God, the second meaning is to be preferred. The words, *through the will of God*, refer to all the providential circumstances of Paul's birth and education, whereby his apostolic mission had been prepared for ; and especially the extraordinary act which completed this preparation, and triumphed over his resistance ; all which Paul sums up in those expressions of the Epistle to the Galatians (i. 15) : " But when it pleased God who separated me from my mother's womb, and called me by His grace. . . ."[1] It is with a feeling of profound humiliation that he emphasizes so expressly this idea of the will of God ; for he feels that it needed unfathomable mercy to snatch him from the obstinate rebellion to which he was giving himself up. But at the same time he is powerfully strengthened in relation

See the development of this idea in Godet *Commentary on Romans* pp. 3-19. (Kregal Publications 1977).

to himself and to the Church, by the assurance that what he is, he is by the will of God. But at the same time he is powerfully strengthened, as regards himself and the Church, by the assurance that it is God who has willed that he should be what he is.

Paul joins with his name that of a Christian, the *brother Sosthenes*. Reuss regards this man merely as an obscure person who no doubt acted as secretary to the apostle. I believe that there are here two errors; the place in our verse ascribed to Sosthenes is wholly different from that which the apostle gives to a simple secretary, as, for example, Tertius (Rom. xvi. 22). Paul uses particular delicacy in his way of mentioning those whom he associates with him in the composition of his letters. In his two Epistles addressed to the Church of Thessalonica, of which Silas and Timothy had been the founders along with him, he mentions them absolutely as his equals, except in so far as he puts himself in the first place; and the first person plural, which he frequently uses, again and again applies, as in ver. 2, to the three taken together. It is nearly the same in Phil. i. 1, where Timothy's name is closely associated in the address with that of Paul, no doubt because Timothy had laboured with him in founding that Church. There is a marked difference between this form and that of the Epistle to the Colossians, where Timothy's name is certainly associated with Paul's, but where it is more profoundly distinguished from it by an appendix added to the latter, in the first place, then by the title of *apostle* given to Paul and the name *brother* to Timothy. This difference arises from the fact that neither the one nor the other having founded the Church, Paul writes here in his character of apostle to the Gentiles, which Timothy does not share. In the letters to the Romans and Ephesians, whom Paul addresses more expressly still as the apostle of the Gentile world, he associates no name with his own. The position given to Sosthenes in our address is therefore somewhat like the place of Timothy in the Epistles to the Philippians and Colossians. Paul makes this brother share to a certain extent in the composition and responsibility of the letter. Sosthenes is perhaps his secretary; but he is more than that: he must be a man enjoying high consideration among the Corinthians, a fellow-labourer with the apostle who, as well as Timothy (2 Cor. i. 1), cooperated in the evangelization of Corinth and Achaia. If it is so, it is probable that we here find the same person who, as chief of the synagogue of Corinth, had played a part in the scene of Paul's appearance before Gallio (Acts xviii. 17). It was he who, after Paul's liberation, as the account of the Acts says, "was beaten by *all*" (the words—*the Greeks* are a gloss), consequently by Jews and Greeks, without Gallio's taking any concern. He took probably a doubtful attitude in this affair, later his position was more decided (see Hofmann). The place assigned him here is consequently, as Heinrici says, a place of honour; it reminds us of that ascribed by Paul to those mentioned in the address of the Epistle to the Galatians (i. 2): "and all the brethren who are with me." Assuredly those brethren were not all his secretaries, but all, in name of the Christian brotherhood, exhorted the Galatians to take to heart the warnings which Paul addressed to them as their spiritual father; so it is that the credit which Sosthenes has with the Church must be added to the superior authority of the apostle. Clement of Alexandria, according to the account of Eusebius (*H. E.* i. 12), made Sosthenes one of the seventy disciples: the statement is without value.

From the author, Paul passes to the readers:

Ver. 2. "To the Church of God, the sanctified in Christ Jesus,[1] which is at Corinth, saints by call, with all that in every place call upon the name of our Lord Jesus Christ, who is[2] theirs and ours."—The term ἐκκλησία, *Church*, formed of the two words, ἐκ, *out of*, and καλεῖν, *to call*, denotes in ordinary Greek language an assembly of citizens called out of their dwellings by an official summons; comp. Acts. xix. 41. Applied to the religious domain in the New Testament, the word preserves essentially the same meaning. Here too there is a summoner: God, who calls sinners to salvation by the preaching of the gospel (Gal. i. 6). There are the summoned: sinners, called to faith thenceforth to form the new society of which Christ is the head. The complement *of God* indicates at once Him who has summoned the assembly, and Him to whom it belongs. The term, *the Church of God*, thus corresponds to the ordinary Old Testament phrase: *Kehal Jehova, the assembly* (congregation) *of the Lord*; but there is this difference, that the latter was recruited by way of filiation, while in the new covenant the Church

[1] B D E F G It. place after θεου (*of God*) the words ηγιασμενοις εν Χριστω Ιησου (*sanctified in Christ Jesus*); T. R. places them, with ℵ A L P Syr., after τη ουση εν Κορινθω (*which is at Corinth*).

[2] ℵ A B D F G omit the τε before και, which is the reading of T. R. with E L P.

is formed and recruited by the personal adherence of faith.

According to the reading of several Mjj. (*Vatic.*, *Clarom.*, etc.), the apostle immediately adds to the words: *the Church of God*, the apposition ἡγιασμένοις ἐν Χριστῷ Ἰησοῦ, *the sanctified in Christ Jesus.* As the Church is composed of a plurality of individuals, the apostle may certainly, by a construction *ad sensum*, join to the singular substantive this apposition in the plural. The received reading separates this substantive from its apposition by placing between the two the words τῇ οὔσῃ ἐν Κορίνθῳ, *which is at Corinth.* This arrangement seems at first sight more natural; but for that very reason it has the character of a correction. It seems to me probable that, thinking already of the moral disorders which stained this Church, the apostle felt himself constrained to characterize the community he is addressing rather morally than geographically. God is holy, and the Church of God ought to be holy like Him to whom it belongs. The perfect participle ἡγιασμένοις indicates not an obligation to be fulfilled, but a state which already exists in them, and that in virtue of a previously accomplished fact. That fact is faith in Christ, which implicitly contains the act of total consecration to God. To embrace Christ by faith is to accept the holiness which He realized in His person; it is to be transplanted from the soil of our natural and profane life into that of His *Divine* holiness. The regimen, *in Christ Jesus*, expresses this idea,—that our holiness is only participation in His in virtue of the union of faith with Him: "For their sakes I sanctify myself," says Jesus (John xvii. 19), "that they also might be sanctified in truth." Several Fathers have applied the expression, *sanctified in Jesus Christ,* to the fact of baptism; their error has been confounding the sign of faith with faith itself.

After having thus characterized the assembly of God as composed of consecrated ones, the apostle adds the local definition: *which is* (which really exists, οὔσῃ) *at Corinth.* He had passed from the unity of the Church to the plurality of its members; he returns from this plurality to the unity which should continue. One feels that his mind is already taken up with the divisions which threatened to break this unity. When we think of the frightful corruption which reigned in this city (Introd. p. 6), we can understand with what inward satisfaction the apostle must have written the words, "the Church of God . . . at Corinth"! Bengel has well rendered this feeling in the short annotation: *Ecclesia in Corintho, lætum et ingens paradoxon.*

Immediately after the words: *sanctified in Christ Jesus,* it is surprising to find: *saints by call,* which seem after the preceding to form a pleonasm. The solution of this difficulty is involved in the explanation of the regimen which follows: *with all those who call upon . . .* This regimen has been connected with the dative τῇ ἐκκλησίᾳ, as if the apostle meant: I address my letter, or I address this salutation, to the Church which is at Corinth, and not only to it, but also to the Christians of the whole world (Chrysostom, Theodoret, Calvin, Osiander, Reuss). But, on the contrary, no apostolical letter has a destination so particular and local as the First Epistle to the Corinthians. Meyer limits the application of the words: *with all who call upon,* like the similar address of 2 Cor. i. 1: "with all the saints who are in all Achaia," and thinks that those referred to here are simply all the Christians scattered throughout the province of Achaia, and who are grouped round the Church of the metropolis; so, after him, Beet, Edwards, and others. But the passage quoted proves exactly the contrary of the conclusion drawn from it. For it shows how Paul would have written here also, if such had been his meaning. Holsten, feeling the impossibility of importing such a restriction, imagines another less arbitrary. He refers the words to the Christians of other Churches, who might be at present staying at Corinth, especially to the emissaries who had come from Jerusalem (*those of Christ*), of whose presence Paul was well aware. But the phrase used is far too general to admit of so limited an application. Mosheim, Ewald think that Paul means by it expressly to include in his salutation all the parties which were formed. But the preposition *σύν, with,* would imply that one of the parties was already separated from the Church itself, while the whole letter proves that they still formed part of it. We must therefore give up the attempt to make the regimen "*with all them who . . .*" dependent on the term: *the Church of God,* and connect it, as is in itself more natural, with the preceding words: "*saints by call.*" The meaning is: "saints in virtue of the Divine call, and that in communion with all them who invoke the name of the Lord in every place." Thus the tautology disappears which is implied in the words: "saints by call," with the preceding: "sanctified in Christ Jesus." There is not here a new synonymous epithet needlessly added to the preceding. The sainthood of the faithful is expressed a second time to connect this new feature with it: that sainthood is the common seal of the members of the Church universal. The words κλητοῖς ἁγίοις are there solely as the point of support for the following regimen: σὺν πᾶσι, *with all them who . . .* This construction also explains quite naturally the two adjectives, πᾶσι, *all,* and παντί, *every* (*place*), which follow. More than once in this letter the apostle will have to censure the Corinthians for isolating their course from that of the rest of the Church, and for acting as if they were the only Church in the world (comp. especially xiv. 36); and therefore in the very outset he associates them with a larger whole, of which they are only one of the members, and with which they ought to move in harmony. Heinrici, while explaining the σύν exactly as we do, thinks he can separate κλητοῖς from ἁγίοις by a comma, and connect the σύν with κλητοῖς alone: "saints, called with all them who . . ." This translation is grammatically forced, and besides it leaves the pleonasm of "saints" and "sanctified" as it was.

Holiness is the normal character *of all them that call on the name of the Lord,* says the apostle. This expression is evidently in his view the paraphrase of the term "believers." A Christian is therefore, according to him, a man who calls on the name of Jesus as his Lord. The term ἐπικαλεῖσθαι is applied in the Old Testament (by the LXX.) only to the invocation of Jehovah (Isa. xliii. 7; Joel ii. 32; Zech. xiii. 9). Immediately after Pentecost, the name for believers was, "they who call on the name of the Lord" (Acts ix. 14, 21; Rom. x. 12, 13); the name of Jesus was substituted in this formula for that of Jehovah in the Old Testament. The very word NAME, applied, as it is in these passages, to Jesus, includes the idea of a Divine Being; so when the Lord says of His angel, Ex. xxiii. 21, "My name is in him," that is to say, He makes this being His perfect revelation. The title *Lord* characterizes Jesus as the one to whom God has committed the universal sovereignty belonging to Himself; and the Church is, in the apostle's eyes, the community of those who recognise and adore Him as such. It is therefore on an act of adoration, and not on a profession of faith of an intellectual nature, that he makes the Christian character to rest. The words: ἐν παντὶ τόπῳ, *in every place,* designate the universality of the Christian Church in point of right (and already, in part, of fact, when St. Paul wrote); comp. 1 Tim. ii. 8. This idea accords with the πᾶσι, *all,* which precedes, and, as we have seen, it agrees with the context. But a large number of commentators endeavour to limit the sense of this expression, by assigning to it as its complement the words following: αὐτῶν καὶ ἡμῶν, "*of them and of us,*" or "*theirs and ours.*" But what would the expression signify: "*their* and *our* place"? De Wette, Osiander, Rückert understand thereby Corinth and Ephesus; Paul would mean: all them that call upon the Lord on your side of the sea, as well as on ours. But to what purpose is this distinction? Besides, the Church of Corinth had already been sufficiently described at the beginning of the verse. Mosheim and Ewald think that by "our place" the apostle means to denote the place of worship of his own partisans, and by "their place" the rooms where the other parties assembled. This explanation is already refuted by our foregoing remarks (p. 44). And Paul would have carefully avoided legalizing in any way the separation which he blamed so severely. Meyer's explanation, followed by Beet and Edwards, seems to me still more forced; the expression, *our* place, denotes the Christian communities of Achaia, in so far as morally the property *of the apostles;* here of Paul and Sosthenes, who preached the gospel in them; and the expression, *their* place, refers to those same communities, in so far as they depended on the Church of Corinth, their metropolis. Does such an exegetical monstrosity deserve refutation? Yet it is surpassed still, if that be possible, by Hofmann's explanation, according to which Paul means that Christians (*them*), more especially the preachers of the gospel (*us*), are found everywhere among those by whom Christ is invoked! We must, with Chrysostom, Calvin, Olshausen, etc., simply give up the attempt to make the complements *of them* and *of us* depend on the word *place;* and leave the phrase, *in every place*, in its absolute and general sense. As to the two pronouns, αὐτῶν and ἡμῶν, *of them* and *of us*, they depend on the word *Lord*, and are the more detailed repetition of the pronoun ἡμῶν (*our* Lord), which preceded: "Our Lord, who is not only *yours*, our readers, but also *ours*, your preachers." There is here, as it were, a protest beforehand against those who, forgetting that there is in the Church only one Lord, say: "As for me, I am of Paul; I, of Apollos; I, of Peter!" "Who is Paul, who is

Apollos, other than *servants* by whom ye believed, by each of them according as *the Lord* gave to him?" (iii. 5, 22, 23). So thoroughly is this the prevailing concern in the apostle's mind, from the very beginning of this letter, that six times, between vers. 1 and 10, he repeats the expression: *of our Lord Jesus Christ.* The received reading, τε καί, instead of the simple καί, may certainly be maintained, though it has against it several important manuscripts; it dwells a little more strongly on the fact that believers have Jesus Christ for *their only* Lord, as well as preachers, and thus better justifies the repetition of the preceding ἡμῶν in these two pronouns.

Ver. 3. "Grace and peace be unto you, from God our Father, and from the Lord Jesus Christ!"—This prayer is the Christian paraphrase of two salutations, the Greek (χαίρειν, Acts xxiii. 26) and the Hebrew ("Peace be to thee").—*Grace* is the Divine good will, bending compassionately toward the sinner to pardon him; toward the reconciled child, to bless him. *Peace* is the profound tranquillity with which faith in this Divine love fills the believer's heart.—Paul does not say: "be to you from God *by* Jesus Christ," but "from God *and from* Jesus Christ," for Jesus is not in his eyes the impersonal channel of the Divine love; He loves with His own peculiar love as brother, as God loves with His love as Father.—By this prayer, the apostle invites the Corinthians to take their place ever anew under the influence of this double source of salvation, the love of the Father and the love of the Son.

We have said that in the address of Paul's letters

there are already betrayed the concerns with which his mind is preoccupied at the time of writing; this is easy to establish in the Epistles to the Romans and to the Galatians, and we have seen the proof of it also in the address we have just studied. Holiness is the characteristic of the members of the Church; the relation of a common life between the particular Church and the Church universal; the dignity of Lord, as competent to Jesus only: such are the traits which distinguish this address from every other; and is it not manifest that they are dictated to the apostle by the particular circumstances of the Church of Corinth, at the time when he wrote?

The Thanksgiving (1:4-9)

The Epistle to the Galatians is the only one in which the apostle passes directly from the address to the handling of his subject, without interposing a thanksgiving. This is due to the tone of abrupt and severe rebuke which characterizes the beginning of the letter. In his other Epistles, before speaking to the Church of what it lacks, of what he would teach or correct in it, the apostle begins by expressing his gratitude for the work already accomplished, and the desires he cherishes for fresh progress to be made. This is what he does here in vers. 4–9. But, as in the addresses, there is in these thanksgivings a great variety, according to the state of each Church. If we compare that which follows with those of the two Epistles to the Thessalonians, the wide difference will be immediately perceived: there, he congratulates the Thessalonians on the work of their *faith*, the labour of their *love*, the patience of their *hope* (1 Thess. i. 3; 2 Thess. i. 3 seq.). Here, there is nothing of the kind: the apostle blesses God for the spiritual gifts, both of *knowledge* and of *speech*, which He bestows abundantly at Corinth. We shall have no difficulty in understanding the reason of this difference.

Vers. 4–6. "I thank my[1] God always on your behalf, for the grace of God which is given you in Jesus Christ; 5. That in everything ye were enriched in Him, in every kind of utterance, and in every kind of knowledge; 6. Even as the testimony of Christ[2] was confirmed in you."—On account of the severity of the rebukes to be found in this letter, some commentators have detected in this thanksgiving a touch of flattery or even of irony. But the whole Epistle shows that the apostle is no flatterer, and irony is excluded by the expression, "I thank my God." Though many things were wanting in the Church of Corinth, the gratitude which the apostle expresses to his God for what He has done in its behalf is nevertheless sincere and earnest; as appears besides from the very measuredness of his commendations shown in the terms he uses.

He addresses his thanks to *his* God: thereby he describes God as the Being in close communion with whom he lives and labours; who, in particular, stood by him in his work at Corinth, and there gave him the most personal proofs of His help and love (Acts xviii. 9, 10); if he uses the word *my* instead of *our* (Sosthenes and I), it is because the matter involves his

[1] ℵ B omit the word μου (*of me*).
[2] B F G read θεου (*of God*) instead of του Χριστου (*of Christ*).

personal relation to God, in which he can associate none of those who labour with him. It is undoubtedly by mistake that the *Sinaït.* and the *Vatic.* have omitted this pronoun *μου.* The first corrector of the *Sinaït.*, who is almost contemporary with the copyist, has supplied it (Edwards).—The word *always* might seem exaggerated; but the apostle's constant concern was the Church in general, and that of Corinth was one of its most important members.—The general term: *on your behalf,* is defined by the more precise phrase, *for the grace of God which . . .*, intended to express the more special subject of the thanksgiving. This grace comprehends the whole state of salvation, with the new life which has been displayed in the Church. It is a mistake, as it seems to me, in many interpreters to limit the application of the word *grace* to the spiritual gifts about to be spoken of: the term is more general.

Ver. 5. With the meaning of the word *grace*, which we have rejected, ὅτι would require to be translated by *in that.* But if we take the word *grace* in the most general sense, ὅτι should be translated by "*seeing that,*" or "*because.*" Indeed, there is here a new fact proving the reality of the preceding. Only from the state of grace could the abundance of gifts arise which distinguishes the Church of Corinth, and which more especially gives occasion to the apostle's gratitude.—The *in everything* is qualified by the two following terms, *knowledge* and *utterance.* The sequel of the Epistle leaves no doubt as to the meaning of these two terms. Chaps. xii.–xiv. will show what a wealth of gifts, both of Christian knowledge and of manifestations in utterance (tongues, prophecies, doctrine), had been bestowed on this Church. We see from viii. 1 and 10, xiii. 2, 8, and 9, that the word γνῶσις, *knowledge*, denotes the understanding of the facts of salvation and of their manifold applications to Christian life. Here it includes the idea of σοφία, *wisdom*, which is sometimes distinguished from it; comp. xii. 8.—The term *utterance* has been applied by de Wette to the rich Christian instruction which the Corinthians had received from Paul's mouth and from which they had derived their knowledge of the gospel. But the term *utterance* must denote a spiritual gift bestowed on the Corinthians, and in connection with the term knowledge. What the apostle has in view, therefore, is those different forms of the new tongue which the Holy Spirit had developed in the Church. The verb ἐπλουτίσθητε denotes their abundance; the word παντί, *every*, their variety; comp. xiv. 26: "When ye come together, each of you hath a psalm, a teaching, a tongue, a revelation, an interpretation." Edwards sees in this aorist an allusion to the present loss of those former riches, as if it should be translated, "Ye *had been* enriched." This is certainly a mistake; the riches remained still, as is shown by chaps. xii.–xiv. The aorist simply relates to the point of time at which the spiritual endowment of the Church took place, when its faith was sealed by the communication of the Spirit. It is not by accident that the apostle only mentions here the speculative and oratorical powers, and not the moral virtues; the *gifts* of the Spirit and not the *fruits* of the Spirit, as at Thessalonica. His intention is not doubtful; for in chap. xiii. 8–13 he himself contrasts the two principal gifts of utterance, tongues, and prophecy, and then knowledge, as things which pass away, with the three things which abide: faith, hope, and love. Here then, side by side with the riches for which the apostle gives thanks, we already discover the defect which afflicts him, but of which he does not speak, because it would be contrary to the object of the passage as one sacred to thanksgiving. This defect stood in relation to the character of the Greek mind, which was distinguished rather by intellectual and oratorical gifts than by seriousness of heart and conscience.

Ver. 6. This verse may be understood in two ways: some (Meyer, Edwards, etc.) regard it as indicating the *cause* of that abundance of gifts which has just been mentioned. They then apply the term ἐβεβαιώθη, *was confirmed*, or rather *affirmed*, to an internal fact: "in consequence of the depth and firmness of faith with which the gospel impressed (affirmed) itself in you." To support this meaning, they rely on the βεβαιώσει of ver. 8; but we shall see that this ground proves nothing, because there the idea of confirmation applies, not to the gospel, but to the persons of the Corinthians. This explanation is not in keeping with the natural meaning of καθώς, *according as*, which indicates rather a mode than a cause. The sense seems to me quite different: the apostle means, not that the wealth of their gifts is due to the depth and solidity of their faith, which would be contrary to the spirit of the whole passage, but that these gifts have been the *mode* of confirming the gospel specially granted to the Church of Corinth. Elsewhere, God could confirm the apostolic preaching otherwise; by miracles, for example, or by moral virtues, fruits of the Spirit; comp. Heb. ii. 3: "The salvation which, having at the first been spoken by the Lord, was *confirmed* unto us by them that heard Him, God Himself bearing witness with them by signs and wonders and by distribution of the powers of the Spirit;" also, 1 and 2 Thess. i. 3 and Gal. iii. 2. The conj. καθώς agrees perfectly with this meaning: "Thus, and not otherwise, did the Divine confirmation of the testimony rendered to Christ take place among you."—The term *testimony* is here used to denote preaching, because this is essentially the attestation of a historical fact (vers. 23, 24). The gen. Χριστοῦ denotes the subject of the testimony, and not its author. It would be otherwise with the gen. θεοῦ, *of God*, if this reading were adopted with the *Vatic.*

Ver. 7. "So that ye come behind in no gift, waiting for the revelation of our Lord Jesus Christ."—In the explanation of the preceding verse, which we have rejected, the ὥστε, *so that*, is made to refer to the verb ἐβεβαιώθη of ver. 6: "Your faith was confirmed in such a way, that in consequence no gift was lacking to you . . ." But in the sense of ver. 6, which we have adopted, this verse being rather an observation thrown in by the way, it is natural to refer the ὥστε to the ἐπλουτίσθητε of ver. 5, which gives a simpler and clearer meaning: "Ye were so enriched, that in point of gifts ye lacked nothing." There is indeed an evident contrast between the two ideas of *being enriched* and *lacking.*—The word ὑστερεῖσθαι, *to lack*, denotes a deficiency either relatively to the normal level which a Church should attain (xvi. 17; Col. i. 24; 1 Thess.

iii. 10), or comparatively to other Churches more richly endowed (2 Cor. xi. 5, xii. 11). The first of these two meanings is evidently the more suitable here. The Corinthians realize, in respect of gifts, *χαρίσματα*, all that can be desired for a Church on the earth. The *ἐν μηδενί* corresponds to the *ἐν παντί* of ver. 5.

The word *χάρισμα*, *gift*, will play a large part in this Epistle. As the form of the Greek term indicates, it denotes in general every concrete product in which grace is embodied. Several commentators (Calvin, de Wette, Meyer) apply the word here to the blessings of salvation in general, as in Rom. i. 11 ; but the evident relation to ver. 5 (comp. the reference of *ὑστερεῖσθαι* to *πλουτισθῆναι*, and that of *μηδενί* to *παντί*) leads us to give a more definite sense to the word *χάρισμα*. According to the two expressions, *knowledge* and *utterance*, it must be applied here to the new spiritual powers with which the Spirit had endowed the members of the Church at Corinth. These various powers, which so often in Paul's writings bear the name of *χαρίσματα*, *gifts of grace*, are certainly the effects of the supernatural life due to faith in Christ ; but they fit in notwithstanding to pre-existing natural aptitudes in individuals and peoples. The Holy Spirit does not substitute Himself for the human soul ; He sanctifies it and consecrates its innate talents to the service of the work of salvation. By this new direction, He purifies and exalts them, and enables them to reach their perfect development. This was what had taken place at Corinth, and it was thus especially that the apostolic testimony had been divinely confirmed in this Church. We see how Paul still carefully avoids (as in ver. 5) speaking of the moral fruits of the gospel, for this was the very respect in which there was a deficiency, and a grave deficiency, at Corinth.

The following words, *waiting for the revelation* . . ., have been very variously understood. Grotius and Rückert have seen in them an indirect reproof to those of the members of the Church who, according to chap. xv., denied the resurrection. But the apostle speaks of waiting for the Lord's *return,* and not of faith in the resurrection. Chrysostom supposes that he wishes to alarm them by thus glancing at the approach of the judgment; but this would not be very suitable to a thanksgiving. Calvin, Hofmann, Meyer suppose, on the contrary, that he wishes to encourage them: "Ye can go to meet the Lord's advent with confidence, for ye possess all the graces that suffice for that time;" or, as Meyer says: "The blessings which ye have received fit you to see the Lord come without fear." But would the apostle thus reassure people whom he saw filled with the most presumptuous self-satisfaction, and given over to a deceitful security? Comp. iv. 6–8, x. 1–22. Reuss supposes that Paul wishes to lead them to put to good account the spiritual aids which they now enjoy. But Paul would have declared this intention more clearly. Mosheim seems to me to have come nearer the true sense, when he finds irony here: "Ye lack nothing, waiting however the great revelation!" Without going the length of finding a sarcasm which would be out of place here, I think that there is really in this appendix, "waiting the revelation . . .," the purpose of bringing this too self-satisfied Church to a more modest estimate. Rich as they are, they ought not to forget that as yet it is only a waiting state: they lack nothing . . . waiting for the moment which will give them everything. As is said, indeed (xiii. 11), all our present gifts of utterance and knowledge have still the character of the imperfect state of childhood, in comparison with that which the perfect state will bring about. There was a tendency among the Corinthians to anticipate this latter state; they already imagined that they were swimming in the full enjoyment of the perfected kingdom of God (iv. 8). The apostle reminds them that real knowledge is yet to come; and this no doubt is the reason why he here uses the term, *the revelation of Jesus Christ,* to denote His advent. He means thereby less to characterize His visible presence (παρουσία), than the full revelation both of Him and of all things in Him, which will accompany that time. In that light what will become of your knowledge, your present prophesyings and ecstasies? Comp. 2 Thess. i. 7; 1 Pet. i. 7, where the use of this term is also occasioned by the context.—The term ἀπεκδέχεσθαι, compounded of the three words, ἀπό, *far from* (here, *from far*), ἐκ, *from the hands of,* and δέχεσθαι, *to receive,* admirably depicts the attitude of waiting.

After expressing his gratitude for what God has already done for his readers, the apostle, as in Eph. i. 17 seq., and Phil. i. 6 seq., adds the hope that God will yet accomplish in them all that is lacking, that they may be able to stand in that great day; such is the idea of the two following verses.

Ver. 8. "Who shall also confirm you unto[1] the end,

[1] D E F G: αχρι τελους, instead of εως τελους.

that ye may be blameless in the day[1] of our Lord Jesus Christ. 9. God is faithful, by whom[2] ye were called unto the fellowship of His Son Jesus Christ our Lord." — The pron. ὅς, *who*, refers of course to the person of *Jesus Christ* (ver. 7). But this name being expressly repeated at the end of the verse, many commentators have been led to refer the pronoun ὅς to θεός, *God* (ver. 4). But this reference would reduce the whole passage, vers. 5–7, to a simple parenthesis; it has besides against it the repetition of the word θεός in ver. 9. If the expression *our Lord Jesus Christ* appears again at the end of the verse, instead of the pronoun, this arises from the fact that the term "the day of Christ" is a sort of technical phrase in the New Testament; it corresponds to the "day of the Lord" in the Old Testament.—The καί, *also*, implies that the work to be yet accomplished will only be the legitimate continuation of that which is already wrought in them. There is undoubtedly an intentional correlation between the βεβαιώσει, *will confirm*, of ver. 8, and the ἐβεβαιώθη, *was confirmed*, of ver. 6. Since God confirmed Paul's preaching at Corinth by the gifts which His Spirit produced there, He will certainly confirm believers in their faith in the gospel to the end.—This end is the Lord's coming again, for which the Church should constantly watch, for the very reason that it knows not the time of it; comp. Luke xii. 35 and 36; Mark xiii. 32. If this event does not happen during the life of this or that generation, death takes its place for each, till that generation for which it will be

[1] D E F G It.: παρουσια, instead of ημερα.
[2] D F G: υφ' ου, instead of δι' ου.

realized externally. The phrase, *in the day of Christ*, does not depend on the verb *will confirm*, but on the epithet ἀνεγκλήτους, *unblameable*. We must understand between the verb and the adjective the words εἰς τὸ εἶναι, as in Rom. viii. 29 ; 1 Thess. iii. 13 ; Phil. iii. 21 (where the words εἰς τὸ γενέσθαι are a gloss) : the end is directly connected with the means. —Ἀνέγκλητος signifies *exempt from accusation*, and many apply the word to the act of justification which will cover the infirmities and stains of believers in that supreme hour, so that, as Meyer says, the epithet is not equivalent to ἀναμάρτητος, *exempt from sin*. It does not seem to me that this meaning suits the parallels 2 Cor. vii. 1, 1 Thess. v. 23 ; for these passages represent believers as completely sanctified at that time. If then they are no longer subject to any accusation, it will not be only, as during their earthly career, in virtue of their justification by faith, it will be in virtue of their thenceforth perfected sanctification. The Greek - Latin reading παρουσία, *advent*, instead of ἡμέρα, *day*, has no probability.

Ver. 9. The asyndeton between the preceding verse and this arises from the fact that the latter is only the emphasized reaffirmation, in another form, of the same idea : the faithfulness of God, as the pledge of the confirmation of believers in their attachment to the gospel. The assurance here expressed by the apostle is doubtless not a certainty of a mathematical order ; for the entire close of chap. ix. and the first half of chap. x. are intended to show the Corinthians that they may, through lack of watchfulness and obedience, make shipwreck of the Divine work in them; the certainty in question is of a moral nature, implying the acquiescence of the human will. As the *ye were called* assumes the free acceptance of faith, so continuance in the state of salvation supposes perseverance in that acceptance. But the apostle sets forth here only the Divine factor, because it is that which contains the solid assurance of this hope.

The words, *by whom ye were called,* sum up the work already accomplished at Corinth by Paul's ministry; comp. Phil. i. 6. We need not with Meyer apply the phrase, *the fellowship of His Son Jesus Christ,* to the state of glory in the heavenly kingdom. The term *κοινωνία*, *fellowship,* implies something inward and present. Paul means to speak of the participation of believers in the life of Christ, of their close union to His person even here below. The form, *Jesus Christ our Lord,* recurs so to speak in every phrase of this preface; it reappears again in the following verse. It is obvious that it is the thought which is filling the apostle's mind; for he is about to enumerate the human names which they dare at Corinth to put side by side with that of this one Lord.

This thanksgiving has therefore, like the foregoing address, a character very peculiarly appropriate to the state of the Church. While frankly commending the graces which had been bestowed on them, the apostle gives them clearly to understand what they lack and what they must yet seek, to be ready to receive their Lord. He now passes to the treatment of the various subjects of which he has to speak with them.

BODY OF THE EPISTLE

1:10-15:58

1

The Parties in the Church of Corinth

1:10-4:21

Ewald has well stated the reason why the apostle puts this subject first, of all those he has to treat in his Epistle. He must assert his apostolical position in view of the whole Church, before giving them the necessary explanations on the subjects which are to follow.

A. *Statement of the fact and its summary condemnation* 1:10-17

Ver. 10. "Now I beseech you, brethren, by the name of our Lord Jesus Christ, that ye all speak the same thing, and that there be no divisions among you, but that ye be perfectly joined together in the same mind and in the same judgment." — The δέ is not adversative: it is the transition particle by which Paul passes from thanksgiving to rebuke. — By the address ἀδελφοί, *brethren*, he puts himself by the side of his readers, and appeals to their affection in view of the serious censure which he has to pass on them.

He rests his exhortation on the revelation made to him and the knowledge which they have of the person and work of the Lord Jesus Christ ; such is the meaning of the term ὄνομα, *the name.* The word *Lord* implies His authority ; the name *Jesus Christ* calls up the memory of all the tender proofs of Divine love displayed in Him who bore the name. It is the eleventh time that the name Jesus Christ appears, and we are at the tenth verse !—The following exhortation bears on three points. The first, τὸ αὐτὸ λέγειν, *to speak the same thing,* is the most external. The phrase includes an allusion to the different formulas enumerated ver. 12. —The two other points relate to the inward conditions of community of language ; the first is negative : that there be no schisms, divisions into different camps, bringing with them opposing watchwords. What a view is here of a Church divided into distinct parties ! The other condition is of a positive nature : it is the perfect *incorporation* of all the members of the Church in a single spiritual organism. The term καταρτίζειν denotes, in the first place, the act of adjusting the pieces of a machine with a view to its normal action ; hence the equipment of a workman for his work (Eph. iv. 12) ; then, in the second place, the rectification of a disorganized state of things, such as the re-establishment of social order after a revolution, or the repairing of an instrument (Mark i. 19 : fishing-nets). Order being disturbed at Corinth, we might here apply the latter meaning. But in this case Paul would rather have used the aor. κατηρτίσθητε δέ than the perfect which denotes the stable condition. The first signification is also somewhat more delicate. Paul does not mean, "that ye be reconstituted," as if he thought them already disorganized, but, "that ye may be in the state of a well-ordered assembly." How so? He indicates this in the two following terms: by the agreement of the *νοῦς* and that of the *γνώμη*. These two words are often distinguished by making the first apply to knowledge, the second to practical life. This distinction, without being false, is not however sufficiently precise; the *νοῦς*, as is shown in ii. 16, denotes the Christian way of thinking in general, the conception of the gospel in its entirety; the *γνώμη*, according to vii. 25, refers rather to the manner of deciding a particular point, what we call opinion, judgment. The apostle therefore desires that there should be among them, in the first place, full harmony of view in regard to Christian truth, and then perfect agreement in the way of resolving particular questions. The conjunction *ἵνα* shows that in his mind the matter in question is rather an object to be attained than a duty which he expects to be immediately realized; it is the state to be aspired after, for the honour of the name of Jesus Christ, whatever may be the sacrifices of self-love and of interest which such an aim may demand of each. After this introduction the apostle comes to the fact which gives rise to this exhortation.

Vers. 11, 12. "For it hath been signified unto me concerning you, my brethren, by them which are of the household of Chloe, that there are contentions among you. 12. Now this I mean, that each one of you saith, I am of Paul; and I of Apollos; and I of Cephas; and I of Christ."—At the moment of enumerating these different parties, the apostle once again unites all the members of the Church under the one common and affectionate address, *my brethren.*—Perhaps the markedly express indication of the source to which he owes this news is intended to exclude in this matter the delegates of the Church who are at this time with Paul. Those of Chloe's household may be the children or slaves of that Ephesian or Corinthian lady (see Introd. p. 21).—The word ἔριδες, *contentions,* denotes bitter discussions which would easily degenerate into *schisms,* σχίσματα (ver. 10).

Ver. 12. Calvin has translated, "I say this *because* . . . ;" but it is more natural to make the τοῦτο, *this,* refer to the following ὅτι : "When I speak of contentions, *I mean this that* . . . " The phrase, *Every one of you saith,* is of course inexact; for every member of the Church did not pronounce the four watchwords. Paul thus expresses himself to indicate that the sin is general, that there is not one among them, so to speak, who has not in his mouth *one* of these formulas. The four are presented dramatically and in the form of direct speech; we hear them, as it were, bandied from one to another in the congregation. Their painful character appears first from the ἐγώ, *I,* put foremost,—there is a preponderance of personal feeling,—then from the δέ, which is evidently adversative: *but,*—there is the spirit of opposition,—finally and chiefly, from the names of the party leaders. Some ancient commentators supposed that the apostle had here substituted the names of eminent men for the obscure names of the real party leaders, to show so much the better how unjustifiable such rivalries are. The passage iv. 6 is that which induced Chrysostom, and others after him, to make so unnatural a supposition. But we shall see that this verse gives it no countenance.

The apostle puts in the forefront the party which takes name from himself; he thereby gives proof of great tact, for by first of all disapproving of his own partisans, he puts his impartiality beyond attack. It has been supposed that in the enumeration of the four parties he followed the historical order in which they were formed; but from the fact that Paul was the founder of the Church, and that Apollos came after him, it does not follow that Paul's party was formed first and that of Apollos second; we must rather suppose the contrary. Paul's partisans had only had occasion to pronounce themselves as such, by way of reaction, against the exclusive partiality inspired by the other preachers who came after him. We have indicated in the Introduction, p. 22 seq., how we understand these opposite groups to have been formed. We cannot concede the least probability to the suppositions of Heinrici, who ascribes to Apollos a Gnostic and mystic tendency, and particularly views on baptism of the strangest kind. From the fact that he arrived at Ephesus as a disciple of John the Baptist, we have no right to conclude, with this theologian, that Apollos established a special bond of solidarity between the baptized and their baptizer like that which, in the Greek mysteries, united initiated and initiator! Heinrici goes the length of supposing that to Apollos and his party is to be ascribed the practice alluded to xv. 29, of baptizing a living Christian in place of a believer who died without baptism! Is it possible to push arbitrariness further? This has been well shown by Hilgenfeld (*Zeitschrift für wissenschaftliche Theologie,* 1880, p. 362 seq.). What distinguished Paul from Apollos, according to iii. 5 seq. and iv. 6, could not be an essential difference, bearing on the substance of the gospel; it could only be a difference of form such as that indicated by the words, "I have planted, Apollos watered, and God gave the increase." By his exegetical and literary culture, acquired at Alexandria, Apollos had gained for Christ many who had resisted Paul's influence; perhaps Sosthenes, the ruler of the synagogue during Paul's stay, was of the number. If it is so, we can better understand how the apostle was induced to associate this person's name with his own in the address of the letter.

We have already said that the existence of a Cephas-party does not necessarily imply a visit of Peter to Corinth. Personal disciples of this apostle might have arrived in the city, or Jewish Christians from Corinth might have met Peter at Jerusalem, and on their return to Achaia they might have reported that this apostle differed from Paul in continuing personally to keep the law, though without wishing to impose it on Gentile converts. The Aramaic name Cephas is perhaps a proof of the Palestinian origin of the party.

As to the last watchword, the Greek Fathers, and Calvin, Mosheim, Eichhorn, Bleek among the moderns, think that it, according to the apostle, gives the true formula by which Paul would designate those whom he approves. Mayerhoff and Ebrard go even the length of thinking that by the word *I*, Paul means to designate himself: "But as for me, Paul, this is my watchword: I am of Christ, and of Christ only!" The symmetry of the four formulas evidently excludes these interpretations. The fourth comes under the censure which falls on the three preceding, "Every one of you saith . . . ," and it is this one above all which gives rise to the following question,—"Is Christ divided?" There was really then a fourth party which claimed to spring directly from Christ, and Christ alone, without having need of any human intermediary. As Paul adds not a single detail regarding this party, either in this passage or in the rest of the Epistle, the field of hypothesis is open, and we shall consecrate to the much discussed question the appendix to be immediately subjoined.

Some commentators seem to us to have exaggerated the character of the division, by supposing that the different parties no longer met in common assemblies, and that the rending of the Church into four distinct communities was an accomplished fact. The contrary appears from the passage xiv. 23, where Paul speaks of the assembling together of the whole Church in one and the same place, and even from the term ἔριδες, *contentions*, which would be too weak in that case. On the other hand, Hofmann has far too much attenuated the importance of the fact mentioned when he reduces it to hostile pleadings in the meetings of the Church, arising from the personal preference of each group for that servant of Christ who had contributed most to its edification. Undoubtedly the external unity of the Church was not broken, but its moral unity was at an end, and we shall see that the disagreement went much deeper into the way of understanding the gospel than this commentator thinks.

Otherwise, would the apostle have spent on it four whole chapters? It has often been attempted to distribute the numerous subjects treated by the apostle in our Epistle among these different parties, as if they had been furnished to him, one by one party, another by another. These attempts have not issued in any solid result. And we must say the same of the most recent attempt, that of Farrar. This critic sees in the Apollos-party the precursors of Marcion and of the Antinomian Gnosticism of the second century; in the Peter-party, the beginning of the anti-Pauline Ebionism of the Clementine *Homilies.* Finally, in the Christ-party, an invasion of Essenism into Christianity, which continued later. The division which Farrar makes of the questions treated by Paul among those different tendencies is ingenious, but lacks foundation in the text of the Epistle.

The party called "those of Christ"

We have already set aside the opinions of those who take the fourth formula to be the true Christian profession approved by the apostle, or the legitimate declaration of a group of believers, offended by the absorbing partiality of the other groups for this or that teacher.

1

The opinion which comes nearest this second shade is that developed by Rückert, Hofmann, Meyer, Heinrici, and to a certain extent by Renan, according to whom the fourth party, pushed by the exclusive preferences of the others, was carried to the opposite extreme, and declared itself independent of the apostolate in general, putting itself relatively to Christ in a position absolutely equal to that of Paul or Peter. "Some," says Renan, "wishing to pose as spirits superior to those contentions, created a watchword sufficiently spiritual. To designate themselves they invented the name 'Christ's party.' When discussion grew hot . . . , they intervened with the name of Him who was being forgotten: I am for Christ, said they" (*Saint Paul*, p. 378). It is for them, it is held, that Paul calls to mind, iii. 22, that if the Church does not belong to the teachers who instruct it, the latter are nevertheless precious gifts bestowed on it by the Lord. Nothing simpler in appearance than this view. An extreme had led to the contrary extreme; partiality had produced disparagement. It was the rejection of apostolical authority as the answer to false human dependence. We should not hesitate to adopt this explanation, if certain passages of Second Corinthians, which we shall afterwards examine, did not force us to assign graver causes and a much graver importance to the formation of this party; comp. especially 2 Cor. x. 7, and xi. 22 and 23.

2

Have we to do, as Neander[1] once thought, with Corinthians of a more or less rationalistic character, with cultivated Greeks who, carried away by enthusiasm for the admirable teachings of Christ, and especially for His sublime moral instructions, conceived the idea of freeing this pure gospel from the Jewish wrapping which still veiled it in the apostolic preaching? In order to make faith easy for their countrymen, they tried to make Jesus a Socrates of the highest power, which raised Him far above the Jesus taught by the Twelve, and by Paul himself. It is against this attempt to transform the gospel into a pure moral philosophy, that it is said the apostle conducts the polemic i. 18–24, and iii. 18–20. This hypothesis is seductive, but the passages quoted can be explained without it, and the Second Epistle proves that the party *those of*

[1] In the first editions of the *Apostolic Age;* later, he adhered to the opinion of Bleek (see above).

Christ had not its partisans at Corinth among converted Gentiles, but in Palestine, among Christians of Jewish origin and tendency.

3

This is recognised by some commentators, such as Dähne[1] and Goldhorn; these seek the distinctive character of this fourth party in the elements of Alexandrine wisdom, which certain Jewish doctors mingled with the apostolic teaching. We shall no doubt discover the great corruptions introduced by the Judaizing heads of the Christ-party into the evangelical doctrine. But it is impossible to establish, by any solid proof whatever, the Alexandrine origin of these new elements.

4

So Schenkel,[2] de Wette, Grimm have pronounced for a more natural notion. According to them, the heads of this party founded their rejection of the apostolic teaching and the authority of their own on supernatural communications which they received from the glorified Christ, by means of direct visions and revelations. Similar claims were put forth a little later, as we know, among the Judaizing teachers of Colosse; why should they not have existed previously in Asia Minor, and thence invaded the Churches of Greece? To support this opinion, there has been alleged chiefly the way in which Paul dwells on that transport even to the third heaven, which had been granted to himself (2 Cor. xii. 1 seq.); and it is thought that he meant thereby to say: "If these men pretend to have had revelations, I have also had them, and still more astonishing." But this would be a mode of argument far from conclusive and far from worthy of the apostle; and we shall see that those teachers probably did not come from the land of mysticism, Asia Minor, but from that of legal Pharisaism, Palestine.

[1] *Die Christus-Partei in der apostol. K. zu Kor.*, 1842.

[2] *De eccl. Cor. primæva faction. turbata*, 1838.

5

This is now recognised by most critics. No doubt we do not see the Judaizing teachers who are concerned here presenting themselves at Corinth, exactly as they did formerly at Antioch and in Galatia. They understood that to gain such men as the Greeks of Corinth, they must avoid putting forward circumcision and gross material rites. But they are nevertheless servants of the legal party as formed at Jerusalem. To be convinced of this, it is enough to compare the two following passages of 2 Cor. x. 7: "If any one trust to himself that he belongs to Christ (Χριστοῦ εἶναι, lit. 'to be Christ's'), let him of himself think this again, that as he is Christ's, so are we Christ's." To whom is this challenge addressed? Evidently to persons who claim to be Christ's by a juster title than the apostle and his partisans, precisely like the men who specially call themselves *those of Christ* in the First Epistle. And who are they? The second passage, xi. 22 and 23, informs us: "Are they Hebrews? so am I. Are they Israelites? so am I. Are they the seed of Abraham? so am I. Are they ministers of Christ? (I speak as a fool); I am more." They were then Jewish believers who boasted of their theocratic origin, and who sought to impose, by means of their relations to the mother Church, on the young Churches founded by Paul in the Gentile world, no doubt with the intention of bringing them gradually under the yoke of the Mosaic law.

But in what sense did such men designate themselves as *those of Christ?*

1. Storr, Hug, Bertholdt, Weizsäcker suppose that they took this title as coming from James, the head of the flock at Jerusalem, known under the name "the Lord's brother;" and that it was because of this relationship between James and Jesus, that they boasted of being in a particular sense men of Christ. But this substitution of Christ's name for that of James is rather improbable, and this explanation could in any case only apply to the few foreign emissaries who came from Palestine, and not to the mass of the Corinthian party which was grouped around them.

2. According to Billroth, Baur, Renan, these people were

the same as "those of Cephas." They designated themselves as *those of Peter* when they wished to denote their human head; as *those of Christ* when they wished to declare the conformity of their conduct with that of the Lord, who had constantly observed the law, and had never authorized the abolition of it, which Paul preached. In reality, the third and fourth party were thus only one; its double name signified, "disciples of Peter, and, as such, true disciples of Christ."

In favour of this identification, it is alleged that in a dogmatic point of view the two first parties, that of Paul and that of Apollos, also formed only one. But we have proved without difficulty the shade which distinguished the partisans of Apollos from those of Paul, and though it did not bear on dogmatic questions, we cannot confound these two parties in one, nor consequently can we identify the last two parties so clearly distinguished by the apostle. Besides, nothing authorizes us to ascribe to Peter a conception of the gospel opposed to that of Paul. We know, from Gal. ii., that they were agreed at Jerusalem on these two points: that believers from among the Gentiles should not be subjected to the Mosaic rites, and that believers from among the Jews might continue to observe them. But we know also from the same passage, that there was a whole party at Jerusalem which did not approve of this concession made to Paul by the apostles. Paul distinguishes them thoroughly from the apostles and from James himself, for he declares that if he had had to do only with the latter, he might have yielded in the matter of the circumcision of Titus; but it was because of the former, to whom he gives the name of "false brethren, brought in," that he was obliged to show himelf inflexible in his refusal. There was therefore a profound difference in the way in which the circumcision of Titus was asked of him by the apostles on the one hand, and by the false brethren on the other. The former asked it of him as a voluntary concession, and in this sense he could have granted it; but the latter demanded it as a thing obligatory; in this sense the apostle could not yield without compromising for ever the liberty of the Gentiles. Consequently, beside Peter's followers, who, while observing the law themselves, conceded liberty to the Gentiles, there was room for another party, which, along with the maintenance of the law for the Jews, demanded the subjection of the Gentiles to the Mosaic system. What more natural than to find here, in *those of Christ*, the representatives of this extreme party? We can understand in this case why Paul places *those of Christ* after those of Peter, and thus makes them the antipodes of his own party.

Far, then, from finding in our passage, as Baur and Renan will have it, a proof of Peter's narrow Judaism, we must see in it the proof of the opposite, and conclude for the existence of two classes of Jew-Christians, represented at Corinth, the one by Peter's party, the other by Christ's.

3. Schmidt has thought that the Judaizers, who called themselves *those of Christ*, were those who allowed the dignity of being members of the kingdom of *Christ*, the Messiah-King, only to the Jews and to those of the Gentiles who became Jews by accepting circumcision. In this explanation the strict meaning of the term *Χριστός*, *Messiah*, must be emphasized. But it seems evident from our two Epistles that the Judaizing emissaries at Corinth were wise enough not to demand circumcision and the Mosaic ritual from the believers there, as from the ignorant Galatians.

4. Reuss, Osiander, Klöpper think those emissaries took the name of *those of Christ*, because they relied on the personal example of Jesus, who had always observed the law, and on certain declarations given forth by Him, such as these, "I am not come to destroy the law, . . . but to fulfil it;" and "Ye have one Master, Christ." Starting from this, they not only protested against Paul's work, but also against the concessions made to Paul by the Twelve. They declared themselves to be the only Christians who were faithful to the mind of the Church's Supreme Head, and on that account they took the exclusive title, *those of Christ*. This explanation is very plausible; but, as we shall see, certain passages of the Second Epistle to the Corinthians lead us to ascribe a quite special dogmatic character to the teaching of *those of Christ;* and it would be difficult to understand how, while wishing to impose on the Corinthians Christ's mode of acting during His earthly life, they could have freed them, even provisionally, from circumcision and the other Mosaic rites.

5. Holsten and Hilgenfeld suppose that the title, *those of*

Christ, originated in the fact that these emissaries had been in personal connection with Jesus during His earthly life. They were old disciples, perhaps of the number of the *Seventy* formerly sent out by Christ, or even His own brothers; for we know from 1 Cor. ix. 5 that these filled the office of evangelist-preachers. Persons who had thus lived within the Lord's immediate circle might disparage Paul as a man who had never been in personal connection with Him, and had never seen Him, except in a vision of a somewhat suspicious kind. There is mention, 2 Cor. iii. 1, of letters of recommendation with which those strangers had arrived at Corinth. By whom had those letters been given them, if not by James, at once the Lord's brother and head of the Church of Jerusalem?

In answer to this view, we have to say that if James acted thus, he would have openly broken the solemn contract of which Paul speaks (Gal. ii. 5–10), and taken back in fact the hand of fellowship which he had given to this apostle. Holsten answers, indeed, that it was Paul who had broken the contract in his conflict with Peter at Antioch; and that after that scene James felt himself free to act openly against him. But supposing—what we do not believe—that Paul went too far in upbraiding Peter for his return to the observance of the law in the Church of Antioch, there would have been no good reason in that why James should retract the principle recognised and proclaimed by himself, that of the liberty of the Gentiles in regard to the law. What has been recognised as true does not become false through the faults of a third.

6. As none of these explanations fully satisfy us, we proceed to expound the view to which we have been led. We shall find ourselves at one partly, but only partly, with the result of Beyschlag's studies, published by him in the *Studien und Kritiken,* 1865, ii., and 1871, iv. We have seen, while refuting Baur's opinion, that there existed even at Jerusalem a party opposed to the Twelve, that of the "false brethren, brought in," whom Paul clearly distinguishes from the apostles (Gal. ii. 4, 6). They claimed to impose the Mosaic law on Gentile converts, while the Twelve maintained it only for Christians of Jewish origin, and the further

question, whether these might not be released from this obligation in Churches of Gentile origin, remained open. We think that this ultra-party was guided by former members of the priesthood and of Jewish Pharisaism (Acts vi. 7, xv. 5), who, in virtue of their learning and high social position, regarded themselves as infinitely superior to the apostles. It is not therefore surprising that once become Christians, they should claim to take out of the hands of the Twelve, of whom they made small account, the direction of the (Christian) Messianic work, with the view of making this subservient to the extension of the legal dispensation in the Gentile world. Such were the secret heads of the counter mission organized against Paul which we meet with everywhere at this period. It had now pushed its work as far as Corinth, and it is easy to understand why the portion of the Church which was given up to its agents, distinguished itself not only from the parties of Paul and Apollos, but also from that of Peter. They designated themselves as *those of Christ,* not because their leaders had personally known Jesus, and could better than others instruct the Churches in His life and teaching,—who in these two respects would have dared to compare himself to Peter or put himself above him?—but as being the only ones who had well understood His mind and who preserved more firmly than the apostles the true tradition from Him in regard to the questions raised by Paul. They were too prudent to speak at once of circumcision and Mosaic rites. They rather took the position in regard to converted Gentiles which the Jews had long adopted in regard to the so-called proselytes *of the gate.* And moreover—and here is where I differ from Beyschlag—when they arrived on Greek soil, they certainly added theosophic elements to the gospel preached by the apostles, whereby they sought to recommend their teaching to the speculative mind of the cultivated Christians of Greece. It is not without cause, that in the Second Epistle to the Corinthians, Paul speaks, x. 5, of "reasonings exalted like strongholds against the knowledge of God," and of "thoughts to be brought into captivity to the obedience of Christ," and that, xi. 3, he expresses the fear that the Corinthians are allowing themselves to be turned away from the simplicity which is in Christ, as Eve let herself be seduced by the cunning of the serpent. Paul even goes the length of rebuking the Corinthians, in the following verse, for the facility with which they receive strange teachers who bring to them *another Jesus* than the one he has proclaimed to them, *a Spirit* and *a gospel* different from those they have already received.[1] Such expressions forbid us to suppose that the doctrine of those emissaries was not greatly different from his own and that of the Twelve, especially from the Christological standpoint (*another Jesus*). There is certainly here something more than the simple legal teaching previously imported into Galatia. It was sought to allure the Corinthians by unsound speculations, and Paul's teaching was disparaged as poor and elementary. Hence his justification of himself, even in the First Epistle, for having given them only "milk and not meat" (iii. 1, 2). Hence also his lively polemic against the mixing of human wisdom with the gospel (iii. 17–20). All this applied to the preaching of *those of Christ*, and not in the least to that of Apollos. We do not know what exactly was the nature of their particular doctrines. It did violence to the person and work of Jesus. Thus is explained perhaps Paul's strange saying, 1 Cor. xii. 3, "No man speaking by the Spirit of God saith: Jesus is accursed!" The apostle is speaking of spiritual manifestations which made themselves heard even in the Church. There were different kinds of them, and their origin required to be carefully distinguished. The truly Divine addresses might be summed up in the invocation, "Jesus, Lord!" While the inspirations that were not Divine terminated—though one can hardly believe it—in declaring Jesus accursed! Such a fact may however be explained when we call to mind a doctrine like that professed by the Judaizing Christian Cerinthus, according to which the true Christ was a celestial virtue which had united itself to a pious Jew called Jesus, on the occasion of His baptism by John the Baptist, which had communicated to Him the power of working miracles, the light from which His doctrines emanated, but which had abandoned Him to return to heaven, before the time of the Passion; so that Jesus had

[1] This seems to me the only possible meaning, whatever Beyschlag may say. The καλῶς ἠνείχεσθε signifies, "Ye took it very well" (when that happened); "it did not revolt you in the least."

suffered alone and abandoned by the Divine Being. From this point of view what was to prevent one pretending to inspiration from exclaiming: "What matters to us this crucified One? This Jesus, accursed on the cross, is not our Christ: He is in heaven!" It is known that Cerinthus was the adversary of the Apostle John at Ephesus; Epiphanius—on what authority we know not—asserts that the First Epistle to the Corinthians was written to combat his heresy. It is remarkable that this false teacher was Judaizing in practice, like our false teachers at Corinth. But it is by no means necessary to suppose that it was exactly this system which Paul had in view. At this epoch many other similar Christological theories might be in circulation fitted to justify those striking expressions of Paul: "another Jesus, another Spirit." Thus the name of Christ, in the title which these persons took, *those of Christ,* would be formulated, not only in opposition to the name of the apostles, but even to that of Jesus.[1] Let us mention, by way of completing this file concerning *those of Christ,* the apostle's last word, 1 Cor. xvi. 22, a word certainly written with his own hand after the personal salutation which precedes: "If any man love not the Lord, let him be anathema!" It is the answer to the "Jesus anathema!" of xii. 3.—We adopt fully, therefore, the words of Kniewel (*Eccl. Cor. vetustiss. dissentiones,* 1842), who has designated *those of Christ* as "the Gnostics before Gnosticism."

There remains only one question to be examined in regard to *those of Christ.* In the Second Epistle to the Corinthians Paul twice speaks of persons whom he designates as οἱ ὑπερλίαν ἀπόστολοι, that is to say, "the apostles transcendentally" or "archapostles" (xi. 5 and xii. 11), and whom he puts in close connection with the *Christ-party.* Baur alleges that he meant thereby to designate the Twelve ironically as authors of the mission carried out against his work by their emissaries

[1] Origen relates, *Cont. Cels.* vi. 2, of the sect of the Ophites, that no one was received into their order until he had cursed Jesus; and of the Gnostic Carpocrates (about the year 135), that he taught that when the question was put to Christians in times of persecution: "Believest thou in the crucified One?" it was allowable to answer: "No;" for it was Simon of Cyrene who was crucified, and not Jesus, and we needed to adhere only to the spiritual Christ. Comp. Volkmar, *Ursprung der vier Evangelien,* p. 45.

arrived at Corinth. We have here, according to him, the most striking testimony of the directly hostile relation between Paul and the original apostles; it was they, and James in particular, who furnished those disturbers with letters of recommendation. On this interpretation rests Baur's whole theory regarding the history of primitive Christianity. But this application is inadmissible for the following reasons:

1. The Twelve had recognised in principle Paul's preaching of the gospel among the Gentiles, and had found nothing to add to it; they had moreover declared his apostleship to have the same Divine origin as Peter's; this is narrated by Paul, Gal. ii. 1–10. How should they have sent persons to combat such a work?

2. If the expression "archapostles," which Paul evidently borrows from the emphatic language of the party recruited by those persons at Corinth, referred to the Twelve, who in that case must have been considered as being an *apostle* in the simple sense of the word? Obviously it could only be Paul himself. His adversaries would thus unskilfully have declared an apostle the very man whose apostleship they were contesting!

3. In the passage, 2 Cor. xi. 5, Paul says, "he supposes he is not a whit behind the archapostles, for though he be rude in speech (ἰδιώτης), he is not so in knowledge." Now it cannot be held that the Twelve were ever regarded at Corinth as superior to Paul in the gift of speech, first because they had never been heard there, and next because they were themselves expressly characterized as ἀγράμματοι and ἰδιῶται (Acts iv. 13).

4. The apostle gives it to be understood ironically (xii. 11 seq.) that there is a point undoubtedly in which he acknowledges his inferiority as compared with the archapostles, to wit, that he has not, like them, been supported by the Church. Now it is certainly of the Church of Corinth that he is speaking when he thus expresses himself; this appears from xi. 20, where he describes the shameless conduct of those intruders toward his readers. As yet the Twelve had not been at Corinth; it is not they, but the newcomers whom Paul designates by this ironical name.

5. How could St. Paul, justly asks Beyschlag, in this same

letter in which he recommends a collection for the Church *of the saints* (that of Jerusalem), designate men sent by that Church and by the apostles, as "servants of Satan whose end will be worthy of their works" (xi. 14, 15)?

Hilgenfeld and Holsten have themselves given up applying the expression archapostles to the Twelve. Agreeably to their explanation of the term, *those of Christ,* they apply it to those immediate disciples of Christ, such as the Seventy or the brothers of Jesus, from whom the party had taken its name, and whom the apostles had recommended to the Corinthians. But this comes nearly to the same, for the brothers of Jesus were at one with the apostles (1 Cor. ix. 5). And besides, how would *those of Christ* have contrasted their leaders as archapostles with Peter himself?

There remains only one explanation. These archapostles are no other than the emissaries of the ultra-Judaizing party, of whom we have spoken. Their partisans at Corinth honoured them with this title, to exalt them not only above Paul, but above the Twelve. We have already explained how this was possible: their object was to break the agreement which was established between the Twelve and Paul; and the letters of recommendation which they had brought were the work of some one of those high personages at Jerusalem who sought to possess themselves of the direction of the Church.

In the following verses, the apostle summarily condemns the state of things he has just described, and defends himself from having given occasion to it in any way. Edwards thinks he can divide the discussion which follows, thus: condemnation of the parties by the relation of Christianity: 1, to Christ, i. 13–ii. 5; 2, to the Holy Spirit, ii. 6–iii. 4; 3, to God, iii. 5–20; 4, to believers, iii. 21–23. But such tabulation is foreign to the apostle's mind. His discussion has nothing scholastic in it. The real course of the discussion will unfold of itself gradually.

Ver. 13. "Is the Christ divided? was Paul crucified

for you,[1] or were ye baptized in the name of Paul?" Several editors (Lachmann, Westcott, and Hort) and commentators (Meyer, Beet) make the first proposition an indignant affirmation: "Christ then among you is rent, lacerated!" But the transition to the following questions does not in that case seem very natural. It is more simple to see here a question parallel to the two following, these being intended to show the impossibility of the supposition expressed by the first. The term *the Christ* denotes the Messiah in the abstract sense, that is to say, the Messianic function, rather than the person who filled the office. The latter would certainly be designated by the name of Jesus or by the word *Christ* without article. How, besides, could we suppose the person of Christ divided into four? Paul means,—is the function of Christ, of Saviour, and founder of the kingdom of God divided between several individuals, so that one possesses one piece of it, another, another? Taken in this sense, the question does not refer only to the fourth party, but to the other three. "Are things then such that the work of salvation is distributed among several agents, of whom Jesus is one, I another?" and so on. Edwards explains thus: "Is not that which is manifested of the Christ in Paul at one with that which is manifested of Him in Apollos, etc. . . . ? Do not these elements form all one and the same Christ?" The meaning is good, but one does not see how in this case the censure applies to the fourth party, which the question, thus understood, seems on the contrary to justify. It is evident the word, Christ, cannot be applied with Olshausen to the

[1] B D read περι υμων, instead of υπερ υμων.

Church, nor with Grotius to the doctrine of Christ.—The form of the first question admitted of a reply in the affirmative or negative; that of the two following (with μή) anticipates a negative answer, serving as a proof to the understood negative answer which is evidently given to the first: "Paul was not, however, crucified for you, was he, as would be the case if a part belonged to him in the work of salvation?" He might have put the same question in regard to Apollos and Cephas; but by thus designating himself he naturally disarms the other parties.—The first question relates to the function of Saviour, the second to that of Lord, which flows from it. Edwards well indicates the relation between the two. The cross has made Christ the head of the body. By baptism every believer becomes a member of that body. The reading of the *Vatic.*, περὶ ὑμῶν, cannot be preferred to that of all the other documents: ὑπὲρ ὑμῶν. This ὑπέρ signifies *in behalf of.* The idea, *in the place of,* which would be expressed by ἄντι, is included in it only indirectly. It is by substitution that the benefit expressed by ὑπέρ has been realized. *To be baptized in the name of . . .* signifies: to be plunged in water while engaging henceforth to belong to Him in whose name the external rite is performed. In the *name* there is summed up all that is revealed regarding him who bears it, consequently all the titles of his legitimate authority. Baptism is therefore a taking possession of the baptized on the part of the person whose name is invoked over him. Never did Paul dream for an instant of arrogating to himself such a position in relation to those who were converted by his preaching.

Yet this would be implied by such a saying as, *I am of Paul.*—And not only could it not be so in fact, but the apostle is conscious of not having done anything which could have given rise to such a supposition.

Vers. 14–16. "I thank God[1] that I baptized none of you but Crispus and Gaius, 15. lest any should say that ye were baptized[2] in my name. 16. I baptized also the household of Stephanas; besides, I know not whether I baptized any other."—Paul's thanksgiving proves that there had been no calculation on his part, when, as a rule, he had abstained from baptizing. The real motive for the course he followed will be given in ver. 17. This is why he is thankful for the way in which God has ordered things. Rückert objects to this reasoning, that if Paul had wished to form a party of his own, he might have done so by getting one of his friends to baptize in his name, as well as by baptizing himself. True; but would he easily have found any one to lend himself to such a procedure? What seems to me more difficult to explain is the supposition itself, on which this passage rests, of a baptism administered in another name than that of Jesus. This idea, which now seems to us absurd, might seem more admissible in the first times of the Church, especially in Greece. In the midst of the religious ferment which characterized that epoch, new systems and new worships were springing up everywhere; and in these circumstances the distance was not great between an eminent preacher like Paul, and the head of a school, teaching and labour-

[1] א B omit τω θεω (*to God*), which T. R. reads with the other Mjj.

[2] א A B C read εβαπτισθητε (*ye were baptized*); T. R. with all the other documents, εβαπτισα (*I baptized*).

ing on his own account. The apostle of the Gentiles, no doubt, passed in the eyes of many as the true founder of the religion which he propagated; and the supposition which he here combats might thus have a certain degree of likelihood. There is no need, therefore, in accounting for this passage, either of Hofmann's hypothesis, according to which there were people at Corinth who boasted of having received baptism at Jerusalem from Peter's own hand,—Paul would thus congratulate himself on not having given occasion to such a superstition,—or for that of Keim and Heinrici, who ascribe a similar superstition to the Apollos-party (see above, p. 65).—The regimen τῷ θεῷ, *to God*, omitted by the *Sinaït.* and *Vatic.*, is unnecessary; it has rather been interpolated than omitted.—Crispus, the ruler of the synagogue at the time of Paul's arrival, had been one of his first converts (Acts xviii. 8); Gaius, his host during one of the stays which followed (Rom. xvi. 23), was also probably one of the first believers. Thus, probably, is explained why Paul had baptized them himself; his two assistants, Silas and Timothy, had not yet arrived from Macedonia, when they were received into the Church. It cannot be held with Beet that Paul deliberately made an exception in these two cases because of their importance: this idea would contradict the very drift of the whole passage. It matters little that in the account given in the Acts the order of events does not agree with what we say here.

Ver. 15. The ἵνα, *that*, refers to the intention of God, who has so ordered the course of things.—It is possible to defend both readings, that of the Alexandrine and that of T. R. The first, *ye were baptized*, might be taken from ver. 15, or be intended to avoid the monotonous repetition of the word *ἐβάπτισα, I baptized.* On the other hand, as Edwards observes, Paul was less afraid of their ascribing a bad motive to him personally, than of their misunderstanding the real meaning of baptism itself; in this sense, the Alexandrine reading suits better.

Ver. 16. The apostle all of a sudden recollects a third exception. Stephanas was one of the three deputies from Corinth who were with Paul precisely at that time.—By the words, *besides I know not . . .*, Paul guards against any omission arising from a new slip of memory. Those who make the inspiration of the Holy Spirit go directly to the pen of the sacred writer, without making it pass through the medium of his heart and brain, should reflect on these words.

Ver. 17. "For Christ sent me not to baptize, but to preach the gospel[1]; not with wisdom of words, lest the cross of Christ should be made of none effect." —Between vers. 16 and 17 the logical connection is this, "If I baptized, it was only exceptionally; for this function was not the object of my commission." The essential difference between the act of baptizing and that of *preaching the gospel*, is that the latter of these acts is a wholly spiritual work, belonging to the higher field of producing faith and giving new birth to souls; while the former rests in the lower domain of the earthly organization of the Church. To preach the gospel is to cast the net; it is apostolic work. To baptize is to gather the fish now taken and put

[1] B reads *ευαγγελισασθαι* instead of *ευαγγελιζεσθαι*.

them into vessels. The preacher gains souls from the world; the baptizer, putting his hand on them, acts as the simple assistant of the former, who is the true head of the mission. So Jesus Himself used the apostles to baptize (John iv. 1, 2); Peter acted in the same way with his assistants; comp. Acts x. 48. Paul certainly does not mean that he was forbidden to baptize; but the terms of his apostolic commission had not even mentioned this secondary function (Acts ix. 15, and xxii. 14, 15). Though he might occasionally discharge it, the object of his mission was different. To the aorist εὐαγγελίσασθαι, the reading of the *Vatic.*, the present εὐαγγελίζεσθαι is to be preferred, which better suits the habitual function.

The connection of the last proposition of ver. 17 with what precedes is not obvious at the first glance. But the study of the following passage shows that we have here the transition to the new development which is about to begin. This transition is made very skilfully: it resembles that of Rom. i. 16, by which the apostle passes from the preface to the exposition of his subject. There might be a more subtle way of appropriating souls to himself than that of baptizing them in his name, even that of preaching in such a way as to attract their admiration to himself by diverting their attention from the very object of preaching: Christ and His cross; now this is excluded by the term *evangelizing* (preaching the gospel), taken in its true sense. Paul means, "I remained faithful to my commission, not only by evangelizing without baptizing, but also by confining myself to evangelizing in the strict sense of the word, that is to say, by delivering my message without adding to it anything of my own." The term *evangelizing* signifies, in fact, to announce good news; it denotes therefore the simplest mode of preaching. It is the enunciation of the *fact*, to the exclusion of all elaboration of reason or oratorical amplification, so that the negative characteristic, *without wisdom of words*, far from being a strange and accidental characteristic added to the term evangelize, is taken from the very nature of the act indicated by the verb. Thus Paul has not only continued steadily in his function as an evangelist; he has at the same time remained faithful to the spirit of his function. He has therefore done absolutely nothing which could have given rise to the formation of a Paul-party at Corinth.—The objective negative οὐ is used because the regimen refers, not to ἀπέστειλε, *sent me*,—in that case the negative would depend on the Divine *intention* in the sending, and the subjective negative, μή, would be required,—but to εὐαγγελίζεσθαι, which denotes the fact of preaching itself.

This second part of the verse contains the theme of the whole development which now follows. The formation of parties at Corinth evidently rested on a false conception of the gospel, which converted it into the wisdom of a school. Paul restores the true notion of Christianity, according to which this religion is above all a fact, and its preaching the simple testimony rendered to the fact: the announcement of the blessed news of salvation (εὐαγγελίζεσθαι). It is thus clear how the second part of the verse is logically connected with the first, the idea of *wisdom of words* being excluded by the very meaning of the term *evangelize*.—The phrase σοφία λόγου, *wisdom of words,* is not synonymous with σοφία τοῦ λέγειν, *the art of speaking well.* The emphasis is rather on the word *wisdom* than on *words.* The former term applies to the matter of discourse; it denotes a well-conceived system, a religious philosophy in which the new religion is set forth as furnishing a satisfactory explanation of God, man, and the universe. The latter bears on the form, and denotes the logical or brilliant exposition of such a system. Most critics think that by this phrase Paul means to allude "to the teaching of Apollos, at once profound and highly flavoured." "The orator preferred to Paul," says Reuss, "was no other than his friend and successor Apollos." We know few commentators who have been able, like Hilgenfeld, to rise above this prejudice, which has become in a manner conventional. As for me, this application seems to be directly contrary to all that Paul himself will afterwards say of Apollos, and to the way in which his teaching is described in the Acts. Paul, in this very Epistle, iv. 4–8, testifies to the closest relation between his own work and that of Apollos. Far from there having been conflict between the two works, that of Paul is represented, iii. 6, under the figure of *planting,* and that of Apollos under that of *watering.* Paul adds, ver. 8: "He that planteth and he that watereth *are one.*" The apostle, on the contrary, characterizes in the following verses the mode of teaching which he would here combat, as belonging to that *wisdom of the world* (ver. 20) which the gospel comes to destroy; he applies to it (iii. 20) these words of a Psalm: "The thoughts of the wise are only vanity;" he accuses it of "destroying the temple of God," and threatens its propagators "with being destroyed" in their turn "by God" Himself (iii. 17, 18); and it is of the teaching of his friend and disciple Apollos that he meant to speak! According to Acts xviii. 27, 28, the whole preaching of Apollos was founded *on the Scriptures*, and not at all on a human speculation which he had brought from Alexandria, as is alleged by those who make him a disciple of Philo. It is even said that "*by the grace* of God he was *very profitable* to those who had believed." The person of Apollos must therefore be put out of the question here: it is impossible even to suppose that all which follows applies to his partisans. We have much more reason to think that those referred to here are the teachers who, under the name *those of Christ*, were propagating strange doctrines at Corinth regarding the person of Christ, and whom Paul accuses, 2 Cor. xi. 2-4, "of corrupting minds from the simplicity which is in Christ," and of beguiling them "as the serpent beguiled Eve."

The systematic and brilliant exposition of the fact of the cross would have the effect, according to Paul's phrase, of κενοῦν, literally *emptying* it. Those who, like Meyer and so many others, apply the foregoing expressions to Apollos, attenuate the meaning of this term as much as possible; according to them, it merely signifies that in consequence of this mode of preaching, the salutary effects of preaching will be ascribed rather to the brilliant qualities of the orator than to the matter of the doctrine, the cross. But this meaning is obviously far from coming up to the idea expressed by the word κενοῦν, *to make void.* Kling comes nearer to the energy of the expression when he refers to the fact that a dialectic and oratorical mode of preaching may indeed produce an intellectual or æsthetical effect, but not transform the egoistical *self*. But if Paul had meant nothing more than this, he would rather have used the word which is familiar to him, *καταργεῖν*, *to deprive of efficacy*. The term *κενοῦν* denotes an act which does violence to the object itself, and deprives it of its essence and virtue. Salvation by the cross is a Divine act which the conscience must appropriate as such. If one begins with presenting it to the understanding in the form of a series of well-linked ideas, as the result of a theory concerning man and God, it may happen that the mind will be nourished by it, but as by a system of wisdom, and not a way of salvation. It is as if we should substitute a theory of gravitation for gravitation itself (Edwards). The fact evaporates in ideas, and no longer acts on the conscience with the powerful reality which determines conversion. The sequel will be precisely the development of this thought.

B. *The nature of the gospel* (1:18-3:4)

The gospel in its essence is not a *wisdom*, a philosophical system; it is a salvation. It is this thesis, summarily formulated in the second part of ver. 17, which the apostle proceeds to develop in the following passage. We have already pointed out, p. 86, the close relation in which it stands to the question that is the subject of this part of the Epistle, that of the parties formed in the Church.

The thesis itself is treated from two points of

view which complete one another: in a first passage, i. 18–ii. 5, the apostle demonstrates it directly; in the second, ii. 6–iii. 4, he prudently limits its application. Undoubtedly the gospel *is* not essentially wisdom; but it nevertheless *contains* a wisdom which is unveiled to the believer in proportion as the new life is developed in him, and which is really the only true wisdom.

The gospel is not a wisdom: (1:18-2:5)

Such, strictly speaking, is the truth which Paul is called to expound to the Corinthians. He demonstrates it to them:

1. By the irrational character of the central fact of the gospel, the cross: vers. 18–25.
2. By the mode of gaining members to, and the composition of their Church: vers. 26–31.
3. By the attitude taken in the midst of them by the preacher of the gospel: ii. 1–15.

Vers. 18–25

Ver. 18. "For the preaching of the cross is to them that perish foolishness; but unto us which are saved it is the power of God."—The *for* announces the proof of the assertion (ver. 17): that to preach the gospel as a word of wisdom would be to destroy its very essence.—The antithesis of the words *foolishness* and *power* is regarded by Rückert and Meyer as inexact, because the opposite of foolishness is wisdom, not force. But these commentators have failed to see that the term wisdom would here have expressed too much or too little: too much for those who reject the gospel, and in whose eyes it can be nothing else than folly; too little for those who are disposed to receive it, and who need to find in it something better than a wisdom enlightening them. As sin is a fact, salvation must be laid hold of above all as a fact, not as a system. It is an act wrought by the arm of God, telling with power on the conscience and on the heart of the sinner: this alone can rescue from ruin a world which is perishing under the curse and in the corruption of sin. —The two datives: τοῖς ἀπολλυμένοις, *to them that perish*, and τοῖς σωζομένοις, *for those who are saved*, have not an exactly similar meaning; the former indicating a simple subjective appreciation, the latter including besides an effective relation, the idea of an effect produced. The participles are in the present, not as anticipating a final, eternal result (Meyer), or as containing the idea of a Divine predestination (Rückert), but as expressing two acts which are passing into fulfilment at the very time when Paul mentions them. In fact, perdition and salvation gradually come to their consummation in man simultaneously with the knowledge which he receives of the gospel.—The addition of the pronoun ἡμῖν, *to us*, is due to the fact that the letter is intended to be read to the believers in full assembly.

This way of treating human wisdom taken by God in the gospel is the fulfilment of threatenings already pronounced against it in the prophetic writings:

Ver. 19. "For it is written: I will destroy the wisdom of the wise, and will set aside the understanding of the prudent."—Isaiah, xxix. 14, had declared at the time when Sennacherib was threatening Judah, that the deliverance granted by Jehovah to His people would be His work, not that of the able politicians who directed the affairs of the kingdom. Was it not they on the contrary who, by counselling alliance with Egypt, had provoked the Assyrian intervention and thus paved the way for the destruction of Judah? It is on the same principle, says the apostle, that God now proceeds in saving the world. He snatches it from perdition by an act of His own love, and without deigning in the least to conjoin with Him human wisdom, which on the contrary He sweeps away as folly.—The verbs in the future, *I will destroy . . . I will set aside*, express a general maxim of the Divine government, which applies to every particular case and finds its full accomplishment in salvation by the cross. Paul quotes according to the LXX., who directly ascribe to God ("I will destroy . . ." etc.) what Isaiah had represented as the result of the Divine act: "Wisdom will perish," etc.—*'Αθετεῖν, to set aside*, as useless or worth nothing. Not only has God in His plan not asked counsel of human wisdom, and not only in the execution of it does He deliberately dispense with its aid, but He even deals its demands a direct contradiction. The following verse forcibly brings out this treatment to which it is subjected in the gospel.

Ver. 20. "Where is the wise? Where is the scribe? Where is the disputer of this age? Hath not God made foolish the wisdom of the[1] world?"—This exclamatory form has the same triumphant tone as in the words of Isaiah of which our passage seems to be an imitation (Isa. xix. 12, xxxiii. 18); comp. in

[1] Τουτου (*of this*) in T. R. is omitted by א A B C D P.

Paul himself xv. 55, and Rom. iii. 27. At the Divine breath the enemy has disappeared from the scene; he is sought for in vain.—Rückert thinks that we should not seek rigorously to distinguish the meaning of the three substantives, that there is here rather a simple rhetorical accumulation. He refers all three to Greek wisdom, with a slight shade of difference in meaning. The emotional tone of the passage might justify this view in any other writer than Paul. But in this apostle every word is always the presentation of a precise idea. The ancient Greek commentators apply the first term, σοφός, *wise*, to Gentile philosophers; the second, γραμματεύς, *scribe*, to Jewish doctors; the third, συνζητητής, *disputer*, to Greek sophists; but, in this sense, the last would be already embraced in the first term. It would therefore be better, with Meyer, to give to the word σοφός a general meaning: the representatives of human wisdom, and to the two last, the more particular sense of Jewish scribe and Greek philosopher. But the term *wisdom*, applying throughout this whole passage to human wisdom represented by the Greeks (ver. 22), I think it more in keeping with the apostle's thought to apply the first term to Greek philosophers, the second to Jewish scribes,—its ordinary meaning in the New Testament; for that of *secretary*, Acts xix. 35, belongs to an altogether special case,—then to unite these two classes in the third term: "those in general who love to dispute," who seek truth in the way of intellectual discussion, by means either of Greek dialectic or Scripture erudition. — The complement, *of this world*, refers undoubtedly to the three substantives, and not only to the last.—The word *αἰών*, *age*, derived either from *ἄω*, *to breathe*, or from *ἀεὶ*, *always*, denotes a period. The Jews divided history into a period anterior to the Messiah—this was what they called *ὁ αἰὼν οὗτος*, *this present age*—and the period of the Messianic kingdom, which they named *ὁ αἰὼν μέλλων*, *the age to come.* But, from the Christian point of view, these two periods are not merely successive; they are partly simultaneous. For the present age still lasts even when the Messiah has appeared, His coming only transforming the actual state of things slowly and gradually. Hence it follows that for believers the two periods are superimposed, as it were, the one above the other, till at length, in consequence of the second and glorious advent of the Messiah, the old gives place entirely to the new.

The second question explains the first. How have the wise of the world thus disappeared? By the way of salvation which God gives to be preached and which has the effect of bringing human wisdom to despair.—The verb *ἐμώρανεν* is usually taken in a declarative sense: "By putting wisdom aside in the most important affair of human life, God has *ipso facto declared* it foolish." But this verb has a more active sense, Rom. i. 22; it would require, therefore, at the least to be explained thus: "He has *treated* it as foolish, by taking no account of its demands." But should there not be given to it a more effective meaning still? "He has, as it were, *befooled* wisdom. By presenting to it a wholly irrational salvation, He has put it into the condition of revolting against the means chosen by Him, and by declaring them absurd, becoming itself foolish." The complement, *of the world,* is not absolutely synonymous with the preceding term, *of this age:* the latter referred rather to the *time,*—the wisdom of the epoch anterior to the Messiah ; the term *world* bears rather on the *nature* of this wisdom,—that which proceeds from humanity apart from God.

But it is asked why God chose to treat human wisdom so rudely. Did He wish to extinguish the torch of reason which He had Himself lighted? Ver. 21 answers this question; it explains the ground of the judgment which God visits on human reason, by the irrational nature of the gospel; to wit, that in the period anterior to the coming of Christ, reason had been unfaithful to its mission.

Ver. 21. "For after that in the wisdom of God the world by wisdom knew not God, it pleased God by the foolishness of preaching to save them that believe."—The γάρ, *for,* does not signify, as Edwards thinks, that the apostle is proceeding to expound the manner in which God has punished wisdom; it introduces the indication of the *ground* why He thought good to deal so severely with it.—'Επειδή, *after that* (ἐπεί), as any one can attest (δή). The δή is added to show that Paul is speaking of a patent fact, on which one may in a manner put his finger. This fact is that of the aberrations to which human reason gave itself up during the times of heathenism, during those ages which the apostle calls, Acts xvii. 30, *the times of ignorance.*

The first proposition describes the sin of reason, and the second—the principal—its chastisement. These two ideas are so developed that the exact correspondence between the sin and the punishment appears from each of the terms of the two propositions. The phrase, *in the wisdom of God*, is not synonymous with the following, *by* (*means of*) *wisdom*. The absence of the complement, *of God*, in the second, of itself shows that the idea of wisdom is taken in the second instance more generally and indefinitely. The matter in question is not a manifestation of the Divine wisdom, but the mode of action followed by human reason, what we should call the exercise of the understanding, the way of reasoning. Hence, also, in this second expression the apostle uses the prep. διά, *by means of*, while in the former, where he is speaking of the wisdom *of God*, he makes use of the prep. ἐν, *in*, which indicates a domain *in which* Divine wisdom has been manifested. It is not difficult to understand what the theatre is of which Paul means to speak, on which God had displayed His wisdom in the eyes of men before the coming of Christ. In the passage Rom. i. 20, the apostle speaks of God's works "in which are visible, as it were, to the eye, from the creation of the world, His invisible perfections, His eternal power and Godhead." In his discourse at Lystra (Acts xiv. 17), he declares that God "has not left Himself without witness before the eyes of men, sending rain from heaven and fruitful seasons, and filling the hearts of men with abundance and joy." In the midst of the Areopagus (Acts xvii. 27), he declares that the end God had in view in distributing men over the face of the earth, was to make them "seek the Lord that they might touch Him as with the hand, and find Him." This universe is indeed, as Calvin says, "a brilliant specimen of the Divine wisdom." In the immense organism of nature, every detail is related to the whole, and the whole to every detail. There we find a perceptible, though unfathomable, system of hidden causes and sensible effects, of efficacious means and beneficent ends, of laws that are constant and yet pliant and capable of modification, which fills the observer with admiration and reveals to his understanding the intelligent thought which has presided over the constitution of this great whole. Man, therefore, only needed to apply to such a work the rational processes, the principles of substance, of causality, and finality, with which his mind is equipped, to rise to the view of the wise, good, and powerful Author from whom the universe proceeds. There was in the work a revelation of the Worker, a revelation constituting what the apostle calls, Rom. i. 19, *τὸ γνωστὸν τοῦ θεοῦ*, "that which is naturally knowable of the Divine person." To welcome the rays of this revelation, and to reconstruct the image of Him from whom it proceeded, such was the noble mission of the reason with which God had endowed man: it should have come by this normal exercise of His gift (*by means of wisdom*) *to know God in His wisdom.* But as Paul expounds, Rom. i. 21, human reason was unfaithful to this mission; man's heart would neither *glorify* God as such, nor even *give thanks to Him,* and reason, thus interrupted in its exercise, instead of rising to the knowledge of the Worker by contemplating the work, deified the work itself. Unable to overlook altogether the traces of the Divine in the universe, and yet unwilling to assert God frankly *as God,* it resorted to an evasion; it gave birth to heathenism and its chimeras.

Some sages, indeed, conceived the idea of a God one and good, but they did not succeed in carrying this vague and abstract notion beyond their schools; the popular deities continued to stand, dominating and falsifying the human conscience. In Israel alone there shone the knowledge of a God, one, living, and holy; but this light was due to a special revelation. We must therefore take care not to include the Jewish revelation, as Meyer and Holsten do, in the meaning of the expression: ἐν τῇ σοφίᾳ τοῦ θεοῦ, *in the wisdom of God.* Not till afterwards, vers. 22–24, will the apostle deal with the Jews, and that in a way absolutely subsidiary, and applying to them a quite different term to that of *wisdom.* As little must we give to the words, *in the wisdom of God,* as is done by Rückert and Reuss, the meaning of our modern phrase, "*In His unfathomable design,* it pleased God. . . ." This interpretation would make the wandering of human wisdom the effect of a Divine decree. Men thus find the doctrine of absolute predestination which they ascribe to the apostle. But how can we fail to see that this would be to exculpate reason at the very moment when the apostle is engaged in condemning it? Finally, it is not in accordance with the thought of the apostle to see in the expression διὰ τῆς σοφίας, *by means of wisdom,* with Billroth and Holsten, the indication of the obstacle which hindered man from arriving at the knowledge of God: "After that, *through an effect of its wisdom,* the world knew not God in . . ." Very far from condemning the exercise of the natural understanding, the apostle on the contrary charges this faculty with turning aside from its legitimate use.

After the ground of the punishment, the punishment itself. The term εὐδόκησεν indicates an act, not of arbitrariness, but of freewill: "He judged good," evidently because it was good in fact. Reason had used its light so ill that the time was come for God to appeal to a quite different faculty.—He therefore presents Himself to man with a means of salvation which has no longer, like creation, the character of wisdom, and which is no more to be apprehended by the understanding, but which seems to it, on the contrary, stamped with folly: a Crucified One! The gen. τοῦ κηρύγματος, *of the preaching*, designates the apostolic testimony as a known fact (art. *τοῦ, the*).—This term includes the notion of authority: God lays down His salvation; He offers it such as it has pleased Him to realize it. There is nothing in it to be modified. It is to be accepted or rejected as it is. It need not be thought with Hofmann and others, because of the prep. διά, *by means of*, that this regimen is the counterpart of διὰ τῆς σοφίας, *by means of wisdom*, in the preceding proposition. It corresponds rather to the regimen ἐν τῇ σοφίᾳ τοῦ θεοῦ, *in the wisdom of God*, in His original revelation which had the character of wisdom. Man not having recognised God in this form by the healthy use of his understanding, God manifests Himself to him in another revelation which has the appearance of folly. The reason why Paul here uses the prep. *by*, to correspond to the *in* of the first proposition, is easily understood. *In* His revelation in the heart of nature, God waits for man; He would see if man, by the exercise of his understanding, will be able to discover Him: "to see whether they will put their hand on Him," as it runs, Acts xvii. 27. It is this expectant attitude which is expressed by the ἐν, *in.* Not having been found thus, God now takes the initiative; He Himself seeks man by the proclamation of salvation. Hence Paul in this case employs the διά, *by means of,* which denotes the prevenient activity.

The term which in the second proposition is the true counterpart of the phrase διὰ τῆς σοφίας, *by means of wisdom* (in the first), is found at the end of the sentence; it is the word τοὺς πιστεύοντας, *them that believe.* The faculty to which God appeals in this new revelation is no longer reason, which had so badly performed its task in reference to the former; it is *faith.* To an advance of love like that which forms the essence of this supreme manifestation, the answer is to be given, no longer by an act of intelligence, but by a movement of confidence. What God asks is no longer that man should investigate, but that he should give himself up with a broken conscience and a believing heart.—Finally, to the two contrasts: *in the wisdom of God and by the foolishness of preaching; by wisdom,* and, *them that believe,* the apostle adds a third: that of the two verbs *know* and *save.* Man ought originally to have known God, and by this knowledge have been united to Him; it was for this end that God revealed Himself to his understanding in an intelligible way. Man not having done so, God now comes to *save* him, and that by means absolutely irrational. Man, first of all, will have to let himself be snatched from perdition and reconciled to God by a fact which passes beyond his understanding. Thereafter he will be able to think of knowing. It would seem to follow from these words of the apostle, that if reason had performed its task of *knowing* God, it would not have been necessary for God to *save* man; a sound philosophy would have raised him up to God. The apostle gives no explanation on this head; but his thought was probably this: if man had risen by his wisdom to the true knowledge and worship of God, this legitimate use of his reason would have been crowned by a mode of salvation appropriate to the laws of this faculty. In the second revelation the Divine wisdom would have rayed forth with more brilliance still than in the first. Thus the character, so offensive to reason, under which the salvation offered to man presents itself in the preaching of the cross, is the consequence of the abuse which reason made of its faculty of knowing. If it had developed itself as an organ of light, the mode and revelation of salvation would have been adapted to its wants. Obviously we cannot know what salvation and the preaching of salvation would have been in such different conditions.

The verse which we have just explained contains in three lines a whole philosophy of history, the substance of entire volumes. As from the standpoint of Judaism the apostle divides history into two principal periods, that of law and that of grace, so from the standpoint of Hellenism he also distinguishes two great phases, that of the revelation of God in wisdom, and that of His revelation in the form of foolishness. In the first, God lets Himself be sought by man; in the second, He seeks man Himself. Such is the masterly survey which the apostle casts over the course of universal history. There was singular adroitness on his part in throwing such a morsel as this development to those Corinthians, connoisseurs in wisdom as they affected to be, and apt to overlook the apostle's superiority. Paul says to them, as it were, "You will have speculation, and you think me incapable of it; here is a specimen, and true also! It is the judgment of God on your past." But at the same time, with what marvellous subtlety of style does he succeed in putting and cramming, as it were, into the two propositions of this verse, all that wealth of antitheses which presented themselves at once to his mind! To construct such a period there needed to be joined to the thought of Paul the language of Plato.

Vers. 22–25 state the historical fact which demon strates the judgment enunciated in ver. 21: The salvation of all, Gentiles and Jews, has really been accomplished by that which is folly in the eyes of the one, and which scandalizes the other.

Vers. 22 and 23. "*For indeed*[1] the Jews require signs,[2] and the Greeks seek after wisdom; 23. but we preach Christ crucified, unto the Jews a stumbling-block, and unto the Gentiles[3] foolishness."—This second ἐπειδή, *for indeed*, should, according to Meyer and Kling, begin a new sentence, the main proposition of which is found in ver. 23: *But as for us, we preach.* The δέ, *but*, would not be irreconcilable with this construction. The δέ is often found in the classics as the sign of the apodosis when this expresses a strong contrast to the preceding proposition (see Meyer); comp. in the New Testament, Col. i. 22. But two reasons are opposed to

[1] All the documents except F G Syr[sch] read και before Ιουδαιοι (*both Jews*).

[2] T. R. with L and Mnn. reads σημειον (*a miracle*).

[3] T. R. reads Ελλησι (*to the Greeks*); but all the Mjj. read εθνεσι (*to the Gentiles*).

this construction: first, the absence of a proper particle to connect this new sentence with the preceding; then the simple logic; for the idea of ver. 22, that Greeks and Jews ask for wisdom and miracles, cannot form a ground for that of ver. 23: that preaching presents a Christ who is to them an offence and folly. The *object* of God, in this mode of preaching, could not have been to scandalize the hearers; in ver. 24 the apostle even expressly adds the opposite thought: to wit, that Christ is to the believers of both peoples power and wisdom. The ἐπειδή of ver. 22 does not therefore begin a new sentence, like that which began ver. 21, and which related to εὐδόκησεν, *it pleased God.* Yet it is not on this account a repetition and amplification of that sentence. The first ἐπειδή (ver. 21) served to explain the rejection visited by God on human wisdom; the second (ver. 22) simply affirms the *reality* of this judgment: "for in reality, as experience may convince you, while men demand wisdom and miracles, we preach to them a Saviour who is quite the contrary, but who nevertheless is to them who receive Him miracle and wisdom." We have not to see, then, in these three verses the development of the words, *them that believe . . .* (Hofmann), nor that of the term, "*foolishness* of preaching" (Rückert, de Wette); they give the proof of the fact of the decree expressed in ver. 21: "It pleased God to save . . ." (Billroth, Osiander, Beet, Edwards). What a strange dispensation! The world presents itself with its various demands: prodigies, wisdom! The cross answers, and the apparent meaning of the answer is: weakness, foolishness! But to faith its real meaning is: power, wisdom! Thus in the gospel God rejects the demands of the world so far as they are false, but only to satisfy them fully so far as they are legitimate.

The apostle divides the ancient world into two classes of men; those whom God has taken under His direction and enlightened by a special revelation, *the Jews;* the others whom He "has left to walk in their own ways" (Acts xiv. 16), the Gentiles, designated here by the name of their most distinguished representatives, *the Greeks.* The two subjects are named without an article: *Jews, Greeks;* it is the category which the apostle would designate.—The particle καί . . . καί, *both . . . and*, indicates that each of those groups has its demand, but that the demands are different. For the Jew it is *miracles*, the Divine materialized in external prodigies, in sensible manifestations of omnipotence. The plural σημεῖα, *miracles*, ought certainly to be read with almost all the Mjj.; the received text reads the singular σημεῖον, *a sign*, with L only. This last reading is undoubtedly a correction occasioned by Matt. xii. 38 and xvi. 1, where the Jews ask from Jesus *a sign* in heaven. Paul's object is not to refer to a particular fact, but to characterize a tendency; this is indicated by the plural, signs, and yet more signs! For it is of the nature of this desire to rise higher and higher in proportion as it is satisfied. "On the morrow after the multiplication of the loaves," says Riggenbach, "the multitudes ask: What signs doest thou then?" Every stroke of power must be surpassed by a following one yet more marvellous.—The Greek ideal is quite different; it is a masterpiece of *wisdom*. the Divine intellectualized in a system eloquently giving account of the nature of the gods, the origin, course, and end of the universe. This people, with their inquisitive and subtle mind, would get at the essence of things. The man who will satisfy Greek expectation will be, not a thaumaturge, making the Divine appear grossly in matter, but a Pythagoras or a Socrates of double power.—Thus we have the two great figures of the ancient world ineffaceably engraved. Let us remark, finally, with what delicacy the apostle chooses the two verbs used to characterize the two tendencies: for the Jew, αἰτεῖν, *ask;* the miracle comes from God—it is received; for the Greek, ζητεῖν, *seek;* system is the result of labour—it is discovered. It is obvious that in this description of the ancient world, from the religious standpoint, the figure of the Jew is placed only for the sake of contrast; the Greeks are and remain, according to the context, the principal figure. It is always wisdom contrasted with the *fact* of salvation.

Ver. 23. As ver. 22 went back on the first proposition of ver. 21, "The world by wisdom knew not God in His wisdom," so ver. 23 (with ver. 24) goes back on the second, "It pleased God to save by . . ." The δέ is strongly adversative. By the ἡμεῖς, *we*, the subject of these verses is also contrasted with that of the previous verse. I mean the preachers of the crucified Christ with the unbelieving Jews and Greeks. Instead of a series of acts of omnipotence transforming the world, or of a perfect light cast on the universe of being, what does the apostolic preaching offer to the world? A Crucified One, a compact mass of weakness, suffering, ignominy, and incomprehensible absurdity! There is enough there absolutely to bewilder Jewish expectation; in the first place, it is a stone against which it is broken. Σκάνδαλον: what arrests the foot suddenly in walking and causes a fall. And the Greek? The term *Christ* seems at first sight not to apply to the expectation of this people. But all humanity, as is seen in Greek mythology, aspired after a celestial appearance similar to that which the Jew designated by the name of *Christ*, after a communication from above capable of binding man to God. So Schelling did not hesitate to say, when paraphrasing ver. 5 of the prologue of John: "Christ was the light, Christ was the consolation of the Gentiles."[1] The apostle can therefore speak also of the Christ in relation to the Greeks. But here again, what a contrast between the desired manifestation and the reality! Must not salvation by the Crucified One be to the Greek, instead of the solution of all enigmas, the most sombre of mysteries?—The participle ἐσταυρωμένον is an attribute, *as crucified*, otherwise it would be preceded by the article; the two substantives, σκάνδαλον and μωρίαν, are appositions.

It might be asked, no doubt, in connection with this verse, whether Jesus, by His numerous miracles, did not satisfy the Jewish demand? But His acts of miraculous power had been annulled, so to speak, in the eyes of the Jews by the final catastrophe of the cross, which seemed to have fully justified His adversaries, and did not suffer them to see in Him any other than an impostor or an agent of diabolical power.

And yet as to this preaching which so deeply shocks the aspirations of men, Jews and Gentiles, so far as

[1] "*Christus war der Heiden Licht; Christus war der Heiden Trost.*"

these are false, it turns out—and daily experience demonstrates the fact—that received with faith, it contains both for the one and the other the full satisfaction of those same aspirations so far as they are true :

Ver. 24. "But unto those [*of them*] which are called, both Jews and Greeks, Christ the power of God, and the wisdom of God."—The αὐτοῖς δέ forcibly separates the called, Jews and Gentiles, from the mass of their fellow-countrymen, while identifying them with it so far as their past life was concerned : "But unto them, those same Jews and Gentiles, once become believers . . ." Those Jews and Greeks themselves who saw in the preaching of the cross only the contrary of what they sought, — weakness, foolishness, — no sooner become believers than they find in it what they asked : power and wisdom.—The term κλητοί, *called*, here includes the notion of *believers*. Sometimes calling is put in contrast to the acceptance of faith ; thus in the maxim, Matt. xxii. 14 : "Many called, few chosen." But often also the designation called implies that of accepter ; comp. i. 1, 2, and Rom. viii. 30 ; and it is certainly the case here, where the term τοῖς κλητοῖς, *the called*, stands for τοὺς πιστεύοντας, *them that believe* (ver. 21). The apostle exalts the Divine act in salvation ; he sees God's arm laying hold of certain individuals, drawing them from the midst of those nationalities, Jewish and Gentile, by the call of preaching ; then, when they have believed, he sees the Christ preached and received, unveiling Himself to them as containing exactly all that their countrymen are seeking, but the opposite of which they think they see in Him.—The accusative Χριστόν might be regarded as in apposition to the *Χριστόν* of ver. 23 (Hofmann); but the phrase, "to preach Christ as Christ," is unnatural; *Χριστόν* should therefore be regarded as the direct object of *κηρύσσομεν*, *we preach* (ver. 23), and the two substantives, *power* and *wisdom*, are not attributes (*as* power, *as* wisdom), but cases of simple apposition, in the same category as *σκάνδαλον* and *μωρίαν*. The apostle here omits the *ἐσταυρωμένον* not without purpose. For the two terms, *power of God* and *wisdom of God*, embrace not only the Christ of the cross, but also the glorified Christ.—The complement, *of God*, contrasts with the power and wisdom of the world, that wisdom and power of a wholly different nature, which on that account the world does not recognise. The *power of God* is the force from above, manifested in those spiritual wonders which transform the heart of the believer; expiation which restores God to him, the renewal of will which restores him to God, and in perspective the final renovation, which is to crown these two miracles of reconciliation and sanctification (ver. 30). The *wisdom of God* is the light which breaks on the believer's inward eye, when in the person of Christ he beholds the Divine plan which unites as in a single work of love, creation, incarnation, redemption, the gathering together of all things under one head, the final glorification of the universe. The believer thus finds himself, as Edwards says, in possession of "a salvation which is at once the mightiest miracle in the guise of weakness [this for the Jew], and the highest wisdom in the guise of folly [this for the Greek]." [1]

[1] Edwards, p. 31.

But how can that which is apparently most feeble and foolish thus contain all that man can legitimately desire of power and light in point of fact? The apostle answers this question by the axiom stated in ver. 25.

Ver. 25. "Because the foolishness of God is wiser than men; and the weakness of God is stronger than men."—The neuter adjectives, *τὸ μωρόν, τὸ ἀσθενές*, do not denote qualities belonging to the being of God Himself, but certain categories of Divine manifestations having the two characters mentioned. If one dared translate thus,—the weak, foolish product of Divine action. And God's masterpiece in these two respects is the cross. The gen. *τοῦ θεοῦ*, *of God*, is at once that of origin and property. The second member of comparison is sometimes completed by paraphrasing,—"wiser than *the wisdom* of men; stronger than *the strength* of men;" but this supposed ellipsis weakens the thought. The apostle means: wiser than men with all their wisdom; stronger than men with all their strength. When God has the appearance of acting irrationally or weakly, that is the time when He triumphs most certainly over human wisdom and power.

What God makes of human wisdom has been clearly manifested by the character of folly which He has stamped on the salvation offered by Christ; it is equally so in the choice God makes of those in whom this salvation is realized by faith in the preaching of it. Such is the idea of vers. 26–31, a passage in which the apostle shows us the most honoured classes of society remaining outside the Church, while God raises up from the very depths of Gentile society a new people of saved and glorified ones who hold everything from Him.

Vers. 26–31

Ver. 26. "For[1] see your calling, brethren, there are among you not many wise men after the flesh, not many mighty, not many noble."—This mode of recruiting the Church confirms the conclusion drawn above from the nature of the gospel. Hence the γάρ, *in fact*, which is certainly the true reading. It was not the leading classes of Corinthian society which had furnished the largest number of the members of the Church. The majority were poor, ignorant, slaves. God shows thereby that He has no need of human wisdom and power to support His work.—The verb βλέπετε should be taken as imperative and not as indicative: "Open your eyes, and see that . . ." This meaning is not incompatible with the γάρ. Meyer rightly quotes Sophocles, *Phil.* v. 1043: ἄφετε γὰρ αὐτόν.—Paul has come near to his readers in reminding them of this fact which touches them so closely; hence the address,—*brethren!*—The word κλῆσις, *calling*, has sometimes been taken in the sense wrongly given to the word *vocation*, as denoting social position. But this meaning is foreign to the New Testament. Paul would describe by it the manner in which God has proceeded in drawing this Church by the preaching of the gospel from the midst of the Corinthian population. Jesus had already indicated a similar dispensation in Israel, and had rendered homage to it: "Father, I thank Thee because Thou hast hid these things from the

[1] Instead of γαρ (*for*), D E F G read ουν (*therefore*).

wise and prudent, and hast revealed them unto babes. Even so, Father, for so it seemed good in Thy sight" (Matt. xi. 25, 26). The fact was not therefore accidental; it belonged to the Divine plan. God did not wish that human wisdom should mix its alloy with His: the latter was to carry off victory alone. Meyer makes πολλοί, *many*, the subject, and σοφοί, *wise*, the attribute: "There are not many who are wise . . . mighty . . ." But in this sense the πολλοί must have been completed by the genitive ὑμῶν, *of you.* It is better simply to understand the verb ἔστε, "*Ye are not* many wise."—In the adjunct κατὰ σάρκα, *according to the flesh*, the word *flesh* denotes, as it often does, human nature considered in itself, and apart from its relation to God. This adjunct has not been added to the two following terms, *mighty . . . noble*, because, as de Wette says, these latter obviously denote advantages of an earthly nature.—**Οἱ δυνατοί**, *mighty*, denotes persons in office; εὐγενεῖς, *the noble*, persons of high birth, descendants of ancient families.[1]

Vers. 27–29. "But God hath chosen the foolish things of the world to confound the wise, and God hath chosen the weak things of the world to confound the things which are mighty; 28. and base things of the world, and things which are despised, and

[1] Hasenklever (*Jahrb. f. prot. Theol.*, 1882, i.) states that, as is proved by the inscriptions in the Catacombs, most of the members of the Primitive Church, at Rome also, belonged to the lower or middle classes (bakers, gardeners, tavern-keepers, freedmen, a few advocates); he observes that the Christians are characterized in *Minutius Felix* (vii. 12) as *indocti, impoliti, rudes, agrestes;* and he rightly regards this fact as the most eloquent testimony in favour of Christianity, which has gained victory over hostile powers, without any external aid, by the sole force of its internal virtue.

things[1] which are not, to bring to nought things that are; 29. that no flesh should glory before God."[2]—The emotion with which the apostle signalizes this providential fact is betrayed by the threefold repetition of the words *God has chosen*, by the thrice expressed contrast between the two opposite terms, *God* and *the world*, and by the emphatic position of the object (thrice repeated) at the beginning of the proposition. The neuter form of the three adjectives, *foolish, weak*, and *vile*, contrasted as it is with the masculines preceding, the *wise*, the *mighty*, the *noble*, is not used accidentally; these neuters indicate a mass in which the individuals have so little value that they are not counted as distinct personalities. So the word τὸ ἀνδράποδον, *the domestic* [thing], is used for slaves. The term ἐκλέγεσθαι does not here denote a decree of eternal predestination, but the energetic action whereby God has taken to Him (the Middle λέγεσθαι) from the midst of the world (ἐκ) those individuals whom no one judged worthy of attention, and made them the bearers of His kingdom. The strong, the wise, etc., are thus covered with shame, because the weak, etc., are not only equal to them, but preferred. In the phrase, *things which are despised*, is concentrated all that disdain with which the ignorant and weak and poor were overwhelmed in the society of heathendom; and the final term, *things which are not*, expresses the last step of that scale of abasement on which those beings vegetated. The subjective negative μή before ὄντα does not deny real

[1] T. R. with B E L P Syr. reads και here (*also* or *even*); this word is omitted by the other Mjj.

[2] T. R. with C Syr. reads αυτου (*Him*) instead of θεου (*God*).

existence, as would be done by *οὐ*, but the recognition of any value whatever in public opinion; all those beings were to it *as non-existent.* The *καί*, which in the received text precedes the last participle, is omitted by most of the Mjj. The meaning *even* would be the only suitable. But how could we explain this *καί*, if it were authentic, otherwise than the previous ones? It is better therefore to reject it. The asyndeton is perfectly in place; it makes this last word the summary, and, so to speak, the accumulation of all the preceding. There is a corresponding gradation in the verb *καταργεῖν*, *to annul* (bring to nought), to reduce to absolute powerlessness, which takes the place of the preceding and less strong term *καταισχύνειν*, *to cover with confusion.* Already the wise and mighty were humiliated by the call addressed to their social inferiors; now they disappear from the scene. And for what end does God act thus? The apostle answers in the following sentence:

Ver. 29. *Ὅπως*, *that thus.* This conjunction denotes the *final* end with a view to which all the preceding *ἵνα*, *that*, indicated only means. The negative *μή*, according to a well-known Hebraism, applies to the verb only, and not at the same time to the subject *all flesh;* for Paul does not mean to say that *some* flesh at least should be able to glory. The word *flesh* is taken in the sense pointed out, ver. 26. No man, considered in himself and in what he is by his own nature, can glory before God, who knows so well the nothingness of His creature. The words, *all flesh*, seem to go beyond the idea of the preceding propositions, where the question was merely of the humiliation of the wise and mighty. But is it not enough that these last be stripped of the right of glorying that the whole world may be so along with them, the weak and ignorant being already abased by their natural condition? As Hofmann says: The one party are humiliated because with all their wisdom and might, they have not obtained what it concerned them to reach, salvation; the other, because if they have obtained it, it is impossible for them to imagine that it is by their own natural resources that they have come to it.

The mode of the *Divine calling*, to which the apostle pointed the attention of his readers, ver. 26, had two aspects: the first, the rejection of things wise and mighty; the second, the choice which had been made of things foolish and weak. The first of these two sides has been expounded, vers. 26–29; the apostle now presents the second.

Vers. 30, 31. "But of Him are ye in Christ Jesus, who, on the part of God,[1] has been made unto us wisdom, as also[2] righteousness and sanctification and redemption; 31. that, according as it is written, He that glorieth, let him glory in the Lord."—Rückert, with his usual precision, asks whether the thought expressed in these two verses is logically connected with the passage as a whole; he answers in the negative, and sees in those two verses only an appendix. We think, as we have just pointed out, that they are on the contrary the indispensable complement of the passage. Vers. 26–29: "See what your calling is not,

[1] T. R. with L Syr. places ημιν (*us*) before σοφια (*wisdom*), while the nine other Mjj. It. place it after that word

[2] F G read: και δικαιοσυνή, instead of δικαιοσυνη τε και.

and understand why!" Vers. 30-31: "See what it is, and again understand why!" The δέ is therefore adversative to the vain boasting of the things that are wise, etc., henceforth reduced to silence; there is opposed the cry of triumph and praise on the side of the things foolish and weak; for ver. 31 evidently forms the counterpart of ver. 29.—'Ἐξ αὐτοῦ, *of Him* (*God*), expresses the essential idea of this conclusion: If things that were not have now become something, it is due to God alone; ἐκ therefore indicates the origin of this spiritual creation; comp. Eph. ii. 9. Ὑμεῖς, *ye*: the things formerly weak, powerless, despised. This pronoun resumes the address of ver. 26. — Calvin, Rückert, Hofmann see in the word ἐστέ, *ye are*, a contrast to the preceding expression: things *which are not.* "It is of God that your transition from nothingness to being proceeds." The words, *in Christ*, would thus express, secondarily, the means whereby God has accomplished this miracle. Others strictly connect ἐξ αὐτοῦ with ἐστέ in the sense of the Johannine phrase: to be of God, to be born of God. But these two explanations have the awkwardness of separating the words ἐν Χριστῷ 'Ιησοῦ from ἐστέ; whereas we know well how frequently Paul uses the form εἶναι ἐν Χριστῷ. It is better therefore, as it seems to me, to translate thus: "It is of Him that ye *are in Christ;*" that is to say: "It is to God alone that you owe the privilege of having been called to the communion of Christ, and of having thereby become the wise and mighty and noble of the new era which is now opening on the world." The following proposition will explain, by what Christ Himself *was*, these glorious effects of communion with Him.—The phrase εἶναι ἐν, *to be in,* denotes two moral facts: first, the act of faith whereby man lays hold of Christ; second, the community of life with Him contracted by means of this act of faith. In this relation the believer can appropriate all that Christ was, and thus become what he was not and what he could not become of himself.—In the proposition which follows, the apostle substitutes for ὑμεῖς, *ye,* the pronoun ἡμῖν, *to us;* and this because the matter in question now is, what Christ is objectively to men, and not the subjective appropriation of Him by believers.—The aor. Passive, ἐγενήθη, is generally regarded (Meyer, Edwards) as equivalent in meaning to the aor. Middle, ἐγένετο, *was, became.* It is, indeed, a form springing up from the dialects, and which was only introduced latterly into Attic Greek. But that does not, we think, prevent there being a difference in the use of the two forms. The passive form occurs in the New Testament only some fifty times, compared with about 550 times that the aor. Middle is used; and it is easy in each of those instances to see the meaning of being made, which is naturally that of the *Passive.* I think, therefore, that we must translate, not, "has been" or "has become," but, *has been made.* This is confirmed by the adjunct ἀπὸ θεοῦ, *on the part of God.* Yet it should be remarked that the apostle has not written ὑπὸ θεοῦ, "*by* God." The ἀπό, *on the part of,* weakens the passivity contained in the ἐγενήθη, and leaves space for the free action of Christ. In using the words ὃς ἐγενήθη, *who has been made* (historically), the apostle seems to have in mind the principal phases of Christ's being: *wisdom,* by His life and teaching;

righteousness, by His death and resurrection; *sanctification,* by His elevation to glory; *redemption,* by His future return.

The received text places the pronoun ἡμῖν, *to us,* before σοφία, *wisdom.* This reading would have the effect of bringing this substantive into proximity with the three following, from which it would only be separated by the adjunct ἀπὸ θεοῦ; and this adjunct again can be made to depend, not on the verb ἐγενήθη, but on the substantive σοφία itself: "wisdom coming from God." In this case there would be nothing to separate it from the three following substantives. But the authority of the mss. speaks strongly in favour of the position of ἡμῖν after σοφία; and the adjunct ἀπὸ θεοῦ depends more naturally on the verb ἐγενήθη; it serves to bring out the idea of the ἐξ αὐτοῦ at the beginning of the verse. It must thus be held that the apostle's intention was clearly to separate the first substantive from the other three, and this has led him to interpose between σοφία and the other substantives the two adjuncts: ἡμῖν and ἀπὸ θεοῦ.—If it is so, it is impossible to maintain the relation which Meyer establishes between the four substantives, according to which they express three co-ordinate notions: 1, that of knowledge of the Divine plan revealed in Christ (*wisdom*); 2, that of salvation, regarded on the positive side, of the blessings which it brings (*righteousness* and *holiness*); 3, that of salvation from the negative view-point, deliverance from condemnation and sin (*redemption*). Meyer rests his view on the fact that the particle τε καί binds the second and third terms closely together, isolating them at the same time from the first and fourth. But regard to philological exactness may have misled this excellent critic here, as in so many instances. Why, in that case, interpose the two adjuncts between the first term and the second? And is it not obvious at a glance that the three last terms are in the closest relation to one another, so that it is impossible to separate them into two distinct groups, co-ordinate with the first? This is what has led a large number of commentators (Rückert, Neander, Heinrici, Edwards, etc.) to see in the three last terms the explanation and development of the first: Christ has become our *wisdom*, and that inasmuch as He has brought us the most necessary of blessings, salvation, consisting of *righteousness*, *sanctification*, and *redemption*. It is easy in this case to understand why the first term, which states the general notion, has been separated from the other three which are subordinate to it. Only this explanation is not in harmony with the special sense of religious *knowledge*, in which the word *wisdom* is taken in the passage. *Wisdom*, as a plan of salvation, is contrasted, ver. 24, with salvation itself as a Divine *act* (δύναμις, *power*). How does it come to be identified here with salvation itself? The word, therefore, cannot denote anything else here than the *understanding* of the Divine plan communicated to man by Jesus Christ. The parallel ver. 24 leads us, I think, to the true explanation which Osiander has developed. According to him, the last three terms are the unfolding of the notion of δύναμις, *power*, as the counterpart to that of *wisdom*. In Christ there has been given first the knowledge of the Divine plan, whereby the believer is rendered wise; then to the revelation there has been added the carrying out of this salvation, by the acquisition of which we become strong. This effective salvation includes the three gifts: *righteousness, holiness, redemption.* The only objection to this view is that the τε καί would require to be placed so as to connect together σοφία on the one hand, and the following three terms on the other, whereas by its position this copula rather connects δικαιοσύνη and ἁγιασμός (*righteousness* and *holiness*), as the second καί connects the third substantive with the fourth. But the omission of a copula fitted to connect the first substantive with the other three may have been occasioned by two circumstances: 1, the two adjuncts which separate the word wisdom from the following three; 2, the difficulty of adding to the copula τε καί, which joins the word *righteousness* with the following, a new copula intended to connect it with the preceding (see Osiander). Then, if it is remembered that the *salvation* described in the last three substantives is only the realization of the Divine *plan* designated by the first (*wisdom*), it will be seen that these may be placed there as a sort of grammatical apposition to the first.

The idea of δικαιοσύνη, *righteousness,* is that developed by Paul in the first part of the Epistle to the Romans, chaps. i.–v. It is the act of grace whereby God removes the condemnation pronounced on the sinner, and places him relatively to Himself, as a believer, in the position of a righteous man. The possibility of such a Divine act is due to the death and resurrection of Christ.—The term ἁγιασμός, *holiness* or *sanctification,* is the Divine act which succeeds the preceding, and whereby there is created in the believer a state in harmony with his position as righteous. It is the destruction of sin by the gift of a will which the Holy Spirit has consecrated to God. This act is that described by the apostle in the succeeding passage of the Epistle to the Romans, vi. 1–viii. 17. I have sought to show in my Commentary on that Epistle, at vi. 19, that the term ἁγιασμός denotes sanctification, not in the sense in which we usually take the word, as a progressive human work, but as the state of holiness divinely wrought in believers. Justification is generally regarded as a gift of God; but sanctification as the work by which man ought to respond to the gift of righteousness. St. Paul, on the contrary, sees in holiness a Divine work no less than in righteousness: Christ Himself is the holiness of the believer as well as his righteousness. This new work is due to His exaltation to glory, whence He sends the Holy Spirit; and by Him He communicates His own life to the justified believer (John vii. 39, xvi. 14). If, then, our righteousness is Christ *for* us, our sanctification is Christ *in* us, Christ *is* our holiness as well as our righteousness.[1] — He is finally our *redemption*, our complete and final deliverance. Such is the meaning of the word ἀπολύτρωσις. The development of this third idea is found, Rom. viii. 18–30. This deliverance, which consists of entrance into glory, is the consummation of the two preceding acts of grace. It is by His glorious advent that Jesus will thus eman-

[1] How evident it is, from this so well-marked distinction between *righteousness* and *sanctification*, that in the eyes of the apostle *righteousness* had the declarative sense, and *sanctification* alone contained the sense of an effectual communication!

cipate justified and sanctified believers from all the miseries of their present state, and give them an external condition corresponding to their spiritual state. Meyer asserts that this meaning of ἀπολύτρωσις would demand the complement τοῦ σώματος, *of the body*, as in Rom. viii. 23. But the term *redemption* embraces much more than the simple fact of the resurrection of the body. It has the wide sense in which we find it, Luke xxi. 28 ; Eph. i. 14, and iv. 30 ; Heb. xi. 35. As to the view of Meyer, who sees in this word only the negative side of moral redemption, deliverance from guilt and sin, it is certainly too weak, and besides this blessing was already implied in the two foregoing terms.—If we so obviously find in the Epistle to the Romans the development of the three last terms, in which the notion of salvation is summed up, we cannot forget that the development of the first, σοφία, occurs immediately afterwards in the same Epistle, in chaps. ix.-xi., which so admirably expound the whole plan of God.—Calvin rightly observes that it would be hard to find in the whole of Scripture a saying which more clearly expresses the different phases of Christ's work.

Ver. 31. In ver. 29 all human glorying has been declared to be excluded; in this, the apostle invites the new people, the wise and mighty whom God has raised up by preaching, to strike up a song of praise, but of praise relating to God alone.—The term κύριος, *Lord*, in the passage of Jer. ix. 23, 24, quoted by the apostle, denotes Jehovah ; but it could hardly fail in the mind of Paul to be applied at the same time to Christ, by whom the Lord has done this work, and who has so often received the title in this chapter.—Here is no commonplace exhortation to glorify the Lord. What we have to see in these words is a hidden antithesis, which is sufficiently explained by the passage, iii. 21–22: "Therefore let no man glory in men; for all things are yours, whether Paul, or Apollos, or Cephas; and ye are Christ's, and Christ is God's." What they have become by the gospel, they owe to the Lord alone, and not to His instruments. For as to what they have been able to do, it is He who has done it by them; therefore it is He only who is to be glorified. The imperative καυχάσθω does not correspond grammatically to the conjunction ἵνα, *in order that.* But the apostle directly transforms the logical conclusion into the moral exhortation contained in the prophetic saying.

This last word sums up the dominant idea of the whole passage from ver. 13: viz. Christ's unique place in relation to the Church. Let others be teachers, He alone is κύριος; for He alone has paid the ransom. To Him alone be the praise!

As God in the salvation of humanity has set aside human wisdom, first of all by the mode of salvation which He has chosen, then by the mode of propagation which He has adopted for the Church, the apostle has also set it aside in his mode of preaching; such is the idea which he develops in closing this passage, ii. 1–5. Thus all is harmonious in the Divine work: the gospel, the work, the preacher.

2:1-5

St. Paul applies to his own ministry at Corinth the principle which he has just laid down, and shows that he has been faithful to it. This is the conclusion of the whole passage.

Vers. 1, 2. "And I also, brethren, when I came to you, came not with excellency of speech or of wisdom, declaring unto you the testimony[1] of God; 2. For I determined not to know[2] anything[3] among you, save Jesus Christ, and Him crucified."—In the first word, κἀγώ, *and I also*, there is contained the connection between this conclusion and the passage as a whole. It does not signify, as de Wette thought: "I, as well as the other apostles," but: "I also, like the gospel itself." Paul has abstained, in harmony with the nature of the gospel, from seeking his strength in the help of human eloquence or wisdom: like Evangel, like evangelist.—The form ἐλθὼν ἦλθον is a frequent expression in Greek (see examples in Edwards), the object of which is to emphasize the verbal notion. The idea the apostle would bring out is that it was with this full-drawn plan that he arrived among them. This method was not the result of a passing state of mind, or of painful experiences he might have made at Corinth in a different way; from his first step in their city, his resolution was taken.—The adjunct καθ' ὑπεροχήν does not bear on the verb ἦλθον, *I came;* it rather explains the mode of preaching than that of

[1] ℵ A C Syr^sch Cop. read μυστηριον (*the mystery* of God). T. R. with the seven other Mjj. It.: μαρτυριον (*the testimony*).

[2] T. R. reads του before ειδεναι (*for* knowing), with L only.

[3] B C P place τι before ειδεναι; the others after.

arriving (Meyer). It therefore qualifies the complex phrase ἦλθον καταγγέλλων, *I came declaring.* The word ὑπεροχή denotes strictly the act of overhanging, or the thing which overhangs; hence superiority, pre-eminence. By Byzantine writers it is used in the sense, "Your Excellency." There is a slight touch of irony in the use of this sonorous and emphatic word. —This exhibition of superiority which he disdained might have been that of philosophic depth (σοφίας), or that of dialectic and oratorical form (λόγου). He would no more have the one than the other.—The term καταγγέλλειν is here chosen deliberately to denote preaching. He came as a man who simply *announces* (καταγγέλλων) a fact. And this is what is expressed by the use of the word τὸ μαρτύριον, *the testimony,* to designate the gospel. The matter in question is not a system of ideas to be exhibited, but merely a testimony rendered to a fact. The genitive θεοῦ is that of the author and not of the object. The idea: the testimony which has God for its subject, would be much too general and would have little ground in the passage. Paul means that he has simply reproduced the testimony which goes forth from God, inasmuch as it is God who, after having effected salvation, has charged him to proclaim it. The reading of the *Sinaït.*, μυστήριον, followed by Westcott and Hort, Edwards, etc., is absolutely misplaced in this context, though Edwards tries to account for it by reference to σοφία. This word μυστήριον has been imported here from ver. 7.—We must note well the two adjuncts, πρὸς ὑμᾶς, *among you,* and ὑμῖν, *to you;* the more that we shall again meet in ver. 2 with the same idea in the *εν ὑμῖν, among you.* On another theatre the apostle would not perhaps have guarded himself with so much care against the danger of lending to the gospel another force than that which properly belongs to it. But arriving at a city like Corinth, where he knew that philosophical and literary curiosity reigned, the apostle had said to himself that, to prevent the Divine work from being corrupted in its essence, preaching must from the first have the simplest character and address itself solely to the conscience. Origen, and in our day Neander, have thought that this resolution was the consequence of the failure which Paul had experienced at Athens when using a more philosophical procedure in his preaching. But the apostle here represents this method as connected with the very essence of the gospel; and it must be remembered that his discourse at Athens was not preaching strictly so called. He had first of all to explain himself in reference to the accusation raised against him, and only after that could he come to the proclamation of salvation; this is what he was about to do at the moment when he was interrupted.

Ver. 2. This verse confirms the preceding (γάρ), supporting it by the idea that this mode of acting was the result of a plan fixed beforehand. The term ἔκρινα, *I judged good,* is well explained by Heinrici by means of Cicero's phrase: *Mihi judicatum est.* Comp. vii. 37; 2 Cor. ii. 1. The apostle does not say, "*I determined* (judged good) not to know . . ." but, "*I did not judge good to know* . . ." He intentionally set aside the different elements of human knowledge by which he might have been tempted to prop up the preaching of salvation. He deemed that he ought not to go in quest of such means. The word τοῦ, *for* or *to the end of*, which the received text reads before the infinitive εἴδεναι, *to know*, emphasizes, a little too much perhaps, the idea of a resolution taken after reflection.—Paul might have used the word *say* instead of *know*. But the latter implies a renunciation, not only outward but inward, of the use of those foreign elements.—By *Jesus Christ*, the apostle understands His manifestation in general, His life, death, and Messianic dignity. Yet, while confining himself to this elementary theme of preaching, he might still have found means to recommend Jesus to the attention and admiration of the wise; in Jesus Himself he believed that he should exhibit only the side that was least attractive to human wisdom, but alone able to save,—*Jesus Christ crucified*,—so much did he dread giving rise to cases of adherence which would have rested only on an intellectual or æsthetical, and consequently superficial, attraction. The ἐν ὑμῖν, *among you*, however, leaves room for the idea that, where he has not to reckon with this danger, he will allow himself to go beyond this limit; comp. ver. 6. But the true servant of Christ thinks of converting before giving himself up to the pleasure of instructing.

In ver. 3, before finishing the development of this idea, the apostle reminds the Corinthians how his *personal attitude* at Corinth corresponded to this humble form which he determined to give to His teaching.

Ver. 3. "And I was with you in weakness, in fear, and in much trembling."—The words καὶ ἐγώ, *and I*, are not the repetition of the κἀγώ of ver. 1; they announce a new feature subordinate to the preceding and in agreement with it. As he did not seek to render his preaching brilliant in matter or form, so in his personal demeanour he did not affect the airs of one assured of success. He felt and showed only one feeling, that of his own weakness. Addressing himself to this Gentile community, he had not, as among Jews, the point of support supplied by the prophecies. On the other hand, he surrendered what might have been his help in his new surroundings — depth of thought and charm of language. What remained to him? Humanly speaking, he felt like one disarmed; hence the ἐν ἀσθενείᾳ, *in weakness* And this feeling of weakness went the length of *fear*, when he weighed the gravity of a work like his, and the responsibility it laid on him. By repeating the prep. ἐν before τρόμῳ, "and *in* trembling," which Paul does not do in the other instances when he joins these two substantives (2 Cor. vii. 15; Eph. vi. 5; Phil. ii. 12), he distinguishes the second from the first more precisely; fear even produced in him a sort of physical tremor. Perhaps he also felt himself humbled by the weakness of his outward appearance (2 Cor. x. 10). All this sufficiently explains the terms of this verse, without the necessity of having recourse to fear of persecutions, of which Chrysostom thinks, or even to the supposition of ill-health, according to Rückert. It is interesting to compare the picture which Paul here traces of his inward frames with the narrative of the external facts of his ministry in Acts xviii. The first of these pictures remarkably completes the second, and explains why the Lord found it necessary to grant to His servant the vision, related Acts xviii. 9, and to say to him, like a friend encouraging his friend: "Fear not; speak and be not silent."—The words *I was with you* embrace not only his public teachings, but his private conversations and all his personal relations.—What a contrast between this humble, even timid, attitude of the apostle, and the bold confidence of the Greek rhetorician stepping before his auditory as a man sure of the success of his person and piece!

Vers. 4, 5. "And my speech and my preaching were not with persuasive[1] words of wisdom,[2] but in demonstration of the Spirit and of power; 5. that your faith should not stand in the wisdom of men, but in the power of God."—The apostle returns from his person to his preaching. *Λόγος*, *speech*, and *κήρυγμα*, *preaching*, have been distinguished in many ways: "My discourses in general, and especially my preaching" (Meyer); or, "My private conversations and my public discourses" (Neander, Rückert, etc.). I rather think that λόγος applies to the matter, and κήρυγμα to the form; the λόγος is the gospel itself; the κήρυγμα is the testimony the apostle renders to it. Neither the one nor the other has been corrupted in his work by the infiltration of human elements or by self-seeking. — The adj. πειθός is not known in classic Greek, in which the word πιθανός is used for *persuasive*. But it is nevertheless regularly formed from the verb πείθω; comp.

[1] Πειθοις (*persuasive*) is read in ℵ A B C D E L P Vulg. Or. Eus., etc. Macar. Chrys. read πιθανοις. Some Mnn. It. Syr[sch] Or. (twice) Eus. (twice) and others read πειθοι (*persuasion*). This reading requires us to read λογων or λογου, instead of λογοις, with some Fathers and Versions.—Λογοις is omitted by F G.

[2] Ανθρωπινης (*human*) is added here by T. R., after A C L P and some Fathers.

φειδός, from φείδομαι; and it is possible that in the apostle's day πειθός belonged only to the spoken language. Some documents have substituted for this adjective the dative πειθοῖ of the substantive πειθώ, *persuasion* (*Itala:* "in *persuasione* sapientiæ verbi"). Heinrici adopts this reading, though it is almost entirely destitute of authorities, because of the fine contrast between this word πειθώ and the following term, ἀπόδειξις. But in that case we should have to read λόγου or λόγων, which are only found in very few authorities, and which are evidently corrections. The adj. ἀνθρωπίνης, *human*, found in the received text, is insufficiently supported.—Instead of endeavouring to satisfy the understanding by means of a system (*wisdom*) ably presented (*persuasive discourses*), the apostle has sought his strength in action of a wholly different nature, in what he calls "the *demonstration of Spirit and of power.*" The word ἀπόδειξις indicates a clearness which is produced in the hearer's mind, as by the sudden lifting of a veil; a conviction mastering him with the sovereign force of moral evidence; comp. xiv. 24, 25.—The gen. πνεύματος, *of Spirit*, is the complement of cause; it is the Divine Spirit alone who thus reveals the truth of salvation; comp. Eph. i. 17, 18. We have to represent this Spirit to ourselves acting at once in him who speaks and in him who hears, in such a way as to make the light pass, through the intervention of the spoken word, from the mind of the one into the mind of the other. The second gen. δυνάμεως, *of power*, is the complement of quality: it denotes the mode of the Spirit's action; it is, so to speak, a taking possession of the human soul, of its understanding and will, by the inward ascendency of the truth. Chrysostom, and in our day, Beet, apply these expressions to the outward miracles which St. Paul sometimes wrought by the power of the Holy Spirit (2 Cor. xi. 12; Rom. xv. 19). Such an interpretation, allowable in the infancy of exegesis, should now be no longer possible. The apostle has just been stigmatizing the going after miracles on the part of the Jews, and we are to suppose him saying here that he sought to render the faith of the Corinthians immovable by the evidence of miracles!

Ver. 5. *Ἵνα, in order that,* indicates the apostle's object in the course he has followed. He was not ignorant that a faith, founded on logical arguments, could be shaken by other arguments of the same nature. To be solid, it must be the work of the power of God, and in order to be that, proceed from a conviction of sin and a personal appropriation of salvation, which the Spirit of God alone can produce in the human soul. The preacher's task in this work lies, not in wishing to act in the place and stead of the Spirit with the resources of his own eloquence and genius, but in opening up the way for Him by simple testimony rendered to Christ.

By these last words, we are brought back to the point of departure of the whole passage, i. 18: the gospel is not a wisdom, but a power; not a philosophy, but a salvation. If the Corinthians were divided into parties, it was because they had failed to know this truth. By making the gospel a system, they had changed the Church into a school, and its ministers into teachers and rhetoricians. Hence it is that St. Paul begins by re-establishing in the mind of the Corinthians the true notion of the gospel. But some of his expressions might lead us to suppose that wisdom was banished from the domain of the gospel. Now this was not what the apostle had meant; and it is this possible misunderstanding which he sets aside in the following passage, where he shows that if the gospel is not essentially wisdom, it nevertheless *contains* a wisdom, and that the true wisdom, superior to all that the human understanding could have discovered.

The gospel contains a wisdom: (2:6-3:4)

The apostle had already declared in passing, i. 23, 24, that for Jews and Gentiles Christ crucified, received by faith, becomes not only the *power of God*, but also the *wisdom of God*. This is the thought which he develops in the passage, which forms in a sense the antithesis, and thereby the complement of the preceding. The first proposition of ver. 6 states its theme, just as the second part of i. 17 contained the summary of the passage i. 18–ii. 5.

Ver. 6. "Howbeit we speak wisdom among them that are perfect, yet not the wisdom of this world, nor of the princes of this world, that come to nought."—The δέ is rather restrictive than adversative. It is intended to limit the idea previously developed, that the cross is not a wisdom. In the case of him who has once experienced the salvation it brings to man, it does not fail to become a light which illumines his understanding and directs his whole life. It is obvious in this sense why the term σοφία, *wisdom*, heads the sentence in the original: it is the essential word, and in a manner the summary, of the passage.

This first proposition has been understood in two very different ways. Some (Chrysostom, Luther, Calvin, Beza, Grotius, Olshausen, Heinrici, etc.) think that Paul, when speaking of *οἱ τέλειοι, the perfect,* means all believers, and that *σοφία, wisdom,* denotes the gospel in the ordinary sense of the word. "But," the apostle says, it is held, "this preaching of the cross, which seems folly to unbelievers, is wisdom in the eyes of believers." This meaning seems to us inadmissible. The term *οἱ τέλειοι, the perfect,* is too special to be taken as the simple equivalent of *οἱ πιστοί, believers.* In ver. 1 of chap. iii. the word *τέλειος* is replaced by *πνευματικός, spiritual,* and the latter is opposed to *νήπιος,* the infant, which cannot speak yet. The same contrast reappears in *τέλειος γίνεσθαι* and *νηπιάζειν,* xiv. 20 ; comp. also Eph. iv. 13, 14 ; Heb. v. 13, 14. Now in all these passages *νήπιος* denotes, not the unconverted, but believers, believers, however, who are only at the first steps of the new life, and whose conversion needs yet to be confirmed. "Ye are yet carnal," says the apostle to the Corinthians, iii. 3, to explain this state of infancy. The word *perfect* has therefore a meaning much narrower than *believer.* It denotes the state of the *mature man,* in opposition to that of the infant. Paul thereby denotes believers who have reached, not absolute perfection (comp. Phil. iii. 12–17), but the full maturity of Christian faith and life. Heinrici objects that in Christianity there is no aristocracy, and Holsten that according to Paul every believer has received the Spirit, and that the Spirit cannot make progress. To the first objection Rückert has already made answer, that every believer being called to that state of maturity, all aristocratic distinctions are *ipso facto* banished. And as to the second, if the Spirit is not open to progress, the believer's life may be gradually penetrated by this perfect principle. Does not the apostle say to the Galatians (iv. 19): "My little children, of whom I travail in birth again until Christ be formed in you." The perfect are therefore in his eyes the most confirmed Christians in whom the new life has attained the normal stature of Christ (Eph. iv. 13, 14).—The form λαλεῖν ἐν is equally incompatible with the interpretation before us. The ἐν, *in*, would in that case mean: *in the eyes of, in the judgment of.* This preposition may sometimes have this meaning with verbs containing the idea of being or appearing; comp. xiv. 11. But with the verb λαλεῖν this sense is inadmissible. The *in* cannot be taken otherwise than in the local sense: *among, in the midst of.* Paul means that when he is in the midst of confirmed believers, mature Christians, he feels himself free to set forth the treasures of wisdom contained in the gospel; comp. Col. ii. 3: "Christ, in whom are hid all the treasures of wisdom and knowledge." For then the question is no longer one of conversion to be wrought or confirmed. He can therefore, as he says, iii. 1, present the gospel, not as the *milk* of babes, but as the *meat* of the strong. This is the meaning which has been recognised by Erasmus, Bengel, de Wette, Rückert, Reuss ("as to philosophy, I preach it to mature men"), Osiander, Neander, Hofmann, Edwards, etc. It is mistaken or obscured in Oltramare's version: "Nevertheless it is wisdom which we teach among the perfect."

To the wisdom which Paul reserved for exposition to

full-grown men in Christ there doubtless belonged what he expounds in passages such as Rom. ix.–xi. (God's plan in regard to the salvation of Jews and Gentiles), in the Epistles to the Ephesians and to the Colossians (the cross as the centre of the history of the universe, as the bond of union between the first and the second creation, as the means of first uniting Jews and Gentiles, and then men and angels, under the sovereignty of Christ, their common head); finally, also in chap. xv. of our Epistle (the Christian eschatology). These admirable designs of God, which have guided and still guide all His dispensations toward men, and whose gradual realization is being effected by the Christian economy, were things which Paul expounded as a teacher, not as a missionary. For they can indeed promote the growth of believers in knowledge and love; but they are not what is needed to convert sinners. It is not the light which rays from the cross which changes the heart, it is the cross itself.

The subject of the verb λαλοῦμεν might be: "I and the other apostles;" but the first verses of chap. iii. show that it is of himself—including, perhaps, his fellow-labourers—that Paul is thinking. His object, indeed, is not to set forth a theory regarding the preaching of the gospel in general, but to justify the manner in which he himself exercised this ministry at Corinth.—The term λαλεῖν is purposely chosen; it denotes communications which are not, like the καταγγέλλειν or the κηρύσσειν, preachings properly so called.—It has been asked whether the apostle meant by the term τέλειος to allude to the position of those *initiated* into the Greek mysteries (τελεταί), and there has been alleged in favour of this supposition the word μυστήριον, *mystery*, which he uses in ver. 7. But in the Epistle to the Hebrews the term τέλειος is used in the same sense as here, and yet nothing is less probable than an allusion to the Greek mysteries in that letter. And as to the word μυστήριον, it refers, in the language of St. Paul, not to a fact into which one man initiates another, but to a plan hidden in God, and which He alone unveils. The word, besides, frequently drops from the pen of the apostle, and that where all allusion to the mysteries would be out of place (Rom. xi. 25, xvi. 25; Eph. iii. 4; Col. i. 27, etc.).

In the following passage the apostle successively develops the three terms embraced in the theme which is stated, ver. 6ª:

Σοφίαν, *wisdom*, vers. 6ᵇ–9.

Λαλοῦμεν, *we speak*, vers. 10–13.

'Εν τοῖς τελείοις, *among the perfect*, vers. 14–16.

Thereafter he concludes by applying all he has just said to his own teaching, iii. 1–4.

VERS. 6ᵇ–9

The apostle describes wisdom, of which he speaks from the viewpoint of its superhuman origin (vers. 6ᵇ and 7), then from that of its impenetrable obscurity to the natural understanding (vers. 8 and 9).—And first, its origin, what it is not (ver. 6ᵇ), and what it is (ver. 7).

This wisdom is not a conception due to the mind of the world, nor even to the genius of its most illustrious representatives. The δέ indicates the resumption of the idea of σοφία, which is about to be developed; comp.

the δικαιοσύνη δέ, Rom. vi. 22.—On αἰών, see on i. 20.—The ἄρχοντες, *princes of this world*, are not, as has been thought by Origen, Ambrosiaster, Bertholdt, the demons. Some have alleged the Johannine expression ὁ ἄρχων τοῦ κόσμου and Eph. vi. 12. But how could Paul say of the demons, in ver. 8, that if they had known Jesus Christ, they would not have crucified Him? Precisely the opposite would be the case. It is equally mistaken to think with others, of the Greek philosophers, who could not be accused of having crucified the Lord (ver. 8). Paul rather means those who in his time directed the national mind of Israel, those who were the authorities in the Sanhedrim, and perhaps, also, of the Jewish and Gentile representatives of political power in Israel, such as Herod and Pilate. These representatives of human intelligence and politics took part directly or remotely in the execution of the Divine plan, without even suspecting it. And so its growing accomplishment goes to make them disappear. The present participle τῶν καταργουμένων, *who are abolished*, is connected by Meyer with the near date of the Parousia, and by Rückert with God's unchangeable decree. It seems to me that it is simpler to regard it as indicating the actual fact: in proportion as the power of the gospel increases on the earth, the representatives of human wisdom lose their dominion, which will end by escaping from their hands altogether.—In the following verse the apostle indicates the true origin of evangelical wisdom.

Ver. 7. "But we speak the wisdom of God,[1] which is a mystery, the hidden wisdom, which God pre-

[1] T. R. with L reads σοφιαν θεου; the others, θεου σοφιαν.

ordained before the ages, unto our glory;"—This verse is the antithesis of the foregoing one (ἀλλά, *but*). The term λαλοῦμεν, *we speak*, is repeated because of the remoteness of this verb in ver. 6.—The gen. θεοῦ, *of God*, is that of origin and possession. The workshop whence this plan has proceeded, where it remains shut up till its revelation, is the mind of God Himself. The ἐν μυστηρίῳ, *in mystery*, or *in the form of mystery*, is naturally joined with the principal term σοφία, *wisdom*, which the apostle aims to distinguish positively, in opposition to the negative definitions of the former verse. The word *mystery* has taken in theological language a meaning which it has not in the New Testament, to wit, a truth which human reason cannot fathom. In Paul's writings it simply signifies a truth or a fact which the human understanding cannot of itself discover, but which it apprehends as soon as God gives the revelation of it. Thus Jesus says, Luke viii. 10: "It is given to you to know the mysteries of the kingdom," and Paul applies the word mystery to things which we perfectly comprehend; for example, Rom. xvi. 25, to the general plan of salvation; Eph. iii. 4, to the calling of the Gentiles; Rom. xi. 25, to the restoration of the Jews; in our Epistle, xv. 51, to the transformation of the faithful at the moment of the Parousia. The term is here contrasted with a system having the spirit of man for its author (ver. 6), and which consequently does not need to be revealed. Many commentators, Erasmus, Rückert, de Wette, Osiander, Meyer, Hofmann, Edwards, Beet, make the adjunct ἐν μυστηρίῳ depend on the verb λαλοῦμεν: "We speak of this wisdom in the form of a mystery;" or, as

Beet says, "in words containing a secret of infinite value, and which only they understand to whom God reveals it, the τέλειοι." But this idea of a speaking on the part of the apostle taking place mysteriously, and, as it were, in secret, is foreign to all we know of his procedure. The sense equally contradicts the use of the term μυστήριον by Paul; for the word refers, not to the relation of one man to another, but to that of God to man.[1] Meyer attempts to meet this last objection; he translates: "We speak this wisdom as being a Divine mystery;" but the phrase λαλεῖν ἐν cannot have this meaning. Other commentators, such as Theodoret and Thomas Aquinas, connect ἐν μυστηρίῳ with τὴν ἀποκεκρυμμένην: "the wisdom hidden in the form of a mystery." But what would this adjunct add to the idea of the participle? And besides, the article τήν would have its natural place *before* the adjunct. The simplest connection is that which we have followed in beginning; it is that which the position of the words itself indicates. The absence of the article τήν before ἐν μυστηρίῳ has been objected; but when the adjunct is closely united in one and the same idea with the substantive on which it depends, the omission of the article is legitimate; comp. the phrase ἡ δωρεὰ ἐν χάριτι (Rom. v. 15).—The epithet τὴν ἀποκεκρυμμένην, *the hidden*, that is to say, which has remained hidden (perfect participle), is not a repetition. It adds to the idea of the *mode*, contained in ἐν μυστηρίῳ, the notion of *time*. This plan, while a secret conceived by God and known to Him alone, might have been revealed much earlier, from the beginning of the existence of humanity; but

[1] See the exegesis on xiv. 2.

it pleased Him to keep silence about it for long ages (*μυστηρίου χρόνοις αἰωνίοις σεσιγημένου*, Rom. xvi. 25; "which was not revealed to other generations as it is now," Eph. iii. 5). It might even be thought that by the article *τήν*, *the*, this long-concealed wisdom is contrasted with another which God had unveiled long before, that of which Paul has spoken, i. 21, which was displayed from the creation of the world in the works of nature (Rom. i. 20).

To these two features which distinguish the wisdom revealed in the gospel from all the products of the human understanding, its higher origin and its non-revelation up to that hour, the apostle adds a third: its saving end in behalf of man, the eternal object of Divine concern.—Some have thought that the term *ὁρίζειν*, *to mark out by limit, to decree*, did not suit the idea of wisdom, and have thought we should understand an infinitive like *γνωρίζειν*, *to make known*: "which God had determined . . . to make known." If this wisdom were only a system or a theory, the verb *ὁρίζειν* might really be applied to it without difficulty. But it should be remembered that the subject in question is a plan to be realized in history, and to which consequently the term *decree* is perfectly suitable. The preposition *πρό*, added to the verb, is afterwards developed in the words, *before the ages*. It is therefore an eternal decree. No doubt eternity is not a *prius* in relation to time; to hold this would be to bring it into time. The *πρό*, *before*, therefore expresses in the inadequate form of temporal priority a superiority of *dignity*, in relation to the decree of creation. The universe exists with a view to man, and man exists with a view to glory. This object, *δόξα*, was the logical *prius* of all that is, of the existence of man himself. These words, *for our glory*, find their explanation in other sayings of the apostle, particularly Rom. viii. 29: "He hath predestinated us to be conformed to the image of His Son, that He might be the firstborn among many brethren;" ver. 17: "Heirs of God and joint-heirs with Christ;" 1 Cor. xv. 28: "That God may be all in all." A society of intelligent and free beings, of men perfectly holy, made capable of reflecting God's glory, and of serving as instruments for His holy action, in filial communion with the Father and in fraternal union with the Son: such was the end which God set before Him in creating the human race. All His particular plans are subordinate to this end. To understand all things from this viewpoint, is the wisdom of which Paul speaks; it is this Divine wisdom which, long kept hidden, is at length unveiled to mankind by the gospel of the cross.

In the two following verses St. Paul *demonstrates* the superhuman and consequently mysterious nature of this wisdom, such as he has just described it negatively and positively in vers. 6, 7. He gives two proofs of it: first, a known fact, ver. 8; next, a prophetic saying, ver. 9.

Ver. 8: "which none of the princes of this world knew; for had they known it, they would not have crucified the Lord of glory;"—The idea of wisdom being that which dominates the entire passage, the pronoun *ἥν*, *which*, should not be made relative to the word *δόξαν*, *glory*, which expresses only a secondary idea, but to the phrase *σοφίαν θεοῦ*, *wisdom of God.*

What proves this wisdom to be a conception superior to all human thought, is the fact that when it was realized in an individual person, the princes of human thought did not discern it; these princes are those spoken of in ver. 6. They had no perception of the glorious destination which God has assigned to humanity, and hence they rejected and crucified Him, who first realized it in His person. The apostle characterizes Jesus Christ as the *Lord of glory.* This title is in keeping with the term δόξα, *glory,* by which he has defined the end of the Divine decree. Glory is the lustre shed by the Divine perfections. This lustre is one day to shine in man, and Jesus Christ, as the first, has realized in Himself that splendour which He is to communicate to all believers. If the representatives of Jewish wisdom and Roman power had understood the higher glory which Jesus was bringing to them, they would undoubtedly have sacrificed that which they possessed. But as they did not discern the former, they chose at any price to maintain their earthly power, and they sought to destroy Him at whose feet they should have abdicated; comp. the parable of the husbandman and the deliberation of the Sanhedrim, John xi. 47. There is an intentional antithesis between the term *crucified,* which indicates the lowest degree of humiliation and suffering, and the title *Lord of glory.* To this proof from fact, the apostle adds the Scriptural demonstration, ver. 9.

Ver. 9: "but as it is written: things which the eye hath not seen, and which the ear hath not heard, and which have not entered into the heart of man, which[1]

[1] A B C read ὅσα instead of ἃ (*which*), as read by all the rest.

God hath prepared for them that love Him."—The grammatical connection of this verse has been variously understood. Erasmus, Estius, Meyer (last ed.), Heinrici, Edwards make ἅ, *things which*, the object of λαλοῦμεν, *we speak*, ver. 7, and consequently in apposition to *the wisdom of God.* But this relation is grammatically forced and logically inadmissible: the apostle does not mean to point out what he speaks among the perfect, but to prove the nature of that wisdom to be sublime and inaccessible to man. Hofmann thinks we should begin a new sentence with ver. 9; the verb on which the ἅ depends would then be ἀπεκάλυψεν, *He revealed*, ver. 10: "What eye hath not seen . . . God hath revealed to us . . ." The δέ of ver. 10 would not be absolutely opposed to this explanation (see on i. 23). But the καθὼς γέγραπται, *as it is written*, would be strangely placed at the beginning of this subordinate sentence. And then, instead of beginning ver. 10 with ἡμῖν δέ, *but unto us*, the apostle ought rather to have written ἀπεκάλυψεν δὲ ἡμῖν ὁ θεός; for the antithesis between the idea of keeping concealed and that of revealing would alone account for the δέ placed at the beginning of the principal sentence. De Wette and Osiander prefer to hold an anacolouthon; the phrase, "things which no eye hath seen," is thrown in, they say, as a description which remains grammatically suspended, "being lost," as de Wette says, "in a mysterious remoteness." It seems to us more natural simply to understand the notion of the verb *to be* in this sense: "It is indeed this very wisdom which is described in the words: Things which the eye hath not seen, etc."—The ἀλλά, *but*, signifies,

"But it could not be otherwise, for Scripture had spoken in these terms." It is difficult to know to what passage of our holy books this quotation refers. Nowhere in the Old Testament are these words literally found. Chrysostom and Theophylact did not know whether they belonged to a prophecy now lost, or if they were taken from Isa. lii. 15 : "They to whom it had not been told shall see, and they who had not heard it shall understand." Origen thought they were taken from an apocryphal writing entitled the Apocalypse of Elias.[1] But nowhere do we find the apostle making similar quotations from uncanonical books, and it cannot be supposed that he would have applied to such books the formula *as it is written*, which would evidently imply the idea of Divine authority. Meyer acknowledges this; only he holds that, by a slip of memory, the apostle, while quoting this apocryphal book, thought he was quoting Isaiah; so also Weiss (*Bibl. Theol.*, p. 274). I cannot see the necessity of so strange a supposition. Jerome already pointed out the true source of this quotation: it is the passage Isa. lxiv. 4 combined with lxv. 17 : "Men have not heard nor perceived, neither hath the eye seen a God beside Thee which worketh for him that waiteth for Him . . ."; and, "The former things shall not be remembered, nor come into mind." Clement of Rome, who, in chap.

[1] We must correct an error which may be caused by the expressions used by Meyer regarding the testimony of Zacharias Chrysopolitanus (of the twelfth century) relative to this declaration of Origen. This author does not say a word to make us suppose "*that he had himself read*" the passage in the apocryphal book of which Origen speaks. Referring simply to that Father, he says: "In nullo enim regulari libro hoc positum invenitur nisi in secretis Eliæ prophetæ" (*Maxima Bibliotheca Veterum Patrum*, t. xix. p. 937).

xxxiv. of his Epistle to the Corinthians, quotes this passage from Paul (with the combination of the two sayings of Isaiah), so well understands it is from the book of this prophet that Paul draws, that he substitutes for the last words of our verse: *τοῖς ἀγαπῶσιν αὐτόν, for them that love Him,* the exact expression of Isaiah (in the LXX.: *τοῖς ὑπομενοῦσιν αὐτόν, for them that wait for Him.* Similar combinations of several prophetic quotations are not rare in Paul's writings; comp. Rom. ix. 33, where are united Isa. xxviii. 16 and viii. 14; and Rom. xi. 26, 27, where Isa. lix. 20 and xxvii. 9 are blended in one).—In the first passage, the prophet, speaking of the work which God will accomplish in favour of His exiled people when He will restore them, says to God: "We can wait until such a God as Thou, like whom is no other, do for us things which surpass all that has been seen and told until now, and all that can be imagined." Or indeed we may suppose that Isaiah transfers himself to the time when all will be accomplished, and that he means: "Never will there have been seen or heard or imagined such things as those which Thou shalt have done for us." No doubt the expression, *come into the mind of man,* taken from Isa. lxv. 17, refers in the context to the memory of things already accomplished, but accomplished merely in prophetic intuition. By combining the three terms *seeing, hearing,* and *entering into the heart,* the apostle wishes to designate the three means of natural knowledge: sight, or immediate experience; hearing, or knowledge by way of tradition; finally, the inspirations of the heart, the discoveries of the understanding proper. By none of these means can man reach the conception of the blessings which God has destined for him. From Irenaeus to Meyer, a host of commentators have applied the ἅ, *things which,* in Paul's sense, to the felicities and glories of heaven. But we have seen, ver. 6[a], that the Divine wisdom of which Paul speaks embraces the kingdom of God in its present form; and the words of ver. 12: "That we might know the things that are freely given to us of God," clearly show that Paul is thinking of the knowledge the believer receives of all the riches of the Divine plans toward him and toward the Church, of what he himself calls, Eph. iii. 18, "their breadth and length, and depth and height." The blessings to come are of course comprehended in such phrases.

The reading ὅσα of A B C has been admitted by Lachmann, Tischendorf, Westcott and Hort, and rightly, as it seems to me, for there is somewhat of enthusiasm in the saying: "those great things which God has prepared." For the *will do,* ποιήσει (LXX.), Paul substitutes the word ἡτοίμασεν, *has prepared,* used also by Clement. The idea is the same, for what God *will do* in the future is precisely what He *has prepared* in the past. The term ἑτοιμάζειν, *to prepare,* recalls the words of Jesus: "the kingdom prepared for you from the foundation of the world" (Matt. xxv. 34), Instead of τοῖς ὑπομενοῦσιν αὐτόν, "for them that wait for Him with perseverance," the apostle substitutes τοῖς ἀγαπῶσιν αὐτόν, *for them that love Him.* This change arises from the fact that the Christian now enjoys the salvation which the Israelite was still waiting for, and is grateful for it to its Author. Thus is exhausted the development of the idea of wisdom (ver. 6[a]).

VERS. 10–13.

With ver. 10 the apostle passes to the development of the second term of his theme: λαλοῦμεν, *we speak.* This wisdom, being God's conception, and inaccessible to the mind of man, how can Paul expound it to his brethren? Vers. 10–12 indicate the means by which he received the knowledge of it; and ver. 13 describes the manner, in keeping with those means, in which he declares it.

Ver. 10. "But[1] God[2] hath revealed them unto us by His Spirit; for the Spirit[3] searcheth all things, yea, the deep things of God."—The δέ is strongly adversative: "This wisdom was hidden, *but* it has been revealed to us." The *for*, which the *Vatic.* reads here, could only refer to the, *we speak*, of ver. 7; but the distance between these two words is too great for this connection to be natural.—The dat. *to us* heads the proposition, to contrast strongly those denoted by this pronoun with the world and its princes to whom the Divine wisdom is veiled. This pronoun neither refers to Christians in general, nor, as Edwards thinks, to the perfect in particular; for the ἡμεῖς, *we*, to whom the revelation is granted, are evidently identical with the *we*, the subject of λαλοῦμεν, *we speak*, in vers. 6, 13. For it is that they may be able to speak that they receive the revelation. Now, in ver. 16, they are expressly contrasted with the τέλειοι, *the perfect*, and

[1] B some Mnn. read γαρ (*for*) instead of δε (*but*).

[2] T. R. with L and Mnn. place ο θεος before απεκαλυψεν; the rest, after.

[3] ℵ A B C here omit αυτου (*of Him*), which is read by T. R. with the rest.

à fortiori with the members of the Church in general. The *we* can therefore only designate the apostles collectively, or Paul himself, with his fellow-labourers. But Paul has no reason to speak here of the other apostles; it is his teaching at Corinth which he wishes to justify (iii. 1–4). It is therefore of himself, and no doubt also of Silas and Timothy (comp. 2 Cor. i. 19), that he is here speaking.—It is natural to place the verb ἀπεκάλυψε, *has revealed*, immediately after ἡμῖν, as is done by almost all the Mjj., and not after the subject ὁ θεός, *God* (T. R.); this is the decisive act from which follows that of the λαλεῖν, *to speak*, ver. 13. —'Αποκαλύπτειν, *to remove the veil*. The text runs, *has revealed to us*, without an object; it is not the thing revealed, it is the act of revelation which Paul would emphasize. By the aorist, he goes back to a determinate point of time, which for him can only be that which he describes, Gal. i. 12, 16. There is undoubtedly a revelation also for the simple believer; comp. Eph. i. 17: "That God may give you the Spirit of wisdom and revelation." But this revelation is only secondary. It is solely the reproduction of the primordial revelation granted to the first interpreters of the Divine thought, and it takes place only through the intervention of the latter. Between the two there is therefore a difference, not only of degree, but of nature and quality. The former, contained originally in the apostolic *declaration*, is now found in the *writings* wherein that declaration is deposited, which are thus the permanent means of which God makes use to effect the latter (John xvii. 20).

The agent by whom God wrought this unveiling in

the mind of the apostle is the Spirit. The pronoun αὐτοῦ, *of Him,* is probably a gloss. The following proposition serves to explain how the Spirit can fill this revealing function: *He searcheth all things.* Instead of ἐρευνᾷ, ℵ A B C read ἐραυνᾷ; an Alexandrine form. Was it the apostle who used it, or the Alexandrine copyists who introduced it? We read—ραυ John v. 39 in ℵ B; vii. 52 in ℵ B T; Rom. viii. 27 in ℵ; xi. 33 in ℵ A B; 1 Pet. i. 11 in ℵ B, and Rev. ii. 23 in A C.—There is no reason for restricting the πάντα, *all things,* to Divine things; on the contrary, the following proposition would in that case be a mere tautology. The Divine Spirit is the luminous principle which possesses and from which proceeds all knowledge; it is in His light alone that everything comes to the light where there are consciousness and intelligence.—The *deep things of God* designate God's essence, then His attributes, volitions, and plans. The operation of *searching,* here ascribed to the Spirit, has been applied by De Wette to the believer who has received the Spirit, or, what comes to the same thing, to the Spirit as dwelling in the Church and acting through believers. The sense would thus be, that through possession of the Spirit, man can penetrate all things, even the deepest purposes of God; comp. ver. 16. But (1) this sense does not accord with the contrast between the verbs *reveal* and *search;* the first is in the past and aorist, and consequently indicates a determinate Divine act, wrought once for all; the second, which is in the present, denotes, on the contrary, a permanent act, which, once the act of revelation is effected, would no longer have any reason for its existence if it was really man's. On the contrary, it is clear that this permanent act of searching, applied to the unceasing activity of the Spirit in God, serves to explain (γάρ, *for*) the revealing function of that Spirit. (2) If Paul meant to speak in ver. 10 of the working of the Divine Spirit dwelling in man to penetrate the Divine decrees, how would he compare this working in ver. 11 with that of man's spirit searching what passes within himself? The two compared relations would be incommensurate. Finally (3), in the passage, xiii. 10–12, Paul declares that here below we know only fragmentarily and as in a dim mirror; how could he say here that the Christian's knowledge extends to all things and penetrates even what is deepest in God? Our passage, therefore, certainly relates to the intra-Divine activity of the Holy Spirit.

Ver. 11. "For what man knoweth the things of man, save the spirit of man[1] which is in him? Even so the things of God hath no man known,[2] but the Spirit of God."—To make intelligible to his readers this inward activity of the Divine Spirit, the apostle invites them to contemplate the working of man's spirit in man himself. For man is made in the image of God, and that precisely in virtue of his spiritual nature. There is in every man a life hidden from all eyes, a world of impressions, anxieties, aspirations, and struggles, of which he alone, in so far as he is a spirit, that is to say, a conscious and personal being, gives account to himself. This inner world is unknown to

[1] F G Orig. omit του ανθρωπου (*of man*).

[2] All the Mjj., with the exception of L, read εγνωκεν instead of οιδεν, the reading of T. R.

others, except in so far as he reveals it to them by speech. Such is the likeness of what passes in the phenomenon of revelation between God and man.—In thus appealing to what we call in philosophical language the fact of consciousness, Paul knows well that he is teaching nothing new. Hence the interrogative form: "What man knoweth . . .?" He adds, when speaking of the spirit of man, τὸ ἐν αὐτῷ, *which is in him*. He did not express himself so when speaking of the Spirit of God. No doubt because he would not have it supposed that in his eyes the analogy was complete. The Spirit is not *in* God, as if God were for him a place.—In the second proposition we must read, with almost all the Mjj., ἔγνωκεν, not οἶδεν, which has undoubtedly been imported from the first sentence. The difference is, as Edwards well puts it, that the latter denotes the knowledge of a fact, the former the knowledge of the inner nature of the thing. The latter is well rendered in Latin by *cognitum habet*. After this short explanation (ver. 11), the apostle, in ver. 12, connects with the principal idea that of the ἀπεκάλυψε, ver. 10: "There was in our favour an act of revelation." And as, in vers. 6, 7, he had contrasted worldly wisdom with Divine wisdom, he contrasts, in ver. 13, the revelation of the Spirit from above with all earthly knowledge.

Ver. 12. "Now we have received, not the spirit of the world,[1] but the Spirit which is of God, that we might know the things that are freely given to us of God:"—This verse is the development of the word *by the Spirit* (ver. 10).—The Divine Spirit is contrasted

[1] D E F G add τουτου (*of this*).

with another, which also has the power of making revelations of another nature, that of *the world.* Beet understands thereby, "the spirit which worketh in the children of disobedience" (Eph. ii. 2); Meyer: the spirit which animates unbelieving mankind, the diabolical spirit. Does the expression used authorize us to go so far? Man, at the time of his creation, received a πνεῦμα; for he participates in the spiritual nature and power which are the essence of God (Gen. ii. 7; John iv. 24). With the Fall, this endowment was not withdrawn from humanity. By its separation from God, the spirit of man became profane, worldly; but it remained in man, as a collective being, as a principle of knowledge and invention, enthusiasm and exaltation. This it is which Pagans called the Muse, and which is concentrated in philosophical and artistic geniuses, communicating to them marvellous insight and words of wondrous power, by which they give tone to their age. And hence the apostle does not scruple himself to quote sayings of the Greek poets, and to designate one of them by the name of *prophet* (Acts xvii. 28; Tit. i. 12). But to whatever degree of power this spirit of the world may rise, it cannot give man the knowledge of the Divine plans, nor make an apostle even of the greatest genius. The expression οὐκ ἐλάβομεν, *we have not received*, signifies, "The spiritual power which has made us what we are, is not that." Comp. an analogous form, Rom. viii. 15.

With this spirit which rises, so to speak, from the heart of the κόσμος, the apostle contrasts the Divine Spirit, literally, *the Spirit which proceeds* (ἐκ) *from God.* This form emphasizes the transcendent character of His inspiring breath. He was in God, and He proceeds from Him to enter into man; comp. Rom. v. 5. This is something different from human inspiration, even when raised to its highest power.—The art. τό, after πνεῦμα, was not strictly necessary (see on ver. 7). But it is put here to remind us of the contrast to the other spirit, the cosmical spirit: "We are certainly neither Platos, nor Demostheneses, nor Homers; but if you would learn what are the thoughts of God toward you, listen to us! The Spirit proceeding from God Himself is He who has revealed them to us."—There is a very marked contrast between the two terms, εἰδῶμεν, *that we might know*, and τὰ χαρισθέντα, *the things which have been* (freely) *given to us.* By this second term Paul understands the gracious blessings of salvation, the gift of the Son, the expiation accomplished by Him, and all the benefits flowing from them: justification, sanctification, final redemption (i. 30). These blessings one may enjoy by simple faith, but without yet measuring all their greatness, because the εἰδέναι, *knowing*, is yet wanting in a certain degree. And hence the apostle asked for the Ephesians (iii. 18) that they might be able "to understand with all saints what is the breadth and length, the depth and height," and for the Colossians (ii. 2, 3), "that they might be brought unto all riches of the full assurance of understanding, to the acknowledgment of the mystery of God and of Christ; in whom are hid all the treasures of wisdom and knowledge." Here, therefore, the εἰδέναι, *knowing*, denotes the account which the believer renders to himself of all that is contained in the τὰ χαρισθέντα, the facts of salvation wrought out for him. It is those higher lights the domain of which we have sought briefly to indicate (see on ii. 6). Between faith in the simple facts of salvation and these more elevated views of the Divine work, there is all the distance which separates the preaching of the *evangelist* from the doctrine of the Christian *teacher*, or, if you will, all the difference which exists between the contents of the gospel history and the teaching of the Epistles.

To this teaching of Divine wisdom, the end of this whole deduction, Paul comes in ver. 13.

Ver. 13. "Which things also we speak, not in the words which man's wisdom teacheth, but which the Spirit[1] teacheth, appropriating spiritual things to spiritual[2] men."—Here is the resuming of the λαλοῦμεν, *we speak*, of ver. 6; it has been prepared for by vers. 10–12: "This hidden wisdom God has revealed to us by His Spirit, and we speak it with words formed in us by this same Spirit. He gives us the form, after having given us the matter." Καί, *also*, prominently brings out precisely this relation between the two operations of the Spirit, *revelation* and *inspiration*. As Paul has contrasted wisdom with wisdom (vers. 6–9), revelation with revelation (vers. 10–12), he now contrasts Divine inspiration with earthly inspiration. By revelation God communicates Himself to man; inspiration bears on the relation of man to man.—The genitives, σοφίας and πνεύματος, *wisdom* and *Spirit*, may, according to Greek usage,

[1] T. R. with E L P adds αγιου (*holy*).

[2] B reads πνευματικως (*spiritually*), instead of πνευματικοις (*to the spiritual*).

depend, not on the subst. λόγοις, *words*, but on the verbal notion expressed by the adjective διδακτοῖς (John vi. 45): "Words taught, not by wisdom, but by the Spirit," and this connection is also that which agrees best with the context. To teach things which the Spirit has revealed, terms are not made use of which man's own understanding and ability have discovered. The same Divine breath which lifted the veil *to reveal*, takes possession also of the mouth of its interpreter when it is *to speak*. Inspiration is, as it were, the language of revelation. Such is the secret of the peculiar and unique style of the Scriptures.—Meyer justly remarks that the term διδακτός, *taught*, while it positively includes the idea of inspiration, nevertheless excludes all mechanical representation of the fact, and implies in the person inspired a living assimilation of the truth expressed.

Very various meanings have been given to the last clause of this verse, according to the different senses in which the word συγκρίνειν may be taken, and according to the two genders, masculine or neuter, which may be ascribed to the adj. πνευματικοῖς, *spiritual*. The rarely used verb συγκρίνειν strictly denotes the act of bringing two things together to compare them and fix their relative value. This is certainly its meaning in the only other passage in the New Testament where it occurs, 2 Cor. x. 12. But in the LXX. this verb frequently takes the meaning of *interpreting*, especially in speaking of dreams (Gen. xl. 8, 16, 22; Dan. v. 15–17), because the interpretation of a dream consists in comparing the image with the idea discovered in it. Several commentators have proceeded on this second meaning;—

Chrysostom: *explaining* Christian doctrines by comparing them with the types of the Old Testament (πνευματικοῖς, neuter); Grotius, on the contrary: *explaining* the prophecies of the Old Testament by comparing them with the doctrines of Christ; Bengel, Rückert, Hofmann: *explaining* the things of the Spirit to spiritual men (πνευματικοῖς, masculine). This third explanation would in the context be the only admissible one. But this meaning of *interpreting* given to συγκρίνειν is at once foreign to the New Testament and to classical Greek.—Erasmus, Calvin, de Wette, Meyer, Osiander seek to come nearer to the real sense of the verb by explaining thus: *joining*, adapting spiritual words to spiritual things (πνευματικοῖς, neuter). It is on this view the justification of the procedure which the apostle has just described in the first part of the verse. To a spiritual body (the wisdom revealed by the Spirit) no other is suitable than a spiritual dress (a language taught by the Spirit). The meaning is excellent; but the last clause would really add nothing to the contents of the previous proposition, and neither in this way is the meaning of the verb συγκρίνειν exactly reproduced. Should not these words form the transition to the development of the third word of the theme (6[a]), *among the perfect*, which will form the subject of the following verses? We must, if it is so, take πνευματικοῖς as a masculine and see in it the equivalent of τέλειοι, *the perfect*; comp. ver. 15 and iii. 1. The word συγκρίνειν has exactly in that case the meaning given it by Passow in his dictionary, a meaning which differs only by a slight shade from the first which we have indicated:

mit Auswahl verbinden, to adapt two things to one another with discernment; which leads us to this explanation: "adapting, applying, appropriating with discernment spiritual teachings to spiritual men." This is precisely the idea which is developed in vers. 14–16, and which will be applied in the final passage iii. 1–4.

This passage has a peculiar importance. It shows that what in Paul's view was the object of the revelation of which he speaks at this point, was not the historical facts from which salvation flows, nor the simple meaning in which they are presented by the preaching used in evangelization; but that it was the Divine plan which is realized through them, their relation to the history of humanity and of the universe, all that we find expounded in the passages quoted above (Eph. and Col., Rom. ix.–xi., 1 Cor. xv.). There we find unveiled the plan of God in all its dimensions (*its length, breadth, depth, height*); all that system of Divine thoughts eternally conceived with a view to *our glory*, of which ver. 7 spoke; the cross, as the centre from which there rays forth in all the directions of time and space the splendour of Divine love. This Christian speculation we have not to make or to seek. It is given: God is its author; His Spirit, the revealer; St. Paul and each of the apostles, in his measure, the inspired interpreter. But this wisdom, revealed to those who are to be its organs, is to be spoken by them only to those who are fit to receive it (vers. 14–16).

Vers. 14–16

We come to the development of the third term: *among the perfect*.

Ver. 14. "But the natural man receiveth not the things of the Spirit of God, for they are foolishness unto him, neither can he know them, because they are spiritually discerned."—It seems at first sight that γάρ, *for*, would have been more suitable than δέ: "We appropriate spiritual things to spiritual men; *for* others would not understand them." But the thought is different. The δέ signifies: "*But*, as to the non-spiritual, we give them nothing of the kind, for we should thereby be doing them more ill than good." Paul here designates the non-spiritual man by the term ψυχικός, *psychical*. This word denotes a being animated with that breath of natural or earthly life (ψυχή) which man possesses in common with all the living beings of creation. It implies here the absence of that breath of higher life which puts moral beings in communication with God, and which Scripture calls τὸ πνεῦμα, *the spirit*. Thus xv. 44, the terrestrial body is called a *psychical* body, inasmuch as it is organized to serve as the dwelling-place and organ of a simple ψυχή, while the future body is called *pneumatical*, spiritual, inasmuch as it is destined to be the organ of a *spirit*. Holsten concludes from this expression of Paul that he denied all possession of the πνεῦμα, *the spirit*, to the natural man. It seems to me that 1 Thess. v. 23 proves the contrary. By putting *body*, *soul*, and *spirit*, parallel to one another, as the three constant objects of Christian sanctification, he shows that in his view these are the three essential elements of the whole human person. Only, before the coming of the Divine Spirit, the spirit in man is rather an aspiration, or, as de Wette says, a *receptivity*, than a power and life. It is simply the organ with which the human soul is endowed for the Divine, the sense destined to perceive and receive it; it is a capacity which the Divine Spirit will change into a real power and a new principle of life when He comes to take possession of it. No doubt *soul,* which is the principle of life common to man and the animals, is in the former endowed with faculties superior to that of all other animated beings. But *spirit* alone puts man into relation with God, and thus forms his really distinctive character among all the animals. The term *psychical* man, which we render by *natural* man, does not therefore exclude the presence of spirit in such a man; it only implies the latent and inactive state of this element, so long as the Divine Spirit has not awakened it to enter into union with Himself and to become through it master of the soul and thereby of the body. In this state man possesses only the natural intelligence with which his soul is endowed, and by means of which he judges things of the present life and is guided in this sphere; it is in this sense that Paul calls him psychical. Meyer thinks that the epithet has not an essentially different sense from the word *carnal,* iii. 1. But in this last passage it is Christians who are spoken of, though weak Christians, *babes in Christ.* Paul would not apply to true believers such strong expressions as those of our verse: "The things of the Spirit are foolishness unto them." Meyer's mistake arises from his not understanding that between ver. 14 and iii. 1 there is by no means a relation of equality. "This wisdom cannot be explained to the psychical man, who has only his natural reason to apprehend it; and as for myself when I was with you, carnal as you still were, though believing, I could not enter on this domain." See also on iii. 16.

The term οὐ δέχεται, *he does not receive,* indicates that in his inner man there is nothing corresponding to this light; it does not penetrate into him. What ravishes advanced believers with joy and admiration leaves him cold, and even produces in him, with all his intelligence in other domains, the impression of something foolish. Why so? Are there two logics: one for the converted, the other for the unconverted? Certainly not. The laws of the syllogism are valid for every sane mind. The difference arises from the fact that the experience of salvation establishes in the believer new premisses, foreign to the natural man's experience. As the egoist cannot believe in the heroism of devotion, and treats it as an impossibility,—not because he has another logic than the man of heart, but because a necessary moral premiss is wanting to him to appreciate the moral fact,—so the purely psychical man, not having made experience of the Divine love, does not possess the premiss necessary for understanding the Divine plan, and with the same understanding as the believer, he calls that *foolishness* which is heaven to the latter.

The apostle adds, *neither can he know them,* as if to say: "If he does not understand them, it is not so much his fault as that of the ill-advised teacher who expounds a Christian philosophy to the man who needs first to have salvation declared to him; who expatiates in the high regions of knowledge, when he should have laboured at the renewing of the heart." Here we see clearly how Paul distinguishes between the simple preaching of salvation and the *wisdom* of which he speaks throughout this whole passage. For certainly he never thought that to the unregenerate there is no need of preaching salvation by the cross, and that it is not their own fault if they do not understand, and so reject it. The use of the adverb *πνευματικῶς*, *spiritually*, has nothing in common with the Alexandrine system of interpretation, according to which those were called *spiritual* who could distinguish in Scripture the profound (allegorical) sense from the grammatical. The word simply means here, "in virtue of spiritual premisses." And the verb *ἀνακρίνειν*, to make an examination, analyze, discern, denotes the analysis made by the *νοῦς* (the understanding) of things transmitted to it, and the judgment resulting from it.

From this Paul could pass directly to the application which he has in view (iii. 1–4). But, as Rückert has well observed, he here interposes a short episode, vers. 15, 16, fitted to pave the way for this application, and to give it its full gravity.

Vers. 15, 16. "But he that is spiritual judgeth[1] all things,[2] yet he himself is judged of no man; 16. for who hath known the mind of the Lord, that he may instruct Him? But we have the mind of the Lord."[3]—Ver. 6 supposed in a preacher the faculty of discerning in each case whether he had to do with a psychical or a spiritual man. This is the faculty which the apostle affirms, ver. 15, and the possession and free exercise of which he claims for himself, ver. 16. The link between vers. 15 and 14 is in the term and idea *ἀνακρίνειν*, *to*

[1] T. R. here reads with B E L P, *μεν*, which is omitted by A C D F G It. Syr^sch^. This ver. is wanting in ℵ.

[2] A C D P read *τα* before *παντα*.

[3] Instead of *κυριου* (*of the Lord*), which is read by B D F G, T. R. reads *Χριστου* (*of Christ*) with ℵ A C E L P Syr.

judge. In virtue of the sway exercised by the πνεῦμα, *the Spirit,* over the psychical faculties of the regenerated man, he is endowed with a superior tact which gives him the power of estimating men and things with certainty. As Edwards says, "If the profane man cannot understand holiness, the holy man can understand the depths of evil." From the higher stage one can look into the lower, but not inversely.—The μέν, which T. R. reads with some Mjj., seems to me to throw rather too much emphasis on the antitheses of the two propositions. I am inclined to suppress it. — Instead of πάντα, some Mjj. read τὰ πάντα, which would here designate the totality of things, absolutely speaking. It is more natural to read πάντα without the article: "All things, each as it presents itself." Several commentators make this πάντα a masculine: *each man.* This sense would be perfectly justified, first by the context, according to which Paul claims for the spiritual man the faculty of discerning in each case with what kind of hearer he has to do, next by the οὐδενός, *none,* which follows, and which is evidently a masculine. But it is nevertheless true that the neuter sense is that which presents itself most naturally to the reader, and it is wide enough to include the other: *all things,* that is to say, every circumstance, every situation, and consequently, also, every person with whom one meets. St. Paul therefore had the right to estimate the spiritual state of the Corinthians, and to judge what suited or did not suit their state.—But, on the other hand, this spiritual man is subject to the scrutiny and sentences *of none.* The masculine sense of the pronoun οὐδενός is evident, since it is only intelligent beings who are capable of judging. From this principle flowed the application which Paul proposed to make to the Corinthians (iii. 1–4); he can judge them, but they are not in a position to judge him.

Ver. 16. "With the humble, more humble; with the proud, more proud," says some one. Never did any one practise this maxim better than the Apostle Paul. Face to face with those who disparage him, he rises to an incomparable height. Jehovah, in Isaiah, addressing ignorant man, threw out this challenge: "Who hath measured the Spirit of the Lord? Who being His counsellor hath taught Him?" Such is the position which the apostle takes up as against his detractors. He quotes this saying after the LXX. (omitting the words of the middle clause, whereas he preserves them, Rom. xi. 34, while omitting the end), and says with them, *who hath known?* instead of, *who hath measured?* Just as the natural man is incapable of judging by his simple reason the ways of God in creation and the government of the world, so is he in no position to appreciate the procedure of the spiritual man. Why so? Because the latter, having the mind of the Lord, stands over against him in the same position as the Lord Himself.—The word συμβιβάζειν signifies strictly, to cause to walk together, and hence, to adjust, combine, conclude (Acts xvi. 10), to demonstrate (Acts ix. 22); it is used in the classics only with the *thing* as object (to demonstrate a thing), while in the LXX. it is used with the *person* as object; and so in them it takes the sense of *instructing*, which it has here.—In the ἡμεῖς, *we*, there is a well-marked contrast to the ὑμεῖς, *ye*, of iii. 1–3. It is obvious how profoundly, in virtue of the revelation he has received, the apostle distinguishes himself from the Church.—The term νοῦς, properly, *understanding*, and hence *mind*, is not synonymous with Spirit. It denotes the mind of God as to the destination of humanity and the best means of realizing it. The Spirit is the agent by whom this mind of God is communicated to the spiritual man.—Of the two readings, *of the Lord* and *of Christ*, the second seems to us preferable; the copyists have been naturally led to substitute Κυρίου (*of the Lord*) for Χρίστου (*of Christ*), to give this passage the form of a regular syllogism: "Who hath known the mind of God? But we know it; therefore no one can judge our mode of acting." But Paul has substituted for, the mind *of the Lord* (of God), the mind *of Christ*, which he tacitly identifies with that of God, because the former is only the reflection of the latter in a human intelligence. By the ἔχομεν, *we hold, we possess*, the mind of Christ is identified in its turn with that of Paul, who knows it by the revelation of the Spirit. Thus the minister of a sovereign could say, after an intimate conversation with his king, I am in full possession of my master's mind. From this moment, therefore, to criticize the servant is to criticize the master.

3:1-4

After demonstrating that though the gospel is not a wisdom, yet it contains one, but one which cannot be expounded except to those who by their spiritual maturity are in a condition to understand it, the apostle applies this truth to his relation to the Church of Corinth. The passage iii. 1–4 is the pendant of ii. 1-5. Edwards well says: I preached to you the gospel as a power (ii. 1-5); I could not preach it to you as wisdom (iii. 1–4).

Vers. 1, 2. "And I also, brethren, could not speak unto you as unto spiritual, but as unto carnal,[1] as unto babes in Christ. 2. I have fed you with milk,[2] not with meat: for hitherto ye were not strong enough, and not[3] even yet are ye."—The apostle, after rising to the height assigned him by the revelation which he has received, severely humbles the presumption of the Corinthians.—The κἀγώ (T. R. καὶ ἐγώ) surprises; it seems as if it should be, "But I," instead of, *And I also.* "This wisdom we have, *but* I could not declare it to you." Yet the *And I also* is easily explained. Paul does nothing more than apply to himself, in his relation to the Corinthians, what he has just said of the relation of the spiritual man to purely natural men. "And I also, as a spiritual man, judged and acted accordingly; comp. the κἀγώ absolutely parallel, ii. 1.—The word ἀδελφοί, *brethren,* serves to soften this personal application.—The *I could not* is an implicit answer to the disdainful charge of his enemies: "He knew not." It was in themselves the obstacle was; his *not being able* was caused by theirs; comp. the "*he cannot* understand," in speaking of the natural man, ii. 14.—Paul no longer uses here ψυχικός, the

[1] ℵ A B C D read σαρκινοις instead of σαρκικοις, the reading of E F G L P.

[2] ℵ A B C P reject the και (*and*), which T. R. reads with the rest.

[3] T. R. with L reads ουτε (*neither*); all the rest read ουδε (*and no more* or *and not even*).

natural man, which would have been too strong. For he did not mean that the Corinthians were entirely destitute of the Divine breath; how could they have been in possession of the χαρίσματα (*gifts*), the presence of which he had recognised in them (i. 5, 7)? Hence it is he uses the term *carnal*, which does not exclude the possession, to a certain degree, of the new life. The Spirit is there, but He has not yet taken a decided preponderance over the instincts of the flesh, the unregenerate nature. By these, indeed, must not be understood merely sensual inclinations. This is plain from ver. 3. For what was there sensual in the divisions which were produced at Corinth? The word *flesh*, which denotes strictly the soft and sensitive parts of the body, denotes also by extension natural sensibility, quick, even purely moral receptivity, for agreeable or disagreeable impressions in general. Thus the man who prefers the intoxicating pleasures of *speaking in tongues* to the holy austerity of prophesying, or the noble simplicity of teaching, is in Paul's eyes like a yet carnal babe; comp. xiv. 20. Consequently those who have found in the different forms in which the preaching of the gospel has appeared in Corinth an occasion for inflating themselves or disparaging others, and thereby tearing the Church into factions, while satisfying their personal vanity, have shown how the flesh, self-complacency, still ruled the new life, and the action of the Spirit in them. Paul would not, however, have called such men *psychical*, as if the Spirit of God were not within them in any sense. Indeed, the psychical man may also be called *carnal*. But there is this difference,—that if in the regenerate man the flesh hinders the action of the Spirit, in the unregenerate man, who possesses only the breath of natural life (the ψυχή), it reigns as lord (Rom. vii. 14–18). The T. R. with some Byz. and Greco-Lats. reads σαρκίκοις, while the Alex. with D read σαρκίνοις. The two adjectives signify *carnal.* But the latter refers to the substance and nature of the being so qualified (2 Cor. iii. 3; Heb. vii. 16), the former to his tendency and activity. The word σάρκινος is rare in the New Testament, while σαρκικός is pretty frequently used. Thus we are not allowed to think that the first has been substituted for the second by the copyists, the more that σαρκικός reappears in ver. 3 almost without a variant. The copyists had therefore no great inclination to substitute for it σάρκινος; while the relation between vers. 1 and 3 could easily lead in ver. 1 to the substitution of σαρκικοῖς for σαρκίνοις. We must therefore read σαρκίνοις in ver. 1, and see in this term, which indicates the hurtful persistence of the state of nature, not so much a reproach as the statement of a fact fitted to explain Paul's conduct when he was among them. This is confirmed by the expression, *babes in Christ,* which he adds as an equivalent term. The word characterizes a state of transition in a sense natural in the development of the believer. Time is needed to become a πνευματικός, as in the natural life there is need of growth to pass from the infant state to that of the mature man. It is obvious how much better than the other the term σάρκινος, carnal in nature, suited the ideas expressed in ver. 1; and how far Meyer is mistaken in regarding it as conveying a more emphatic rebuke than the term σαρκικός in ver. 3.

Ver. 2. The figures used by the apostle relate to the term *babes.* *Milk,* according to ii. 2, denotes the preaching of Jesus crucified, with its simplest contents and its most immediate consequences, expiation, justification by faith, the sanctification of the justified believer by the Holy Spirit, what saves by converting and regenerating. *Meat* represents what Paul has just called *wisdom,* the contemplation of the Divine plan in its entirety from its eternal predestination to its final consummation. The same figure occurs Heb. v. 12 and vi. 2, but with this difference, that there the persons in question are former Hebrews, and that the rudiments of religious knowledge (milk) are not exactly the same for those who were formerly Jews as for those who were formerly heathen.—The apostle says (literally), *I have given you to drink,* and that in relation to the two substantives, though the figure only corresponds to the first. It is a usual inaccuracy; comp. Luke i. 64.—The words, *Ye could not yet,* naturally refer to the time of Paul's first stay. Meyer, Edwards think that it is unnecessary to understand an infinitive (to bear meat); perhaps they are right; it is in this sense that I have translated, "Ye were not strong enough."—Paul adds (what is still more humiliating) that this weakness characterizes even their present condition. The οὐδέ, *and no more* or *not even,* which is the reading of almost all the Mjj., is harder than the οὔτε, *neither,* of the T. R. This second reading is more delicate. I should not be surprised if the οὐδέ had been substituted for the οὔτε, because the τε wanted its correlative particle.—Billroth was the first to ask how this saying agrees with chap.

xv. of our Epistle, where the apostle enters into such profound details respecting Christian eschatology. I think that the *Ye are not able* did not exclude an excursion into the domain of wisdom, when positive negations demanded it. And perhaps, as Rückert supposes, the apostle thought good to seize this opportunity to show his detractors how far he could rise when it pleased him to spread his wings.

Vers. 3, 4. "For ye are yet carnal:[1] for whereas there is among you envying and strifes,[2] are ye not carnal, and walk as men? 4. For while one saith, I am of Paul; and another, I of Apollos, are ye not men?"[3]—The apostle here uses, according to the great majority of the documents, the term σαρκικοί, carnal by acts. The matter in question is no more a simple state of weakness which continues in spite of regeneration, but a course of conduct which attacks the new life and tells actively against it.—The form ὅπου, *there where*, borrowed from the notion of place, is used here, as often, in a logical sense.—Ζῆλος has most frequently in the New Testament an unfavourable sense: heat, jealousy; thence springs ἔρις, *strife*, which is only the manifestation of the ζῆλος in words.—The third term in the T. R., *divisions*, seems to be unauthentic; perhaps the enumeration of the works of the flesh, Gal. v. 20, gave rise to this interpolation.—Such a state can only arise from self-complacency, either on the part of the leaders or their adherents; and that is *the flesh*. What completes the proof that such a state is a fruit

[1] D F G, σαρκινοι; all the rest σαρκικοι.

[2] T. R. adds here, with D E F G L It. Syr. Ir. Chrys. etc.: και διχοστασιαι (*and divisions*).

[3] T. R. with L P Syr.: σαρκικοι (*carnal*), instead of ανθρωποι (*men*).

of man's natural heart, is the analogy presented by the Church thus divided with the spectacle offered in the midst of the Greek people by the rival schools of philosophy. And doubtless that is what the apostle means by the expression : *walking according to man*, that is to say, following a conduct after the manner of man left to himself. No doubt a wholly different meaning could be given to the term, *walking according to man*, did we explain it by the following verse. It would signify : to make oneself dependent on a man, a party leader. But this meaning would depart somewhat from the idea which rules in this passage : the influence of the carnal mind on the conduct of the believer.

Ver. 4. The two examples the apostle gives in this verse are intended to prove that what he blames in the divisions which have been formed, is not any hostility they may have to his person, but the fact of those divisions themselves. And hence he puts forward his own party and the nearest to his own, that of Apollos. It follows that Paul starts from the fact of the most intimate harmony between him and Apollos, and that every attempt to apply to the ministry and party of this evangelist the foregoing polemic against worldly wisdom should be abandoned.—Instead of the received reading, *Are ye not carnal?* which is a surprise, as simply repeating the question of ver. 3, there is read in most of the Mjj., *Are ye not men*, or rather, *Are ye not* (human) *beings?* A question which seems stranger still. We must undoubtedly explain it by the preceding expression : *walking according to man.* " Are ye not falling back from the higher state to which faith had raised you, into the state of the natural man? Are ye not becoming again what ye were before being in Christ?" Meyer quotes as an analogous form the word of the *Anabasis*: ἄνθρωπός εἰμι, "I am a man," meaning: I am only a weak and fallible man. It is in the same sense that it is said, Gen. vi. 3, "They are but flesh." Hofmann rather sees in this question an appeal to the feeling of their dignity as men. But the question thus understood, to have a logical connection with the preceding proposition: "While one saith . . . ," would require to be put thus, "Are ye men?" The οὐκ or οὐχί is superfluous in this sense.—The placing of the μέν would lead us to suppose that he who pronounces the first watchword is the same person as pronounces the second (δέ); there is here an inaccuracy common in the classic style (see Meyer). This μέν must be logically put to the account of Paul in explaining the fact, not to the account of the interlocutor whom he brings on the stage.

Ver. 4 expresses the result of the whole foregoing development, and forms the transition to the following passage. In order to attack the spirit of rivalry with effect, and the divisions which had invaded the life of the Church, Paul had gone to the very root of the evil: the false way of regarding the gospel itself. He had shown that the preaching of the gospel was, not the exposition of a new religious speculation, but the good news of a fact, and that a fact absurd in the eyes of reason: the salvation of humanity by a Crucified One; and now he deduces therefrom the true notion of the Christian ministry and of the part it has to play within the Church.—Holsten and others think that the apostle turns at this point to the partisans of Apollos to upbraid their infatuation for this teacher. This we think is an error arising from a misunderstanding of vers. 4 and 5. We shall see that this special intention is foreign to the true sense of the following passage.

C. *The true nature of the Christian ministry* (3:5-4:5)

In this passage, Paul expounds :

1. The place of preachers, in relation to the Church (vers. 5–20).

2. The place of the Church, in relation to preachers (vers. 21–23).

3. He closes, as at the end of the two previous passages (ii. 1–5 and iii. 1–4), by applying the truth expounded to his own relation to the Corinthians (iv. 1–5).

Vers. 5–20

In order to show what, in a religious organization like that which the gospel creates, is the place of preachers, the apostle takes two examples : Apollos and himself ; and he develops what he means to expound regarding the true place of Christian preachers, by applying it more specially to those two principal agents of the Divine work at Corinth.

Ver. 5. "What[1] then is Apollos ?[2] And what is[3] Paul ? Ministers[4] by whom ye believed, and that, as

[1] T. R. reads τις with C D E F G L P Syr. Cop. ; ℵ A B It. read τι.

[2] T. R. with L Syr. puts the question relating to Paul before that relating to Apollos.

[3] ℵ A B C P here read εστιν, which T. R. omits with D E F G L It.

[4] T. R. reads αλλ' η (before διακονοι) with L P Syr.

the Lord gave to each."—There is no difficulty, whatever Hofmann may object, in connecting the *then* with the previous verse, provided we see in this verse the conclusion and consequently the summary of all that goes before from i. 17 and even from i. 12 : "Now if, in virtue of the very nature of the gospel (which is a salvation, not a system), its preachers are not what you make them when you say : I am of Paul or of Apollos, what are they *then?*" Rückert regards this question as an objection raised by an interlocutor of the apostle. But it belongs to the train of his argument; it is the theme of the whole following passage. Besides, Paul indicates such interruptions more precisely (xv. 35).—The Greco-Lat. and Byz. MSS. read τίς : *who* are they (as individuals)? The Alex. read τί : *what* are they (as to their office)? The second reading is more in keeping with the context. It is no doubt, as Meyer thinks, the personal names which have led to the substitution of the masculine for the neuter.—T. R. places the question relating to Paul *before* that which concerns Apollos, probably under the influence of the preceding verse and of i. 13. But the apostle has not here the same reason as formerly for putting himself first. For he is no longer dealing with a personal preference to be condemned; here he begins a matter of doctrine.—The ἀλλ' ἤ, *other than*, in T. R. is probably a gloss; the answer is more direct: *ministers.* Such is the great word, that which without any roundabout states the nature of the position : not heads of schools, not founders of religious societies, as having a work of their own, but simple *employés* labouring on the work of another. This situation of ministers is characterized by two features: "*By whom* ye have believed." As Bengel well says: "*By* whom, and not *in* whom;" simple agents (διά). The *ye believed* applies also to Apollos, though the Church was already founded when he arrived at Corinth; for he had increased the number of believers and contributed to sustain the faith of those whom Paul had led to believe.—***Καί***, *and that;* and moreover: Neither do those agents who labour on another's account do anything at their own hand. This is the second feature and, in a sense, the second form of their dependence: *as the Lord gave to each.* The following verse shows that Paul is here thinking of the kind of work which the Master commits to each labourer, while rendering him fit for it by personal gifts which He confers on him and by the special commission which He gives him.—The ἑκάστῳ, *to each,* is placed by inversion, as in vii. 17 and elsewhere, before the conjunction, to bring out clearly the *distinction* between those different tasks. For hereby is completed the idea of dependence: All *for* a master, as all *by* this master! This master is denoted by the term ὁ **Κύριος**, *the Lord,* in opposition to the preachers who are only διάκονοι, *servants.* This Lord, according to Chrysostom, de Wette, Meyer, is God; comp. ver. 6. But in general in the New Testament, when the term **Κύριος** does not belong to an Old Testament quotation, it denotes Jesus Christ. This is particularly the case in the first chapter of this Epistle. And ver. 6 proves nothing in favour of the opposite sense, for the action of Jesus and that of God, though distinct, are not separate. Comp. xii. 5, where the functions of ministers are also put in relation to Christ, as Lord of the Church, and their efficacy in relation to God, as the last source of all power.

Vers. 6, 7. "I planted, Apollos watered, but God gave the increase; 7. So then neither is he that planteth anything, neither[1] he that watereth, but God that giveth the increase."—The asyndeton between ver. 6 and the preceding one arises from the fact that the verse reaffirms in a new form the last proposition of ver. 5, of which it is only the development. In the two functions of *planting* and *watering*, there reappears in specialized form the idea of distribution contained in the "*as* the Lord gave *to each*." In respect of Corinth Paul had received the mission of planting, that is to say, of founding the Church; Apollos, that of watering, that is to say, of developing the Church already founded. And if the labour of the one and the other had had some true success, it was due solely to the concurrence of God. As Edwards says: "God is the source of life in the physical as in the moral world. Man can indeed put the seed in contact with the soil; but life alone makes it spring and grow; and this life is not only beyond the power but even beyond the knowledge of man." The imperfect ηὔξανεν denotes a Divine operation, which was in process at the very time when Paul and Apollos were labouring.—The apostle wishes decidedly to take away all individual and independent worth from the labour of the two workers whom he has chosen as examples, in view of a Church which tends to falsify the position of its ministers. This choice then has a

[1] ℵ C: ουδε instead of ουτε.

perfectly natural explanation : was it not by speaking of himself and his friend that he could, with least scruple, remind them of the humble position of Christ's ministers, by leaving it to the Church itself to make application of the truth to the other workers whom it exalted ?

Ver. 7. What harvest would have sprung up from the labour of the two workers without the life which God alone could give ? What then are those workers ?—There is ordinarily understood as the predicate of the last proposition : *is everything.* But why not simply retain the preceding predicate : *is anything?* If in this work God alone is anything, is not this equivalent to saying that He is *everything?* The reading οὐδέ, *nor any more,* in two Alex., insists perhaps too specially on applying the idea of nothingness to Apollos.—This first development, vers. 5–7, is directed against the folly of raising servants to the rank of masters. The following combats the opposition which it is sought to establish between them by comparing them with one another, and taking the liberty of rating their respective merits.

Ver. 8. " Now he that planteth and he that watereth are one, but every man shall receive his own reward according to his own labour."—The δέ is here a particle of transition, but with a shade of contrast : " *Now,* despite this difference of functions (pointed out, vers. 5–7), these ministers are one." This unity is not that of their common nothingness (Bengel : " Neuter æque *quidquam* est "), nor that of the part of simple servants (de Wette, Meyer, Heinrici, etc.) ; it is that of the work on which they labour together. To understand what Paul means by this unity, it is enough to consider the foregoing figures (vers. 6, 7). Between two gardeners, one of whom plants and the other waters one and the same garden, who would think of setting up any rivalry? Would not the labour of the one become useless without that of the other? What folly, then, to disparage the one and exalt the other!

But yet there will one day be—the second δέ is adversative—a difference established between them: the difference of the reward they will receive, which will depend on the degree of their fidelity in their respective labours. This idea, expressed in the second part of the verse, is that which Paul proceeds to develop in the passage, vers. 10–15. Of course it is the Master who will pass this estimate; it will take place at the day of judgment. And so what folly it is to anticipate it by comparisons made beforehand! The terms ἴδιος μισθός, *his own reward*, and ἴδιος κόπος, *his own labour*, recall the saying, Gal. vi. 5: "Every man will bear his own burden." The estimate of the fidelity of each servant will not rest on the comparison of it with another's, but on the labour of each compared with his own task and his own gift. Now who else than God could pronounce such a sentence? And not only has He alone the power, but He alone has the right. This is what is brought out in ver. 9.

Ver. 9. "For we are labourers together with God; ye are God's husbandry, God's building."—It is not without reason that in the original the word θεοῦ, *God's*, heads the three propositions of this verse. God alone is Judge, for He is the proprietor in whose service all this work is done. It is therefore a mistake in

Holsten and others to refer the *for* to the idea of the unity of the workers (ver. 8[a]). It bears on what immediately precedes (ver. 8[b]). The worker's responsibility in this labour is presented in two aspects; and first from the standpoint of the servant's own position: συνεργοὶ θεοῦ, *labourers together with God.* It is grammatically inexact to apply the preposition σύν, in the word συνεργοί, to the community of labour existing among the workers themselves: "fellow-labourers in God's service" (Bengel, Olshausen, Heinrici). This sense is connected with the false explanation which regards *for* as a confirmation of the unity of the workers among themselves (ver. 8[a]). According to Greek usage, the regimen of σύν, in the composite συνεργός, is expressed by the following complement: comp. Rom. xvi. 3, and Phil. i. 24, συνεργὸς ἡμῶν (*the fellow-worker with us*). The meaning therefore is: "We are at work with God Himself." Some have shrunk from this bold idea of making Christ's minister in the Church the fellow-labourer of God. And yet what else is said by ver. 6? In every sermon, in every instance of religious instruction, in every pastoral visit, is not the pastor the agent by means of whom God works in souls? But, perhaps, with a complement like θεοῦ, *of God,* there must be added to the idea of joint labour that of dependence. The meaning would then be: "*God's* day-labourers, working *with* Him." Consequently it is His to pay the workmen, and to value their labour! Is it not His goods that are in question? To Him belongs the Church, *His* field, *His* house. The word γεώργιον is not fully rendered by the term *field;* this would rather be expressed by ἀγρός (Matt. xiii. 24; Luke xiv. 18) The term γεώργιον embraces the idea of cultivation along with that of the field; and therefore we translate "God's *husbandry*." It is nearly the same with the term οἰκοδομή, which is unknown to classic Greek down to Aristotle (Edwards). It is taken here rather in the sense of a building *in course of construction* (οἰκοδόμησις) than in the sense of a building finished (οἰκοδόμημα); for, according to the context, the workmen are still at work. It is therefore to a Divine possession that the workers put their hand! We feel that the apostle has passed to a new idea, that of the responsibility of the workers. What gravity attaches to such labour! To cultivate a field the harvest of which is *God's!* To build the house which *God* Himself is to inhabit! God alone can estimate such labour, and He will not fail to do so. Vers. 10–15 describe this responsibility and the inevitable judgment which will hallow it. It is less to the Church than to preachers themselves that the immediate sequel is addressed. For several of them at Corinth were certainly not innocent of what had happened. The use of a second figure, that of *building* after that of a *field* (used in vers. 6–8), is due to the feeling of the apostle that the latter does not suffice to depict what he is about to express. He needs one which lends itself better to the dramatic exposition of the *two opposite results* which human labour may have.

But before indicating this difference between the two kinds of building, the apostle thinks good to put his own work out of the question. For it is ended, and—as the result has proved—well ended.

Ver. 10. "According to the grace of God which is given unto me, as a wise master builder, I laid[1] the foundation, and another buildeth thereon; but let every man take heed how he buildeth thereupon!"—The apostle first looks backwards (*I laid*), in order to put himself out of the question; hence the asyndeton.—*The grace given him* is that of founding the Church among the Gentiles, particularly at Corinth, with the totality of gifts which he received for this mission, and the use of them which he has been enabled to make. The phrase, *according to the grace* . . ., softens the eulogy which he seems to award himself in speaking, as he does here, of his work at Corinth.—One might see in the words, *as a wise master builder*, nothing more than an idea analogous to that expressed in Matt. vii. 24–27. Paul would then simply mean: "I did not build on ground without laying a foundation; as a good architect, I provided a foundation for the building." But the idea of prudence, or better still, of ability, contained in the term *σοφός*, seems rather to relate to the *manner* in which he laboured in laying the foundation, than to the simple act itself of laying it. He took care to avoid factitious modes of procedure, means borrowed from human eloquence and speculation; he deliberately confined himself to bearing testimony to the fact of salvation, leaving the Holy Spirit to act, and refraining from entering before the time into the domain of Christian speculation; his wisdom, as a founder, was to make no account of wisdom; comp. ii. 1–5, and iii. 1–4.—The *master*

[1] ℵ A B C read *εθηκα*, instead of *τεθεικα*, the reading of T. R. with D E L P.

builder is not only he who draws the plan of the building,—in this sense the title would revert to God,—but also the man who directs its execution.—The perfect τέθεικα, which is read in the received text, might appear preferable to the aorist ἔθηκα of the Alexandrines; for the foundation, once laid, remains. But the aorist, which denotes the act done once for all, better contrasts Paul's work with the subsequent labours which are still going on.—These labours are denoted by the term ἐποικοδομεῖν, "*building on* (the foundation laid)." The ἄλλος, *another*, is referred specially to Apollos. Two things should serve to set aside this idea: first, the present ἐποικοδομεῖ, *builds upon;* for, at the time when Paul wrote, Apollos was no longer at Corinth; then the word *each* which follows, and which shows that the ἄλλος, *another*, is a collective term. The word, in fact, denotes the whole body of individuals who, as prophets, teachers, or speaking in tongues, had laboured, since Paul's departure, in developing the Church founded by him. Apollos was one of them, and he certainly belongs, in Paul's view, to the number of those who had built with materials of good quality, ver. 14; comp. vers. 6, 7. The end of the verse is an admonition addressed to all these workers, and prepared for by all that precedes from ver. 8^{b}. The πῶς, *how* (that is to say: with what sort of materials), is the theme of the whole following development.

Ver. 11. "For other foundation can no man lay than that is laid, which is Jesus[1] Christ."—The γάρ, *for*, announces an explanation of the warning contained in

[1] T. R with some Mnn. reads ο before Χριστος (*the* Christ).

the βλεπέτω, *let him consider well.* The γάρ refers, not to ver. 11 taken separately,—this verse is only a reservation, and, so to speak, a μέν relatively to the following δέ,—but to the whole passage, vers. 12–15. The apostle means that his work, all that has been his, has been relatively simple. He has had nothing else to do than take the foundation laid by God Himself in the person of the living Christ, dead and risen again, and lay it in the heart by preaching, as the foundation of Christian faith and salvation. The participle κείμενον, *which is laid*, refers to God's work, and the verb θεῖναι to the labour of the preacher who founds the Church by testifying of this work. If the preacher would lay another foundation, it would be the beginning of a new religion and a new Church, but not the continuation of the Christian work. Now Paul is speaking here of preachers assumed to be Christians.—But the work of those who have to construct the building on the foundation laid is not so simple; and hence they should take good care as to the way in which they do it.

Vers. 12, 13. "But if any man build upon this foundation[1] gold,[2] silver,[3] precious stones, wood, hay, stubble; 13. every man's work shall be made manifest; for the day shall declare it, because it shall be revealed by fire, and the fire[4] shall try every man's work of what sort it is."—The δέ is adversative: "My work, the part assigned to me, is done, and well done. *But* let those who labour now take heed what they

[1] א A B C omit τουτον (*this*), the reading of T. R. with D E L P It. Syr.

[2] א B: χρυσιον instead of χρυσον.

[3] א B C: αργυριον instead of αργυρον.

[4] A B C P read αυτο (after το πυρ), which is omitted by א D E L It.

do!" The εἰ might be taken interrogatively: Is it that? as sometimes. But it is simpler to translate it in its ordinary sense of *if*, and to find the principal proposition at the beginning of ver. 13.—The guidance of converted souls is a much more delicate work than the labour bestowed on their conversion; in fact, it is easy to employ materials in the work of their spiritual development which shall be more hurtful than useful. Now the Church is God's house, God's habitation, and into such a building no materials should enter save such as are worthy of its sublime destination. Oriental palaces and temples presented to the eye only the most precious materials: marble, jasper, alabaster (*precious stones*), besides gold and silver in profusion. This is what is still seen at the present day when one penetrates into the interior of the dwellings of rich Oriental merchants. The houses of the poor, on the contrary, are built of wood and of earth hardened with straw, and covered with thatch.—The diminutives χρυσίον and ἀργύριον differ from χρυσός and ἄργυρος (in T. R.) only in this that they denote specially either an ingot, or a piece of gold or silver.

God, the owner of the Church which is to become His dwelling, is represented here as a Lord who has contracted with numerous builders each charged with a part of the building. They are of course held bound to employ only materials appropriate to such an edifice, and to the dignity of him who means to make it His habitation. Most modern commentators think that the three kinds, whether of good or of bad materials, represent the *doctrines* taught by preachers, the didactic developments added by them to the fundamental truth of the gospel, that of salvation. This, with shades of difference, is the opinion of Clement of Alexandria, Erasmus, Luther, Beza, Calvin, Grotius, Neander, de Wette, Meyer, etc. But is not this to forget that the edifice to be built is not a book of dogmatics, but the Church itself, composed of living personalities? Other commentators have been led by this reflection to apply the figure of the various materials to the different classes in the membership of the Church: so Pelagius, Bengel, Hofmann; preachers, according to this view, are regarded as responsible for the good or bad composition of the churches which they instruct and guide. But if Paul could censure those preachers for having tolerated unworthy members or allowed them to make their way into the Church, could he have accused them of having voluntarily introduced them into it, as would be implied by the figure of the bad materials employed in the work? And could preachers of this kind end with being saved (ver. 15)? The good or bad materials can therefore neither represent the doctrines preached, true or false, nor the members of the Church, worthy or unworthy. There remains only one interpretation, which is to a certain extent that of Origen, Chrysostom, Augustine, and, in our day, of Osiander. The apostle means to speak of the religious and moral fruits produced in the Church by preaching. The spiritual life of the members of the flock is, in a certain measure, the teaching itself received, assimilated, and realized in practice. Either the pastor, by his preaching, his conversation, his example, the daily acts of his ministry, succeeds in developing among his flock a healthy religious life, drawn from communion with

Christ, abounding in the fruits of sanctification and love; and it is this strong and normal life which St. Paul describes under the figure of precious materials; or the pastor, by his pathetic discourses, his ingenious explanations, succeeds indeed in attracting a great concourse of hearers, in producing enthusiastic admiration and lively emotions; but all this stir is only external and superficial; with it all there is no real consecration to the Saviour. This faith without energy, this love without the spirit of sacrifice, this hope without joy or elasticity, this Christianity saturated with egoism and vanity: such are the wood, hay, stubble. The apostle himself sets us on the way of this explanation when in chap. xiii. he calls faith, hope, and love "the three things *which remain;*" these then are the materials which will survive intact the trial by fire.—It was for the successors of Paul and Apollos to judge whether they had continued in the spirit which had animated the authors of the work. Chaps. xii.–xiv. show plainly enough that it was not so.—It would be a mistake to think that the gold, silver, precious stones represent three different stages of the Christian life. As, in the figure, these three kinds of materials have their normal place side by side with one another in the temple or palace, they must be taken to represent the different forms of spiritual life which are produced in souls by healthy evangelical preaching.

The apostle had declared, ver. 8, that each would be appraised and recompensed according to the nature of his work. He now points out when and how this discrimination will take place.

Ver. 13. The same figure continues. The edifice before being inhabited by the Master must pass through the proof of fire, in which the materials of bad quality will be reduced to ashes, but from which the good materials will come forth intact.—Commentators are mostly at one in our time in applying the *day* of which the apostle speaks to the epoch of the Lord's advent. Grotius thought of the meaning of the Latin *dies* in the phrase *dies docebit:* "time will show." Neander also held that the history of the Church is the grand means of putting to the proof the doctrines of teachers. Calvin, adopting a similar interpretation, understands by *the day* the time when true Christian knowledge comes out in its clearness; as happened, for example, at the epoch of the Reformation. But it is impossible to prove that this meaning, with its different shades, can be that of the term *the day.* Others have applied it to the date of the destruction of Jerusalem, because this event was particularly suited to dissipate in the Church the Jewish opinions which Paul was combating; but what Paul combats in this whole passage is worldly wisdom rather than theocratic prejudices. St. Augustine thought of the day of affliction which puts to the proof the reality of the inner life; and Hofmann, of Antichrist's great persecution, which will bring victory to the good, defeat to the bad. It seems that such was the meaning already given to our passage by the author of the *Διδαχὴ τῶν δώδεκα ἀποστόλων* (*the doctrine of the twelve apostles*) in the second century; for in chap. xvi. the warning, "Watch," is first founded on the calamities of the last days, and next the author adds: "Then will appear, like a Son of God, the seducer of the world, and the race of men will come εἰς τὴν πύρωσιν τῆς δοκιμασίας (*into the burning of trial*)," words which can only be taken from our passage. But, when that day is referred to in Scripture, it is more distinctly qualified; comp. Eph. vi. 13 (*the evil day*); Heb. iii. 8 (*the day of temptation*); 1 Pet. ii. 12 (*the day of visitation*); Rev. iii. 10 (*the hour of trial*), etc. It is therefore more natural to abide by the first meaning: the day of Christ, when the separation will be made between believers themselves; comp. i. 8, iv. 5.—The manifestation which will take place at that time will be effected by means of *fire*. Many, and Meyer himself, seem to take this word in its literal sense, quoting as parallel 2 Thess. i. 8, where the Lord is represented as coming from heaven with flames of fire. But it must not be forgotten that the building to be proved exists only figuratively, and that consequently the fire which is to put it to the proof can only be also a figurative fire. The term therefore can only denote here the incorruptible judgment pronounced by the omniscience and consuming holiness of the Judge who appears. His Spirit will thoroughly explore the fruit due to the ministry of every preacher. When, in the Apocalypse, the judgment is described which the Lord passes on the Seven Churches, it is said in connection with that of Thyatira (ii. 18): "These things saith the Son of God, who hath eyes like unto a flame of fire." The look of a holy man may become an insupportable fire to the wicked, how much more that of the Lord! This penetrating look will then separate between what is real, solid, indestructible, and what is only transient, apparent, factitious. The subject ordinarily assigned the verb ἀποκαλύπτεται, *is manifested,* is that of the preceding proposition, *the day:* "The day of Christ is manifested with fire or by fire. But then it seems no more possible to take the term fire in the figurative sense. Others take as subject that of the first proposition of the verse, the *work:* "The work is manifested by means of fire." But this sense leads to an intolerable tautology with the following proposition; the apostle does not so repeat himself. Bengel and Osiander understand as subject, *the Lord;* but to reach this subject we must go back to ver. 11; then it is difficult to suppose that Paul would have said: "The Lord is manifested with fire." Is it not better to take ἀποκαλύπτεται in the impersonal sense? "For it is by fire that manifestation takes place," that is to say, that things are manifested as what they really are. This proposition enunciates not a fact, but a principle; hence the verb in the present ἀποκαλύπτεται, which contrasts with the two futures the preceding (δηλώσει) and the following (δοκιμάσει).—The ὅτι, *because,* supposes the principle recognised, that judgment, of which fire is the emblem, accompanies the day of the Lord.

From this principle flows the consequence enunciated in the last proposition. — If the pronoun αὐτό is authentic, which is read after πῦρ by the *Vatic.* and three other Mjj., it may be taken as relating to the fire: "the fire *itself,*" that is to say: the fire in virtue of its own proper nature; or what seems simpler, it should be taken in relation to the work, ἔργον, and made the object of δοκιμάσει: "the fire will attest it, the work, so as to bring out what it is" (ὁποῖόν ἐστι).

—The double result of this putting to the proof is described in vers. 14, 15.

Vers. 14, 15. "If any man's work shall abide which he hath built thereupon, he shall receive the reward; 15. if any man's work shall be burned, he shall suffer loss [of reward]; but he himself shall be saved, yet so as through fire."—Μενει is generally taken as a future (μενεῖ, *shall abide*), because of the future which follows κατακαήσεται, *shall be burned.* But there is no force in this reason; the act of burning is instantaneous; hence the future, which refers to a definite time, while that which abides, abides always: the thought expressed by the present μένει. The μισθὸν λήψεται, *shall receive the reward*, might be rendered in this everyday form: When it shall have been recognised that the work was of good quality, his cheque will be paid to him. This reward cannot be salvation; for the faithful workman was already in possession of this supreme blessing when he was labouring. We have to think then of more particular privileges, such as the joy of being the object of the Master's satisfaction: "Good and faithful servant!" then the happiness of seeing invested with glory the souls whom a faithful ministry has contributed to sanctify; finally, the possession of a glorious position in the new state of things established by the Lord at His Parousia: "Thou hast gained ten pounds; receive power over ten cities" (Luke xix. 17).

Ver. 15. To understand the picture which the apostle draws of the opposite result, we must undoubtedly suppose the workmen occupying the portion of the building which has been committed to them, and to which they are putting the last touch. In proportion as the fire, set to the building, consumes the combustible materials of which the bad workman has made use, the latter of course finds himself in danger of perishing along with his work; if he is saved, it can only be by escaping through the flames, and thanks to the solidity of the foundation.—The second future κατακαήσεται, *shall be burned,* is an ancient form (Homer, Hesiod) which had been replaced by the first future καυθήσομαι, and which reappears in the later Greek writers. By the perishable *work* of this labourer, Paul understands the Christian life without seriousness, humility, self-denial, personal communion with Christ, which has been produced among the members of the Church by the ministry of a preacher solely concerned to move sensibility, to charm the mind and please his audience.—The *loss,* ζημία, with which he is threatened, consists above all in the proved uselessness of his labour and in its destruction, which will take place under his own eyes. With what pain will he contemplate the merely external fruits of his brilliant or profound preaching passing away in smoke! Then he will see himself refused the reward of the faithful servant, the honourable position in, Christ's kingdom, to which he imagined himself entitled: the payment of his cheque will be refused him.

But the apostle adds that this worker *shall be saved.* Chrysostom and the old Greek commentators understood the word *save* here in the sense of keep: "kept in Gehenna to suffer for ever." But the pronoun αὐτός establishes an evident contrast between the reward lost and the person saved; then the verb σώζειν, *to save*, is always taken in a favourable sense; Paul would have required to say in the sense indicated τηρηθήσεται, *shall be kept;* finally, the διὰ πυρός, *through fire*, is not identical with ἐν πυρί, *in fire*. The apostle certainly means, that though this workman has put bad materials into the building, yet because he built on the foundation he will not be given over to condemnation. But if he reaches salvation, it will only be through the furnace, like one who is obliged, in order to save his life, to pass through the flames. This furnace comprehends all the terrors of this judgment: the shame of this revelation, the horror caused by the look of the offended Judge, the grief of seeing the work on which he congratulated himself reduced to nothingness, and the souls whom he thought he had built up incapable of undergoing the last trial, and lost partly through his fault . . . ! "I have searched myself and I have found myself," said a dying pastor; "this is all the punishment God reserves for me." Were not these the first kindlings of the fire of which the apostle here speaks?

Some Catholic commentators have thought to find in the words, *as through fire*, a proof in favour of the doctrine of purgatory, and the Council of Florence, in 1439, based the dogma on this passage (Edwards). This is to forget,—1. that the fire is allegorical like the building; 2. that it is only teachers who are in question; 3. that the trial indicated is a means of valuation, not of purification; 4. that this fire is lighted at Christ's coming, and consequently does not yet burn in the interval between the death of Christians and that advent; 5. that the salvation of the worker, of which Paul speaks, takes place not *by*, but *in spite of* the fire.

There is something more serious than to build badly, and that is to do violence to what is already built. Such is the relation between the following passage, vers. 16–20, and the preceding. Hofmann well states this transition: "Paul passes from those who took upon them, without serious reflection, to continue his work at Corinth, to those who did not fear to destroy the fruit of his labour." Only it need not be said: of *his* labour; for he has not given himself out as one of the ἐποικοδομοῦντες, of those who have raised the building on the foundation laid. We must therefore speak of the work done, and successfully done, after Paul's ministry. To whom are we to ascribe such labour if not to Apollos, who had watered what the apostle had planted? As, then, it was impossible to apply to this teacher the figure of the bad workman in the previous picture, it is still more impossible to apply to him the figure of the destroyers in the following representation. And since the labour of demolition, about to be spoken of, is attributed to that same human wisdom spoken of in chap. i., we find the opinion confirmed which we had expressed in explaining the chapter, viz. that it had no reference whatever to the ministry of Apollos.

Vers. 16, 17. "Know ye not that ye are a temple of God, and that the Spirit of God dwelleth in you? 17. If any man destroy the temple of God, him[1] will God destroy;[2] for the temple of God is holy, which temple ye are."—The asyndeton between vers. 15 and

[1] A D E F G Syr^{sch} read αυτον, instead of τουτον, the reading of T. R. with ℵ B C L P.

[2] D E F G L P read φθειρει (*destroys*), instead of φθερει (*shall destroy*), the reading of T. R. with ℵ A B C.

16 is to be remarked; it is as if, on occasion of what the apostle has just said about bad workers, a sudden view took possession of his heart, that of the gravity of the act of those workmen who not only build badly, but who destroy what is already constructed. Everything in this abrupt transition betrays emotion; the interrogative form: Know ye not . . . ? which appeals to the conscience of the Church and to the livelier feeling which it should have of its own dignity; the phrase, *temple of God*, forming a step higher than the simple *building* (ver. 9); finally, the two analogous gradations, that of the first φθείρειν, *destroy*, rising above the act of bad *building thereon*, and that of the second φθείρειν, denoting the punishment, rising above the simple fact of ζημιοῦσθαι, *suffering loss* (of reward).—We must avoid translating, "*the* temple of God." The Church of Corinth is not the universal Church. The absence of the article before ναός, *temple*, makes this word the indication of a simple quality: "Ye are a temple of God; ye partake of the sacred character of such a building!" This applies to every believer at Corinth, and at the same time to the Church as a whole. And how do they all possess such a dignity? The following proposition explains: God dwells in Christ, and Christ by the Holy Spirit dwells in the believer. The Father and the Son, according to the promise of Jesus, thus make, by the Spirit, "their abode in him" (John xiv. 23). The same figure: Eph. ii. 19–22; 1 Pet. ii. 4, 5.—The adjunct ἐν ὑμῖν, *in you*, may signify within you or in the midst of you. The context speaks rather in favour of the second meaning, since Paul is addressing the Church as such. But as

God dwells *among* believers only on condition of dwelling *in* them, the second meaning implies the first. Is the apostle thinking of the temple of Jerusalem, for which henceforth the Church, the true spiritual temple, is to be substituted? Possibly. Now if it was a sacrilege to profane the shadow, what will it be to do violence to the body (Col. ii. 17)!

Ver. 17. Again an asyndeton. Ver. 16 was the minor of the syllogism of which ver. 17 is the major: "Ye are a temple . . .; he is destroyed who destroys a temple . . ., therefore . . ." The conclusion which is self-evident is understood.—The future φθερεῖ, *shall destroy,* is no doubt the true reading, though the present φθείρει might also be defended as the present of the idea, and consequently of certain realization. In ver. 15, notwithstanding the loss of the reward (the ζημιοῦσθαι), the salvation of the workman was reserved; here, it is excluded. The punishment increases with the guilt: "As thou has treated the house of God, thou shalt be treated." The Greco-Lat. reading, αὐτόν, *him,* emphasizes the *identity* of the man who has destroyed and who is destroyed. But the Alex. and Byz. reading, τοῦτον, *him,* this man, is at once better supported and more forcible.—The following proposition gives us to know the wherefore of this severe treatment; the dignity of the building to which this sacrilegious workman does violence. The force of the proof rests on the attribute ἅγιος, *holy.* What is holy, that is to say, consecrated to God, partakes of the inviolability of God Himself.—The apostle finding it superfluous to enunciate the conclusion in full, contents himself with suggesting it by the last words:

"a holy temple, which ye are." The plural pronoun οἵτινες is a case of attraction from the following ὑμεῖς. This relative pronoun of quality is to be connected not with ναός only, nor with ἅγιος only, but with the entire phrase, ναὸς ἅγιος, *holy temple.*

To what persons did this warning and threatening apply? Evidently to those who had laboured at Corinth in such a way that they had ended with disorganizing the Church, poisoning its religious and moral life, and compromising the Divine work so happily begun and carried forward in that great city. Here it is, as it seems to me, that we find the full explanation of the end of chap. ii., where Paul spoke of the *psychical* or natural man, distinguishing him from the yet carnal Christian (iii. 1–4). The majority of the Church of Corinth belonged to the second category; but there was certainly a minority in it whom the apostle ranked in the first. It was they whom he had in view in the last two so severe verses of chap. ii.: the man who has only his natural understanding; and it is to them he returns in the verses immediately following, where he again, as in chap. i., puts worldly wisdom on its trial. We have already said: these various passages, as it seems to us, can only concern *those of Christ*, as they are unmasked in the Second Epistle. But why does the apostle address this warning not to the guilty themselves, but to the Church: "Know ye not that *ye are* a temple of God," and all that follows? It is because he wishes to excite the whole Church to a holy indignation, and to call forth within it a vigorous reaction against the authors of these troubles; comp.

the appeal to the vigilance of believers, Phil. iii. 2: "Beware of evil workers." In the following verses, Paul shows the source of the evil, as he had already pointed it out in chap. i., in order to open the eyes of both.

Ver. 18. "Let no man deceive himself; if any man thinketh that he is wise among you, let him become a fool in this world, that he may become wise."—Again an asyndeton, testifying to the emotion which fills the apostle's heart.—The illusion, to which he points in the first words of the verse, according to some, is the security in which those teachers live, not suspecting the danger which they run (vers. 16, 17). But the words εἴ τις δοκεῖ, *if any man thinketh*, imagines, claims, lead us rather to connect the idea of *self-deceiving* with what follows. There are people who have claims to wisdom, and who display their eloquence within the Church. Edwards concludes from the ἐν ὑμῖν, *among you*, that if they were among them, they were not of them; otherwise Paul would have said, τίς ὑμῶν. The fact that those people were strangers may be true, but the term used does not necessarily say so. Its meaning is rather this: "If any individual whatever, Corinthian or other, while preaching the gospel *in your assemblies*, assumes the part of the wise man and the reputation of a profound thinker (iv. 10), let him assure himself that he will not attain to true wisdom till he has passed through a crisis in which that wisdom of his with which he is puffed up will perish, and after which only he will receive the wisdom which is from above." This crisis of death to false wisdom is what the apostle characterizes by the words: *let him become a fool!*

To renounce this imaginary wisdom, which is only a human conception, to own his ignorance in what concerns the great matter of salvation, and, after taking hold of Christ crucified, who is foolishness to the wise of this world, to draw from Him the Divine wisdom which He has revealed to the world, such is the only way of realizing the claim expressed in the words, " thinketh he is wise."—Does the phrase, *ἐν τῷ αἰῶνι τούτῳ*, *in this world*, belong to the preceding or the succeeding proposition ? in other words, does this adjunct qualify the idea of being wise in the Church, or that of becoming a fool ? In the former case the words would characterize a preacher who tries to gain the reputation of wisdom among Christians by putting himself forward in the midst of them as the *representative of the wisdom of the world.* In the latter case Paul would say : " If thou claimest to be a wise man in the Church, well ! But in that case begin with humbling thy reason, accepting the foolishness of the cross, and with thus becoming a fool *in the eyes of the wise of the world*, and then thou shalt be able to become really the organ of Divine wisdom in the Church." Notwithstanding the able pleading of Rückert in favour of the former meaning, we think, with Hofmann, that the second deserves the preference. The antithesis between the *among you* and the *in this world* stands out more precisely, and the sense is simpler. —The following verses justify the necessity of dying to the wisdom of the world. Of old has not God, the only wise, charged it with foolishness ? Two scriptural declarations are alleged in proof.

Vers. 19, 20. "For the wisdom of this world is

foolishness with God. For it is written, 'He that taketh the wise in their craftiness.' 20. And again, 'The Lord knoweth the reasonings of the wise, that they are vain.'"—The first passage declares the powerlessness of the wisdom of the world to reach the ends at which it aims, consequently its vanity from the standpoint of utility. It is taken from Job v. 13. The devices of the wise themselves become the net in which God takes them, so that they are forced in the end to confess that the more subtle, the more foolish they have been. The verb δράσσειν, *to close the fist upon* (from δράξ, *the fist*), is much more expressive than the word καταλαμβάνειν used by the LXX. to render the Hebrew term. The apostle likewise improves the translation of the LXX. by substituting for φρόνησις, *prudence*, the word πανουργία, from πᾶν and ἔργον, the capacity for doing everything, not in good, but in evil, to attain the end in view.

Ver. 20. This passage is taken from Ps. xciv. 11. It proclaims the emptiness of human wisdom, not now as to its result, but as to its very essence. The Hebrew and the LXX. say, "the thoughts of *man.*" The apostle says, *of the wise*, because it is through them that mankind exercise their understanding.—The verb *knowing* has two objects in the original texts (Hebrew and Greek), as is often the case; first, the object known, the thought; then what God knows of those thoughts: that they are vain. We cannot render this forcible turn of expression in French.[1]—The apostle here judges human wisdom only from the point of view

[1] [Our Authorized English Version imitates the Hebrew and Greek. —Tr.]

of the discovery and attainment of salvation. He certainly respects every sincere effort to discover the truth (Phil. iv. 8); but salvation is a thought of God superior to all the discoveries of human wisdom (ii. 6–8).

Though he had addressed the whole Church (ver. 17 : *Ye are* . . .), it was those who encouraged disorders whom the apostle had indirectly threatened in the foregoing verses. The three following verses contain the direction which it remains to him to give to the Church itself as to its conduct toward Christ's true ministers. They are therefore the conclusion of the passage begun ii. 5.

Vers. 21–23

Ver. 21. "So then, let no man glory in men, for all things are yours."—The apostle began by reminding the Corinthians of what preachers are in relation to the Church : *servants* (ministers) of the one Lord; then, in a passage which may be regarded as an episode, he put before the eyes of the Church and of ministers themselves the grave responsibility incurred by the latter (vers. 10–20). Now he concludes; this is shown by the particle of transition ὥστε, *so that;* we can only translate it here by *so then,* because of the following imperative. We shall see that this same conjunction is ordinarily used in this Epistle to announce the practical conclusion to be drawn from a foregoing statement of doctrine; comp. vii. 38, xi. 33, xiv. 39, xv. 58.—On the imperative after ὥστε, see on i. 31.—*To glory in a person* can only mean : to boast of one's relation to him, to take honour from belonging to him, as a servant or a disciple takes glory from the name of an illustrious master. It is an allusion to the formulas: "I am of Paul, . . . Apollos, . . ." etc. Far from its being believers who belong to their teachers, it is much rather these who belong to them; and not only their teachers, but *all things.* Stoic wisdom had said: *Omnia sapientis sunt,* because the wise man can make use of everything, even of what is adverse to him. The believer can say so with a yet loftier and surer title, because he belongs to God, who puts all things at the service of His own. It is in this sense that Paul says, Rom. viii. 28: "All things work together for good to them that love God." As he develops it in the same passage, God, in His eternal plan, has disposed all things with a view to the salvation and glory of those who He knew beforehand would believe on His Son. The contents of this πάντα, *all things,* are detailed in the following enumeration, which has been called, not without reason, "the inventory of the possessions of the child of God," and in which death itself figures.

Vers. 22, 23. "Whether Paul, or Apollos, or Cephas, or the world, or life, or death, or things present, or things to come, all are yours; 23. and ye are Christ's, and Christ is God's."—In the front are placed the names of the three teachers who had been made party chiefs, and in connection with whom all this instruction is given. To express his conclusion, Paul has only to give back the three formulas. Instead of saying, "I am Paul's," the Corinthian should say, "Paul is mine." The Church is the end; the ministers are the means. Peter, with his personal memories of the life of Jesus, Apollos, with his knowledge of the Scriptures and the irresistible charm of his eloquence, Paul, with his superior knowledge of God's plan for the salvation of the world and his incomparable apostolic activity, are not masters to whom the Church should bow as a vassal, but gifts bestowed on it, and which it is bound to turn to advantage, without despising one or going into raptures over another. Paul cannot, of course, give back the watchword of the fourth party in the same way; for in itself this formula exactly expressed the truth. We shall see, by and by, how he brings it back to its true meaning.

These three gifts represent one and the same idea, that of the ministry, that is to say, in general, gifts of a spiritual order. In contrast to them Paul names *the world*, the totality of beings who, outside the Church, may tell on the lot of believers, or of the Church itself. Animate or inanimate, the creatures obey Christ who has received power over all things, and, through Him, the Church, which is His body (Eph. i. 22).—Of the powers acting in the world there are two, of formidable and mysterious greatness, which seem to decide the course of the universe, *life* and *death*. The first comprehends all phenomena which are characterized by force, health, productiveness; the second, all those which betray weakness, sickness, decay. From the one or other of these two forces proceed all the hostile influences of which the believer feels himself the object. But he knows also that he is not their puppet; for it is Christ his Lord who guides and tempers their action. Chrysostom, Grotius, and others have restricted the application of these two terms, *life* and *death*, to the teachers of the Church. But the apostle, on the contrary, would have them taken in their widest generality.—To these two pairs, that of the spiritual order and the terrestrial order, and that of life and death, the apostle adds a third in relation to time, *things present*, and *things to come.* The participle τὰ ἐνεστῶτα, strictly: what is imminent, here, as often, in contrast to "things future," takes the sense of *things present.* It comprehends all that can happen us in the present state of things, and as long as we form part of it; while *the things to come* denote the great expected transformation, with its eternal consequences. Then the apostle sums up his enumeration by reproducing the bold paradox with which he had begun: "Yea, I tell you, *all is yours.*" It is easy to see what the apostle wishes: to exalt the consciousness of this Church, which is degrading itself by dependence on weak human instruments (ἀνθρώποις, ver. 21), to the height of its glorious position in Christ. He strives to restore it to self-respect. It is the same intention which comes out in the following words.

Ver. 23. We might be tempted to give the words, *and ye are Christ's*, a restrictive meaning: "Ye are His alone, not your teachers'." But in the two analogous propositions, that which precedes and that which follows, Paul certainly does not mean: "All things are only yours," and "Christ is only God's." It is not restrictions we have here, but strong affirmations; the thought is not limited, it rises. "All things are the Church's, because it belongs itself to Christ, and depends on Him." It is in this saying, *and ye are Christ's*, that allusion is found to the fourth party. It is not merely a few presumptuous people, puffed up with conceit of their own wisdom, who can say: *And as for me, I am Christ's;* this is the privilege of the whole Church.—And, as if to put the last stroke to the annihilation of all human glory, Paul denies it even in the person of that Lord in whom all mankind might legitimately glory: *and Christ is God's.* As the Church possesses all things because it depends on Christ, Christ possesses all things because He depends on God; comp. xi. 3. God in Christ, such then for man is the one subject of glorying (i. 31). It has been asked, from the first ages of the Church, whether these words referred to Christ as man, or as a Divine Being. The old commentators and several of the Fathers, even Athanasius (see Edwards), applied them to the eternal relation between the Son and the Father. This is done also by Meyer, Kling, etc. Hence would follow the subordination of the Son to the Father, even within the Trinity. Others, Augustine, Calvin, Olshausen, de Wette, Edwards, apply them to Christ only in His humanity, in order to maintain the essential equality of the Father and the Son. It must be remembered, above all, that they refer to the Lord in His present state of glory, for it is as glorified that He is the Head of the Church. But this itself proves that the first explanation is not less true than the second; they are as inseparable from one another as the two states, the human and Divine, in the person of the exalted Christ. That is to say, we apply the notion of dependence contained in Paul's expression, not only to the Lord's humanity, but also to His Divinity. Is not this implied besides in the names of *Son* and *Word* used to denote His Divine being? And is not Beet right in affirming that only this notion of the essential subordination of the Son to the Father enables us to conceive the unity in the Divine Trinity? The meaning therefore is, that as to His one and indivisible person as Son of God and Son of man, Jesus receives all from the Father, and consequently belongs to Him wholly. It is on this absolute dependence that His universal sovereignty rests.

As soon as the Church of Corinth rises to the view of these relations, what will become of the miserable desire among its members to magnify themselves and to turn what may be wanting to others into a ground of self-satisfaction? How will it be possible for one, when he contemplates the absolute dependence in which the Son abides relatively to the Father, still to glory in himself or in another? Each believer will possess everything, even the eminent teachers who enable him to make progress, as gifts from His hand.

After thus making the Corinthians ashamed of their guilty infatuations, it only remains to the apostle to check the rash judgments in which some indulge respecting him: this is what he does in the following passage, which closes this section.

4:1-5

Ver. 1. "Let a man so account of us as of ministers of Christ and stewards of the mysteries of God."—After explaining what preachers *are not,* to show that no man should make himself dependent on them, the apostle declares *what they are,* to withdraw them from the rash judgments of the members of the Church. He does so first by continuing to speak of himself and

Apollos (*us;* comp. vi. 6), then he speaks singly of himself (*me*, v. 3).—The word οὕτως, *thus*, which begins this passage, has been understood in the sense of *so then.* Thus taken, it would connect this passage with the preceding, announcing a consequence drawn from it. But vers. 21–23 had already drawn the consequence (ὥστε, ver. 21) from the preceding exposition. And the logical relation between what follows and what precedes would rather be that of contrast. The end of ver. 23 had raised the readers to such a height, that the apostle does not care to connect with it what follows by any particle whatever, and continues by an asyndeton. It seems to me indeed, as to Rückert, that the οὕτως is nothing else than the antecedent of of the ὡς, *as*, which follows; comp. John vii. 46; Eph. v. 33; James ii. 12, etc. The meaning is: "*See how* you ought to regard us."—The word ἄνθρωπος might be translated by the French pronoun *on;* perhaps it is better rendered by *each;*[1] comp. xi. 28. Edwards sees in the use of the word an imitation of the Hebrew *Isch.* Bengel thinks that the term is intended to contrast man's judgment with that of God. I think the apostle wishes it to be felt that he is addressing the Church in the person of *each* of its members, and recalling to their minds the notion of ignorance and weakness attached to the condition of man.—The term ὑπηρέτης, which we translate by *minister*, strictly denotes a man who acts as rower under the orders of some one (ὑπό and ἐρέσσω); he is a man labouring freely in the service of others: it here denotes the acting and laborious side of the Christian ministry. The term

[1] [Our English translation renders literally.—Tr.]

οἰκονόμος, *steward*, dispenser, denotes, among the ancients, a confidential slave to whom the master intrusts the direction of his house, and in particular the care of distributing to all the servants their tasks and provisions (Luke xii. 42). This second term designates preachers as administrators of a truth which is not theirs, but their master's. It relates to the inward and spiritual side of the work of the ministry.—The trust administered by them is *the mysteries of God.* This term *mystery,* in the singular, denotes the plan of salvation in general (see on ii. 7). In the plural, it relates to the different designs included in this plan. The plural is here connected with the idea of distribution associated with that of steward. Perhaps Paul makes allusion to the choice which Apollos and he required to make among the manifold materials of Christian teaching, in order to use in every case only those which were appropriate to the state of the Corinthians (iii. 2).—The genitives *of Christ* and *of God,* which are certainly related to those of iii. 23, remind us that preachers, as labouring in the active service *of Christ,* the Head of the Church, and charged with distributing to it the truths *of God,* have to give account before these supreme authorities and not before the members of the Church. They go where Christ sends them, and deliver what God has given them. They are not to be judged *in this respect.* The only thing that can be asked of them, is to be faithful in the way in which they fulfil the missions confided to them, and in which they conform their teaching to the measure of light which they have received.

Ver. 2. "Now what[1] remains[2] to require[3] of stewards is, that a man be found faithful."—The meaning of the received reading (ὃ δὲ λοιπὸν ζητεῖται . . . ἵνα) is this: "As to what may be required moreover (λοιπόν, *for the rest*) of stewards, it is that . . ." According to this reading, the apostle means: the ministry of teaching being once confided by God to a man, the question is no longer if he is more or less eloquent, more or less profound, more or less captivating,—God, who chose and sent him, has alone to do with all these questions,—but only if he is *faithful*, that is to say, if he gives out conscientiously what is committed to him, if he puts all the gifts and powers with which he is endowed into the service of this task; if, as a devoted servant, he has only one interest, the cause of his Master. He can only be called to account for the conscientious use of what he has received.—This clear and natural meaning suits the context and leaves nothing to be desired. But several Mjj. of the *three* families present different readings. Some (A C D F G P) read ὧδε λοιπὸν ζητεῖτε, which would signify: "For the rest in these circumstances seek in stewards that each be found faithful . . ." This meaning is inadmissible. In such a sentence two things, it is plain, are mixed up: an exhortation addressed to particular persons, the Corinthian readers (*seek*), and a general principle (*in stewards; each*, τίς). The *Sinaït.* attempts to remedy this awkwardness

[1] T. R. reads ο δε (*now that which*) with E L and the most of the Mnn., while ℵ A B C D F G P It. Syr. read ωδε (*in these circumstances*).

[2] After λοιπον, ℵ reads τι (*something* or *what is it which?*).

[3] T. R. with B L Mnn. It. Syr. reads ζητειται (*it is sought*), while ℵ A C D E F G P read ζητειτε (*seek*).

by introducing after λοιπόν a τι, which can only be taken in an interrogative sense: "In these circumstances, moreover, *what* else seek ye in stewards, than that each . . . ?" The meaning is good in itself; only, instead of *in stewards*, there would need to be *in us.* For if this question expresses a consequence to be drawn from ver. 1, as the word ὧδε would demand *in this state of things*, it would require to be *in us* (*these* particular *stewards*), and not *in stewards* in general. The τις following is likewise suitable only to a maxim.—There remains the reading of B: ὧδε λοιπὸν ζητεῖται ἵνα: "In this state of things, the only thing sought (λοιπόν, the only thing which remains) in stewards is that . . ." This reading, though admitted by most commentators of our day, is no more admissible than the preceding, and for the same reason. The ὧδε, *in this state of things*, can relate only to the case of ver. 1, and consequently to the ministers denoted by the ἡμᾶς, *us* (Paul and Apollos), while the words: *in stewards*, give to this saying the character of an entirely general rule of conduct. We must therefore return to the reading and sense of the T. R. This is one of those cases in which all the presumptions of external criticism are of no avail, whatever may be said against exegetical reasons. It is easy enough to explain what has given rise to the corruption of the text in part of the documents of the three families, and so early as in the old versions. The beginning was made by substituting for ζητεῖται, *is sought*, the imperative ζητεῖτε, *seek*, either to continue the series of the preceding imperatives (καυχάσθω, λογιζέσθω), and to give to the sentence a hortative turn (the same error as in most of the Mjj., Rom. v. 1: ἔχωμεν, and 1 Cor. xv. 49: φορέσωμεν), or as a mistake arising from the pronunciation of αι (in ζητεῖται) as ε. The imperative once admitted, led to the change of ὃ δέ into ὧδε to make this verse an application of the idea of the preceding verse.—*Λοιπόν, moreover*, that is to say: beyond what God and Christ give to their agents; comp. the expressions: "the grace given unto me," iii. 10, and the ὡς ἔδωκεν, iii. 5.—The relation between the two ideas of *seeking* and *finding* is evident. It is this relation which justifies the use of the conjunction ἵνα, *that*. Men seek with the view of finding.—The idea of the verse therefore is: that the only thing for which the steward is responsible, is his fidelity. Now this is the very point on which man's judgment is incompetent, vers. 3–5.

Vers. 3, 4. "But with me it is a very small thing that I should be judged, of you or of a human tribunal; yea, I judge not mine own self. 4. For I know nothing against myself; yet am I not hereby justified; but[1] he that judgeth me is the Lord."—The two previous verses related to preachers in general, especially to Apollos and Paul. From this verse, the application becomes wholly personal to Paul. For in what he proceeds to declare, the apostle can evidently make no affirmation except in so far as concerns himself.—'Εμοί: "*with me* (at least)." Paul cannot know whether Apollos thought like him on this point.—The preposition εἰς, which indicates motion, or tendency to a point, is slightly incorrect, with the verb of rest, ἔστι. It indicates the progressive reduction to a minimum of

[1] Instead of ο δε, ℵ reads ο γαρ (*for* He).

value, in proportion as the apostle weighs the judgments which are passed on him at Corinth. These unfavourable judgments become more and more with him the last thing which disquiets him.—The *that* (ἵνα) does not entirely lose the notion of aim: Paul has no interest whatever *with a view to the fact that* these judgments exist or do not exist. —The term ἀνθρωπίνη ἡμέρα, which we render by *a human tribunal,* literally signifies *a human day,* a day of human assizes. The word *day* is used in the same way in the Latin phrase *diem dicere.* —These last words contain a softening of what Paul had just said of the small value which he attaches to the judgments of certain Corinthians. The same indifference he feels in regard to all human judgment in general.—The term ἀνακρίνειν denotes rather the examination than the judgment; but as the examination issues in a sentence, and as we have no verb to render the strict sense, we must translate by the word *judge.*—Once on this way, the apostle goes to the very end. He does not himself feel adequate to judge himself with certainty. The ἀλλά indicates the gradation: "I refuse not only the judgment of others, *but also* that of myself;" comp. 2 Cor. vii. 11. He feels that in his inner man there are unexplored recesses which do not allow him to discover thoroughly the real state of things, the full integrity of his own fidelity, and consequently to pronounce a valid sentence on himself.

Ver. 4. His inmost conscience does not upbraid him with any unfaithfulness; but for all that (ἐν τούτῳ), he is not yet justified, that is to say, found irreproachable, by Him who searches the hearts and reins (ver. 5). It is usually objected that in this so simple sense, held by Chrysostom, Calvin, de Wette, Osiander, Edwards, the term δικαιοῦσθαι, *to be justified,* is taken in a purely moral sense, quite different from the ordinary dogmatic sense which it has in Paul's writings. That is not exact. The meaning of the word *to be justified* remains at bottom always the same: to be declared just. Only this declarative act is applied to another period, and given forth under other conditions than in the use which the apostle ordinarily makes of it. The time in question here is the day of judgment, not the hour of conversion; and consequently the condition of justification is not faith only, but holiness and fidelity, fruits of faith. At the time of conversion a man is declared just without yet being so; in the day of judgment, to be declared such he must be so in reality. The declarative sense of the word justify remains therefore as the basis of the use which the apostle here makes of the term; it is exactly the same in the passage Rom. ii. 13. — Melanchthon, Calvin, Rückert, Meyer, Beet maintain the application of the term to justification by faith in the ordinary sense of the word. The following is the wholly different explanation which they give of the verse: "It is to no purpose that I feel myself guilty of nothing; it is not thereupon that my justification rests, but on Christ alone." Rückert and Meyer allege in particular the position of the words ἐν τούτῳ, *in this,* after the negative οὐκ, a position which makes the negative, instead of bearing on the verb, bear on ἐν τούτῳ; it is not therefore the *being justified* which is denied, but the *being justified on this* (ground), that is to say, through the fidelity of which Paul is conscious. He means: "I am justified not by this, but by something else." His system was well enough known, Rückert thinks, to make every one comprehend what was the other understood way. But Osiander rightly answers, that in this case, what Paul affirms so energetically is a thing which is understood of itself. Who could imagine that the apostle thought of founding on his present apostolical fidelity the absolution of all the sins of his past life? Then it would be strange if in opposition to the means of justification, which he so expressly excludes, he purely and simply should understand that which he maintains. Finally, vers. 3 and 5 manifestly transporting us to the day of judgment, we are obliged to refer ver. 4 also to that time. As to the position of the ἐν τούτῳ (*for this*) after the negative, it is intended to emphasize the idea of *for this* in the sense of "*even* for this," without there necessarily being a contrast to any other way of justification.—According to an explanation not infrequent in Catholic writers, the apostle is supposed here to express the uncertainty in which he is plunged as to his state of grace, and to teach thereby even the impossibility of the Christian's attaining the assurance of salvation here below, unless by an exceptional revelation. Calvin has already set aside this misunderstanding. Paul denies the competency of any human judge whatever, even himself. But if he did not obtain from God the full approbation after which he aspires, and to which he hopes he has a right, it would not follow in his view that his salvation was thereby compromised. Has he not just affirmed that the workman who has built with bad materials, but on the true foundation, shall not perish, but lose only the reward of his work? How, then, should he put his own state of grace in doubt for some unfaithfulness which remained unperceived even by his conscience? Though blameable in one point, he would not therefore be rejected.

If the meaning which we reject had been the one Paul had in view, he must have gone on to say: "*For* it is the Lord who *justifieth* me." He says on the contrary, thinking of the judgment: "*Now* it is the Lord who maketh *the examination.*"—The *Sinaït.* reads γάρ instead of δέ, which gives an excellent meaning: "I am not justified by the fact of my good conscience; *for* He who maketh the only valid examination, is the Lord." But the δέ, however, better emphasizes the distinction between this Judge, whose examination alone is competent, and the fallible man who claims to pose as judge.—The pres. participle ἀνακρίνων indicates the permanent function, the office. "He is the investigator of my life."

Ver. 5. "Therefore judge nothing before the time, until the Lord come, who even[1] will bring to light the hidden things of darkness, and will make manifest the counsels of the hearts: and then shall every man have praise of God."—This verse is, as it were, the full period put to the personal application which Paul has just made in vers. 1–4. The ὥστε, *so that,* therefore corresponds to that of iii. 21. There the meaning was: *therefore* no infatuation!—Here: *therefore* no

[1] D E F G It. omit και (*even*).

judgment!—The τι is rather a qualifying pronoun than the indication of the object of κρίνετε: "Do not pass any judgment!"—The words, *before the time,* are explained by what follows: *till the Lord come,* the true Judge. This character which belongs to Him exclusively is explained by the two following relative propositions. In fact, the infallible judgment of a human life supposes two things: the revelation of the acts of that life in their totality, even the most unknown, and the manifestation of the inner springs of the will, in the acts known or unknown. This is what Paul means by the two phrases: "*the things of darkness*" and "*the counsels of the hearts.*" The hidden acts, which will be brought to light, are not only the bad, but also the good (Matt. vi. 3, 4, 6; 1 Tim. v. 23–25). It is the more necessary to have regard to the last here as there is no question afterwards except that of *praise.*—The inner springs and feelings are what determine the true quality of actions in the eyes of God; it is therefore on the complete knowledge of them that the just appreciation of a human life rests.—The καί before φωτίσει, which we have translated by *even,* which others render by *also,* has been variously understood. Osiander, Rückert: "He will come not only to judge, but *also* to set in light." This sense is inadmissible; for the second of these deeds should not follow but precede the first. Meyer: "Among other things, at His coming, He will *also* do this (set in light)." But why allude to other things, and what are those things? Hofmann establishes a correlation between the two καί in the sense of: *both . . . and . . .,* or of: not only . . ., but also. But why emphasize so strongly the hardly appreciable shade between the two almost synonymous verbs? It seems to me that the first *καί*, rendered by *even*, bears on the two following verbs, and contrasts the whole portion of the life *known* by other men with that which the Lord only knows and which He will then manifest. The second *καί*, *and*, serves only to connect the two parallel and equivalent verbs.—The *and then* brings out the gravity of this time of complete revelation; it contrasts it with the premature judgments of the Corinthians (*before the time*). —*Praise:* the true praise, that which will run no risk of being changed into a sentence of condemnation by a higher tribunal, like the premature praises which the Corinthians decreed to their favourite teachers. What a sting lay in this last word addressed both to the frivolous admirers and to the self-sufficient orators who had excited this profane enthusiasm! From the passage about to follow, iv. 18–21, we shall be able to gather to what point things were already going at Corinth in this painful direction.

D. *Pride the first cause of the evil* (4:6-21)

Here is the final and general application of the whole first part, relating to the divisions which had arisen in the Church. The apostle, after reminding the Corinthians of the true nature of the gospel, and deducing as a consequence that of the Christian ministry, makes palpable the vice which is eating into them: spiritual pride. He passes here from the defensive to the offensive; he has justified himself against the frivolous and rash criticisms of the

Corinthians; he proceeds now to their judgment.—Ver. 6 is the transition from the foregoing exposition to the practical conclusion.

Ver. 6. "Now these things, brethren, I have presented, by way of applying them to myself and to Apollos for your sakes; that ye might learn in us not[1] to go beyond this limit:[2] that which is written; that no one of you be puffed up for one against another."—By the address, *brethren*, Paul puts himself by the side of his readers. The verb *μετασχηματίζειν* properly signifies: to present a thing or person in a form different from its natural figure, to transform, disguise. It is in this sense that it is applied to Saul in the LXX., 1 Sam. xxviii. 8 (Heinrici); comp. also 2 Cor. xi. 13, 14. St. Paul means that in the preceding passage (from iii. 5) he has presented, while applying them to himself and Apollos, the principles regarding the ministry which he was concerned to remind them of, in view of certain preachers and of the Church, which misunderstood them. He did not wish to designate those preachers by name, lest he should shock susceptibilities already awakened. He explains this method, which he thought himself called to use in the delicate circumstances, by the words δι' ὑμᾶς, *for your sakes*, which here signify: "the more easily to gain your acceptance of the truth thus presented." Expressions like these: "Paul is nothing, Apollos is nothing" (iii. 7), applied to other leading persons at Corinth, would have seemed injurious, while in the

[1] T. R. reads *φρονειν* after *γεγραπται* with L P Syr.; all the rest omit it.

[2] T. R. reads *υπερ ο* with D E F G L Syr[sch]; ℵ A B C read *υπερ α*.

form used by Paul the truth declared lost all character of personal hostility. Hence it follows that the word ταῦτα, *these things,* applies solely to the last passage concerning the ministry, and not at all to the previous passages regarding the nature of the gospel. It is therefore a mistake to find here a proof in favour of applying to Apollos or his partisans the polemic against human wisdom in the first two chapters. The passage rather shows how thoroughly Paul felt himself one with Apollos, seeing he could treat him as a second self, and distinguish him so pointedly from the teachers who opposed him at Corinth.

After explaining the method used by him in the previous statement of doctrine, he points out the object of this teaching. In speaking thus of himself and his friend, he meant to indicate a limit they should never cross in estimating preachers whom the Lord gives them. All glory is to be refused to man in the spiritual work of which he is the agent. The T. R. gives as the object of μάθητε, *that ye may learn,* the infinitive φρονεῖν, to think of, aspire: "that ye may learn not to go in your thinking beyond . . ." But, according to the authority of the MSS., this word is probably a gloss; Hofmann thinks it borrowed from Rom. xii. 3. Rejecting it, the meaning remains the same; but the turn of expression is briefer and more pointed: that ye may learn the: not going beyond *what is written* (Greco-Lat. and Byz.), or *the things which are written* (Alex.). But of what is the apostle thinking in this ὃ or ἃ γέγραπται? The words might relate to what Paul himself has just written in the foregoing passage. In this case we must adopt the

Alex. reading, ἅ, *the things which;* for the form, *what* (ὅ) *is written,* would naturally apply to the Old Testament. But even with the Alexandrine form the application of the words to the preceding passage is far from probable. Would not Paul rather have said: ἃ προέγραψα or ἃ προεγράφη, *what I have,* or *what has been written before?* comp. Eph. iii. 3.—Or it has been thought that Paul was here referring to the words of Scripture which he had quoted above (iii. 19, 20; i. 31). But those quotations were too remote to lead the readers to understand such an allusion. Bengel, Meyer, Kling, Edwards refer the words, *what is written,* to the Old Testament in general, that supreme law of human thought, which takes all glory from man and ascribes all success to God. But a quotation so vague and general is far from probable. It seems to me, as to several modern commentators, that we must here see a proverbial maxim, in use perhaps in the Rabbinical schools: "Not beyond what is written!" The article τό, *the,* which precedes the words, seems in fact to give them this quasi-technical character; comp. the article τό, Rom. xiii. 9 and Gal. v. 14, thus used before well-known formulas. The meaning would then be: that ye may all retrace your steps in connection with what I have just told you of ourselves (Apollos and me), within the limit of a healthy appreciation: "Not beyond what Scripture says (Scripture which everywhere teaches the nothingness of man)!" This meaning thus amounts to the same as the previous explanation.

This first *that,* which is the explanation of *for your sakes,* must be a means in relation to a second more remote end. The meaning of the last proposition seems to me to come out clearly from the contrast between the two prepositions, ὑπέρ, *in favour of*, and κατά, *against*. The apostle has in view those members of the Church who were captivated by one teacher to the disparagement of another. The apostle calls this infatuation a *being puffed up*, because in exalting another man, one takes credit to himself for the admiration which he feels; one glories in being able to appreciate a superiority which others fail to know; the pride of the head of the party thus becomes the pride of the whole. The last words, *against another*, may refer either to this or that other teacher who is despised, or this or that other member of the Church who does not share the same infatuation, or who feels a quite different one. The contrast between the two adjuncts, *for the one* and *against the other*, seems to me to decide in favour of the first meaning. The pronoun εἷς, *one*, is used instead of τίς, *anyone*, with the view of isolating more completely the individual who poses as judge, and thereby breaks the unity of the body. And when this *one* is *each one*, what becomes of the Church?—It is difficult to explain the form of the word φυσιοῦσθε. If it is the indicative, this mood does not agree with the conjunction ἵνα, *that;* and if it is the subjunctive, the regular contraction would be φυσιῶσθε. This dilemma has driven Fritzsche and Meyer to give to ἵνα the meaning of *where;* which would signify, "a state of things in which." But this meaning would be superfluous, and the word ἵνα is nowhere used in this way in the New Testament; even in classic Greek this use is found only in poetry. It must therefore be held either that in this case the apostle used an incorrect contraction, but one which might be common in later Greek or in the spoken language, or that he used the indicative mood with the conjunction *ἵνα*. This takes place often enough with verbs in the future, when it is wished to emphasize the reality of the action dependent on the *that*. By applying this construction here in the present, Paul would remind them forcibly that the fact, which ought not to be, is *really* passing at the time at Corinth. The same form reappears, Gal. iv. 17 (ζηλοῦτε for ζηλῶτε), and again in the case of a verb in οω; this circumstance might incline us to the first explanation.—The following verse proceeds to show all there is to be condemned in such a puffing up.

Ver. 7. "For who maketh thee to differ? And what hast thou that thou didst not receive? And if thou didst receive it, why dost thou glory as if thou hadst not received it?"—Here is the standard indicated by the *It is written*. For one of the fundamental truths of Scripture is that the creature possesses nothing which is not a gift of the Creator.—Sometimes the three questions of this verse have been applied solely to the party chiefs and not to the members of the Church. But the apostle does not distinguish so strictly between the admirers and the admired; for the line of demarcation between teachers and taught was not so exactly drawn then as it was afterwards.—The first question refers to the superiority claimed by each eminent member of a party relatively to those of the other parties. The apostle asks this man, who thinks himself superior to others, to whom he ascribes the honour of the privileged position he has gained. For this meaning of *διακρίνειν, to distinguish,* comp. xi. 29; Acts xv. 9. What is the answer expected? Some think it is: *nobody.* They rely on the fact that the answer to the second question is certainly: *nothing.* The apostle's object, on this view, is to deny even the superiority of which this individual boasts. But in this sense should not the apostle have written τί (*what* is it that?) rather than τίς (*who* is he that?)? Others think that the answer understood is *God:* "He that maketh thee differ from others by superiority of gifts, is not thyself, but God." This sense is certainly better. But thereby the question becomes almost identical with the following one. Is it not better to state the answer thus: "*not thyself.*" There is thus in the following question a gradation indicated by the δέ. Indeed, this second question bears on the qualities which are matters of pride to the individual, his gifts, lights, eloquence, and the answer is: "absolutely *nothing.*" The third question implies the conclusion to be drawn from the other two. The καί may be regarded as independent of εἰ: "If *really*" (Hofmann, Holsten). But it may also form with εἰ a single conjunction in the sense of *though:* "How, *though* having received, dost thou boast as if thou hadst not received?" This is the most natural meaning; comp. Edwards.—In this interrogative form thrice repeated, and in the individual apostrophe, *thou,* the emotion, the indignation even, which fills the apostle, shows itself strongly. He is revolted at the thought of those empty pretensions, so contrary to the humility which faith should inspire. At this point the spectacle of the sin of the Church passes before his view with such liveliness that his discourse all at once takes the form of a long sarcasm. He thinks he sees before him the old Pharisaism raised again in the forms of the Christian life. His burning irony does not take end till ver. 13, where it is extinguished in grief.

Ver. 8. "Now ye are full; now ye are rich; ye have reigned as kings without us; and I would to God[1] ye did reign, that we also might reign with you!"—The asyndeton is a new evidence of emotion. The ἤδη, *now*, placed foremost, repeated, and that in the same place in the second proposition, well expresses the movement of this whole passage: "Now already!" Paul and the other apostles are still in a world of suffering; but at Corinth the Church already lives in full triumph.—The *fulness* denotes the imperturbable self-satisfaction which characterized the Corinthians. It is all over among them with that poverty of spirit, that hungering and thirsting after righteousness, those tears of repentance, which Jesus had made the permanent condition of life in Him (Matt. v. 1–4). They are people who have nothing more to ask, all whose spiritual wants are satisfied; they have reached the perfect life!—The expression, *riches,* no doubt, alludes to the abundance of spiritual gifts which distinguished this Church above all others, and which Paul himself had recognised in the outset (i. 5, 7). The rebuke applies, not to the fact of their possession of gifts, but to the feeling of pride which accompanied it.—The aorist is substituted for the perfect, because the fulness is a state which remains, while the acquisition of riches is the initial

[1] D F G omit γέ.

and momentary fact.—The ἐβασιλεύσατε signifies, *ye have become kings.* The advent to royalty is expressed by the aorist; for the aorist of verbs in ευω denotes, not the state, but entrance into the state. This royalty is, of course, that of the Messianic epoch, when the faithful are to reign with Christ. This condition of things glorious seems to have already begun at Corinth. No more obscurity, no more infirmity! The Church swims in full celestial state. Unspeakable delights, sublime illuminations, miraculous powers, captivating sermons: it lacks nothing.—The words χωρὶς ἡμῶν, *without us,* have been understood in the sense of "in our absence," or "without our co-operation;" as if Paul would say: "Grand things have passed at Corinth since we left you!" But in this explanation it is forgotten that the regimen *without us* takes the place, in this third proposition, of the ἤδη, *already,* which began the first two, and this leads to a meaning still more telling: "Without our having part in the elevation which is granted to you. Ye are rich, ye are kings; we others are not so happy. . . . We still drag out the miserable existence of this nether world!" The *without us* paves the way for ver. 9.—The last words are thus easily explained: "And would to God this grand news were true, that ye were really on the throne! For in that case, it is to be hoped that we should soon be seated with you." This σύν, *with,* corresponds precisely to the χωρίς, *without us,* in the preceding proposition.—The γε, as always, is restrictive: "If *this one* wish were realized, all the others would be satisfied." The restriction might also be understood in this sense: "If at least it were enough to desire it to secure that it should be!" This meaning seems to me less natural.—The second aorist ὄφελον (for ὤφελον), *I owed*, and hence *it would need*, is often used as a conjunction with the ellipsis of the following εἰ (*if*) to express *utinam;* the following verb is in the indicative, as dependent on the understood εἰ.

Ver. 9. "For I think that[1] God hath set forth us apostles, as the last, as appointed to death, for we are made a spectacle unto the world, both to angels and to men."—Most modern commentators make the irony stop here; they take the verb δοκῶ seriously: "*I deem* that our position is full of sufferings." But the *for* rather leads us to suppose that the irony continues. There was in the thought of being associated *later* in the kingship, which the Corinthians already enjoyed, something very strange when it was applied to the apostles, the founders and guides of the Church; for was it not they who seemed entitled to enter on possession of kingship before all other Christians? Hence the words, *for I think.* "Ye outstrip us in the kingdom of God; for I think that God has assigned us the last place, us the apostles!" To justify this ironical supposition, the apostle in what follows draws a picture of the reproaches and sufferings of the apostolic life, contrasting them with the royal airs which certain of the Corinthians assume. Some understand the words τοὺς ἀποστόλους ἐσχάτους in the sense of "the last of the apostles," as if Paul alone were spoken of; comp. xv. 9: "I am the least of the apostles," and Eph. iii. 8: "To me who am the least of all saints." Paul thus designates himself, it is said, either as the last called to the apostle-

[1] T. R. with E L P reads ὅτι after γὰρ.

ship, or as formerly a persecutor. But why should Paul put the plural here if he was speaking of himself personally? comp. vers. 3 and 4. Besides, to express this idea he must have used one or other of these forms: τοὺς ἐσχάτους ἀποστόλους, or τοὺς ἀποστόλους τοὺς ἐσχάτους, or τοὺς ἐσχάτους τῶν ἀποστόλων. Finally, the idea thus expressed would be opposed to the spirit of the context; for the peculiarity of being last of the apostles would be the very thing to justify God's supposed way of acting towards him, whereas Paul wishes to bring out the absurd character of such a supposition. We must therefore take τοὺς ἀποστόλους, *the apostles*, as in apposition to ἡμᾶς, *us*, and ἐσχάτους, *the last*, as the attribute of ἀπέδειξεν, *He hath set forth*: "He hath set us forth, us the apostles, as the last." By the words *us the apostles*, Paul understands, not only himself, or himself and his fellow-labourers, but himself and the Twelve who still share with him both the labours and the reproaches of the testimony borne to Christ. May there not be in this extension of the thought to the Twelve (as in the analogous passage, xv. 11), an evidence of the contempt with which *those of Christ* treated the Twelve no less than Paul? (See pp. 71, 79.)—The word ἀπέδειξεν (Beza: *spectandos proposuit*) indicates public exposure either to honour or reproach. The following words, *as condemned to death*, are explanatory of the attribute, *the last*. Down to the end of the verse the apostle is alluding to the gladiators who were presented as a spectacle in the games of the amphitheatre, and whose blood and last agonies formed the joy of a whole population of spectators. The passage xv. 32 seems to prove that the figure was once at least a reality in apostolic life.—The term θέατρον, *spectacle*, is in keeping with this public exhibition. The κόσμος, *world*, here denotes the whole intelligent universe which plays the part of spectator. It is subdivided (comp. the two καί, *both . . . and . . .*) into *men* and *angels*. By the former we need not understand merely unbelievers, persecutors, but all mankind, hostile or in sympathy. And by angels should not be understood, with some, only bad angels, with others, only the good. The bad are not excluded, that of course; the good are naturally embraced in the term, as appears to follow from Eph. iii. 10.—Instead of the past ἐγενήθημεν, *we were*, or *we became*, it seems as if the present ἔσμεν, *we are*, were required. But the aorist serves to designate this mode of existence as the lot which *was assigned* them once for all. "It seems truly that it was *God* who arranged things thus: the Church on the throne, and the apostles under the sword!"

Ver. 10. "We are fools for Christ's sake, ye are wise in Christ; we weak, ye strong; ye honourable, we despised." —The contrast between the two situations enunciated in vers. 8 and 9 is expressed in ver. 10 in three antitheses, which are, as it were, so many blows for the proud Corinthians. These words are addressed especially to the principal men of the Church, but at the same time to all its members who share in the pretensions of these proud party leaders. And, first, as to *teaching*, the apostles had to face the reputation of foolishness which the gospel brings on them, while at Corinth there is found a way of preaching Christ so as to procure a name for wisdom, the reputation of profound philosophers and of men of most reliable judgment (φρόνιμος).—*Διά, on account of* (for Christ's sake). As a Rabbin he might have become as eminent a savant as Hillel, as celebrated as Gamaliel; for Christ he has consented to pass as a fool. The Corinthians know better how to manage; they make the teaching even of the gospel (*ἐν Χριστῷ, in Christ*) a means of gaining celebrity for their lofty wisdom.

The second contrast relates to *conduct* in general. They come before their public with the feeling of their strength; there is in them neither hesitation nor timidity. The apostles do not know these grand lordly airs. Witness the picture, chap. ii. 1–5, where Paul describes his state of trembling at Corinth. Finally, the third antithesis relates to the *welcome received* from the world by the one and the other. The Corinthians are honoured, fêted, regarded as the ornament of cultivated circles; there is a rivalry to do them honour. The apostles are scarcely judged worthy of attention; nay, rather reviled and calumniated. In this last contrast the apostle reverses the order of the two terms, and puts the apostles in the second place. This is by way of transition to one or two traits of detail in the apostolic life which he is about to draw. Indeed the word *ἄτιμοι, despised,* is the theme of the following verses.

Vers. 11–13. "Even unto this present hour we both hunger and thirst, are naked,[1] buffeted, without certain dwelling-place; 12. labour, working with our own hands. Being reviled, we bless; being persecuted, we

[1] ℵ B C D E F G P read γυμνιτευομεν, instead of γυμνητευομεν which T. R. reads with L.

suffer it; 13. being defamed,[1] we intreat; we are made as the filth of the world, the offscouring of all, even until now."—The first words, *even to this present hour*, reproduce the thought of the whole passage: "As for us, up to this hour, we are little aware that the dispensation of triumph has already begun." The following enumeration bears, in the first place, on the privations and sufferings of all kinds endured by the apostles (vers. 11, 12[a]). To the want of suitable food and clothing there is sometimes added bad treatment; the word κολαφίζεσθαι may denote either blows with the fist or with the palm of the hand. Besides, as the rule, want of a fixed dwelling-place, of a home. Finally (ver. 12[a]), the manual labour imposed on Paul, especially the voluntary obligation to gain his livelihood by his own work (ix. 6).

The enumeration goes on by indicating the humble and patient conduct of the apostles in the midst of these sufferings (vers. 12[b]–13[a]). Three particulars form a double gradation: insults with sneering (λοιδορεῖσθαι), persecutions in a judicial form (διώκεσθαι), calumnies which assail honour (δυσφημεῖσθαι). The T. R. reads βλασφημούμενοι; but as the verb δυσφημεῖσθαι is much more rarely used in the New Testament, and as it is found in almost all the Mjj., it deserves the preference. —To sneering the apostles reply with *blessing*. The word εὐλογεῖν in the New Testament signifies *to wish well*, and that in the form which alone can render the wish efficacious, that of prayer.—To ill-treatment they reply by *suffering* (ἀνέχεσθαι, *to exercise self-control*);

[1] ℵ A C G read δυσφημουμενοι instead of βλασφημουμενοι, which T. R. reads with all the rest.

they do not even complain. Finally, they oppose to calumnies kindly *intreating;* they beseech men not to be so wicked, to return to better feelings, to be converted to Christ.

But with this way of acting what do they get from the world? They become the object of its more complete disdain. This is what is expressed by ver. 13[b]. The term περικάθαρμα, *filth,* denotes literally what is collected by sweeping all round the chamber (περί); and περίψημα the dirt which is detached from an object by sweeping or scraping it all round. These two figures therefore represent what is most abject. It has been sought to give to these two terms a tragical meaning, that of an *expiatory victim,* a sense in which they were sometimes taken among the Greeks. At times of public calamity, a criminal was chosen who was devoted to the angry gods to appease their wrath. This man, who was, as it were, the defilement of the people incarnate, bore the curse of all and perished for all. He was designated by the terms κάθαρμα or περίψημα. The formula with which the priest hurled him into the sea was this (according to Suidas): περίψημα ἡμῶν γενοῦ, ἤτοι σωτηρία καὶ ἀπολύτρωσις ("be our expiatory victim, and so our salvation and deliverance"). Did Paul mean to allude to the religious sense of the two terms which he uses? I do not think so; the saying thus understood would take an emphasis which hardly suits the sorrowful humility of the whole passage.—The plural of the first substantive relates to the different apostles, while the second substantive in the singular makes them one mass, an object of contempt, which is still more forcible. The adjuncts *of the world* and *of all* both indicate the totality to which the apostles naturally belong, but from which they are distinguished as being the most contemptible it contains. To the plural, *sweepings* (filth), there corresponds the singular, *of the world;* and to the singular, *the offscouring*, the plural, *of all:* They are what Paul says: each for all, and all for each.—The last words, *even until now*, betray yet once more before closing the feeling of sorrowful irony which inspired the whole passage. They are the counterpart of the ἤδη, *now*, with which he had begun, and they sum it up likewise as a whole. Rückert cannot approve of the sarcastic tone of this passage. He says, frankly (pp. 124, 125): "This passage of Paul's has always produced on me a repulsive impression. . . . There are found in it undeniable traces of wounded personal feeling, of irritation caused him by the loss of the consideration which he enjoyed at Corinth . . . everywhere there reigns concern about his own personality. I am pained to have to pass such a judgment on this great man; but he too was human . . ." This eminent commentator has not considered,—1. that as against proud infatuation, the weapon of ridicule is often the only efficacious one; 2. that the indignation which inspired this passage bore on a state of things which was not only an attack on the apostle's person, but a mortal danger to the spiritual life and the whole future of the Church; 3. that the following words, expressive of incomparable fatherly tenderness and solicitude, do not well agree with those wholly personal feelings, which he ascribes so daringly to the apostle.

Vers. 14–21 are the conclusion of all the apostle has written from i. 12. He first makes an explanation about the severe manner in which he has just spoken to them. It is not resentment or enmity which has inspired his words, it is the painful solicitude he feels for them (vers. 14–16).

Ver. 14. "I write not these things to shame you, but as my beloved sons I admonish[1] you."—Ἐντρέπειν, *to turn one back upon himself*, and hence: to cause shame. The apostle no doubt spoke to them in a humiliating way; but his object was quite different from that of causing them shame; he wished to lead them with a firm hand into another way. It is somewhat different in vi. 5 and xv. 34; here he has positively the intention of making them ashamed.—We need not read with some Mjj., νουθετῶν, *admonishing you*. This form is imitated from the preceding participle. It is a new proposition: "This is what I really do when speaking to you thus." Νουθετεῖν, in a manner: to bring back the mind to its place; to lead one back to a calm and settled frame.—Paul has the right and it is his duty to act thus, for he is their spiritual father. He is himself the only one of their preachers who merits the name; this is what is brought out by the pronoun μου: "*my children*." The following verse justifies the pronoun with its exclusive bearing.

Vers. 15, 16. "For though ye should have ten thousand tutors in Christ, yet have ye not many fathers; for in Christ Jesus I have begotten you through the gospel. 16. I beseech you therefore:

[1] ℵ A D P read νουθετων (*admonishing*), instead of νουθετω (*I admonish*).

be ye imitators of me."—In ver. 15, Paul presents the almost ridiculous figure of a flock of pupils placed under the rod of several thousands of tutors. There is an allusion to that host of teachers who had risen up at Corinth after the departure of Paul and Apollos, and to whom was addressed the warning in iii. 12--15, regarding those who continued a building once founded. The pedagogue (tutor) among the Greeks was the slave to whom a child's education was committed till he reached his majority; literally: he who guides the child to school.—*'Αλλά*: here, like the *at* of the Latins. It was Paul to whom God had given to *beget* the Corinthians to that new life which the others only promoted; comp. a similar figure, Gal. iv. 19. This term γεννᾶν, *to beget*, applies not only to the ministry of preaching, but to the intense labour of the whole man which is carried out in his personal relations and in the act of prayer. — It should be remarked that Paul prefixes to the idea of his labour the two qualifications: *in Christ Jesus* and *by the gospel*. It was in virtue of the communion and power of Christ, and by means of the gospel which he received from Him, that he was able to produce this spiritual creation. He thus excludes beforehand every appearance of boasting in what he says of himself in the last words: ἐγὼ ἐγέννησα.—But if it was Christ who acted with His power and word, it was nevertheless through him, Paul (ἐγώ, *I*), that He produced this creation. Hence Paul's right and duty to exhort them, and even to admonish them as he does.

Ver. 16. A father has a right to expect that well-born children follow his steps; hence the *therefore*.

The apostle is thinking particularly of the absence of all self-seeking and self-satisfaction, of the abnegation and humility of which they had an example in him. The νουθετεῖν (ver. 14) referred especially to their past, and to all that was blameworthy in it; the παρακαλεῖν applies to the future, and to the good which ought to appear among them. The word γίνεσθε, *become* (be), reminds them how far they have gone astray. — To help them on the way of return to a new course, Paul sends them one of his most faithful fellow-labourers, whom he hopes soon to follow himself (vers. 17–21).

Ver. 17. "For this[1] cause have I sent unto you Timothy, who is my beloved son and faithful in the Lord; he shall bring you into remembrance of my ways which be in Christ,[2] even as I teach everywhere in every Church."—We need not take the aorist ἔπεμψα in the sense of the Greek epistolary past, when the author, transporting himself to the time when his letter shall be read, speaks in the past of a present fact. The passage xvi. 10, 11, proves that the apostle means, *I have sent*, for Timothy had really started when Paul was writing, though he was not to arrive till after the letter; comp. Acts xix. 21, 22. How do such coincidences prove the accuracy of the narrative of the Acts!—In calling Timothy *his son*, he alludes to his conversion of which he had been the instrument, no doubt during his first visit to Lystra; comp. 2 Tim. i. 2. By this title he gives him, as it were, the position of an elder son relatively to the Corinthians, who, as younger children, should take rule from him.

[1] ℵ A P add to τουτο (*this*) αυτο (*this very*).
[2] ℵ C Mnn.: εν Χριστω Ιησου.

He characterizes him as *beloved*, which recommends him to their affection, and as *faithful in the Lord*, which is his title to their confidence. The term πιστός is used, like our word *faithful*, in the active sense: one who believes, or in the passive sense: one who may be believed, who should be trusted. It is the second sense which at least prevails here; he will be to them a sure counsellor in the things of the Lord. —His mission is *to bring them into remembrance.* This phrase, designedly chosen, distinguishes the part of Timothy from that of the apostle, and insinuates at the same time that the Corinthians are not ignorant, but that they have only forgotten.—What does the apostle understand by *his ways which be in Christ?* Is it the way in which he regulates his own conduct? But the words, "As *I teach* everywhere," do not suit this meaning. Meyer thinks that the words, *as I teach,* may be applied to the way in which he acted when carrying out his office as a preacher. This is an inadmissible makeshift. Or should we, on the contrary, apply the phrase, *my ways in Christ*, to the contents of the apostolic preaching? This meaning is no less forced. It only remains, as it seems to me, to apply the καθὼς διδάσκω, *as I teach*, to the apostle's practical teaching (as it is summed up Rom. xii.–xiv.), to the true method of Christian life: the humility, abnegation, self-forgetfulness, consecration to the Lord, which ought to characterize a true believer. This is the course which Paul himself has followed since he was in Christ (my ways in Christ); and it was this mode of acting pursued by the apostle which he inculcated in all the Churches. The word καθώς, *even as*, brings out the harmony between his life and this teaching.—The words *everywhere* and *in every Church* seem to be tautological. But the first signifies: *in* every sort of country, in Asia as in Greece. Timothy, who had followed him in all his journeys, could bear witness to this. *In every Church* signifies: *in each Church* which I found. He seeks to impress the same direction on these new communities; there is always the call to come down by humility, not to be exalted by boasting. No doubt there was the disposition to believe that Paul was imposing exceptional demands on the Corinthians. But no; they are the same as are accepted and practised by each of his Churches; comp. i. 2, xiv. 33, 35, 36. Timothy, who has himself witnessed all these foundations, will be able to certify them of the fact.—But this sending of Timothy might lead them to suppose that the disciple was a substitute for the apostle, and that after this visit the latter would not think of coming himself. This conclusion had already been expressly drawn, some had even made a triumph of it at the expense of the apostle. He had doubtless been informed of this by the three deputies, and it is to this insulting supposition that the final passage refers, vers. 18–21.

Ver. 18. "But some are puffed up, as though I would not come to you."—The δέ is adversative: "*But* do not proceed to conclude therefrom that . . ." The present participle ὡς μὴ ἐρχομένου, "as if I were not *coming*," has been explained by supposing that Paul here is quoting verbally the saying of his adversaries: "He is not *coming!*" This is far-fetched; the present is simply that of the idea; comp. xvi. 5.—Who are those *some*, so ready to interpret the steps taken by the apostle in a sense unfavourable to his character? The partisans of Apollo, answer many. There is nothing to lead us to this idea. On the contrary, we find, 2 Cor. x. 9, 10, a statement which is manifestly related to this: Paul's adversaries charged him with seeking to terrify the Church by threatening letters of excessive severity, but not daring to appear himself to bear out the energy of his language by his presence, because he was well aware of his personal weakness and insufficiency. It cannot be doubted that the people of this stamp were already at Corinth at the date of the First Epistle to the Corinthians and were passing such judgments. Now these people, as we know from Second Corinthians, were *those of Christ* (x. 7 and xi. 23). Such then were the men who, even at the date of the first letter, were allowing themselves to accuse the apostle so gravely. Perhaps, however, by the word *some* should rather be understood those of the Corinthians who had been led away, than those strangers themselves; in his First Epistle, Paul seems not yet inclined to come to close quarters with the latter.—The word *are puffed up* refers to the air of triumph with which this party hasted to proclaim the grand news in the Church: "Timothy is coming instead of Paul; Paul is not coming."

Vers. 19, 20. "But I will come to you shortly, if the Lord will; and will know, not the speech of them which are puffed up, but the power. 20. For the kingdom of God is not in word, but in power."—The δέ is again adversative: "But this malicious forecast will be falsified." The γνώσομαι, *I will know*, is the language of a judge proceeding to make an examination. This term has already a threatening solemnity; it gives a forewarning of the judgment about to follow (ver. 21).—Paul contrasts *the word*, here the fine discourses, the eloquent tirades, the profound deductions, which called forth the plaudits of the hearers, with *the power;* by which he designates the effectual virtue of the Divine Spirit which brings back souls to themselves, makes them contrite, leads them to Christ, and begets them to a new life. Paul will find out whether, with this abundance of talk which makes itself heard in the assemblies (chap. xiv.), there is found or there is lacking the creative breath of the Spirit. He is at home in this field; he will not be deceived like those poor dupes who have been misled at Corinth.—*Them that are puffed up:* all those self-inflated creatures, under whose eyes scandals are passing which they cannot or will not repress, who have only an insipid Christianity, and to whom applies the figure of salt without savour. Chap. v., ver. 2 in particular will show clearly what was already in the apostle's mind.

Ver. 20. The maximum of ver. 20 explains the necessity of such a judgment. It is impossible to refer the notion of the *kingdom of God*, as Meyer would have us, to the Messianic future. Paul is certainly speaking of the kingdom of God in the spiritual sense in which it already exists in the souls of believers. There, where the will of God has become the ruling principle, and where man's will is only the organ of the former, God reigns from the present onwards; comp. Rom. xiv. 17. This spiritual presence of the kingdom of God in the heart is what paves the way for its future appearing.—The most eloquent words do not guarantee the possession of this spiritual state, and cannot produce or advance it in others. What manifests its existence, is power to make hearts fertile in fruits of submission to the will of God.—Paul's work at Corinth will not be confined to taking knowledge of the evil; acts will follow as may be needed.

Ver. 21. "What will ye? That I come unto you with a rod, or in love, and with a spirit of meekness?"[1] —It is as if Paul said to them: "Peace or war: choose!" The emotion caused by this challenge, so boldly thrown out, explains the asyndeton. The preposition ἐν, *in*, is applied in classic Greek, as here, to denote the use of a weapon.—The figure ῥάβδος, *rod*, is connected with that of father, used above. It is the emblem of the disciplinary power with which the apostle feels himself armed.—There is something startling in the antithesis: *or with love.* Supposing he required to use the rod, would he not do so in love? Certainly; but if there is love in the act of striking, there is also something else: hatred of evil. And this will have no occasion to show itself, except in so far as there shall be something to correct. Let us add that the Greek term ἀγάπη denotes the love of complacency which is expressed by approving manifestations.—Some have unaerstood the phrase, *spirit of meekness*, as if it were, with a *disposition* of meekness. But it is impossible wholly to make abstraction of the Divine breath in the use of the word πνεῦμα, *spirit.* Paul knows well that the meekness he will use, if it is in

[1] The MSS. write πραυτης or πραοτης.

his power, will not be natural good-naturedness, but the fruit of the Spirit, of which he himself speaks Gal. v. 23.

Already in these last verses we can discern the idea of *discipline* rising, which will be the subject of the following chapter. One is struck also at the degree of audacious hostility to which his adversaries in the Church had gone, in daring to express themselves in regard to him as they were doing (ver. 18), and in giving occasion to the use of so menacing a tone. But, as has been well observed by Weizsäcker, Paul does not wish for the present to open hostilities. He throws out a word in passing, then he resumes the course of his letter.

The first part of the Epistle is closed. The divisions which had arisen revealed to Paul the deep corruption which the gospel had undergone in this Church. He understood it: teachers are not changed into heads of schools, except because the gospel has been changed into a system. To ascend then to the true notion of Christianity, in order to deduce from it that of the Christian ministry, and to restore the normal relation between this office and the whole Church, such was his first task. The flock once gathered under the shepherd's crook, he may with hope of success attack the particular vices which had crept into it. These first four chapters are thus the foundation of the whole Epistle.

2

Discipline (5:1-13)

A large number of commentators think that Paul here passes to the vice of impurity. But it is not till vi. 12 that he really attacks this vice. As to chap. v., they confound the occasion with the subject. The occasion is an act of impurity; but the subject treated, and that in consequence of the laxity which the Church had shown in regard to this scandal, is the duty of every living Church to take action against sin when it manifests itself openly within its pale.

It is impossible with the large number of the unconverted who become members of the Church, and with the sin which the converted themselves still bear in them, that evil should not sometimes break out in the Christian community. But the difference which should ever remain between the Church and the world is, that in the former sin should not manifest itself without falling under the stroke of rebuke and judgment. "There is a Holy One in the midst of thee," said the prophet Hosea to Israel. A Holy One lives also in the Church, and from Him there go forth, in every true Church which has life and not merely the name to live, a protest and reaction against all notorious wickedness. This reaction, the work of the Holy Spirit who proceeds from Christ, is discipline. Where it is weakened, the Church is in the same measure confounded with the world.

The chapter which we proceed to study is the classical passage of the New Testament on the subject; if the apostle has put it here, it is because the subject belongs, on the one side, to the ecclesiastical questions treated in chaps. i.–iv., and on the other to the moral questions which will be treated, chaps. vi.–x. It is therefore the natural transition between the two domains of ecclesiastical or collective life and the moral life of each member.—In vers. 1–5, Paul speaks of discipline in special connection with the particular case which obliges him to treat the subject, to pass thereafter to the condition of discipline in general (vers. 6–8); the passage, vers. 9–13, is an appendix.

CHAP. 5:1-5

Ver. 1. "In general, it is reported that there is fornication among you, and such fornication as is not found even among the Gentiles,[1] that one hath his father's wife."—The first word, ὅλως, has been variously explained. It signifies *totally*, and hence *in general* or *summarily*, but never *certainly*, as some have sought to understand it here. If this adverb qualifies ἀκούεται, *it is reported*, we may explain, "it is reported *everywhere*." But Paul would have found a clearer term to express this idea. Or we might understand it, "People talk generally of fornication among you;" but the sequel, καὶ τοιαύτη, *and such fornication*, . . . does not at all suit this meaning. The adjunct ἐν ὑμῖν, *among you*, cannot, of course, depend on ἀκούεται, *it is reported*; it must necessarily be referred to an οὖσα, *being*, understood: "It is reported *that there is* fornication among you." If it is so, the meaning of ὅλως is determined by the gradation following: καὶ τοιαύτη, *and even such*: "The vice of fornication exists *in general* among you,

[1] T. R. with L P Syr. reads ονομαζεται (*is named*) after εθνεσιν.

and it is even such a case as would scandalize the Gentiles themselves." The word ὅλως is used, vi. 7, exactly in the same way.—The verb *ὀνομάζεται, is named,* in T. R., is a gloss taken from Eph. v. 3. The word is wanting in most of the Mjj. We have simply to understand *ἐστί.*—Instead of saying, *his father's wife,* Paul might have used the word *μητρυιά, step-mother;* but the former expression brought out more strongly the enormity of the act. This is also expressed forcibly by the position of the pronoun *τινά* between the two terms *wife* and *father.* Was the father still living? We can hardly think so; the act would be too odious.[1] The marriage of a son with his step-mother was forbidden among the Jews under pain of death (Lev. xviii. 8). The Roman law equally forbade it. It is therefore probable that this union had not been legally sanctioned. Of the impression produced by such acts, even among the heathen, when they did exceptionally take place, we may judge from the words of Cicero in his defence of Cluentius: "O incredible crime for a woman, and such as has never been heard of in this world in any other than her solitary case!"—It appears from the whole chapter that the man only was a Christian; for if the woman had not been still a heathen, would not Paul have judged her as severely as the man? And what has been the conduct of the Corinthians in view of such a scandal?

Ver. 2. "And ye are puffed up, and have not rather mourned, that he that hath done[2] this deed might be

[1] The passage 2 Cor. vii. 12 ought not to be quoted in proof, as is often done. The term *αδικηθεις* can only refer to Paul himself.

[2] ℵ A C read *πραξας,* instead of *ποιησας,* which all the rest read.

taken away[1] from among you."—Even this fact has not sufficed to disturb the proud self-satisfaction which he has already rebuked in the Corinthians in the previous chapter, or to make them come down from the celestial heights on which they are now walking to the real state of things.—The word πεφυσιωμένοι, *puffed up*, goes back on the words, iv. 6 (φυσιοῦσθε), and especially ver. 19 (τῶν πεφυσιωμένων). What have they done, those grand talkers, in view of this monstrous scandal? This is what the apostle called "having speech but not power." Should not this moral catastrophe have opened their eyes to the fallen state in which their Church lay? Calvin admirably says: "*Ubi luctus est, ibi cessat gloriatio.*"—A living Church, which had in it the δύναμις of its Head, would have risen as one man, and gone into a common act of humiliation and mourning, like a family for the death of one of its members. This is what is expressed by the verb πενθεῖν, *to conduct a mourning.*—The aorist ἐπενθήσατε cannot merely designate a feeling of inward grief. It shows that Paul is thinking of a positive, solemn deed, of something like a day of repentance and fasting, on which the whole Church before the Lord deplored the scandal committed, and cried to Him to bring it to an end.

The words, *that might be taken away*, are referred by most commentators to the excommunication which the Church would not have failed to pronounce upon the guilty one as the result of such an act of humiliation. Calvin says without hesitation, "The power of excommunication is established by this passage." But

[1] T. R. with L reads εξαρθη, instead of αρθη.

it seems to me that neither the conjunction *that* nor the passive *might be taken away* is suitable to an act which the Corinthians should have done themselves. The *that* rather indicates a result which would be produced, independently of them, in consequence of the mourning called for by the apostle. It is the same with the passive form *might be taken away.* If Paul had thought of an exclusion pronounced by the Church itself, he would have said: "That ye might take away;" or, better still, "Ye have not mourned, and then taken away the offender." At the most he would have said, "Ye have not mourned, *so that* (ὥστε) he might be taken away." Whether we refer the ἵνα to the intention which would have dictated the mourning (Meyer, Edwards), or to that of the apostle who calls for it (de Wette), we do not sufficiently account for it, any more than for the passive form *might be taken away.* It must be confessed, it seems to me, that in Paul's view he who does the act of taking away is different from him who mourns, though the mourning is the condition of his intervening to strike. This is what the Corinthians should have known well, and this is precisely the reason why they should have mourned that he whose part it was to take away might act. The mysterious arm, which, if the Church had felt its shame, would have removed it by striking the guilty one, can only be the arm of God Himself. To the grief and prayer of the Church He would have responded in a way similar to that in which He had acted, on the words of Peter, toward Ananias and Sapphira, or as He was acting at that very time at Corinth, by visiting with sickness, and even with death, the profaners of the Supper (xi. 30–32).—Hofmann sees that in the ordinary construction these expressions cannot apply to an act done by the Church. And, as he does not suppose that the term can designate anything else than excommunication, he begins a new sentence with *ἵνα*, regarding this conjunction, with Pott, as the periphrasis of an imperative: "Let such a man be taken away from among you (by a sentence of excommunication)!" No doubt the *ἵνα*, *that*, is sometimes used thus. But it is hard to see how such an order would harmonize with what follows, where Paul relates what he has done to make up for what the Corinthians had not done. Besides, this construction would here be entirely unexpected and far from natural. The ἐξαρθῇ of the T. R. is taken from ver. 13. The reading should be ἀρθῇ, with most of the Mjj.—The verb αἴρειν, or ἐξαίρειν, is ordinarily used in Leviticus and Deuteronomy to denote the capital punishment inflicted on malefactors in Israel; comp. also the ἀπαρθῇ, Matt. ix. 15, and parallel, applied to the Messiah's violent death.—In saying *from among you*, Paul is certainly thinking of the way in which he had characterized his readers at the beginning of his letter: "Sanctified in Christ Jesus, saints by call." How could one guilty of adultery and incest have a place in such an assembly!—The term τὸ ἔργον τοῦτο has a certain emphasis: "An act such as this." The reading πράξας, in three Alex., might be preferred, because the verb πράσσειν is pretty often used in an unfavourable sense, in opposition to ποιεῖν (see John iii. 20, 21; v. 29, etc.). But ποιεῖν better expresses than πράσσειν the accomplishment of the deed.—After characterizing both the guilty pride and softness of the

Church, the apostle contrasts with them his own mode of acting.

Ver. 3. "For I verily, as[1] absent in body, but present in spirit, have decided already, as though I were present, [to deliver over] him that hath so done this deed . . ."—The *for* is thus explained: "Such is what you ought to have done; *for*, as for me, this is what I have done. The μέν, to which there is no corresponding δέ, serves to isolate Paul, putting him in contrast to the Church, and so strengthens the force of the ἐγώ, *I*: "I, for my part, while you . . . !"—The first ὡς, *as*, is rejected by the majority of the Mjj., perhaps wrongly; it has been thought incompatible with the following ὡς before the second παρών. But these two ὡς may have their distinct value. The first bears strictly on the second participle: *present in spirit*. It signifies: "So far as absent in body, no doubt, but really present spiritually." It is the *as* which serves to express the *real* character in which the person acts; the second signifies, on the contrary, *as if*. Paul would bring out this contrast: "As for you who were present, you did nothing; and as for me, distant from you though I am, yet living spiritually among you, this is how I acted!" The word *already* has great force here, whether it signifies, "while you remained inactive, you wise and eloquent preachers;" or whether Paul rather means, "before even arriving among you."—The verb κέκρικα may be rendered by *I have judged*, or *I have decided*. Not being able to say [in French] *judged to deliver*, we have used the second term; but in a passage of a judicial character like this the verb ought to express

[1] ℵ A B C D P omit the ὡς (*as*), read by T. R. with E F G L It.

rather the idea of a sentence pronounced than of a simple resolution taken. This is undoubtedly what has led Hofmann and Edwards to give this verb for its direct object the following accusative: τὸν κατεργασάμενον, *him who has thus acted.* Now, as the verb παραδοῦναι (ver. 5) can be nothing else than the object of κέκρικα, we must hold in this case a mixture of two constructions, "I have judged this man," and "I have judged to deliver him over to Satan." This rather forced interpretation seems to me unnecessary. It is simpler to make τὸν κατεργασάμενον the object of παραδοῦναι, and τὸν τοιοῦτον (ver. 5) the grammatical repetition of the object, a repetition occasioned by the interposition of ver. 4. — But the important question is, whether the παραδοῦναι, *the act of delivering over,* the object of *I have judged,* or *decided,* should be regarded as the result of a future decision which Paul proposes to be taken by the Corinthians themselves, or whether he thinks of it as a decision already taken and decreed between God and him. Commentators agree in holding the first sense. Paul waits, they say, till, in consequence of the decision which he has taken by himself, the Church of Corinth shall assemble and pronounce a sentence in keeping, if one may so speak, with his premonition. This meaning is open to certain doubts. Would not Paul say in that case: "I have decided that the man *should be delivered over,*" and not: "I have judged *to deliver him over*"? It might therefore be supposed that the judicial assembly of which the apostle speaks has already taken place at the time of his writing, and that the three deputies represented the Church in his presence. Thus the three acts would be naturally explained: κέκρικα, συναχθέντων, παραδοῦναι. But the participle συναχθέντων would in this sense require rather to be placed before κέκρικα, and the idea of a purely *spiritual* presence would rather apply to the Church than to Paul. We must therefore return to the ordinary explanation. Only there is not the faintest hint of making the pronouncing of the sentence dependent on the vote of the assembly which is to be held at Corinth, as if the apostle's decision could be annulled by the contrary opinion of a majority. For his part (μέν), everything is decided, and with his apostolical competency he has judged to deliver over [the offender]; there will be joined to him, in the assembly which he convokes to take part in this terrible act, whoever wishes and dares.—The apparent pleonasm, οὕτω τοῦτο, "who has *so* done *this*," has been variously explained. The word *so* is said to signify, "as a Christian," or "with the aggravating circumstances which you know," etc. It seems to me that we have here one of those circumlocutions in which judicial sentences delight. The protocol of a tribunal would be precisely expressed in this way. The object is to exactly define the deed, with all the circumstances known or unknown which make it what it is: its publicity, the shamelessness of its author, etc. In fact, these last words of ver. 3 contain, as it were, the *preamble* to the sentence delivered; and, in what immediately follows, everything bears a very pronounced judicial character.—But the essential thing with the apostle is not that the sentence be delivered, it is that it be so with the assent of the Church. For his aim, besides the saving of the guilty one, is to awaken the conscience of the whole community, its energetic protest against the scandal which it has witnessed till now in silence. And such is the intent of ver. 4, which indicates three things: 1. the assembly which is to take place; 2. its competency; 3. its power of execution. We are thus reminded of a tribunal prepared for the sentences delivered by it.

Vers. 4, 5. "Ye and my spirit being gathered together in the name of the[1] Lord Jesus Christ,[2] 5. to deliver with the power of our[3] Lord Jesus[4] such an one unto Satan for the destruction of the flesh, that the spirit may be saved in the day of the Lord Jesus."[5] —The tribunal is formed of the Christians of Corinth assembled in Paul's spiritual presence; his competency is the *name* of Jesus Christ, under whose authority the sentence is given; his ability to execute is the *power* of Jesus Christ.—There are four ways of connecting the two subordinate clauses, *in the name of* . . . and *with the power of*, with the two verbs, *being gathered together* and *delivering*. The first two make the two clauses bear on the same verb, either on *being gathered together* (Chrysostom, Theodoret, Calvin, Rückert, Holsten), or on *delivering* (Mosheim, etc.). According to the last two, they are distributed between the two verbs; some ascribing the first clause, *in the name of*, to the last verb *deliver*, and the second clause, *with*

[1] ℵ A here omit ημων (*our*), which is read by T. R. with all the rest, It. Syr.

[2] A B D reject the word Χριστου (*Christ*).

[3] All the Mjj., except P, here read ημων (*our*).

[4] ℵ A B D P omit Χριστου (*Christ*), which is read by T. R. with E F G L.

[5] So T. R. with ℵ L; B omits Ιησου (*Jesus*); P Or. read ημων after κυριου (*our Lord*).

the power of, to the first verb, *being gathered together* (Luther, Bengel, de Wette, Meyer, Kling, Edwards); the others making each clause bear on the verb which immediately follows it: *in the name of* on *being gathered together*, and *with the power of* on *delivering* (Beza, Olshausen, Ewald, Hofmann, Heinrici). I have no hesitation in preferring this last construction. Independently of the position of the words, which suits this meaning better than it does any of the others, the decisive reason seems to me to be the conformity of the notion of each clause with that of the verb it qualifies. Is it a judicial assembly which is in question, the important thing is its competency; and this is what is indicated by the ἐν ὀνόματι . . ., *in the name of* . . ., as qualifying *being gathered together*. Is it, on the contrary, the execution of the sentence which is in question, what is important is force, power *de facto;* and this is exactly what is expressed by the ἐν δυνάμει, *with the power of* . . ., as qualifying *to deliver*. This construction seems to me also to be confirmed by the striking parallel Matt. xviii. 18–20, a saying which must have been present to Paul's mind in this case: "Verily I say unto you, whatsoever ye shall bind on earth shall be bound in heaven. . . . Again I say unto you, that whatever two or three of you shall agree to ask on the earth, it shall be done for them of My Father. For where two or three *are gathered together in My name* (συνηγμένοι εἰς τὸ ἐμὸν ὄνομα), there am I in the midst of them." This promise certainly served as a ground for the actual conduct of the apostle. The moment has come for the Church to do what Jesus called *binding;* it has to judge. This judgment is to be pronounced by the faithful *gathered together in His name,* as many of them as will be found *to agree* in view of an interest of this kind, should there be only *two or three.*—The *name* denotes the person of the Lord in so far as it is revealed to the hearts of believers, recognised and adored by them.—Perhaps we should, with the documents, reject the word *Christ,* and preserve only the name *Jesus,* which calls up the historical personality of Him who has promised to be invisibly present at such an act. It is on this promised presence that the authority of the assembly which does it rests. The pronoun *ye* does not necessarily embrace the whole of the Church, for the matter in question here is not a vote by a majority of voices; it is a spiritual act in which, from the very nature of things, only the man takes part who feels impelled to it, and each in the measure in which he is capable of it. Two or three suffice for this, in case of need, Jesus Himself says; for the means of action in such discipline is agreement in prayer. How could all this apply to a decree of excommunication, pronounced after contradictory debating, and by a majority of voices, perhaps a majority of one? The things of God do not admit of being thus treated.

The most mysterious expression in this so mysterious passage is the following: καὶ τοῦ ἐμοῦ πνεύματος, *and my spirit.* At this assembly, which is to take place at Corinth, Paul will be present by his spirit (ver. 3). It would seem that what Paul here affirms of himself ought to be applied to Jesus. But it must not be forgotten that if Jesus is the Head of the Church in general, Paul is the founder and father of the Church of Corinth, and that in virtue of his personal union to Jesus, the spiritual presence of the Lord (Matt. xviii. 20) may become also that of His servant. In chapter xii. of the Second Epistle to the Corinthians, Paul does not himself know whether it was with or without his body that he was present at a scene in paradise.

The words σὺν τῇ δυνάμει, *with power*, cannot be connected with the participle συναχθέντων, *being gathered together*, whether we make Christ's power a sort of third member of the assembly, or whether we regard this power of Christ as sharing in the judgment in so far as it must carry it into execution. The first meaning needs no refutation; the second is an over-refinement. This regimen, on the contrary, is quite naturally connected with παραδοῦναι: "to deliver with the power of Christ Himself." There is nothing here opposed, as Edwards thinks, to the natural meaning of σύν. Certainly this preposition does not denote the means *by* which (διά, ἐν); but it can perfectly denote a co-operating circumstance, as in the phrases σὺν θεῷ or σὺν θεοῖς πράττειν, to do with the help of God; comp. Heinrici, ad h. l. Human action does not become efficacious except in union with Divine power.—The *repetition* of the words, *of our Lord Jesus* (or *Jesus Christ*), at the end of the verse, belongs to the forms of language used by the ancients in their formulas of condemnation or consecration (*devotio*). The object of *deliver* is briefly repeated by the τὸν τοιοῦτον, *such an one*, a form which brings out once more the odious character of his conduct.

The obscure expression παραδοῦναι τῷ Σατανᾷ, *to deliver to Satan*, is found only elsewhere in 1 Tim. i. 20: "Hymenæus and Alexander, whom I have delivered unto Satan, that they may learn not to blaspheme."—It has been understood in three ways. Some have found in it the idea of *excommunication* pure and simple (Calvin, Beza, Olshausen, Bonnet, Heinrici, etc.). Calvin thus briefly justifies this sense: "As Christ reigns in the Church, so Satan outside the Church. . . He then, who is cast out of the Church, is thereby in a manner delivered to the power of Satan, in so far as he becomes a stranger to the kingdom of God." But the insufficiency of this sense has been generally felt. Why use an expression so extraordinary to designate a fact so simple as that of exclusion from the Church, especially if, as those commentators hold, Paul had just designated the same act by a wholly different term (ver. 3)? Still, if the use of the term had a precedent in the forms of the synagogue! But Lightfoot has proved that this formula was never in use to denote Jewish excommunication. We have besides already called attention to the fact that the δύναμις, *the power*, of the Lord was not necessary to the execution of a sentence of excommunication. And how could this punishment have prevented Hymenæus and Alexander from blaspheming? Is it not possible to blaspheme, and that more freely, outside than within the Church? Finally, it remains to explain the following words: *for the destruction of the flesh*; we do not think it is possible on this explanation to give them a natural meaning.—Moreover, from the earliest times of exegesis down to our own day, the need has been felt of adding another idea to that of excommunication, viz. *bodily punishment*, regarded either as the proper consequence of excommunication (Calov), or as a chastisement over and above, added to excommunication by the Apostle Paul. To the Church it belongs to exclude from its membership; to the apostle to let loose on the excommunicated one the disciplinary power of Satan to punish him in his body (so nearly Chrysostom, Theodoret, Rückert, Olshausen, Osiander, Meyer). This sense certainly is an approach to the truth; but why seek to combine the idea of excommunication with that of bodily punishment? The former is taken from ver. 3, from the *αἴρειν ἐκ μεσοῦ*; we have seen that it is not really there. But what is graver still is, that it would follow from this explanation that the sécond chastisement, bodily punishment, would be inflicted on the incestuous person in consequence of the Church's neglecting to inflict on him the first. In fact, it follows from ver. 3 that the apostle's intervention in this matter was rendered necessary by the lax toleration of the Christians of Corinth. In these circumstances the apostle could no doubt inflict the penalty which the Church should have pronounced, but he could not decree an aggravation of punishment; for the fault of the Church added nothing to that of the culprit. In this respect the first explanation would still be preferable to this second. The latter nevertheless contains an element of truth which we should preserve, and which will constitute the third (Lightfoot, Hofmann, Holsten): the idea of a *bodily chastisement*, of which Satan is to be the instrument. Such is the punishment which Paul inflicts at his own hand,

and in virtue of his apostolic power, and which corresponds to the αἴρειν ἐκ μέσου, *taking away from among,* to the cutting off which the Church had not sought to obtain from God. Satan is often represented as having the power to inflict physical evils. It is he who is God's instrument to try Job when he was stricken with leprosy. It is he, says Jesus, who for eighteen years holds bound the poor woman who was bent double, and whom He cured on the Sabbath day (Luke xiii. 6). Paul himself ascribes to a messenger of Satan the thorn in the flesh, of which God makes use to keep him in humility (2 Cor. xii. 7). It is Satan who is the murderer of man in consequence of the first sin (John viii. 44), and he has the dominion of death (Heb. ii. 14). It is not hard to understand how a painful, perhaps mortal, punishment of this kind might bring the blasphemy on the lips of a heretic to an end. It is obvious how it might bring back to himself and to God a man who was led away by the seduction of the senses. Suffering in the flesh is needed to check the dominion of fleshly inclinations. The only difference between this chastisement decreed by the apostle, and that which the Corinthians should have asked from above, is, that the Church would have referred the mode of execution to God, while Paul, in virtue of his spiritual position superior to that of the Church, feels at liberty to determine the means of which the Lord will make use. For "he knows the mind of the Lord" (ii. 16). It will perhaps be asked how Satan can lend himself to an office contrary to the interests of his own kingdom. But we know not the mysteries of that being, in which the greatest possible amount of blindness is united to the most penetrating intelligence. "Malignity," says M. de Bonald, "sharpens the mind and kills sound sense." Was it not the messenger of Satan whom God used to preserve Paul from pride, and who kept him in that consciousness of his weakness by means of which the Divine power could always anew manifest itself in him?

The apostle adds: εἰς ὄλεθρον τῆς σαρκός, *for the destruction of the flesh.* Those who apply the foregoing expression to excommunication are embarrassed by these words. Calvin takes them as a softening introduced into the punishment, a carnal condemnation importing simply a temporal and temporary condemnation, in opposition to eternal damnation. This interpretation of the genitive σαρκός is its own refutation. Others think of the ruin of the worldly affairs of the excommunicated person, in consequence of his rupture with his former customers, the other members of the Church. How is it possible to ascribe such a thought to the apostle! The only tenable explanation is that which is found already in Augustine, then in Grotius, Gerlach, Bonnet: the destruction of the flesh, in the *moral* sense of the word, that is to say, of the sinful tendencies, in consequence of the pain and repentance which will be produced in the man by his expulsion from the Church. But,—1. Might not this measure quite as well produce the opposite effect? Thrown back into the world, the man might easily become utterly corrupt. 2. The term ὄλεθρος, *destruction, perdition,* would here require to denote a beneficent work of the Holy Spirit; that is impossible; see the threatening sense in which the word is always taken in the other passages of the

New Testament: 1 Thess. v. 3 and 2 Thess. i. 9 (ὄλεθρος αἰφνίδιος, αἰώνιος, *destruction sudden, eternal*); 1 Tim. vi. 9 (ὄλεθρος καὶ ἀπώλεια, *destruction and perdition*). Paul means here to speak of a real *loss* for the man, according to the uniform meaning of the word ὄλεθρος. The matter in question is the destruction of one of the elements of his being with a view to the salvation of the other, which is the more precious. When Paul wishes to express the moral idea of the destruction of sin, he uses quite other terms: *to reduce to impotence*, καταργεῖν (Rom. vi. 6); *to cause to die, kill*, νεκροῦν, θανατοῦν (Col. iii. 3; Rom. viii. 13); *to crucify*, σταυροῦν (Gal. v. 24); terms which have a different shade from ὄλεθρος. 3. The opposite of σάρξ, *the flesh*, in the following words, is πνεῦμα, *the spirit*. Now this second term cannot simply denote spiritual life, to which the expression *being saved* would not apply; it can only denote the substratum of that life, the spirit itself, as an element of human existence. Hence it follows that neither does *the flesh* denote fleshly life, but the flesh itself, the substratum of the natural life. —The flesh must therefore be taken in the sense of the earthly man, or, as Hofmann observes, of the *outward man*, in Paul's phrase (2 Cor. iv. 16: "If our outward man perish . . ."). It is in this sense that the word *flesh* itself is taken a few verses before (ver. 11), in the saying: "That the life of Jesus may be manifested *in our mortal flesh;*" so Phil. i. 22 (τὸ ζῆν ἐν σαρκί) and Gal. ii. 20 (ὃ νῦν ζῶ ἐν σαρκί). The apostle might have two reasons for using the term *flesh* here rather than *body;* in the first place, σάρξ expresses the natural life in its totality, physical and psychical; and next, the body in itself is not to be destroyed (chap. xv.). It is therefore the destruction of the earthly existence of the man which Paul meant to designate by the words ὄλεθρος τῆς σαρκός; and M. Renan is not wrong in saying: "There can be no doubt of it; it is a condemnation to death that Paul pronounces." The sudden death of Ananias and Sapphira offers an analogy to the present case, not that Paul is thinking of so sudden a visitation; the expression he uses rather indicates a slow wasting, leaving to the sinner time for repentance.

This destruction of the flesh has in view *the saving of the spirit, in the day of Christ.* Some versions translate: "that *the soul* may be saved . . .," as if the soul and spirit were in Paul's eyes one and the same thing. The passage 1 Thess. v. 23 proves the contrary. "The *soul* is, in man as in the lower animals, the breath of life which animates his organism; but the *spirit* is the sense with which the human soul is exclusively endowed to experience the contact of the Divine and apprehend it." This higher sense in the soul once destroyed by the power of the flesh, connection is no longer possible between the soul and God. This is undoubtedly what Scripture calls the second death. As the first is the body's privation of the soul, the second is the soul's privation of the spirit. This is why the apostle wishes at any cost to save the *spirit* in this man, in which there resides the faculty of contact with God and of life in Him throughout eternity. It need not be said that the spirit, thus understood as an element of human life, can only discharge its part fully when it is open to the working of the Divine Spirit.—The words, *in the day of the Lord*

Jesus, transport us to the time when Jesus glorified will appear again on the earth to take to Him His own (xv. 23); then will be pronounced on each Christian the sentence of his acceptance or rejection. These last words appear to me to confirm the explanation given of the phrase, *destruction of the flesh*. For if this denoted the destruction of the fleshly inclinations in the incestuous person, the awaking of spiritual life which would follow would not take place only at Christ's coming, it would make itself felt in him in this present life.—Rückert has very severely judged the apostle's conduct on this occasion. He is disposed, indeed, to make good as an excuse in his favour the impetuosity of his zeal, the purity of his intention, and a remnant of Judaic prejudice. But he charges him with having given way to his natural violence; with having compromised the salvation of the guilty person by depriving him, perhaps, if his sentence came to be realized, of time for repentance; and finally, with having acted imprudently towards a Church in which his credit was shaken, by putting it in circumstances to disobey him. We do not accept either these excuses or these charges for the apostle. The phrase *deliver to Satan*, being foreign to the formulas of the synagogue, was consequently, also, foreign to the apostle's Jewish past. The alleged violence of his temperament does not betray itself in the slightest in the severity of his conduct. The apostle here rather resembles a mother crying to God for her prodigal son and saying to Him: My God, strike him, strike him even to the death, if need be, if only he be saved! As to the Church, Paul no doubt knew better than the critic of our day how far he could and ought to go in his conduct toward it. —Another critic, Baur,[1] has taken up and developed the observations of Rückert, confirming them by the Second Epistle. In the passage 2 Cor. ii. 5–11, he sees the proof that the apostle's injunctions had not been executed, that the sentence pronounced by him against the incestuous person had not been followed with any effect, and that the apostolical power which he claimed was consequently nothing but an illusion; that after all, in short, nothing remained to the apostle but piteously to beat a retreat, "presenting as his desire what was done without his will," and putting on the appearance of pardoning and asking favour for the guilty one from the Corinthians, who pardoned the delinquent in spite of him.—This entire deduction assumes one thing: to wit, that the passage 2 Cor. ii. 5–11 refers to the affair of the incestuous person. But the close relation between this passage and that of vii. 12 demonstrates that it is nothing of the kind, and that all that Paul writes in chap. ii. refers to an entirely different fact, to a personal insult to which he had been subjected at Corinth, and which had taken place posterior to the sending of the first letter.[2] And supposing even that the passage of chap. ii. related to the incestuous person, what would it tell us? That the majority of the Church (οἱ πλείονες, *the larger number*) had entered into the apostle's views as to the punishment

[1] *Der ap. Paulus*, i. pp. 234, 235.

[2] In any attempt to maintain the reference of 2 Cor. vii. 7 seq. to the affair of the incestuous person, the word ἀδικηθείς, *he to whom a wrong has been done* (ver. 12), must be referred to the guilty man's father, as if such an act could be ranked in the category of injustices! Besides, does not the very fact of the incest necessarily suppose the father's death? See Hilgenfeld, *Einleitung*, pp. 284, 285.

of the culprit; and that the latter had fallen into such a disheartened state that his danger now was of allowing himself to be driven by Satan from carnal security to despair. If such was the meaning of the passage, what would it contain that was fitted to justify the conclusions of Baur, and the awkward light in which they would place the conduct and character of the apostle?

The apostle has terminated what concerns the particular case of the incestuous person. From this point onwards the subject broadens; he shows in the general state of the Church the reason why it has so badly fulfilled its obligations in this particular case (vers. 6–8).

Vers. 6–8

Ver. 6. "Your glorying is not good; know ye not that a little leaven leaveneth[1] the whole lump?"—There are two ways of understanding the connection between the following passage and that which precedes: either the apostle continues to dwell on the disciplinary obligation of the Church,—and we must then regard the *leaven* to be taken away as either the incestuous person, or rather the vicious in general,—or it may be held that Paul, after upbraiding the Church with its negligence, seeks to guide its finger to the true cause of the mischief: the want of moral sincerity and firmness. This is the state which must be remedied without delay. Then reaction against the presence of the vicious will take place of itself. The first words are better explained in the second sense, for they relate to

[1] D reads δολοῖ (It. *corrumpit*).

the present state of the Church in general. I have translated καύχημα by *vanterie* (boasting), as if it had been καύχησις (the act of boasting), because we have no word in French to denote the *object* of boasting.[1] Chrysostom thought the word should be applied to the incestuous person himself, assuming that he was one of the eminent men in whom the Church gloried. Grotius and Heinrici have reproduced this explanation. It seems to us untenable: the Church was satisfied with its state in general, and in particular with the wealth of its spiritual gifts, on which Paul himself had congratulated it (i. 5–7), and of which chaps. xii.–xiv. will furnish proof. But this abundance of knowledge and speech was no real good except in so far as it effected the increase of spiritual life in the Church, and the sanctification of its members. As this was not the case, the apostle declares to them that their ground of self-satisfaction is of bad quality; a being vainly puffed up (iv. 19): "Ye are proud of the state of your Church; there is no reason for it!" He thus returns to the idea of ver. 2.—This judgment is called forth by the softness of their conduct in regard to the evil which shows itself among them. Should they who are so rich in knowledge fail to know the influence exercised on a whole mass by the least particle of corruption which is tolerated in it?—Paul clothes his thought in a proverbial form (Gal. v. 9). *Leaven* is here, as in many other passages (Matt. xiii. 33; Luke xii. 1), the emblem of a principle apparently insignificant in quantity, but possessing a real penetrating force, and that either for good (Matt. xiii. 33) or for evil (Matt. xvi. 6; Gal.

[1] [Our English *boast* is used in both senses.—Tr.]

v. 9). Does Paul understand by this *little leaven* (the literal sense), the incestuous person or any other vicious member of the same kind, whose tolerated presence is a principle of corruption for the whole community? This is the meaning generally held. Or is he rather thinking of evil in general, which, when tolerated even in a limited and slightly scandalous form, gradually lowers the standard of the Christian conscience in all? It does not seem to me likely that Paul would designate as a *little* leaven a sinner guilty of so revolting an act as that in question (ver. 1), or other not less scandalous offenders. It is therefore better to apply this figure to all sin, even the least, voluntarily tolerated by the individual or the Church. This meaning, held by Meyer, de Wette, Hofmann, Gerlach, is confirmed by vers. 7 and 8.

Vers. 7, 8. "Purge out[1] the old leaven, that ye may be a new lump, as ye are unleavened. For even Christ, our Paschal lamb, hath been sacrificed.[2] 8. Therefore let us keep the feast, not with old leaven, neither[3] with the leaven of malice and wickedness; but with the unleavened bread of purity and truth."—If the figure applied to the incestuous man or to the vicious, the word ἐκκαθάρειν, *to purify by removing*, would apply to an act such as the: *taking away from among* (ver. 2), and the: *delivering to Satan* (ver. 5); and the words: *that ye may be a new lump*, would signify: that ye may present the spectacle of a Church renewed by the absence of every vicious member. But the

[1] T. R. with C L P here add ουν (*therefore*).

[2] T. R. with L P Syr. reads υπερ ημων (*for us*).

[3] C Or. read μη instead of μηδε.

epithet *old*, given to leaven, and ver. 8 show that leaven is here taken in an abstract sense: "the leaven which consists of natural malignity and perversity." The exhortation to *purging* applies therefore to the action of each on himself, and of all on all, in order to leave in the Church not a *single* manifestation of the old man, of the corrupt nature, undiscovered and unchecked.

The οὖν, *therefore*, of T. R. ought, according to most of the Mjj., to be suppressed. It only goes to weaken the vivacity of the imperative. It is well known that among the Jews, on the 14th Nisan, the eve of the first and great day of the feast of Passover, there was removed with great care all the leaven (*pain levé*, raised bread) which could be found in their houses; and in the evening, along with the celebration of the Paschal feast, the sacred week began, during which nothing was eaten but cakes of unleavened bread. Leaven represented, according to the particular ceremonial of this feast, the pollutions of the idolatry and vices of Egypt with which Israel had broken in coming forth from it. As Israel had providentially carried to the desert that night only unleavened bread, the permanent rite had been borrowed from the historical circumstance (Ex. xii. 39, xiii. 6–9). The apostle spiritualizes the ceremony. As the Israelites at every Passover feast were bound to leave behind them the pollutions of their Egyptian life, in order to become a new people of God, so the Church is bound to break with all the evil dispositions of the natural heart, or that which is elsewhere called *the old man*.—The desired result of this breaking on the part of each one with his own known sin, will be the renewing of the whole Church : *that ye may be a new lump.* Another allusion to Jewish customs. On the eve of the feast, a fresh piece of dough was kneaded with pure water, and from it were prepared the cakes of unleavened bread which were eaten during the feast. The word νέον, *new,* does not signify : new as to quality (as καινόν would do), but *recent,* as to time. The whole community, by this work of purification wrought on itself, should become like a piece of dough newly kneaded. Has not the awakening of a whole Church been seen more than once to begin with submission to an old censure which weighed on the conscience of *one* sinner ? This confession drew forth others, and the holy breath passed over the whole community.

The phrase which follows, *as ye are unleavened,* has greatly embarrassed commentators, who have explained it as if it were, " ye should be," which grammatically is inadmissible. Chrysostom thinks of final sanctification, others of baptismal regeneration,—meanings equally impossible. In saying, *ye are,* the apostle thinks of what they are, not in point of fact, but of right ; the idea is the same as in Rom. vi. 11 : death to sin and life to God, virtually contained in faith in the dead and risen Christ. For the believer nothing more is needed than to become what he is already (in Christ). He must become holy in fact, as he is in idea. — Grotius has proposed to give to ἄζυμος, *unleavened,* the active meaning belonging to the adjectives ἄσιτος, ἄοινος (abstaining from bread, from wine) ; according to him, Paul characterizes the

Corinthians as persons who no longer feed on leavened bread (in the spiritual sense). But this term cannot be twisted from the definite meaning which it has in the Jewish ritual, and which is perfectly appropriate. They ought to become individually the organs of a new nature, which is in accordance with their true character as beings unleavened so far as they are believers.—The proof that this is what they are in point of right is given in the sequel.

From the time when the Paschal lamb was sacrificed in the temple, no leaven bread was allowed to appear on an Israelitish table; and this continued during the whole feast. Similarly the expiatory death of Christ, containing the principle of death to sin, there begins with His death in the case of the Church and of each believer the great spiritual Passover, from which all sin is banished, as leaven was from the Jewish feast. Every Christian is an *azyme* (unleavened one).—The particle καὶ γάρ, *for also*, has for its characteristic the connecting of two facts of an analogous nature (*also*), the second of which is the ground of the first (*for*): this is exactly the case here.—The work πάσχα, strictly speaking, *passing*, denoted God's passing over Egypt, on the night when He smote the first-born and spared the houses of the Israelites sprinkled with the blood of the lamb. The word was afterwards applied to the lamb itself; in this sense it is taken here.—The words *for us*, read by T. R., are omitted in the majority of the Mjj.—By the complement ἡμῶν, *our*, Paul contrasts the Christian Passover with that of the Jews. As the latter began with the slaying of the lamb, ours began with the bloody death of Christ; Χριστός is in apposition to *πάσχα*. The practical consequence of His death thus understood, and of the new state in which it places believers, is drawn in the following verse.

Ver. 8. The Christian's Paschal feast does not last a week, but all his life. In an admirable discourse Chrysostom has developed this idea: "For the true Christian, it is always Easter, always Pentecost, always Christmas." Such is the sense in which the apostle exhorts the Corinthians to keep the feast.—The words, *not with old leaven*, signify, in accordance with what precedes: not by persisting in the corrupt dispositions of the old man.—The particle *μηδέ*, *nor any more*, according to Edwards, does not introduce an additional thought, but only the explanation of the preceding allegorical phrase. I do not think this meaning possible. The *μηδέ* seems to me intended to bring out a special feature in the general idea in direct connection with present circumstances; so, or nearly so, de Wette, Rückert, Meyer, etc. The word *κακία* denotes rather corruption of the nature or state, and the word *πονηρία*, deliberate malice of the will. In the context, the first of these terms relates to a corrupt state of the soul, which does not allow it to be indignant against evil, but leaves it to act toward it with lax toleration; the second goes further: it denotes active connivance and protection. These two vices, both proceeding from the leaven of the old nature, had been prominently manifested in the Church's conduct towards the incestuous person. With these dispositions Paul contrasts those which should characterize the renewing of the purified mass.

The two complements εἰλικρινείας and ἀληθείας are, like the two preceding, genitives of apposition : " unleavened bread consisting of . . ." The word εἰλικρίνεια, according to the most probable etymology, πρὸς εἵλην κρίνειν, to judge by the light of the sun, denotes proved transparency, and so the purity of a heart perfectly sincere before God, to which all sympathy with evil is completely foreign. This pure crystal is the opposite of κακία, the corrupted nature.—The second term, *truth*, ἀλήθεια, denotes righteousness in its active form, inflexible firmness, constancy in maintaining all that is revealed to the conscience as good, and consequently in struggling against evil without making the smallest compromise ; it is the opposite of πονηρία. Hofmann has taken up the unfortunate idea—and he has been followed by Heinrici — of explaining the charge of malice contained in this verse by the misunderstanding, to some extent voluntary, on the part of the Corinthians, which Paul now proceeds to rectify. The apostle does not condescend to such petty recriminations.

Must it be concluded from these verses that the apostle wrote this letter at the time of the Passover ? The figures used do not, as we have seen, contain anything which does not admit of explanation independently of all connection with the actual celebration of the Passover. Yet it is certain, that if we hold this feast and the composition of our letter to have been simultaneous, the choice of the figures, which come on us somewhat abruptly, is more naturally explained. This induction is confirmed by xvi. 8 : " I will tarry at Ephesus until Pentecost." And as Acts xx. 6 shows that St. Paul, as well as the Churches founded by him, observed the Passover and celebrated it at the same time as the Jews, we shall not assuredly be going beyond his thought if we find in the words, "Let us keep the feast," an *allusion* to that which was being celebrated at the time in the Churches.

A second question often discussed is the following: May the words, "Christ, our Passover, has been sacrificed," be regarded as a testimony in favour of John's narrative, according to which Jesus died on the day (14th Nisan) when the Paschal lamb was sacrificed, and not, as it has been thought necessary to conclude from the synoptics, on the afternoon of the 15th Nisan? It seems to me that the name Paschal lamb, given to Jesus by St. Paul, does not depend in the least on the day or hour when He died. His relation to the Paschal lamb lies in the essence of things, and does not depend on a chronological coincidence. But there is one aspect in which Paul's words cannot be well understood, as it appears to me, except from that point of view which the narrative of John brings into light. The feast of unleavened bread began on the 14th in the evening, after the slaying of the lamb. Now this relation, which forms the basis of our passage, would be disturbed if Jesus, in Paul's view, did not die till the afternoon of the 15th, after the feast of unleavened bread had already lasted for a whole day.—After pointing out to the Church what it should have done, the apostle gives it to understand the reason why it has not done so: it is because the old leaven has regained the upper hand in its moral life, and that it requires to undergo a complete renovation. This said, the subject of discipline is finished; if Pauls adds a few more observations, it is to dissipate a misunderstanding arising from a passage of his on the subject in a letter which he had previously addressed to them.

Vers. 9–13

Vers. 9, 10. "I wrote unto you in my epistle not to company with fornicators; 10.[1] not altogether with the fornicators of this world, or with the covetous and[2] extortioners or with idolaters; for then must ye needs[3] go out of the world."—Paul begins with recalling the terms of which he made use (ver. 9); then he sets aside the false sense which had been attached to them (ver. 10), and states his real judgment (ver. 11); finally, he justifies his judgment in vers. 12, 13.—*Ἐν τῇ ἐπιστολῇ*, literally, *in the Epistle*, the one you know. It is vain for Chrysostom, Erasmus, Lange, to allege that Paul alludes to vers. 2, 6, and 7 of this same chapter, or for Lardner to attempt to find here the announcement of what is about to follow, vers. 10–13. It is easy to see that nothing in what precedes contained the direction given here, and that the ἔγραψα, *I wrote*, can only refer to the rectification of an idea which had been fathered on Paul, and which had been reported to him. A correspondence between Paul and the Church had certainly preceded our Epistle; comp. vii. 1: "Now concerning the things whereof ye wrote unto me." In 2 Cor. vii. 8, Paul refers, using the same expression, to

[1] T. R. with L P reads και (*and*) ου παντως.
[2] T. R. with E L Syr. reads η (*or*), instead of και (*and*).
[3] T. R. with P: οφειλετε (*ye need*), instead of ωφειλετε (*ye would need*).

a previous letter. Had there not been dogmatic reasons for denying the possibility of the loss of an apostolic document, this meaning would not have been contested. —The term *to company* (mingle) *with*, *συναναμίγνυσθαι*, strictly denotes living in an intimate and continuous relation with one,—*σύν* emphasizing the intimacy, and *ἀνά* the repetition of the acts. Does the rupture demanded by the apostle refer to the conduct of Christians in private life, or to ecclesiastical communion? In any case, the Corinthians could not have thought of an ecclesiastical rupture with people with whom no ecclesiastical bond existed. Did they not apply Paul's regulation to sinners who were yet outside of the Church? We may see in 2 Thess. iii. 14 how the expression " not to company with " is synonymous with *στέλλεσθαι ἀπό*, *to hold aloof from*, of ver. 6; and in that context the term certainly refers to private life. Finally, if the matter in question here were the ecclesiastical relation, the apostle would not have to say to believers, " Do not company with the vicious," but, " Do not allow the vicious to company with you." This precept of Paul's is parallel to that of John, Second Epistle, ver. 10: " If any one bringeth not this teaching, receive him not into your house, and give him no greeting."

Ver. 10. The *καί*, *and*, which begins this verse in the T. R., is too little supported to be authentic.—The words *οὐ πάντως τοῖς πόρνοις* naturally have the effect of an explanatory apposition added to the *πόρνοις* at the end of ver. 9, in this sense: " When I spoke of fornicators in my letter, I did not thereby mean all the fornicators of this world in general." After all attempts to explain this *οὐ πάντως* differently, it seems to me that this is the interpretation which holds good. Only, it logically implies that by the phrase, *the fornicators of this world,* Paul denotes, not only those who are without the Church, but those also who profess the gospel. It is the only way of explaining the *οὐ πάντως*, which is not the absolute negative, like *πάντως οὐ*, *absolutely not,* but, on the contrary, a restricted negative (*not absolutely, not entirely*): I wrote to you to break with fornicators, not with fornicators in general, which would oblige you to go out of the world, but with those only who profess the gospel. This is the meaning adopted by Neander, Hofmann, and others. It is objected that the phrase, the fornicators *of this world,* must be exclusive of those *of the Church.* Why so? The idea is simply, "not generally with all the fornicators living with you in this world." Such is evidently the meaning of the word *world* in the following sentence. Meyer has thought that it is to mark the difference between these two meanings given to the word *world* that Paul rejects the *τούτου*, *this,* in the following sentence. But it may also be to avoid an awkward and useless repetition. As to those who, like Meyer, de Wette, Edwards, hold that *the fornicators of this world* must here be necessarily contrasted with those of the Church, they are thrown into embarrassment by the *οὐ πάντως*, and they apply it solely to the *limitation* of relations with these fornicators: "I meant you not to have relations too complete (*πάντως*) with non-Christian fornicators," which would authorize restricted relations, without which life in the world would be impossible. But this meaning is not natural; for what Paul here distinguishes is not the greater or less degree of intimacy in relations to impure heathen; he is contrasting with the relation to impure heathen, which he authorizes, the relation to impure Christians, which he forbids.—We do not take account here of the interpretations which separate *οὐ* from *πάντως*, connecting the former with the verb *ἔγραψα*, and the latter with the verb *συναναμίγνυσθαι*,—a separation far from natural,—nor of that of Rückert, who understands *οὐ πάντως* almost as if it were *πάντως οὐ*, *absolutely not*, though Paul knows perfectly the use and meaning of this form; comp. xvi. 12. However this may be, the view of the apostle remains substantially the same: the rupture which he demands is not applicable to the vicious in general, but only to those who lay claim to the name of Christians.—To libertinism Paul adds *covetousness* as to earthly goods, and that in the two forms of *πλεονεξία*, which, to have more, uses fraudulent and indelicate processes, like usury, and that of *ἁρπαγή*, injustice by violent means. These two words are connected, not by *ἤ*, *or*, but by *καί*, *and*, as two species of one and the same genus.—*Idolaters*, as such, would seem to be an impossibility in the Church; but there might be Corinthians who, after believing, had kept up habits of idolatry; and chap. viii. will show us that many of them could not bring themselves to give up the banquets to which they were invited in idol temples. These three vices, fornication, covetousness, idolatry, are related, as Estius and Edwards observe, the first to the individual himself, the second to his neighbours, the third to God.

It is evident that in a city like Corinth, to break off all connection with persons of these three categories would have been for a man to condemn himself to live as a hermit. This is probably what the Corinthians had retorted with a measure of irony; and so the apostle, no less than they, rejects an idea so absurd. The majority of the Mjj. read ὠφείλετε, *ye would need*, which gives a simple sense. T. R. with P and Chrysostom reads ὀφείλετε, *ye need*, a form which is also, though less easily, intelligible: "Since, if it is so, ye need . . ." Calvin, starting from this reading, has given the sentence a quite different meaning: "For ye need really to separate yourselves from the world (morally)." But the particle ἄρα, *then*, indicates, on the contrary, a consequence from what precedes.—And now Paul establishes his true thought.

Ver. 11. "But now I have written unto you not to keep company, if any man that is called a brother be a fornicator, or covetous, or an idolater, or a railer, or a drunkard, or an extortioner; with such an one, no, not to eat."—The words *but now* can only express a logical contrast. The νῦν contrasts Paul's true thought, which remains, with his thought as it was disfigured by the Corinthians, which is relegated to the past.—The emphasis is on the words, *who is called a brother;* as Paul goes on to say in ver. 12, he has not to exercise discipline on those who do not profess the faith. But when a man, who parades the title of Christian, exhibits this profession side by side with vice, the Church is bound to protest against this lying union, and with this view, so far as depends on it, to break off all relations with such a man. This is the way to tear from him the mask with which he covers himself to the shame of the Church and of Christ Himself.—The six following terms have been grouped, either in threes (Meyer) or in three pairs (Hofmann), with more or less ingenuity. It seems to me that, as in the enumeration Rom. i. 29 seq., we have here rather an unstudied accumulation than a classification, strictly so called. It may be said that in such cases disgust excludes order. To the four terms of ver. 10 Paul adds two new ones: λοίδορος, a man who speaks rudely, who calumniates, and μέθυσος, *the intemperate man*.—We have already shown that the *not to company with* indicates the rupture of private relations. But should not the last words, *with such a man, no, not to eat*, be applied to the rupture of the ecclesiastical relation by his exclusion from worship and from the Holy Supper? The word μηδέ, *nay, no more, not even*, does not allow this explanation of συνεσθίειν, *to eat with*. For this act is thus characterized as a matter of less gravity, and Paul could never so speak of the Holy Supper. Among the ancients, for a man to receive any at his table was much more a sign of intimacy than in our day; and the apostle is unwilling that by the sign of so close a personal relation the idea should be authorized that the vicious man is acknowledged by other Christians as worthy of the name. Meyer, indeed, admits that the phrase, *no, not to eat with* . . ., can only refer to the believer's private table. But by an argument *à fortiori*, he concludes that it applies with still more certainty to the Holy Supper. Theodoret had already argued in the same way: "Not to eat, with stronger reason not to hold communion with him." In such a matter it is dangerous to proceed by way of logical deduction. In arguing thus, account is not taken of this difference, that the table prepared in my house is my own, while the Holy Supper is the Lord's Table.

I am therefore responsible for those whom I admit to the former, but not for those who appear at the latter. It appears from xi. 28, 29, that the Lord thinks good to leave each one liberty to eat and drink his condemnation at the holy table, and will not prevent him from doing so by external means. The parable of the tares already suggested such a course, the only one in keeping with God's regard for human liberty. The apostle justifies the distinction which he has just made between believers and unbelievers.

Vers. 12, 13. "For what have I to do to judge them also[1] that are without? do ye not judge them that are within? 13. But them that are without, God judgeth. And[2] put away[3] from among yourselves that wicked person."—The first question is the justification (*for*) of ver. 10: "We have not to judge unbelievers." The second is the justification of ver. 11: "But we have to judge believers."—Our competency to exercise discipline does not extend further than the solidarity established by confession of the common faith. This general truth the apostle expresses in his own person (μοί, *mine*), as is often done in stating moral maxims (vi. 12, for example); this form does not therefore assume, as has been sometimes thought, that the word κρίνειν, *to judge*, has here a particular meaning, applicable exclusively to the apostle; for example, that of laying down disciplinary rules: "The rules which I prescribe to you on this subject are not to be applied

[1] T. R. with D E L here adds και (*also*).

[2] T. R. with E L Syr. reads και (*and*), while this word is omitted in the other 8 Mjj.

[3] T. R. with E L reads εξαρειτε (*ye will take away*), instead of εξαρατε (*take away*), read by the 8 other Mjj.

to those who are without." This sense of κρίνειν is inadmissible. In any case, had it been the part which he had to take personally on which Paul wished to lay stress, he would not have used the enclitic form (μοι), but the full form (ἐμοί). He speaks of himself, not as an apostle, but as a Christian; and what he says applies consequently to every Christian. Every Christian has individually the mission to exercise the judgment of which he speaks in ver. 11. We have already pointed out the profound analogy which prevails between this chapter and the disciplinary direction given to the apostles by the Lord (Matt. xviii. 15–20). We find in the latter (in ver. 17) the same use of the singular pronoun, which strikes us here in the language of the apostle; only the pronoun is in the second person, because it is Jesus who is addressing the believer: "Let him be to *thee* as a heathen and publican." It is therefore every believer who is bound freely at his own hand to pronounce this rupture of relations with the unbelieving brother which Paul prescribes to the Church in general. For if it is in itself the duty of all, it cannot be other in point of fact than a completely individual act.—T. R. with 3 Mjj. reads: "What have I to do to judge those *also* (καί) that are without?" This καί may, after all, be authentic: "The competency which I have in regard to my brethren, should I not *also* extend to others?" The Jews called the heathen *chitsonim, those without* (Lightfoot, *Hor. hebr.*, p. 6). The apostle borrows the name from them to designate, not only the heathen, but the Jews themselves; comp. the analogous term used by Jesus, Mark iv. 11. In all the synagogues dispersed throughout heathen countries careful watch was kept over the respectability of the members of the community. Should the Church in this point remain behind the synagogue?—The term *judge* can only be explained in the context by what precedes. It can only therefore refer to the means which have just been indicated, viz. private rupture.

The second question (ver. 12[b]) is in the same relation to ver. 11 as the first (ver. 12[a]) to ver. 10. "I have not the task of judging them that are without; but have not you that of judging them that are within, the vicious among believers, and that in name of the faith which they profess along with you?" We are called to remark the emphasis put on the word ὑμεῖς, *ye*, in opposition to θεός, *God*, the subject of the following proposition.

Ver. 13 justifies by a remark, and moreover by a Scriptural quotation, the distinction laid down in ver. 12. There are two domains, each subject to a different jurisdiction: the Christian judges the Christian; the man of the world is judged by God. It is needless to say that this contrast is only relative. The unfaithful Christian is also judged by God (xi. 30–32); but he has at the same time to do with another judge, the Christian community to which he belongs; while the non-Christian can sin without being subjected to any judgment of the latter kind. It seems at the first glance as if this saying were in contradiction to that of our Lord: "Judge not. . . . Why seest thou the mote in thy brother's eye?" (Matt. vii. 1–3). But when Jesus speaks thus, the judgment which He would exclude is that of secret malevolence, which condemns precipitately, on simple presumptions, or putting a malignant construction on motives. St. Paul is equally averse to such judging, xiii. 7. The judgment he lays on the Christian as a duty is that of charity, which, in view of notorious facts, seeks the best means to bring a brother back to himself who is self-deceived as to his spiritual state, and to save him (ver. 5). The former of these judgments is accompanied with a haughty joy, the other is an act of self-humiliation and mourning (ver. 2). The first proposition of ver. 13 might be made the continuation of the second question of ver. 12: "Do not ye judge . . . and does not God judge?" But the affirmative meaning seems simpler.—The verb *κρινει* might be a future (*κρινεῖ*): "God *shall judge;*" the words would then refer to the last judgment. But, after the presents *κρίνειν, κρίνετε,* the verb is rather a present (*κρίνει*), the present of the idea and competency: "It is God who is their Judge."—The final proposition, containing a Scripture quotation, is usually separated from what immediately precedes, to form, as it were, a last peremptory order summing up the whole chapter. It is clear that in this sense the *καί, and* (before the imperative *ἐξάρατε* or the future *ἐξαρεῖτε*), is out of place. It is omitted therefore in the Alex. and Greco-Latin readings, which evidently proceed on this interpretation. But what is overlooked in adopting this sense is the close connection established by the last words: *ἐξ ὑμῶν αὐτῶν, from among yourselves,* with what *immediately* precedes (vers. 12, 13[a]): "Thou shalt take away the wicked, not from human society, as if thou hadst to judge also them that are without, but *from the midst of thyself,* from those that are within." Such then is the *Scriptural justification* of the distinction laid down by Paul, vers. 10–13[a], between the judgment of *those without* and of *those within.* As Israel was bound to cut off the malefactor, not from heathen nations, but *from its own midst,* so with the Church. From this point of view we cannot but adopt the καί, *and,* of the T. R. and of the Byzantines, to which must be added the support of the Peschito, a support by no means to be despised, notwithstanding all that Westcott and Hort say: "*And finally,* you remember the Bible rule . . . !" This is the final proof.—The same reason which led to the suppression of the καί, *and,* no doubt led also to the change of the future ἐξαρεῖτε, *ye shall take away,* into the aor. imperative ἐξάρατε, *take away!* Once this last word was held to be the summary of the chapter, it is evident the imperative alone was suitable. If, on the contrary, the explanation here proposed is the true one, the future ought to be preserved, as giving more literally the formula quoted; comp. Deut. xvii. 7–12, xxii. 21, xxiv. 7. It has been suspected that the reading ἐξαρεῖτε, *ye shall take away,* was borrowed from these passages; but the text of the LXX. has in all these sentences the sing. ἐξαρεῖς, *thou shalt take away.* Why should the Byzantine copyists have transformed it into a plural? —The term *take away,* like that of *judge* (ver. 12), should be determined by what precedes. The means of execution, of which the apostle is thinking, can only be the two indicated by himself, that of mourning, ver. 2, which appeals to the intervention of God (with or without the παραδιδόναι), and that of the personal rupture, indicated ver. 11, which plunges the sinner into isolation. Such are the weapons of Christian discipline, which correspond to Israelitish stoning; Paul knows no others, when once the first warnings have failed. The very act of *delivering to Satan*, which he does as an apostle, not without the co-operation of the Church, is not essentially different from the judgment which it should itself have carried out according to ver. 2.—Rückert, who always takes a very close grip of questions, does not think that the term τὸν πονηρόν, *the wicked*, can possibly designate any other than the incestuous person. These last words would thus be the summary of chap. v.: "Exclude that guilty one!" But then, how explain the two passages, vers. 6–8 and 9–13[a], which seem to deviate from the subject properly so called? The first, according to him, is intended to prove the *necessity* of the exclusion; the second, its *possibility*; then, lastly, would come the final order, as an abrupt conclusion. This is able, but inadmissible. The passage vers. 6–8 has a wholly different meaning, as we have seen. The passage vers. 9–13 is introduced, not by a logical connection, but by an accidental circumstance, the misunderstanding on the part of the Corinthians. The τὸν πονηρόν, *the wicked*, does not therefore refer in the least to the incestuous man personally, but, as in the precepts of Deuteronomy, to the whole category of the vicious who are within. Paul does not return to the case of the incestuous man, but continues to treat the general subject of discipline to which he had passed from ver. 6.

Ecclesiastical Discipline.

Let us briefly study the few passages of the New Testament which bear on this subject.

Matt. v. 22.—Jesus here distinguishes three judicial stages: the judgment (κρίσις), the Sanhedrim, and the Gehenna of fire. These phrases are borrowed from the Israelitish order of things, in which they denote the district tribunal, the superior court, and, finally, the immediate judgment of God. If we apply these terms to the new surroundings which are formed about Jesus, and regard the first as brotherly admonition, the second as that of the heads of the future community of which the little existing flock is the germ, the third as God's judgment falling on the incorrigible sinner, we shall have a gradation of punishments corresponding, on the one hand, to the received Israelitish forms, and, on the other, to the passages of the New Testament, including that which we are explaining.

Matt. xviii. 15–20.—Here is the fullest passage. Jesus begins with *admonition;* there are three degrees of it: 1. *personal,*—as it is a private offence which is in question, the offended man takes the initiative; then 2. it takes a graver character by the addition of *two witnesses;* 3. it is the whole assembly together which admonishes the culprit. In the second place, admonition is followed by *judgment;* the dealing of the Church having failed, the offended person and every member of the congregation regard the brother, now recognised to be guilty, as a heathen or publican, which, in Jewish language, signifies that they break off all personal connection with him. Finally, the Church does not yet abandon the guilty man; it prays that he may repent, or, if not, that God may punish him visibly. Two or three brethren are sufficient to carry out this appeal to God effectually. The last stage, final perdition, is not here mentioned by Jesus; but it had been indicated by Him in the saying Matt. v.

2 Thess. iii. 6, 14, 15.—The first stage, that of warning, is here satisfied by the apostle's own letters; comp. 1st Ep. iv. 11, and 2nd Ep. iii. 6–12. The second stage, that of judgment, begins at ver. 14. It is the σημείωσις, the *public declaration,* probably a communication from the rulers of the flock regarding what has taken place, and the invitation to the congregation to break off private relations with the culprit, without however ceasing to love him, and to act accordingly by praying for him and seeking to bring him back. The

apostle stops here, like Jesus, in the second passage of Matthew.

Rev. ii. 19–22.—A false prophetess, whom the bishop has not checked, is to be punished by a disease sent by the Lord. This threat corresponds to the judgment whereby Paul gives over the incestuous person to Satan; and John's position in delivering this message is not without analogy to Paul's in our chapter. With this punishment coming directly from the Lord might be compared the punishment drawn down by profane communions, of which mention is made in chap. xi. of our Epistle. But we would not anticipate the explanation of the passage.

It is clear that the means of excommunication cannot be supported by any passage of the New Testament, but that the Church is not for all that defenceless against the scandals which arise within it. After admonitions, if they are useless, it has two arms: 1st. humiliation, with prayer to God to act; and 2nd. private rupture. The use of these means depends on individual believers, and may dispense with all decision by way of a numerical majority. And how much ought we to admire the Lord's wisdom, who took care not to confide the exercise of discipline to such uncertain hands as those of the half plus one of the members of the Church. To be convinced of this, it is enough to cast our eyes on the use which the Church has made of excommunication. There is not on the earth at this hour a Christian who is not excommunicated: Protestants are so by the Roman Church; the Roman Church by the Greek Church, and *vice versa;* the Reformed by the Lutherans, who refuse to admit them to their Holy Supper; the Darbyites by one another. Is there not then enough here to cure the Church of the use of this means? "The weapons of our warfare," says St. Paul, 2 Cor. x. 4, "are not carnal, but are powerful by God." It is certainly probable that the incestuous member of the Corinthian Church, visited with judgment from above, and abandoned for the time by all his brethren, did not present himself at the love-feast and the Holy Supper. And even at this hour it is hard to believe that a scandalous sinner, with whom the most of his brethren have broken, and for whom they besiege the throne of God, would have the audacity to present himself with them at the holy table; but if he chooses, he should have it in his power as Judas had. If the Church lives, the Lord will show that He also is living. Excommunication may have been a measure pedagogically useful at a time when the whole Church was under a system of legality. Now the Church has recovered consciousness of its spirituality; ought not its mode of discipline to follow this impulse, and return to the order of primitive spiritual discipline?

3

Lawsuits (6:1-11)

The subject of discipline, though connected with the domain of ecclesiastical life, trenched on the sphere of moral questions. We come now to the subjects which belong exclusively to the latter sphere.

As the apostle had dealt with discipline, first from the standpoint of the special case which had raised the question, then, more generally, he acts in a similar way in regard to the subject which is now to follow. He treats of lawsuits between Christians,—1. in vers. 1–6, from the special standpoint of recourse had to heathen tribunals; and 2. in vers. 7–11, from the more general viewpoint of the lack of righteousness and charity which such conflicts between brethren imply.

Meyer alleges that there is no logical relation between this subject and the preceding; he founds on the asyndeton between the last verse of chap. v. and our ver. 1. But the absence of any particle fitted to connect these two verses is much rather the evidence of a very profound bond of feeling between the two passages. For by this form the second becomes, as it were, a reaffirmation of the ideas expounded in the first. And, in point of fact, does not Paul here, as in the former passage, combat in this proud Church the total lack of care for its own dignity before God and men? "Not only do ye not judge those whom you have a mission to judge (*them that are within*); but, moreover, ye go to have yourselves judged by those who are beneath you (*them that are without*)!" The basis of these two passages is therefore the same: it is the idea of the judicial competency of the Church in relation to its own members, but applied to two wholly different sins. Edwards understands the thing nearly in the same way. "He has just expounded the greatness and power of the Church; and now he asks if one could be found among them who would dare to do violence to the majesty of Christ who dwells in it."

Vers. 1–6

Ver. 1. "Dare any of you, having a matter against another, go to law before the unjust, and not before the saints?"—The word τολμᾶ, *dares he,* heads this passage, exactly because it appeals vigorously to Christian dignity: "What! there is one who has this miserable courage!" One needs courage to degrade himself. The pronoun τίς, *some one,* does not mean that there are many who are in this case; but there are too many if there is one. A single such case casts reproach on the whole Church. The Jews, who had the feeling of their theocratic nobility, had not recourse in their litigations to heathen tribunals; a system of arbitration established among them decided such questions; and the Corinthians had not Christian honour enough to rise to the same level!—For the moment the apostle leaves out of account the fact of the κρίνεσθαι, *getting judged, having a suit;* he will return to it, ver. 6. Here he fixes solely on the *way* in which these affairs are treated at Corinth.—The article τόν, *the,* before ἕτερον, *other*, serves strongly to individualize the adverse party in every case.—The heathen, of whom the official judges form part, are designated, not as usual by the term ἄπιστοι (*those who do not believe*), but by the term ἄδικοι, *unjust.* The apostle would make palpable the contradiction there is in going to ask justice of those who are themselves devoid of justice. The prep. ἐπί here signifies *in presence of;* as in the phrases ἐπὶ δικαστῶν, τοῦ δικαστηρίου (Plato, Demosthenes). Christians receive the title of honour οἱ ἅγιοι, *the saints.* They are people whom a Divine consecration has profoundly separated from the unjust and sinful world, and who ought therefore to possess within them the standard of justice. Had not Daniel seen the judgment given *to the saints* of the Most High? (vii. 22).

Vers. 2, 3. "Or[1] do ye not know that the saints shall judge the world? And if the world shall be judged by you, are ye unworthy to judge the smallest matters? 3. Know ye not that we shall judge angels? much more things that pertain to this life."—The T. R. is mistaken in omitting the *or* at the beginning of the question. Its meaning is: "Or if you affect to justify this mode of action, are you then ignorant that . . . ?" By the formula, *do ye not know,* which occurs no less than ten times in our Epistle, the apostle alludes to the doctrines he had delivered to the Church at the time of its foundation. Here it applies to a very special point of Christian eschatology, and from the

[1] T. R. omits ἢ (*or*) with E L.

example it may be concluded how detailed was the instruction which the Churches received from the apostle. The verb κρινοῦσι should evidently be taken as a future, *shall judge*, as well as the κρινοῦμεν, *we shall judge*, of the following verse. *The world*, which is to be judged by the saints, can only designate those who have rejected the appeal which had been addressed to them by the gospel.—The Greek Fathers have sought to spiritualize this notion of judgment by reducing it to the moral contrast, which will burst into view at the day of judgment, between Christian holiness and the pollution of other men (Matt. xii. 41); or there has been found in it the general notion of the kingdom and glory of believers yet to come (Flatt). But the idea of a real judicial act is demanded by the context. Lightfoot, Vitringa have thought that this was the announcement of a time when, the gospel having become supreme, courts of law would be composed of Christians; as if *the world* of which the apostle speaks in this passage could be Christendom! We have already quoted the saying of Daniel, according to which the world is to be judged by the saints. Jesus seems to apply this notion in a special way to the apostles (Matt. xix. 28): "In the regeneration which is to come, then ye shall be seated on twelve thrones, judging the twelve tribes of Israel." The Apocalypse extends this privilege to all believers (ii. 26, 27, and xx. 4).—Billroth has proposed to make the whole second part of the verse also dependent on: *Do ye not know . . .?* "Do ye not know that . . . and that it is unworthy of you to appear before the lowest tribunals (those of the heathen)?" But this construction is complicated, and the word ἐλάχιστα, *the least,* does not lend itself well to this meaning; comp. the parallel expression, βιωτικά, *the things of this life,* in the following verse. The second proposition of ver. 2 is therefore also a question: "Are not ye, the future judges of the world, worthy to pronounce on things which have only the slightest value?" The present κρίνεται, *is judged,* expresses not an actual fact, but a principle.—The adjunct ἐν ὑμῖν, literally *in you,* may be explained by the idea of the accused's presence in the circle formed by the tribunal. But this meaning is far from natural, especially when the accused is such as *the world!* It is better to understand: "in your person, which has become (by Christian sanctification) the rule of absolute justice;" which amounts to saying: *by you;* comp. the ἐν, Acts xvii. 31. The complement κριτηρίων ἐλαχίστων is often translated by *the least things to be judged.* Meyer is perhaps right in saying that usage does not admit of this meaning; but it is not exact to allege that the word κριτήριον can signify nothing except "a tribunal." It has many and varied meanings besides (see Passow: means of judgment; court of justice; place of judgment). Consequently we are entitled to give it here an analogous sense such as the context naturally demands, viz. a *sentence delivered:* "How should ye, who are invested with so high a competency, be unworthy to deliver sentences of a greatly inferior order?"

Ver. 3 does not present a new argument; it is the previous one raised to its culminating point. For the angels also, according to Paul, form part of the κόσμος, the *world* (see on iv. 9). Again we have the phrase:

Do ye not know? but without the particle ἤ, *or*, precisely because here is the continuation of ver. 2. The more striking the fact indicated in this verse,—the judgment of angels by the saints,—the more entitled is the apostle to express his wonder that his readers can be ignorant of it or can act as if they were in ignorance.—Meyer maintains that the word *angels*, used simply, denotes in the New Testament only *good* angels. It is one of those statutes which this excellent commentator loves to set up as a barrier against the caprice of exegetes, but the yoke of which need not be taken up without check. I think that the explanation of the idea contained in the first part of this verse is found in our Epistle itself, xv. 24. If it is so, Paul can only be speaking here of higher powers of *wickedness.* This meaning is also that which best accords with the meaning of the word *the world* (ver. 2). According to Meyer and Hofmann (who applies the word at once to good and bad angels), the judgment to which good angels shall be subjected will bear on the degree of fidelity with which they have discharged their office as *ministering spirits* to believers (Heb. i. 14); but nowhere in Scripture is there mention of a judgment of the elect angels. And in any case, we must not overlook the absence of the article before the word *angels:* "beings belonging to the category angel." Paul does not mean to designate these or those angels; he wishes to awake within the Church the feeling of its competency and dignity by reminding it that beings of so exalted a nature shall one day be subjected to its jurisdiction.

It is remarkable that in the parables of the tares and

of the drag-net, it is the angels who effect the division between men (wheat and tares, good and bad fishes); while in our passage, it is sanctified believers who judge angels. It seems as if God would glorify Himself in each of these orders of His creatures by means of the other.—Let it also be borne in mind that in Daniel's description (chap. vii.) there is not a word said of the judgment of the angels by the saints; this is a detail absolutely peculiar to Paul, and which, like that mentioned 1 Thess. iv. 15, rests no doubt on a personal revelation.

The last words, *much more things of this life*, need not be regarded as the continuation of the previous question, as is done by Tischendorf; it is the conclusion in the form of an exclamation. The form μήτι γε is found nowhere else in the New Testament. The simplest way of explaining it is to understand the verb λέγωμεν; *ne* (μή) *ullo quidem* (γε) *modo* (τι) *de rebus ad vitam pertinentibus* (βιωτικά) *loquamur;* "Not to speak even of earthly things; they follow *as a matter of course*, after what has been said of angels!" So far as sense is concerned, this is very much the same as our rendering: "much more." The γέ has here, as usually, the effect of emphasizing the preceding word (μήτι), so as to set aside every other supposition.

Ver. 4. "If then ye have judgments of things pertaining to this life, set them *to judge* who are least esteemed in the Church!"—Here is the practical conclusion from the foregoing argument; in its form there is a touch of irony. The μέν already suggests that after what Paul is about to say, he will have something more to add of a graver character: the unsuitableness of law processes in themselves (ver. 6 seq.). It appears to me that the *καθίζετε* ought to be taken as imperative: "Set up!" as it has been by the old Greek commentators, the *Vulgate*, Calvin, Beza, Bengel, Hofmann, Edwards. "If it is needed to have judgments on earthly things, set up the least of you, those who pass for the least intelligent: they will be good enough for this want." Luther and most moderns (Olshausen, de Wette, Rückert, Meyer, Heinrici) have rejected this sense and taken the verb *καθίζετε* as interrogative or exclamatory, applying the words, "those who are least esteemed in the Church," to the heathen tribunals before which the Christians of Corinth went to crave justice: "Do you then choose as your judges those who . . . ?" or: "You set up as your judges those who . . . !" This meaning seems to me inadmissible: 1. because of the *οὖν*, *then*, the natural meaning of which cannot in this case be preserved; 2. the term *set up* cannot, without doing violence to the meaning of the word, signify: to take as judges men already constituted such by others; 3. the phrase, *them who are nothing esteemed in the Church*, cannot in the apostle's view apply to heathen. But Paul may well apply the term with a touch of irony to designate those of whom small account is made in their assemblies: "Do not go and seek your first orators to make them arbiters in such cases, but take the least among you." Ver. 5 very naturally connects itself with this meaning.

Vers. 5, 6. "I speak to your shame: is it so that there is[1] not a wise man among you, no not

[1] Instead of *ἐστι*, which T. R. reads with D E F G, the reading *ἐνι* is found in ℵ B C L P.

one,[1] that shall be able to judge between his brethren? 6. But brother goeth to law with brother, and that before the unbelievers."—The first words of ver. 5 may bear on what precedes; in that case they signify: "I am certainly not opposed to your choosing capable men as arbiters; I have only spoken as I have done (ver. 4) to make you ashamed, by showing how little importance I attach to those wretched interests for which you do not scruple to compromise the honour of the Church." But the following οὕτως takes a more serious and definite meaning, if the first proposition is connected with what follows, ver. 5: "*Thus then*—I say this to your shame—in your Church of wise men, not a wise man capable of pronouncing on such affairs!" The proper reading is οὐκ ἔνι (abbreviation of ἔνεστι), *there is not there.*—The Alex. read: *not a wise man;* the Greco-Lat.: *not a single wise man;* the T. R.: *no wise man, not even one;* the last reading is preferable, at least in point of sense.—The aorist διακρῖναι here signifies: to decide summarily, settling the question with a stroke of the pen. It is a case of arbitration, not a law process.—The expression ἀνὰ μέσον τοῦ ἀδελφοῦ is evidently incomplete; the ἀνὰ μέσον, *between,* supposes a regimen formed of two terms: between a brother (the plaintiff) and his brother (the accused); comp. Gen. xvi. 5; Ex. xi. 7 and xxvi. 33 (in the LXX.). Either the second term was understood, or it might be supposed that by an elliptical form of the word *his brother* was put for: "*the claim* of his brother."

[1] T. R. with L reads σοφος ουδε εις; א B C Or.: ουδεις σοφος; F G P: ουδε εις σοφος.

The word διακρῖναι, *to distinguish, decide,* would then signify: to separate between the true and the false in this claim. In any case the meaning is: "No law pleading! The word of an arbiter, let that be final!" In this mode of expression there is a sort of disdain for the object of contention.

Ver. 6 is the exclamatory conclusion of the foregoing development. The ἀλλά is not a particle of gradation; it is simply the *but* adversative. To understand the contrast which it marks, we must take exact account of the difference in meaning and tense between the two verbs of ver. 5 and ver. 6, διακρῖναι and κρίνεσθαι. The former denotes the summary verdict of an arbiter: hence the aorist; the latter puts us face to face with all the lengthy processes and windings of a lawsuit: hence the present. — And that with a brother and before a heathen tribunal! What a scandal! what a shame to the Church!

Vers. 7-11

Provisionally the apostle had passed over in silence the fact itself of the discussion of selfish interests between Christians, to condemn only their having recourse to the judicial intervention of heathen. In the first words of ver. 6, only, he had touched the deeper evil, that of such disputes at all between brethren. He now comes to this sin, the first occasion and cause of the other.

Vers. 7, 8. "Nay, already[1] it is altogether a defect

[1] T. R. reads ουν (*therefore*) after ηδη μεν, with A B C E L P Syr^sch; this word is omitted by ℵ D.

in you[1] that ye have lawsuits one with another. Why not rather take wrong? why not rather be defrauded? 8. Nay but ye yourselves do wrong and defraud, and that[2] your brethren!"—Here is the second charge which he brings against them, the fact of lawsuits in themselves. This charge essentially includes two. The ἤδη μέν, *already*, indicates the one; the ἀλλά of ver. 8 the other. And first, ver. 7, it is bad to have a lawsuit about a wrong which one considers to have been done to him by a brother. Why not bear a wrong? The *therefore* of the T. R. has no meaning; it ought to be suppressed.—The term ἥττημα, from ἡττᾶσθαι, *to remain beneath*, denotes a defeat when it is used in reference to a fight, and a deterioration or deficiency when applied to a state of things. The latter is the only meaning which is suitable here. There is a moral deficiency among them on this point compared with what they should be as Christians; ὅλως, *in general;* that is to say: "without dwelling longer on the particular fact which I have condemned above." We must certainly reject ἐν, *among*, before ὑμῖν, *you:* "It is a deficiency *on your part*, pertaining to you."—The reflex pronoun ἑαυτῶν is used here as it often is instead of the reciprocal pronoun ἀλλήλων; this form brings out the close solidarity in consequence of which a brother pleading against a brother pleads in a sense against himself.—The two questions which close the verse justify the idea expressed by the word ἥττημα. There is a defect in acting thus; for there is something better to be done: viz. to bear. There is there-

[1] The εν of T. R. is found only in the Mnn.

[2] T. R. reads ταυτα (*these things*), with L; all the rest: τουτο (*this*).

fore a lack of charity. Paul himself says, xiii. 4: "Charity suffereth long." *Μᾶλλον, rather;* that is to say, rather than enter into a lawsuit. Paul does not say that a Christian should do nothing to secure himself against injustice. But if it must come to a lawsuit, he advises *rather* to bear the wrong. Is he alluding to the precepts of Jesus in His Sermon on the Mount, Matt. v. 39–42? It seems very probable. The thought which Jesus undoubtedly meant to express in these paradoxical forms is this: Love, infinite as God, is ready, so far as itself is concerned, to bear everything. If therefore in practice it sets limits to this absolute patience, it is not from regard to itself, as if its endurance were at an end; but it is for the good of that very being with whom it has to do, so that it is in this case its own limit, in other words, it has no limit outside of itself.—The two verbs ἀδικεῖσθαι and ἀποστερεῖσθαι are in the Middle: to let oneself be wronged; to let oneself be robbed. The former refers to injustices in general, the latter to wrongs in regard to property.

Ver. 8. But there is more: to account for a lawsuit, there is needed something else than the lack of charity on the one hand; there must be a graver want still on the other, the want of justice. To speak of maltreated, robbed, is to speak of maltreating, robbing. Hence the gradation expressed by ἀλλά: *But much more!* The ὑμεῖς, *ye,* coming first, expresses indignation: "It is ye, Christians, who . . . !" The, *and that,* indicates a new gradation: the want of justice betrays a more odious character when it assails one nearer our heart, a brother!—It is easy to see why certain copyists have substituted ταῦτα (the two acts mentioned) for τοῦτο.—It really seemed that the Corinthians, since they had received grace, thought themselves freed from all moral responsibility; it is this dangerous security which the apostle attacks in what follows.

Vers. 9, 10. "Or know ye not that the unrighteous shall not inherit the kingdom of God? Be not deceived: neither fornicators, nor idolaters, nor adulterers, nor effeminate, nor abusers of themselves with mankind, 10. nor thieves, nor covetous, nor[1] drunkards, nor revilers, nor extortioners shall[2] inherit the kingdom of God."—The particle ἤ, *or*, signifies, as it usually does in this formula: "Or, if you think you can act thus without danger . . . ." The Corinthians seemed to imagine that their religious knowledge and Christian talk would suffice to open heaven to them, whatever their conduct otherwise might be. But how do they fail to understand that by falling back into sin, from which faith had rescued them, they themselves destroy the effect of their transition from heathenism to the gospel?—The *unrighteous* are placed first and separately named; for righteousness is the matter now in question (ver. 8).—The notion of the *kingdom of God* is here taken in the eschatological sense, that is to say, from the standpoint of the final consummation of this Divine state of things; and the verb κληρονομεῖν, *to inherit*, is an allusion to the inheritance of Canaan given to Israel as

[1] ℵ A C P read ου, instead of ουτε (*nor*), which is the reading of T. R. with B D E L Syr.

[2] T. R. with L P here reads ου, which is rejected by all the rest.

a type of the blessedness to come.—The μὴ πλανᾶσθε, *do not deceive yourselves*, shows clearly that seductive arguments were in circulation by which the vicious succeeded in quieting their consciences.—The warning is generalized, as in chap. v. 9–11. The first five terms in the following enumeration relate more or less directly to the vice of impurity; the following five to the spoliation of another's goods.—Idolatry was closely connected with licentiousness in morals (see on chap. v. 11).—The effeminate, μαλακοί, are either those who give themselves up to some unnatural vice, or all in general who pamper their body; *abusers of themselves*, ἀρσενοκοῖται, are those who give themselves over to monstrous vices (Rom. i. 27). There is in the latter term the idea of activity; in μαλακοί rather that of passivity.

Ver. 10. The apostle closes the enumeration with ἅρπαγες, *extortioners;* this last term leads back to the principal subject of the whole passage, the ἀδίκειν and the ἀποστερεῖν.—In one of the last terms, for οὔτε, *nor*, the apostle substitutes οὐ, *not*, as if the feeling of repulsion rose in him with the accumulation of terms: "No, in spite of all your reasonings, it will be of no avail! The drunkard shall not enter . . ."—The kingdom of God is a holy state of things, it receives none but sanctified members.

Ver. 11. "And such were some of you, but ye are washed, but ye are sanctified, but ye are justified in the name of the[1] Lord Jesus Christ,[2] and by the Spirit of our God."—Paul has been addressing the feeling of fear; he now appeals to the higher motive, that of

[1] B C P add ημων (*our*). [2] T. R. omits Χριστου (*Christ*), with A L.

Christian honour. He thus returns to the feeling which had dictated the first word of the passage, τολμᾷ τις, *has any one the courage?*—The vices he has just enumerated belong to a past from which a series of Divine facts have separated them for ever. These facts are, first, baptism, then the consecration and reconciliation to God of which baptism is the symbol. Such a fathomless depth of grace is not to be recrossed!—**Καί**, *and* it is true.—There is in the verb ἦτε, *ye were*, more than the recalling of polluting acts; the term identifies their person with the pollutions to which they gave themselves up.—But, by the τινές, *some*, the apostle restricts the application of his saying, not only in the sense which Reuss ascribes to the words (one who was guilty of *one* of those vices, another of *another*), but so as to bring out that there was, after all, among them a goodly number of men who before their conversion had lived exempt from all those external pollutions. Billroth has made τινές an attribute, and connected it as such with ταῦτα in the contemptuous sense, "such a set of men!" This would have needed ταῦτά τινα, or τοῖοί τινες (Meyer).

The following verbs denote the three acts which constituted the entrance of believers into their new state. They are joined together by the ἀλλά of gradation: *but moreover* (2 Cor. vii. 11); from which it does not follow that the order in which these acts are placed is necessarily one of chronological succession, it may equally be one of moral gradation. For the apostle's intention is to bring out by each stroke, with more and more marked emphasis, the contrast between the former state of believers and the new state into which these acts had brought them.

All are at one in applying the first of the three verbs to *baptism.* In fact, outwardly speaking, it was the act which had transferred them from the state of heathens to that of Christians, from the condition of beings polluted and condemned to that of beings pardoned and purified. The Middle form of the verb ἀπελούσασθε, *ye washed yourselves*, expresses the freedom and spontaneity with which they had done the deed; comp. the ἐβαπτίσαντο, x. 2 (in the reading of the *Vatic.*); Edwards also compares Acts xxii. 16.—The term *bathe, wash,* is explained by the two following terms. Baptism, when it is done in faith, is not a pure symbol; two purifying graces are connected with it, *sanctification* and *justification.* The verbs which express these two facts are in the passive; for they signify two Divine acts, of which the baptized are the subjects. The two verbs in the aorist can only refer both of them to a deed done once for all, and not to a continuous state. This is what prevents us from applying the term *sanctify* to the growing work of Christian sanctification. This word here can only designate the initial act whereby the believer passed from his previous state of corruption to that of holiness, that is to say, the believer's consecration to God in consequence of the gift of the Spirit bestowed on him in baptism; comp. Acts ii. 38; 2 Cor. i. 21, 22; Eph. i. 13. They entered thereby into the community of saints which is presided over by Jesus Christ, the Holy One of God.—The verb *sanctify* is placed before *justify*, because, as Edwards says: "Paul, wishing to contrast the present moral condition of believers with their former state, lays special emphasis on the characteristic of sanctification." This is also the feature which most directly applies to the passage vers. 7–10.—From the fact that the term *justify* is placed second, many, even Meyer, have concluded that it could not here have its ordinary Pauline meaning, and that instead of imputed righteousness it must denote exceptionally the internal righteousness which God infuses into the hearts of believers during the course of their life. But this meaning is, whatever Meyer may say, incompatible with the use of the aorist (ye *were* justified), a tense which necessarily denotes the initial moment of the new state of righteousness, the transition from the state of corruption to that of regeneration. Besides, it would be impossible to distinguish from this point of view the meaning of the two acts sanctifying and justifying, and to understand how they could be joined, or rather contrasted, with one another by an ἀλλά of gradation: *but moreover.* It is therefore, also, wholly mistaken when Catholic theologians, and even Protestants, like Beck, make use of this passage to deny the notion of justification as the imputation of righteousness in Paul's writings. When an entire dogmatic view is thus made to rest on the succession of two terms, it should be remembered that the inverse order is given in i. 30. We have already indicated the reason why Paul emphasizes sanctification in the first place: it is to point out clearly the contrast between the normal state of the Christian and the degrading vices which were invading the Church; comp. i. 2. But thereafter he feels the need of ascending to the hidden foundation of this sanctifying action of the gospel, to the state of justification in which the believer is put by it. The question at the outset of the passage was whether Christians did not possess in themselves the standard of righteousness, by means of which they might regulate their mutual differences. From this point of view Paul had called the heathen *οἱ ἄδικοι, the unrighteous.* By closing with the idea of the justification bestowed on believers, he points to them as the true possessors of righteousness, first in their relation to God, and thereby in all the relations of life.

But what is it that gives to baptism such efficacy, that, when it is celebrated with faith, it is accompanied with such graces, and draws a line of demarcation so profound between two states in the believer's life? The apostle indicates the answer in the last words of the verse: *in the name of the Lord Jesus and by the Spirit of our God.* It seems to me that there is an unmistakable allusion in these words to the formula of baptism: "In the name of the Father, of the Son, and of the Holy Spirit." In the two passages we find the three names whose invocation constitutes the peculiar characteristic of this institution.—The construction of the sentence does not allow us to apply the first of these clauses exclusively to the one of the last two verbs, the other to the other (Flatt). It seems to me equally impossible to connect them both with the last verb, as Rückert and Meyer propose. I think that both together apply to the first verb, ἀπελούσασθε, *ye were washed*, and therefore to the two following verbs, which, as we have seen, are merely epexegetical of the first. As this verb expressly points to the ceremony of baptism, these two subordinate clauses reproduce the formula of invocation which was pronounced when the rite was celebrated. The *name of Jesus* denotes the revelation of His person and work, which has been granted to the Church. It is because of this knowledge that the Church carries out this act of spiritual purification on those whom it receives as its members.—The *Spirit* of God is the creative breath which accomplishes the new birth in the heart of the man baptized, and thus separates him from the pollutions of his past life. I cannot possibly understand why Meyer alleges that this second clause cannot apply to the verb ἀπελούσασθε as well as the first. Is not the action of the Spirit in the heart of the baptized, whereby he deposits in it the principle of consecration, the purifying act by way of excellence ? (Titus iii. 5). By adding *of our God*, the apostle expresses the idea of the fatherly and filial relation formed by Christ between God and the Church, and in virtue of which He communicates to it His Spirit. The apostle never fails, while paying homage to the two Divine agents, Christ and the Spirit, to ascend to the supreme source of all this salvation, even God, who reveals Himself in Jesus, and gives Himself by the Spirit.—Hofmann has taken the strange fancy to connect these two clauses with ver. 12: "In the name of Christ, and by the Holy Spirit, all things are lawful to me." But if the maxim, *All things are lawful to me*, had been qualified from the first in this way, Paul would not have needed to limit its application afterwards, as he does on two successive occasions, and by two different restrictions in ver. 12 (see Meyer).

The formula of baptism in the Apostolic Church.

The idea has often been expressed, that the formula of baptism in the Apostolic Church was not yet that which is mentioned Matt. xxviii. 19: "In the name of the Father, of the Son, and of the Holy Spirit," and that it was limited to the invocation of the *name of Jesus* (Acts ii. 38, viii. 16, x. 48, xix. 5). The passage which we have been studying does not appear to me to favour this view. For, as we have pointed out, the mention of the three Divine names contained in the formula Matt. xxviii. 19, is supposed by the terms used by the Apostle Paul. The idea even of God as Father seems implied in the pronoun *ἡμῶν, our* God.—There is another fact which seems to me to confirm this result; that which is related Acts xix. 1–6. Paul asks some disciples who have not yet heard speak of the Holy Spirit: "in what (*εἰς τί*) then (*οὖν*) they have been baptized?" The logical relation, expressed by *then*, between the ignorance of those persons in regard to the Holy Spirit and the apostle's question regarding the baptism which they have received, would not be intelligible if the mention of the Holy Spirit had not been *usual* in baptism as it was celebrated by the Apostolic Church. Now if the name of Jesus and that of the Holy Spirit were solemnly pronounced in baptism, that of God could not be wanting. Hence I conclude that the phrase: *to baptize in the name of Jesus,* frequently used in the Acts, is an abridged form to denote Christian baptism in general. This conclusion is confirmed by the fact that in the *Teaching of the Twelve Apostles* the Trinitarian formula found in Matthew is used side by side with the abridged form of the Acts; comp. vii. 1 and ix. 5.

4

Impurity (6:12-20)

It has sometimes been imagined that the apostle was here resuming the subject of chap. v., from which he had allowed himself to be diverted by the question of lawsuits. But we have seen that the subject of chap. v.

was not impurity at all, but discipline, treated in connection with a case of impurity. Lawsuits followed, by a transition which we have explained (vi. 1). And now Paul continues to treat of the moral disorders which he knows to exist in the Church. If the manner in which he enters on the subject in ver. 12 has been thought somewhat abrupt, it is because account has not been taken of the connection between the maxim: *All things are lawful to me,* and the warning of ver. 9: *Be not deceived.* It is perfectly obvious that some at Corinth were indulging in strange illusions as to the consequences of salvation by grace, and even went the length of putting the practice of vice under the patronage of the principle of Christian liberty.—Neander has thought that in beginning as he does in ver. 12, the apostle proposed immediately to treat the subject of meats consecrated to idols, a subject in connection with which he repeats (x. 23) the same maxim, and that he was led away from the second part of ver. 13 to deal with impurity, to resume the subject of offered meats later (chaps. viii.–x.). The truth involved in this view is, that from this point the idea of Christian liberty is that which prevails to the close of chap. x.; comp. Holsten, *Ev. des Paulus,* p. 293. But the order in which the subjects are linked to one another in this Epistle is the fruit of too serious reflection to allow us to hold such an interruption. And the relation which we have just pointed out between ver. 12 and vers. 9 and 10, where impurity holds the first rank in the enumeration of the vices mentioned, shows clearly that the apostle knew the goal at which he was aiming.

Ver. 12. "All things are lawful unto me, but all

things are not expedient; all things are lawful for me, but I will not be brought under the power of any."—Paul himself had no doubt uttered this maxim at Corinth more than once: "All things are lawful to me," applying it to acts indifferent in themselves, but which the Mosaic law had forbidden, on account of its pedagogic nature. When the question was as to the use of certain meats, or observance of certain days, or any other external prescription, the apostle said without scruple in such a case: "All is lawful to me." This saying had not been forgotten; it suited only too well the free disposition of the Greek mind. And perhaps the perverted application which certain members of the Church made of it was ascribed even to the apostle himself. Did this maxim figure in the letter which the Corinthians had addressed to him? In any case, there is something striking in the repetition of the words in our verse; it is intended to stigmatize the abuse of the dictum stupidly employed to justify evil. —Paul therefore means: "All things are lawful undoubtedly, and I have no thought of retracting what I have said." Then follow two restrictions which have a touch of irony: "All is lawful to me . . ., unless indeed it be doing evil to myself or my neighbour by the use of my liberty." The term *συμφέρειν, to contribute to the good,* is completed (x. 23) by *οἰκοδομεῖν, to edify;* there accordingly it applies to good in general, while *οἰκοδομεῖν* applies specially to the good of our neighbour. Here the good of our neighbour is not in question, but that of the acting subject himself; the following proposition brings out another and more special trait. Then the apostle repeats the same dictum, as if to ridicule the unintelligent and mechanical use of it; and he limits its application by the second restriction, which applies, like the first, to the individual himself: "All is lawful to me, unless it be using my liberty to the extent of alienating it." There is an evident connection between the word ἔξεστι, *is lawful*, and the term ἐξουσιασθήσομαι, *I will let myself be brought under the power*. The regimen ὑπό τινος is certainly neuter: "by *anything;*" not, "by *any one*." The reference is to everything which is included in the πάντα, *all things*, which precedes.—The pronoun μοι, *to me*, is used as in v. 12, to give the proposition the force of an axiom: *Vim habet gnomes*, says Bengel. Similarly the ἐγώ, *I*, used in the following proposition: I no longer really possess that which possesses me. This saying of the apostle reminds us of the adage of the Stoics: *Mihi res, non me rebus submittere conor*. Paul here puts himself at the standpoint of simple common sense. The reasonable use of my liberty cannot go the length of involving my own loss of it, or of rendering me a slave by reducing me to a thing. Thus Paul has beaten the adversary on his own ground. He has brought him to contradict himself by showing him that his principle, applied without discernment, is self-destructive. The second restriction: "I will not make myself the slave of anything," is developed in vers. 13–16.

Vers. 13, 14. "Meats are for the belly, and the belly for meats, and God shall destroy both it and them. But the body is not for fornication; but for the Lord, and the Lord for the body. 14. Now God hath raised up the Lord, and will also raise up[1] us[2] by His power."—Several commentators have thought that the contrast set up by Paul in these two verses, between the act of eating and the impure use of the body, was called forth by certain statements in the letter of the Corinthians, in which they justified this vice by assimilating it to the other bodily wants, such as that of eating and drinking. Rückert has combated this opinion, for the reason that the Church could not have gone the length of systematically justifying vice; and besides, would not Paul have repelled such an assertion with the liveliest indignation? But without any allusion to the letter of the Corinthians, he might say: "All is lawful; for, according to the principle laid down by Jesus, it is not what enters into a man that defiles him; this domain of food-taking has nothing in common with moral obligation and our eternal future; but it is wholly otherwise with impurity."—The apostle distinguishes two opposite elements in our bodily organism: the organs of nutrition, which serve for the support of the body, and to which, by a Divinely established correlation, there correspond the external objects which serve as meats. The morally indifferent character of this domain appears from the fact of its approaching destruction: God will abolish those functions in the day of the redemption of our bodies. But it is not so with our bodies strictly so called, with the body for which Paul exclusively reserves the name, and which he identifies with our very personality. This is the

[1] The T. R. with ℵ C E K L reads εξεγερει (*will raise up*); A D P Q: εξεγειρει (*raises up*); B: εξηγειρεν (*raised up*).
[2] The υμας (*you*) of the T. R. is a simple error.

permanent element in our earthly organism, that which forms the link between our present and our future body. Now this element, the essential form of our personality, is that which is involved in the vice of impurity. And hence the profound difference between impurity and the natural functions of physical life. There exists between our body and the Lord Jesus Christ a moral relation analogous to the material and temporary relation which exists between the stomach and meats. The body is *for Christ,* to belong to Him and serve Him, and Christ is *for the body,* to inhabit and glorify it.

Ver. 14. In consequence of this sublime relation, the body will not perish. As God raised up Christ, He will also raise the body which has become here below the property and sanctified organ of Christ. The apostle says, "will raise *us* also;" he thus expressly identifies our personality with the body which is to be its eternal organ.—The readings *raises* and *raised* are evidently erroneous. The former would be the present of the idea, which does not suit here; the latter would refer to the spiritual resurrection (Eph. ii. 5, 6), which is stranger still to the context. The idea of the future resurrection of this earthly body, like to that in which Christ lived, is fitted to impress us with the reverence due to the future organ of our glorified personality.—The last words, *by His power*, perhaps allude to some doubts in regard to the possibility of the fact.—It is remarkable that Paul here places himself in the number of those who *shall rise again,* as elsewhere he ranks himself with those who shall be *changed* at Christ's coming again. He had no fixed idea on this point, and he could have none, the day of Christ's coming being to him unknown.

Ver. 15. "Know ye not that your[1] bodies are the members of Christ? Shall I then take the members of Christ, and make them the members of an harlot? Let it not be so!"—Paul had just said that the body is not for fornication, but for the Lord. In the first proposition of this verse he justifies the *for the Lord,* to deduce from it as a conclusion in the second the *not for fornication.* Baur and Scherer see here a *petitio principii,* inasmuch as the term *harlot* already implies the guiltiness of fornication, which is precisely the point to be proved. But the apostle is not treating the question from the standpoint of rational morality; he starts from Christian premises: *Know ye not . . . ?* Now the relation between Christ and the believer, implied in faith, gives him logically the right to reason as he does.—As the Church in its totality is the body of Christ, that is to say, the organism which He animates with His Spirit, and by which He carries out His wishes on the earth, so every Christian is a member of this body, and consequently an organ of Christ Himself. By means of the Spirit of Christ which dwells in his spirit, and by means of his spirit which directs his soul and thereby his body, this body becomes as it were the body of Christ, the executor of His thought; hence the practical conclusion: This organ of Christ must not be taken from Him to be given to a harlot. Therein is a double crime: on the one hand, a revolt, an odious abduction (ἄρας); on the other, an act of ignoble self-debasement and the ac-

[1] א A read ημων (*our* bodies).

ceptance of a shameful dependence. And hence the apostle's cry of indignation : *Let it not be so !—Ποιήσω,* perhaps the deliberative subjunctive aorist: "Shall I choose to make . . . ?" or simply the future indicative : "Shall I make ?" The second meaning is better: one does not deliberate in regard to such an act.—But do not the expressions, "members of Christ" and "members of an harlot," contain something of exaggeration ? This is what the light-minded Corinthians might ask, and it is to this objection that vers. 16 and 17 give answer.

Vers. 16, 17. "Or[1] know ye not that he which is joined to an harlot is one body [with her]; for the two, it is said, shall be one flesh. 17. And he that is joined unto the Lord is one spirit [with Him]."—The ἤ, *or*, is certainly authentic; as always it signifies, "Or indeed, if you deny what I have just said, are you then ignorant that . . . ?" The proof of the truth of the expression used (*members of an harlot*) is given by means of the Biblical words, Gen. ii. 24. Are these words in the narrative of Genesis the continuation of Adam's discourse, or a remark added by the author himself, as happens in several other cases (Gen. x. 9, xv. 6, xxxii. 32; see Hofmann) ? It matters little; for the declaration can have value in the eyes of the sacred historian only in so far as it is the expression of a Divine truth.—The reg. *with her* is omitted in Greek after the word *one body.* This ellipsis arises from the fact that the nominative ὁ κολλώμενος and the dative τῇ πόρνῃ are morally regarded as forming one and the same logical subject of the proposition. The words

[1] D E K L 50 Mnn. omit the η (*or*) before ουκ.

οἱ δύο, the two, were added to the original text by the LXX., whom St. Paul here follows.—The subject of the verb *φησίν, says he,* may be either Adam, or Moses, or Scripture, or God Himself; or finally, as is shown by Heinrici, the verb may be a simple formula of quotation like our: *It is said.* This form is frequently found in Philo.—The expression *one flesh* finds its confirmation in the extraordinary fact that from this union there may proceed a new personality. Therein is contained, for the reflecting mind, the undeniable proof of the profoundly mysterious character of such a union; it appears like the continuation of the creative act.

Ver. 17 is not, as has sometimes been thought, foreign to the argument as a whole. As ver. 16 justifies by a Biblical quotation the strong expression of ver. 15: "Shall I make them the members of an harlot?" so ver. 17, framed as it were on the words of Genesis, justifies the equally strong expression of ver. 15: "Taking the members of Christ;" comp. xv. 45.—We again find here the ellipsis of ver. 16; the "with Him" is understood after the words *one spirit,* as if to say that the believer's union with Christ culminates in the existence of one and the same spirit, and consequently in the possession and direction by Christ of the believer's whole person, soul and body.—According to Holsten (p. 466 seq.), the assimilation of these two unions is so untenable logically, that vers. 15–17 can only be an ancient gloss intended to remove the obscurity of ver. 13. I think it is better to seek to penetrate the depth of the apostolic thought than arbitrarily to recompose the text according to our own ideas.

Under the sway of this holy view (ver. 17), the apostle, at the thought of the crime of fornication, utters, as it were, a cry of horror (ver. 18[a]); then he finishes his demonstration.

Ver. 18. "Flee fornication! Every sin that a man doeth is without his body; but he that committeth fornication sinneth against his body."—Anselm has well expressed the meaning of the first sentence of the verse: "If we must *fight against* other sins, we must *flee from* fornication;" witness Joseph's example.—The asyndeton betrays the apostle's emotion.

Thus far (vers. 13–17) the thought developed by Paul had been that of the *dependence* arising from impure intercourse: "I shall not make myself the *slave* of anything" (ver. 12[b]). For a man to give to a degraded person a right over him by such a union, is not this to place himself in the most ignoble kind of dependence? From this point Paul passes to the development of the first thought of ver. 12: "All things are not *expedient*," and he shows the injury which the fornicator inflicts on his own body.—He here enunciates a distinction between fornication and other sins, which it is difficult to understand. How are passion, falsehood, intemperance, suicide, sins committed *without the body*, while fornication is one in the body? Rückert and de Wette acknowledge their inability to find a meaning for this contrast; Calvin and Neander see in it no other idea than that of the greater guiltiness which attaches to the sin of fornication. According to Meyer, Paul means that in other sins some external matter is necessary, while fornication proceeds entirely from within. Hofmann, after criticising those different explanations, gives one which is stranger still, and almost unintelligible: The man who commits any other sin does not keep in his body the matter of his sin (the drunkard, the suicide); while the impure person makes his very body the subject of his sin, and continues in his bodily life identified with the being to which he has given himself.—It seems to me that the contrast stated by Paul is to be explained only from the point of view at which ver. 13 placed us. The apostle means to speak of the body strictly so called, of the body in the body; he contrasts this living and life-giving organism with the external and purely physical organism. We possess a material body, the matter of which is being perpetually renewed; but under this changing body there exists a permanent type, which constitutes its identity. In chap. xv. 50, where Paul is teaching the resurrection of the body, he declares that "flesh and blood cannot inherit the kingdom of God." He therefore distinguishes between the organism composed of flesh and blood, which forms the outward wrapping of the man, and the body strictly so called, one with the person which animates this wrapping. It is the same distinction as we have found in vers. 13, 14 of our chapter. Now it is to this inner body that the sin of the fornicator penetrates; it is by and against this inner organism that he sins, while other sins only reach its wrapping, the external body. The εἰς, in so far as it is contrasted with the prep. ἐκτός, *outside of*, ought to signify *in;* but it differs nevertheless from the simple ἐν, *in*, in that it also denotes the *injury* which the body receives from it; hence the meaning of *against* which is added to that of *in.* Thus we understand the οὐ συμφέρει of ver. 1. Yet bodily injury is not the thing of which Paul is thinking. The sequel shows in what the punishment consists. The body thus profaned had a sublime destiny, and of this it is deprived by the violence done to it.

Vers. 19, 20. "Or know ye not that your body[1] is the temple of the Holy Spirit which is in you, and which ye have of God? And ye are not your own; 20. for ye are bought with a price; therefore glorify God in your body."[2]—The ἤ, *or*, signifies, "Or if you deny the fatal violence done to your body by fornication, you are ignorant of the holy dignity to which it is destined, and of which it is deprived by this sin. The fornicator sins and robs his body of the honour of being the temple of God."—According to Rom. viii. 11, the presence of the Holy Spirit in the believer is the pledge of a glorious resurrection for his body. To renounce this dignity of being a temple and organ of the Holy Spirit by the fact of fornication, is therefore to expose himself to lose this resurrection.—The phrase, *which ye have*, or, *which ye hold from God*, is intended to emphasize strongly the superhuman origin of that Spirit whom the believer receives, and the dignity of the body in which this Divine Guest comes to dwell. We must not translate: which ye have *by* God, as if ὑπό were used; ἀπό denotes the origin and essence.—It would not be unnatural to make the last proposition, *And ye are not your own*, also dependent on the inter-

[1] L Cop. and several Fathers read τα σωματα υμων (*your bodies*).

[2] T. R. with K L P Syr. here adds: και εν τω πνευματι υμων ατινα εστι του θεου (*and in your spirit, which are God's*).

rogative verb, *Know ye not that . . .?* But Hofmann rightly objects that the ὅτι would require to be repeated. It must therefore be regarded as a forcible affirmation: "And (because of the communication of the Spirit) ye do not any more belong to yourselves, and have consequently no longer right to dispose of your body at will." And this taking possession of the believer by the Holy Spirit is not only an act of power on God's part, it is founded on right. This is what is explained by the first proposition of the following verse.

Ver. 20. The taking possession is legitimate; for there was the payment of a purchase price. We must not therefore translate: "bought at a *great* price." The greatness of the price does not matter here. It is the fact of payment only which Paul would emphasize.—The particle δή is untranslateable; it implies the perfect evidence, and consequently urgency, of the fulfilment of the duty mentioned.—The phrase *glorify God* does not signify merely: not to dishonour Him; it means to display positively in the use of our body the glory and especially the holiness of the heavenly Master who has taken possession of our person. Man has lost, in whole or part, since his fall, the feeling which was so to speak the guardian of his body, that of natural modesty. Faith restores to it a more elevated guardian: self-respect as being bought by Christ the organ of the Spirit and temple of God. This is modesty raised henceforth to the height of holiness.—The words which follow in the T. R., *and in your spirit . . .*, are an interpolation added with a liturgical and hortatory aim.

The three essential ideas of the passage are therefore :—

1. That the use of Christian liberty as respects the body is naturally restricted by the danger of using that liberty so as to alienate it and destroy ourselves.

2. That fornication involves the Christian in a degrading physical solidarity, incompatible with the believer's spiritual solidarity with Christ.

3. That it renders the body unfit for its Christian dignity as a temple of God, and so for its glorious destination.

It appears from this entire development that contempt of the body goes side by side with abuse of the body, while respect for the body will always be the best means of ruling it. And so the whole of Scripture, from the first page of Genesis to the last of Revelation, pays homage to the dignity of the human body.

5

Marriage and Celibacy (7:1-40)

Some commentators begin the second part of the Epistle here. According to them, the apostle up to this point answered the reports which had been made to him *viva voce* (i. 11 and v. 1); now he takes up the letter of the Corinthians to answer the questions it contains. It is certain that in ver. 1 the subject which he proceeds to treat is presented in reply to a question which had been addressed to him. A similar formula occurs viii. 1, xii. 1, xvi. 1, 12 ; and it is natural to hold that in each of these cases it introduces a subject raised by the letter of the Corinthians. Nevertheless the difference between verbal reports and epistolary communications would be too external to have determined the general arrangement of our Epistle. It is impossible to overlook a moral relation between the matter about to be treated in this chap. vii. and that of fornication, treated in the second half of chap. vi. It is easy to establish a still closer connection with what precedes. In ver. 12 of chap. vi. there had been put the question of Christian liberty and its limits. It was from this point of view that the apostle had treated the subject of fornication. Now the question of marriage (chap. vii.), as well as that of sacrificed meats (chaps. viii.–x.), and even, up to a certain point, that of the behaviour of women in meetings for worship (chap. xi.), all belong to this same domain. If then it is true that the apostle here passes to the questions put to him by the Corinthians, it must be acknowledged, on the other hand, that he does not do so without establishing a logical and moral connection between the different subjects which he treats in succession.

The questions examined in this chapter, the preference to be accorded to celibacy or marriage, as well as others subordinate to it, must have been discussed at Corinth, since the apostle's advice was asked about them. There were therefore in the Church partisans of celibacy and defenders of marriage. Did this division coincide in any way with that of the different parties? The attempt has been made to prove this. Schwegler regards the admirers of celibacy as Judeo-Christians of Essenian tendency, and identifies them with the party of Peter. But Peter himself was married (ix. 5; Mark i. 30). Others — Ewald, Hausrath, for example — have supposed that they were members of the party which designated itself *those of Christ,* and that they alleged against marriage the example of Jesus. But this example was too exceptional; and in any case Paul would have required to rebut this argument. The general current of the Jewish mind recommended and glorified marriage. We might therefore take them to be members of the Pauline party, who rested their argument on the apostle's example, and on some mistaken saying which he had uttered during his stay at Corinth. But there is nothing in chap. vii. leading to this supposition.—Grotius thought that the opponents of marriage at Corinth were men of culture, who, influenced by certain sayings of the Greek philosophers, regarded marriage as a vulgar state and one contrary to man's independence. But the apostle in his answer makes no allusion to such an idea, and the sayings of the Greek sages, which might be quoted, have rather the effect of whimsical utterances called forth by the troubles of family life, than of a serious theory. It seems simpler to hold that the opposition to marriage at Corinth proceeded from a reaction against the licentious manners which reigned in that city. New converts often go beyond the just limit of opposition to the life of nature, and easily lose sight of the Divine basis of human relations. The history of the Christian Church is full of examples of such extreme tendencies. It is easy therefore to understand how among the most serious Christians, especially among Paul's converts, men should be found, who, disgusted with all that belonged to the relations between the two sexes, proclaimed the superiority of the celibate life.

It was certainly one of the most delicate tasks for him whom God had called, not only to create the Church among the Gentiles, but also to direct its first steps in the new way which opened before it, to show the young Churches what they ought to reject and what they might preserve of their former life. So we shall see in this very chapter the apostle enlarging the question, and applying the solution which he gives in regard to marriage to other social relations in connection with which analogous difficulties were raised. The apostle needed all the wisdom which God had bestowed on him when entrusting him with his mission (Rom. xii. 3), and all the natural subtlety of his understanding, to resolve the questions proposed to him, without compromising the future of individuals and of the Church. Thus, as to marriage, he could not forget that the conjugal bond was a Divine institution; he had himself just quoted vi. 16, the saying on which the sacred and exclusive character of this relation rests. But, on the other hand, he contemplated the ideal of a Christian life freed from every bond and wholly consecrated to the service of Christ, and every day he felt from his own experience the value of such a state. The question must therefore have presented itself to his mind in two aspects equally grave, neither of which could be sacrificed to the other, and yet aspects apparently contradictory. The task was thus at once important and difficult.—He begins by treating of the *formation* of the marriage bond, vers. 1–9; then he takes up questions relative to the *loosing* of the bond, vers. 10–24; finally, he deals with the preference to be given to celibacy or marriage in the case of *virgins* and *widows*, vers. 25–40.

Vers. 1–9

Notwithstanding the intrinsic excellence of celibacy, marriage should be the rule in practice. Such is the general meaning of this first passage.

Vers. 1, 2. "Now concerning the things whereof ye wrote unto me,[1] it is good for a man not to touch a woman; 2. but, to avoid fornication, let every man have his own wife, and let every woman have her own husband."—The form περὶ δέ, *now concerning*, is common in the classics (see Heinrici, p. 60). Paul thereby intimates that he is passing to a new subject, but one which has already been raised. The περὶ ὧν ought certainly to be grammatically expanded in this way: περὶ ἐκείνων περὶ ὧν ἐγράψατέ μοι λέγω τάδε.—The δέ, *now*, lightly marks the contrast between the questions which Paul had treated at his own hand and those which were put to him by the letter of the Corinthians.—The pronoun μοί has been added rather than omitted by the copyists; there was no reason for rejecting it.—In what sense are we to take the word καλόν, *it is good?* Jerome, the great partisan of celibacy, took it in the moral sense: "it is *holy* . . . ;" and he did not fear to draw from it the conclusion: "If it is good not to touch, then it is bad to touch."

[1] א B C omit μοι (*to me*).

The logic of this argument is by no means unassailable. Anyhow, this consequence does not agree with the true notion of marriage according to St. Paul. To evade it, some have given the word καλόν, *good*, a purely utilitarian sense: "It is *expedient* . . ." And the possibility of this sense seems clearly to result from the comparison of Matt. v. 29 with xviii. 8, where in the same saying of Jesus the term συμφέρειν is used the first time, and καλόν the second. But the question is whether the word συμφέρειν itself has in the mouth of Paul and Jesus a purely utilitarian sense. In any case, it is not so in our Epistle, where, in the passages vi. 12 and x. 23, and in ver. 35 of our chapter, the word συμφέρειν certainly contains the notion of *moral* utility. With stronger reason ought it to be so with the word καλόν. In the well-known epithet καλὸς κἀγαθός, by which the Greeks designated the man every way honourable, man *as he should be* in all respects, the first adjective expressed the idea of beauty linked to that of goodness, the high propriety which distinguishes moral worth. Such, it seems to me, is the notion which the apostle would here express by the word καλόν. He proclaims aloud that the state of celibacy in a man is absolutely becoming and worthy, has nothing in it contrary to the moral ideal. There were assuredly at Corinth persons who maintained the contrary. This first verse has often been taken as a concession: "*No doubt* it is well to . . . *but*" (ver. 2). In this case, Paul must have said: καλὸν μέν. It becomes then a positive declaration, independent of what follows. Thereafter will come the restriction indicated by δέ.—In speaking thus, Paul felt himself supported by a decisive example, that of Jesus Christ, the realization of supreme moral beauty in human form, and moreover by the saying of Jesus, Luke xx. 34, 35: "The children of this world marry and are given in marriage; but they which shall be accounted worthy to obtain that world, and the resurrection from the dead, neither marry nor are given in marriage," a saying from which it followed that the splendour of the ideal shines still more perfectly in the person of the celibate than of the married Christian. No doubt there might have been quoted in objection to the apostle the words of God Himself: "It is not good that man should be alone," οὐ καλὸν εἶναι τὸν ἄνθρωπον μόνον (Gen. ii. 18). But the answer would not have been difficult. The believer who lives in union with Christ is no longer in the same position as the natural man. He has in the Lord that complement of his personal life, which the latter seeks in marriage.—No doubt that does not prove—and St. Paul, we shall see, does not seek to affirm—that celibacy in itself is *holier* than married life. The point in question is one of dignity, propriety. The apostle means simply to assert that there is nothing unbecoming in a man's living in celibacy.—The expression μὴ ἅπτεσθαι, *not to touch*, does not refer, as Rückert has thought, to the conduct of those united in marriage; it is at a later stage (vers. 3–5) that Paul treats this point. He wishes to tranquillize unmarried persons who are uncertain about the line of conduct they have to follow. The expression used is probably borrowed from the letter of the Corinthians. Holsten thinks that the expression also applies to illicit relations. But in chap. vi. Paul had completely exhausted this subject.

After clearly reserving the honourableness of celibacy, Paul passes to the practical truth which he is concerned to establish, the general necessity of marriage. For, as Reuss says, "his object is rather to protest against ascetic exaggerations than to favour them.'

Ver. 2. The δέ is adversative: "*but*, honourable as celibacy is, it should not be the rule." — The plural *fornications* refers to the numerous acts and varied temptations which abounded at Corinth. — When he says, *every man*, *every woman*, Paul of course understands the exception pointed out in ver. 7, and the case which he will treat specially vers. 25–38 (virgins). — Baur, Rothe, Scherer, Holsten, and even Reuss[1] accuse the apostle of proceeding on a view of marriage much inferior to the moral ideal of the relation. It would seem that he regards it only as a makeshift intended to remove a greater evil. But it is forgotten that the apostle is not here framing a theory of marriage in general; he is answering precise questions which had been put to him, and of whose tendency and tenor we are ignorant. In our very chapter, ver. 14 proves clearly that he knows the moral side of the relation perfectly; the same is true of the words xi. 3, which make marriage the analogue of the most exalted of all things: the relation between Christ and the human soul; nay,

[1] "It must be granted that this argument, dictated no doubt by a very laudable prudence, does not reveal a very elevated conception of marriage and of its moral aim."

even of the relation between God and Christ. Reuss acknowledges "that in other Epistles, marriage is spoken of from a less contemptuous point of view;" comp. Eph. v. 25–27. Now, as it is improbable that Paul modified his conception of marriage, and as the passages of our Epistle quoted above show that in fact there is nothing of the kind, it must be concluded that in this exposition the apostle desired to keep strictly within the limits traced out for him by the questions of the Corinthians on the subject.—But still, that marriage may correspond to the end pointed out, the life in this state must be in accordance with its nature. This is the meaning of the vers. 3–5, which are a short digression; after which the apostle follows up in ver. 6 the idea of ver. 2.

Vers. 3–5. "Let the husband render unto the wife her due,[1] and likewise also the wife unto the husband. 4. The wife hath not power of her own body, but the husband; and likewise also the husband hath not power of his own body, but the wife. 5. Defraud ye not one the other, except it be with consent, for a time, that ye may give[2] yourselves to prayer,[3] and come together[4] again, that Satan tempt you not for your incontinency."—The reading of the T. R., *due benevolence*, is a paraphrase substituted for Paul's real words, *the debt*,

[1] T. R. with K L Syr. reads την οφειλομενην ευνοιαν (*the due benevolence*); all the other Mjj. It.: την οφειλην (*the debt*).

[2] T. R. with A L: σχολαζητε, instead of σχολασητε, which is the reading of the other Mjj.

[3] Before τη προσευχη (*to prayer*), T. R. with K L Syr. reads: τη νηστεια και (*to fasting and*), which is omitted by the other Mjj. It. Or. and other Fathers.

[4] T. R. with some Mnn. only reads συνερχεσθε; K L P Syr.: συνερχησθε; the eight other Mjj. It. Or.: ητε.

with the view of avoiding what might be offensive in the latter in public reading. This verse confirms us in the idea that among some of the Corinthians there existed an exaggerated spiritualistic tendency, which threatened to injure conjugal relations, and thereby holiness of life.

Ver. 4. This verse justifies the direction given in the preceding. By the conjugal bond, each spouse acquires a right over the person of the other. Consequently each alienates a portion of personal independence. Hence precisely the καλόν of celibacy.

Ver. 5. In this verse there is reproduced the direction given in ver. 3, but in a negative form: *Defraud not,* to exclude expressly the contrary opinion, and at the same time to *limit* this prohibition, nevertheless under certain conditions fitted to remove the danger of the restriction. The interruption of the conjugal relations authorized by the apostle may take place on three conditions: 1. mutual consent; 2. temporary duration; 3. the aim of securing spiritual meditation; and the particle εἰ μή τι ἄν, *unless it is,* by which Paul authorizes the exception, is immediately determined by two restrictions, one of which gives it a purely contingent or *doubtful* (ἄν) character, the other a limited (τι) character.—To *prayer* T. R. adds *fasting;* but this is an interpolation arising from later ecclesiastical usages.—The reading συνέρχεσθε or συνέρχησθε, in the Byz. documents, instead of ἦτε, is due to the same cause as the variant of ver. 3.—Among the Jews, also, it was customary to prepare by temporary separation for acts of particular solemnity (Ex. xix. 15; 1 Sam. xxi. 4; comp. Josh. vii. 13, etc.). The spirit, by asserting its dominion over the senses, becomes more conscious of its own proper life, and by this concentration on itself, opens more profoundly to the communications of the higher world.—All these restrictions are suggested to the apostle by a double fear; on the one hand, the natural incontinence of his readers (ἀκρασία from ἀκρατής, one who is not master of himself), and on the other, the working of Satan, who fans carnal desires with his breath, and thus brings about from the smallest occasion the cause of a fall. These occasions were frequent at Corinth; there was one especially, of which the apostle will afterwards speak, participation in idolatrous banquets.

Vers. 6, 7. "Now I speak this by permission, not of commandment. 7. But[1] I wish that all men were even as I myself; yet every man hath his proper gift of God, one[2] after this manner, and another[2] after that."—The remark which the apostle makes in ver. 6 might be applied to the foregoing prohibition: "Defraud not . . .;" or, as is done by Tertullian, Origen, Jerome, Calvin, to the precept: "that ye come together again." But this precept had been given only accidentally, and the ground for it had been too strongly stated to admit of its being afterwards presented as a simple counsel, and not as a positive rule. Meyer and Beet make this remark bear on the restriction: "Except it be for a time." Meyer paraphrases thus: "If I recommend you to keep apart only for a time, it is not an absolute command I give on the subject, it is

[1] T. R. with B K L P Syr. reads γαρ (*for*), while ℵ A C D F G It. read δε (*now* or *but*).

[2] T. R. reads ος μεν and ος δε with K L, while the rest read ο μεν and ο δε.

a simple counsel. But you may, if you think good, remain in this state of separation, provided it be with common consent." But, in the first place, this meaning is overturned by the same reasons as the preceding, from which it is not essentially different. Then what right have we to separate one of the three conditions (*common consent*) from the other two? Are they not put on exactly the same footing in ver. 5? Far from wishing by ver. 6 to attenuate the importance of the limits traced in ver. 5, the apostle aims, on the contrary, throughout this whole passage to combat a too pronounced ascetic tendency which threatened to prevent marriage, or to turn it aside from the end for which the apostle claims it as a general rule. If it is so, the remark of ver. 6 can only refer, as has been clearly seen by Beza, Grotius, de Wette, Hofmann, to the essential idea of the passage, as stated in ver. 2, and as it is to be restated in a new form in ver. 7: the general duty of marriage. Vers. 3–5 have only been a digression intended to maintain in the normal state the practice of marriage. The apostle now returns to the principal idea (ver. 2): "In speaking as I do, I do not for a moment mean to give you an apostolical command to marry. I give you a simple counsel, founded on the knowledge I have of your weakness."—The verb συγγινώσκειν, *to know with*, denotes the sympathetic feeling with which one appropriates the thought or state of another, condescension, accommodation, and even pardon. The substantive συγγνώμη consequently expresses an advice in which one takes account of circumstances. It was precisely in this sense that the apostle had laid down as a rule the married state.

Ver. 7. The received reading γάρ, *for*, rests on the *Vatic.*, the Peschito, etc. Its meaning is easy: "I certainly did not mean to enjoin you to marry; for my desire is rather . . ." But all the other Mjj., the *Itala*, and several Fathers read δέ, *but*, which is more difficult, and for that very reason more probable, and which can also be justified: "I commit you in general to marriage, *but* that is not my wish, absolutely speaking; on the contrary . . ." It seems as if instead of the indic. θέλω, *I wish*, the optative would have been required. But this would only have expressed a contingent wish, whereas the indicative expresses a real wish of the apostle, though he gives up its fulfilment for reasons independent of his wish. As Osiander observes, the form θέλω has in it something subjective. —Is the phrase, *all men*, which does not signify merely all Christians, as Osiander still thinks, determined by the near prospect of the end of the world? This is unnecessary. Absolutely speaking, Paul can only desire for every man what he has found best for himself; but no doubt on the condition that there be no essential difference between him and others.—From the words, *as I myself*, it may be inferred with certainty that Paul was not married, and quite as certainly that he was not a widower. For how could he have expressed the desire that all men were widowers! See on ver. 8.—The καί, *also*, after *as*, strengthens the idea of the resemblance which he would like to see existing between him and other men (Rom. i. 13; Acts xxvi. 29).

But the preference which Paul gives to celibacy meets with an obstacle in practice. There is a difference among men of which account must be taken.

Jesus had already pointed it out (Matt. xix. 10–12), and He had Himself drawn from the fact the practical consequences relating to the subject before us. There are men whom their natural temperament, in the first place, and then a spiritual grace which takes possession of this particular disposition, render capable of living in the state of celibacy without struggle and without inward pollution. Agreeably to this saying of Jesus, Paul desires that when one has the privilege of possessing the glorious faculty of consecrating himself without encumbrances to the service of God and men, he should not sacrifice it.—The expressions, *one after this manner, and another after that,* denote respectively, aptitude for life in celibacy, and aptitude for married life. It should be observed that these two aptitudes bear, both alike, the name of *gift*, *χάρισμα*. And we can thus put our finger on the error into which Reuss falls, when he says: "If abstention, life in celibacy, is a particular gift of God's grace, it is evident that something is wanting to the man who does not possess it." The apostle is innocent of this erroneous conclusion. For he declares that there is not *one* single gift, but *two* different gifts. If the one is the gift of celibacy for the kingdom of God, the other is that of marriage, also for the kingdom of God. Meyer, it is true, alleges that the apostle is here expressing an abstract maxim, and that the two *οὕτως*, *thus*, do not properly apply either to celibacy or marriage specially. But what matters? If it is a general maxim, it is in any case stated here only with a view to its application to the two positions compared in the passage. Hence it follows that there is no less need of a gift of grace to use marriage Christianly than to live Christianly in celibacy.

In vers. 1–7 Paul laid down two principles: the intrinsic honourableness of celibacy (vers. 1 and 7[a]), and the preference which must as a rule be given to marriage (vers. 2 and 7[b]). He now draws, vers. 8 and 9, the consequences of these two principles; and first, ver. 8, the consequence from the first; then, ver. 9, that from the second.

Vers. 8, 9. "I say then to the unmarried and widows, it is[1] good for them if they abide even as I. 9. But if they cannot contain, let them marry; for it is better to marry[2] than to burn."—The δέ, *then,* indicates the transition from the grounds to the final sentence.—On καλόν, *good,* see on ver. 1. The αὐτοῖς, *for them,* is remarkable; used without regimen, the word καλόν would have been too absolute; it might have seemed to ascribe a moral superiority to celibacy.—The contrast between ταῖς χήραις, *widows,* and τοῖς ἀγάμοις, *the unmarried,* has led Erasmus, Beza, etc., to regard the latter as embracing only widowers. But there is no ground for thus restricting the meaning of ἀγάμοι; the word naturally comprehends also young unmarried men. On the other hand, Meyer extends the meaning of the word too far when he brings under it also virgins. The latter will have their chapter for themselves (ver. 25 seq.). It would even be altogether unsuitable to apply to them what is said in ver. 9. Why, finally, would the apostle have joined them with unmarried men

[1] T. R. with E K L reads εστιν (*is*), which is omitted by all the rest.

[2] ℵ A C read γαμειν instead of γαμησαι, which T. R. reads with all the rest.

and widowers, instead of joining them with widows? —The reason why widows are mentioned separately, while widowers are confounded with bachelors, is this, widowhood creates, in the case of the woman, a more special position than in that of a man; a widow differs much more socially from a virgin than a widower from a young man. Besides, the masculine χῆρος, *widower*, is in Greek an adjective rather than a substantive, while the opposite is the case with the feminine χήρα, *widow*.—From these last words, *if they abide even as I*, Luther, Grotius, etc., have concluded that Paul must have been a widower, but erroneously. The idea of *abiding* as Paul, according to the true meaning of ἀγάμοι, may embrace perseverance in celibacy, as well as perseverance in the state of widowhood (see on ver. 7). Clement of Alexandria also alleged that Paul was a widower; but it was neither on the ground of a tradition nor on account of this verse. Eusebius cites this Father's opinion (*H. E.*, iii. 24); he justified it by the passage Phil. iv. 3, where he erroneously ascribed to the word σύζυγος the meaning of spouse.[1]

Ver. 9. It is a good thing (καλόν) to remain free from every bond, if one can do so without sinning; but if sin is to be the result, it is better to marry; for sin is an evil, while marriage is not. — The compound word ἐγκρατεύεσθαι includes three ideas: *to possess in oneself* (ἐν) *the power of* (κρατεῖν) *controlling oneself* (the middle form). It is the opposite of the ἀκρασία of ver. 5.— The aor. imper. γαμησάτωσαν, *let them marry*, has something about it abrupt and dry: "Let them marry and

[1] "Paul does not fear, in one of his letters, to address his own wife" (σύζυγον).

have done with it!" The aor. ἐγάμησα in later Greek sometimes takes the place of the primitive aor. ἔγημα, which is found Luke xiv. 20.—The term *πυροῦσθαι, to burn*, does not at all apply to the torments of hell, as Tertullian and Pelagius thought. Paul by this word denotes every painful exercise of soul; comp. 2 Cor. xi. 29; here: the fire of inward lusts in conflict with conscience. Comp. the ἐξεκαύθησαν of Rom. i. 27, notwithstanding the difference of situation.

The fundamental question regarding the formation of the marriage bond is resolved. The apostle now examines the questions relating to the *maintenance* or *breach* of this bond. He here encounters two different positions. The first is that of the married who both belong to the Church (vers. 10, 11); the second, that of the married of whom one only is a Christian (vers. 12–16). There follows an appendix relating to some analogous questions (vers. 17–24).

Vers. 10–24

Vers. 10–16.

The rules to be followed in the case of two Christian spouses (vers. 10, 11).

Vers. 10, 11. "But unto the already married I command, not I, but the Lord, that the wife depart[1] not from the husband, 11. that if she is parted, she ought to remain unmarried, or be reconciled to her husband, and that the husband do not put away his wife."—The γεγαμηκότες, *married*, are contrasted, on the one hand, with those who are widowers or bachelors (vers. 8, 9), and on the other, with the τοῖς λοίποις, *the others*,

[1] T. R. with ℵ B C K L P: χωρισθηναι; A D E F G: χωριζεσθαι.

or *the rest* (ver. 12); as these are also married, those of ver. 10 can only be regarded as spouses living in Christian marriage on both sides, and *the others*, of ver. 12, as living in mixed marriage (a Christian spouse with a Jewish or heathen spouse). To understand the apostle's mode of expressing himself, we need only call to mind that this letter was intended to be read in the assembly of the Church; consequently, when the apostle said: "Those who are in the state of marriage" (γεγαμηκότες, the perfect), he could only thereby designate two spouses who were both Christians.—The verb παραγγέλλω, *I command*, sometimes includes, along with the idea of commanding, that of transmitting; perhaps it is so in this passage: "As to this command, I do not give it to you myself; I transmit it to you."—What are the meaning and bearing of the distinction which Paul establishes in the words, *not I, but the Lord?* The simplest supposition is that he means to speak here of a command given by Jesus Himself during His earthly sojourn. And what confirms this meaning is, that we really find this precept in our Gospels proceeding from the mouth of Jesus, just as we read it here; comp. Matt. v. 32, xix. 9; Mark x. 11; Luke xvi. 18. Not that I hold that the three first Gospels were already composed and circulated in the Churches at the time when Paul wrote; rather he derives his knowledge of this saying from the oral tradition which proceeded from the apostles. Baur has objected that if Paul had meant to cite a positive command of the Lord, he must have used the past παρήγγειλεν (*He commanded*), and not the present. But the command of Jesus is regarded as abiding for the Church throughout all time. No doubt it might also be that the apostle meant to say he had received this command by way of revelation. But the fact that we find it expressly given in our Gospels by the Lord proves that this is the saying to which he alludes.—And what is the effect of the distinction which Paul establishes between what the Lord commands and what he himself prescribes (ver. 12)? Does he mean that his apostolical commands are less infallible than those of the Lord? But this would be to sap apostolical authority with his own hands, and the words, xiv. 37, where he calls certain prescriptions in regard to worship a commandment of the Lord, would certainly not confirm this distinction. He means rather to establish the difference between the commands given expressly by the Lord, which have consequently indisputable force for the whole Church, and those which emanate from himself, and which, as such, are law only for the Churches founded by him and subject to his apostleship. So the former required only to be cited; they had no need of being demonstrated to any one who professed faith in Christ. The latter, on the contrary, assumed the acknowledgment of Paul as an apostle of the Lord; the apostle therefore felt himself called to expound the reasons which justified them; comp. vers. 14 and 16.

In quoting the words of Jesus, Paul omits the limitation put by the Lord on the command not to separate: "unless it be for adultery." Luke and Mark likewise omit it in the account of this discourse. The reason is that it was taken for granted; for in this relation adultery is equivalent to death; and such a crime was not to be thought possible in the Christian community.

—The wife is placed first, because it is from her, as the weaker party, that the inclinations for separation oftenest come. The apostle says, in speaking of her, χωρισθῆναι, *to be separated*, while in the end of the following verse, in speaking of the man, he says ἀφιέναι, *to send away*, or *let go*. The reason perhaps is because the man is in his own home, and remains there, whereas the woman leaves the domicile.

Ver. 11. The first part of the verse is a parenthesis; for the proposition begun in ver. 10 finishes with the last words of ver. 11. The apostle anticipates the case in which, notwithstanding his, or rather the Lord's, prohibition, a Christian woman has left her husband: ἐὰν δὲ καί, *but if even* (with and in spite of this prohibition). Such a violation of the Lord's words have been regarded as inadmissible. Hofmann therefore supposes that it is solely deeds already consummated at the time when Paul wrote his letter that are in question; and Holsten concludes from this same alleged impossibility that the parenthesis, ἐὰν δὲ . . . καταλλαγήτω, is only a later interpolation. All this is unnecessary. Paul could perfectly anticipate the case in which, notwithstanding this prohibition, a wife, outraged by the bad treatment of which she was the victim, would go off abruptly in a moment of lively irritation. Fearing to do more harm than good by doing violence to the state of things, Paul accepts the situation. But first he seeks to prevent a second and still graver evil from being added to the first, and that by a new marriage of the separated wife, a marriage which Jesus called adultery; then he recommends a reconciliation as soon as possible. It has been asked whether the interdict against a new marriage applied also to the case in which one of the spouses had been guilty of adultery; and next, whether in this case the prohibition applied to the injured party as well as to the criminal spouse. Catholic law absolutely forbids divorce, even in the case of adultery, while Protestant law in these circumstances allows it. And, as to second marriage, Protestant law likewise permits it, but only to the innocent party. The refusal of divorce in the case of adultery seems to us to transgress the meaning of the Lord's words; for by these adultery is implicitly put on the same footing as death. And, as to the right of remarriage granted to the innocent party, it does not seem to me at all contrary to the text of Scripture. But what seems to me absolutely irreconcileable with the Lord's words, is the readiness with which Protestant pastors, becoming the agents of a purely civil legislation, consent to bless *in the name of the Lord* marriages contracted between persons whose first marriage had not been dissolved for the only reason authorized by the Lord, so that this new union, according to His positive declaration, is adultery. To bless on His part what He Himself characterizes so severely is a strange way of acting in His name. The State may have excellent reasons for not imposing on human society in general such rules as in their severity go beyond its moral level (Matt. xix. 8); but the Church has reasons not less valid for refusing to follow it in this region contrary to the will of its Master. Of course this faithful conduct of the Church demands, as a consequence, the distinction between State legislation and Church legislation. After this parenthesis, the apostle finishes the quotation of the Lord's words, by adding what concerns the husband. On the term *ἀφιέναι*, *to put away*, see on ver. 10. For the rest, the two sexes are put on the same footing. Among the Greeks, the wife could separate freely from her husband.

Vers. 12, 13. "But to the rest, speak I,[1] not the Lord: If any brother hath a wife that believeth not, and she be pleased to dwell with him, let him not put her away; 13. and the woman which[2] hath an husband that believeth not, if he[3] be pleased to dwell with her, let her not put away her husband."[4]—Those whom the apostle calls *the rest*, in contrast to the spouses of ver. 11, can only be the married who do not both belong to the Church, and only one of whom was present at the reading of this letter. The sequel will leave no doubt of this interpretation. It is clear that neither the apostle nor the Church would have authorized a marriage between a member of the Church and a Jew or heathen; but one of two spouses might have been converted after marriage; hence the possibility of mixed marriages. Jesus could not have thought of giving a direction for such cases; so the apostle declares that he has no command to transmit from the Lord on this subject. It is therefore himself, Paul, who must regulate the case, drawing its solution, by way of deduction, from the essence of the gospel. It seems to me even that the expression, *I, not the Lord*, excludes not only any positive ordinance uttered

[1] T. R. with D E F G K L puts εγω (*I*) before λεγω (*I speak*); A B C P Syr[sch] put it after.

[2] T. R. with 6 Mjj.: ητις (*who*); ℵ D F G P: ει τις (*if a*).

[3] T. R. with E K L Syr.: αυτος; all the rest: ουτος.

[4] T. R. with K L P: αυτον (*him*); all the rest: τον ανδρα (*the husband*).

by the Lord during His life, but even any special revelation proceeding from Him on the subject. It does not follow, however, that he puts himself in this respect on the same footing as any other Christian. How, if it were so, could he say with authority in ver. 17 : " So ordain I in all the Churches " ? He knew himself to be enlightened, as an apostle, with a wisdom superior to ordinary Christian wisdom, and that even in cases in which he had neither an external revelation (ver. 10), nor an inward revelation properly so called (xi. 23) to direct him.

Two cases might present themselves in mixed marriages: Either the heathen spouse consented to remain with the Christian spouse ; this is the case treated vers. 12–14. Or he refused ; this is the case treated vers. 15, 16.

On the first supposition, the Christian spouse, whether husband or wife, ought to remain united to the Jewish or heathen spouse; for the consent of the latter implies that he will not annoy the Christian in the discharge of her religious obligations.—The term ἀφιέναι, *put away,* is here applied to the wife as well as to the husband, perhaps because, as Bengel finely observes, in the eyes of the Church the Christian wife is, despite her sex, the nobler of the two ; or, more simply, because, in case of the heathen desiring to remain with his wife, it is she who would *speak the leave-taking* (give the *congé*) if she refused. This direction given for the first case, the apostle is careful to justify it, precisely because this is his ordinance, and not the Lord's.

Ver. 14. " For the unbelieving husband is sanctified

in the wife,[1] and the unbelieving wife is sanctified in the brother;[2] since otherwise were your children unclean; but now are they holy."—The essential idea is that expressed by the word put at the head of the first and second proposition: ἡγίασται, *is sanctified.* The use of this term is no doubt occasioned by the fear which the Christian spouse might have of contracting defilement by remaining united to a heathen or Jewish spouse. So some interpreters have given the word a a purely negative, or, what amounts to nearly the same, a Levitical and ritual sense. Paul, it is said, means: marriage in this condition does not become an impure state, does not affect the Christian with defilement similar to that which was produced under the law by the touch of a dead body, for example. But this meaning, held by Rückert, as being purely negative, is too weak to correspond to the positive term ἡγίασται; and besides, resting on the theocratical idea of an external and ritual purity, it is not in keeping with the spirit of the New Testament. Others, with different shades, take this term as expressing the hope of sanctifying influence which the Christian spouse will in the end exercise over the heathen or Jewish spouse; so Olshausen: the Christian spirit will distil on him; de Wette, Neander: he will be placed under the beneficent influence of his spouse and of the Church. But the perfect ἡγίασται, *has been put in a state of holiness*, cannot designate a hoped-for result; and ver. 16 precisely contradicts the certainty of such a

[1] D E F G It. Syr^{sch} add τη πιστη (*believing*).

[2] T. R. with K L Syr. reads ανδρι (*the husband*); all the rest: αδελφω (*the brother*).

result. Meyer and Reuss seek to evade these difficulties by making ἡγίασται here signify: "He is associated, affiliated to the Church by the conjugal bond which unites him to his spouse." But do we not thus come back to the idea of a purely ceremonial holiness, a consecration wholly objective and external? Hofmann thinks that we must here abstract from all influence over the person of the non-Christian spouse, and apply the idea of holiness only to the *bond* between the two spouses, to their conjugal relation as such. This amounts to saying, as in the first interpretation, that such a union is pure for the two spouses. But if this idea had been that of Paul, he would have expressed it in a less involved way. To get at his thought in this verse, we must take account of the perfect passive and of the preposition ἐν, *in*. The latter indicates that the heathen or Jewish spouse has his holiness *in* the person of his spouse, and the perfect passive indicates that the communication of this holiness or consecration to God is regarded by Paul as already finished. As the believer is consecrated to God in the person of Christ, and as by faith in Him he gains his own consecration in His (see on i. 2), so the non-Christian spouse is sanctified in his Christian spouse by his consent to live with her. This consent is in his relation to his Christian spouse what faith is in the believer's relation to Christ. By consenting to live still with his spouse, the Jewish or heathen spouse also accepts her holy consecration and participates in it. Thus it is so long as he persists in this consent. The apostle of course reckons on the sanctifying influence of such a situation; but the use of the perfect and of the preposition ἐν, *in*, show that the point before him here is not strictly and above all that sanctifying influence, but the position of consecration in which the non-Christian spouse is at once placed by his determination to remain united to his Christian spouse.

Is this consecration of the one in the person of the other really tenable? Certainly; and the apostle proves it by an analogous moral fact and one universally admitted in the Church. The conjunction ἐπεί, *since*, is frequently used to mean: "since, *if it were otherwise*, this is what would happen" (*da sonst*, Passow); comp. for this meaning in the New Testament Rom. xi. 22: "since otherwise (that is to say, if thou persevere not) thou also shalt be cut off;" and in our own Epistle, v. 10 and xv. 29: "since otherwise (if there be no resurrection), what shall they do . . . ?" It is the same in profane Greek; comp. the numerous examples quoted by Passow. The ἄρα, *then*, announces an explanatory inference: "since if you refuse to acknowledge as true what I have just affirmed . . ." M. L'Hardy, in his book, *Le baptême des enfants* (1882), has disputed this universally admitted meaning of *since otherwise*, and has attempted to substitute for it the meaning, *seeing that, considering that.* The idea, according to him, is this: "Ye ought not to separate (ver. 13), first, because the unbeliever is sanctified in the believer (ver. 14[a]); and next, *from the consideration that*, if separation takes place, your children, deprived of family life, will be impure; whereas, if you remain united, they will be holy." We should thus have here a second reason to justify the μὴ ἀφιέτω, *let her not put him away*, of ver. 13. But in this sense the connecting particle with what precedes would be not ἐπεί, but καὶ δέ, *and moreover*; then the ἐπεί, *since*, can in any case only bear on the verb which immediately precedes, ἡγίασται, *is sanctified*, twice repeated, and not on the remoter imperative of ver. 13. It is in this case an argument whereby the apostle demonstrates the truth of the affirmation enunciated in the first part of the verse: *he is sanctified*.

The expression, *your children*, may be understood in two ways. It may be applied—and it seems at first sight the most natural meaning—only to children born of mixed marriages. So Chrysostom, Flatt, Bonnet, L'Hardy, and others. But from ver. 12, Paul, in speaking of spouses placed in this condition, has used the third person. Why would he pass all at once to the second while addressing the same persons: τέκνα ὑμῶν, *your* children? Then would the argument have been conclusive? Would a mother, who doubted the consecration of her husband by means of her own faith, have admitted more easily the state of consecration belonging to her children by means of her maintaining that conjugal life of whose purity she was distrustful? It is therefore more probable that the expression, "*your* children," contains, as Beet says, "an appeal to all Christian parents." Paul addresses them all (ὑμῶν, *you*) as present at the time when his letter is read in the congregation. The argument is this: "If it is a thing admitted by you all, that notwithstanding their original pollution, your children, who are not yet believers, are nevertheless already consecrated and holy in the eyes of God, and that in virtue of the bond which unites them to you, their parents, why would you make a difficulty about recognising also that an unbelieving husband may be regarded as consecrated to God in virtue of his union with his believing wife, and that by the fact of his desire to remain united to her?" So de Wette, Rückert, Olshausen, Neander, Meyer, Osiander, Hofmann, Heinrici, Edwards. By the form, *since otherwise*, this reasoning becomes an argument *ad absurdum:* "If you deny this participation of the non-Christian spouse in the consecration of the Christian spouse, you ought, if you are to be consequent, to declare your own children impure, to regard them as polluted beings, heathen children, which your Christian instinct refuses to believe." To give more force to this reasoning, Paul changes the ἡγίασται, *is sanctified*, into ἅγιά ἐστιν, *are holy*. This second term is stronger than the first. The verb, in the perfect passive, indicated a position in which the subject is placed in the person of another, whereas the adjective ἅγια, *holy*, expresses a real quality inherent in the subject, though the latter has not yet any share in the act (faith) which seems to be its condition. Now if this characteristic is indisputable in the judgment of Christian feeling, with stronger reason ought the privilege designated above to be so.—The term ἀκάθαρτα, *impure*, here signifies: yet plunged, like children of heathen parents, in their natural impurity.—The νῦν δέ, *but now*, brings out the contrast between the true, only tenable idea, and the absurd supposition conditionally stated.

But what exactly are we to understand by this word ἅγια, *holy?* If ἀκάθαρτα, *unclean*, cannot in this case designate either an external and ritual defilement, like those which were contracted under the Old Testament, or a personal moral defilement, since it is infants who are spoken of, and can only consequently apply to natural corruption; in like manner the word *holy* cannot designate here either a simply Levitical purity, for we are no longer under the Old Testament, or free and personal holiness, like that of regenerated believers. Is it possible then to discover an intermediate between these two alternatives? De Wette, Olshausen, Osiander, Neander, Edwards think that the reference is to the Christian influence of parents by means of their prayers, instructions, example (*practical power*, Edwards). But this explanation carries us to the future, and to a very uncertain future (see ver. 16); whereas the verb ἐστί, *are*, denotes a real and present fact. The Reformers, from their viewpoint of absolute predestination, did not shrink from giving the fullest meaning to the word ἡγίασται.[1] According to Calvin (*Instit.* iv. 16, pp. 310–312), the children of Christians are holy from their birth, in consequence of supernatural grace. For this idea of the inward sanctification of the children of Christians from their birth, Beza substitutes that of their assured regeneration in consequence of their election. But it is not by denying liberty that any one will come to understand the notion of holiness in St. Paul. Calvin thinks of a holiness bestowed by *supernatural grace* on the children of Christians from their entrance into life. But do the facts confirm this

[1] See in Edwards the development of this point.

theory? Others, like M. Ménégoz,[1] explain the idea of the apostle by that of the solidarity and organic unity of the family. But does this law hold also in the spiritual domain? Hofmann understands, holy *in the eyes of the parents,* "who do not see the sin with which the child is born, but only the gift of God which they have received in the child." But how can we discover here the meaning of the word *holy?* Bonnet and L'Hardy start from the use of this word, Rom. xi. 16: "If the root be holy, so are the branches;" and they think that as there remains in the family of Abraham, even when rejected, a predisposition to the service of God, so the blessed effects of the covenant of grace extend from Christian parents to their children, because these are "the fruits of a blessed union in God." Here, then, we have "a natural holiness, one of position."[2] Beet, in an analogous sense, adduces the words, Ex. xxix. 37: "Whatsoever touches the altar of God shall be holy." Children laid by the prayer of the parents on the altar of God become a holy thing; and so it is with the husband whom his Christian wife presents to God.—In my opinion there can be no doubt that the matter in question here is a transmitted grace, a consecration of the child to God resulting from the Divine offer of salvation under which it is put from its birth, whether it afterwards accept or reject it. But even in this case the assertion, *are holy,* still seems extravagant. There is something so firm and precise about it, that one involuntarily seeks a positive fact on which to support it. Certainly, since it is

[1] *Revue chrétienne*, Avril 1884; *Le Baptême des enfants.*
[2] L'Hardy, pp. 495, 514.

children and non-believers who are in question, it is allowable to hold by a notion of holiness which approaches that of the Old Testament; but in this sense the need of an external objective fact, to account for such a declaration, makes itself the more felt. This fact can only be, as it seems to me, the baptism of the Corinthian children in regard to whom the apostle expresses himself so categorically. No doubt the gravest German commentators find in this very saying an indisputable proof against the practice of infant baptism in the Churches founded by Paul. "If," it is said, "Christian children had been already introduced into the Church by baptism, their position would no longer have any analogy to that of the heathen spouses of whom St. Paul speaks in the first part of this verse, and he could not logically conclude from the former to the latter. His argument is valid only in so far as both alike lie outside at once of faith and baptism." But this objection rests on the idea that baptism is here regarded by Paul as the *principle* of the holiness ascribed by him to the children of Christians. From this point of view it would indeed differ totally from that which Paul, by his *is sanctified* (ver. 14[a]), can allow to non-Christian spouses. But if Paul regards the baptism of those children, not as the source, but as the *proof of the fact*, the seal of their state of holiness, the whole thing is changed. He means, not that they are holy because of their baptism, but that their baptism was the sign and proof of the fact of their state of holiness. And whence, then, arises this holiness which rises superior in them from their birth over natural corruption, and which rendered them fit to receive baptism, though they had not yet personal faith? As Jewish children did not become children of Abraham by circumcision, but as it was descent from their parents, children of Abraham, which made them fit to receive circumcision, so it is with the children of Christians. Their consecration to God does not depend on their baptism; but their fitness for baptism arises from the solidarity of life which unites them to their parents, and through them to the covenant of grace founded in Christ, and in which these live. Until Christian children decide freely for or against the salvation which is offered to them, they enjoy the benefit of this provisional situation, and are placed with all belonging to the family in communication with the holy forces which animate the body of Christ. And this is a state superior, though analogous, to that of the non-Christian spouse, who, in virtue of keeping up his union with his Christian wife, is not himself received into the covenant (ἅγιος, *holy*), but yet regarded as destined to enter into it (ἡγιασμένος, *sanctified*, consecrated, in the person of his wife, a member of the Church). If this second result were impossible, the first would be still more so.

Infant Baptism, in relation to the passage, vii. 14

German commentators are almost unanimous (except Hofmann, who here follows a way of his own) in regarding infant baptism as incompatible with these words of the apostle. The latest English critics (Edwards, Beet), though knowing the German works, do not adhere to the conclusion drawn in them, and do not believe the words to be incompatible with the ecclesiastical practice of baptizing infants. For my part, I do not find Paul's expressions intelligible except on the supposition that this practice existed.

In his interesting and able work already quoted, Professor Ménégoz has proposed an intermediate way. According to him, when Paul baptized whole families, Jewish or heathen (Acts xvi. 15, 33, xviii. 8; 1 Cor. i. 16), it is indisputable that the children were included. But 1 Cor. vii. 14 proves, he thinks, on the other hand, that in Christian families the children born after the baptism of the parents did not receive it themselves, which M. Ménégoz explains by supposing that their baptism was regarded as included in that of their parents. They were looked on "as baptized in the womb of their mother." It was not, according to him, till later and gradually that baptism was extended to the children of Christians themselves, because this rite being the mode of enlisting into the Church, it could not in course of time be refused to the descendants of Christians without effacing the line of demarcation between them and the world.

This hypothesis, intended to reconcile the two classes of passages, which M. Ménégoz thinks he finds in the New Testament, seems to me inadmissible. According to it, there were in Paul's Churches two classes of Christians: the one baptized, those who had passed from heathenism or Judaism to Christianity; the other unbaptized (except in the person of their parents), those who were born of parents already Christian. But where in the New Testament is there a trace of such a difference? Does not the apostle say: "We *all* (ὅσοι, as many as there are) who were baptized in Christ . . . ?" The same expression, Gal. iv. 27, and in our own Epistle, xii. 13: "We all (ἡμεῖς πάντες) were baptized into one Spirit to form one body." These expressions show that baptism was regarded as the external bond of all the members of the body of which the Spirit was the soul. And why, if M. Ménégoz' supposition was well founded, was not the baptism of children born of parents not yet Christian regarded as involved in that of their parents, as well as that of the infants born after their conversion, unless we are prepared to ascribe to the Church, and to Paul himself, the most grossly materialistic ideas? Has not M. Ménégoz himself very properly reminded us of the fact that, according to the notions of antiquity, the father's religion determined that of the family? His personal baptism should therefore have sufficed for all in the one situation as well as in the other. Finally, I think I have shown that the passage, 1 Cor. vii. 14, in favour of which so strange a hypothesis is proposed, not only does not require, but excludes it.

But does not ecclesiastical history protest against our exegetical result as false? With the exception of two passages, the one from Origen, the other from Tertullian, it is silent on the point before us. Now, of these two passages, that of Origen is positive in favour of the apostolic origin of infant baptism (*Comment. in epist. ad Rom.* t. v. 9): "The Church learned from the apostles that it ought to give baptism to infants." In the second, Tertullian, after his going over to Montanism (*De baptismo*, c. 18), dissuades parents from baptizing their children; which proves that the practice existed in his time, but that Tertullian himself did not regard it as apostolical. These facts are insufficient, from the historical point of view, to authorize a sure conclusion either on the one side or the other. It is therefore for exegesis to enlighten history rather than the reverse.

The apostle now passes to the opposite case, that of the Christian spouse whose heathen partner does not consent to live with her.

Vers. 15, 16. "But if the unbelieving depart, let him depart; a brother or a sister is not under bondage in such things; but God hath called us[1] in peace. 16. For what knowest thou, O wife, whether thou shalt save thy husband? and how knowest thou, O man, whether thou shalt save thy wife?"—The rule to be followed in this case is given in ver. 15; the reason follows in ver. 16. The Christian spouse should in this case consent to a separation which she could not refuse without going in the face of incessant conflicts. The word, *let him depart*, throws back the

[1] ℵ A C K read υμας (*you*) instead of ημας (*us*), which is the reading of T. R. and all the rest, It. Syr.

whole responsibility on the non-believer. The expression ἐν τοῖς τοιούτοις might signify, *in such circumstances* (the refusal of the heathen spouse). But the plural leads more naturally to the sense, *in such things, in this kind of matters.* The apostle is no doubt thinking of the transient element in earthly relations in general, when compared with the eternal interests which alone can bind the believer absolutely. He has probably already in view the other analogous relations with which he proceeds to deal in this connection from ver. 17. The words ἐν εἰρήνῃ, *in peace,* have often been understood as if they were εἰς εἰρήνην, "to peace." But if this had been Paul's idea, why not express himself so? He means rather that the call to faith which they accepted, bore from the first a pacific character, for it consisted in the offer of peace with God; and consequently the stamp of peace ought to be impressed on all their earthly conduct. Chrysostom regarded this last remark as intended to restrict the liberty of separation granted in the previous words; in this sense: "Nevertheless consider well that it is to peace thy Master has called thee, and see yet whether thou couldest not maintain the union." But as Edwards says, if the non-believer has left the Christian, how is it possible to exhort the latter to live in peace with the former? Is it not clear that by persisting to impose her presence, the Christian spouse would put herself directly in contradiction to the spirit of peace? For this conduct could not fail to issue in a state of perpetual war. The δέ is adversative: *but.* It contrasts with the subjection, which is denied, the duty of living in peace, which is affirmed. One might also, like Beet, translate the δέ in the sense of, *and moreover;* this would give a gradation: "And not only are ye not subject in this case . . ., but moreover there is a duty to . . ."—The difficult question in regard to this verse is to determine whether the *is not under bondage* includes, besides the right of separation, that of remarriage for the Christian spouse. Edwards cites the fact that this was the opinion of Ambrosiaster, whereas the Council of Arles (314) decided the question in the opposite sense. Among Protestants, *malicious desertion*—such is the judicial name for the χωρίζεσθαι on the part of one of the spouses—is regarded in general as equivalent to adultery, and consequently as authorizing a new marriage. I do not think that it is possible exegetically, as Edwards proposes, to decide the question in the latter sense, for, as Meyer observes, the οὐ δεδούλωται simply authorizes separation, without containing, either explicity or implicitly, the idea of a new union. In any case, in application to our present circumstances, it must not be forgotten that separation between a Christian and a heathen spouse is not subject to the same conditions as separation between two Christian spouses. For the latter, the rule has been given, and that by the Lord Himself, vers. 10, 11.

The two questions of ver. 16 have been frequently understood, from Chrysostom to Tholuck, in a sense opposed to liberty of separation: "What knowest thou whether thou shalt not save . . .?" Edwards has proved by several examples, taken from classic Greek, the *grammatical* possibility of taking εἰ in the sense of *whether;* comp. moreover in the LXX. Joel ii. 14;

Jonah iii. 9. But, as he rightly says, the context is decidedly opposed to this interpretation. It would assume that meaning of the preceding proposition which we have been obliged to reject; and so understood, the saying would demand of the Christian, with a view to a result very problematical and rendered almost impossible by the refusal of cohabitation on the part of the heathen spouse, an altogether disproportionate sacrifice.

VERS. 17–24

To illustrate the spirit of the prescriptions which he has just given, and to trace at the same time the line of conduct to be followed in certain analogous cases which occurred in the life of the Church, the apostle widens the question, and shows that the general viewpoint which he has taken, to solve the questions relating to marriage, commands all the relations of the Christian life. The following passage is therefore a digression, but one intended to elucidate more completely the subject treated. In ver. 17 the principle is laid down on which all such questions depend; in vers. 18 and 19 this principle is applied to a first example; it is repeated in ver. 20, then applied to a second example, vers. 21–23; finally, it is repeated anew by way of conclusion, ver. 24.

Ver. 17. "Save this,[1] that as the Lord[2] hath distributed[3] to every man, as God[4] hath called every one, so

[1] Some Mnn. and Fathers read η μη (*or not*), instead of ει μη (*if not*), which is the reading of all the Mjj.

[2] T. R. with K L here reads ο θεος (*God*), instead of ο κυριος (*the Lord*), which is the reading of the other eight Mjj.

[3] ℵ B: μεμεριχεν, instead of εμερισεν.

[4] T. R. with K L here reads ο κυριος (*the Lord*), instead of ο θεος (*God*).

let him walk; and so ordain I in all the Churches."—The particle εἰ μή, *unless*, or, *if it is not so*, has been explained in a multitude of ways. Some have connected it with the preceding verse, in this sense: "What knowest thou whether thou shalt save thy wife, *or not?*" But there would have been needed at least ἢ εἰ μή, or better, ἢ μή; and it is certainly from this that there has arisen the reading ἢ μή, *or not*, which is followed by Chrysostom and others, but which has no authorities in its favour. Besides, why not add this *or not* also to the first question? (de Wette). This addition, finally, would be most superfluous. Rückert would be disposed to make εἰ μή (supplying σώσεις, *thou shalt save*) a new proposition: "But if thou knowest not whether thou shalt save thy wife, here in any case is the rule to be followed." This meaning would be admissible, but an adversative particle would have been indispensable. Beza takes εἰ μή in the sense of ἀλλά, *but*, which cannot be supported grammatically.—Already by the words ἐν τοῖς τοιούτοις, *in such things*, the apostle had betrayed his intention of extending the treatment of the question proposed to other analogous subjects. This transition is indicated by the particle εἰ μή, *unless that*, which marks his return to the general rule from which he had been forced to deviate in the exceptional case treated, vers. 15 and 16. The principle, on which rested the two directions given to spouses, vers. 10, 11, and 12–14, was to remain as Christians in the situation where marriage had previously placed them. After the exception to this rule which he authorized, vers. 15 and 16, the apostle returns, by the particle, *unless that*, or, *saving the case that*, to the line of conduct indicated in the outset, and which he now states in a perfectly general way in ver. 17 : every believer ought to remain in the earthly situation in which the call to salvation found him. This is the meaning held by most modern interpreters (de Wette, Osiander, Meyer, Hofmann, etc.).—The authority of the Mjj. hardly allows us to admit the received reading, according to which the subject of the first clause is ὁ θεός, *God*, and that of the second, ὁ κύριος, *the Lord*, evidently Jesus Christ; comp. viii. 6. This reading is, however, the most natural, for in the first proposition the subject in question is external circumstances over which *God* presides, and in the second the calling to salvation which is undoubtedly often ascribed to God, but which may also be attributed to *Christ*. Hofmann, too, prefers this reading to that of the majority of the Mjj., which reverses the order of the two subjects. With this last reading it must be held that Christ is regarded here as directing from the midst of His glory the course of things on the earth. For it does not seem to me possible to apply, as Reiche and Heinrici do, the verb ἐμέρισεν, *has distributed* (μεμέρικεν, of ℵ B, is probably a correction after κέκληκεν), to the share of *spiritual* graces bestowed on each believer. The *assigned portion* in which each should continue can only be, according to the context, the circumstances, analogous to the state of Christian or mixed marriage, in which the believer was providentially placed at the time of his conversion: "The position in which thou didst hear and receive the Divine call is also that in which thou shouldest continue to live" (περιπατεῖν, *to walk*). A situation which could not prevent salvation from being realized in us, will not be incompatible with life in salvation.—The two *everys* are, by a strong inversion, placed before the conjunction which begins the proposition to which they belong. Thereby the apostle would emphasize the idea that there are as many particular positions as individuals called, and that each of them is their Divinely distributed lot which they ought not to change at will.

But Paul would not have it thought at Corinth that the principle here laid down is invented by him with a view to some present and special application which he contemplates within that Church. As to the rule, he lays it down in all the Churches founded by him, whose conduct amid such delicate questions he is called to direct. The word **διατάσσομαι**, *I ordain*, contains two ideas: that of a summary decision (**διά**), and that of apostolical competency (the middle, **τάσσομαι**, *I regulate in my sphere*).—The word *all* must of course be limited to the Churches dependent on his apostleship; comp. xiv. 37. The rule laid down in this verse is therefore this: the calling to the gospel ought not to be a reason with the believer for changing his outward situation. This principle well shows with what a conviction of its victorious power the gospel made its entrance into the world. It did not fear to confront any earthly position, lawful in itself; but it faced them all with the certainty of being able to penetrate and sanctify them by its spirit. As Edwards says: "The gospel introduces the principle of order as limiting that of liberty in the present life. It does not make slaves of us, but it does not plunge us into anarchy. It is not despotic; but neither is it revolutionary."

The apostle cites and deals with two examples: the state of circumcision or uncircumcision, and that of slavery or freedom.

Vers. 18, 19. "Is any man called being circumcised, let him not become uncircumcised; is any called[1] in uncircumcision, let him not be circumcised. 19. Circumcision is nothing, and uncircumcision is nothing, but the keeping of the commandments of God is everything."—Whether we give to the two verbs in the indicative the interrogative or affirmative sense matters little; it is here the hypothetical indicative. —The apostle is alluding to a custom which was introduced among the Hellenistic Jews, of practising a surgical operation intended to disguise their state of circumcision. They wished thereby to escape either persecution, or ridicule, in the public baths or games. These renegades were called *meschoukim, recutiti.* Epiphanius ascribes the invention of the process to Isaiah. Mention is made of it in the Book of Maccabees (i. 11, 15) and in Josephus (*Antiq.* xii. 5. 1). This difference, circumcision or uncircumcision, which had played so decisive a part from the religious standpoint of the Jews, was reduced to nothing by the gospel, which absolutely subordinates the ritual to the moral side of things. The coming of Christ inaugurated a new era, in which holiness alone remains; comp. Rom. ii. 29. In the expression *commandments of God* there are embraced the moral contents of the Jewish law and of the example and teachings of Jesus,

[1] T. R. with E K L: εκληθη, instead of κεκληται.

as well as the directions of His Spirit. Paul in like manner elsewhere contrasts with circumcision and uncircumcision the *new creature* (Gal. vi. 15), or *faith acting by love* (Gal. v. 6); comp. Rom. xiii. 9, where the whole law is summed up in love. It is evident that Paul is here speaking of the end to be realized, not of the means indispensable to its attainment.

Ver. 20. "Let every man remain faithful to the calling wherewith he was called."—Literally: "Let every man abide in the calling wherewith he was called." The word κλῆσις, *call*, *vocation*, cannot denote the earthly state or profession; it is applied here as elsewhere, to the call to salvation. The pronoun ῇ with ἐκλήθη would suffice to prove this: "the call *with which* he was called." Only the idea of the call must be taken to embrace all the external circumstances which furnish the occasion and determine the manner of it. What a difference between the manner of calling in the case of one circumcised and of one uncircumcised! Now this earthly situation, appointed by God, must not be left at one's own will. What was the means of thy call will not fail to exercise thy fidelity.—This maxim, which closes the treatment of the first example, serves as a transition to that of the second.

Ver. 21. "Thou wast called being a slave, care not for it; but if therewith thou mayest be made free, use it rather."—Here in this domain is the extreme case which can be conceived. Few situations could appear so incompatible with Christian holiness, dignity, and freedom as that of a slave. But a multitude of evidences proves that Christianity had quite specially found access to persons of this class. But, abnormal as this position may appear, it will not remain beyond the victorious influence of the gospel. The spiritual elevation which faith communicates, places the believer above even this contrast: slave, free.—There is something heroic in the word of the apostle: *care not for it.* "Do not let this position weigh either on thy conscience or on thy heart!" Hofmann applies these words, not to the state of slavery, but to the counsel which the apostle has just given, in this sense: "Do not torment thyself with the counsel I give thee; it should not prevent thee from accepting thy liberty, if an opportunity of recovering it presents itself." This explanation is not natural. For it is evident that it was his enslaved condition which would above all fill a Christian in this position with concern. The anxiety which Paul's order could cause him was only an effect of that which the position itself caused.

The second part of this verse has been understood in two diametrically opposite senses. The ancient Greek exegetes, and, among the moderns, de Wette, Meyer, Osiander, Kling, Reuss, Renan, Heinrici, Holsten, Edwards, Jean Monod (in a pamphlet published in connection with the American War on the subject of slavery[1]), among translators, Rilliet, Oltramare, Segond, Weizsäcker, think that the apostle means: "But, though thou mayest become free, use rather (slavery)." Calvin, Neander, Hofmann, Bonnet, Beet give this meaning, on the contrary, to the apostle's words: "But nevertheless, if thou canst become free,

[1] *Saint Paul et l'esclavage*, par J. A. Monod. Toulouse, 1866.

The author is not M. Jean Monod, Professor at Montauban, but is the Rev. Jean-Adolphe Monod.

profit by it (by accepting the advantage which is offered thee)."

The reasons ordinarily alleged in favour of the first interpretation are: 1. The conjunction *εἰ καί*, which signifies *even if, although:* "But *although* thou mightest become free, remain a slave." 2. Ver. 22, which more naturally justifies the idea of remaining a slave. 3. The whole context, which rather calls for encouragement to remain what one is than to change his state. Renan compares Paul's counsel thus understood with the words of the sages of the time: "The Stoics used to say like St. Paul to the slave: Remain what thou art; think not of freeing thyself." According to this interpretation, the Christian slave would be invited to refuse, should the case occur, the liberation which was offered him, and "to regard his state, to use Reuss' expression, as a means of education to salvation and as a special sphere of activity assigned to him." But these reasons are far from seeming to me decisive. The form *εἰ καί* has not always the sense of *even if* or *though.* The two elements of which it is composed may remain distinct, so that the *εἰ* continues an *if*, and the *καί* an *also.* This is established by Passow by many examples (ii. 1540).[1] We see this in our Epistle (iv. 7), and even in our chapter, in vers. 11, 28, where the meaning of *though* would be absolutely illogical, and where the *εἰ καί* evidently signifies: *If therewith,* if however. A new fact (*καί*) presents itself, which gives a new aspect to the case. It is precisely

[1] "In the form εἰ καί," says he, "καί may be separated from εἰ and no longer bear on the whole, but on a single term of the hypothetical proposition."

so in our passage: "But if *therewith* (besides the internal liberty which thou possessest, or thy tranquillity of soul, thy οὐ μέλεσθαι), thou canst also become outwardly free . . ." (καί applying to δύνασαι γένεσθαι). It might even be asked whether, in the other sense, Paul would not have required to say: καὶ εἰ, *and even if.* On the connection with ver. 22, see below. Finally, as to the context, it agrees perfectly with the second explanation, if this counsel be regarded as a *restriction* brought into the general rule. This is what is naturally indicated by the ἀλλά, *but,* for in the other sense it would require to be taken as an ἀλλά of gradation: *but moreover;* which is rather forced. We here find a restriction parallel to that of vers. 15 and 16, which was also introduced by an adversative particle (εἰ δέ, *but if*). As, in these verses, the Christian spouse was authorized to deviate from the general rule and to separate from the heathen spouse who refused to remain with her; so in our verse the Christian slave, after having been exhorted to bear without a murmur the state of slavery, is authorized to take advantage of any opportunity which occurs of exchanging it for freedom: "But if, therewith, thou mayest be made free . . ."

The reasons which appear to me to decide in favour of this meaning are the following: 1. The natural regimen of χρῆσαι, *make use of,* after the words which immediately precede, *If thou mayest be made free,* is certainly: "make use of the possibility." It is much less natural to go to the preceding sentence to borrow the idea of slavery. 2. The μᾶλλον, *rather,* which some oppose to this meaning, is on the contrary much more naturally explained if the apostle has in view the acceptance of liberty. He was well aware that the slave's situation might be such that he could legitimately prefer to remain in it. Hence it is that to his counsel to accept he delicately adds the word *rather*, which takes away from his words everything of an imperative character: "I would have thee in this case to incline *rather* to liberty." From the rule so forcibly inculcated: to remain in his position, there might in fact arise this misunderstanding, that a slave should not think himself free to profit by an offer of emancipation; this is what the apostle wishes to avoid. 3. Could Paul reasonably give to the Christian slave the advice to remain a slave if he could lawfully regain his freedom? Is not liberty a boon? Is it not the state which accords with the dignity of man? one of the features, the fundamental feature perhaps, of God's image in man? No doubt the Christian slave possesses inward liberty; for the Lord has set him free, not only from condemnation and sin, but also from the yoke of external circumstances, which he can henceforth accept as a gift of God. Nevertheless it remains true, that enjoying liberty, he will be able as a rule to give himself more efficiently to the service of God. What would be said of a prisoner who should refuse liberation, alleging that in his prison he enjoys moral liberty? Or of a sufferer, who, being able to recover health, should refuse to do so for the reason that on his couch he possesses spiritual life? The apostle had too much wisdom from above, and also too much natural good sense, to give himself up to such exaggeration, which belongs to an unhealthy asceticism.

Heinrici points out, rightly no doubt, the much more gentle and humane form which slavery had taken at that period. This is true : the master had no longer the right of life and death over his slave ; but nevertheless he had the disposal of his person. And if the Christian could find strength in communion with Christ to overcome the temptations attached to such dependence, what an exaggeration would it be to bind him to reject an opportunity providentially offered of becoming free, and escaping from the cause of such conflicts ! 4. Moreover, the apostle has himself clearly enough expressed his judgment on this question in the Epistle to Philemon ; and all the torture to which Meyer subjects his words (see in his *Commentary*) does not avail to show that the apostle did not really and positively claim from Philemon the emancipation of Onesimus, who had become his brother by the common faith : "Knowing that thou wilt do even beyond what I say" (Philem. ver. 21). This passage may certainly be called the first petition in favour of the abolition of slavery. It is not by violent means, like servile wars, it is by the spirit which breathes in such words that Christianity has made and still makes the chains of the slave to fall. And as St. Paul could not contradict himself on this point, we may be assured that his thought was no other than this: "But if therewith (while consenting to live in the state of slavery, enjoying moral liberty) thou mayest become free, take advantage of it."

Vers. 22, 23. "For he that was called in the Lord being a slave, is the Lord's freedman ; likewise [1] he that

[1] T. R. with K L adds και (*also*) after ομοιως.

was called being free is Christ's slave. 23. Ye were bought with a price : become not the slaves of men!"—According to most commentators, ver. 22 is intended to justify the counsel to prefer servitude. Edwards: "A reason why the Christian slave should continue a slave rather than accept liberty." The reasoning in itself would be admissible : "The slave being spiritually free, and the free believer morally a slave, the contrast is neutralized; why make a change of state?"—But this verse may quite as well justify the counsel of ver. 21, as we have understood it; not in the sense that the first proposition of ver. 22 would justify the first counsel of ver. 21, and the second proposition the second. For in this case the second proposition would not answer the purpose, for the Christian slave called to liberty is not in the position of the free Christian who becomes the slave of Christ. It must be borne in mind that the second part of ver. 21 was a restriction arising in connection with the first, a sort of parenthesis; after which Paul returns to the general idea. We must therefore disentangle the thought common to the two propositions of ver. 22, and apply it to the passage as a whole : If in Christ slaves become free, and the free slaves, then neither slavery nor liberty is to be dreaded for the believer! Slavery will not take away from him his inward liberty, for he is Christ's freedman; and liberty will not plunge him into licence, for he has become Christ's slave. The consequence is, that the Christian slave may either remain a slave, or become free, without harm. For, in the latter case, he enters the class of the free who become the Lord's slaves.

The expression ἐν κυρίῳ κληθείς does not signify: called to communion with the Lord, but: called by a call addressed in the Lord.—The gen. κυρίου here is at once that of cause and of possession. The sentence of emancipation was pronounced by the Lord; by it He delivered this spiritual slave from the power and condemnation of sin; thenceforth this freedman belongs to Him as His servant.

Ver. 23. The second person plural which comes in here shows that the apostle is addressing the entire Church without distinction. If some from being slaves have become free, and the others from being free have become slaves, it is because a purchase has been made; this purchase, so far as it is a ransom, has freed the slaves, and, as a purchase price, it has brought the free into servitude.—But how is the warning which follows connected with the mention of the great fact of redemption? Some have thought that Paul meant thereby to prevent the free men of Corinth from selling themselves as slaves for the service of Christ (Michaëlis, Heydenreich). But no trace is found of such conduct, and in any case the transition to so new an idea would be denoted by some particle or other.—Monod compares this saying with a passage of the letter of Ignatius to Polycarp (c. 4), where the former writes of male and female servants: "Let them not desire to be set free at the charge of the common treasury, lest they should be found the slaves of their lust." Paul, he thinks, is reminding Christians thus redeemed that they ought to take care to maintain their independence over-against the Church, or those who have rendered them this service. But how can we bring ourselves to apply to such a purchase the solemn expression, *bought with a price?* comp. vi. 20. Besides, Paul addresses this recommendation, as we have seen, to the whole Church. This last reason equally forbids us to accept the opinion of Chrysostom (*De Virgin.*, c. 41), quoted by Edwards, according to which Paul recommends slaves not to serve *servilely*, but as exercising their spiritual liberty; comp. Col. iii. 23.—Rückert, Hofmann, compare this warning with iii. 21: "Let no man glory in men;" they think that Paul is inviting the Church to shake off the yoke of the party leaders spoken of in the first chapters. Nothing appears in the context which could call forth such a warning here, and how should Paul immediately return from this strange thought to the general rule, ver. 24? Meyer's solution seems to me the most natural. Paul, he thinks, wishes to combat the docility of the Church towards certain agitators who were urging believers, in consequence of their conversion, to change their external situation. Indeed, Meyer rightly observes that unless we assume such a tendency, this whole digression (vers. 17–24) lacks a basis. Perhaps it was above all in regard to questions about slavery and liberty that those men sought to impose their opinions on the other members of the Church. Let the severe saying, iv. 15, be remembered: "Though ye should have ten thousand tutors in Christ . . . !"—The apostle concludes by reproducing in a summary form the general principle already twice stated, vers. 17, 20.

Ver. 24. "Brethren, let every man wherein he was called, therein abide before God."—The principal idea is not that of abiding *before God* in that state; it is abiding *in that state,* and that *before God.* By these last words, Paul reminds his readers of the moral act which has the power of sanctifying and ennobling every external position : the eye fixed on God, *walking* in His presence. This is what preserves the believer from the temptations arising from the situation in which he is ; this is what raises the humblest duties it can impose on him to the supreme dignity of acts of worship. — Hofmann seeks to give to ver. 24 a different meaning from that of vers. 17, 20, by referring the two pronouns ᾧ and τούτῳ to the person of the Lord. But the parallelism with vers. 17, 20 is obvious at a glance ; and the repetition is easily justified by the importance of the principle enunciated.

In fact, this principle has been of incalculable importance in the development of the Church. It is by means of it that Christianity has been able to become a moral power at once sufficiently firm and sufficiently elastic to adapt itself to all human situations, personal, domestic, national, and social. Thereby it is that without revolution it has worked the greatest revolutions, accepting everything to transform everything, submitting to everything to rise above everything, renewing the world from top to bottom while condemning all violent subversion. Whence has the apostle derived this principle in which there meet the most unconquerable faith and the most consummate ability ? "I say unto you by the grace given unto me ;" so Paul expressed himself when opening a series of purely practical prescriptions, Rom. xii. 3. Wisdom from on high did not less direct Paul the pastor than Paul the teacher. And then it is probable that he was not unacquainted with the Master's homely saying: "And she put the leaven into the meal, until the whole was leavened." The Holy Spirit had given him the commentary on this short parable.[1]

VERS. 25–40

In this third part of the chapter, the apostle discusses the question of marriage as it relates to virgins (25–38), adding at the end a word in regard to widows (39, 40). No doubt in the first part of the chapter (vers. 1-9) he was occupied with the formation of the marriage-bond, and it might appear that the question of the marriage of virgins comes under this head. But the grounds which he had made good in this passage, as to celibates, widowers, and widows, did not altogether apply to virgins; and then, according to ancient custom, it was the father who decided the lot of these last. Hence Paul reserved to himself the opportunity of addressing parents on this subject in a separate passage. The advice which he gives, and then develops, is this: Parents, if circumstances allow it, will be right in preferring celibacy for their daughters (vers. 25, 26), and that for these two reasons: the difficulties of the present situation (vers. 27–31); the advantage which will accrue from it to their Christian activity (vers. 32–38).

Vers. 25–31: The present state of things.

[1] Is there not room for surprise that a Christian society can exist, which, while regarding St. Paul as an apostle of the Lord and an organ of the Divine Spirit, has adopted the method of immediately snatching away new converts from the duties of their natural position to launch them upon the world as agents in a work of evangelization? Is not this the antipodes of the principle thrice stated by the apostle?

Ver. 25. "Now concerning virgins, I have no commandment of the Lord; but I give my judgment, as one that hath obtained mercy of the Lord to be faithful."—The form of transition used by the apostle would lead us to suppose that he is replying to a special article of the letter of the Corinthians (comp. ver. 1); questions had certainly been put to him on the subject which he proceeds to treat.—If we compare vers. 27, 28, 29, where the apostle addresses young men, a reason might be found for applying the word παρθένος, *virgin*, with Bengel, to bachelors as well as to spinsters. Rev. xiv. 4 has been quoted for this wide meaning. But the uniform use of the word in classic and sacred literature does not authorize this meaning. In the passage of the Apocalypse it is an adjective, and ought probably to be taken in a moral sense. The entire sequel, vers. 32–38, proves that it is of maidens Paul meant to speak, and that if he says a word about young men, it is only in passing and to show that radically he makes no difference, in what he says here, between the two sexes. The principle which guides him is and remains this: to abide in the position where the Divine call found us.—The expression *commandment of the Lord* cannot denote, as in ver. 10, an order that proceeded from the mouth of Jesus during His earthly life. The form οὐκ ἔχω, *I have not*, would not be suitable in this sense, a commandment of Jesus not being Paul's personal property, but belonging to the whole Church. Paul therefore does not possess, either by way of tradition or of revelation, an order emanating from Jesus on this point.—But, as the Corinthians may desire to know his personal opinion, he does not refuse to communicate it to them. He rests the value of his counsel on the mercy of which he has been the object, a mercy which has made him a man worthy to be believed. The word πιστός, *faithful,* has, as we have seen, iv. 17, two closely connected meanings: one *who believes* firmly, and one *who may be trusted.* The second meaning appears in the context the more natural: "I have no infallible direction, coming from the Lord, to give you. But through the grace shown to me, I find myself in a position to give you a good advice." Comp. ver. 40.

Hence it follows that Paul does not give the counsel immediately to be mentioned in virtue of his apostolic authority, but as a simple Christian. The words are very instructive, as showing with what precision he distinguished apostolical inspiration from Christian inspiration in general, making the former not only the highest degree, but something specifically different from the second. He thus, with a consciousness perfectly assured, traced the limit between what he had directly received by way of revelation, with a view to his *apostolic* teaching, and what he himself deduced from Christian premisses by his own reflections, as any believer may do under the guidance of the Spirit. We thus see what is implied in his view by the title of *apostle,* under the guarantee of which he places the contents of his Epistles. He was not of the mind—as is sought to persuade the Church in our day—that his gospel was only the result of his meditations and researches.—After this preface, he states the advice he has to give.

Ver. 26. "I think therefore that this state is good

for the present distress, seeing that it is good for man so to be."—This verse has been translated in a multitude of ways. As Paul seems to say two things at the same time, Rückert, Meyer, Edwards hold some incorrectness. After dictating the words: "I think this, that it is good because of the present distress," Paul, they say, forgot that he had already expressed the idea: that this is good, and repeated it by mistake, saying, "that it is good for man so to be." This is to hold a strange idea of the way in which Paul composed; and besides, did he not read over his letters before despatching them? Nor would it be possible to understand why in the second proposition he added the word ἀνθρώπῳ, *for man*, and substituted the verb εἶναι for ὑπάρχειν. Reuss holds an explanatory repetition: "My advice is, that this is good because of the difficult times which are coming; that it is good for man so to live." But to what purpose this repetition? and why the two changes which we have indicated? Holsten sees in τοῦτο, *this*, a pronoun representing by anticipation the idea of the second part of the verse: "I think that *this* (τοῦτο), [to wit] that it is good for man so to be, is good on account of the present necessity." Heydenreich and Heinrici take the ὅτι as a pronoun (ὅ τι), which leads to this meaning: "I think this, that [for virgins], on account of the present necessity, *all that is good* for man [to wit] so to be (to remain virgin) is good." The construction proposed by Hofmann surpasses, if possible, even these violences: "I think this: that it is good—because on account of the present necessity, it is good for man—so to be (to remain virgin)." There is, in my view, only one construction admissible, that proposed by de Wette; it is as simple in form as suitable in sense: "I think therefore that this (the state of virginity) is good on account of the present difficulties, seeing that in itself it is good for man so to be." The idea is this: "If, in general, celibacy is a state good for man (ἄνθρωπος, man or woman), now is the time for applying this principle, especially in regard to virgins, on account of the difficulties of the present time."—The pronoun τοῦτο, *this*, is not the object of νομίζω, *I think*, but the subject of the infinitive ὑπάρχειν; it relates to the state of celibacy, the idea of which was contained in the term παρθένων, *virgins*, ver. 25.—The verb καλὸν ὑπάρχειν denotes a goodness in point of fact, while καλὸν εἶναι, in the following proposition, denotes goodness of essence. The difference of expression is explained by the regimen διὰ τὴν ἐνεστῶσαν ἀνάγκην, *on account of the necessity*, of the *present*, or *imminent*, distress; an expression which gives to the καλόν of celibacy the character of suitableness. Hofmann has carried this regimen to the following proposition, beginning with ὅτι, *because*. But the idea of distress belongs rather to the first proposition, which is intended to characterize the present time as particularly inviting to celibacy.—The word ἐνεστώς strictly signifies *imminent* (comp. 2 Thess. ii. 2), or *present* (iii. 22; Rom. viii. 38; Gal. i. 4). The *imminent* tribulation denotes, it is held, the time of distress which is to precede the end of the world (Luke xxi. 25–27), what Jewish theology called *dolores Messiæ*, the crisis of the painful birth-pangs of the Messianic kingdom, the reign of the man of sin (2 Thess. ii.). Such is the meaning held by Meyer, Osiander, Edwards, etc. Others give ἐνεστῶσα the meaning of *present;* so Calvin and Grotius, who apply present distress, — the former to the troubles inseparable from married life; the latter to the sufferings of this earthly life in general. But the phrase *the present distress* is too precise to admit of such vague explanations. While holding the sense of *present,* which is the most common, it seems to me that we must apply the term *necessity,* or *distress,* to the whole state of things between the first and second coming of Christ. In Paul's view the *last times* began with Pentecost. From that date the character of human existence is one of incessant and painful tension, of struggle between the new life, which sprang up with the appearing of Christ, and the life of the old world, which is departing, but which will not pass away till the Lord's return. On the painful character of this whole period, comp. Luke xii. 51: "I am come, not to give peace on earth, but war;" and so xvii. 22. And how much more acute will the crisis be when persecution will emerge on this ground of trouble and suffering! It seems to me that ver. 28 speaks in favour of this explanation. No doubt in using the expression *present distress* to characterize the earthly future of the Church, the apostle had no idea that there could be a time when the world would be outwardly Christianized and Christianity secularized. Like the author of the Apocalypse, he saw the struggle of the two hostile principles going on increasing in intensity till the final crisis. If history has followed another course, and if the war already kindled in the apostolic time has given place to a false peace, this is due in great measure to the weakening of the heavenly virtues of the Church.

As it always is in the human domain, which is that of liberty, the Divine plan has been realized in this respect only in an abnormal way.

Under those conditions which were already difficult at the time when the apostle wrote, and which were to become always more so, the unmarried maiden would have, according to him, a much easier path than the woman burdened with a family. The second proposition adds to the reason drawn from the *present* situation a more general reason, which is no other than the opinion already given on celibacy, vers. 1 and 7ª. The ὅτι, *because*, signifies, " celibacy is preferable at this time for virgins, *because* in general it is preferable for man." The *permanent* (εἶναι) and *general* (ἄνθρωπος) judgment forms the basis of the *present* (ὑπάρχειν) and *particular* (παρθένοι) counsel.—The *so to be* may denote either the state of virginity (τοῦτο) or the state in which man naturally finds himself. The second sense agrees better with the term ἄνθρωπος, which includes the two sexes.

Ver. 26 therefore embraces two propositions, the first of which contains the particular counsel called for by the circumstances, the second the indication of the general preference to be given to celibacy. It is these two propositions which are taken up again and developed in the sequel, the first in vers. 27–31, the second in vers. 32–38.

Vers. 27, 28. "Thou art bound to a wife, seek not to be loosed; thou art loosed from a wife, seek not a wife. 28. But and if thou marry,[1] thou hast not sinned; and if a virgin marry, she hath not sinned; nevertheless such shall have trouble in the flesh; but I

[1] T. R. with K L: γημης; ℵ A: γαμηση; B P: γαμησης.

would spare you."—The apostle would not, however, have ver. 26[a] understood in the sense of a *moral* superiority granted to celibacy. He therefore expressly repeats what he had said in ver. 10 (from a somewhat different standpoint): He who is bound, whether as affianced or as married, ought not, with a view to realizing a higher sanctity, to break the bond. I do not think that there is ground for restricting the application of these first words to the *affianced*, as Hofmann does. —If one were to take the term λέλυσαι, *art thou loosed*, in the strictness of the letter, it would apply only to widowers and those divorced. But the context proves that, as Origen had already understood it, the word here signifies in general: *If thou art free from bond*, and that it refers also to celibates.

Ver. 28 is meant to prevent a misunderstanding to which the second part of ver. 27 might give rise. What Paul says here is not a command; if one act differently he will not sin.—The form ἐὰν καί evidently means, as in vers. 11 and 21, *if therewith*, if nevertheless, and not *though*.—On the two forms γήμῃς and γαμήσῃς, see on ver. 9. Edwards remarks that if we read γαμήσῃς, we have here the two forms in the same verse.—The *flesh* strictly denotes the organ of physical sensibility; but the meaning of the word extends very often to moral sensibility.—The term *trouble*, literally, *tribulation*, must denote the same thing as *the present necessity*, ver. 26, so: the state of permanent conflict in which the Church is with the world till the perfect establishment of the kingdom of God. As long as this state of things shall last, Christian parents who are tender and faithful will have to suffer much for themselves and for their children in a community which is strange to God. The *οἱ τοιοῦτοι* denotes those who marry in spite of this counsel.—There is a sort of paternal solicitude in the words, *but I spare you.* The path of celibacy which he recommends will be that in which they shall have least to suffer. St. Augustine makes a singular mistake in giving these words the meaning: "I spare you the enumeration of the troubles of family life."

But, in all that precedes, Paul has not yet gone to the root of the matter. What is of importance is not: marrying or not marrying; but a habit of soul in keeping with the situation indicated above. And as in vers. 17–24 he had extended his point of view and generalized the question, so as better to justify his counsel to remain in their present state, so in vers. 29–31 he explains, while applying it to various analogous cases, his true view in regard to celibacy and marriage in present circumstances.

Vers. 29–31. "But this I mean, brethren,[1] the time is henceforth limited,[2] that they even that have wives be as though they had none; 30. and they that weep, as though they wept not; and they that rejoice, as though they rejoiced not; and they that buy, as though they possessed not; 31. and they that use this

[1] T. R. here reads *οτι* (*that* or *because that*), with D E F G It. Syr.; the other six Mjj. omit it.

[2] The Mnn. present three principal readings:—

T. R. with E K L: *συνεσταλμενος το λοιπον εστιν ινα* . . . (*the time is limited, as to what remains, that* . . .).

א A B D P: *συνεσταλμενος εστι το λοιπον ινα* . . . (*the time is limited that, as to what remains,* . . .).

F G It. Vulg. Tert.: *συνεσταλμενος εστι, λοιπον εστιν ινα* . . . (*the time is limited; it remains that* . . .).

world,[1] as not abusing it : for the fashion of this world passeth away." — The formula τοῦτο δὲ φημί, which begins ver. 29, does not announce a simple explanation, as a τοῦτο λέγω would do. The term φημί has a certain solemnity : " Now here is my real view, the most essential thing which I have to declare to you." —By the address : *brethren,* he draws near to them as if to gain an entrance into their minds for this decisive thought, with the particular applications they are to draw from it, each for himself. If, with T. R., we should read ὅτι before ὁ καιρός, it would require to be translated by *because,* and τοῦτο referred to what precedes (ver. 28) ; but the following sentence would become extremely heavy, on account of the two conjunctions ὅτι and ἵνα, which follow one another. We must therefore reject ὅτι. The participle συνεσταλμένος (from συστέλλειν, to furl sails, to pack luggage, to reduce into small volume, to shorten a syllable, etc.) may be taken either in the moral sense (straitened, pressed with trouble, 1 Macc. iii. 6 ; 2 Macc. vi. 12), or in the literal sense (reduced to small volume, concentrated, abridged). As the first meaning cannot well apply except to persons, the second is here preferable ; only it must be remarked that Paul does not use the word χρόνος, which denotes time in respect of its duration, but καιρός, time in respect of its character, season, opportunity. The apostle therefore means not that the present epoch will embrace a greater or less number of years, but that the character of the epoch is its being contained between precise limits which do

[1] T. R. reads, with E K L P, τω κοσμω τουτω ; D F G : τον κοσμον τουτον ; ℵ A B : τον κοσμον.

not admit of its being extended indefinitely. These limits are, on the one side, the coming of Christ which took place recently, and on the other, His coming again, which may be expected any hour, and which will be the close of the καιρός. There is therefore no longer anything assured in the present existence of the world; it is profoundly compromised since the coming of Christ, who created thenceforth a higher sphere of existence; hence it follows that human life has no longer a future, except one limited and precarious; comp. Phil. iii. 20: "Our citizenship is in heaven." We are in *the last hour* (ἐσχάτη ὥρα ἐστί, 1 John ii. 18), of which no one knows how long it will last (Mark xiii. 32); for that depends on God, and also in part on the faithfulness of the Church, and on the conduct of the unbelieving world.—Of the three readings which we have given in the note, that of the T. R., supported by three Byz., signifies: "The time is limited as to what remains, that . . ." The reading of the four older Mjj. signifies: "The time is limited, that for the future (τὸ λοιπόν) . . ." That is to say, that the time for the future ought to be otherwise used than it has been in the past. The third, that of F G, signifies: "The time is limited; it remains (it follows therefrom) that . . ." This last ought to be rejected without hesitation; for the expression λοιπὸν ἵνα cannot signify: it follows that. In the Alex. reading we must accept the inversion of the τὸ λοιπόν, and bring it into the proposition of ἵνα. The emphasis put by this construction on τὸ λοιπόν is justified no doubt by the contrast between the remaining future and the past which has already elapsed. But the inversion is harsh, and the first reading, that of the Byz., seems to me preferable. Its meaning is very simple: "The time is limited as to what remains." The time which mankind have yet to pass is limited by the coming of Christ. And so, whereas unbelievers regard the world as sure to last indefinitely, the Christian has always before his eyes the great expected fact, the Parousia; hence there arises in him a wholly new attitude of soul, that which the apostle characterizes in the following words. The: *in order that,* shows that this new attitude of the heart is willed of God as the proper consequence of the character assigned to the present epoch. We must take care not to make the *ἵνα* depend on the verb *φημί*: "*I declare* this *to you in order that* . . ." This inward disposition of believers springs much more naturally from the character of the epoch in which they live, than from Paul's declaration, which is addressed only to some of them. The anticipation of Christ's coming is that which transforms the mode of regarding and treating all earthly positions.—The *καί,* which follows *ἵνα,* should be translated by *even: Even* the married ought in their attitude of soul to return to the state of celibates. By their detachment from the things of this earth, which are about to fail them, and their attachment to Christ, who is coming again, they recover that state of inward independence which they lost by marrying. Externally bound, they become free again as to their moral attitude; comp. the slave, ver. 22[a].

Ver. 30. Here is depicted the spiritual detachment in its application to the various situations of life. As nothing in this world has more than a waiting character, the afflicted believer will not be swayed by his pain; he will say to himself: It is no more worth the trouble! The man who is visited by joy will not be intoxicated by it; he will say to himself: It is but for a moment. He who buys, will not seize and hold the object he has got too keenly (κατέχειν, *to hold firmly*); for he will look upon himself as always ready to give it up. It is not meant that the believer will not rejoice or be afflicted or care for what he has. But, as Edwards well says: "Excess is prevented, not by the diminution of the joy or of the grief, but by the harmony of both. Joy and grief becoming more profound harmonize in a sadness full of joy and a joy full of sadness."

Ver. 31. The phrase *using this world* is a formula in which are embraced marriage, property, commerce, political, scientific, and artistic activity. The believer may use these things, provided it is constantly in a spirit which is master of itself, detached from everything, looking only to Christ.—It is a mistake here to translate the term καταχρῆσθαι in the sense of *abusing;* for there never is for any one a time of abusing. To the notion of the simple χρῆσθαι, *to make use of,* the preposition κατά adds, as in the preceding verb, a shade of tenacity, carnal security, false independence. He who uses the world, in these different domains, while keeping his eye constantly fixed on the future, ought to preserve the same inward calm as one might who had broken with the whole train of earthly affairs. The Alex. read the regimen in the accusative (τὸν κόσμον); this construction is found only in the later Greek, and that with the compound καταχρῆσθαι. —

The last words justify the disposition of detachment which the apostle recommends. They do not express merely the commonplace thought: that visible things are transitory in their nature. Undoubtedly Edwards is right in saying: "Every change proves that the end will come;" but we must not forget that this proposition is connected by γάρ, *for*, with the preceding: "The time is limited." This relation obliges us to apply the παράγει, *passeth away*, to the near coming of the Lord, who will transform the present fashion of the world, that is to say, of external nature and human society. The term τὸ σχῆμα, *the fashion*, the external state of a thing, proves that the world itself will not disappear, but that it will take on a new mode of existence and development; comp. Rom. viii. 19–22 and Matt. xix. 28.

The apostle has just developed the term *the present distress* (ver. 26[a]), and expounded the reason for the preference to be given to celibacy for virgins, taken from present circumstances. He passes to the more general reason stated in ver. 26[b]: "It is good *in itself* for man so to be."

Vers. 32–38: The general suitableness of celibacy.

Vers. 32, 33. "But I would have you without carefulness. He that is unmarried careth for the things that belong to the Lord, [seeking] how he may please[1] the Lord. 33. But he that is married careth for the things that are of the world, [seeking] how he may please[1] his wife."—The subject is no longer merely the exceptional anxieties which the education and care of

[1] T. R. with K L P reads αρεσει (*will please*); all the rest: αρεση (*may please*).

a family may cause parents, in a time dangerous for the Church. Paul has especially in view here the *moral* difficulties which the conjugal relation brings with it at all times. The δέ is the transition from the one of these ideas to the other. The term, ἄγαμος, *unmarried,* includes, as in ver. 8, bachelors and widowers. With the view of illustrating the general truth which he would apply to virgins, the apostle shows first that it applies also to men. The affirmation : *careth for the things of the Lord,* is not absolute. It is not always so, it is true ; but nothing prevents the Christian celibate from acting thus.

Ver. 33. The aorist γαμήσας signifies : *from the time he is married.* The step once taken, what follows is the necessary result. But it is no blame which Paul thereby throws on marriage ; it is a fact which he states to justify the greater *difficulty* a married man experiences in realizing in this state entire fidelity to the Lord. The unmarried man has only one question to put to Himself : how shall I act to please the Lord ? The married man is obliged to take into account another will than that of the Lord and his own, a will which he should consult and which must be gained for his plans. There are, besides, earthly interests to manage ; for they concern the future of her who shares with him the burden of the family. This care is not a sin, otherwise marriage would be a morally defective state ; it is a sacred obligation, a duty at once of delicacy and justice, which the husband contracted by marriage. With the same measure of fidelity, the married man will therefore have a double difficulty to surmount, from which the celibate is exempt, that of getting his wife to accept the moral decisions which he feels bound to take, and that of not sacrificing his Christian walk to the earthly fortune of his family. — These reflections are true, practical, sensible, in accordance with the experience of life, and they do not in the least justify the charge brought against the apostle of degrading marriage. If the married believer comes out of these difficulties victorious, he will not be either more or less holy than the unmarried believer.—All this is only an introduction; in the following verses, the apostle reaches the subject strictly so called; for it is of virgins he is now speaking.

Ver. 34. "[1]The married[2] woman also is divided. The unmarried[3] virgin careth for the things of the Lord, that she may be holy both in body and in spirit; but she that is married careth for the things of the world, [seeking] how she may please[4] her husband."— The text, at the beginning of ver. 34, has been extraordinarily handled and re-handled. This arises, no doubt, from the uncertainty which copyists felt in regard to the verb μεμέρισται, *is divided.* Should it be made the end of ver. 33, or the beginning of ver. 34? On this there depended also in part the question of the καί (*and*) before the verb. The verb may certainly be

[1] The και (*and*) at the beginning of the verse is found in ℵ A B D P Syr^sch. T. R. omits it, with E F G K L It.

[2] The και (*and*) before η γυνη (*the woman*) is omitted by T. R. with D E.

[3] The words η αγαμος (*the unmarried*) are read twice in ℵ A, after η γυνη (*the woman*) and after η παρθενος (*the virgin*); and once only, after η γυνη (*the woman*), in B P, and after η παρθενος (*the virgin*) in D E F G K L It. Syr.

[4] T. R. with K L P: αρεσει; the rest: αρεση.

connected with the preceding sentence; in this case it ought to be preceded by *καί*: "He who is married cares for the things of the world, how he may please his wife; *and he is divided* (in himself)." It will be objected that such an addition destroys the parallelism with ver. 32; but there was no observation to be made on the result of the harmony between the will of the celibate and that of the Lord, whereas it is otherwise in the case of ver. 33. This meaning is that adopted by Neander, Hofmann, Edwards, Lachmann, Westcott, and Hort. Only one cannot help asking why the apostle did not likewise add an analogous reflection when concluding the case of the married woman in ver. 34. The parallelism between the two members of the sentence is rigorous, and seemed to demand it. It is better, therefore, to join the verb *μεμέρισται* (with or without the *καί*) to ver. 34. But in this case, what is the subject of the verb *is divided?* And how are we to read and punctuate the following words? One reading gives the epithet *ἡ ἄγαμος*, *unmarried, twice*, first after the word *ἡ γυνή*, *the woman*, and then after the word *ἡ παρθένος*, *the virgin;* another, only after the first of these words; a third, only after the second. Not only does the majority of the documents support this third reading; but its representatives are found in the three families of Mjj., and the two oldest versions testify in its favour, so that we ought to receive it as the most probable. The true text seems to us to be: *Μεμέρισται καὶ ἡ γυνὴ [καὶ] ἡ παρθένος ἡ ἄγαμος μεριμνᾷ* . . . But the question is, how far we are to extend the subject of *μεμέρισται*, *is divided.* Many think that the subject is double: *Both the wife and the virgin are divided.* Then the new sentence would begin with ἡ ἄγαμος, *the unmarried.* We should require to take the verb *is divided* in the sense of *is different* (so Chrysostom, Luther, Mosheim, etc.), or, what comes to nearly the same thing, in the sense of *going in opposite directions* (Theodoret, Meyer, Beet): "There is a difference between the wife and the unmarried woman." But after the idea of a division of the same person by opposite cares had been so forcibly advanced in ver. 33, it is unnatural to give to the verb μερίζεσθαι, *to be divided,* the sense of *to differ,* all the more that the verb is in the singular, and that, notwithstanding all Meyer's subtle explanations, one would expect the plural (μερίζονται), as is shown by the paraphrase of Theodoret, who instinctively falls into the plural (μεμερισμέναι εἰσὶ ταῖς σπουδαῖς). This verb in the singular can only apply to one whole divided into several parts (comp. i. 13; Mark iii. 25, 26, etc.). Although, then, the Latin and Syriac versions, and almost all the Latin Fathers give this meaning, it appears to me difficult to accept it.—There remains, as it seems to me, only one possible explanation: that which assigns to μεμέρισται as its subject the following term only: *the woman,* ἡ γυνή, reading the καί: *The woman also is divided* (evidently *the married woman*). Ver. 33 had just shown the married man divided within himself by different anxieties. It is absolutely the same with the married woman, adds the apostle; and he establishes it in the sequel of the verse, presenting first by way of contrast the description of the virgin who consents to remain so. The beginning of the following proposition is therefore ἡ παρθένος, *the virgin.* The καί before this word ought either to be understood in the sense of *also* (like the bachelor, ver. 17), or rejected. It may easily have been added under the influence of the widespread interpretation which made the following substantive a second subject of μεμέρισται.—The apostle forcibly brings out the contrast between the married woman who is inwardly divided, and the virgin whose happy inward harmony the apostle proceeds to point out. The apposition ἡ ἄγαμος, *the unmarried*, is not a pleonasm; it signifies: "the virgin *who remains* unmarried." She takes counsel only of the will of the Lord, without being obliged to put herself at one with the will of a human master; she has consequently only one perfectly simple aim to pursue, that which is indicated by the ἵνα, *in order that*, which follows. The word ἁγία, *holy*, is equivalent here to the term *consecrated*, that is to say, entirely devoted in her body and spirit to the service of the Lord. As to the words: *in her body*, we must compare ver. 4, where it is said of the married woman that she has not power over her own body. As to *the spirit*, compare what follows, where it is said of the married woman that she is under obligation to take account of her husband's will, as well as of earthly necessities. It is an ideal full of nobleness and purity which floats before the eyes of the apostle, when he thus describes the life of the Christian virgin being able to give herself up, without the least distraction, to the task which the Lord assigns her. He will give scope to this impression still more fully in ver. 35. In the last proposition of the verse, the apostle returns to the other alternative, that of marriage, and develops the first words of the verse: *The woman is divided.* The aor. γαμήσασα signifies: from the moment when she did the act of marrying. In English we should rather join these two propositions by a conjunction: "While the virgin cares for . . . the married woman cares for . . ."

Ver. 35. "And this I speak for your own profit, not that I may cast a snare upon you, but for that which is comely, and that ye may attend upon[1] the Lord without distraction."—Paul feels the need of defending himself from the charge which might be brought against him of giving scope to an individual preference, and of letting his private position influence his directions as an apostle. In all that he has just said, he has had in view nothing but the real advantage of those who have consulted him: the simplest and easiest possible consecration of their whole life to the Lord, without any concern to divert them from it.—The word βρόχος denotes the noose thrown in the chase to capture game. Some have thought that Paul meant that while thus recommending celibacy, he did not seek to make them fall into impurity. But would he have needed to set aside such a suspicion? The figure of *throwing a net over them* contains a wholly different idea: "I do not claim to make slaves of you, to hamper your liberty by forcing you to live to my taste, and according to my personal sympathies; but this is what I have in view." And he then expounds the ideal of Christian celibacy in the elevated and pure light in which he contemplates it, that is to say, as a state of supreme comeliness through the consecration

[1] T. R. with K reads: ευπροσεδρον; L: προσεδρον; the rest: ευπαρεδρον.

of body and spirit to the Lord.—*Τὸ εὔσχημον* denotes perfect fitness. Natural innocence raised to heavenly saintship through union with Christ, such, in the eyes of the apostle, is the incomparable adornment of the virgin. This first term refers to state; the second rather to action. The reading by far most widely spread is *εὐπάρεδρον*, a term compounded of three words: *ἕζομαι, I seat myself; παρά, by the side of,* and *εὖ, well, honourably.* The word therefore calls up the figure of a person nobly seated at the Lord's side. But two Byz. documents read,—the one *εὐπρόσεδρον,* the other *πρόσεδρον,* an expression if possible still more beautiful, the preposition *πρός* adding to the idea of *παρά, beside,* that of *being turned toward* (John i. 1): the state, that is, of a person seated beside the Lord, with his eye turned to Him. Of the two adjectives *πάρεδρος* and *πρόσεδρος,* the most frequently used is *πάρεδρος*; it is translated by assessor, colleague, disciple, etc. The word *πρόσεδρος* scarcely figures in Greek literature; a reason for giving it the preference, all the more that to the idea of assiduity it adds a notion of tenderness which is foreign to the other. Let us add that in Hellenistic Greek, which must have been especially familiar to the apostle, the use of the word *προσεδρία* is established to denote assiduity (3 Macc. iv. 15). These reasons will have some weight with those who think that in view of the different texts they ought to preserve their liberty of judgment.—The neuter of the two adjectives may be regarded as the equivalent of the verb in the infinitive (with the article); only by the form which the apostle chooses the act becomes in a sense a quality inherent in the subject.—The *εὖ, well,* in the two adjectives, expresses the propriety, the dignity, the moral beauty of this position, and of the activity of the Christian virgin; here is the excellence, the *καλόν*, of celibacy, the utility, the *συμφέρον* of which has been described in vers. 34, 35. Finally, the adverb so full of gravity, *ἀπερισπάστως*, literally, without dragging in different directions, without distractions, closes this development with a last word which sums it up in its entirety; comp. the *ἕως ἄρτι*, iv. 13. The term reminds us of the double solicitude which divides the heart of the married woman: on the one side, concern for the will of the Lord; on the other, concern about the will of her husband and the exigencies of the world.

It is difficult to think that Paul, in writing these exquisite lines on the position of the young Christian, had not in view the picture drawn, Luke x. 39–42, of Mary of Bethany seated at the Saviour's feet and hearing His words. As has been pointed out, the *μεριμνᾷ* of Paul (ver. 34) corresponds to the *μεριμνᾷς* of Luke, the *εὐπρόσεδρον* to the *παρακαθίσασα*, and the *ἀπερισπάστως* to the *περιεσπᾶτο* and the *τυρβάζῃ*.

The apostle has concluded the exposition of his reasons. The *present* excellence of celibacy for the virgin arises from the greater *facility* of life which it will procure for her; and to this advantage another is added, which belongs to the state of celibacy *in general:* the perfect *simplicity* of the task for which the unmarried Christian lives.

From these considerations Paul finally draws the practical conclusion. He puts two cases, as he had done in regard to married Christians, vers. 12, 15, and gives his decision as to the one (ver. 36), and as to the other (ver. 37); after which he sums up his judgment (ver. 38).

The first case:

Ver. 36. "But if any man think that he behaveth himself uncomely toward his virgin, if she pass the flower of her age, and need so require, let him do what he will; he sinneth not; let them marry."[1]—Paul introduces his advice by δέ, *but*, because this counsel is in contrast to the thought expressed, ver 35. The antithesis of ἀσχημονεῖν to τὸ εὔσχημον is manifest.—The verb ἀσχημονεῖν may have the active or passive sense: *to behave uncomely toward any one*, or: *to be the object of unsuitable treatment.* Of these two meanings the first only agrees with the preposition ἐπί which follows, and which indicates the object of the action; comp. also xiii. 5. But it might be a question whether the verb should not be taken here in an impersonal sense: "that there is no uncomeliness for his virgin." I know no example of this usage; but the *if she pass the age*, which has embarrassed Hofmann, would fall in better with this meaning than with the active sense. The proposition ἐὰν ᾖ would then be the logical subject of ἀσχημονεῖν. Several commentators (de Wette, Meyer, Edwards even) think that the dishonour of which Paul speaks is that which the virgin contracts by allowing herself to be drawn into evil. But the apostle's thought is far removed from such a supposition; and he would have expressed it by saying: "if any one *fears*," and not: "if any one *thinks*." He is speaking solely of that sort of shame which attached to the position of spinster, still more among the ancients than among us;

[1] D F G: γαμειτω (*let her marry*).

comp. Ps. lxxviii. 63, and a passage quoted by Heinrici (p. 213).[1]—With the words: "If she pass the flower of her age" (ὑπέρακμος), we must, of course, understand without marrying.[2]—The meaning of the word οὕτως, *thus, so,* is explained by the beginning of the verse and by the contrast to ver. 26; it is the state of marriage, whereas in ver. 26 the context would show that it was the state of celibacy. Hofmann, after Theophylact, makes the proposition καὶ οὕτως the principal one: "If any one . . ., well! so it must be." But there would be a glaring tautology with the three following propositions, and there would be no ground for the καί. The καί here signifies, *and consequently.* The ὀφείλει, *it must be,* follows first from the father's judgment, determined by the general prejudice, and next from the circumstances (the desire of the daughter and mother) which press in favour of a consent, which nothing but the firmly opposed conviction of the father could prevent. Under these conditions, things *must* take their course.—In what follows the apostle means: "He might, no doubt, have done better for his child's happiness; but he has not made himself liable to any reproach." Holsten thinks that the subject of ἁμαρτάνει is the virgin; but it is the father who is regarded as acting throughout the whole passage.—The subject of γαμείτωσαν, *let them marry,* is, quite naturally, the virgin and the young man who asks her in marriage.

[1] *Phalaridis epist.*, p. 130: "For it is regarded by men as very shameful that a daughter remain at home beyond the time fixed by nature."

[2] Holsten gives this word a strange and unexampled meaning; he sees in it the idea of an over-excited sensibility (υπερ, in Paul's writings). Hence for the father the οφειλειν! This meaning is the less necessary because the father was already inclined to give his consent.

For there is no reason to suppose that the apostle is alluding, as Rückert has thought, to a definite couple, about whom the Corinthians had addressed a question to him.

The second case:

Ver. 37. "Nevertheless, he that standeth stedfast in his heart, having no necessity, but hath power over his own will, and hath so decreed in his own[1] heart that[2] he will keep his virgin, doeth[3] well."—This long sentence, loaded with incidental propositions, fully represents all the turnings which the father's original wish will have to take in order to reach at length a definite conclusion. This whole domestic drama has for its point of departure a *firm conviction*, already formed in the father's mind, that celibacy is preferable to marriage for his child; ἕστηκεν ἑδραῖος, *he has become and remains firm.* The participle μὴ ἔχων ἀνάγκην, *not underlying constraint*, qualifies the finite verb ἕστηκεν; it therefore signifies, the father has become and remains firm because there is nothing to hamper his liberty, neither the fear of opinion nor the character and indomitable will of the virgin, nor too ardent a wish on the part of the mother. The second finite verb ἔχει is not parallel to the μὴ ἔχειν; the construction, which has nothing irregular, gives it as its subject simply the ὅς, the subject of the first verb. After measuring himself with all the difficulties of the situation, and finding none of them insurmountable, the father remains *master of his own*

[1] ℵ B P: ιδια καρδια (*his own heart*); T. R. with the others: καρδια αυτου (*his heart*).

[2] ℵ A B P omit the του before τηρειν.

[3] ℵ A B: ποιησει (*will do*); T. R. with the other Mjj. It. Syr.: ποιει (*doeth*).

deliberate will, and may thus—here is the third verb —at length *take the* final *resolution* henceforth to refuse every offer for his daughter. These long circumlocutions do not at all suppose in him an arbitrary will which takes account of nothing but itself. On the contrary, they imply the fact that before taking the final decision, everything has been heard, examined, weighed. — The art. τοῦ before τηρεῖν is omitted in the Alex. reading. It presents a difficulty, which speaks in favour of its authenticity, as Meyer acknowledges. For the rest, if we take the word τηρεῖν, *to keep,* in its true sense, the difficulty vanishes, and the τοῦ, which expresses an *aim,* finds an explanation. In fact, the verb *to keep* does not signify, to maintain his daughter as a virgin (making παρθένον an attribute), but *to keep* her *for* the end to which she is consecrated (the service of Christ). Hence it follows that the act τηρεῖν is not an explanatory apposition to τοῦτο, *this,* which was clear enough of itself, but a definition of the end: "and who has decided *this* in his heart (not to marry his daughter), *with a view to* keeping her."— The words τὴν ἑαυτοῦ παρθένον, literally, "*the* virgin belonging to himself," *the object* of τηρεῖν (see ver. 36), express the feeling of solicitude which guides this father: "the cherished being who has been providentially confided to him."

The principal sentence, which consists of only two words, contrasts by its brevity with the whole series of parentheses which have preceded. It is the simple fact in which all the anterior deliberations issue. — Must we read with the Alex. ποιήσει, *will do,* or, with the other Mjj. and the two ancient versions, *Itala* and

Peschito, ποιεῖ, *doeth?* Meyer himself abandons the Alex. reading, and rightly. The present agrees better with the parallel term οὐχ ἁμαρτάνει, *sinneth not*, of ver. 36. The future has probably been imported here from the following verse, where it has rather fewer authorities against it and more internal probability.—The apostle closes this discussion by the brief and striking summing up of his view:

Ver. 38. "So then he that giveth in marriage[1] doeth[2] well, but[3] he that giveth not in marriage[4] will do[5] better."—We again find here one of those ὥστε, *so that*, with which Paul, in this Epistle, loves to formulate his final judgment on a question which he has finished treating.—There is in Greek, before the words *he that giveth in marriage*, καί, *both*, which serves to co-ordinate the subjects of the two parallel propositions: "both . . . and . . ." This particle was suggested to Paul, on beginning his sentence, by his feeling of the equality of the two subjects in their *doing well*, their καλῶς ποιεῖν. But as he proceeds in the expression of his thought, the idea of equality gives place to that of superiority in the second father, and he substitutes at the head of the second proposition, as we have it in the received reading, the δέ, *but*, which expresses a contrast or a gradation, for the καί, *and*, which was in his original intention. It is easy to see how the reading of the Byz., notwithstanding its apparent

[1] T. R. with L P: εκγαμιζων; all the rest: γαμιζων.—Besides, T. R. with K L omits την παρθενον εαυτου (*his virgin*).

[2] B: ποιησει (*will do*), instead of ποιει (*doeth*).

[3] T. R. with K L P: ο δε (*but he . . .*); all the rest: και ο (*and he . . .*).

[4] T. R. with K L P: εκγαμιζων; all the rest: γαμιζων.

[5] א A B: ποιησει (*will do*); T. R. with the other Mjj. It.: ποιει (*doeth*).

incorrectness, corresponds better with the movement of the apostle's thought than the Alex. and Greco-Latin reading.—There is room for hesitation between the received reading, *ἐκγαμίζων*, and the Alex. reading, *γαμίζων*. But there can be little doubt that the words *τὴν ἑαυτοῦ παρθένον* (א A) or *τὴν παρθένον ἑαυτοῦ* (B D), *his virgin*, which are omitted by the T. R., are a gloss. It was easy to add them to fill in the ellipsis of the object, but there was not the slightest reason for rejecting them, if they had existed in the text. Meyer therefore rightly judges that here again the Alex. text is corrupt. There is thus room for supposing that *ἐκγαμίζων* is the true reading. In any case, it better expresses the feeling of self-deprivation on the part of the father.—The reading of the *Vatic.* alone, *ποιήσει*, *will do*, in the first proposition, is certainly a mistake. On the other hand, the future may well be held to be the true reading in the second proposition, since two other Alex. here agree with the *Vatic.* It was, no doubt, to complete the parallelism that the future was introduced into this MS. in the preceding member of the sentence, and even by some into ver. 37. The present was preferable in ver. 37, which contained a general maxim. But here there is something prophetic, and consequently encouraging, in the future: "This father will see that he has taken the better course."

This *well* and *better* sum up the whole chapter. The *well* proves that in the eyes of Paul there is neither defilement nor even inferiority of holiness in marriage, and that the *better* is uttered by him from the prudential point of view, either as to the sufferings avoided or as to the more complete personal liberty for the service of Christ. St. Paul could speak of this position from experience. What would have become of his ministry among the Gentiles on the day when he should have exchanged his independence as a celibate for the duties and troubles of family life? It may be objected, no doubt, that if Paul's principle became a generally observed maxim, the existence of the race would be compromised. But the apostle knew well that Christians will always be a minority in human society, and that among Christians themselves there will not be more than a minority possessing the special gift of which he spoke in ver. 7.

Vers. 39, 40 : widows.

It has been asked why Paul returns to widows, after having already given in vers. 8 and 9 the direction which concerns them. Reuss supposes that Paul forgot what he had said in these verses, or that he judged it suitable to inculcate it anew. But in the verses quoted, Paul had only spoken of widows jointly with celibates and widowers. Now their social position was so far different from that of the latter, that he might judge it necessary to add a special explanation regarding them. According to ancient ideas, there was no doubt as to the legitimacy of a second marriage for widowers; but it was otherwise with widows. It is known how much perseverance in widowhood was honoured among the Jews; comp. Luke ii. 36 and 37; from this to the condemnation of a second marriage was not far. And we also know that among the heathen a sort of contempt was expressed for the *mulier multarum nuptiarum,* and that they went the length of inscribing this title of honour on the tombstone of a woman: *univira.*[1] In the second century of the Church we hear even Athenagoras call a second marriage, whether of man or woman, a decent adultery. Probably, therefore, among the questions put to the apostle in regard to marriage, there was one which bore on this particular point. The general answer given (vers. 8, 9) required, therefore, to be more specialized and confirmed; and this answer being only a particular application of all that he had just expounded in regard to virgins, could not be placed elsewhere than here. The only difference on this point between virgins and widows is, that in the case of widows everything is referred to their own wish, without any more question of the father's.

Vers. 39, 40. "A wife is bound[2] as long as her husband liveth; but if[3] her husband be dead, she is at liberty to be married to whom she will, only in the Lord. 40. But she is happier if she abide as she is, after my judgment. Now[4] I think that I also have the Spirit of God."—*Γυνή,* without article: a wife in opposition to a virgin,—*Is bound:* to her husband, as long as he liveth. The regimen *νόμῳ, by the law,* has no doubt been borrowed from Rom. vii. 2.—Paul limits the liberty which he concedes to the widow by the restriction, *only in the Lord.* In this context the meaning of the words can only be: on the basis of communion with Christ, consequently with a member of the Christian society. This is the meaning now

[1] See Heinrici, p. 214.

[2] T. R. reads, with E F G L P Syr.: νομω (*by the law*); this word is omitted in ℵ A B D Fa.

[3] F G L add και after εαν δε.

[4] Instead of δε (*now*), B reads γαρ (*for*).

generally held. The words would be superfluous, if we made them signify, with Chrysostom, Calvin, and others: honourably and piously. Reuss objects to the meaning, "with a Christian," that the same reservation should have been made also in the case of virgins. But in regard to the latter Paul had not said: *to whom she will.* For in that case there was the paternal will which watched over their lot.

Ver. 40. By the word *happier* the apostle sums up the two reasons, the one general, the other particular, whereby from ver. 25 he had justified his preference given to celibacy for the Christian virgin. There is therefore no question of a superior holiness in this world, or a more glorious position in the next, attributed to this state.—The apostle on this point does not arrogate more to himself than a *view*, an *advice*, the value of which every one can appraise at his pleasure. It is evident how far he was removed from that exaltation which makes fanatics take all their ideas for revelations. Nevertheless he certainly claims an inspiration, such as that which all Christians share, and consequently he traces to the direction of the Divine Spirit the advice which he has just expressed. But we must beware, as we have already said, ver. 10, of concluding from this, with several (comp. in particular Reuss, p. 197), that he did not claim, besides this, revelations of a wholly special kind, going beyond what was granted to the Church in general. In other cases he is careful to affirm, in regard to directions which he gives, that they proceed *from the Lord;* comp. xiv. 37, and also the expression vii. 17. If he thus expresses himself in connection with simple directions about public worship or Christian practice, how much more conscious was he of being the organ of a Divine revelation of a wholly personal kind when the matter in question was the very essence of his religious teaching, *his gospel!* We are led, therefore, to distinguish here three degrees of authority,—1. The direct commands *of the Lord*, which He gave during His sojourn on the earth, and which Paul merely quotes without discussing their grounds (ver. 10). 2. The *apostolic* commands of the apostle, which are imposed on Churches subject to his jurisdiction, and which he gives them as the organ of a higher illumination attached to his special mission. As to these he is careful to expound their reasons, being unwilling to ask his brethren to give a *blind* obedience (vers. 12–17); comp. x. 15. 3. The directions which he gives as a *simple Christian*, which he himself declares to be purely optional, and which he leaves to the judgment of every believer (ver. 25). Far from confounding these different degrees, and assimilating, for example, the second with the third, we should recognise and admire the precision with which the apostle distinguished them and could draw the practical consequences of the distinction.—The word δοκῶ, *I think*, is not in the least, as Chrysostom and others have thought, a modest way of affirming his inspiration. It is evidently, especially if account be taken of the κἀγώ, *I also*, an ironical expression: "Now I hope, however, even if my apostolical authority is disputed among you, that you will not deny to me the possession of the Divine Spirit, such as you recognise in all Christians, and specially in the numerous spiritual guides to whom you give your confidence" (iv. 15).

There are few chapters of the apostle which have drawn down on him such severe judgments.

In connection with the passage vers. 29–31, it has been asserted that his morality itself was "the plaything of a shortsighted Christology." What we have found in the passage are practical directions in which St. Paul takes account of the relation between the world and the Church on to the Parousia, a relation which may in the course of time be more or less strained, but which in any case renders it always difficult for Christian spouses to educate and guide a family. What pious parents have not had painful experience of the fact? In truth, the apostle did not foresee the armistice which would be established for a time between the two hostile societies; but the conflict between the opposing principles which animate them has never ceased, and, in proportion as the last times approach, it will again become more and more what it was in apostolic times. Paul's ethics do not therefore depend on a chronological error; they rest on the just appreciation of the Church's position in the world down to the coming of the Lord.

It is objected to this same passage that every believer is placed in it face to face with the Parousia, as if this event were to terminate his own life. But, in speaking thus, Paul only does what the Lord Himself did. Jesus very expressly set aside the idea of the nearness of His return (Matt. xxv. 5; Mark xiii. 35; Luke xii. 45, xiii. 18–21, xxi. 24; Matt. xxiv. 14; comp.

Mark xiii. 32); and yet this is how He speaks to His disciples (Luke xii. 36): "Be ye like men looking for their lord, when he shall return from the wedding, that when he cometh and knocketh, they may open to him immediately." This is because, in fact, death is to every believer a personal and anticipated Parousia. The saying of Jesus is therefore for all on to the last day a moral truth, but this truth is only relative, till the promise be accomplished in its strict sense to the last generation. So it is with the sayings of Paul.

Again, it has been alleged that Paul here taught the religious and moral superiority of celibacy, and while some have praised him for so doing, others have sharply reprimanded him.[1] His accusers charge him with nothing less than putting himself in manifest contradiction to the saying of Jesus, which he quotes himself, and to God;[2] and what is more astonishing is, that they claim to be thereby doing no violence to his apostolic infallibility. Indeed, does not Paul himself declare that he is here speaking as a simple Christian, not as an organ of Divine revelation?—But is it credible that Paul, an intelligent man, should not have noticed the contradictions between his advice and the declarations of God and of Jesus Christ, while the author of the writing quoted discerned them so easily? Or that Paul, having seen these contradictions, should

[1] In particular Mme de Gasparin in her work on *Les Corporations Monastiques*.

[2] The work quoted, ii. p. 422: "The Lord declares: It is not good for man to be alone! Paul declares: It is good for man not to marry! Paul says: I command them, yet not I, *but the Lord:* Let the woman not depart (ver. 10)! And scarcely has he traced these infallible sayings, when, of his own authority, he overturns them: Let her depart (ver. 15)!"

have audaciously faced them, and that without even attempting to say a word to resolve them? The fact is, that all that the author writes on this subject proceeds on the erroneous opinion, that Paul ascribes a superiority in *holiness* to celibacy. This is what he does not do for an instant, as we have seen, not even in the passage vers. 32–34.

Sabatier, in *l'Apôtre Paul*, p. 142, has reproduced, as Reuss and Scherer had done, the judgment of Baur, according to which Paul had formed at this period a gross idea of the conjugal bond. "In the Epistles of the captivity," says he, "we shall see St. Paul reaching a broader appreciation of marriage and of domestic life." We shall set over against this judgment the views of a very independent-minded German critic, Heinrici, who thus expresses himself (p. 136): "We have here (ver. 14) the proof that the apostle recognises the *moral character* of marriage and of its relation to the kingdom of God." If with this verse we join ver. 16 and xi. 3, it will be seen which of the two judgments is based on the facts. *To save, to sanctify*, such is certainly the higher end of the marriage union from the Christian point of view, according to the author of the Epistles to the Corinthians.

6

The Use of Meats offered to Idols, and Participation in the Sacrificial Feasts (8:1-10:33)

The apostle passes to a new subject, which, like the preceding, seems to be suggested to him by the letter of the Corinthians, and belongs to the domain of Christian liberty. The believers of Corinth and the other Greek cities found themselves in a difficult position in regard to the heathen society around them. On the one hand, they could not absolutely give up their family and friendly relations; the interests of the gospel did not allow them to do so. On the other hand, these relations were full of temptations and might easily draw them into unfaithfulnesses, which would make them the scandal of the Church and the derision of the heathen. Among the most thorny points in this order of questions were invitations to take part in idolatrous banquets. The centre of ancient worships was the sacrifice; it was in this religious act that all the important events of domestic and social life culminated. As in Judaism (comp. Deut. xxvii. 7, the peace-offerings), these sacrifices were followed by a feast. All that remained of the victim's flesh, after the legs, enclosed in fat, and the entrails had been burned on the altar (see Edwards), and after the priest had received his portion, came back to the family which offered the sacrifice, and these consecrated meats were eaten either in the apartments or sacred wood belonging to the temple, or in the worshipper's house; sometimes, also, they were sold in the market. And as the sacrifice usually took place in connection with some joyful circumstance, relatives and friends were invited to the feast, among whom it might easily happen that there were Christians. So also, when those meats were sold in the market, a Christian might find himself exposed to the eating of them either at his own house or that of others.

Now various questions might be raised on this subject. And first of all, Is it allowable for a Christian to be present at a feast offered in the temple of an idol? Some, in the name of Christian liberty, answered: Yes! They boldly took advantage of the adage: All things are lawful for me (vi. 12, x. 23). Others said: No! for in such a region one subjects himself to the danger of malign and even diabolical influences. The scruples of the more timorous went further: Even in a private house, even in one's own house, is it not dangerous to eat of that meat which has figured on the idol's altar? Has it not contracted a defilement which may contaminate him who eats it? Not at all, answered others. For the gods of the heathen are only imaginary beings; meat offered on their altar is neither more nor less than ordinary meat.

The latter were certainly of the number of those who, at Corinth, called themselves Paul's disciples. Must we thence conclude, with Ewald and others, that the former were solely Christians of Jewish origin, who styled themselves Peter's disciples? There is nothing to prove this. It is even somewhat difficult to maintain, as we shall see, in view of certain passages of chap. viii., that these sticklers were mainly Christians of Jewish origin. Several commentators, last among them Holsten, rather regard those timid Christians, and rightly I think, as believers of Gentile origin, who could not free themselves all at once and completely from the idea in which they had lived from infancy, that of the reality and power of the divinities which they had worshipped. They might be confirmed in this view by the Jewish opinion, of which traces are found still later in the Church, that idols represented evil spirits. As to Jewish Christians, the passage Rom. xiv. shows that in any case we ought not to exclude them wholly. These were men whom the gospel had only as yet half freed from their national prejudices, particularly from that which held the heathen deities to be so many diabolical personalities.

The solution of these questions bristled with difficulties. The one party held strongly to their liberty, the other not less seriously to their scruples. The apostle must avoid favouring either superstition in the latter or libertinism in the former. He needed all his practical wisdom and all his love to trace a line of conduct on this subject which would be clear and fitted to unite hearts, instead of dividing them.

It has been asked why he did not here simply apply the decree of the Council of Jerusalem (Acts xv.), which called on the Gentile believers of Syria and Cilicia to give up the use of meats offered to idols, out of regard to the repugnance of Jewish Christians. And some have even gone the length of alleging the apostle's silence as an argument against the historical reality of the decree. But (1) this decree, from its very nature, could only have a temporary value, and it soon came out at Antioch, in connection with Peter's sojourn (Gal. ii.), what practical difficulties stood in the way of its application. (2) At the time and in the circumstances in which Paul had accepted it, this apostle did not yet hold his normal position in the Church. His apostolical authority had just been recognised with difficulty by the apostles. In Syria and Cilicia he was not yet on his own domain, for it was not he who had founded the Church there. But it was now entirely different in Greece; and it would have been to derogate from his apostolical position, as well as from his evangelical spirituality, to resolve a question of Christian life by means of an external decree like an article of law. It was from the spirit of the gospel that, in virtue of his apostolical authority and wisdom, he must derive the decision which the Church needed. (3) It was the more important for Paul to act thus because he had above all at heart to form the conscience of the Corinthians themselves, and to educe spontaneously from it the view of the course to be followed: "I speak unto you as unto wise men; judge yourselves what I say" (x. 15). It is precisely because of this method followed by the apostle that the discussion contained in these three chapters may still be so useful to us, though referring to wholly different circumstances. Paul on this occasion ascends to the first principles of Christian conduct, and we have only to gather them up to apply them to our own circumstances. (4) Finally, this subject presented a host of complications which could not be resolved by the summary decree of Acts xv., and which demanded a detailed examination.

The following is the order adopted by the apostle: He first treats the question by putting himself at the viewpoint of love. A Christian ought not to ask: What suits me best? but: What will most surely contribute to the salvation of my brethren? (viii. 1–ix. 22). Then the apostle passes to a second consideration: that of the salvation of the man himself who is called to act. He must take care while using his liberty not only not to destroy others, but also not to destroy himself (ix. 23–x. 22). Finally, he concludes by recapitulating the whole discussion, and laying down some practical rules in regard to the different particular cases which might present themselves (vers. 23–33).

A. The Question considered from the Viewpoint of our Neighbour's Salvation (8:1-9:22)

The apostle proves that if there is a knowledge which all equally possess (vers. 1–6), there remains a difference of degree which imposes duties on one class relatively to others (vers. 7–13); then he shows by his own example how such obligations ought to be discharged (ix. 1–22).

1. *The knowledge common to all* (vers. 1-6)

Vers. 1–4. "Now, as touching things offered to idols, we know that we all have knowledge,—knowledge puffeth up, but love edifieth. 2. If[1] any man think that he knoweth[2] anything, he knoweth[3] nothing

[1] א A B P here omit the δε (*but* or *then*), which T. R. reads with all the rest.

[2] T. R. reads, with K L, ειδεναι (*savoir*, *to know* a fact), instead of εγνωκεναι (*connaître*, *to know* a person or thing), which is the readingof all the rest.

[3] T. R. with E K L: εγνωκε; all the rest: εγνω. The latter omit ουδεν (*nothing*), which is added by T. R. with the same three.

yet[1] as he ought to know. 3. But if any man love God, the same is known of Him — 4. as concerning therefore the eating of those things that are offered in sacrifice to idols, we know that an idol is nothing in the world, and that there is no God[2] but one."—We might take the preposition περί, *on the subject of*, with its regimen as a sort of title: "As to what concerns consecrated meats. . . ." In that case we must understand: "This is what I have to say to you;" comp. vii. 1. But we might also make this preposition depend on the verb οἴδαμεν, *we know*, or finally, on the expression γνῶσιν ἔχομεν, *we have knowledge;* in this sense: "We know that on the subject of meats offered in sacrifice we all have knowledge." In itself this last meaning might be suitable; but in ver. 4, where the sentence is taken up again (after an interruption), the words: *we have knowledge*, are omitted, and the περί, *on the subject of*, can only be explained there, and consequently also in ver. 1, in one of the two first meanings. The first construction is likewise set aside by ver. 4, where the περί can only depend on the verb which follows it, οἴδαμεν, *we know*. We are thus perforce brought to the second construction: "On the subject of meats . . . we know."—After such a verb as *we know*, it is more natural to give ὅτι the meaning of *that*, than the meaning of *because*. This sense is confirmed by ver. 4, where it is evidently the only one possible.—Several (Flatt, etc.) have supposed that these first words: *On the subject of . . . we know that . . .*,

[1] ℵ A B P: ουπω (*not yet*), instead of ουδεπω (*not even yet*), the reading of T. R. with the rest.

[2] T. R. with K L Syr. here adds ετερος (*other* god).

were taken word for word by the apostle from the letter of the Corinthians. The most advanced members of the Church, they hold, expressed themselves thus: "We know that every one is sufficiently enlightened on this subject, and consequently we are perfectly free to use our liberty in the matter." Paul afterwards shows (ver. 7), they continue, that this affirmation is far from being exact. But, if it were so, we must also ascribe to the Corinthians vers. 4–6, which are a continuation of the sentence begun at ver. 1; now it is evident that it is Paul who speaks in these verses. The subject of *we know* is therefore, first of all, Paul and Sosthenes, who address the letter, but at the same time the Corinthians, whom the authors include with them in the same category. Perhaps the Corinthians had written something similar to these opening words; and Paul chooses to emphasize it as his own affirmation: "Yes, undoubtedly, we know, as you love to repeat that . . . ;" comp. the similar maxim reproduced by Paul, vi. 11.—As this beginning of the sentence is taken up again, ver. 4, it must necessarily be held that a parenthesis begins in ver. 1 and continues to the end of ver. 3. The only question is where this parenthesis begins. Luther, Bengel, Olshausen, Heinrici, Edwards, etc., think that it opens with the conj. ὅτι, to which they give the meaning *because.* We have already set aside this meaning of ὅτι, and we add that the following asyndeton: "knowledge puffeth up . . .," would be far from natural so soon after the beginning of a parenthesis; two successive interruptions of the thought are inadmissible. The parenthesis therefore does not begin till the second proposition of the verse: "Knowledge puffeth up. . ."—*All* denotes in Paul's view all those who composed the Church. They had in baptism abjured the errors of polytheism, and accepted what the Church taught regarding the only true God. They had therefore all a certain measure of knowledge. How can Edwards go astray so far as to see in this πάντες, *all*, an allusion to the other apostles and to the decree of the Council of Jerusalem?

But, at this word knowledge, the apostle all at once stops short; and he gives himself up to a brief digression on the uselessness and nothingness of a certain kind of knowledge, as well as on the true nature of that for which this fair name should be reserved. "Knowledge, yes, every one has it; but when it is only in the head, and the heart is empty of love, knowledge produces only a vain *inflation*, presumption, vanity, lightness." With this idea of inflation the apostle contrasts that of *edification*, that is to say, of a solid and growing building; fulness, that is, reality, in opposition to emptiness and appearance. *Love* alone can produce in him who knows, and, through him, in his brethren, serious moral progress. Love alone draws from God the real knowledge of Divine things, and teaches him who receives it to adapt it to the wants of his brethren.

Ver. 2. The asyndeton of ver. 2 (the δέ of the T. R. should, it appears, be rejected) does not indicate a new interruption. It is that frequent asyndeton which announces the more emphatic reaffirmation of the previous thought: "Yes, that knowledge devoid of love and of power to edify, when we look at it more nearly, is not even a true knowledge." The expression εἰ τὶς δοκεῖ, *if any one thinketh he knoweth,* indicates an empty pretence; real knowing, on the contrary, is denoted by the words, *as he ought to know.* The reading should certainly be, with almost all the Mjj., ἐγνωκέναι, instead of the εἰδέναι of T. R.; as Edwards says, the second of these terms signifies: *to know* a fact, while the former signifies: *to be thoroughly acquainted with,* to have penetrated the thing. Now this second meaning is the only one which is suitable here.

It matters little whether we read with the Alex. οὔπω, *not yet,* or with the Greco-Lat. and the Byz. οὐδέπω, *not at all yet.* As to the pron. οὐδέν, *nothing,* of the T. R., it ought certainly to be suppressed (with the majority of the Mjj.). It weakens the idea instead of strengthening it. It is not the knowledge of this or that which the apostle denies to the man who is full of self and empty of love; it is the very possibility of knowledge. One can only know by assimilating the being to be known, and one can only assimilate him by renouncing self to give himself to him. Love, therefore, is the condition of all true knowledge, and that above all, when, as here, it is God and His thought and will which are in question; comp. 1 John iv. 8: "He who loveth not, knoweth not God; for God is love."

Ver. 3 is the antithesis of ver. 2: Without love, no knowledge (ver. 2); with love, true knowledge (ver. 3). But why, instead of: "The same knoweth God," does the apostle say: *The same is known of God?* Does he mean to deny the first of these two ideas? Assuredly not. But he clears, as it were, this first stage, which is self-understood, to rise at a bound to the higher stage, which supposes and implies it. To be known of God is more than to know Him. This appears from Gal. iv. 9: "But now, having known God, or rather being known of Him." In a residence, every one knows the monarch; but every one is not known by him. This second stage of knowledge supposes personal *intimacy*, familiarity of a kind; a character which is foreign to the first. We need not therefore seek to give the expression, "to be known of God," an exceptional meaning, which was done by Erasmus: "he is *acknowledged* of God as His true disciple;" and by Grotius: "He is *approved* of Him." Beza went even the length of giving to the passive ἔγνωσται, *is known*, the sense of a Hebrew Hophal: "he *is* rendered knowing, put in possession of the knowledge of God." The word *know* is here taken in the same sense as in Ps. i. 6: "The Lord knoweth the way of the righteous," a passage which Heinrici rightly compares. The eye of God can penetrate into the heart that loves Him and His light, to illuminate it. In this light an intimate communion is formed between him and God; and this communion is the condition of all true knowledge,—of man's being known by God as of God's being known by man.—The pronoun οὗτος, *this same*, does not refer to God, but to man; it signifies: "This same truly," in opposition to those πάντες, *all*, to whom the privilege of knowledge was so freely ascribed at Corinth (ver. 1).

After this digression, for which there was only too much reason, the apostle returns to the thought which he had begun to enunciate, ver. 1.

Ver. 4. The οὖν, *therefore*, indicates, as it does so frequently, the resuming of the interrupted sentence; but with this difference, that for the *fact* of knowledge (the γνῶσιν ἔχειν) Paul substitutes as the object of the *we know* the *contents* of the knowledge.—The term βρῶσις, the *act of eating*, which he here introduces (it did not occur in ver. 1), has in it something disdainful; it emphasizes the lower and material character of the act in question.—The contents of the knowledge which Paul ascribes to all Christians, are the monotheistic creed, as it is summed up in the two following propositions. And first the nothingness of idols; οὐδέν might be an adjective: "*no* idol." In that case we must apply the term idol to the false deity itself. None of those *deities* worshipped by the heathen has any existence in the circle of real beings (*the world*). So Meyer, de Wette, etc. But, says Edwards, it is doubtful whether εἴδωλον, the *idol*, can denote the false God, without the image representing it; the examples quoted do not prove this. He explains thus: There is not in creation any visible image of God; the only real image of God is that which is in heaven: Christ (Col. i. 15; 2 Cor. iv. 4). But one feels at once how foreign this thought is to the context. The subject in question for the time is God; only afterwards will Paul come to Jesus Christ, as the only *Lord* (ver. 6). What has led some to make οὐδέν an adjective, is the following οὐδείς, which evidently signifies *no*. But why should the construction of the two propositions be the same? The οὐδέν ought to be taken as a predicate: "That an idol *is nothing* in the world." It must be remembered that the statue was judged by the heathen to be the dwelling and agent of the god himself, so that the apostle means: If in the world of beings you seek one corresponding to the statue and person of Jupiter, Apollo, etc., you will find *nothing.*—In the following proposition, the word ἕτερος, *other* (which is found in the T. R.), must be rejected.—There was certainly not a single Christian at Corinth who had not subscribed to these two propositions; and the apostle may have borrowed them from the Church's own letter. He himself confirms while explaining them, but at the same time completing and prudently limiting them in the two following verses.

Vers. 5, 6. "For though there be that are called gods, whether in heaven or in earth, as there be gods many, and lords many, 6. but to us there is but one God, the Father, of whom are all things, and we in Him, and one Lord, Jesus Christ, by[1] whom are all things, and we by Him."[2]—*Καὶ γάρ, and indeed.* Paul affirms, in harmony with the Corinthians, that whatever may be the multiplicity of gods worshipped by the heathen, the Christian recognises only one God, Him whose character he here defines, and but one Lord, the Mediator between God and men. "The imagination of the Greeks," says Beet, "filled with divinities the visible and invisible heavens, and on earth, mountains, forests, and rivers." These are the λεγόμενοι θεοί, the beings designated by the name of gods and worshipped as such, but who, as the epithet indicates, have only the *name* of deity. The two

[1] B only reads δι' ου (*on account of whom*), instead of δι' ου (*by whom*).

[2] In some Fathers and Mnn. there is found the addition: "And one Holy Spirit, in whom are all things."

propositions which begin, the one with εἴπερ, *even though*, the other with ὥσπερ, *as indeed*, have been very variously understood, according as the two verbs εἰσί, *are*, which stand at the head of both, have been taken to denote a logical or a real existence. In the view of Rückert, Olshausen, Meyer, Kling, Hofmann, real existence is to be understood in both cases in this sense : "Even if (εἴπερ) the gods of mythology really exist (a supposition which is not absurd), agreeably to the fact that (ὥσπερ) there really exist gods and lords in abundance (the angels in their different orders enumerated by Paul, Eph. i. 21 ; Col. i. 16 ; comp. Deut. x. 17 and Ps. cxxxvi. 2, 3), even if such gods really exist, yet there is for us, Christians, only one God and one Lord." But it is not easy to explain clearly the relation between these two real existences, the former of which on this understanding is put as hypothetical, and then the second as certain, and which nevertheless both relate to one and the same subject. Others, like Chrysostom, Calvin, Beza, Neander, de Wette, regard these two existences as imaginary. "Even though (εἴπερ) the heathen worship a multitude of fictitious gods, as one may see, indeed (ὥσπερ), that according to them, every place is full of gods and lords. . . ." But de Wette himself cannot help seeing the useless tautology of these two propositions of really identical meaning. Commentators of a third view, like Grotius, Billroth, understand the former of the two εἰσί, *are*, in the sense of a real existence, the latter in that of an imaginary existence : "Even though there really exists a host of beings, such as the sky, the sun, the moon, the earth, the ocean, which are made gods, as it may be seen in fact that among the heathen these are deities." But with what view would the apostle thus insist on the reality of the creatures which heathenism had deified? If, as is exact, one of the two verbs should denote a real, the other a fictitious existence, is it not much more natural to interpret in the latter sense that one of the two εἰσί (*are*), which is accompanied by the participle λεγόμενοι, *called?* For this apposition undoubtedly does not force us (comp. 2 Thess. ii. 4) to attribute an imaginary character to these gods, but it permits and leads to it. In this case the following would be the meaning of the verse: "Even though there are in abundance beings called gods, and worshipped as such, with whom the imagination of the heathen peoples both heaven and earth (Jupiter, Apollo, Mars, Ceres, Bacchus, Nymphs), as in fact (ὥσπερ) there really exist—we must not be deceived on the point—gods many and lords many. . . ." By these last words the apostle means, that if the particular mythological deities are only fictions, there is yet behind these fictions a reality of which we must take account. In x. 20 he expressly declares, that "what the Gentiles sacrifice they sacrifice to demons;" not, certainly, that he regards the god Jupiter as one demon and the god Apollo as another; but in heathenism in general he recognises the work of malignant spirits, who have turned man away from God, and filled the void thus formed in the soul with this vain and impure phantasmagoria. It is in the same sense that he describes demons, Eph. vi. 12, as "rulers of the present darkness;" that he calls Satan, 2 Cor. iv. 4, the *god of this world* who blinds the unbelieving; and that Jesus

Himself calls him the *Prince of this world* (John xii. 31, xiv. 30). The term, *gods many*, refers to the heads of this kingdom of darkness; the term, *lords many*, to the inferior spirits, the subordinate agents; comp. in our Epistle xv. 24.—If criticism, such as is practised in our day, had the least interest in setting our Epistle in opposition to that of the Romans, how easy would it be for it to maintain by means of this passage, either that they proceed from two different authors, or that the apostle's ideas had become changed in the interval between the one and the other! In point of fact, the explanation which the apostle gives of the origin of heathenism in the Epistle to the Romans (chap. i.) is purely psychological, and leaves wholly out of account all influence exercised by superior beings. But the two explanations hold true together and complete one another. The apostle emphasizes in each Epistle that which is of importance to the subject he is treating; in Romans, where he wishes to bring out the corruption of mankind, he shows the *moral* origin of idolatry: how this great collective sin proceeded from the heart of man; in our Epistle, where he has in view certain practical rules to be drawn for the conduct of the Corinthians, he emphasizes the diabolical influence which concurred to produce heathenism. Is there not a lesson of prudence and wise reserve to be drawn from this fact for so many other analogous cases? It will be seen afterwards with what view the apostle here presents simultaneously these two aspects of the truth: on the one side, the nothingness of heathen divinities; and, on the other, the diabolical reality which is hidden under this empty phantasmagoria.

The first point of view will justify the liberty allowed in regard to the eating of offered *meats;* the second, the absolute prohibition against taking part in the idol *feasts.*

Ver. 6. With these fictitious, and yet, in a certain sense, real gods and lords, Paul forcibly contrasts by the adverb ἀλλά, *but,* and the pronoun ἡμῖν, *for us,* put first, the only God and the only Lord recognised by the Christian conscience. The title *the Father,* added to the word *God,* is taken in the absolute sense in which it embraces His Fatherhood both in relation to Christ and to us. The apostle here adds two notions: the proceeding of all things from God alone (ἐξ οὗ, *of whom*), and the moral consecration of believers to Him alone (εἰς αὐτόν, *for Him*). In such a context he cannot be intending to describe thereby His greatness and perfection; but he means that nothing of all that forms part of the universe created by such a Being (offered meats in particular) can defile the believer (x. 25, 26). How could that which is made by God prevent him from being and remaining for God what he ought to be? (see Hofmann).

As God, the Father, is contrasted with the principal heathen deities, *Christ, the Lord,* is so with the secondary deities who served as mediators between the great gods and the world. What Paul means is, that as the world is *from* God, and the Church *for* God; so the world is *by* Christ, and the Church also *by* Him.

The former of the two propositions relative to Christ: *by whom are all things,* can only apply, as is recognised by all the critics of our time, de Wette, Heinrici, Reuss, Meyer, and even Pfleiderer and Holtzmann, to the work of creation. Baur thinks that the διά may be referred in the first proposition, as well as in the second, to the work of redemption. But the ἡμεῖς, *we*, of the second proposition evidently contrasts Christians, as objects of redemption, with τὰ πάντα, *all things*, as objects of another work, which, as is shown by the previous proposition, can only be creation. Holsten, alone, cannot bring himself to this avowal. In the words, *all things by Him*, he finds only the idea of the government of all things by the glorified Christ. But the *by Him* corresponds to the *of Him* (ἐξ αὐτοῦ) of the previous proposition, and can consequently apply only to the same work, that of creation, of which God is the author and Christ the agent. It is the same thought as in Col. i. 15–17, where the ἐν corresponds to our διά, and as in John i. 3, where the δι' αὐτοῦ expresses the creation of all things *by* the Logos. The idea which Holsten finds in this proposition would, besides, be out of all relation to Paul's object, which is to show that a meat divinely created cannot separate man from God. The *Vaticanus*, instead of δι' οὗ, reads δι' ὅν, *on account of whom;* evidently the mistake of a copyist.—In the second proposition the word ἡμεῖς, *we*, contrasted with *all things*, shows that the subject in question is the spiritual creation accomplished by Christ, the work of salvation. These words have their commentary in Col. i. 18–22, as the preceding in Col. i. 15–17. They form the counterpart of the second preceding proposition relating to God. In the physical order we are *of* God and *by* Christ; in the spiritual order we are *by* Christ and *for* God.

We have already pointed out more than once how,

notwithstanding the diversity of forms, the views of Paul coincide with those of John. We have just seen this in connection with the regimen δι' οὗ, which so vividly reminds us of the δι' αὐτοῦ of John i. 3. This connection is equally striking if we compare from the Christological viewpoint this saying of Paul with John xvii. 3. In the two passages, the personal distinction between God and Christ is strongly emphasized, though the community of nature between both appears from this very distinction, and from all the rest of the books where these sayings are contained. Reuss maintains that there are in the Gospel of John two opposite theories going side by side; but we must in that case say the same of the writings of the Apostle Paul, whose rigorous logic no one disputes. In point of fact there is no contradiction in either; for both emphasize with the full consciousness of what they affirm the subordination of the Son in the unity of the Divine life; see on iii. 23.

Here we have one of the passages which establish the complete unity of the apostle's Christology in his first letters, and in those of his imprisonment (Col., Eph., Phil.). "Let there be an end then," says Gess rightly (*Apost. Zeugn.*, ii. p. 295), "to the assertion that the Christology of the later Epistles is contrary to that of Paul; according to which Christ, it is held, is nothing more than the ideal or celestial man, and that though one is forced to allow that our passage makes Him the mediator of the creation of the universe!"

Thus far, St. Paul would say, we are all at one, but here now is the point where difference begins, and this difference impresses the Christian who loves, with regard and sacrifices toward those whose judgment differs from his.

2. *Difference in knowledge, with the practical obligations arising from it* (vers 7–13).

Ver. 7. "Howbeit there is not in every man that knowledge. Some, through the habit[1] which they have to this[2] hour of [believing in] the idol, eat the meats as offered to the idol, and their conscience being weak is defiled."—The strong contrast indicated by the ἀλλ' οὐκ, *but not,* and by the place given at the opening of the sentence to the ἐν πᾶσιν, *in all* (opposed to ἡμῖν, *to us,* ver. 6), may be paraphrased as follows: "But this monotheistic knowledge possessed by us all has not yet unfolded in the consciousness of all its full consequences." At the first glance the opening words of this verse seem to contradict the assertion of ver. 1 ("we know that we all have knowledge"), and it was this supposed contradiction which led several critics to refer the words of ver. 1 only to the enlightened Christians of Corinth (Beza, Flatt, etc.), or to these with the addition of the apostle (Meyer). Ver. 7 in this case would refer to the weak Christians only, and would agree without difficulty with ver. 1. But in thus escaping from one contradiction, we fall into another. How, on this view, can we explain the πάντες, *all,* of ver. 1, having regard to the οὐκ ἐν πᾶσιν, *not in all,* of ver. 7? The *all* of ver. 1 would necessarily require to have been qualified by some restriction.

[1] ℵ A B P Cop. Cyr. read συνηθεια (*the habit*), while T. R. with D E F G 4 Mnn. It. Syr^sch Vg. reads συνειδησει (*the consciousness*).

[2] The two words εως αρτι (*to this hour*) are placed by T. R. with A L P after του ειδωλου, while ℵ B D E F G It. Syr^sch Cop. put them before.

Besides this, as de Wette observes, the apostle has just unfolded in ver. 6 the contents of the knowledge, and he has done so as speaking not in the name of some, but of *all* Christians (*we*, in opposition to the heathen). The apparent contradiction between vers. 1 and 7 must therefore be resolved differently. Account must be taken of two differences of expression. In ver. 1: *we all have;* here: *in all there is not;* in ver. 1: [some] *knowledge*, a certain knowledge (γνῶσις without article); in ver. 7, [the] *knowledge* (γνῶσις with the article): "All have the monotheistie knowledge in general (a certain knowledge, ver. 1); but *the* precise knowledge which is in question here (to wit, that heathen deities do not exist, and consequently cannot contaminate either the meats offered to them or those who eat them), this knowledge is not *in all*, has not yet penetrated the conscience of all to the quick, so as to free them from every scruple." How many truths do we possess, from having learned our catechism, the practical conclusions of which we are yet far from having drawn! How many people ridicule belief in ghosts, whom the fear of spirits terrifies when they find themselves alone in the night! The idolatrous superstitions are numerous which still exercise their influence on our monotheistic Christendom.—The *strong* among the Corinthians did not make this distinction between theoretic knowledge and its practical application; and hence it was that they thought themselves entitled to set aside all consideration for the weak: "Freedom to eat meats offered to idols follows logically from the monotheistic principle common to all; so much the worse for those of us who want logic! We are not called to put ourselves about for a brother who reasons badly." This was strong in logic, but weak in ἀγάπη (*love*). And hence it was that the apostle had introduced at the beginning of this chapter the short digression on the emptiness of knowledge without love.

There is room for hesitating between the reading of the T. R. : τῇ συνειδήσει, *through conscience*, after the Byz. and Greco-Lat.'s, the *Itala* and the *Peschito*, and that of the Alex. and of a later Syriac translation : τῇ συνηθείᾳ, *through habit*. Meyer, Heinrici, Holsten have returned, contrary to Tischendorf's authority (8th edition), to the received reading. They allege its difficulty. But is it not very improbable that the word συνήθεια, so rare in the New Testament (it is found only twice), has been substituted for the term συνείδησις, which occurs in this same verse and twice besides in this chapter? (vers. 10 and 12). As to the sense, συνείδησις, *conscience*, would denote the inward conviction of the *reality* of the idol, which in such persons has survived their conversion. The term συνήθεια denotes the *habit* which they have of regarding the idol as a real being. The words ἕως ἄρτι, *till now*, especially placed, as they are in most Mjj., before τοῦ εἰδώλου, apply naturally, not to the verb, but to the substantive which precedes, and agree perfectly with the notion of habit : a habit (which lasts) till now even after the new faith should have put an end to it. If this is the true reading, the conclusion is almost necessary that the persons in question were of heathen origin. The old prejudice, under the dominion of which they had lived, resisted logic. They could not imagine that the powers they had so long revered under the names of Zeus, Mars, Minerva, etc., had not some reality. Hence the meats offered on their altar could no longer be simple meats; they must have taken something of the malignant character of those beings themselves. And therefore the Christian who eats them in this character (ὡς εἰδωλόθυτον, *as sacrificed*) is *ipso facto* polluted.—What does the apostle mean by the expression *weak conscience?* The term συνείδησις, *conscience*, strictly denotes the *knowledge* which the *Ego* has of itself, as willing and doing good or evil (the moral conscience), and of itself in what it thinks and knows (the theoretical conscience).[1] It is the moral conscience which is here in question. It is weak, because a religious scruple, from which the gospel should have set it free, still binds it to beings which have no existence and hinders it from acting normally. Probably those former heathen, while adhering to belief in one God, still regarded their deities of other days, if not as gods, at least as terrible powers. The apostle adds that this conscience will be *defiled*, if the person eats of those meats in this state. In fact, this act remains upon it as a stain which separates from the holy God the man who has committed it while himself disapproving of it.

Vers. 8, 9. "Now meat commendeth[2] us not to God: for[3] neither,[4] if we eat, are we the better; neither,[4]

[1] See the development of this subject in Holsten, *Evangelium des Paulus*, t. i. p. 311.

[2] T. R. with D E L P reads παριστησι (*commendeth*), while ℵ A B Cop. read παραστησει (*will commend*).

[3] ℵ A B omit γαρ (*for*).

[4] We have followed in the order of these two propositions the reading of ℵ D E F G L P It. Syr.; the inverse order is followed by A B.

if we eat not, are we the worse. 9. But take heed lest by any means this liberty of yours become a stumbling-block to them that are weak."[1]—The transition between this verse and the foregoing is as follows: By eating such meats thou mayest therefore lead the weak brother to defile himself (ver. 8); but as for thyself thou hast nothing to gain, any more than thou hast to lose, by not eating. The conclusion is obvious.—The verb *παριστάναι, to present,* is often used of the presenting of offerings to God; comp. Rom. xii. 1, vi. 13, etc.; and if we read the verb in the present with the T. R., it is the most natural sense: "It is not in the power of meats to add anything to or take anything from the value which our consecration to His service has in the sight of God." If we read the future with the Alex., we must, like Holsten and others, apply the verb to the day of judgment; comp. 2 Cor. iv. 14; Rom. xiv. 10: "Meats will not make us stand before God in that day." This meaning is much more foreign to the context; for the threat will not come till later (vers. 11, 12). The parallels quoted in its favour prove nothing, the verb *present* being used in a wholly different relation. Here we have a general maxim, with which the present is in keeping.—Bengel, Meyer, Hofmann, in order to explain more easily the connection of this proposition with the two following alternatives, give the verb a morally indifferent meaning: "Meats determine our relation to God neither for good nor evil (*neque ad placendum, neque ad displicendum,* Bengel)." This sense would be more natural in the philosophical style

[1] T. R. with L: *ασθενουσιν*; all the rest: *ασθενεσιν*.

than in biblical language. The meaning which we have given may be suitable in the two following propositions; the privation of that which has no relation, causes no loss.—The order of the two following propositions in A B (see critical note) is condemned by the other Mjj. and by the ancient versions.—Calvin, Mosheim, and others have seen in this verse an objection of the Corinthians: "Meats not being able to procure either approval or condemnation, we may consequently act at will." Paul, they say, answers in ver. 9. But this argument would rather be opposed than favourable to the conduct of the strong. For if those meats neither caused them gain nor loss, but may through them cause their brother to sin (ver. 7), it is evident that they ought to abstain in cases where this last result may be produced. The consequence of ver. 8 therefore is, that no importance whatever is to be attached to those meats in themselves. Hence ver. 9: But there is importance in not causing one's brother to sin by means of those meats.

Ver. 9. The δέ is adversative: *but.* The term βλέπετε, *consider well,* is opposed to the lightness with which the Corinthians used their right.—In the word, ἐξουσία, *power, right,* here *liberty,* there is an allusion to the favourite formula of the strong at Corinth: "All things are lawful for me." The connection must be observed between ἐξουσία and ἔξεστι.—The pronoun αὕτη, *this liberty,* strongly contrasts this power, which is in itself an advantage, with the evil effects which it may produce when imprudently exercised.—And now from these general considerations the apostle comes to their application.

Vers. 10, 11. "For if any man see thee,[1] which hast knowledge, sit at meat in the idol's temple, shall not the conscience of him which is weak be emboldened to eat those things which are offered to idols? 11. And[2] so through[3] thy[4] knowledge thy weak brother[5] perisheth,[6] for whom Christ died."—The *for* indicates that here is the danger Paul had in view when he said: *Take heed!* in ver. 9.—This *any man* is one of the *some* of ver. 7.—The reading σέ, *thee,* must evidently be preferred to that of the Mjj., which omit this pronoun.—The term εἰδωλεῖον, the situation in which the idol is set up, is not common in classic Greek; it is not even mentioned in Passow's large dictionary. . It was formed by Jewish writers (1 Maccab. i. 47, x. 83) on the model of the words βακχεῖον, ποσειδωνεῖον, temple of Bacchus, Neptune, etc.; the apostle no doubt uses it to avoid the word ναός (Edwards).—It is far from probable that one formerly a Jew would be found within the enclosure of an idolatrous temple, and still less that the sight of a Christian partaking of such a banquet would have inspired him with the desire to eat meats offered to the idol; this spectacle, on the contrary, would have filled him with horror. The weak brother is therefore, as we have said, rather a former heathen.—The term οὐκ

[1] B F G omit σε (*thee*).

[2] T. R. with D E F G L Syr. reads και (*and*); ℵ B: γαρ (*for*); A P: ουν (*therefore*).

[3] T. R. with L reads επι (*upon*); the rest εν (*in, through*).

[4] B omits σῃ (*thy*).

[5] T. R. with L P places the word αδελφος (*brother*) after ασθενων (*weak*), while the rest read ο αδελφος (*the brother*) and place these words after γνωσει (*knowledge*).

[6] T. R. with E F G L Syr. reads απολειται (*will perish*); ℵ B D P: απολλυται (*perishes*).

οἰκοδομηθήσεται, *will be edified,* [emboldened], is used with evident irony. It suffices to call to mind that the more advanced believer should by his superior knowledge have edified the other by enlightening his conscience and emancipating him from his false scruples, whereas by his imprudence he leads him to trample upon his conscience, and thus substitutes false edification for the true: he enlightens and strengthens him to his loss! Fine edification! It may appear surprising that Paul here lets the conduct of the strong Christian pass without calling his attention to the evil which he may do himself by taking part in such a banquet in such a place. But the apostle never wanders from his subject. His subject here is the self-denial imposed by love to our neighbour. He will afterwards (x. 15–21) treat the other side of the question, that concerning the danger to which the strong believer exposes himself.

Ver. 11. If we read *for,* with the two oldest Mjj., this particle refers to the ironical term *will be edified* [emboldened]: "edified, *for* as the fruit of it he perishes!" But it seems to me more natural simply to read, with all the other Mjj. and the *Peschito, καί,* in the sense of: *and so.* As to the tense of the verb, the present, *perisheth,* in the Alex. should be preferred to the future, *shall perish,* of the T. R. The apostle is thinking of the immediate effect: "He is from that moment in the way of perdition." An unfaithfulness, however small it may appear, separates the believer from his Lord; by interposing between the branch and the stock, it interrupts the communication of life which ought to take place from the one to the other. From that moment spiritual death commences, and if this state continues and becomes aggravated, as is inevitable in such a case, eternal perdition is the end of it; comp. Rom. xiv. 15. Every word of this verse has a force of its own: *cause to perish;* what success! A *weak brother;* what magnanimity! Through *knowledge*, which ought to have been used for his advancement; what fidelity in the use of grace received! A *brother* over whom thou shouldest have watched as over the apple of thine eye; what love! A man for love of whom *Christ* gave Himself to die; what gratitude!—It is this last particular, the sin against Christ, which the apostle more especially emphasizes as the gravest of all, in the following verse.

Vers. 12, 13. "But when ye sin so against the brethren, and wound their weak conscience, ye sin against Christ. 13. Wherefore, if meat make my[1] brother to offend, I will eat no flesh while the world standeth, lest I make my brother to offend."—Every violence done to a brother's conscience, even though he should not thereby be drawn into a deed of unfaithfulness, is a sin committed against Christ, whose work so painfully accomplished we compromise. Here again there is a marked force in every term: τύπτειν, strictly speaking, *to strike;* συνείδησις, *conscience*, the most sacred of things; ἀσθενοῦσα, *weak*, tottering with weakness, and consequently claiming the greatest regard; εἰς Χριστόν, *against Christ*, the highest of crimes.

Ver. 13. This thought of ver. 12 tells so vividly on the apostle's heart, that it inspires him with a sort of vow whereby he is ready to devote his whole life.

[1] D F G It. omit μου (*my*).

The διόπερ, *wherefore*, sums up all the grounds previously indicated, in particular that of ver. 12: *against Christ.*—Instead of, *a* [kind of] meat, we ought logically to read, *this* [kind of] meat, or a [kind of] *flesh.* But the apostle generalizes the idea; though in the second part of the verse, by the use of the expression: *flesh*, he returns to the particular case. He employs the first person, because the sacrifice in question is one which a man may impose on himself, but which he has no right to impose on others. He would rather abstain from flesh all his life than by using it cause one of his brethren to fall even once.—Holsten well sums up the idea of the chapter thus: The strong sought the solution of the question from the standpoint of knowledge and its rights; the apostle finds it from the standpoint of love and its obligations.

The last words of this chapter evidently form the transition to the following passage, in which Paul continues to present to the Corinthians his own example, by reminding them of the great and constant voluntary sacrifice with which he accompanies the exercise of his apostleship. As Calvin observes to perfection (and such is the real transition from chap. viii. to chap. ix.): "*Quia in futurum pollicendo non omnibus fecisset fidem, quid jam fecerit, allegat.*" To the contingent sacrifice of ver. 13 he adds, as a still more convincing example, the sacrifice which he has already made, and which he renews daily, his renunciation of all recompense from the Churches founded by him.

The Use of Meats offered to Idols—*continued*

3. *The example of abnegation given by Paul*

(9:1-22)

It is easy, from what we have just said, to understand the link which connects the following passage with the question treated by the apostle. It is nevertheless true that the subject which he proceeds to handle receives so considerable a development, that it is difficult to resist the idea that he had special reasons for expounding it here with so many details. This supposition is confirmed by the allusions to a secret hostility against his apostleship, which occur in abundance in the first three verses of the chapter, and still more clearly by a passage in the Second Epistle, where the odious accusations of his adversaries, in regard to this disinterested conduct on the part of the apostle, are dragged to the light of day. We see, in fact, from 2 Cor. xii. 11–18, that instead of admiring St. Paul's abnegation, his enemies at Corinth turned it into a weapon against him, alleging that if he did not make his Churches maintain him, it was because he did not feel himself to be the equal of the true apostles, and that, moreover, he found other ways of indemnifying himself for the self-denial which he seemed to exercise.

Our First Epistle to the Corinthians already assumes all this; but for prudential reasons Paul as yet lets it barely appear. In vers. 1–3 he establishes the reality of his apostleship; then he deduces from it, vers. 4–14, his apostolical right to maintenance. He afterwards explains, vers. 15–18, the real motive which had led him to decline the exercise of this right; finally, in vers. 19–22, he shows how the principle of abnegation which he has just professed extends to his whole mode of acting in the exercise of his ministry.

Vers. 1–3

Ver. 1. "Am I not free?[1] am I not an apostle? have I not seen Jesus[2] our Lord? are not ye my work in the Lord?"—These accumulated questions betray the emotion which seizes the apostle as he approaches this delicate subject. Before showing why he has renounced his rights, he must prove that those rights exist, and, to this end, that he is truly an apostle. If, with the T. R., we begin with the question: *Am I not an apostle?* it can only signify: "Am I not free to use the rights which this office confers on me?" But this question would come rather abruptly after the preceding verse, and the two last questions of the verse connect themselves much more directly with the idea of apostleship than with that of liberty. We must therefore begin with the latter, according to the Alex.: "*Am I not free?*" This question is also more naturally connected with the last idea of the previous chapter.

[1] T. R. with D E F G K L It., etc., places these two questions in inverse order; we have followed the order of ℵ A B P, several Mnn. Syr^{sch} Cop.

[2] T. R. with D E K L P Syr. Cop. reads Ιησουν Χριστον.

We shall find the apostle closing (vers. 19–22) with the same idea of Christian liberty with which he had begun. This liberty of Paul's is liberty to eat sacrificed meats, and in general to free himself wholly, when he thinks good, from Jewish usages (vers. 19, 20).—From his liberty as a Christian, Paul passes, in the second question, to his apostolic dignity and to the rights which he possesses as an apostle. The verb οὐκ εἰμί, *am I not*, is placed before the predicate in the two questions, because it is on the idea of *being* that the emphasis lies: "Am I not *really?*" An *apostle* is one sent immediately by the Lord, who alone can confer such a mandate. But the call to the apostleship implies a personal meeting with Christ, and hence the third question: *Have I not seen . . . ?* When, at Jerusalem, it was wished to elect an apostle to take the place of Judas, the two candidates were chosen among those who had companied with Jesus, "from the baptism of John to the ascension, to be witnesses of His resurrection" (Acts i. 22). If Paul had merely heard the good news, like all other believers, from the lips of the Twelve, whatever might have been his gifts, he could never have claimed the title of an apostle. And hence the term: *I have seen*, in this context, cannot refer either to any instance in which Paul might have seen Jesus at Jerusalem during His earthly ministry, or to a simple vision which the Lord might have granted him. This term can only designate the positive historical fact of the appearing of Jesus on the way to Damascus. It was never believed in the primitive Church that an accidental meeting with Jesus, or a vision, such as that of the dying Stephen, could give a right to the title of apostle; comp. xv. 8 and Acts xxii. 14.—The Alex. reject the word *Christ* to retain only the word *Jesus*, and rightly; for we have to do here with the historical personage who appeared to Paul, with Him who said to him: "I am Jesus whom thou persecutest." The title *our Lord* denotes this Jesus as Head of the Church, who alone is entitled to confer the apostleship; comp. Gal. i. 1 and Acts i. 26.—But the Lord's appearing to Paul was known mainly, if not exclusively, from his own account; to deny it his adversaries had only therefore to cast doubt on his sound sense or good faith. Hence the apostle adds a new proof of his apostleship, borrowed from the experience of the Corinthians themselves, the founding of their Church by him, Paul; this is the subject of the fourth question. The force of this argument is less in the fact itself of the founding of the Church than in the Lord's co-operation powerfully manifested in the course of this work. The words ἐν κυρίῳ, *in the Lord*, bear on the whole question, and not only on the words ἔργον μου, *my work*; they are the true point of support for the conclusion to be drawn. We know from the passage ii. 1–5 the weak, unarmed, trembling condition in which the apostle felt himself when he founded this Church. So this work could be attributed only to Christ's power acting through his weakness and itself touching hearts. It is to this experience of Christ's co-operation in the work of His servant that Paul appeals in the two following verses, which are specially connected with this last question, and state the conclusion of it.

Vers. 2, 3. "If I be not an apostle unto others, yet doubtless I am to you: for the seal of mine apostleship[1] are ye in the Lord; this is my answer to them that do examine me."—The datives *unto others* and *to you* are not only datives of appreciation (in the judgment of), but also datives of relation, as Rückert observes. Though Paul had not been related as an apostle to any other Church, yet as truly as the Church of Corinth was a Church founded by him, he possessed in his relation to it this title of apostle. It was the *seal* officially put by the Lord Himself on his apostolic mission, and it would have been somewhat strange if those who were themselves the living proof of his apostleship should put Paul in the position of proving it to them.

The asyndeton between vers. 2 and 3 announces a reaffirmation under strong feeling of the idea of ver. 2. The emotion is explained by the last words: *them that examine.* Paul's apostleship is the subject of an examination at Corinth! At Corinth a discussion is raised regarding the nature of the appearance whereby Christ conferred on him the apostleship! There is a tendency, perhaps, to represent him, even as in Galatia, as a disciple of the apostles who has revolted against his masters! It is allowable to suppose that these words do not apply to the members of the Church themselves, those of whom Paul has just said that they are his living defence, but to the foreign emissaries who have arrived at Corinth. Comp. Gal. i., where Paul replies to similar accusations.—The pronoun *αὕτη* brings into bold relief this idea of defence: "As to *this* defence, it is yourselves, you, the work of the Lord by me." After having thus established the reality of his apostleship, at least in relation to this Church, he draws

[1] T. R. with D E F G K L reads *της εμης*; ℵ B P: *μου της*.

the inference from it: his right is to be maintained by the Church of Corinth and the others which he has founded.

Vers. 4–14

Vers. 4–6. "Have we not right to eat and to drink?[1] 5. Have we not right to lead about a sister as wife, as well as the other apostles and the brethren of the Lord and Cephas? 6. Or I only and Barnabas, have not we power to forbear[2] working?"—Paul uses the plural (*we have*), because he is thinking also of Barnabas, who acted in this respect in the same way as himself (ver. 6); perhaps he means also to include Silas and Timothy, who had laboured with him in founding the Church of Corinth, joining him in his mode of living; comp. ver. 11: "*If we have sown* among you spiritual things. . . ." The terms *eat* and *drink* receive from the context this special meaning: to eat and drink at the Church's expense. The eating of sacrificed meats is no longer in question. The interrogative μή assumes the negative answer: "It is *not however* (μή) possible that we have *not* (οὐκ) the right. . . ?"

Ver. 5. The right of Paul and Barnabas, as apostles of the Lord, is demonstrated down to ver. 14 by a series of arguments, the first of which, vers. 5, 6, is taken from the example *of the other apostles* and of the *Lord's brothers.* Not only were these personally maintained by the Churches they visited, but each of them had his wife with him, who shared in this

[1] T. R. with A E K L P: πιειν (*drink*); B: πειν; ℵ D F G: πιν.

[2] T. R. with E K L reads του before μη εργαζεσθαι, which is omitted by all the rest.—Vulg. Tert. Hil. Ambros. omit μη (*to act thus*).

advantage. The Greek text signifies: "a sister as wife." The Vulgate translates: "a wife as sister;" it is obvious in what interest. "Clement of Alexandria, at the end of the second century, makes no difficulty about recognising the fact that all the apostles were married (*Strom.* iii. p. 448); Ambrosiaster (probably the Roman deacon Hilary in the fourth century) declares (2 Cor. xi. 2) that all the apostles, except John and Paul, had wives" (see Heinrici, p. 240).—The term περιάγειν, *to lead about*, can apply only to habitual missionary journeys. This little word dissipates to some extent the obscurity in which the book of Acts leaves the career of most of the Twelve. It reveals to us also what an important part the brothers of Jesus played in the early propagation of Christianity. They must have occupied the first rank among the evangelists, who came immediately after the apostles (Eph. iv. 11). These brothers of Jesus were, according to the Gospels, four in number: James, Joses, Simon, and Jude (Matt. xiii. 55 and parallels). An ancient tradition makes them elder brothers of Jesus, the issue of a first marriage of Joseph. Later it was sought to identify two or even three of them with the apostles of the same name; they were held to be cousins of Jesus, sons of a brother of Joseph, called Alphæus. After his death, Joseph and Mary took them into their house to bring them up with Jesus; this is what led to their being called His brothers. The eldest, James, was the Apostle James, son of Alphæus (Matt. x. 3); Simon, the last but one, was the Apostle Simon Zelotes (Matt. x. 4; Luke vi. 15); and the youngest, Jude, was the Apostle Jude Lebbæus, or Thaddæus (Matt. x.

3; Luke vi. 16). This ingenious combination falls to pieces before the two sayings, John vii. 5, where, some months before the Passion, it is said of the brothers of Jesus, "that they did not believe in Him,"—they were not therefore of the number of the Twelve,—and Acts i. 13, 14, where, even after the Ascension, they are still placed outside the circle of the apostles. Our passage, too, has been relied on to identify them with the Twelve. For, it is said, since Peter is mentioned along with the apostles, though he was one of them, it may well be so with the brothers of Jesus. But it is not necessary to give to the two καί, *and*, in our verse an identical meaning. We may explain it: "the other apostles, *as well as* (first καί) the brothers of Jesus, *and specially* (second καί) Cephas." As to the brothers of Jesus, therefore, there are only two suppositions possible: either that they were, according to a tradition already quoted, brothers of Jesus by the father, or that they were his later-born brothers. It is well known what an ascendancy in the Church was given to the eldest of them, James, by the fact of his being the Lord's brother; comp. Gal. i. 19, and ii. 1–10; Acts xv.—The Gospels positively inform us that Peter was married (Matt. viii. 14). Tradition calls his wife sometimes Concordia, sometimes Perpetua. Peter is expressly mentioned, because he occupied the first rank among the apostles and evangelists; his was the example *par excellence*.

Ver. 6. The conj. ἤ, *or*, has here the meaning which it so frequently has in Paul's writings: "*Or indeed* in the opposite case would it happen that . . . ?"—No doubt Barnabas had not been called to the apostleship by the Lord, in the same way as Paul (ver. 1); but, by his co-operation in the work of the apostle of the Gentiles, he was included, as it were, in his apostleship. Yet there remains an important difference between him and Paul, a difference which comes out in a characteristic way, by the application of the adjective μόνος, *only*, exclusively to Paul. It is exactly the same relation as is supposed by Gal. ii. (comparing especially vers. 8, 9).—The term *working* receives a determinate sense from the context: gaining one's livelihood by his work. Some Latin authorities omit the negative μή and translate: *to do so*, that is to say, to live at your cost. This meaning of the word ἐργάζεσθαι is impossible.

To this historical argument, taken from the *example* of the apostles, Paul adds a second, borrowed from *common right*.

Ver. 7. "Who goeth a warfare at his own charges? who planteth a vineyard, and eateth not the fruit[1] thereof? or[2] who feedeth a flock, and eateth not of the milk of the flock?"—The gospel is profoundly human; it welcomes all that is in conformity with nature in its normal state. Thus Paul appropriates without hesitation the principle contained in the three examples quoted, which he takes from common life. The principle is this: The man who consecrates his labour to a work, ought to be able to live by that work. The soldier leaves his trade for war; his support is due to him from the man in whose service he fights; ὀψώνια, *pay*, strictly the cooked meats taken along with

[1] T. R. with E K L Syr. Cop. reads εκ του καρπου (*of its fruit*); the eight other Mjj.: τον καρπον (*the fruit*).
[2] B D E F G Sah. omit η (*or*).

bread; hence: pay in kind, then also in money.—The vine-dresser bestows all his life on the care of the vine of his employer (Matt. xx. 1-7); he ought to partake of its fruit. The reading of T. R.: *of its fruit* (ἐκ τοῦ καρποῦ), is more exact in point of sense; but it is probably a correction of the other better supported reading, τὸν καρπόν, *its fruit*, an expression which does not necessarily signify that the whole of the fruit comes to him, as if he were proprietor. The three examples, of the soldier, the vine-dresser, and the shepherd, present themselves all the more naturally to the apostle's mind, because the people of God are often described in the prophets as an army, a vine, a flock.—Next, Paul corroborates this argument taken from human right by a third, which he borrows from *Divine right*.

Vers. 8, 9. "Say[1] I these things as a man? or saith not the law the same[2] also? 9. For it is written in the law of Moses, Thou shalt not muzzle[3] the ox that treadeth out the corn. Doth God take care for oxen?"—God had commanded the Jews, Deut. xxv. 4, that when harvest came, the ox, while treading the corn which it had contributed to produce by the painful labour of ploughing, should not be muzzled, and thereby prevented from enjoying, conjointly with man, the fruit of its toil. Among the heathen no scruple was felt about acting differently, and hence God expressly forbids this practice to His people.

[1] D E F G It. Vulg. read λεγω, instead of λαλω, which is read by T. R. with all the rest.

[2] T. R. with A L P reads η ουχι και ο νομος ταυτα λεγει; ℵ A B C D E Cop.: η και ο νομος ταυτα ου λεγει; F G: η ει και ο νομος ταυτα λεγει.

[3] T. R. with ℵ A C E K L P: φιμωσεις; B D F G: κημωσεις.

God's object in acting thus was evidently to cultivate in the hearts of His people feelings of justice and equity. This moral object appears not only from the prohibition in itself, but also from all the other injunctions which accompany it in chaps. xxiv. and xxv. of Deuteronomy: the command to restore to the poor man his garment, taken as a pledge, immediately after sunset (xxiv. 10–13); to pay to the poor labourer his wages on the same evening (vers. 14, 15); not to put the child to death with the guilty father (vers. 16–18); always to leave, when gathering the harvest, a gleaning for widows and strangers (vers. 19–22); not to subject the criminal to more than forty stripes (xxv. 1-3), etc. Does not this whole context show clearly enough what was the object of the prohibition quoted here? It was not from solicitude for oxen that God made this prohibition; there were other ways of providing for the nourishment of these animals. By calling on the Israelites to exercise gentleness and gratitude, even toward a poor animal, it is clear that God desired to inculcate on them, with stronger reason, the same way of acting toward the human workmen whose help they engaged in their labour. It was the duties of *moral beings* to one another, that God wished to impress by this precept.—The expression: *according to* [as a] *man*, is opposed to the law, which possesses a Divine authority. Here the apostle employs the term λέγω, *to declare, ordain*, whereas in speaking of his own saying, he had simply used the word λαλῶ, *to express*.

Ver. 9. We ought probably to prefer the reading of the *Vaticanus*, κημώσεις, to that of the T. R., φιμώσεις. The meaning is the same, but the second reading is no doubt derived from the LXX. The verb κημοῦν signifies more specially to close the mouth *by a muzzle*, while φιμοῦν signifies to close the mouth in general, by any means whatever.—The mode of treading out corn in the East is this: over the ears spread out on the threshing-floor there are made to pass horses or oxen, or sometimes a small wain drawn by these animals, and on which the driver stands.—When Paul asks if God *takes care for oxen,* it is clear that he is not speaking of God as Creator, but of God as giving the law (ver. 8), *in ferendâ lege,* as Calvin says; for in the domain of creation and Providence "He does not neglect even the smallest sparrow" (Calvin). As we have seen, it was on the heart of the Israelite that He sought to impress this prohibition.

Ver. 10. "Or saith He it not altogether for our sakes? Yea, for our sakes, no doubt, this is written: that he that plougheth should plough in hope; and that he that thresheth should partake of the object hoped for."[1]—The meaning of the ἤ, *or*, is this: "Or, if it cannot be for the sake of oxen that God has spoken thus, is it not absolutely for us, that is to say, with a view to man's heart to train it to generous feelings?" The πάντως may signify *entirely, absolutely* (not at all on account of oxen); but it may also, as in Luke iv. 13, have the meaning of *certainly*.—The sequel shows that the understood answer is strongly affirmative: "Yea, absolutely for us! for it is for us that it was written

[1] There are three readings: 1. The Western or Greco-Latins D F G It.: της ελπιδος αυτου μετεχειν (*to partake of his hope*). 2. The Alexandrine in ℵ A B C P Syr. Sah. Cop.: επ' ελπιδι του μετεχειν (*in the hope of partaking*). 3. The Byzantine in T. R. with E K L: της ελπιδος αυτου μετεχειν επ' ελπιδι (*with the hope of partaking of his hope*).

that . . ." The δι' ἡμᾶς, *for us,* signifies that in thus legislating, it was man's moral good, and not the satisfying of oxen, that God had in view. The ἡμᾶς, *us,* has sometimes been taken as referring to the ministers of the gospel. There is nothing to justify this restricted application. In this case we should have required ὑπὲρ ἡμῶν, *in our favour.* The opposite of oxen is men, and not apostles. Paul does not, therefore, in the least suppress the historical and natural meaning of the precept, as is thought by de Wette, Rückert, Meyer, Reuss, Edwards, and so many others. He recognises it fully, and it is precisely by starting from this sense that he rises to a higher application. In the conduct which God prescribes to man toward this animal, which serves him as a faithful worker, Paul finds the proof of the conduct which man should with stronger reason observe toward his human servants, and with still stronger reason the Church toward its ministers. This entire gradation would crumble instantly were the lowest step of the scale suppressed, that which was directly present to the mind of Moses; a fact which was understood by the apostle as well as by those who criticize him. Far from arbitrarily allegorizing, he applies, by a well-founded *a fortiori,* to a higher relation what God had prescribed with reference to a lower relation.—The *for* [yea] bears, as it does so often, on the understood affirmative answer. And the reasoning is this: "The precept has not its full sense except when applied to a reasonable being. For it is not oxen that can be encouraged during the toil of ploughing by foreseeing the joy of harvest. The human workman, on the contrary, can calculate beforehand the share in the result of his labour which will be granted to him, and be sustained by this hope. This is what God would have His people understand by forbidding them to deprive the ox of enjoying the result of his labour on the happy day of harvest."—It is possible, as many do, to explain the ὅτι in the sense of *because* : " It was written, because this is how it is just that the case should be in all relations ; " or we may translate by the simple *that*, which makes the following clause the subject of ἐγράφη, *it was written*. In this sense Paul would regard the clause dependent on ὅτι as the simple paraphrase of the word : *Thou shalt not muzzle* . . . , in Deuteronomy ; but this, ver. 10, contains a wholly new idea. In any case, it would be very forced to give to this ὅτι the meaning of : " to demonstrate that . . .," as Edwards proposes.

This apostolic paraphrase of the Mosaic command is generally ill understood, and that because the two acts of *ploughing* and *treading out* are regarded as two parallel examples ; they are taken to mean two works, of which Paul declares that both should be done with the expectation of recompense. With such an idea it becomes impossible to understand the words and reasoning of the apostle. According to a view common in the Scriptures, the act of ploughing is a hard and painful labour, and consequently the man who gives himself to it needs encouragement. This encouragement is the hope that he shall one day participate in the produce of harvest. There is nothing painful, on the contrary, in the act of treading out ; it belongs to the harvest day, and consequently to the hour of joy, to the festival by which the ploughman is recompensed for his toil. On this entire order of ideas, comp. Ps. cxxvi. 5, 6: "They that sow in tears shall reap in joy. He that goeth forth and weepeth, bearing precious seed, shall come again with rejoicing, bringing his sheaves." And if this is true in regard to man, it ought to be so also in regard to the being of an inferior order who shares his labour and pain. But it cannot be so with the ox which has ploughed with him, except on condition that no muzzle is applied to deprive it of its portion at the time of the festival, hindering it from tasting the fruit which it has contributed to produce.

The two acts, then, of ploughing and treading out are so far from being related as two examples in juxtaposition, though they are constantly regarded in this light, that the former alone is considered as a labour; the latter is the recompense rightly expected by the workman who has done the former. The understanding of this suffices to make it plain that the reading preserved by the Greco-Latin Mjj. is the only one which corresponds to the apostle's thought: "He that plougheth should plough with hope (this is what sustains him in his painful toil), and (when the day of harvest has come) at the time when he treads out, he ought not to be cheated of the hoped-for boon (as would be the case if he were muzzled on that day)." Having been at the toil, he ought also to be at the recompense, enjoying the harvest. The Alexandrine copyists having, like the commentators in general, understood the two acts of ploughing and treading as two equally painful labours, which are both entitled to the expected recompense, thought that they should apply the notion of hope also to the act of treading, whereas it applied only to ploughing; hence their reading: "And he that treadeth out [should tread], *with the hope of partaking.*" The Byzantines, after beginning like the Westerns, were led astray by the already corrupted Alexandrine text, and added, like them, to the end of the second proposition the words: ἐπ' ἐλπίδι, *in hope*, which, as we have seen, have no meaning when applied to him who threshes. The application to the relation between the apostle and the Church which he founded is thus perfectly clear. The time comes when the apostle, after painfully ploughing and sowing, is entitled to partake of the harvest, by receiving from the community once formed what is needful for his maintenance. To refuse him this fruit of his painful labour at this time would be to act contrary to the spirit of the Mosaic precept, to convert the rightful expectation of the faithful workman into a deception.

This passage rightly understood is singularly instructive. It is difficult to suppress a smile when listening to the declamations of our moderns against the allegorizing mania of the Apostle Paul, or when we find even an Edwards imagining that he who ploughs is the labourer who founds a church, and he who threshes represents the subsequent labourers who build it up! Paul does not in the least allegorize either in the sense of Edwards or in any other. From the literal and natural meaning of the precept he disentangles a profound moral truth, a law of humanity and equity, and drawing from its temporary wrapping this permanent lesson, he applies it with admirable exactness to the case in hand.—Moreover, we have to gather from the study of this passage a very important lesson as to the preservation of the text. All our great modern critics, Lachmann, Tischendorf, Tregelles, Westcott and Hort, think the preference should be given as a rule to the readings of the ancient Alex. Mjj., and one is thought lagging behind the age if he does not follow them with docility in this path. Now here is a case where the corruption of the text in these documents is patent, and where it is easy to discover the false idea which produced the corruption. Is exegesis to be held bound, as Westcott and Hort would demand, to close its eyes to the light, and hold by a decidedly corrupt text, because it has on its side the *Vaticanus* and the *Sinaïticus?* The interpreter of the Holy Scriptures is not at liberty to subordinate his common sense to the arbitrariness, the ignorance, or the negligence of the ancient copyists.

The two following verses do not so much contain new arguments in favour of the apostolic right established by Paul, as subsidiary reflections, intended to show better how the precept founded on human analogies (ver. 7) and on biblical right (8–10) applies still more rigorously to the apostle and his fellow-labourers than would at first sight appear.

Ver. 11. "If we have sown unto you spiritual things, is it a great thing if we should reap[1] your carnal things?"—When the vine-dresser and the shepherd partake of the fruit of their labour, when the ox eats the corn while treading it out, the part thus allowed to the worker is taken from the very produce of his labour, and consequently his part is of the same nature as that

[1] T. R. with ℵ A B K: θερισομεν; C D E F G L P It.: θερισωμεν.

produce. It is not so with the wages of the preacher What he receives is greatly inferior in value to what he has given. It follows that his right to be supported is still more indisputable than would appear if we held to the preceding examples.—The plural: *we have sown*, can refer only to the three founders of the Church of Corinth, Paul, Silas, and Timothy (2 Cor. i. 19).—The dative ὑμῖν, *for you*, is the dative of favour; they are the soil which has benefited by the seed scattered with so much labour. To this dative corresponds the genitive ὑμῶν, *of you*, on your part, which indicates the origin of the wages. It seems to us that we must read with the Alex. the subjunctive θερίσωμεν, rather than the indicative θερίσομεν. The Greco-Lats. have substituted the latter for the former because of the εἰ, *if*, which did not seem to be in keeping with the subjunctive mood. But it is precisely the opposite which is true, for the harvest in question exists only in thought, according to Paul, and he does not in the least ask that it should be realized.—To this first *à fortiori* the apostle adds a second.

Ver. 12. "If others be partakers of this right over you, are not we rather? Nevertheless we have not used this right; but suffer all things, lest we should hinder[1] the gospel of Christ."—As to this right of support the Corinthians granted it to others, after Paul left them; how would they deny it to him and to those (*us*) who were the first to bring them salvation? —The apostle alludes to workers who came afterwards, and when the Church was already founded. They were either Corinthian teachers or Judaizing intruders. The

[1] ℵ D L: εκκοπη; all the rest: εγκοπη.

passage 2 Cor. xi. 20 leaves no doubt as to the manner in which the latter turned their ministry in the Church to advantage: "If any man bring you into bondage, if he devour you, if he take of you, . . . ye bear it." These strangers, then, fleeced the Corinthians at will, and Paul and his companions did not possess the right which they declined to exercise! Hofmann thus establishes the contrast, rather, it is true, according to the apostle's thought than his words: "We have the right, and we do not use it; they have not the right, and they use it."—The expression τῆς ἐξουσίας ὑμῶν has been variously understood. Some have given the word the meaning of οὐσία, *possessions*, goods: "If others share *your possessions*." But the term has never this meaning in the New Testament, and it has a wholly different one in the second part of this same verse. Ewald and Holsten reach the same meaning, but by another way: they understand by ἐξουσία ὑμῶν the full liberty which the Corinthians have to dispose of their earthly goods. This meaning is equally inapplicable in the second part of the verse. We must simply, with de Wette and Meyer, make ὑμῶν the genitive of the object (as in Matt. x. 1): "the right or power *over you;*" that is to say, the right of having ourselves supported by you. Olearius had conjectured the reading ἡμῶν: "*our* right over you." Rückert was disposed to accept this correction. But it is not necessary, and xi. 10 shows with what liberty Paul uses this term ἐξουσία.—The second part of the verse is strictly speaking an anticipation; for Paul has not yet closed his exposition of the reasons on which his apostolic right rests (see vers. 13, 14); and it is not till ver. 15 that he develops the idea, enunciated here in advance, of his renunciation of his right. But the eagerness of his adversaries to secure payment of their ministry, would seem to lead him immediately to contrast with their love of comfort his own disinterestedness.—The apostle, in consequence of his renunciation of all payment, had to suffer, not only every kind of privations (nakedness, hunger, thirst), but also all kinds of labours and watchings; see the description 2 Cor. xi. 24–27, where he contrasts his kind of life with that of the Judaizing emissaries. The verb στέγω, strictly *to cover*, and that so as to receive the blows intended for another, consequently signifies also *to bear*. Holsten well: "I bear all the labours of life without having recourse to your help." Heinrici gives to this word the meaning of *self-restraining*, patiently keeping silence; but this meaning seems to us less natural than the preceding.—Of the two readings ἐκκοπή (mutilation, cutting off) and ἐγκοπή (notch, hindrance), the second is preferable; the first term would be too strong. In speaking of a hindrance to be removed, Paul is thinking, no doubt, of the false judgments which might be called forth, especially in Greece, by a preaching of the gospel, which, like the teaching of itinerant philosophers and rhetoricians, should be recompensed with payment in any form whatever. He was concerned to exalt the dignity of his message by making it gratuitous. The term εὐαγγέλιον has here, as most frequently in the New Testament, the verbal sense: the *act* of preaching.—After this anticipation, called forth by the contrast he presented to his adversaries, he resumes the demonstration he had begun, and closes it with the two most decisive arguments.

Ver. 13. "Do ye not know that they which minister about holy things live of the temple? and they which wait[1] at the altar are partakers with the altar?"—In heathen as well as in Jewish worship, it was customary for those who were employed in the sacred ceremonies, to live on the product of these rites. This was a matter so thoroughly received, that Rückert thinks he can apply the two terms used in ver. 13 (*minister*, *wait upon*) to those heathen and Jewish worships, and that Hilary (Ambrosiaster) has applied the first to heathen and the second to Jewish worship. But by the expression: *Do ye not know?* Paul seems to appeal to a Divine authority; he means probably, therefore, to speak only of Jewish worship. The term *temple*, also, can hardly refer to any other edifice than the only one which in Paul's eyes deserved the name, the temple of Jerusalem; see on viii. 10. Finally, in this sense the expression: *even so*, ver. 14, would become somewhat unsuitable; for the apostle could not put on the same level the authority of heathen customs and that of the Lord. It is therefore with reason that most commentators refer these two examples to Jewish worship, with this difference only, that according to Meyer and others, the two propositions refer to the priests, while according to others,—Chrysostom, for example,—the first refers to the Levites, the second to the priests; or finally, according to a third class, the first denotes the Levitical order as a whole (Levites and priests together), and the second, the priests only. This last meaning seems to me the only admissible one. *To minister about holy things*,

[1] T. R. with A L: προσεδρευοντες; the other nine: παρεδρευοντες.

in the first proposition, is a very general expression comprehending all the acts and all the individuals devoted to the temple service; whereas *serving at the altar* applies to none but to priests, who alone offered the victims on the altar. It is well known that the Levites lived by their employment by means of the tithes and offerings paid by the people, and that in like manner the priests lived by the altar, first by means of the tithe which the Levites paid to them, and then specially by the portion of the victims which was reserved for them. It is this last custom which explains the term συμμερίζεσθαι, *to partake with* the altar. Finally, the apostle reaches the unanswerable argument: the positive order of the Lord Himself.

Ver. 14. "Even so hath the Lord ordained that they which preach the gospel should live of the gospel."—Rückert does not think that we have here a new argument; he regards it as only the application to the Christian Church of what was common among Jews and Gentiles (ver. 13). But the apostle could not possibly have presented the consequence of a Jewish or Gentile usage as a positive command of the Lord. We must therefore understand the οὕτω καί in the sense of: *And so also.* This is the last fact which completes the proof of the apostles' right. When Paul says: *hath ordained,* he is thinking of a saying of Jesus; it is that of Matt. x. 10 and Luke x. 7. He knew it from apostolic tradition, as he did that which he has already quoted vii. 10. It is somewhat remarkable that in 1 Tim. v. 18 this command of Jesus is connected, as in our passage, with that of Deuteronomy cited in ver. 10.—By the dative τοῖς καταγγέλλουσιν, *to them who preach,* Paul does not mean that it is *to the* preachers the command is given; it is the dative of favour: *for them.* The expression: *live of the gospel,* may apply, according to time or place, to free gifts or to a regular salary. It is only the principle which is of importance.—According to St. Paul, the Lord has established in His Church a class of members occupying a particular position. While other believers realize the new life in the exercise of a secular profession which affords them a livelihood, they renounce every secular occupation to consecrate all their time and powers to the development of the spiritual life in others; and consequently the Church to which they thus consecrate their life is bound to provide for their material support, as Jesus provided for the maintenance of His disciples from the day when He commanded them to leave their nets, and said to them: "I will make you fishers of men." Such is the foundation of the institution of the Christian ministry. The object of Jesus in establishing it was not to institute a new priesthood, a human mediatorship between God and the Church; but neither did He wish to abandon the development of His work to the spontaneous zeal of the faithful. He has avoided these two opposite rocks, and confined Himself to instituting a *ministry* to preach and have the cure of souls, the members of which live *for* the gospel, and consequently ought also to live *of* the gospel. But woe to the man who claims to live *of* the gospel without living at the same time *for* the gospel!—Paul has reminded his readers that he was really an apostle (vers. 1–3), and then demonstrated by five arguments of increasing force the right which therefore belongs to him and his fellow-labourers (vers. 4–14). He now reaches the idea which he had in view from the beginning: that of the voluntary sacrifice which he has made of this right (vers. 15–17). In ver. 15 he expresses the fact of the sacrifice itself; in vers. 16–18, the reason which impels him to act thus.

VERS. 15–18

Ver. 15. "But I have used[1] none of these things: neither have I written these things, that it should be so done unto me: for it were better for me to die, than that any man[2] should make my glorying void."[3]—Paul contrasts the sacrifice which he has made of his right, and consequently of his well-being and ease, with the selfishness of those of the Corinthians who, without any self-restraint, used their liberty in regard to sacrificed meats.—The aorist ἐχρησάμην, in the T. R., would refer to the initial act of renunciation; the perfect κέχρημαι, in almost all the Mjj., denotes the permanent state of privation founded on the act. This reading is preferable.—The expression: *these things*, may refer to the manifold *rights* which are comprehended in that of being supported (comp. vers. 4, 5), or to all the numerous *reasons* alleged, from ver. 4 onwards, to justify this right. "I have used none of them," signifies in this second case: "I have not made them good." After such an enumeration, the second

[1] T. R. with K: εχρησαμην; all the rest: κεχρημαι.

[2] T. R. with C K L P reads ινα τις (*that any one*); F G: τις (*any one*); ℵ B D: ουδεις (*no one*).

[3] T. R. with K: κενωση (*should make void*); all the rest: κενωσει (*shall make void*)

meaning is more natural.—It is remarkable that Paul, after speaking in the first person plural, vers. 4–6, here passes to the first person singular. This is because in what follows, the matter in question, as we shall see, is a fact absolutely personal, the consequences of which do not concern the others except as his fellow-labourers in the work of the apostleship among the Gentiles. —But Paul will not have it supposed that he has written all this long demonstration, that in the future a different treatment should be observed toward him than that which has hitherto prevailed. The word *οὕτω, so,* signifies in the context: "*As I might be entitled to require,* and as in fact is done for others;" comp. the similar elliptical *οὕτω,* vii. 26 and 40. The *ἐν ἐμοί* here signifies, as often: *in regard to me* (Matt. xvii. 12). It is so far from being the desire of the apostle to induce the Church to make a change in this respect, that he would rather be deprived of his ministry by death, than discharge it on any other condition than its being gratuitous. The reading of the T. R. is simple, provided we allow a very common inversion in the words *τὸ καύχημά μου,* which belong to the proposition of *ἵνα*; comp. iii. 5, and 2 Cor. ii. 4. Thus the meaning is: "Than the fact that as to my cause of glorying, any one should deprive me of it." This cause of glorying is certainly the fact of preaching the gospel gratuitously. "I should like rather to be taken from my work by death, than to do it without having this cause of glorying." But there exist two readings different from this; and first that of the two ancient Alex. (*Vatic.* and *Sinaït.*) and of the *Cantabr.*; see the critical note. Those who bind themselves to the readings of these MSS. are greatly embarrassed by such a text. Meyer, in his second edition, explained the ἤ in the sense of *than*, and held an aposiopesis: "Than this that as to my cause of glorying. . . . No! no man shall make it void." This construction is excessively forced. Edwards, without being disposed to justify it, accepts it from want of having anything better to propose. Meyer himself, since the date of his fourth edition, no longer gives to the ἤ the sense of *than*, but that of *or*, and he thus explains: "It is better for me to die (than to preach the gospel without having this ground of boasting); *or*, if I must still live, no one shall make void my ground of glorying (by preventing me from continuing to act as I have hitherto done)." Every one must feel how wire-drawn this meaning is in comparison with the simple sense expressed by the received reading; and in any case, after the comparative μᾶλλον, *rather*, it is unnatural to give to the conjunction ἤ any other meaning than that of *than*. The other divergent reading from that of the T. R. is that of the two Greco-Lats., F G: "Or, as to my ground of glorying, who shall be able to make it void?" But this question does not logically agree either with the preceding or the following sentence; then the order of the words would be far from natural in this sense; finally, the ἤ ought after μᾶλλον to signify *than*, rather than *or*. Lachmann puts a period after ἀποθανεῖν, as Ambrosiaster had already done: . . . *magis mori. Nemo gloriam meam evacuabit.* Then, himself perceiving the impossibility of this interpretation, he proposes to read νή, instead of ἤ, in the sense of a solemn affirmation: "By my ground of glorying, no one will make it void," a sense more impossible still. Holsten, after proposing some conjectures (κενῶσαι or ἐξουδενῶσαι), despairs of restoring the authentic text. Rückert likewise concludes his excellent discussion by saying: "The result to which I come, therefore, is that we do not know what Paul himself wrote, but that of all proposed to us, the best is the received reading." Klosterman (*Probleme im Aposteltexte*, 1883) concludes for the meaning of the text F G, but by putting the following verse in the mouth of one who he supposes attempts to make void the apostle's ground of glorying by alleging that he preaches, not from moral motives, but from constraint. Such interpretations do not call for discussion. In my view, it was evidently the Greco-Latin documents which in ver. 10 had preserved the true reading, and it is no less clear that here it is the Byzantines (supported in this case by Cod. *Ephrem* and by the *Peschito*) which we ought to follow. There is nothing impossible in admitting the required inversion. Only it is better to read the future κενώσει, *shall make void*, than the subjunctive κενώσῃ. The copyists finding that the indicative did not agree with the ἵνα, replaced this conjunction either by the interrogative pronoun τίς (F G) or by the pronoun οὐδείς (Alex.). Others (Byz.) transformed the indicative into the subjunctive. As to the ἵνα, *in order that*, it does not lose its signification of an end to be reached. This end is, making void the subject of Paul's glorying, an end which he ascribes to the man who should wish to induce him to accept a salary.

And why would the apostle prefer no longer to preach at all, and even *to die*, to exercising a paid ministry of the gospel? It is because the act of preaching in itself contains nothing which furnishes him with a ground of glorying. For to fill this office is with him a matter of necessity; it is an: I must!

Ver. 16. "For though I preach the gospel, I have nothing to glory of:[1] for necessity is laid upon me; for[2] woe is unto me, if I preach not the gospel!"—Many have taken the first proposition as a general maxim. Paul would say, that in itself the act of preaching is not a cause of glorying to the preacher, whoever he may be. But why not, if he discharges this task with all his heart and in love to his Lord? For we shall immediately see what in Paul's sense is to be understood by a ground of glorying. Besides, in a passage of so personal a character as this, the first person singular can only designate Paul himself. If to him personally the act of preaching the gospel is not a ground of glorying, it is because this is a task which he is *forced* to discharge. In fact, if he does not do it, the threatening of a terrible condemnation hangs over his head. When dictating these words: "Woe to me if I do not . . .," the apostle is no doubt thinking of the Lord's threatening: "It would be hard for thee (it would cost thee dear) to kick against the pricks" (Acts ix. 5). What a difference between an apostleship thus conferred and that of the Twelve, who had become attached to Christ by an act of free faith! Their call, with such a preparation and ground, and the ministry which followed it, were a work of free will; while he,

[1] ℵ D E F G read χαρις (*grace*), instead of καυχημα (*ground of glorying*), which T. R. reads with A B C K L P Syr. Cop.

[2] T. R. reads δε (*then*) with K L Syr., instead of γαρ (*for*), which is the reading of all the rest.

Paul, had been, as it were, seized with living force in the way of obstinate unbelief, and constrained by threatening to obey the call. Such an apostleship in itself offers nothing satisfying to the heart of him who is invested with it. By καύχημα, *a cause of glorying*, we are not here to understand a cause of boasting; such a thought would belie the apostle's entire evangelical conception. The word is well explained by Heinrici: "the joyous feeling of the moral worth of one's own action." This is not the Pharisaical pride of *merit* connected with the work. It is the grateful heart which needs to feel that it is doing something *freely* to correspond to the love of which it has been the object. The reading χάρις, *favour*, in the Greco-Lat. and the *Sinaït.*, would only have meaning if we understood it in the same sense as Luke vi. 32, 33: a *title* to Divine favour. But the close relation between this verse and the preceding speaks for the received reading and demands the term καύχημα.—Though the δέ after οὐαί ("*but* woe . . .") may be logically defended, the γάρ, *for*, being better supported and offering a simpler logical connection, should be preferred: No ground of glorying, for there is constraint; and there is constraint, *for* damnation awaits me if I withdraw from the task.

Ver. 17. "For if I do this thing willingly, I have a reward: but if against my will, it is a dispensation which is committed unto me."—The γάρ, *for*, signifies that the second part of ver. 16 really proves the affirmation enunciated in the first, to wit, that Paul has no cause of glorying in the act of preaching, if he does so by constraint.—The first of the two propositions contains a simple supposition, stated in passing to form a contrast with the second, which alone expresses the real fact. As Heinrici well says: "If I preach the gospel willingly—*which is not the case*—I have a reward." The second proposition signifies, on the contrary: "But if I do so by constraint—*as is really the case*—it is a dispensation committed . . ." In the first proposition the apostle could have used the optative πράσσοιμι ἄν: If *I should do so* of good-will . . . He has preferred the indicative πράσσω, *if I do so*, probably because he knows that this case, denied so far as he is concerned, is in fact realized in the case of others: "If, like those who freely became preachers (the Twelve, ver. 5), I preach of my own good-will." The words μισθὸν ἔχω signify: "I have right in this case to a recompense." This term *recompense*, μισθός, is correlative to καύχημα, cause of glorying. The second denotes Paul's action, whereby he can give to his work a character of freedom; the other, the advantage which should accrue to him from it. We shall see in ver. 18 what this advantage is.—The two terms ἑκών and ἄκων (*willing* and *unwilling*) do not refer, as some have thought, to the subjective disposition with which the apostle usually filled this ministry: "If I preach with ardour . . . or if I preach against my will." Thus understood, the two propositions of the verse would not fall into the context where the subject is preaching gratuitously. Paul is speaking of the manner in which he was *charged* with the apostleship. As the term ἑκών alludes to an apostleship freely accepted, the term ἄκων refers to the constraint which characterized the origin of his, the ἀνάγκη of ver. 16.

The last words, οἰκονομίαν πεπίστευμαι, literally: *it is a stewardship with which I am charged*, signify: I must by all means fulfil it. The construction is the same as Rom. iii. 2. These words contrast the situation of a slave with that of the freeman. Among the ancients, stewards belonged to the class of slaves (Luke xii. 42, 43). Now a slave, after completing his task, has no recompense to expect; he would simply have been punished had he not done it. The sense is therefore: "I do slave's work, nothing more." Such was the position made for Paul by the mode of his calling to the apostleship; and it would remain what it is, servile, if he were content to preach the gospel like the other apostles. But this is precisely the position which he will not have, and to which he would prefer death itself. He would feel himself related to his Lord, not as a slave, but as a freeman, a friend; and hence it is that because this element of free-will had been lacking in the origin of his apostleship, he introduces it afterwards; how? This is what is explained in ver. 18.

Ver. 18. "What is[1] my[2] reward then? [It is] that, when I preach the gospel, I may make the gospel[3] without charge, that I use not the right which belongs to me in my preaching."—According to Meyer, the understood answer to the question: "What is my reward?" is negative: "I have none; I receive no reward." And the sequel signifies, according to him: "And it is so willed of God that I may render the preaching of the gospel free of charge, which alone can

[1] D F G It.: εσται (*shall be*), instead of εστι (*is*).
[2] T. R. with B D F G L P It. reads μοι; ℵ A C K: μου.
[3] T. R. with F G K L P Syr. here adds του Χριστου (*of the Christ*).

procure me a true recompense." Idea and construction, all is forced in this explanation. That of Hofmann is equally far-fetched. All of his explanation I can understand is, that he continues the question to the end of the verse: "What is the reward which could lead me to make the preaching of the gospel free of charge?" But the meaning which he gives to this question is beyond my comprehension. Paul's question after what precedes has a very simple meaning: "If the apostleship in itself gives me no ground of glorying because it is forced upon me, and if consequently it does not assure me of any reward, what shall I do after all to obtain that reward without the hope of which it would be impossible for me to labour?" The answer follows: "The way which presents itself to me, is to make the preaching of the gospel without charge. Thereby I do at least something which was not imposed on me; I introduce into my apostleship that element of freedom which was wanting at its origin, and I thus establish, as far as in me lies, a sort of equality between me and the apostles who attached themselves freely to Christ." We have here a feeling of exquisite delicacy, and, if one may so speak, of transcendent modesty, which is far from having been always understood. Baur, especially, has thought that there is here the idea of the merit of works, which Paul had cherished during the time of his former Pharisaism. The apostle imagines, he thinks, that he can do more than is strictly obligatory, and thereby procure supererogatory merit before God. But Paul wishes simply to escape from the position "of the unprofitable servant who does only what he is obliged to do" (Luke xvii. 10).

He wishes at any price to pass from the servile state to that of a freeman acting from gratitude. The apostle does not for a moment suppose, when he thus speaks, that love goes beyond moral obligation rightly understood, but only that love is more than the legal and purely external fulfilment of duty. This latter secures against punishment; but it does not introduce the servant into his master's intimacy. It is strange to hear the apostle accused of going back to his old Pharisaic viewpoint in the very passage where he expresses most forcibly the insufficiency of the external work, and the imperious need of a spiritual relation to his God. The proposition beginning with the ἵνα, *in order that,* is the grammatical subject of the understood proposition containing the answer to the question: "What, then, is my reward?"—"It is that *I may make* without charge . . ." This ἵνα, *in order that,* is not altogether equivalent to a simple ὅτι, *that;* it indicates the aim as ever requiring to be attained anew.—The word μισθός, *reward,* denotes, as is shown by the end of the verse, the advantage which Paul gains for the preaching of the gospel by the gratuitousness with which he follows it. This useful result for the kingdom of Christ is the *reward* which corresponds to the internal feeling of elevation (καύχημα) which is imparted to him by the position as a free servant, thus acquired.—The form εἰς τὸ μὴ καταχρήσασθαι, *so as not to use* . . ., is almost equivalent to a Latin gerund: in not using. We need not here, any more than in the passage vii. 31, give to καταχρῆσθαι the sense of *abuse.* The κατά simply strengthens the notion of *using:* to use to the utmost. Paul means that there remains of his right a portion which he does not use, that this remnant, which he declines to use, may impress on his ministry the character of free-will which is wanting to it by nature (from the mode of its origin).

There is, perhaps, no passage in the apostle's letters where there are more admirably revealed at once the nobility, delicacy, profound humility, dignity, and legitimate pride of his Christian character. Serving Christ cannot give him matter of joy except in so far as he has the consciousness of doing so in a condition of freedom. And this condition he must gain by imposing on himself a mode of following the apostleship more laborious for himself, but more favourable to the propagation of the gospel, than that used by the other apostles, on whom the office of preacher was not imposed. But for this very reason we also understand how personal and exceptional this renunciation was which the apostle practised, and that it would be unjust to set it up as a model for the ordinary preachers of the gospel. Finally, let us call to mind that we have not here to do with an arbitrary renunciation imposed by Paul on himself with the view of inflicting meritorious and, in a sense, expiatory suffering. Paul had discerned how useful and even indispensable to the honour of the gospel this mode of acting was, especially in Greece. It was the one way of distinguishing the preaching of salvation from that venal eloquence and wisdom on which the rhetoricians lived.

With ver. 18 Paul has closed the digression relative to apostolic payment. But his abnegation is not confined to that; it extends to his entire conduct in his ministry. In all respects he acts on this principle:

to give up his liberty from regard to others, so far as it can contribute to save them.

Vers. 19–22

Ver. 19. "For though I be free from all, I made myself servant to all, that I might gain the more."—Paul formulates the general principle on which is founded the particular self-denial of which he has just spoken, and which guides all his conduct. Thus the *for* finds its natural explanation. By the term *free*, Paul returns to the question of the first verse, the theme of the whole passage.—Most commentators of our day take πάντων in the masculine sense : *from all men.* But the preposition ἐκ, *out from,* is not very suitable in this sense ; it would rather require ἀπό. 'Εκ supposes a domain from which one goes forth. Paul has therefore in view all the legal prescriptions relating to meats, days, forbidden touchings, and in general everything in religion and morals which belongs only to the external form. As to himself, he felt that he was no longer subject to any restriction of the kind. Yet he consented to accommodate himself to the prejudices of any man, rich or poor, great or small, who held to any of these observances, and that for the very reason that in his eyes they were indifferent ; he was infinitely less afraid of sacrificing his liberty than of using it so as to compromise the salvation of one of his brethren. We must therefore take πᾶσιν, *to all*, in the masculine sense as certainly as we take πάντων in the neuter sense (see on ver. 22).—The pronoun ἐμαυτόν, *myself,* indicates the apostle's action on himself, necessary to effect this deliberate subjection. — The words τοὺς πλείονας, *the more*, have been variously explained. Rückert: as many as possible; Neander, Edwards: more than I should have gained without that; de Wette, Meyer, Holsten: the greater number of those to whom I preach; Heinrici: more than those whom I had gained by acting otherwise; Hofmann, Alford: in greater number than those who have been converted by others. The most natural meaning seems to me to be: to gain *them* (these πάντες) *in greater number* than I should have done by acting otherwise. Account is thus taken both of the article and of the comparative.—The word *gain* should not be taken in the sense which has become almost technical, in which we say: to gain one to the faith or to the gospel. The term is taken in its purely natural meaning. The apostle regards the salvation of a soul converted by him as a personal gain; for he identifies his possessions with those of Christ. What he gains for Christ is a part of his μισθός, his reward.—The following verses are the development of the word ἐδούλωσα, *I made myself servant.*

Vers. 20–22. "And unto the Jews I became as[1] a Jew, that I might gain Jews; to them that are under the law, as under the law, though myself not under the law,[2] that I might gain them that are under the law; 21. To them that are without law, as without law, being not without law to God, but under the law through Christ,[3] that I might gain them[4] that are without law;

[1] F C omit ὡς.

[2] This clause is omitted by T. R. with D^gr. K the most of the Mnn. Syr^sch. It is found in ℵ A B C E F G P It. Vg. Sah.

[3] T. R. with K L: θεῳ, Χριστῳ (*in relation to God, to Christ*); ℵ A B C D F G P It.: θεου, Χριστου (*of God, of Christ*).

[4] T. R. omits τους with F G K L.

22. To the weak became I as weak,[1] that I might gain the weak: I am made all[2] things to all, that I might by all means save some."[3]—We might regard *the Jews* and *those who are under the law* as forming only one class of persons, under two different aspects: first in their national, and then in their religious relation. The first term would refer to their language, dress, etc.; the second, to their dependence on the law. But this distinction is somewhat far-fetched. Is it not better to understand by the first term those who were Jews by origin, and to include in the second, with those same Jews, all the proselytes of Gentile origin who accepted the yoke of the Mosaic law?—While, on the one hand, the apostle inflexibly refused every concession in favour of the law, to which an obligatory character could be attached (Gal. ii. 3–5), he was, on the other hand, equally pliable and accommodating toward any one who might be scandalized by entire independence of legal observances. Thus are explained the circumcision of Timothy (Acts xvi. 3), the vow of Cenchrea (xviii. 18), and the docility of the apostle in regard to the request of James relative to the Nazarite vow at Jerusalem (xxi. 26). The absence of the article before *'Ιουδαίους* arises from the fact that Paul wishes to designate not the individuals, but the category: Jews. The word *νόμος*, *law*, is without article, because what is expressed here, as Holsten says, is the notion of the genus or kind. The omission of the words: *though not without law*, in the Byz., arises probably from the

[1] T. R. with C D E F G K L Syr. omits *ως* (*as*), which ℵ A B read before *ασθενης*.

[2] T. R. with E K L P reads *τα* before *παντα*.

[3] Instead of *παντως τινας*, D E F G It. read *παντας*.

mistake of a copyist whose eye passed on from the second ὑπὸ νόμον to the third. The proselytes to whom, as well as Jewish Christians, the second part of the verse relates, forms the transition to the Gentiles, ἄνομοι, *without law* (ver. 21).

Ver. 21. The term: *them that are without law*, is not taken in the sense: rebels to law, as in 2 Thess. ii. 8. Its meaning is simply privative: those who are not subject to a law. Paul has made himself like them by taking the freedom secured by Christ from all legal observances which do not come under the permanent moral law. But, while affirming this, he declares himself subject, in his inmost life, to the true law, the Divine will which has become through Christ his personal will. The T. R. reads with K L the datives θεῷ and Χριστῷ, while the Alex. and Greco-Lats. read the genitives θεοῦ and Χριστοῦ. By the dative, Paul says that he is not without law *relatively to* God in virtue of the inner law, according to which he lives by the fact of his union with Christ. The genitive rather indicates a relation of possession, which in this case cannot well apply to anything except to the law itself. "Not without feeling myself bound by a *law of God*, seeing that, on the contrary, as Christ's possession, I carry the law in me." It must be confessed that the meaning of the first reading is much simpler and more normal. But to explain the two readings one might conjecture an intermediate one: θεοῦ in the first clause, Χριστῷ in the second. In any case, Paul distinguishes three moral states: a life *without* law, that of the Gentile; a life *under* the law, that of the Jew (Rom. vii.); and a life *in* the law, that of the believer (Rom.

viii.). In the first state the will is given up to its natural tendencies; in the second, it is subject to a rule which controls it from without, and which it obeys only by constraint; in the third, the human will is identified by the Spirit of Christ with the Divine law; comp. Jer. xxxi. 33.—For the absence of the article (if we reject τούς with the T. R.), see on ver. 20.

Ver. 22. I think with most commentators, that *the weak* in this verse denotes Christians who are yet slenderly confirmed, such as those mentioned in chap. viii. No doubt the term *gain* does not apply to them in the same sense as to the Jews and Gentiles of whom Paul has been speaking; but the consequence of their weakness, if one should scandalize them, by making them return to their Gentile or Jewish life, might yet be to *destroy* them, as is shown by passages of the Epistles to the Corinthians and to the Hebrews. Paul did not regard them as gained till they were secured against such relapses. Edwards rightly remarks, that we have here exactly the three categories of persons whom Paul mentions in concluding this part, x. 32: "Jews, Greeks, and the Church of God."—The ὡς, *as*, before ἀσθενής, is probably an addition. The apostle may well say that he became weak when he adopted a line of conduct resting on scruples which he did not share.

The last words of the verse sum up the entire passage; they correspond to the first of ver. 19. Not being able to cite all the particular subjects of accommodation, Paul comprehends them in a general expression: τὰ πάντα, *all things*. Here we have very certainly the neuter employed side by side with the masculine τοῖς πᾶσιν, *to all*, confirming our interpretation of the πάντων, ver. 19. The words πάντως τινάς, *absolutely some*, signify: "in any case some at least of the mass," that is to say, of the multitude of the unbelieving or indifferent whom he met in the capitals of the heathen world where he proclaimed the gospel. No observance appeared to him too irksome, no requirement too stupid, no prejudice too absurd, to prevent his dealing tenderly with it in the view of saving souls.—The word *save*, which he here substitutes for *gain*, clearly shows what he understood by this gain; the salvation of his brethren, this formed his riches!

Thus Paul's conduct was as far removed from the licence or insolent superiority of the liberals of Corinth as from the timorous servility of the weak Christians. Free in respect of everything, he made himself the slave of all from love. What firmness of principle, and at the same time delicacy of conduct, what a combination of strength and gentleness, elevation and humility! How had this fiery steed been tamed and trained by his skilful rider! While preserving his nobility and high spirit, he had acquired the most admirable adaptability. It seems to me difficult to believe that when thus describing his conduct, Paul had not in view the charge of versatility which his adversaries brought against him (2 Cor. i.). As in the previous passage he had indirectly rectified the consequences which his adversaries drew from his refusal of payment, he wishes here to explain to the Church the alleged inconsistencies with which he was charged in his conduct as to Mosaic observances. It was no matter of inconstancy or guile (1 Cor. ii. 15 seq.), but of love.

Thus far the apostle has claimed of believers the renunciation of their rights from regard to the salvation of their neighbour. Now he presses the proud and intractable Corinthians more forcibly, by showing them that it is not their neighbour's salvation only that is at stake in this matter, but also their own. This new and more pressing consideration is developed on to x. 22.

B. The Question considered from the Viewpoint of the Salvation of the Strong themselves (9:23-10:22)

As Paul concluded the preceding development by giving his own example, he introduces the following in the same way. In vers. 23–27 he shows the danger which he himself ran, if he ventured to deviate from the austere path of voluntary renunciation. Then, in chap. x. 1–11, he presents a second example to the Corinthians, that of the people of Israel when they had come out of Egypt, whose numerous chastisements in the wilderness were called forth by their loose abandonment to their lusts. Finally, vers. 12–22, he applies these examples to the present situation of the Corinthians.

1. *The example of the apostle* (vers. 23–27)

Ver. 23. "Now then I do all things[1] for the gospel's sake, that I might be partaker thereof also."—The δέ, *then*, is progressive; it marks the transition from

[1] T. R. with K L Syr. reads τουτο (*this*); all the rest, παντα (*all things*).

interest taken in the salvation of our brethren to care for our own. To understand this verse, we need not construe it in the way in which it is usually done, as if the verb *I do* had two regimens; the first, *for the gospel,* and the second, *that I might . . .,* the latter being regarded as explaining the former. The explanation would not square sufficiently with the term to be explained. There is, it seems to me, only one motive, that which is indicated by the *that,* the salvation of Paul himself. This will appear if we paraphrase as follows: "If I act thus for the gospel, it is that I myself might be partaker thereof." Those sacrifices which he makes for the preaching of the gospel (διὰ τὸ εὐαγγ.), he makes that he may himself share in the salvation which he preaches; comp. ver. 27, which is the key of all that precedes. This life of self-denial, then, is the only condition on which Paul founds the hope that he may one day be welcomed by the Judge and receive the crown from His hand.—If we read τοῦτο, *this,* with T. R., the reference is to the general principle of conduct expounded above. If, with the Alex. and the Greco-Lats., we read πάντα, *all things,* the word refers to the various applications of the principle which have been enumerated. The last reading seems preferable. — The Greek expression literally means: *fellow-partaker of the gospel.* The apostle means: partaking with all other believers in the blessings which it confers, and in those which it promises. Paul would not at any price be deprived of the salvation and glory made sure to other preachers by the freedom with which they perform their task. These words should open the eyes of the Corinthians, who will deny themselves nothing, to the danger to which they thus expose themselves. Edwards explains Paul's phrase in the sense: "to be a partaker of the *spirit* of the gospel." Certainly Paul does not think that the reward promised to the faithful can be separated from the possession of the evangelical spirit. But ver. 27 constrains us to think specially of salvation, and of the salvation, present or final, which the gospel promises. Ver. 19 expresses in a positive form the same idea as ver. 27 does negatively.

To illustrate this terrible thought, the apostle borrows a figure from the most exciting spectacle which Greek life presented. Every two years there were celebrated near Corinth the Isthmian games, which, like the other public games of Greece, such as the Olympic and Nemæan games, included the five exercises of leaping, throwing the discus, racing, boxing, and wrestling. All Greece witnessed these competitions with the warmest interest, and the athlete who was proclaimed the victor received the admiration and homage of the whole nation; see the description given by Beet, p. 157 seq. It is quite probable, as the same author says, that, during the two years Paul had passed at Corinth, he had himself witnessed the Isthmian games, at least once.—Paul makes use here only of the two exercises of racing and boxing.

Ver. 24. "Know ye not that they which run in a race, run all, but one receiveth the prize? So run, that ye may obtain."—In the application, the *goal* is no more identical with the *prize*, than in the actual case. The goal is perfect holiness; the prize is glory, the crown of holiness. Of course, in mentioning the fact that out of a number of runners only one reaches the goal first, and obtains the prize, the apostle does not mean, that of the multitude of Christians only one will be saved. What he desires to inculcate by the figure is, that to succeed in the Christian race, one must labour for his salvation with the same energy and the same resolution to reach the goal of holiness, as this one victor to reach the goal of the race. Like him, the Christian must learn to forget everything else, that he may see only the goal to be reached. They are not very many, Paul means, who, while calling themselves Christians, run after this manner! The word οὕτω, *so*, may be regarded as a particle of inference: "*so then* run, that ye may obtain." But it may also be made the antecedent of the conjunction ἵνα: "Run *in such a way that* . . ." There is more vivacity in this second meaning of οὕτω. This little word, rightly understood, seems intended to cheer and stimulate the runners. It is objected, that instead of the ἵνα, *that*, a ὥστε, *so that*, would have been needed. But the ἵνα brings out better the aspiration of the runner after victory.—When the apostle speaks of this *one*, does he allude to his own mode of acting? Possibly (vers. 26, 27). In any case they ought to beware, those Corinthians — fond of their ease and obstinately attached to their rights and liberties—lest they be in the end like those slack runners who lose the prize. To win, it is not enough to run, it is needed to run *well* (Rückert). This idea is the transition to the following verse.

Ver. 25. "Now, whoever strives for the mastery abstains from everything: they to obtain a corruptible crown; but we an incorruptible."—Edwards rightly says: "This verse reminds the Corinthians of two things: first, the difficulty of winning, and next, the infinite value of victory." The participle *every man striving* relates, not to the time when the athlete is already in the lists, but to the time when he enrols himself among those who are to take part in the competition. During the ten months before the day of the games, the competitors lived in sustained exercises and with special self-denial, abstaining from everything that could exhaust or weight the body. For the Christian, whose conflict is a matter, not of a day, but of the whole life, abstinence, the condition of progress in sanctification, is consequently an exercise to be renewed daily.—The abstinence of the athletes did not relate only to criminal enjoyments, but also to gratifications in themselves lawful; so the Christian's self-denial should bear, not only on guilty pleasures, but on every habit, on every enjoyment which, without being vicious, may involve a loss of time or a diminution of moral force.

Should any complain of this condition of final triumph, Paul reminds them that the athletes make such sacrifices with a view to a passing honour, whereas they have in prospect eternal glory. The pine crown which the judge put on the victor's head in the Isthmian games, while it was the emblem of glory, was at the same time the emblem of the transitory character of that glory. For the spiritual victor there is reserved an unfading crown!

Vers. 26, 27. "I therefore so run, not as uncertainly; so fight I, not as one that beateth the air: 27. But I buffet[1] my body, and lead it captive: lest, when I have preached to others, I myself should be rejected."—The particle τοίνυν, *conformably thereto*, does not occur elsewhere in Paul's writings; it forcibly expresses a consequence inevitably resulting from what precedes: "In virtue, then, of this state of things in which there is nothing to be changed."—The word *run* denotes the progress made in Christian sanctification; comp. Phil. iii. 13, 14.—As to the οὕτω, it is evidently here the antecedent of ὡς.—The adverb ἀδήλως has sometimes been taken in the passive sense: "Without being seen, remarked," like a runner who is lost in the crowd of other athletes. The apostle would thus expressly designate himself here as the *one* who attracts the attention of the spectators, by outstripping the other runners. This meaning would be admissible if such an expression were not rather pretentious. It is better to give the adverb the active sense: "Without seeing the goal, and consequently the course, clearly, as when one walks in the dark; so: deviating to right and left." This meaning is more in keeping, as we shall see, with that of the following figure: *beating the air*, which has an analogous signification, as is proved by the parallelism of the two propositions. Paul alludes to that sterile activity of the sages and orators of Corinth, who neglect the true end of Christian life, sanctification and final salvation, and are concerned only to charm their hearers, to enjoy themselves with them, and to lord it over them. As for him, he runs with his eye

[1] T. R. with ℵ A B C D reads υπωπιαζω (*I buffet*); F G K L P read υποπιαζω (*I subject*); and D[c] with several Fathers: υποπιεζω (the same meaning).

firmly fixed on the goal. — Next, to bring home this obligation still more forcibly to his readers, he refers to a second and more formidable kind of contest, boxing. Here there is not only running, but striking and being struck. And the blows, to be effective, must not be lost on the air ; they must fall on the adversary. The term *beat the air* has sometimes been taken as an allusion to the kind of gymnastics in which the athletes engaged to prepare themselves for the contest, and which was called *sciomachy*. But we are here in the heat of the contest itself. The allusion therefore, if there was one, could only in any case be very indirect.

Ver. 27. The apostle explains by his own example who the adversary is on whom these redoubled and redoubtable blows are to fall ; it is his own body. He does not say his flesh, as if he wished here to lay stress on the characteristic of sin in the body ; no, it is the organism, as such, that he curbs and bends by all sorts of exercises and austerities to make it a pliable instrument. There is room for hesitation between the two readings ὑπωπιάζω, *I buffet* (the verb strictly signifies : to strike under the eyes, so as to make blue wounds), and ὑποπιάζω or ὑποπιέζω, to grip so as to put under. This second reading would suit the following verb : to lead captive ; but the first agrees better with the foregoing verb : *to give blows with the fist*. By this figure the apostle describes all the privations which he imposes on his body, all the labours to which he condemns it throughout the entire course of his life, and that especially in consequence of his refusing all payment and obliging himself to provide with his hands for his maintenance ; comp. 2 Cor. vi. 4, 5, xi. 23–27 ; Acts xx. 34, 35.—

The word δουλαγώγω, *to lead captive*, continues the figure. As the victor led the vanquished round the arena, amid the plaudits of the spectators, so Paul, after breaking the opposition of his body, leads it like a submissive servant before the face of the world in the labours of the apostleship.

And let not this be taken as a work of supererogation, fitted to confer on him some peculiar merit and a higher degree of glory! In his eyes, there is no luxury in the question, it is a simple necessary. Were he to act otherwise, he should be afraid, he who has stimulated others, of being himself finally rejected. One can hardly avoid seeing in the term κηρύσσειν, to fill the office of herald, to publish, an allusion to the function of the man whose duty it was to sound the trumpet and so summon the athletes to begin the contest. Such is the figure of what the apostle was doing for the Gentile peoples by the preaching of the gospel. Rückert, it is true, objects, that, in the public games, the herald himself did not enter the lists. Comparisons always halt somewhere; otherwise they would imply not comparison, but identity. The Christian ministry presents this exceptional character, that he who fills it has two tasks to perform simultaneously: that of calling others to salvation, and that of securing his own. Heinrici has thought that the point here was the approbation or disapprobation which the herald might deserve by the way in which he proclaimed the name and eulogy of the victors, after the combat. This is to press the figure beyond all measure.—The term ἀδόκιμος, *non-acceptable*, to be rejected, comes, grammarians say, from δέχομαι, *to receive*. This term also belonged to the language of the public games. Before admitting candidates to the honour of competing in the circus, they were subjected to a preparatory trial, called *δοκιμασία*, by means of which there were set aside all those who were not fit to enter the lists. Could Paul be alluding to this custom? It seems to me improbable. His concern is not about the trial for *entrance* into the contest, but about the exit trial. The terms *δόκιμος* and *δοκιμή* are so frequently used by the apostle, that it is unnecessary to explain the use of them here by an allusion which would be so far from appropriate. It is his salvation, the welcome to be received by himself from the Judge, which the apostle sees to be at stake, and with a view to which he thinks it his duty to use such severity toward his own body.

Such is the mode in which the apostle seeks to awake feelings of salutary fear and serious watchfulness in those self-infatuated Corinthians, who, on the ground of their superior knowledge and alleged emancipation, forgot the regard which they owed to the salvation of their brethren, without imagining that by this conduct they were compromising their own.

The better to inculcate the manner in which they should act, he seeks at that very moment to make himself a Greek to the Greeks, borrowing from their national life the figures most fitted to strike their imagination.—It has often and justly been remarked, how frequent these figures, borrowed from the contests of the stadium, are in the authors of the New Testament Epistles (Phil. iii.; 2 Tim. iv.; Heb. xii., etc.), while they are wholly strange to the discourses of Jesus in the Gospels. Have we not here a proof of the fidelity with which the original form of the latter has been preserved to us? Why, if they had been composed later, and after the Gospel had penetrated into the Greek world, should not such figures so familiar to Greek thought appear in them?

2. *The example of the Israelites* (10:1-11)

This passage is the continuation of the foregoing. What the apostle has just indicated as a possibility for himself, he now points out as a reality in the history of the Jewish people. In them we have a nation who, after having been the object of the most ample favours from God, favours even which were perfectly analogous to those we enjoy as Christians, nevertheless perished because of its failure in self-renunciation. In fact: 1, the Israelites having come out of Egypt had all participated in the extraordinary favours which accompanied this deliverance, vers. 1–4; 2, and yet they almost all perished in the wilderness, ver. 5; 3, such is the image of the lot which threatens the Corinthians if they act in the same manner, vers. 6–11.

The analogy between this passage and the preceding is striking: this nation, that had come out of Egypt to get to Canaan, corresponds to the runner who, after starting in the race, misses the prize, for want of perseverance in self-sacrifice. The one runner whom the judge of the contest crowns is the counterpart of the two faithful Israelites, to whom alone it was given to enter the Promised Land.

But in the following passage we have no longer to do with a simple comparison; it is more serious; we enter into the realities of history. The apostle, as has been remarked here, becomes a Jew to the Jews, as he had formerly become a Greek to the Greeks.—Vers. 1–4. He begins by recalling the favours bestowed on the Jews in and after their deliverance from the Egyptian captivity, and he compares these favours with those enjoyed by Christians. For the salvation founded by the ministry of Moses in Israel is one and the same work with the salvation brought in by Christ; and the laws of Divine action, which directed the former of these deliverances, are exactly the same as those to which final salvation is subject.

Vers. 1, 2. "Indeed,[1] brethren, I would not that ye should be ignorant, how that all our fathers were under the cloud, and all passed through the sea; and were all baptized[2] into Moses in the cloud and in the sea."—The connecting particle δέ, *then,* in the T. R. would indicate a gradation which the preceding remarks easily explain: "And there is more here than a simple figure, such as that of the games." This reading is therefore quite suitable; the other, found in the Alex. and Greco-Latins, γάρ, *for,* is also suitable; the *for* bears especially on the last idea of the foregoing verse, the being found worthy of rejection. "And *indeed* the danger exists; what happened to our fathers is the proof of it." This second connection is simpler.—In saying: *I would not that ye should be ignorant,* the apostle would not insinuate that they do not know the account of the exodus from Egypt; he means that he is afraid they

[1] T. R. with K L Syr. reads δε (*then*), instead of γαρ (*indeed*), which is the reading of the nine other Mjj.

[2] T. R. with B K L P: εβαπτισαντο; ℵ A C D E F G: εβαπτισθησαν.

do not sufficiently understand the meaning and bearing of the events to which he here refers.—Meyer has concluded from the expression: *our fathers,* that Paul is here speaking as a Jew, and in the name of Jewish Christians. But by the address: *brethren,* he has just comprehended the whole Church in one and the same body. He therefore sees in the Christian Church the outgrowth of the ancient Israelitish community. Indeed, according to Romans, chaps. iv. and xi., the Church is grafted on the patriarchal trunk; and, in virtue of this spiritual relation, the fathers of the Jewish people are also those of the Christian household. —The prominent place which he gives to the word πάντες, *all,* as well as its repetition in vers. 2, 3, and 4 (five times), show that we have here the essential idea of the passage: "Those people who *almost all* perished, began with being *all* blessed of the Lord." This is the counterpart of ix. 24: "All run, but one obtains the prize."—The verb in the imperfect, ἦσαν, *were,* denotes a state which is prolonged, while the crossing of the Red Sea having been an event of the day is denoted by the aorist (διῆλθον).—The preposition ὑπό, *under,* is construed with the accusative, because it has not merely a local sense here, but expresses the moral notion of protection: they were *under the shelter* of the Divine presence manifested by the cloud.

Ver. 2. After stating the fact, this verse indicates its religious signification and bearing; it was a true *baptism* which was conferred on them all. As the baptized person enters the water and receives the sprinkling on his head, and as this water by the sacramental words becomes to him the pledge of salvation, so the Israelites, placed under the cloud and crossing the sea, possessed the visible pledge of Divine blessing and salvation. This miraculous crossing separated them thenceforth from Egypt, the place of bondage and idolatry, exactly as the believer's baptism separates him from his former life of condemnation and sin. In this parallel there is no petty and Rabbinical typology; everything is well grounded from the moral point of view. The material water did not play any part in the passage of the Red Sea: it is not said either that it rained from the cloud on the Israelites, or that they had their feet plunged in the water. The crossing was to them as baptism is to the believer, the threshold of salvation. This spiritual analogy is expressed by Paul in the words: *and were all baptized into Moses.* By following their God-given leader with confidence at that critical moment, they were closely united to, and, as it were, incorporated with Moses to become his people, in the same way as Christians in being baptized on the ground of faith in Christ become part of the same plant with Him (Rom. vi. 3–5); they are thenceforth His body.—There is room for hesitation between the two readings ἐβαπτίσαντο (the middle), *they had themselves baptized,* and the passive ἐβαπτίσθησαν, *they were baptized.* In favour of the middle form, it can be said that the copyists could easily have substituted for it the passive form, which is more generally used in the New Testament in speaking of Christian baptism. Then the apostle required to bring out in this context the idea of faith in Moses as the *active* principle of the conduct of the Israelites.—Here, probably, with the words of the Old Testament, of which the apostle is thinking, we have the only passage of Scripture in which a man is presented as the object of faith ; comp. Ex. xiv. 31 : "And they believed the Lord, and His servant Moses." No doubt faith, according to the scriptural view, can only have a Divine object, God Himself, His word, His promises, His work ; but when a servant of God is absolutely identified with the Divine will and work, as Moses was, then the absolute confidence which attaches to that which is Divine may also be extended to him. Without faith in the *Divine* mission of Moses, Israel would not have followed him to the wilderness.—The preposition ἐν has rather the instrumental sense (*by*) than the local (*in*).

But the Jews not only received a baptism, they partook also of a Holy Supper :

Vers. 3, 4. "And did all eat the same spiritual meat; 4. And did all drink the same spiritual drink ; for they drank of that spiritual Rock that followed them ; and that Rock was Christ."—As the Holy Supper serves to maintain in salvation those who have entered into it by the faith professed in baptism, so the Israelites also received, after the initial deliverance, the favours necessary to their preservation. These benefits, corresponding to the bread and wine of the Supper, were the *manna* daily received, and the *water* which God caused to issue from a rock in two cases of exceptional distress. The epithet πνευματικός, *spiritual*, cannot refer to the *nature* of these two Divine gifts ; for they were material in substance. We may interpret it in two ways : either in the sense of *typical*, if we regard the material gift as the figure of a higher and future one ;

or in the sense of *supernatural*, in so far as these gifts were the immediate products of creative energy, regarded as proceeding from the Divine Spirit (Gen. i. 2; Ps. xxxiii. 6). I doubt whether examples can be quoted sufficient to establish the first of these two meanings; Rev. xi. 8, the only passage adduced by Edwards, is not convincing. The second meaning, on the contrary, is in harmony with biblical language in general and with that of the apostle in particular, though Holsten alleges the contrary; comp. Gal. iv. 29. Moreover, it must be considered that the first meaning, by lowering the gifts made to the Israelites to the level of mere figures, would so far diminish the force of the argument; while the second, by representing them as miraculous gifts, gives it additional solidity: Heavenly food, and He did not save them! Supernatural water, and those who drank it perished under condemnation! — The pronoun *τὸ αὐτό, the same* (food), does not refer, as is thought by Calvin and Heinrici, to the identity of these gifts with those bestowed on Christians. The one point in question is the relation of the Israelites to one another. *All* partook *equally* of this miraculous nourishment; and two were saved!

Ver. 4. Paul here refers to the two events related Ex. xvii. 6 and Num. xx. 11. The miraculous character of the water which came from the rock is explained by the following proposition (*for*); it follows from the spiritual nature of the rock whence it flowed. The word *spiritual* cannot therefore have here a meaning exactly similar to that which it had in the foregoing propositions. There this epithet denoted the supernatural origin of the material gifts. Applied, as it is here, to the *source* of the miraculous water, it can only designate the *nature* of the rock; for it is this nature which explains the creative energy that was inherent in it and the supernatural effects it could produce. To produce this supernatural water, there was needed a rock Divine in its nature.—Several commentators, Rückert, Baur, de Wette, Meyer (1st edns.), have thought that Paul was here appropriating the Rabbinical fable, according to which a material rock rolled over hill and dale across the desert beside the camp of the Israelites, so as to supply them with the water they needed; it was Miriam, Moses' sister, who above all was said to possess the secret of getting this water. But how can we imagine for a moment the most spiritual of the apostles holding and teaching the Churches such puerilities? In any case, even if he meant to allude to so ridiculous a fable, which we greatly doubt, he has done so in such a way as to make palpable the wide divergence between the Rabbinical opinion and his own. In fact, the object of the two epithets ἀκολουθούσης and πνευματικῆς, *accompanying* and *spiritual*, is certainly to distinguish exactly the invisible and spiritual Rock of which he himself speaks, from the material rock spoken of in Exodus, that of which the Lord said to Moses the first time: "I will stand before thee there upon the rock in Horeb, and thou shalt smite the rock, and there shall come water out of it," and the second time in the wilderness of Sin: "Take the rod . . . and speak to the rock . . ., and thou shalt bring forth water from the rock." These two rocks already stood there when Israel arrived in these localities, and they remained there when Israel left them. Paul, therefore, can only mean one thing: that behind these material and immoveable rocks, there was one invisible and moveable, the true giver of the water, to wit, the Christ Himself. If anyhow such is the meaning of the narrative of Exodus, in Paul's view, where is place left for a third sort of rock at once spiritual and material and of a nature wholly incomprehensible? The imperfect ἔπινον, *drank,* indicates duration, a repetition of similar cases; and this because the spiritual Rock was always present in the mysterious cloud which accompanied Israel. This is what the apostle expresses when he adds: *and that Rock was Christ.* Meyer, after abandoning his first explanation, adopts the view, since his 4th ed., that these words constrain us to hold that Paul regarded the Rock as a visible and real manifestation of the Christ, who accompanied Israel in the cloud, according to the words of the Targum of Isaiah (xvi. 1) and of Philo, who say that "the rock was *wisdom.*" But the idea of the incarnation of the Christ in a rock is so contrary to the spirit of St. Paul, that one cannot entertain it seriously, and ver. 9 represents the Christ in the wilderness acting as the representative of Jehovah, from the midst of the cloud! Is it not perfectly simple to explain this figure of which Paul makes use, by the numerous sayings of Deuteronomy, in which the Lord is called the Rock of Israel: "The Rock, His work is perfect" (xxxii. 4); "Israel lightly esteemed the Rock of his salvation" (ver. 15); "Of the Rock that begat thee thou art unmindful" (ver. 18), etc., and by all those similar ones of Isaiah: "Thou hast not been mindful of the Rock of thy strength" (xvii. 10); "in the Lord is the Rock of ages" (xxvi. 4)? Only, what is special in the passage of Paul is, that this title of Rock of Israel, during the wilderness history, is ascribed here, not to Jehovah, but to the Christ. The passage forms an analogy to the words John xii. 41, where the apostle applies to Jesus the vision in which Isaiah beholds Adonai, the Lord, in the temple of His glory (ch. vi.). Christ is represented in these passages, by Paul and John, as pre-existent before His coming to the earth, and presiding over the theocratic history. In ch. viii. ver. 6, Paul had designated Christ as the Being *by whom* God created all things. Here he represents Him as the Divine Being who accompanied God's people in the cloud through the wilderness, and who gave them the deliverances which they needed. We have the same view here as appears in the *angel of the Lord*, so often identified in Genesis with the Lord Himself, and yet distinct from Him, in the Being who is called in Isaiah the *angel of His presence* (lxiii. 9), and in Malachi the *angel of the covenant, Adonai* (iii. 1), the Mediator between God and the world, specially with a view to the work of salvation. It is easy to understand the relation there is between the mention of this great theocratic fact and the idea which the apostle wishes to express in our passage. The spiritual homogeneity of the two covenants, and of the gifts accompanying them, rests on this identity of the Divine head of both. The practical consequence is obvious at a glance: Christ lived in the midst of the ancient people, and the people perished! How can you think yourselves, you Christians, secure from the same lot!—It is clear that there is no good ground for holding, as Holsten does, the second part of this verse to be interpolated. It enters perfectly into the course of the argument.—Reuss alleges that with such a conception of history as the apostle here expresses, "one comes very near seeing nothing more in it than pure allegories, and not realities." It seems as if this critic would like to make St. Paul the forerunner of his own critical system. He forgets that it is one thing to derive a moral application from an accomplished fact, and another to assert that the fact itself is only an illustration of the moral idea.

It has been justly observed that in this passage we find for the first time the combination of the two sacred acts of baptism and the Lord's Supper, as forming a complete whole: the one representing the grace of entrance into the new life, the other the grace by which we are maintained and strengthened in it. The combination of these two acts, under the particular name of *sacraments*, is not therefore an arbitrary invention of dogmatic.

The Israelites, after their exodus from Egypt, all received Divine favours analogous though inferior to those which Christians themselves enjoy; and, notwithstanding, what a judgment!

Ver. 5. "But with most of them God was not well pleased: for they were overthrown in the wilderness."—Ἀλλά: notwithstanding so great favours.—*They were overthrown* . . ., an allusion to Num. xiv. 29: "Your carcases shall fall in the wilderness." What a spectacle is that which is called up by the apostle before the eyes of the self-satisfied Corinthians: all those bodies, sated with miraculous food and drink, strewing the soil of the desert!

Vers. 6–11. From these facts the apostle derives this lesson: The greatest blessings may issue in the greatest judgments.

Ver. 6. "Now these things were our examples, to the intent we should not lust after evil things, as they also lusted."—*These things:* this rejection, this curse after such blessings.—*Examples for us;* strictly: *examples of us,* that is to say, of what will happen to ourselves if we follow their example.—The use of the plural (ἐγενήθησαν) follows by attraction from the predicate τύποι.—The word τύπος, *type,* which comes from τύπτω, *to strike,* strictly denotes an impression in which an already existing image is reproduced. But, strange to say, in the history of the kingdom of God, the figure which serves to produce the impression does not appear till after the impression itself; it has indeed a pre-existence relatively to it, but only in the Divine mind. In history, the derived impression appears first, on one of the lower stages of revelation, and the model figure does not appear till a more advanced epoch of the kingdom of God.—*That we should not lust after* . . . Literally: "that we should not be *lusters* of evil things." The noun (ἐπιθυμητής) denotes the permanent disposition, the inward vice, while the particular acts are denoted by the verb in the aorist (ἐπεθύμησαν).—The word ἐπιθυμία, *lust,* expresses, as is shown by its composition, the motion of the soul (θυμός) toward (ἐπί) a good thing which God does not give, egoistical and discontented aspiration.—By *evil things* are to be understood the enjoyments which God does not grant, either because they are evil in themselves, or because, perfectly legitimate as they are, God requires them to be sacrificed in the service of love or for the sake of watchfulness. The phrase: *desirous of evil things*, includes all the following *sins*, and reveals their common cause, just as the phrase *to be overthrown* sums up all the *judgments* which are about to be enumerated. —These examples are four in number; two refer to pleasures which God refuses, vers. 7, 8; two to the feelings of irritation and rebellion excited by this refusal, vers. 8, 9.

Vers. 7, 8. "Neither be ye idolaters, as were some of them; as[1] it is written, The people sat down to eat and drink, and rose up to play. 8. Neither let us commit fornication, as some of them committed, and fell in one day three and twenty thousand."[2]—The μηδέ, *neither*, connects this proposition closely with the preceding; we pass from lust to the acts in which it seeks its satisfaction.—The example quoted is that of the worship of the golden calf, and of the profane feast which followed it, Ex. xxxii. The verb παίζειν, strictly: *to play*, is specially used of dancing.

Ver. 8. The danger of fornication was always connected with idolatry. At Corinth, therefore, it might easily follow participation in the sacrificial feasts.—The example quoted is that mentioned in Num. xxv., where, according to Balaam's treacherous advice, the Israelites were enticed to a sacrifice offered by the Midianites to the god Baal-Peor, and where they let

[1] T. R. with C D K P: ως; the rest: ωσπερ.
[2] Two Mnn. Syr. Armen.: εικοσι τεσσαρες (*twenty-four thousand*).

themselves be drawn into this sin.—The Old Testament relates (ver. 9) that 24,000 perished of the plague, inflicted by the wrath of the Lord. St. Paul speaks only of 23,000. We might admit a slip of memory. But the figure 24,000 is exactly reproduced in Philo and Josephus and the Rabbins. Are we to suppose that Paul did not know his sacred history so well as they? The same fact prevents us from supposing a variant in the text of the Old Testament. May we not here suspect a piece of Rabbinical refinement, similar to the: *forty stripes save one*, spoken of in 2 Cor. xi. 24? To avoid the risk of exaggeration, it had become the habit, in oral teaching we may suppose, to speak of 23,000 instead of 24,000 (see Calvin).—The transition from the second person (*that ye become not*, ver. 7) to the first (*that we commit not*) seems to arise from the fact that the second danger was much more common than the first, and might apply to Christians in general.

Vers. 9, 10. "Neither let us tempt the Christ[1] as[2] some of them tempted Him, and were destroyed[3] of serpents; 10. Neither[4] murmur ye as[5] some of them murmured, and were destroyed of the destroyer."—The first of the two sins against which the Corinthians are indirectly put on their guard in these verses, is evidently the discontent which they feel on account of

[1] T. R. with D E F G It. Syr^{sch} Sah. reads τον Χριστον (*the Christ*); ℵ B C P: τον κυριον (*the Lord*); A: τον θεον (*God*).

[2] T. R. with E K L adds και (*also*).

[3] T. R. with Greco-Lat. and Byz.: απωλοντο (*perished*); A B: απωλλυντο (*were perishing*).

[4] T. R. with A B C K L P Syr.: γογγυζετε (*murmur*); ℵ D E F G: γογγυζωμεν (*let us murmur*).

[5] ℵ B P: καθαπερ (*absolutely as*), instead of καθως (*as*).—T. R. with B L reads και after καθως or καθαπερ.

the self-denial required by their Christian call. The example quoted is that of the Israelites dissatisfied with the food to which they are reduced in the wilderness, and who are punished by the scourge of the fiery serpents (Num. xxi. 5 seq.).—The expression *to tempt God,* so often used in Scripture, signifies : to put God to the proof, to try whether He will manifest His goodness, power, and wisdom either by succouring us from a danger to which we have rashly exposed ourselves, or by extricating us from a difficulty which we have ourselves wilfully created while reckoning on Him, or by pardoning a sin for which we had beforehand discounted His grace. This, according to the biblical view, is one of the greatest sins man can commit. The Jews committed it in the wilderness by their murmurs, because they sought thereby to challenge the display of Divine power in the service of their lusts. The Corinthians in their turn committed it by pushing to its utmost limits the use of their Christian liberty in regard to heathen feasts. Could our Christianity, said they, really forbid to us those pleasures? Is not God able to keep us from falling even in such circumstances? And even if we should fall, would not His grace be ready to pardon and raise us again? They thus claimed to make God move at their pleasure, even should it be necessary to work miracles of power or mercy to save them.—Of the three readings τὸν κύριον, *the Lord,* τὸν Χριστόν, *the Christ,* and τὸν θεόν, *God,* the last should be set aside without hesitation; it has only the Alexandrinus in its favour; it is a correction following the usual biblical phrase *to tempt God.* The other two come to the same thing in point of sense; for the term *the Lord* always denotes Christ in the New Testament when it is not found in a quotation from the Old. It might be said in favour of the reading *the Lord*, that it explains more easily the other two; but in favour of *the Christ*, we have, first, the agreement of the two Greco-Latin and Byzantine families, then the more extraordinary form and the greater difficulty of the expression, finally, its appropriateness in the application of the saying to the Corinthians and the comparison of ver. 4. This reading is also preferred by Osiander, Reuss, Heinrici, Hofmann, etc. For the meaning of it, see on ver. 4.

Ver. 10. Here is the fourth trespass of which St. Paul speaks: the murmuring against Moses and Aaron. The fact which he cites is that related Num. xvi.; the revolt of Korah, Dathan, and Abiram, in consequence of which a sudden plague destroyed the despisers of the servants of the Lord. Some have thought of the event related Num. xiv., where, in consequence of the report of the spies sent to Canaan, the people murmured and rebelled. But this sin was not followed by any immediate judgment; it became the occasion of the sentence pronounced on those who were more than twenty years of age when they came out of Egypt, a sentence which was executed only slowly during their whole journeying in the wilderness. The intervention of the destroying angel indicates a sudden and mortal plague; this circumstance is certainly not mentioned in the narrative of the punishment of Korah and his companions; but it is supposed by the term *maggēpha, the plague*, ver. 48 (Hebrew text, xvii. 13), which

St. Paul interprets by Ex. xii. 23. In quoting this example, he certainly has in view the irritation felt by a party among the Corinthians against himself, his fellow-labourers, and those of the leaders of the flock who along with them disapprove of taking part in heathen rejoicings. This party chafed at their severity, which gave rise to so painful a situation for Christians in relation to their friends, and they asked, as Korah and his followers did in respect of Moses and Aaron, Whether the authority they exercised over the Church was not a usurpation?—Of the two readings *murmur* and *let us murmur*, the first ought to be preferred, in the first place, because the second probably arises from an assimilation of this verb to the verbs of vers. 8 and 9; and next, because we have here an admonition altogether special, applicable only to the Church of Corinth, like that of ver. 7, where already the second person was used. — The imperfect ἀπώλλυντο, *were perishing*, is preferable to the aor. ἀπώλοντο, *perished;* it makes us witnesses, as it were, of the mournful scene.

Ver. 11. "Now all [1] these things happened [2] unto them for ensamples: [3] and they are written for our admonition, upon whom the end of the world is come." [4]—This verse is the summary of all the foregoing examples; a fact which leads us to prefer the reading of the *Sinaït.* and of the Greco-Lats., which preserves and even places foremost the word πάντα, *all.* —The two readings τύποι, "as *types*," and τυπικῶς,

[1] T. R. with C K L P Syr. reads: ταυτα δε παντα; א D E F G: παντα δε ταυτα; A B: ταυτα δε.

[2] Two readings: συνεβαινεν and συνεβαινον.

[3] T. R. with D E F G L: τυποι; א A B C K P: τυπικως.

[4] T. R. with A C K L: κατηντησεν; א B D F G: κατηντηκεν.

typically, have the same meaning; but the second is to be preferred, first, because it is read in MSS. of the three families; and next because the word τυπικῶς occurs nowhere else. The substantive τύποι has probably come from ver. 6.—Of the two readings συνέβαινον and συνέβαινεν, the first goes better with τύποι, the second with τυπικῶς.—The apostle does not mean that these facts did not really happen, as has been insinuated, but that they had a bearing beyond their immediate signification. The Scripture compilation of the facts of sacred history has the same end as the history itself. The same God who directed the latter willed that it should be committed to writing with a view to those who should live in the final epoch of the world, and for whom those facts, without Scripture, would be as though they were not.—The word νουθεσία signifies: *rebuke, correction*, 2 Tim. iii. 16, 17. This is what the Corinthians needed at that time.—Τὰ τέλη τῶν αἰώνων, literally *the ends of the ages*, is a term corresponding to the *acharith hajjamim, the end of the days*, in the prophets; comp. the expressions *the last times* (1 Pet. i. 20), and *the last hour* (1 John ii. 18). It is the dispensation of the Messiah which for us falls into two periods, confounded in one in the view of the prophets, that of His purely spiritual kingdom and that of His kingdom of glory. Paul is here speaking of the former. *The ages*, αἰῶνες, denote the whole series of historical periods, and the term "*the ends* of the ages," shows that the Messianic period itself will contain a series of phases.—The verb καταντᾷν, *to meet*, represents the ages which follow one another in the final dispensation, as coming to meet the living. We must prefer the perfect κατήντηκεν of the Alex. reading to the aorist of the T. R.; Paul does not mean to speak of the meeting itself, but of the whole state of things constituted by this constant approach of the end. This final period is the most solemn of all, for it is during its course that the laws of the Divine kingdom, imperfectly manifested in former periods, display their conclusive effects. Formerly blessings and judgments, all have only a provisional and figurative character. With the final period of history, everything, whether for weal or woe, takes a decisive, eternal value. This is why everything which happened in former times took place with a view to us to whose lot it has fallen to live at this last hour (ἡμῶν εἰς οὕς).—The apostle did not himself know the duration of this final period, which in his mind coincided with the development of the Church; but the phrase: *the ends of the ages*, shows that he did not regard it as so short as is commonly alleged; see on vii. 29.

3. *The application of these examples to the Church of Corinth* (vers. 12–22)

The parallel which the apostle had proposed to draw between the Israelites and Christians is closed. He now makes the practical application of it to the spiritual state of the Corinthians, an application which has, in the first place, a general character (vers. 12, 13), but which soon passes more specially to the important point which Paul has in view from ix. 23, participation in the sacrificial banquets (vers. 14–22).

Vers. 12, 13. "Thus, then, let him that thinketh he

standeth take heed lest he fall! 13. There hath no temptation taken you but such as is common to man: but God is faithful, who will not suffer you to be tempted above that ye are able; but will with the temptation also make a way to escape, that ye[1] may be able to bear it."—The ὥστε, *so that*, which we render by *thus then*, indicates that this exhortation to watchfulness is the inference to be drawn from the foregoing examples. There is here in the term δοκεῖν, *to think*, a notion, not of illusion, but of presumption. Paul allows indeed that the person addressed by him *is standing*, for he afterwards speaks of the danger he is in of falling; but the very claim to be standing may lead to neglect of vigilance, and thereby to a fall.—Ἑστάναι, perfect infinitive contracted for ἑστακέναι or ἑστηκέναι. The two figures *to be standing* and *to fall* do not represent the state of grace or condemnation, but the state of fidelity or sin; comp. Rom. xiv. 4.

Ver. 13. This verse is undoubtedly one of the most difficult of the whole Epistle, at least as to the logical connection joining it to what precedes and to what follows. This is very apparent when we study the commentaries. Many commentators (Meyer, Heinrici, Holsten, Beet) find here an encouragement fitted to soften the severity of the warning of ver. 12, in this sense: "And it is easy for you with watchfulness not to fall; for your previous temptations have not hitherto exceeded your strength, and should they be even greater, the faithfulness of God is a pledge to you that they will not go beyond it in the future." The absence of the particle δέ at the beginning of the verse seems

[1] The υμας, *you*, in the T. R. is only found in K.

to me incompatible with this meaning. Besides, the Corinthians had more need of being admonished than tranquillized. Finally, and above all, the asyndeton with the preceding context leads us rather to expect an emphatic reaffirmation of the need of vigilance, than an encouragement. This has been felt by the ancient Greek commentators, Chrysostom, etc., and several moderns, such as Bengel, Olshausen, Rückert, Neander, and, to a certain extent, Edwards. The meaning, according to them, is this: "Take so much the more heed as you are not yet out of danger. Up till now you have not been very greatly tempted" (Edwards: "It has not yet gone" the length of blood, of persecution; Heb. xii. 4); "but how will it be if there should come on you stronger temptations than the former? God no doubt will still protect you, but on condition that you watch." But is not this whole series of ideas very complicated? Then the force with which the faithfulness of God is expressed in the second part of the verse is not in keeping with so threatening a sense. The following, as it seems to me, is the true order of the apostle's thoughts: "If you should fall thus (ver. 13), you would be without excuse; for the temptations which have met you hitherto have not been of an irresistible nature, and as to those which may come on you in the future, God is always ready to sustain you and to save you in time from peril." The conclusion is drawn in ver. 14: "Wherefore beware of throwing yourselves into temptations to which you are not exposed by God Himself, and to which you would certainly succumb." This meaning seems to me to be nearly that of Hofmann. The Corinthians must be made to understand that they run no risk of sinning and falling away from faith, if they have only to encounter the temptations which God allots to them, but that they have no pledge of victory whatever in the case of temptations into which they throw themselves with light-heartedness. The passage is therefore at once an encouragement in respect of the former, and a grave warning in respect of the latter.

The term πειρασμός, *proof, temptation,* comprehends all that puts moral fidelity to the proof, whether this proof have for its end to manifest and strengthen the fidelity—it is in this sense that God can tempt, Gen. xxii. 1; Deut. xiii. 3;—or whether it seeks to make man fall into sin—it is in this sense that God cannot tempt, James i. 13, and that the devil always tempts. It may also happen that the same fact falls at once into these two categories, as for example, the temptation of Job, which on the part of Satan had for its end to make him fall, and which God, on the contrary, permitted with the view of bringing out into clear manifestation the fidelity of His servant, and of raising him to a higher degree of holiness and of knowledge. There are even cases in which God permits Satan to tempt, not without consenting to his attaining his end of bringing into sin. So in the case of David, 1 Chron. xxi. 1; comp. with 2 Sam. xxiv. 1. This is when the pride of man has reached a point such that it is a greater obstacle to salvation than the commission of a sin; God then makes use of a fall to break this proud heart by the humbling experience of its weakness. Such undoubtedly is the meaning in which we are to say: "Lead us not into temptation." These remarks will find their application in the immediate sequel.—It is possible to refer the term ἀνθρώπινος, *human*, to the *origin* of the temptation. There is not one of your temptations which did not proceed from man, either from the evil heart and its natural lusts, or from the example of other sinners. The temptations of which Paul thus speaks, would be opposed either to those which come from God, or rather to those which have Satan for their author. And indeed the context might lead us to think of the diabolical temptations to which the Corinthians did not fear to expose themselves when they took part in those feasts where the breath of Satan diffused an atmosphere all impregnated with idolatry and sensuality; "God has never put you into positions so diabolical; it is yourselves who seek them." This meaning would be natural enough in the context; but the following words of the verse would in this case seem intended to encourage the Corinthians to brave such dangers by the promise of Divine succour, which it is impossible to hold. It is better, therefore, with most commentators, to apply the epithet *human* to the *nature* of the temptation: "A temptation proportioned to the strength of man;" but without isolating man from God, for God only can give man victory even in the slightest temptation. And to account more fully for this unprecedented expression, must we not contrast it with an *angelic* temptation? Suppose the Corinthians, impatient of the apostle's exactions, should in their ill-humour express themselves thus: "We should require to be angels to live as he demands!" "No," Paul would answer; "I do not ask of you superhuman sacrifices in the name of your Christian profession.

Your faith has not put you into a situation which a weak man cannot bear; but God is faithful, and He measures the temptation to the amount of strength." Then the apostle adds, that if the situation became difficult to such a degree as to appear utterly intolerable, the faithfulness of God would show itself by putting an end to such a situation. Thus everything seems to me to find its natural connection.—The words ὑπὲρ ὃ δύνασθε, *beyond what ye are able*, come as a surprise. Has man then some power? And, if the matter in question is what man can do with the Divine help, is not the power of this help without limit? But it must not be forgotten, that if the power of God is infinite, the receptivity of the believer is limited: limited by the measure of spiritual development which he has reached, by the degree of his love for holiness and of his zeal in prayer, etc. God knows this measure, Paul means to say, and he proportions the intensity of the temptation to the degree of power which the believer is capable of receiving from Him, as the mechanician, if we may be allowed such a comparison, proportions the heat of the furnace to the resisting power of the boiler. It is evident from the words: *with the temptation*, that God co-operates with it in the sense we have spoken of above, and this is precisely the reason why He can also bring it to an end at any moment He chooses.—The *issue*, ἔκβασις, may be obtained in two ways. Either God by His providence can put an end to the situation itself, or by a ray of light from on high He can rid the believer's heart of the fascinating charm exercised over him by the tempting object, and change into disgust the seductive attraction which it exercised. Of the two ways, the struggle to the death between inclination and duty issues in the victory of the believer. The conclusion is this: "Victory being assured over the temptations which God sends you, seek not to throw yourselves into those which He does not send" (ver. 14).

Hofmann rightly observes, that nothing rendered the breach of the converted heathen with his past and with his surroundings so conspicuous as his refusal to take part in the sacrificial feasts. And so, many Corinthians sought to persuade themselves that they might harmonize this participation with their Christian profession. Had they not declared the nothingness of idols? Such a feast, therefore, had no longer for them the character of a sacrifice; it was a purely social act, to which the great maxim of Christian liberty in regard to external things applied: "All things are lawful for me." Paul well knew that here was the most difficult sacrifice to be obtained. Accordingly with what prudence does he proceed! His whole handling of the question is a masterpiece of strategy. In chaps. viii. and ix. he treats the Corinthians as *strong;* only for the sake of their brethren does he ask them to deny themselves meats offered to idols; he encourages them by describing the sacrifices which he has made and is daily making for the Churches and the gospel. Then suddenly (ix. 23) he passes to an entirely new order of considerations: "And if I act thus," he adds, "it is also for the sake of my own salvation, which I should certainly compromise by acting otherwise." Then he demonstrates the reality of this danger by the case of the Israelites who drew down on themselves the Divine condemnation by revolting against the self-denial which the wilderness life imposed on them. "Do ye also, therefore, fear to fall by refusing to God the sacrifices which He asks of you!" At this point, after having gradually enclosed them in his net, he all at once ties the knot so long prepared for, and finally pronounces in ver. 14 the decisive word:

Vers. 14, 15. "Wherefore, my dearly beloved, flee far from idolatry. 15. I speak as to wise men; judge ye what I say."—The address so full of tenderness: *my dearly beloved,* expresses how much it costs him to be obliged to impose on them a sacrifice which he knows to be so painful.—*Διόπερ, precisely on this account:* because you can reckon on God's help in the temptations which He appoints to you Himself, but not in others.—The expression: *flee far from,* is certainly used designedly. In a similar passage, vi. 18, Paul had used the verb *flee* simply with the substantive as its object. If he here interposes the preposition ἀπό, *far from,* it is to tell them, not only to flee idolatry itself (that would have been superfluous), but to flee far from all that approaches it or might lead them into it. The sacrificial feasts were not quite idolatry, but they bordered on it and might lead to a fall into it.

Ver. 15. Then he appeals to their own judgment. For he would have the decision to proceed from their conscience. The Corinthians boast of wisdom; he appeals to this very wisdom. The second proposition of this verse has sometimes been taken as the object of the verb of the first: "I pray you as intelligent people to judge what I say." But it is much more natural to take as the object of the verb *I say* the whole argument which follows in the passage, vers. 16–22: "I proceed to expound my thought to you; judge yourselves what I advance." On the term φημί, see on vii. 29. He would impose nothing on them; but he proceeds to submit to them certain premisses which they cannot gainsay, and from which there will follow a consequence, which they cannot refuse, without rejecting those premisses themselves.

The following passage rests on these principles: that any religious act whatever brings us into communication with the spiritual world, that this exercises a power, and that the nature of the influence thus exercised depends each time on the character of the invisible Being to which the worship is thus addressed. Thus the Holy Supper brings the believer under the influence of Christ (vers. 16, 17); the Jewish sacrifice brings the Israelite into contact with the altar of Jehovah (ver. 18); and the heathen sacrificial feast brings man under the influence of the demons whose arts have given birth to idolatry.

Vers. 16, 17. "The cup of blessing which we bless, is it not the communion of the blood of Christ? The bread which we break, is it not the communion of the body of Christ?[1] 17. Seeing that there is only one bread, we, being many, are one body: for we are all partakers of one bread."[2] — The Holy Supper is, in the New Testament, the corresponding action to the feast which completed the peace-offering in the Old. The sacrifice once offered, the Jewish wor-

[1] D F G read: κυριου (*of the Lord*), instead of Χριστου.
[2] D E F G It. here add και του ενος ποτηριου (*and of the one cup*).

shipper with his family celebrated a sacred feast in the temple court, in which the priest participated, and in which the part of the victim not consumed on the altar was eaten in common. It was in a manner the pledge of reconciliation which the Lord gave to the sinner on his restoration to grace. So the victim sacrificed is eaten by the believer in the Lord's Supper in token of reconciliation, and the result of this act is the formation of a real communion on the part of the worshipper, first with the victim (ver. 16), then also with all the other worshippers (ver. 17).

As in the second proposition of ver. 16 the accusative ἄρτον, *the bread*, is an attraction arising from the following ὅν, Meyer, Hofmann, Holsten, etc., have thought that it must be so also with τὸ ποτήριον, *the cup*, in the first proposition. But this reason would only be valid if the proposition relative to the bread was placed first; reading the text as it stands, it is impossible to take τὸ ποτήριον otherwise than as a nominative.—The genitive εὐλογίας, *of blessing*, must contain an allusion to the famous cup of the Paschal feast, which bore the name of *cos habberakia*, the *cup of blessing;* it was the third which the father of the family circulated in the course of the feast; he did so while pronouncing over it a thanksgiving prayer for all God's benefits in nature and toward Israel. Jesus had reproduced this rite in the institution of the Holy Supper, but substituting, no doubt, for the Israelitish thanksgiving a prayer of gratitude for the salvation, higher than the deliverance from Egypt, which He was about to effect by His death, the foundation of the new covenant. The meaning therefore is: "The cup over which the Lord uttered the thanksgiving which we repeat when we celebrate this ceremony." Some give the genitive εὐλογίας an active meaning: "The cup which produces blessing." Heinrici compares, in an analogous sense, Ps. cxvi. 13: "the cup of salvation," and Isa. li. 17: "the cup of fury;" he thus explains this complement: "The cup which contains the blessing of Christ." This meaning is less natural in itself; and next, it does not answer to the meaning of the corresponding Hebrew expression. There is only one reason that might lead us to accept it, the desire to escape a tautology with the following phrase: *which we bless.* We could not escape from this awkwardness if, with Meyer, we regarded this last expression as only the explanatory paraphrase of the τῆς εὐλογίας, *of blessing.* Such a repetition would be superfluous. Besides, Paul would have required to say in this case ὑπὲρ οὗ *(for which)*, and not ὅ, "*which* we bless." This pronoun in the accusative shows precisely that these words contain a new idea. It was not only God that was blessed *for* this cup, the symbol of salvation; but the cup itself was blessed as representing that which Christ had held in His hand when He instituted the Supper and said, "This cup is the new covenant in My blood." The complement: *of blessing*, expresses the idea: "May God be blessed for this cup!" and the words: *which we bless,* this: "May this cup be blessed to us!" Comp. the phrase Luke ix. 16: *He blessed the loaves.* It was by this blessing or consecration of the cup as a figurative sign of the blood of redemption that the cup became to the consciousness of the Church the means of participation in the blood of Christ.—The plural: *we bless*, alludes to the *amen* whereby the Church appropriated the formula of consecration. In the age of Justin (middle of the second century), it was the presbyter, presiding over the assembly, who performed this act; we cannot say whether it was so already in the apostle's time. The *Didache* (*Διδαχή*) *of the Twelve Apostles*, describing the ceremony of the Supper (chap. ix.), tells us nothing on this head.

In the principal proposition, the notion of *being* (*ἐστί*) is certainly not the essential idea in Paul's view, as if he wished to insist and to say: "is *really*." In this sense the word *ἐστί* would have required to be placed first both times, before the predicate *κοινωνία*, *the communion*. The emphasis is on the predicate: *the communion*. By this term *κοινωνία*, does the apostle mean to designate a material participation in the blood of Christ, or a moral participation in its beneficent and salutary efficacy for the expiation of sins? In the former case we must hold, that as the instantaneous effect of the consecration, a physical act is wrought, either in the form of a transubstantiation, which makes wine the very blood of Christ, or in that of a conjunction of the blood with the wine of the Supper. But if the real blood of Christ was in one of these two forms offered to the communicant, this so essential element of the rite would certainly have been wanting the first time it was celebrated when Jesus instituted it; for His blood being not yet shed could not be communicated to the apostles. The reference, therefore, could only be to the blood of His glorified body. But the Apostle Paul expressly teaches that blood, as a corruptible principle, does not enter as an element into the glorified body (xv. 50). The two theories, Catholic and Lutheran, seem to us to be overturned by this simple observation.—On the other hand, the apostle's words cannot merely denote, as some commentators have supposed, the profession of faith made by the communicant in the expiatory virtue of Christ's blood, and the thanksgiving with which he accompanies this profession. What does Paul wish to prove by appealing here to the analogy of the Holy Supper? He wishes to demonstrate, by the salutary influence which the communion exercises over the believer's heart, that demons exercise a pernicious one over him who takes part in the heathen sacrificial feasts. The Holy Supper is not, therefore, according to the apostle's view, a simple act of profession and thanksgiving on the believer's part. It is, at the same time, a real partaking of the grace purchased by Christ, and which He communicates to the devout soul of the communicant. This conception is a sort of intermediate one between the two opposite views which we have just set aside, a conception of the kind which Calvin sought to formulate. Especially as to the cup, the communion is an effectual partaking in the expiation accomplished by the blood of Christ and in the reconciliation to God which is thus assured to us; it is our taking in possession that remission of sins, of which Jesus Himself spoke when handing the cup, and by which we are placed in the pure and luminous atmosphere of Divine adoption.

The accusative τὸν ἄρτον, *the bread*, is explained by attraction of the following pronoun ὅν (Matt. xxi. 42). It is occasioned by the fact that the bread is here contemplated in its close relation to the act as a whole; the bread only appears as broken.—The words are not used in connection with the bread, nor with the thanksgiving, nor with the act of consecration, but solely with the breaking of it. It is so, undoubtedly, to avoid repetition; for the bread also was consecrated with thanksgiving. This appears from the passage of Justin in which he calls the Holy Supper: ἡ εὐχαριστηθεῖσα τροφή, the Eucharistic nourishment, for which thanks are given, as well as at a yet earlier period, from the *Doctrine of the Twelve Apostles,* in which there is express mention of the double thanksgiving for the cup and the bread in the primitive Jewish Christian Churches.—The plural κλῶμεν, *we break,* either suggests the moral participation of the whole church in this act which the president performed in memory of Jesus breaking the bread for the disciples, or it supposes a form such as prevails in the Churches where every communicant himself breaks off a piece of the bread which passes from one to another. The term κοινωνία, *communion,* is repeated in connection with the bread; it is, in fact, the notion which unites the two acts in one, and from which has arisen the ordinary name of the sacrament, the *communion.*—Holsten thinks he can apply this word to the relation formed between believers by participation in the Supper. This is to do violence to the term which denotes the inner side of the participation of believers in the sacrament; comp. i. 9. The idea of the relation between communicants will not come till ver. 17, as a corollary from the idea of their union with Christ. It is to get at the same meaning of κοινωνία that some commentators, such as Erasmus, Zwingle, etc., have here applied the term σῶμα Χριστοῦ, *the body of Christ*, to the Church, the community of those who believe in Christ. This explanation is as untenable as Holsten's. It is incompatible with the parallel proposition relative to the *blood* of Christ; in this connection it is quite certain that the body of Christ can only denote the physical organism which Christ possessed here below, an organism represented by the bread broken in the Supper, and of which the blood, taken literally, was the life. The believer's communion with the body of the Lord adds a new element to communion with Christ, founded on participation in His blood; the latter is participation in a benefit purchased *by* Him, that of reconciliation; the former is participation in His person, the assimilation of the very substance of His being. In the blood, represented by the cup, we contemplate and apply to ourselves *Christ dead for us;* in the body, represented by the bread, we appropriate *Christ living in us.* Our communion with this body broken for us, and then glorified, is therefore of a more intimate, more direct, more living nature than communion with the blood. St. Paul himself has expressed this profound fact in all its force and reality in the words: "It is no more I that live, but Christ that liveth in me" (Gal. ii. 20). No doubt this fact is above all of a spiritual nature; it is His holy person whom His Spirit makes to live in us; but this spiritually holy person is at the same time a corporeally glorified person, and Paul himself teaches us that we are in a living relation to it, similar to that by which our natural descent unites us to the first Adam (xv. 48, 49). Participation in His glorified body thus follows from communion with His holy person by the power of the Spirit. If it is so, we find here, though Holsten seeks to show the contrary, the same group of thoughts as in John, when, in chap. vi., Jesus speaks of the necessity of eating His flesh and drinking His blood to have life and *to be raised again at the last day* (vers. 39, 40, 44, 54). It is true, John uses the word *flesh* rather than body. But this is because he means to designate the substance as related to the idea of *eating*, which is naturally the dominant one in the context (following the multiplication of the loaves); whereas Paul speaks of the *body*, as an organism, and that in relation to the notion of *breaking*, which is particularly prominent both in this passage and in xi. 24. This shows no difference of view, but only of relation.—It has been asked why in our passage the cup is placed before the bread, while in chap. xi., and in the institution of the Holy Supper, we find the opposite order. Meyer answers: Because the idea of bread afforded a transition to that of the flesh of the Jewish and heathen sacrifices, immediately to be spoken of; Hofmann: Because wine played the principal part in heathen feasts, and so required to be put first. Edwards, nearly the same: Perhaps because the sacrificial meals were rather *συμπόσια* than *συσσίτια*. I incline to think that Paul, speaking here in name of the Christian consciousness, puts the blood first, because it is expiation which faith appropriates in the first place; while the bread is placed second, because it represents the communication of Christ's power and life, which follows faith in reconciliation by His death. The opposite order was required by the circumstances of the institution of the Supper; see on chap. xi. 24 seq.

Ver. 17. From the communion of every believer with the Lord, Paul deduces the communion of believers with one another; we shall see with what view. This verse may be construed grammatically in three ways. The first and most obvious would be to make the ὅτι, *seeing that*, relate to the preceding verse, while understanding the verb ἐστί in the first proposition: ". . . is the communion of the body of Christ, seeing that there is only one bread." Then, taking this construction as granted, it might be applied also to what follows: "(and) seeing that therefore we are one body, we who are many." So Meyer, Osiander, etc. According to this interpretation, the communion of Christians with one another would be here alleged to prove the communion of Christians with their Head in the Holy Supper. The construction is not tenable: 1, because the existence of two parallel propositions not connected by καί, *and*, would be without example in Paul's writings; 2, because the verb ἐστί, *is*, could not be understood in the first proposition; it would require to be expressed as corresponding to the ἐσμέν, *we are*, in the second; 3, because the proof would be defective. The communion of Christians with Christ in the Holy Supper cannot be demonstrated by the communion of Christians with one another, because this second fact is much less evident to the Christian consciousness.—The second construction also makes the ὅτι, *seeing that*, dependent on ver. 16, but makes the two substantives *one bread* and *one body* two coordinate predicates of *the many*: "seeing that we, *the many*, are one bread, one body;" so Holsten. What a strange mode of expression: *we are one bread!* The more so, as Meyer observes, that the term *bread* can only be taken here in a figurative sense; otherwise there would be a tautology with the following proposition: "We are all partakers of one bread." But if the word *bread* is taken the first time in its mystical sense, why add to it the expression: *one body?* In no sense can the apostle conclude from the fact that all communicants partake of one bread, that they all become that bread!—We must therefore have recourse to a third construction, the only admissible one, as it seems to us; it is that followed by the Vulgate, Calvin, Beza, Rückert, Hofmann, Heinrici, etc. The conjunction ὅτι, *seeing that,* is the beginning of a new sentence; and the subordinate proposition: "*seeing that* there is one bread," is regarded as dependent on the following proposition, which is the principal: "Seeing that there is one bread, we, being many, are one body." The logical nexus which unites these two propositions is explained by the following sentence: *For we are all partakers of the same bread.* The communicants, by all receiving a piece of the same bread, are thereby bound, morally speaking, however numerous they may be, into one spiritual body; for this bread of which they all partake has been solemnly consecrated to represent one and the same object, the body of Jesus. The bond which thus unites them to Jesus as their common Head, unites them also to one another as members of the same body. Here is a subsidiary consideration which the apostle adds to the main argument, indicated in ver. 16. And indeed, by taking part in the heathen sacrificial feasts, the Corinthians would not only separate themselves from Christ, to whom they were united in the Supper; they would also break the bond formed by this same ceremony between them and the Church, the body of Christ.—In the use of this term σῶμα, *body*, Paul passes from the literal sense (the Lord's body), ver. 16, to the figurative sense (the Church), ver. 17; this passage is natural because of the close relation between the two notions. If we become one and the same spiritual body with one another, it is because we all participate by faith in that one and the same body of Christ, with which we enter into relation in the Supper.—The verb μετέχειν, *to partake*, is usually construed with a simple genitive; it takes here the preposition ἐκ, *of, from*: "We all receive (a piece which comes) *from* the same bread." This term differs from the more inward expression κοινωνία, *communion*, in that it denotes external participation in the bread of the Supper. It is obvious that we cannot, with Rodatz and Heinrici, understand the words *one body* in the sense of: "one body *with Christ*." For the matter in question in ver. 17 is the breaking of the bond which unites believers to the Church as a whole.

The apostle quotes as a second example the Jewish sacrificial feasts.

Ver. 18. "Behold Israel after the flesh: are not they which eat of the sacrifices in communion with the altar?"—Israel is placed here by way of transition from the Church to the heathen. There were also among the Jews sacrificial feasts celebrated in the temple precincts, over which God Himself was held to preside, in consequence of the communion established with Him by the expiatory sacrifice; comp. Lev. viii. and Deut. xii., where are found the prescriptions regarding the peace offerings. — The special call for the attention of the readers contained in the imperative βλέπετε, *behold,* arises from the fact that a usage is in question which is stranger to their sphere than the preceding. By the qualifying κατὰ σάρκα, *after the flesh,* Paul means to bring out the external character of the Israelitish worship, in opposition to the spiritual worship of the true Israel, the Church.—It is no doubt under the influence of the same thought that he says: "In communion with the *altar,*" rather than in communion with Jehovah. By sacrifice the guilty Israelite was replaced within the theocratic organization, of which the altar was the centre, rather than in communion with God Himself. As an analogous expression, Heinrici quotes the description of Philo, who calls the Israelitish priest κοινωνὸς τοῦ βώμου. The Epistle to the Hebrews shows why the blood of the victims could do no more.—It is evident that an Israelite who had eaten his part of the victim at Jehovah's table, and had thus made fast the bond which united him to the theocracy, could not thereafter take part in a heathen ceremony without committing a moral enormity. In the following verses the apostle gives the application of these examples.

Vers. 19, 20. "What say I then? that the meat offered to the idol is anything? Or that an idol is anything?[1] . . . 20. But the things which they sacrifice,[2] they sacrifice to demons, and not to God. Now I would not that ye should be in communion with demons."—The way in which Paul had just cited the two previous examples evidently assumed that he ascribed a diabolical influence to the sacrificial feasts of the heathen; now this idea seemed to be in contradiction to chap. viii. 4, 6, where it had been declared that the gods of the heathen are not real divinities, and that the meat offered on their altar is consequently neither more nor less than simple meat, like any other. Paul therefore anticipates the objection which he foresees: "Art thou not now, contrary to thy previous declarations, allowing a disturbing influence to meats devoted to idols, and consequently, a Divine reality to the idols themselves?" In the order of questions, I follow the reading of the *Vatic.* and the *Cantabrig.*, for it seems to me logical that Paul should begin with the question relating to the meat offered, to ascend therefrom to the question relating to the idol. I admit, however, that the opposite order may also be justified.—The omission of the question relating to the idol in the *Sinaït.*, etc., is one of those many lacunæ, especially in this MS., which are caused by the recurrence of the same letters at the distance of a few words. In the first question: *That the meat offered to the idol is anything?* the word *anything*

[1] The T. R. with K L Syr. reverses the order of the two questions.—The MSS. ℵ A C read only the second, that relative to the idol.—The MSS. B D F P It. Cop. present the text reproduced in the translation.—F G have a peculiar and absolutely inadmissible text.

[2] T. R. with C L reads both times θυει, instead of θυουσιν, and adds with ℵ A C K Syr. τα εθνη (*the Gentiles*), which is omitted by all the rest.

signifies anything exceptional, having power to exercise a particular influence. In the second question: *That an idol is anything?* the *anything* signifies anything real. Sometimes the word τί has been taken as an adjective: "That any idol *whatever* is, that is to say exists" (εἴδωλόν τι ἔστιν, instead of εἴδωλόν τί ἐστιν). But the τί would be superfluous in this sense. It is more natural to take it as the predicate in the two questions.

Ver. 20. The apostle does not even take the trouble of stating the negative answer which he gives to these two questions; he passes directly to the affirmation which concerns him: Jupiter, Apollo, Venus, certainly, are not real beings; but Satan is something. Behind all that mythological phantasmagoria there lie concealed malignant powers, which, without being divinities, are nevertheless very real, and very active, and which have succeeded in fascinating the human imagination, and in turning aside the religious sentiment of the heathen nations to beings of the fancy; hence the idolatrous worships, worships addressed to those diabolical powers and not to God.—The subst. τὰ ἔθνη, *the Gentiles,* is omitted by the *Vatic.* and the Greco-Lats.; it is certainly an explanatory addition. This neuter substantive, once introduced, dragged into the T. R. the singular θύει, instead of the plural θύουσιν.—The subject of this latter verb is understood; it is self-evident.—The term δαιμόνιον, *demon,* which occurs nowhere else in Paul's writings except in 1 Tim. iv. 1, has quite another meaning in the New Testament than in the classics. In the latter it is synonymous with θεῖον, something Divine. Plato in the *Symposium,* says that "demon is something intermediate between God and mortals;" and, in another passage: "That the demons interpret to the gods the things of men, and to men the things of the gods." Imported into biblical language by the version of the LXX., the word there denotes the fallen angels, so often spoken of in Scripture. Thus Deut. xxxii. 17, the LXX. translate the words: *jize-bekou laschschédim . . .*, ἔθυσαν δαιμονίοις καὶ οὐ θεῷ (*sched* probably denoting in Hebrew idols, from *schad*, to rule). The Jews identified heathen divinities with the demons themselves; thus it is that the LXX. translate in Isa. lxv. 11, the phrase: "to prepare a table for the host of heaven," by: "to prepare a table for the demon." The pagan Plutarch (*De defectu orac.*, chap. xiii.) ascribes to wicked spirits all that was barbarous and cruel, for example, human sacrifices in heathen religions. We may compare also Ps. xcvi. 5: "For all the gods of the heathen are demons" (in Hebrew *idols*), and Baruch, chap. iv.: "They sacrifice to demons, not to God." It is in this Jewish acceptation that the term is used here. But the words of the apostle do not imply the idea that every false god worshipped by the heathen corresponds to a particular demon; they signify merely that heathen religions emanate from those malignant spirits, and that consequently the man who takes part in such worship puts himself under their influence. "How was it possible," says Heinrici, "to sit at such a feast, to be sprinkled with the holy water, to obey the prescription of sacred silence, to take part in the joy of the hymns and dances which filled the interval between the sacrifice and the banquet, and finally to be given up to the joy of the feast which crowned the festive day to the glory of the false god, without acting as a worshipper of the heathen divinity?" The diabolical character of idolatry could be masked to a certain extent in Greek heathenism by the charm or majesty of the forms; but is it not clearly unveiled in modern heathen religions, particularly in Hindoo and African forms of worship, in which God's holy image has come at last to give place completely to hideous and ignoble figures? Besides, the inspiring sentiment of these worships is solely that of fear.

The δέ is progressive: "*Now* I would not." This authoritative form is accounted for by the solicitude of love. A father cannot allow his children to deliver themselves into bad hands.

Vers. 21, 22. "Ye cannot drink the cup of the Lord, and the cup of demons: ye cannot be partakers of the Lord's table, and of the table of demons; 22. or do we provoke the Lord to jealousy? are we stronger than He?"—Edwards thinks that the matter in question here is an impossibility in point of *fact*. The heart cannot at the same time receive the holy inspirations of Christ and the impure influences of demons. But in that case the apostle would have used words of a more inward and spiritual character than *cup* and *table*. The impossibility is rather one of *right*: "You cannot morally, that is to say, without self-contradiction, and drawing down on you a terrible judgment, take part at the same time in two worships so opposite to one another." *The cup of demons* is an expression easily understood, when we remember that in the solemn feasts of the ancients the consecration of the banquet took place with that of the cup, accompanied by the libation in honour of the gods. The first cup was offered to Jupiter; the second to Jupiter and the Nymphs; the third to Jupiter Soter. To participate in these three cups which circulated among the guests, was not this to do an act of idolatry, and to put oneself under the power of the spirit of evil, as really as the Jew by sacrificing put himself under the influence of Jehovah, and the Christian by communicating under that of Christ? Materially, no doubt, it was possible to act thus, but not without criminal inconsistency. And what proves that this is the meaning of the: *Ye cannot*, is the fact that, in the sequel, Paul expressly states that the Corinthians already venture to act thus; for he declares the fate which awaits them if they persist (ver. 22).

Ver. 22. The ἤ is taken in its usual sense in Paul's writings: "*Or* if, notwithstanding." In other words: "Or if you will persist in acting thus, do you know what you are doing, and to what you expose yourselves? You provoke in the heart of God that more terrible fire than the fire of wrath, which is called jealousy!" What is the hatred vowed against a declared enemy in comparison with the fury which falls on an unfaithful spouse? The term *παραζηλοῦν, to excite to jealousy*, is taken from Deut. xxxii. 21: "They have provoked me to jealousy by that which is not God" (idols put in the place of God). The text says briefly: "Do we provoke to jealousy?" Holsten regards this indicative as inadmissible, and thinks the meaning of the subjunctive to be indispensable: "Would we provoke (παραζηλῶμεν)?" He therefore takes the termination ουμεν to be an irregular subjunctive form, like that which is supposed to be found in iv. 6 and Gal. iv. 17 (see on the first of these passages). But the supposition seems to me unnecessary. The indicative signifies: "Are we truly acting thus?" The form supposes that it was really being done; and this is certainly what is proved by the saying viii. 10, which has by no means the effect of a supposition without reality.—The apostle alludes to the maxim whereby the strong Corinthians justified their carnal conduct: "All things are lawful for us." — The communicative form: *Do we go the length of . . . ?* Are we . . . ? serves to soften the severity of the merciless irony: *stronger than God . . . ?* The term *κύριος*, *Lord,* might be applied to God, as is usually the case in passages quoted from the Old Testament. But I rather think, with de Wette, Meyer, Hofmann, following the vers. 4, 9, and 21, that in this case Paul applies it to Christ.

And now, after having adjusted this burning question, the apostle reverts in a calmer tone to the less difficult one, of the use of offered meats, giving a few very simple and precise practical rules on the subject, which flow from the principles laid down in the foregoing chapters. Vers. 23 and 24, 32 and 33, prove that these injunctions are specially addressed to the strong (see Heinrici and Holsten).

C. Rules for the use of those who eat Meats offered to Idols (10:23-11:1)

Ver. 23 forms the transition to this third passage, which is, as it were, the recapitulation of the whole matter treated in these three chapters.

Ver. 23. "All things[1] are lawful, but all things are not expedient: all things[1] are lawful, but all things edify not."—The apostle here repeats the adage already enunciated, vi. 12, applying it, however, to a wholly different matter. We must beware of concluding from this repetition, as has been done, that the whole intermediate part has only been a digression. Such a subordinate position would not be in keeping with the gravity of the subjects treated. What meets us in these words is simply a sort of dictum which had come to be used at Corinth on all occasions, without discernment and without taking sufficient account of the limitations enjoined by watchfulness and charity. The logical bond between this rash affirmation of Christian liberty and the thought of ver. 22 is obvious.—The term *all things* applies to external acts, in themselves indifferent, such as using this or that kind of food. The pronoun μοι, *for me*, ought probably to be omitted in this sentence, as well as in the following, with the majority of authorities, not, however, without remarking that this pronoun is read in the two propositions of the verse, not only in K L and the *Peschito*, but also in the *Coislinianus* (H), a MS. of the sixth century, transcribed from the autograph MS. of Pamphilus of Cæsarea.—The same meaning is usually given to the two verbs συμφέρει, *is expedient*, and οἰκοδομεῖ, *edifies*. But this would be a pure tautology. It seems to me probable, from ver. 33, that the former applies to spiritual good in general, including our own (comp. ix. 23–xi. 22), and the second more specially to our

[1] T. R. with K L Syr. reads μοι (*for me*) after παντα in both propositions.

neighbour's (comp. viii. 1–ix. 22).—Such is the general principle ; it will be repeated at the close (ver. 31) in different terms. Ver. 24 reproduces it immediately in a negative form, in order to exclude the great obstacle to its realization.

Ver. 24. "Let no man seek his own, but each[1] his neighbour's good."—It is the idea of οἰκοδομεῖν, *edifying*, which rules in this verse. It is not necessary to understand the adverb μόνον : "Let no man seek *only* . . ." The exclusion is absolute, because it condemns every pursuit of self-interest which is inspired by egoism : "Let no man seek his own enjoyment or advantage ; but let him in his conduct always take account of the interest of others."—In the application of this rule to the particular subject with which Paul is dealing, two cases might present themselves to the Christian : that of a meal in his own house (vers. 25, 26), or that of a meal in a strange house (vers. 27–30).

Vers. 25, 26. "Whatsoever is sold in the shambles, eat, asking no question for conscience sake : 26. for the earth is the Lord's, and the fulness thereof."—A Christian whose conscience is free from every scruple as to the eating of offered meats, sends and buys meat at the shambles ; he has not to ask whether it is or is not sacrificial meat ; it is pure in itself, like everything God has created. The term μάκελλον, *shambles*, is connected with the Latin *macellum*, and with the old French word *mazel*. The proper Greek word would have been κρεοπώλιον. — The last words, διὰ τὴν συνείδησιν, *for conscience sake*, are naturally connected with μηδὲν

[1] The word εκαστος, *each*, in the T. R. is read only in E K L Syr.

ἀνακρίνοντες. Edwards also explains it in this way, applying it, however, to a strong conscience: an enlightened and firm conscience is a reason *for* abstaining from all inquiry. Holsten, on the contrary, alleges that the conscience here, as in the rest of the passage, can only be that of the weak Christian, of which the strong Christian needs not take account when he is eating alone at his own house. But, in these two senses, Paul would have added, as in ver. 29, some qualification or other to indicate of which conscience he meant to speak. The simplest view is to hold that he is thinking of *conscience*, absolutely speaking, as in our expression: for conscience sake. The falsest interpretation is that of Chrysostom, Erasmus, etc.: "Making no inquiry, and that in order that, if you come to learn that it is meat which has been offered to idols, you may not have the burden of it on your conscience." This meaning would suppose that the direction is addressed to the weak.

Ver. 26. This is a quotation from Ps. xxiv. 1, a passage which, by proclaiming that all that fills the world comes from God and belongs to Him, saps the prejudice of the weak at Corinth at the root. By quoting this saying from the Old Testament, Paul wished to raise the weak to the height of the strong. Heinrici makes the interesting remark that these words of the Psalmist are used among the Jews as a thanksgiving at table.

The second case, that of an invitation to the house of a heathen: vers. 27–30. Again, two alternatives must be distinguished; in the first place, the case of a feast at which no observation is made by any of the guests regarding the meats which are presented.

Ver. 27. "If[1] any of them that believe not bid[2] you, and ye be disposed to go; whatsoever is set before you, eat, asking no question for conscience sake."—The reading δέ, *but*, may be supported as contrasting this new case with the foregoing; but the two cases may also be simply put in juxtaposition without particle, according to the reading of the Alex.—There is much delicacy in the: *and ye be disposed* . . . Paul does not forbid acceptance of the invitation; for family bonds ought to be respected; they may even become, in the case of the believer, a means of advancing God's kingdom. But, while speaking as he does, and expressly referring the decision to the Christian's conscience, he yet makes him feel the need of reflection; for many dangers might accompany such invitations to heathen houses, even in a private dwelling, where the meal was always accompanied with certain religious ceremonies. The words εἰς δεῖπνον, *to a feast*, in the Greco-Lat. reading, are certainly a gloss. For the διὰ τὴν συνείδησιν, see on ver. 25. Holsten gives to these words the meaning: "The strong believer need not make inquiry, and that because of the conscience of the weak brother, present or not present, who might be offended if it turned out as the result of the inquiry that the meat had been offered to idols." The same reasons as we have given at ver. 25 seem to us to exclude this meaning.

The second alternative, vers. 28–30: the case in

[1] T. R. with C E H K L Syr. reads δε (*but*) after ει (*but if*).
[2] D E F G It. read εις δειπνον (*to a supper*) after των απιστων.

which the question is raised as to the origin of the meats offered at a feast.

Vers. 28, 29. "But if any man say unto you, This is offered[1] in sacrifice, eat not, for his sake that showed it, and for conscience[2] sake. 29. Conscience, I say, not thine own, but of the other: for to what purpose can my liberty be judged by another's conscience?"—The τίς, *any one,* of ver. 28 cannot, as Grotius thinks, denote the same person as the τίς of the foregoing verse, the heathen who invited the Christian. He would not be designated by an indefinite pronoun. It must therefore be one of the guests. Are we to suppose him, as has been thought by Chrysostom, de Wette, etc., a malicious heathen, who wishes by the remark to embarrass the Christian, or a serious heathen wishing to call his attention to the mistake he is about to commit without knowing it (Ewald)? But in these two cases the duty of the believer would have been, not to abstain, but, on the contrary, to partake of the meat while stating the motive of his conduct, and justifying his freedom from all scruple in regard to idols in which he does not believe; it was an excellent opportunity for expounding his faith. The person in question, therefore, is a sincere Christian, whose conscience is still hampered with scruples, and whom his strong brother is bound to treat with consideration. In this way, the following words: *For his sake that showed it, and for conscience,* are easily explained. The two motives refer to the same person, remaining,

[1] T. R. with C D E F G K L P ειδωλοθυτον; but ℵ A B Syr^sch Sah. read ιεροθυτον.

[2] T. R. with K L here repeats the words of ver. 24: του γαρ κυριου η γη και το πληρωμα αυτης.

however, distinct. The first is directed against the influence which the example might exercise over the weak Christian, by leading him to eat against his conscience; the second, to the shock which his conscience will infallibly undergo on seeing the strong believer eat, even supposing he should resist the example which is set him. The repetition of the quotation from Ps. xxiv. at the end of ver. 28, in the T. R., is evidently due to an interpolation. The only meaning which could be given to the words here would be this: "There is on the table plenty of other meats which thou mayest use." But such a reflection is far from natural.

Ver. 29. The apostle expressly declares that such a sacrifice by no means implies that the strong believer renounces his conviction and right; his conscience remains independent of his brother's, though he voluntarily subordinates his conduct to the other's scruple. —The reason which the apostle gives for this conduct has been differently understood. Meyer and de Wette think that Paul means: "For on what ground should I subject your conscience to the judgment of your neighbour's? You preserve, therefore, so far as you are yourselves concerned, your entire liberty." But the conjunction ἱνατί does not signify: For what reason, with what right? This compound conjunction, after which we must understand γένηται, literally signifies: *that what good may come about?* The meaning is therefore: "For what advantage can there be in my liberty being condemned . . . ?" We have in the parallel discussion of Rom. xiv. a perfectly similar saying, which leaves no doubt as to the meaning of this. Paul there says, ver. 16: "That your good be not evil spoken of (blasphemed)!" This good is the liberty of the strong, and Paul asks of them not to make such a use of it as will provoke the disapproving judgment of the weak. Here he asks, besides, what advantage such a judgment, imprudently provoked, can have; what edification it can afford either to the Christians present, or to the non-Christians, who become witnesses of the mutual contradictions between believers, and of the condemnations which they pass on one another. The question put in ver. 29 is reproduced still more clearly in ver. 30.

Ver. 30. "If[1] I with thanksgiving be a partaker, why am I evil spoken of for that for which I give thanks?"—The asyndeton of itself proves that this verse reaffirms and explains the idea of the foregoing. It brings out still more forcibly the absurdity of the strong Christian's conduct by the revolting contradiction which would arise between the thanksgiving with which he partakes of the food offered to him, and the wounding of the conscience testified by the blame of the weak. What! that for which a believer gives thanks, the other converts into a ground of defamation against him! This is what is expressed by the word *βλασφημεῖν*. "What sort of religion is that?" the heathen would say, who were witnesses of both actions. The apostle concludes by stating generally the principle which, in such matters of Christian liberty, ought to be the supreme guide of the believer's conduct:

Vers. 31, 32. "Whether therefore ye eat, or drink, or whatsoever ye do, do all to the glory of God. 32. Give none offence neither to the Jews, nor to the

[1] T. R. adds δὲ (*but*), with some Mnn. only

Greeks, nor to the Church of God;"—Here again we have both the συμφέρειν and the οἰκοδομεῖν (the promotion of good in general, and our neighbour's edification in particular), which Paul had recommended, ver. 23; only he here expresses himself in a more concrete way; first positively, ver. 31, then negatively, ver. 32. In questions which are not in themselves questions of good or evil, and which may remain undecided for the Christian conscience, the believer ought to ask himself, not: What will be most agreeable to me, or what will best suit my interest? but: What will contribute most to promote God's glory and the salvation of my brethren?—God's glory is the splendour of His perfections, particularly of His holiness and love, manifested in the midst of His creatures. The question for the Christian is therefore translated into this: What will best make my brethren understand the love and holiness of my heavenly Father?

Ver. 32. To this positive criterion another of a negative character is added. Will not my brother's conscience be shocked by the use I make of my liberty, if I act in this or that way? The apostle mentions the three circles of persons of which the Christians of Corinth ought to think in a case of uncertainty: first, the *Greeks*, who are here put for the heathen in general; next, the *Jews*, who are intentionally placed between the heathen and the Church; and, finally, Christians, whom he calls the *Church of God*, to emphasize the preciousness of the least of the members of such a body, in virtue of his being God's property. The believer should avoid both what may prevent those without from entering and what may alienate and drive out those who are already saved.

Paul concludes by reminding them how this principle guides all his conduct.

Ver. 33–xi. 1. "even as I please all men in all things, not seeking mine own profit, but the profit of the many, that they may be saved. XI. 1. Become imitators of me, as I am of Christ."—In chap. ix. the apostle had developed at length the example of self-denial, which he was constantly giving to the Church by submitting to the necessity of earning a livelihood for himself, and in general, by becoming subject, when it was necessary, to the legal observances, from which he felt himself set free by faith in Christ. In concluding this whole passage, in which he has asked the Corinthians to make many sacrifices which are painful to them, he once more refers to his example, because he knows that we are not at liberty to ask sacrifices from others except in proportion to those which we make ourselves.—The phrase *to please others* may denote a vice or a virtue. That depends on the object proposed, whether to gain our neighbour's good graces selfishly, or to gain the attachment of our neighbour so as to win him for God. These are the two cases Paul contrasts with one another in this verse, in order to exclude the first, in so far as his own conduct is concerned; comp. Gal. i. 10. The: *in all things,* comprehends of course only the things which belong to the province of Christian liberty. — The *many* is opposed to Paul as an individual, and their salvation to his individual interest (ἐμαυτοῦ, *of myself*).

XI. 1. Christ alone is the perfect model; each

believer is a model to his brethren only in so far as he is a copy in relation to Christ.—Paul has in mind especially the absolute self-denial which was the basis of our Lord's earthly life, Rom. xv. 1–3.—It is only the fact expressed in the second part of the verse which gives the apostle the right and liberty to write the first. To be quite exact, we must understand in the second proposition not the verb *be,* but the verb *become,* used in the first.—The imitation in question is not a slavish one. As Paul was not in circumstances identical with those of Christ, so the Corinthians were not in circumstances altogether analogous to those of Paul. What he asks of the Church is, that it allow itself to be guided by the spirit of self-denial which animates himself, as he is guided by the spirit of self-sacrifice which was the soul of Christ's life.

We have already cast a glance over the course followed by the apostle in treating this delicate subject. It was needful to limit the use made of their liberty by many of the Corinthian Christians, and among them no doubt, by those who directed the opinion of the Church, without placing them again under the yoke of an external law, and while bringing them to understand themselves the necessity of the sacrifice. This sacrifice wounded their vanity as much as their love of pleasure. It is easy to see the extreme prudence with which the apostle required to conduct this discussion. He begins by stating the point about which all are agreed, the monotheism which excludes the reality of idols. He leaves aside for the moment the frequenting of idolatrous feasts, appealing only to charity for weak brethren. He encourages the strong by his example, deters them by that of the Israelites. After this preparation, he strikes the great blow. Then he concludes calmly with some simple and practical rules in regard to the eating of meats, rules which admirably establish harmony between the rights of liberty and the obligations of charity.—Justly does Rückert exclaim, as he closes the analysis of the passage: "Truly I could not conceive a more prudent or better calculated course; we have here a masterpiece of true eloquence." Pity, only, that this eminent exegete does not stop there, but thinks he must ascribe to the apostle's eloquence, in this case, a certain character of craftiness. Evidently in the course followed by the apostle we are bound to recognise the wisdom of the serpent; but it does not for a moment exclude the simplicity of the dove. For prudence is throughout ever in the service of the love of truth and of zeal for the good of individuals and of the Church.

7

The Demeanour of Women in Public Worship (11:2-16)

The apostle has just treated a series of subjects belonging to the domain of the Church's moral life, especially in connection with Christian liberty (chaps. vi.–x.). He now passes to various subjects relating to *public worship*, beginning with that which lies nearest the domain of liberty: the external demeanour of women in public worship. Then will follow the disorders which have crept into the celebration of the

Holy Supper and into the administration of spiritual gifts. Such are the three subjects Paul conjoins in the closely connected chaps. xi.–xiv.

The ancients in general laid down a difference between the bearing of men and that of women in their appearances in public. Plutarch (*Quæst. Rom.* xiv.) relates that at the funeral ceremony of parents, the sons appeared with their heads covered, the daughters with their heads uncovered and their hair flowing. This author adds by way of explanation: "To mourning belongs the extraordinary," that is to say, what is done on this occasion, is the opposite of what is done in general. What would be improper at an ordinary time becomes proper then. Plutarch also relates that among the Greeks it was customary for the women in circumstances of distress to cut off their hair, whereas the men allowed it to grow; why so? Because the custom of the latter is to cut it, and of the former to let it grow (see Heinrici, pp. 300, 301). According to several passages from ancient authors, while the long hair of the woman was regarded as her best ornament, the man who, by the care he bestowed on his hair, effaced the difference of the sexes, was despised as a voluptuary. The Greek slave had her head shaved in token of her servitude; the same was done among the Hebrews to the adulteress (Num. v. 18; comp. Isa. iii. 17). In regard to acts of public worship there existed a remarkable difference between the Greeks and the Romans. The Greek prayed with his head uncovered, whereas the Roman veiled his head. The ancients explain these opposite usages in various ways. Probably in the Roman rite there was expressed the idea of the scrupulous reverence which should be brought into the service of the deity, while the Greek rite bespoke the feeling of liberty with which man should appear before the gods of Olympus. The Jewish high priest officiated with his mitre on his head, and the Jew of the present day prays with his head covered, no doubt in token of reverence and submission. It appears from all these facts what an intimate relation the feeling of the ancients established between the worshipper's demeanour, as regards the noblest part of his being, the head, and his moral and social position. "The point here was not only," as Heinrici well says, "a matter of decorum." His conduct in this respect corresponded to a profound religious feeling.

This is the point of view at which we must place ourselves to understand the following discussion. St. Paul was accustomed to say: "In Christ all things are made new; there is neither male nor female, neither bond nor free, neither Greek nor Jew." How easy was it from this to jump to the conclusion: Then there is no longer any difference, especially in worship, where we are all before God, between the demeanour of the male and that of the female. If the male speaks to his brethren or to God with his head uncovered, why should not the female do so also? And with the spirit of freedom which animated the Church of Corinth, it is not probable that they had stopped short at theory. They had already gone the length of practice; this seems to be implied by vers. 15, 16. The apostle had learned it, not from the letter of the Corinthians, to which he does not here make any allusion (as in viii. 1), but probably from the deputies of the Church.

He begins with a general commendation in regard to the manner in which the Church remains faithful to the ecclesiastical institutions he had established among them.

Ver. 2. "Now I praise[1] you, that ye remember me in all things, and keep the ordinances, as I delivered them to you."—The *now* is progressive; it is the transition to the new subject. Edwards takes it adversatively (in contrast to the expression *imitators of me*): "*But*, if you do not imitate me in everything, I acknowledge that in these things you observe my instructions." This connection does not seem to me natural.—The word παραδόσεις here certainly denotes the traditions relating to ecclesiastical customs, and not doctrinal instructions; these will come to be treated xv. 3.—The μου, *me*, seems to me to be the complement of the μέμνησθε, *ye remember*; the πάντα is in that case an adverbial qualification: *in all things*, on all points. Rückert thinks he can make πάντα the direct object of the verb, and μου the complement of πάντα: "You remember all that proceeds from me." But, not to speak of the usual construction of the verb (with the genitive), there would be something harsh in the expression πάντα μου (*all things of me*). Finally, the other construction more delicately expresses the personal remembrance of which Paul feels himself to be the object on their part.—But there was a point on which the apostle had not expressly pronounced in his oral teaching, probably because the occasion had not occurred, no woman having made trial in his presence of the right of speaking, and that with her head uncovered. Things had changed since his departure.

[1] T. R. with D E F G K L It. Syr. here reads ἀδελφοί (*brethren*).

VERS. 3–6

Ver. 3. "But I would have you know, that the head of every man is the[1] Christ; and the man is [the] head of the woman; and God [the] head of the[2] Christ."—The δέ is adversative: *but;* Paul proceeds to a point to which the eulogy he has just passed does not apply.—One is tempted to ask, as he reads the following sentences, why the apostle thinks it necessary to take things on so high a level, and to connect what is apparently so secondary a matter with relations so exalted as those of man with Christ, and of Christ with God. To explain his method, we must bear in mind the pride of the Corinthians, who thought they knew everything, and whom the apostle wishes, no doubt, to teach that they have yet something to learn: "*I would have you know.*" It is likely enough, from ver. 16, that the ultra-liberals of Corinth spoke with a certain disdain of the ecclesiastical prescriptions left by the apostle, and that in the name of the Spirit some claimed to throw his rules overboard. Paul would give them to understand that everything hangs together in one, both in good and in evil; that unfaithfulness to the Divine order, even in things most external, may involve an assault on the most sublime relations, and that the pious keeping up of proprieties, even in these things, is an element of Christian holiness. Hence he begins with placing this special point in the life of the Church under the light of the two holiest analogies that can be conceived, and in which he shows the revelation

[1] ℵ B D F G omit ὁ (*the*) before Χριστος.
[2] T. R. with C F G K L P omits του (*of the*) before Χριστου.

of a Divine order. Those who criticise him presumptuously will thus be able to understand whence he derives the rules which he lays down in the Church.

There exist three relations, which together form a sort of hierarchy: lowest in the scale, the purely human relation between man and woman; higher, the Divine-human relation between Christ and man; highest in the scale, the purely Divine relation between God and Christ. The common term whereby Paul characterizes these three relations is κεφαλή (hence our word *chief*), *head.* This figurative term includes two ideas: community of life, and inequality within this community. So between the man and the woman: by the bond of marriage there is formed between them the bond of a common life, but in such a way that the one is the strong and directing element, the other the receptive and dependent element. The same is the case in the relation between Christ and the man. Formed by the bond of faith, it also establishes a community of life, in which there are distinguished an active and directing principle, and a receptive and directed factor. An analogous relation appears higher still in the mystery of the Divine essence. By the bond of filiation, there is between Christ and God communiön of Divine life, but such that impulse proceeds from the Father, and that "the Son does nothing but what he sees the Father do" (John v. 19).—The relation between Christ and the man is put first. It is, so to speak, the link of union between the other two, reflecting the sublimity of the one and marking the other with a sacred character, which should secure it from the violence with which it is threatened. The only question is whether, as has been thought by Hofmann, Holsten, etc., the point in question is the natural relation between Christ and man, due to the dignity of the pre-existing Christ as creator (Hofmann), or as the heavenly Man, the prototype of earthly humanity (Holsten),—or whether, as is held by Meyer, Heinrici, etc., Paul means to describe the relation between Christ and men by redemption. The expression: *every man*, seems to speak in favour of the first sense; and the passages viii. 6 and x. 4 might serve to confirm this meaning. Christ as having been the organ of creation, is the head of every man created in His image, believing or unbelieving. But vers. 4 and 5 seem to me to prove that Paul is thinking not of man in general, but of the Christian husband. "Every man . . ., every woman who prays, who prophesies . . .," this can only apply to believers. It is from ver. 7 that Paul passes from the spiritual order to the domain of creation in general. What is true in the first sense, is that every man is ordained to believe in Christ and to take Him for his head, that is to say, to become a *Christian* husband.—The article ἡ is to be remarked with κεφαλή in the first proposition (it is wanting in the other two). This arises, no doubt, from the fact that the man may have many other heads than Christ; the article serves to point out Christ as the only normal head. In the other two relations, this was understood of itself.

This relation belonging to the kingdom of God has for its counterpart in the family the relation between husband and wife. Paul is here thinking chiefly of the natural and social relation, in virtue of which the husband directs and the wife is in a position of subordination. But this natural relation is not abolished by the life of faith; on the contrary, it takes hold of it and sanctifies it. Must we conclude, from the term used by Paul, that the Christian wife has not also Christ for her head, in respect of her eternal personality? By no means; salvation in Christ is the same for the wife as for the husband, and the bond by which she is united to Christ does not differ from that which unites the man to the Lord. The saying: "Ye are branches, I am the vine," applies to the one sex as much as to the other. But from the standpoint of the earthly manifestation and of social position, the woman, even under the gospel economy, preserves her subordinate position. There will come a day when the distinction between the sexes will cease (Luke xx. 34–36). But that day does not belong to the terrestrial form of the kingdom of God. As long as the present physical constitution of humanity lasts, the subordinate position of the woman will remain, even in the Christian woman. As the child realizes its communion with the Lord in the form of filial obedience to its parents, the Christian mother realizes her communion with the Lord in the form of subordination to her husband, without her communion being thereby less direct and close than his. The husband is not between her and the Lord; she is subject to him *in the Lord;* it is *in Him* that she loves him, and it is by aiding him that she lives for the Lord. If from the social standpoint she is his wife, from the standpoint of redemption she is his sister. Thus are harmonized these two sayings proceeding from the same pen: "In Christ there is neither male nor female," and: "The husband is the head of the wife."

These two relations, that of Christ to the man, and that of the man to his wife, rest on a law which flows from the nature of God Himself. In the oneness of the Divine essence there are found these two poles, the one directive, the other dependent: God and Christ. Paul evidently desires to rise to the highest point, above which we can conceive nothing. Some, like Heinrici, Edwards, etc., think that this expression: *the head of Christ,* can only apply to the Christ incarnate. But if the relation were thus understood, one of the two essential features would be wanting, indicated by the term head, and which characterize the two preceding relations: *community* of life and nature. We cannot, therefore, confine this saying to the Lord's human nature, and we think there is no ground for shrinking from the notion of subordination applied to the Divine being of Christ; see on iii. 23. This idea of the subordination of Christ, conceived as a pre-existent being (viii. 6, x. 4), springs out of the terms *Son* and *Word,* by which He is designated, as well as from the very passages where the divinity of Christ is most clearly affirmed (Col. i. 15; Heb. i. 2, 3; John i. 1, 18; Rev. i. 1). Holsten thinks that he escapes all difficulty by bringing in here the idea of Christ as the heavenly *Man,* according to the discovery made by Baur by means of the passage xv. 45 seq. It is very certain that had it not been found in that passage, nobody would have extracted it from the one we are explaining. For the examination of this conception ascribed to Paul, we shall therefore refer to the passage quoted.

Thus, then, in the apostle's view, the relation between husband and wife in marriage is a reflection of that which unites Christ and the believer, as this again reproduces the still more sublime relation which exists between God and His manifestation in the person of Christ. Paul certainly could not say more in the Epistle to the Ephesians to express a higher notion of marriage than these words. M. Sabatier, expounding the idea of marriage in the Epistle to the Ephesians, says: "Husband and wife form an indissoluble organic unity." Exactly; but can this "indissoluble unity" be more forcibly expressed than by comparing it, as Paul does in our passage, to the unity of Christ with the believer and of God with Christ? M. Sabatier adds, still expounding the contents of Ephesians: "The one does not reach the fulness of existence without the other." Certainly; but is not this exactly what Paul teaches here in vers. 11, 12: "The man is not without the woman in the Lord, nor the woman without the man." And on such grounds a progress is alleged as having taken place in Paul's ideas on marriage, in the interval between the Epistle to the Corinthians and that to the Ephesians!

After recognising, as a principle which controls all community of life, Divine and human, that duality of factors, the one active, the other receptive, which forms the basis of marriage, the apostle passes by an asyndeton to the application which he wishes to make of it to the case in question at Corinth.

Vers. 4–6. "Every man praying or prophesying, having his head covered, dishonoureth his head. 5. But every woman that prayeth or prophesieth with her head uncovered dishonoureth her head: for that is even all one as if she were shaven. 6. For if the woman be not covered, let her also be shorn: but if it be a shame for a woman to be shorn or shaven, let her be covered."—Chrysostom has concluded from ver. 4, as Edwards also does, that the men too, at Corinth, did violence to their proper dignity by being covered. But it is not probable that abuses arose in that direction, especially in Greece (see above, p. 104). The demeanour which becomes the man is only mentioned to bring out by contrast that which alone is becoming in the woman.—The two acts of *prophesying* and *praying* will be again brought together in chap. xiv., where we shall speak of them more specially Let us only say here, that in chap. xiv. (comp. especially vers. 14–17) prayer is more or less identified with *speaking in a tongue*, a gift which is treated conjointly with prophecy. This observation leads us to suppose, as Baur has already done, that by the prayer of which Paul speaks, in our vers. 4, 5, he means chiefly a prayer *in a tongue*, that is to say, in ecstatic language. The phrase κατὰ κεφ. ἔχειν is elliptical: "having down from the head," that is to say, wearing a kerchief in the form of a veil coming down from the head over the shoulders.—In the last words: *dishonoureth her head*, the word *head* has often been understood literally (Erasmus, Beza, Bengel, Neander, Meyer, etc.): By veiling the head made to appear uncovered, he covers it with shame. But why in this case prefix to ver. 4 the reflection of ver. 3: "The head of every man is Christ"? If this remark had a purpose, it should be to prepare for the idea of ver. 4, and consequently to justify the application of the term *head* to Christ Himself; which does not prevent us from holding, with many critics, that there is here a delicately intended play on words: "By dishonouring his own head, the believer, who covers himself, dishonours Christ also, whose glory he ought to be." Indeed, as Holsten says, every man who, in performing a religious act, covers his head, thereby acknowledges himself dependent on some earthly head other than his heavenly head, and thereby takes from the latter the honour which accrues to Him as the head of man. The head uncovered, the brow open and radiant, the look uplifted and confident, the noble covering of hair, like, as some one has said, "to a crown of extinct rays,"[1] such are the insignia of the king of nature, who has no other head in the universe than the invisible Lord of all. If, then, he is not to impair the honour of his Lord, he must respect himself by not covering his head.

Ver. 5. But precisely because the woman is in a position contrasted with that of the man, in so far as she has *here below* a visible head, she would dishonour this head by affecting a costume which would be a symbol of independence. And since the woman does not naturally belong to public life, if it happen that in the spiritual domain she has to exercise a function which brings her into prominence, she ought to strive the more to put herself out of view by covering herself with the veil, which declares the dependence in which she remains relatively to her husband. As Heinrici says, it can only be to the shame of her husband if a wife present herself in a dress which belongs to the

[1] "A une couronne de rayons éteints."

man. By uncovering her head (in the literal sense) she dishonours her head (in the figurative sense).—Here a difficulty arises. The apostle, by laying down for the woman the condition of wearing the veil, seems decidedly to authorize the act to which this condition applies, that is to say, he permits the woman to pray and to prophesy in public. Now in chap. xiv. 34 he says, absolutely and without restriction: "Let your women keep silence in the Churches." This apparent contradiction has led Hofmann, Meyer, Beet, and others to the idea, that, in our chapter, Paul had in view only gatherings for family worship (Hofmann) or private meetings (Meyer), composed exclusively of women (Beet). But it is impossible to hold that the apostle would have imposed the obligation of the veil on a mother praying while surrounded by her husband and children. Neither is it possible to see how the idea of Meyer and of Beet could be reconciled with ver. 10 of our chapter (*because of the angels*). Besides, ver. 16 naturally implies that Paul is thinking of public worship (*the Churches of God*). Finally, in vers. 34 and 35 of chap. xiv., he is not distinguishing between different kinds of assemblies; but he is contrasting assemblies in general with the time when husband and wife find themselves alone together at home: "Let the women keep silence in the Churches . . ." (ver. 34), "let them ask their husbands at home" (ver. 35).—Heinrici proposes to restrict the prohibition laid on women, in chap. xiv., to the tokens of admiration which they liked to give to those who spoke in tongues, or also to the curious questions which they put to the prophets, thus of course disturbing the decorum of the assemblies. Some writers in England have even supposed that in chap. xiv. Paul simply means to forbid women to indulge in the whisperings and private conversations which would break the stillness of worship. But it is impossible so to restrict the meaning of the word λαλεῖν, *to speak*, in chap. xiv., applied as it is in that chapter to all the forms of public speaking. Besides, the prohibition, if it had one of these meanings, should have been addressed to men as much as to women. What the passage in chap. xiv. forbids to women, is not ill-speaking or ill-timed speaking, it is *speaking;* and what Paul contrasts with the term speaking, is *keeping silence* or asking *at home.* —It might be supposed that the apostle meant to let the speaking of women in the form of prophesying or praying pass for the moment only, contemplating returning to it afterwards to forbid it altogether, when he should have laid down the principles necessary to justify this complete prohibition. So it was that he proceeded in chap. vi., in regard to lawsuits between Christians, beginning by laying down a simple restriction in ver. 4, to condemn them afterwards altogether in ver. 7. We have also observed the use of a similar method in the discussion regarding the participation of the Corinthians in idolatrous feasts; the passage, viii. 10, seemed first to authorize it; then, afterwards, when the time has come, he forbids it absolutely (x. 21, 22), because he then judges that the minds of his readers are better prepared to accept such a decision. But this solution is unsatisfactory, because it remains true that one does not lay down a condition to the doing of a thing which he intends afterwards to forbid absolutely.—It has also been thought that the term λαλεῖν, *speaking*, should be taken in chap. xiv. solely in the sense of *teaching*. Thus the woman might prophesy or pray in an unknown tongue; but she must never indulge in teaching. But it is impossible to accept so limited a meaning of the word λαλεῖν in a chapter where it is used all through to denote both prophetical speaking and speaking in tongues. This solution is not, perhaps, radically false, but it is impossible to deduce it from the word *speaking* in chap. xiv. in contrast to the terms *prophesying* and *praying* in chap. xi.—I rather think, therefore, that while rejecting, as a rule, the speaking of women in Churches, Paul yet meant to leave them a certain degree of liberty for the exceptional case in which, in consequence of a sudden revelation (*prophesying*), or under the influence of a strong inspiration of prayer and thanksgiving (*speaking in tongues*), the woman should feel herself constrained to give utterance to this extraordinary impulse of the Spirit. Only at the time when she thus went out of her natural position of reserve and dependence, he insisted the more that she should not forget, nor the Church with her, the abnormal character of the action; and this was the end which the veil was intended to serve. Moreover, Paul does not seem to think that such cases could be frequent. For in chap. xiv. *prophetesses* are not once mentioned along with prophets, and yet the name προφῆτις was familiar in the Old Testament, and is not wanting in the New (Luke ii. 36; Rev. ii. 20). Probably in making the concession which we find in this passage, the apostle was thinking only of married women. The question could hardly have been even raised as to young women. Reuss says: "In Greece a woman of character did not appear in public without a veil." How much more must it have been so with unmarried persons! And if Paul had extended to the latter the permission implied in his words, he would still less have suppressed in their case the condition of the veil imposed on the former.

In the last words of ver. 5, Paul likens the woman who appears in public with her head uncovered to one who has her head shaven. This was never found among the Greeks, except in the case of women who were slaves; among the Jews, only in the case of the woman accused of adultery by her husband (Num. v. 18). A similar usage seems to have prevailed among other nations besides. — The subject of the proposition, according to most, is understood: *every woman that speaketh with her head uncovered* (see Meyer). But is it not simpler to make *ἓν καὶ τὸ αὐτό, one and the same thing*, the subject of *ἐστί*: "One and the same [condition] is the woman's who is shaven [as hers who is not veiled]." The verb *ξυρέω*, or *ξυράω*, or *ξύρω*, signifies *to shave* to the skin.

Ver. 6. To impress the revolting character of such a course, the apostle supposes it pushed to extremity. There is something of indignation in his words: "If this woman has effrontery enough to do the first of these acts, well and good, better also do the second!" The repulsive character of the one should make that of the other felt. The word *ξυρασθαι* is usually accented, as if it were the present infinitive passive of *ξυράω* (*ξυρᾶσθαι*). But why should it not be regarded as the aorist infinitive middle, like *κείρασθαι*, of the form *ξύρω* (*ξύρασθαι*)? See Passow. There is a gradation from the one of these verbs to the other: To cut the hair or even to shave the head.—The word *αἰσχρόν*, *shameful*, includes the two notions of physical ugliness and moral indecency.

Vers. 7–12

Thus far the apostle has been arguing from the parallel between the subordinate position which Christian principle ascribes to the woman (ver. 3), and the receptive position of the man relatively to Christ, and of Christ Himself relatively to God. Now he shows that the conclusion he has drawn from this double analogy is confirmed by the mode of the woman's creation. For in the apostle's eyes the kingdom of nature does not proceed from another God than that of grace. On the contrary, it is in the sphere of redemption that the Divine thoughts, which are only sketched in the kingdom of nature, reach perfection.

Vers. 7–9. "The man indeed, being the image and glory of God, ought not to cover his head: but the[1] woman is the glory of the man. 8. For the man is not taken from the woman; but the woman from the man. 9. And the man indeed was not created for the woman; but the woman for the man."—The *γάρ*, *for*, leads us to expect a confirmation drawn from a domain other than the preceding. The omission of the article before the words *εἰκών*, *image*, and *δόξα*, *glory*, gives these two substantives a qualitative significance.—The meaning of the first is that man, by his sovereignty over the terrestrial creation, visibly reflects the sovereignty

[1] T. R. with ℵ C E K L omits the article *ἡ*.

of the invisible Creator over all things. We here find the idea of man's lordly position in nature, as it is expressed Gen. i. 26–28, and celebrated in Ps. viii.—The second, *glory of God*, expresses the honour which is shed on God Himself from this visible image which He has formed here below, especially when man, carrying out his destiny, voluntarily renders Him homage for his high position, and adoringly casts at His feet the crown which God has put on his head. Analogous to this is the meaning in 2 Cor. viii. 23, where the deputies of the Churches are called *the glory of Christ*, because they make the Lord's work, in the Churches they represent, shine before the eyes of those to whom they are delegated.—The man existing in this double character (ὑπάρχων), as image and glory of God, ought not to veil this dignity by covering himself when he acts publicly. This would be in a way to tarnish the reflection of the Divine brightness with which God has adorned him, and which ought at such a time to shine forth in his person. But in virtue of the very same law, the woman ought to act in an opposite way. If, in the discharge of such an office, the veil is opposed to the man's sovereignty, it is from that very fact in keeping with the woman's condition. She, indeed, was created as the *glory of the man*, because, as is said in the following verses, she was taken *from* him and formed *for* him (vers. 8, 9). It is an honour, the highest of all undoubtedly, for one being to become the object of another's love and devotion; and the more the being who loves and is self-devoted is exalted in talent and beauty, the more is this honour increased. Can there therefore be a greater glory to man than to possess, as a loving and devoted helpmeet, a being so admirably endowed as woman! All the perfection that belongs to her is homage rendered to the man, from whom and for whom she was made, especially when she consecrates herself freely to him in the devotion of love. Critics have been exercised, and justly, about the reason why the apostle has not in the second case repeated the term *image*. De Wette has thought that had he made woman the image of man, the apostle would have denied to her the possession of God's image. Meyer thinks that this expression would wrongly imply, on the part of the woman, a certain participation in the sovereignty of the man. The second ground seems to me truer and more in keeping with the context. The *image* of the husband in the family is not the wife, but the son. It is he who is heir of the paternal sovereignty.—The inference from this relation in regard to the woman's demeanour will be drawn in ver. 10.

Vers. 8, 9 serve to prove the expression: *glory of the man*. In ver. 8 the narrative of Genesis (ii. 22, 23) is referred to, according to which the man did not appear as proceeding from the woman; but inversely. And why so? For a reason (γάρ) which is at the same time a new proof (καί) of the expression: *glory of man*, in ver. 7. The woman proceeded from the man because she was intended to serve as his helper, and to complete his existence.—The διά, *on account of*, alludes to the saying of Genesis (ii. 18): "It is not good for man to be alone: let us make a helpmeet for him."—The practical conclusion, ver. 10:

Ver. 10. "For this cause ought the woman to have

a sign of power on her head because of the angels."—*For this cause:* because she was formed *from* him and *for* him.—Literally it is: "the woman ought to have on her head *a power.*" This term *power* has been understood in many ways; but they are not worth the trouble of enumeration, the meaning is so clear and simple. *Power* is put here for a *sign of power,* and of power not exercised, but submitted to. The woman ought to wear on her head the sign of the power under which she has been placed. It is a frequent way of speaking in all languages, to use the sign of a thing to denote the thing itself, for example the sword for war, the crown for sovereignty. But it is rarer to find, as here, the thing itself put for the sign; but examples are also found of this other form of metonymy; thus when Diodorus, describing the statue of the mother of the Egyptian king Osimandias, says that she has three kingships on her head, he means, evidently: three diadems, symbols of three kingships; or when the same historian gives the name ἀλήθεια, *truth,* to the ornament which the Egyptian priests wore to symbolize their possession of this highest good.—The difficulty of the verse lies in the last words: *because of the angels.* Have we here a second reason? In that case it would require to be connected with the preceding (as was indicated by the word *for this cause*) by some such particle as: *and, and also,* or *and besides.* Is it, on the contrary, the same reason presented in another form? But in that case it is difficult to understand the relation between such different modes of expression to convey the same idea. Heinrici, who has thoroughly felt this difficulty, seeks to resolve it by maintaining that the angels are here mentioned because they were God's agents in the work of creation, of which mention was made vers. 8, 9, and therefore sure to be particularly offended by a mode of acting opposed to the normal relation established in the beginning between man and woman. This solution is certainly not far from the truth. Only it seems to us that we must set aside the idea of the intervention of angels in the work of creation. They no doubt beheld that work, according to Job xxxviii. 7, with songs of joy, but without any co-operation on their part being indicated. We are called rather to bear in mind, that, according to Luke xv. 7, 10, the angels in heaven hail the conversion of every sinner; that, according to Eph. iii. 10, they behold with adoration the infinitely diversified wonders which the Divine Spirit works within the Church; that, according to 1 Tim. v. 21, they are, as well as God and Jesus Christ, witnesses of the ministry of Christ's servants; finally, that, in this very Epistle (iv. 9), they form along with men that intelligent universe which is the spectator of the apostolical struggles and sufferings. Why, then, should they not be invisibly present at the worship of the Church in which are wrought so large a number of those works of grace? How could an action contrary to the Divine order, and offending that supreme decorum of which the angels are the perfect representatives, fail to sadden them? And how, finally, could the pain and shame felt by these invisible witnesses fail to spread a sombre shade over the serenity of the worship? In Christ heaven and earth are brought together (John i. 52). As there is henceforth community of joy, there is also community of sorrow between the inhabitants of these two spheres. The Jews had already a similar sentiment in their worship. This is what has led the Greek translators to say (Ps. cxxxviii. 1): "I will praise Thee before the angels," instead of: "I will praise Thee before Elohim." This explanation is more or less that of Chrysostom and Augustine; it is that of Grotius and of most of the moderns (Rückert, de Wette, Meyer, Osiander, etc.). Edwards thinks it is as models of humility in general life, and not only in worship, that the angels are here proposed as an example to Christian women; but the preposition διά, *because of*, expresses a different relation from that of example. It is rather to the presence of the angels that it calls our attention. — There has often been reproduced, in recent times, an idea which occurs so early as in Tertullian: Paul is held to be speaking here of the evil angels whose passions might be excited by the view of unveiled women. Or, thinking of angels in general, there has been found in our passage an allusion to Gen. vi. 1-4 (Kurtz, Hofmann, Hilgenfeld). But if good angels are in question, they have many other opportunities of seeing woman unveiled than in Christian worship; and if evil angels, this temptation makes no change in their state. Besides, there is no special indication leading us to find here an allusion to Gen. vi.—Storr, Flatt, etc., have taken the ἄγγελοι to be *spies* sent by the heathen to watch Christian worship (Jas. ii. 25); Clement of Alexandria: *the most pious* members; Beza: the *prophets* of the Church; Ambrose: the *pastors* (Rev. i. 20). Such significations are now only mentioned as matters of history.

Baur and Neander, finding it impossible to connect with the reason indicated by the words : *for this cause,* the reason contained in these : *because of the angels,* have proposed to suppress the last words as a later interpolation. Holsten goes further ; he extends this supposition to the whole of ver. 10, but for a different reason. Giving to this verse a meaning almost the same as that of Hofmann (allusion to Gen. vi.), he concludes therefrom, very logically, as it seems to me, that such a saying cannot be ascribed to the apostle. Only the premiss (the meaning ascribed by him to the verse) is false, consequently also the conclusion which he draws from it. As the documents present no variants, the authenticity of the verse may be regarded as certain.

After having thus declared the natural dependence of woman in relation to man, the apostle yet feels the need of completing the exposition of this relation by exhibiting the other side of the truth ; this he does in vers. 11, 12.

Vers. 11, 12. " If, however, the woman is not without the man, neither is the man without the woman,[1] in the Lord ; 12. for as the woman is of the man, even so is the man also by the woman ; and all things of God." —The subordination of the wife to her husband is tempered in Christ by the oneness of the spiritual life which they both draw from the Lord. The one is not without the other, and that evidently as believers ; there is community of prayer between them, the constant exchange of spiritual aid and active co-operation.

[1] T. R. with A L Syr. reverses the order of the two parallel propositions.

The words *in the Lord* refer not to God, but, as usual in the New Testament, to Christ; the mention of God only comes later, in ver. 12. It does not seem to me that there is sufficient reason for finding here, with Holsten, an allusion to the softening which the gospel has introduced into the wife's subordination, as it was laid down in Genesis; the reason alleged in ver. 10 rather carries us back to the order of nature which is recognised and sanctioned by the gospel.—The order of the propositions followed by the T. R., contrary to the great majority of the Mjj., is evidently mistaken.

Ver. 12. The *for* indicates that the relative equality of the two sexes in Christ was already prefigured, so to speak, by a fact belonging to the order of natural life. So it was that the *for* of ver. 7 served to give a reason for the wife's moral subordination by a fact drawn from the inferior domain. If, so far as creation goes, the woman is of the man,—this is the proof of her dependence (ver. 8),—on the other hand, as to the conservation of the race, the man is of the woman, and this decisive fact in the life of humanity, restores equality to a certain extent between the two sexes. The natural order makes woman not only man's spouse, but also his mother; therewith all is said. We see here with what wisdom the apostle could apply to the domain of spiritual life, not only the scriptural types, but also the hieroglyphics of nature. And thus are explained to us the last words of the verse: "*And all things are of God.*" He is the Author of nature as well as of grace, and He has laid in the first the outlines, so to speak, of the Divine thoughts, which he realizes perfectly in the second.

Vers. 13–16

The apostle concludes by appealing to the natural impression which ought to follow from a particular feature in the physical conformation of the man and the woman. This last argument is strictly connected with the last words of ver. 12.

Vers. 13–15. "Judge in yourselves: Is it comely that a woman pray unto God uncovered? 14. Doth not[1] nature itself[2] teach you, that, if a man have long hair, it is a shame unto him? 15. but if a woman have long hair, it is a glory to her: for her hair is given her[3] for a covering."—After appealing to the sacred analogies mentioned in vers. 3-6, and to the relation established by creation between the sexes (vers. 7–12), Paul finally takes to witness a fact nearer to us, inherent in the human person itself. We here come to a formula similar to that with which he had closed the previous discussion x. 15: "Judge of yourselves!" These words appeal to the instinct of truth which ought to exist in his readers themselves.—The following question finds its solution in vers. 14, 15, where the fact is stated which should serve as the basis of their judgment.—The addition of the words τῷ Θεῷ, *to God*, is difficult to explain; for it appears as if it were precisely in speaking to God that the woman could speak without impropriety unveiled. But let us remember that we are here in full public worship, and that it is at the moment when the woman's voice is uttering the

[1] T. R. with E K L reads, before ουδε, η (*or*), which is omitted by all the rest.

[2] T. R. with C L reads αυτη η φυσις; all the rest: η φυσις αυτη.

[3] T. R. with ℵ A B reads αυτη (*to her*) after δεδοται; the rest omit it.

deepest impressions and the holiest emotions of adoration and love, that a feeling of holy modesty ought to constrain her to secure herself from every indiscreet and profane look. For the very reason that she is speaking *to God*, she ought in this sacred act to veil her figure from the eyes of men. These words: *to God*, are therefore, whatever Holsten may say, perfectly in place.

Ver. 14. The ἤ, *or*, of the T. R. might be suitable so far as the sense goes: "*Or indeed*, if you answer my question in the negative, does not nature teach you . . . ?" This use of the ἤ is frequent in Paul. But for this very reason the particle might easily have been introduced; the authorities in its favour are weak.

Ver. 14 must therefore be regarded as directly answering the question put in ver. 13: "After all I have said to resolve the question, is there not another master whose voice you ought of yourselves to hear, and who will teach you that . . . ?" This master is *nature*, ἡ φύσις, a word which here can neither signify moral instinct nor established usage. It follows indeed from ver. 15 that Paul is thinking of the physical organization of woman. If we receive the reading of the T. R., αὐτὴ ἡ φύσις, *even nature*, the idea is: "That which seemed unable to teach us anything in such a domain." But if we follow the other reading, ἡ φύσις αὐτή, *nature itself*, the meaning is rather: "itself, without me, without my teaching."—Hofmann and Heinrici understand the following ὅτι in the sense of *because*, and make the διδάσκει an intransitive verb: "Does not nature itself instruct you?" But the ὅτι after such a verb as διδάσκειν naturally signifies *that*, and all the more because the ὅτι at the end of ver. 15 really signifies *because*, and serves to explain the bearing of the two preceding ὅτι: "Does not nature itself show you *that* . . . and *that* . . ., *seeing that* . . . ?" By not giving the man long hair, like the woman's, nature itself has shown that an uncovered head, and an open brow, suit his dignity as king of creation. The hair of the man is a crown, while, as the following verse adds, that of the woman is a veil.

Ver. 15. By giving to the woman a covering of hair, which envelopes her, in a manner, from head to foot, nature itself has shown that it is suitable to her to withdraw as much as possible from view, and to remain concealed. This long and rich hair is given to her ἀντὶ περιβολαίου, *in place of a veil*. This substantive does not merely denote, as κάλυμμα would do, an ornament for the head; it is a vestment enveloping the whole body, a sort of peplum. It is a natural symbol of reserve and modesty, woman's most beautiful ornament. —It has been objected, not without a touch of irony, that for the very reason that nature has endowed woman with such a covering, she does not need to add a second and artificial one (Holsten). But this is to mistake the real bearing of the apostle's argument. All is spiritual in his view. He means that nature, by constituting as it has done each of the two sexes, has given both to understand the manner in which they will fulfil their destiny; for man, it will be public and independent action; for woman, life in domestic retirement and silence. Whoever has the least appreciation of the things of nature, will recognise the profound truth of this symbolism.—The Greco-Lat. and Byz. reading omits the αὐτῇ at the end of the verse. The meaning is not affected by the omission (contrary to Holsten).

Notwithstanding the unanimity of the Mjj. and Vss. in favour of the text of this passage, Holsten has thought right to propose a whole list of rejections; that, for example, of vers. 5^b and 6, of ver. 10, and even of vers. 13–15. We have refuted this critic's objections when it seemed to us necessary. They arise from certain general ideas about the passage, which we think false; the first: that Paul has in view only husbands and wives who are *Christians;* the second: that if the wife is bound to speak veiled it is only in presence of *her own* husband, to whom she ought to show, that while fulfilling this function, she does not forget her dependence on him; the third: that on reaching the last section (vers. 13–15), the text passes, in a far from logical way, from the domain of moral obligation—which is Paul's true standpoint—to that of social propriety, which, according to Holsten, is the interpolator's standpoint. But (1) from the outset, and even in ver. 3, it is of the difference of the sexes as such that the apostle is thinking. He is speaking of man and woman in general, regarding young men and young women as naturally destined for marriage. The whole female sex is in his eyes created with a view to its subordination to the male sex, as Tertullian well says (see Heinrici): "*Si caput mulieris vir est, utique et virginis, de quâ fit mulier quæ nupsit.*" (2) It is not because of her husband only that the woman who speaks in public ought to continue veiled; it is as a woman, and to maintain in her own consciousness and in that of the Church her permanent character of dependence. (3) The passage vers. 13–15 does not give a reason which lies outside of moral obligation. Woman's physical constitution is a revelation of the Creator's will regarding her. Not to conform to this indication, is not merely to offend social propriety, it is to transgress the will of the Creator. Thus fall all Holsten's objections against the authenticity of the text of our passage.

The apostle closes with a sentence which seems to say: Now, enough of discussion; let us have done with it.

Ver. 16. "But if any man seem to be contentious . . . we have no such custom, neither the Churches of God."—Holsten and others regard this saying as a kind of confession that the apostle feels the insufficiency of the proofs which he has just alleged. But such a supposition would do violence to his moral character, and Paul's words do not really signify anything of the kind. They simply prove that there are at Corinth controversial spirits, who, on such a subject, will never tire of arguing and raising objections indefinitely. That does not mean that, as to himself, he does not regard the question as solved and well solved. — The word δοκεῖν is used here in the same sense as iii. 18, x. 12, Gal. vi. 3, to denote a vain pretence. Undoubtedly nobody takes glory from a fault, such as love of disputation (φιλόνεικος); but Paul means to say: "If any one wishes to play the part of a man whom it is impossible to reduce to silence, who has always something to answer . . ." This was one of the natural features of the Greek character.—The principal proposition does not correspond logically to the subordinate one beginning with *if;* we must understand a clause such as this: "Let him know that . . ." or: "I have only one thing to say to him, namely, that . . ." I cannot understand how eminent critics, such as the old Greek expositors, then Calvin, de Wette, Meyer, Kling, Reuss, Edwards, could imagine that the custom of which the apostle speaks is that of disputing! The love of disputation is a fault, a bad habit, but not a custom. To call the habit of discussion an ecclesiastical usage! No. The only custom of which there can be any question here is that on which the whole passage has turned: women speaking without being veiled. Paul means that neither he, nor the Christians formed by him, nor in general any of the Churches of God, either those which he has not founded or those properly his own, allow such procedure in their ecclesiastical usages; comp. xiv. 36, 37, where the idea simply indicated here is developed.—The material proof of this assertion of Paul's is found in the Christian representations which have been discovered in the Catacombs, where the men always wear their hair cut short, and the women the palla, a kerchief falling over the shoulders, and which can be raised so as to conceal the face (Heinrici, p. 324).—The complement *of God* is intended to bring out the dignity and holiness of all these Churches, and consequently the respect due to their religious sentiment, which contrasts with the presumptuous levity of the Corinthians.

We hope we have justified the thought expressed by the apostle regarding the social position of woman, as well as the particular application which he deduces from it. Holsten thinks that whatever may be said, the apostle thereby puts himself in contradiction to the principle so often enunciated by him: "In Christ there is neither male nor female," and on this account when he came to the end of the passage, he felt, as it were, the ground going from under him. But the apostle's personal conviction, as he expresses it here, was certainly very deliberate; the loyalty of his character forbids us to doubt it. Was this conviction solely a matter of time and place, so that it is possible to suppose, that if he lived now, and in the West, the apostle would express himself differently? This supposition is not admissible; for the reasons which he alleges are taken, not from contemporary usages, but from permanent facts, which will last as long as the present earthly economy. The physical constitution of woman (vers. 13–15) is still the same as it was when Paul wrote, and will continue so till the renewing of all things. The history of creation, to which he appeals (vers. 8–12), remains the principle of the social state now as in the time of the apostle; and the sublime analogies between the relations of God to Christ, Christ to man, and man to woman, have not changed to this hour, so that it must be said either that the apostle was wholly wrong in his reasoning, or that his reasons, if they were true for his time, are still so for ours, and will be so to the end. As to the parity of man and woman in Christ, it is clear, and that from this very passage, that Paul means to speak of their relation to Christ in redemption, and not of the social part they are called to play.

8

Disorders in the Celebration of the Lord's Supper (11:17-34)

The disorder which Paul has just described and combated was a small matter in comparison with that to which he now passes. The style of his language, too, becomes more severe. The apostle begins by applying to the assemblies for worship what he said about the prevailing discussions at Corinth, in the first four chapters (vers. 17–19); then he passes to the principal ground of rebuke, that which refers to the celebration of the Holy Supper (vers. 20–34).

VERS. 17–19

Ver. 17. "Now in this that I command[1] you I praise[1] you not, that ye come together, not for the better, but for the worse."—There is evidently a contrast between this preface and the preamble to the foregoing passage (ver. 2). There the apostle praised the Corinthians for their general fidelity to the ecclesiastical institutions he had transmitted to them; there was, however, an exception to be made of the special subject which he was about to treat, vers. 4–16. Here the tone becomes that of positive blame. This blame is not in contradiction to the preceding eulogium; for it does not bear on their neglect or corruption of an institution, but on the profane spirit brought to the celebration of one of the most important acts of worship. — Of the four readings given in the note, two may be set aside without hesitation, that of B, which puts the two verbs in the participle, and that of D, which puts them both in the indicative; these readings have no meaning. That of four Mjj.: "This I command you while not praising you for that . . .," can only be maintained by referring *τοῦτο*, *this*, to what follows, and in particular, as Heinrici thinks, to the

[1] T. R. with ℵ E K L P reads *παραγγελλων ουκ επαινω*; A C F G Syr^sch: *παραγγελλω ουκ επαινων*; B: *παραγγελλων ουκ επαινων*; D: *παραγγελλω ουκ επαινω*.

historical proof which is about to be given of the importance of the Holy Supper (vers. 23, 24). But the principal idea is the contrast between the blame now expressed and the eulogium of ver. 2, and this contrast leads us more naturally to make the verb *praise* the principal verb (οὐκ ἐπαινῶ, *I do not praise*), and the verb *command* the secondary verb (participle παραγγέλλων, *commanding you*); thus the meaning is: "While simply recommending you to take account of the direction I have just given (vers. 1–16), I cannot praise you in the matter of which I am about to speak." Holsten objects that we should in this case require the aor. παραγγείλας, *after having enjoined this on you;* and he is disposed to make the word παραγγέλλων an interpolation, which is wholly arbitrary, for all the MSS. read the two verbs. And why could not Paul use the present when speaking of the injunction which he has just given at that very time? Does it not remain in his letter for the moment when it shall be read at Corinth? We must therefore also refer τοῦτο, *this,* not to ver. 16, as Edwards will have it, but to the important command contained in the preceding passage, in regard to women, and to translate nearly as Reuss does: "While giving you this warning, I cannot praise you in the matter of which I now proceed to speak."—The apostle thus characterizes the transition from a simple recommendation to positive blame: *I do not praise you.* This is an evident litotes, as in ver. 22.—Then comes a rebuke which relates to all the meetings for worship held by the Church of Corinth: "In general your assemblies are not blessed; from the way in which you hold them, they throw you back rather than help you forward; they are the opposite of what they should be."

Vers. 18, 19. "For first of all, when ye come together in[1] the Church, I hear that there be divisions among you; and I partly believe it. 19. For there must even be sects among you,[2] that[3] they which are approved may be made manifest among you."—The apostle now gives the reason for the severe words: "I do not praise you." The: *for first of all*, announces a first rebuke in regard to the divisions in their assemblies (vers. 18, 19), and leads us to expect a second to be indicated by a: *then again;* but this formula, corresponding to the *first of all*, is found nowhere in the sequel. Where does this second rebuke begin? Meyer, Osiander, Heinrici think that it points to the abuses in the exercise of spiritual gifts treated in chaps. xii.–xiv.; that if there is not found at the beginning of chap. xii. the ἔπειτα δέ, *then again*, which should correspond to our πρῶτον μέν of ver. 18, this may arise from the fact that the long development of chap. xi. had made the apostle forget the form used at the beginning of the passage (ver. 18). Edwards prefers to place the expected *secondly* in ver. 34, where, according to him, it is logically implied in the τὰ δὲ λοιπά, *the rest.* Hofmann thinks that there is no *secondly* to be sought in the sequel, since πρῶτον signifies here, as often, not *firstly*, but *principally;* comp. Rom. iii. 2. This last assertion might be established if πρῶτον stood alone; with the μέν it is less easily

[1] T. R. reads with some Mnn. only τη (*the*).
[2] D F G It. here omit εν υμιν (*among you*).
[3] B D read και (*also*) after ινα (*in order that*).

admissible. And how should the *divisions* be represented as the essential point in what follows? The meaning of Edwards can as little be admitted. The words: "The rest *will I set in order* when I come," do not contain any threatening, any announcement of rebukes to be addressed to them. Meyer's meaning falls to the ground for this reason: that the divisions, σχίσματα, mentioned vers. 18, 19, are not put by the apostle in any connection with the disorders in the Holy Supper, which are explained by a wholly different cause. Consequently the two subjects cannot have been combined in one by Paul, and both embraced in the πρῶτον μέν of ver. 18. We have therefore simply, with Olshausen, de Wette, Rückert, to place the understood *then again* at ver. 20, where the rebukes begin relating to the celebration of the Supper. And such is the meaning to which we are led by the close study of the relation between the three terms συνέρχεσθε, *ye come together* (ver. 17), συνερχομένων ὑμῶν, *when ye come together* (ver. 18), and συνερχομένων οὖν ὑμῶν, *when therefore ye come together* (ver. 20). Meyer thinks that the second συνερχομένων (ver. 20) is the repetition of the συνερχομένων (ver. 18). Hence it is he combines in one and the same rebuke the blame bearing on the divisions and that which applies to the profanation of the Supper. This is his error. The second συνερχομένων is not the repetition of the first, but of the συνέρχεσθε, *ye come together*, of ver. 17: "You come together for the worse, and that chiefly because of your divisions (vers. 18, 19), then again because of the way you celebrate the Supper." Here is the second rebuke, developed from ver. 20 to ver. 34. Meyer asks why, if it is so, the first rebuke is found so briefly treated? Quite simply, because this matter of divisions had already formed the subject of the whole first part, chaps. i.–iv., and Paul needs only here to refer to it, while applying to their meetings for worship what he had said of the malign influence exercised by such divisions over the life of the Church in general.—The two συνερχομένων are therefore parallel to one another, and both rest on the συνέρχεσθε of ver. 17. Only the first of these participles points to their assemblies merely in a passing way, while the second, referring as it does to the subject about which the apostle is now most seriously concerned, the profanation of the holy table, is emphasized by the οὖν, *therefore;* this particle shows that he is returning to the thought which had mainly suggested to him the εἰς τὸ ἧττον συνέρχεσθε, *ye come together for the worse* (ver. 17).

The first thing which Paul has to blame in their assemblies for worship, is the *divisions* which break out among them.—The τῇ before ἐκκλησίᾳ in the T. R. should be rejected. The meaning is not: in the *church,* but: in *church:* "when you come together in a general assembly of the Church." The point in question is the manner, not the place; comp. xiv. 23. The form of the phrase seems incorrect; for it is not at the time when their divisions break out that the apostle hears of them. This finds its explanation the instant we refer the present participle συνερχομένων, not to the time, but to the manner of meeting.—The news might have reached him either by the house of Chloe (i. 11), or by the deputies of the Church (xvi. 15).—The: *and I partly believe it,* is very delicate. Paul would admit that the state of things has been described to him in certain respects worse than it is. But when a Church is in the moral state in which that of Corinth is, it must inevitably become a theatre of discord. This necessity is of the same kind as that indicated by Jesus when He said: "It must needs be that offences come" (Matt. xviii. 7), that is to say: given such a world as ours.—In the following verse the moral reason is explained which renders these discussions providentially necessary.

Ver. 19. When a Church is forming, or when in a Church already established a revival takes place, there is a sort of fascination exercised over a great number of individuals who adopt the gospel preaching, or the new ideas, less from a serious and personal moral need than from a spirit of opposition or innovation, or from a proneness to imitation. Hence, at the end of a certain time, the necessity for a process of purifying; this is carried out by a separation due to the fermentation which follows from the contact of the heterogeneous elements within the same mass. The effect of this action is to show in clear light those members of the Church who are serious and genuine, and to separate them definitely from those who have believed only superficially and temporarily. This experience, made over and over again since then by the Church, is that which the apostle foresaw as an inevitable phase in the development of the flock at Corinth. The δεῖ, *there must*, is a heightening of the ὑπάρχειν, the existence as *matter of fact* (ver. 18); see on vii. 26. The apostle thinks that the fact *is*, because he knows that it *must be*. He knows even that there is something graver to be expected. For the καί, *even,* which follows the δεῖ, *it must be that,* intimates a second gradation strengthening the first. This new gradation bears, as is proved by the position of the καί, on the substantive αἱρέσεις, in its relation to the σχίσματα, *divisions,* of ver. 18. Indeed, it is wholly in vain that Meyer seeks to identify these two terms. No doubt the word αἵρεσις may have a very softened sense, in respect of its etymological signification: *choice, preference* (from αἱρεῖσθαι). But in the New Testament it has always a very forcible meaning; so Gal. v. 20, where it is placed after διχοστασίαι, *dissensions,* and that evidently as a gradation above this already strong enough term; so also Acts v. 17 and xv. 5, where it denotes the opposite parties of the Sadducees and Pharisees among the Jewish people; finally, xxiv. 5 and xxvii. 28, where the Christian community is designated by this term as a special party in the midst of this same people. In all these cases the external division evidently rests on internal opposition, on profound and trenchant doctrinal differences. And it is also in this sense that the word αἵρεσις ought to be taken here, as has been recognised by Calvin, Beza, Rückert, Edwards. The context also imperatively demands this forcible meaning. To the simple divisions which arise from personal preferences or aversions, Paul foresees that there will succeed divisions of a far more profound nature, founded on opposite conceptions of Christian truth. He believes what is told him of the first, because he even expects the second. There will arise among them false doctrines, *heresies,* according to the meaning which the Greek term has taken in later ecclesiastical language, and thence will follow much graver disruptions than the present divisions. The σχίσματα resemble simple rents in a piece of cloth; but the αἱρέσεις are rendings which remove the fragment and break the unity of the piece. The Second Epistle to the Corinthians shows in how brief a period this anticipation of the apostle was realized.

The καί, which is read in B D after ἵνα, *that*, and which could only be rendered by *also*, gives no precise meaning, and should be rejected.—Of the two ἐν ὑμῖν, *among you*, the first is omitted by D F G, the second by C. They ought to be preserved, both of them. The first applies to the Corinthians the consequence from the moral necessity affirmed in this first proposition; the second puts to them, as it were, a question: "How many will there be found in your Church of these δόκιμοι?"—The δόκιμοι are those who at such crises prove their Christian character by a wisdom and maturity of judgment which mark them in the eyes of all with the seal of Divine approbation; comp. ix. 27. It is with a view to the manifestation of such genuine Christians, that the whole crisis has been permitted (ἵνα, *that*).—The apostle passes to the second subject of rebuke:

Vers. 20–34

Vers. 20, 21. "When ye come together therefore[1] into one place, this is not[2] to eat the Lord's Supper. 21. For in[3] eating every one taketh before other his

[1] D F G omit ουν (*therefore*).
[2] D F G: ουκετι (*this is no more*), instead of ουκ εστιν (*this is not*).
[3] D E F G: επι τω instead of εν τω.

own supper : and one is hungry, while the other is full."—On the connection with what precedes, see on ver. 18. Here would stand the ἔπειτα δέ, *but next*, if Paul had expressed it. This preamble, ver. 20, is not without solemnity. The very first words make us feel that we are coming to a grave matter.—The term ἐπὶ τὸ αὐτό, *into the same place*, denotes, like the words ἐν ἐκκλησίᾳ, *in Church* (ver. 18), a meeting of the whole Church gathered together in the same place ; comp. xiv. 23. So it assembled to celebrate the Supper. This rite was preceded by a feast in common, called δεῖπνον, *supper*, a term from which it follows that the celebration took place in the evening. It was thus wished to reproduce, as faithfully as possible, that feast of the Lord at which He instituted the Supper, and which took place on the last evening of His life. Those feasts, of which the Holy Supper formed the close, were called *agapæ*, that is to say, *love-feasts* (Jude, ver. 12). Each one brought his quota. And certainly, according to the idea of this institution, all the provisions should have been put together and eaten in common by the whole Church. But selfishness, vanity, sensuality had prevailed in this usage, and deeply corrupted it. These agapæ had degenerated at Corinth into something like those feasts of friends in use among the Greeks, where men gave themselves up to drinking excesses, such as we find sketched in the *Symposium* of Plato. And what was still graver, and which had certainly not been witnessed even at heathen banquets, each was careful to reserve for himself and his friends the meats which he had provided ; hence it was inevitable that an offensive inequality should appear between the guests, becoming to many of them a source of humiliation, and contrasting absolutely with the spirit of love of which such a feast should have been the symbol, as well as with the rite of the Supper which formed its close. Chrysostom supposes that the agape took place after the Holy Supper; evidently a mistake. It was not till later that this different order was introduced, till at length the meal itself was totally abolished.—*This is not to eat the Lord's Supper*, says Paul. We need not here take ἐστί, as many have done, in the sense of ἔξεστι, *it is allowed, it is possible,* as if Paul meant that in these circumstances it is no longer morally possible to celebrate the communion rightly. It is simpler to understand the words in this sense: "To act as you do (ver. 21), can no more be called celebrating the Supper; it is indeed to partake of a feast, but not that of the Lord." The adj. κυριακόν, *the Lord's,* reminds us that it was He who founded the feast, who gives it, who invites to it, who presides over it.—The following verse explains the severe judgment which has just been expressed regarding this way of celebrating the agape.

Ver. 21. By the way in which they act, they change the sacred feast into an ordinary supper, which has no longer anything in common with the sacred feast which it should recall. It is on the προ, *before,* in the verb προλαμβάνειν, that the emphasis lies: "You make haste to take the provisions you have brought *before* it has become possible to make a general distribution of them, and without sharing them with your neighbours."—The epithet ἴδιον, *his own,* expresses the right in virtue of which the owner thinks he can act thus.—The words ἐν τῷ φάγειν indicate the moment when the feast begins, following the act of worship which had certainly preceded: when the feasting is reached, including the supper, and then the holy sacrament.—The words: *one is hungry,* refer to the poor who are present.—The verb μεθύειν usually signifies to be intoxicated; but it may also be applied to eating, in the sense in which we say to eat his fill, and so to form a contrast, as is the case in this passage, to πεινᾷν, *to be hungry.* The word μεθύειν certainly shows that the pleasure of good cheer and drinking went the length of intemperance, just as in those friendly feasts at which Greek gaiety and frivolity took free course. — Now follow the rebukes which such conduct deserves.

Ver. 22. "Have ye not then houses to eat and to drink in? or despise ye the Church of God, and shame them that have not? What shall I say to you? Shall I praise[1] you? In this point, I praise you not." —One feels in the lively succession of these accumulated questions the indignant emotion which fills the apostle as he calls up the scene before him. The γάρ, *for,* refers to an idea which is understood: "It ought not so to be, *for* have you not . . . ?" Paul points out three principal sins in this conduct. First, the feast itself so celebrated; the agape, with the Holy Supper terminating it, is not a meal taken for support; it is a religious rite expressly instituted, and that for a religious purpose. If any one wishes to satisfy his hunger, he has the means of doing so otherwise. We learn from this first rebuke how thoroughly distinct in the apostle's eyes was the feast of the Supper from a common feast, even when taken in the most Christian

[1] B F G It. read επαινω instead of επαινεσω.

spirit and hallowed by thanksgiving. To hold, as Vinet somewhere has done, that every Christian meal should become a Holy Supper, is an ultra-spiritualistic error, the thoroughgoing application of which would inevitably compromise the existence, first, of the ministry, then of the Church itself. The second rebuke refers to the want of respect to an assembly like the Church; the third to the offence in particular given to a portion of its members, the poor who are humiliated.—The formula μὴ . . . οὐκ signifies: "It is not so however that you have not?" The other two questions, closely connected as they are, might contain only one rebuke, in the sense that the dishonour to which the Church was subjected consisted precisely in the humiliation of its poor members; for the whole body feels the contempt with which one of its members is treated. But it is better to regard the two ideas as distinct. There is first contempt inflicted on the Church, as such, in this transformation of one of the most solemn acts of its worship into a means of gross and sensual enjoyment; the complement *of God* brings out the gravity of this profanation more forcibly. Then comes the humiliation inflicted on the poor; it appears in all its force if we take the expression μὴ ἔχειν, not only in the sense of poverty in general, but as having a direct application to the present case: Those who have nothing, that is to say, no food with them.—The question: *What shall I say?* indicates the embarrassment the apostle feels when he would characterize such conduct without using terms too severe. There is a litotes full of irony in the last words: *Shall I praise you?* Then returns the tone of the most sorrowful earnestness: "*In this I praise you not.*" We think, with Meyer and Holsten, that the words ἐν τούτῳ, *in this*, must be connected with the following verb *I praise you not*, rather than with the preceding, *shall I praise you?* as is done by Heinrici and many others. "On other points I can praise you (ver. 2), but on this, not!"

To make the Corinthians blush at their profane spirit, the apostle brings them face to face with the scene of the institution of the sacrament. But his object, in relating this solemn event, is not merely to contrast with their selfish and frivolous disposition the spectacle of Christ's sufferings and devotion. Paul, in going back on the solemn institution of the Supper by the Lord, wishes above all to bring home to them the difference between this feast and a feast intended to satisfy bodily wants. Here is a religious rite, a true ceremony, for it was positively instituted.

Vers. 23–25. "For I have received of the Lord that which also I delivered unto you, That the Lord Jesus, the night in which He was betrayed,[1] took bread:[2] 24. and when He had given thanks, He brake it, and said,[3] This is My body [which is] for you;[4] this do in remembrance of Me. 25. After the same manner also He took the cup, when He had supped, saying, This cup is the New Testament in My blood: this do ye, as

[1] T. R. with L P: παρεδιδοτο; all the rest: παρεδιδετο.

[2] D F G: τον αρτον (*the bread*), instead of αρτον (bread or *a* bread) [loaf].

[3] T. R. with K L P Syr. here reads: λαβετε, φαγετε (*take, eat*); all the rest omit these words.

[4] T. R. with E F G K L P Syr. here reads κλωμενον (*broken*); D: θρυπτομενον (*bruised*); Sah. Cop.: διδομενον (*given*); א A B C read simply το υπερ υμων.

oft as ye drink it, in remembrance of me."—The *for* shows that the account of the institution, which follows, is meant to justify the various rebukes expressed in ver. 22. First of all, Paul establishes on an immovable foundation the authority of his narrative. It comes *from the Lord*, and without any other middle party than the apostle himself.—The ἐγώ, *I*, is put at the head to give the readers an assurance of the truth of the narrative: This is what I hold, *I* from a good source, from the Lord Himself.—But it is asked in what way this account could have been delivered by the Lord to the Apostle Paul, who was not of the number of the Twelve present at the institution of the Supper. The usual answer is this: The apostle had knowledge of the fact from the apostolical tradition; and to prove this mode of transmission, reliance is placed on the use of the preposition ἀπό, which does not denote, as παρά would do, direct transmission, but which simply points to the first source from which the account proceeded. Thus, according to Reuss, "Paul here speaks of a communication made to him by older disciples, but not of an immediate revelation." But the question arises in this case, what means the *I* placed first in the sentence: "*I*, even I have received of the Lord"? If he is speaking of no other communication from the Lord than that which he gave as the author of the rite in question, or that which, through the apostles as its channels, conveyed this account to Paul, thousands of Christians, and hundreds of evangelists, might have said as much as St. Paul; and instead of saying: "*I* have received," Paul, if he was not to be guilty of charlatanism, ought simply to have said: "We have received of the Lord." In the passage xv. 3, where he is really summing up the apostolical tradition, he avoids using the pronoun ἐγώ which characterizes our passage. If the account of the institution of the Supper really came to Paul from the Lord, it could only be in the way of direct revelation. The preposition ἀπό, which strictly denotes the first origin, is not opposed, as is constantly repeated, to this interpretation; comp. Col. i. 7, iii. 24; 1 John i. 5, where the communication implied in the ἀπό is as direct and personal as possible. And if it is objected, that to express this last idea παρά would have been necessary, which specially denotes direct transmission, it is forgotten that this preposition is virtually found in the verb παρέλαβον, *I received from.*[1] By using the two prepositions ἀπό and παρά the apostle brings out at once the purity of the origin and the purity of the transmission of his account. Heinrici quotes several passages in which the term παραλαμβάνειν is applied to initiation into the mysteries, for example in Porphyry: παραλαμβάνειν τὰ Μιθριακά, *to be initiated into the mysteries of Mithras.* This meaning would certainly suit here. The apostle then would say that the Lord Himself initiated him into the knowledge of this important act of his life. But we have no need of such a comparison to account for the choice of the term used by the apostle.—Bengel, Olshausen, Rückert, Meyer, de Wette, Osiander, have recognised that the only possible meaning of the passage was that of direct

[1] Comp. for the use of the παρά denoting direct communication in the composition of the word παραλαμβάνειν, Gal. i. 9, 12; Philip. iv. 9; 1 Thess. ii. 13; 2 Thess. iii. 6.

instruction given to the apostle by the Lord; comp. Gal. i. 12. It is objected that revelation bears on doctrines, not on historical facts, and it is asked what purpose such a miracle would have served, since Paul could know from ecclesiastical tradition the fact which he here relates. But we find in the Acts a revelation, containing at least the sketch of a historical fact (ix. 12), and several visions in which the Lord conversed with Paul, as friend with friend (xxii. 17 seq., xxiii. 11). If these accounts are not mere tales, we should conclude from them that revelation may also bear on particular historical facts. Now in the present case such a communication was a necessary condition of the apostle's independence and dignity. For he was not a simple evangelist, delegated by men (Gal. i. 1), but a founder of Churches, the apostle chosen for the heathen world, as the Twelve were for the Jewish people, and consequently dependent only on the Lord; and when he instituted in his Churches a rite of such decisive importance as the Supper was, he required to be able to do so without appealing to any human authority, but supported, like the Twelve, by the Lord Himself. As we study the account immediately following, we shall prove the truth of this observation. The manner in which the Lord communicated this fact to him, we know not, and can only refer to Gal. i. 11, 12.

The words: *that which also I delivered unto you*, guarantee the purity of transmission. The *καί*, *also*, expresses the identity between the accounts of Jesus to Paul, and of Paul to the Corinthians.—As he enters on the narrative, Paul adds to the title *Lord* the name *Jesus*, to carry back the thought of his readers to His earthly person, and so call up the scene of the institution.—If Paul mentions the detail, that it was *night* when Jesus instituted the Supper, it was no doubt to compare with that time the hour when the Church celebrated the rite. Every similar night which shall follow should reproduce the emotions of that original night, and borrow from it something of its deep solemnity. The sad character of that night is brought out by the words: *in which He was betrayed.* Nine Mjj., belonging to the three families, read the verb in the form of παρεδίδετο, which is adopted by Tischendorf. In fact, the later Greek writers tended more and more to assimilate the conjugation of the other classes of verbs in μι to the conjugation of verbs in ημι; or should we see in this strange form the imperfect of a compound of δίδημι (formed from δέω, *to bind*), a word which appears once in the *Anabasis?* The sense would be: "on the night on which they bound Him." But neither the imperfect nor the preposition παρά agrees with such a meaning.—The article introduced by the Greco-Lat. reading before ἄρτον must be rejected. The word literally signifies *a bread;* one of the cakes of unleavened bread placed on the table.

Ver. 24. The thanksgiving of the father of the family at the Paschal feast, referred to the blessings of creation and to those of the deliverance from Egypt. That of Jesus no doubt referred to the blessings of salvation, and the founding of the New Covenant.—Though the breaking of the bread was necessary to its distribution, Jesus nevertheless performed this act as a symbol of what awaited Himself.—The words of the T. R.: λάβετε, φάγετε, *take, eat,* are an interpolation taken from the accounts of Matthew and Mark. This order is here implied in the act of breaking the bread and holding out the piece.—The τοῦτο, *this*, denotes the piece which He has in His hand. What is the relation between this bread and the body of Jesus? Does the word *is* denote homogeneity of substance, so that the material of bread gave place at that moment to that of the body of Jesus, as Catholics understand it? But if it is the earthly body of Jesus which is in question, it is difficult to conceive how the bread could have become the very substance of the hand which offered it. Or might it be His glorified body? But this body was not yet in existence. It must therefore be said, on this view, that the first Holy Supper was as yet only the institution of the rite, not the real rite, and that now it is the invisible and glorified body of the Lord which takes the place of the bread, or, according to the Lutheran idea, accompanies the bread. But how is it possible to apply either of these two notions to the *blood* of the Lord? We know from xv. 50 that blood is not an element which can belong to a spiritual and glorified body, whether the Lord's or ours (xv. 49). In any case the Lord would have required to say, not: *This* is, but: "*This will be* My body, when the time comes." And even so the Lutheran conception would not be justified, for *being*, in the present or future, does not signify accompanying. The simplest explanation is this: Jesus takes the bread which is before Him, and presenting it to His disciples, He gives it to them as the *symbol* of His body which is about to be given up for them on the cross, and to become the means of their salvation; the verb *be* is taken in the same sense as that in which we say, as we look at a portrait: it *is* so and so!—The reading of the T. R. κλώμενον, *broken*, which is found in the Greco-Lats. and the Byzs., seems at first sight probable; it is defended by Hofmann. In the other reading: *My body which is for you*, τὸ ὑπὲρ ὑμῶν, there is something extremely bare. But is it not probable that this very bareness, which is more tolerable moreover in Aramaic than in Greek, is that which occasioned the interpolation of the participle? It was so natural to borrow it from the preceding verb ἔκλασε. This view is confirmed by the readings διδόμενον, *given*, and θρυπτόμενον, *bruised*, which are found in some documents. There has evidently been a wish to supply either from Luke (διδόμενον), or freely (θρυπτόμενον), the participle which seemed to be wanting.—If the Alex. reading is adopted, the meaning is this: "My body, which *is there* for you," for your salvation, like this bread placed on the table for your nourishment.

The following words: *This do in remembrance of Me*, are only found in Luke's account of the institution; they are wanting in Matthew and Mark. But these words are of great importance, for it is really on them alone that the idea of the Holy Supper, as a permanent rite, is based. Without them this act might be regarded as having been done by Jesus once for all. Evidently the apostles did not so understand it, for from the first they introduced the regular celebration of the sacrament (Acts ii. 42). We do not the less on that account maintain the importance of Paul's independence, and of the originality of his narrative. — The τοῦτο, *this*, cannot refer, like the previous one, to the piece of bread; what would be meant by the ποιεῖτε, *do?* It embraces the whole preceding action: the breaking of the bread on the part of Jesus, and the eating on the part of the disciples. This act in its entirety is to be constantly repeated in the gatherings of believers.—The word *do* applies to the apostles, not merely as apostles, but also as believers; they are present both as founders of the Church, commissioned to give over this ceremony to it, and as its representatives, who shall soon be called to celebrate the feast with it.—The words: *in remembrance of Me*, certainly contain an allusion to the lamb slain in Egypt, the blood of which had saved the people, and in memory of which the Passover was celebrated. In Ex. xii. 14, it was said: "This day shall be to thee *for a memorial (lezikkaron).*" Jesus therefore means: "When you shall hereafter celebrate this sacred feast, do it no longer in memory of the lamb whose blood saved your fathers, but in memory of Me and of the sacrifice which I am about to make for your salvation." There is ineffable tenderness in the expression of Jesus: *in remembrance of Me.* As Darby finely observes (in his little work on *Public Worship*), the expression: *memory of Me*, twice repeated, makes the Holy Supper still more a memorial of our *Saviour* than of our *salvation.* Each time this feast is celebrated, the assembly of the disciples of Jesus anew presses around His beloved person. It is clear that the Holy Supper is, as Zwingle thought, a commemorative feast, and that it was most unjust on Luther's part to pronounce on him a moral judgment of condemnation for this view, which might be perfectly sincere. The believing and grateful remembrance of

Jesus is most certainly the part of man in this feast. His ποιεῖν, His *doing*, in this holy action, is the inward disposition of grateful remembrance. This is what was wanting in the frivolous and empty religious demonstrations of the Corinthians. But while recognising this side of the truth in Zwingle's idea, we at the same time put our finger on his error. Side by side with the human *doing*, there is in the Holy Supper the Divine *doing*. In the religion of spirit and life, a ceremony of pure commemoration cannot exist. Every rite celebrated according to its spirit must contain a grace, a Divine gift. And what could be the gift bestowed on the believer in the Holy Supper, if not that which the rite so strikingly symbolizes, the most intimate union with the Lord Himself? How could He who said: "Where two or three are gathered together in My name, I am in the midst of them," fail to communicate Himself spiritually to His own in a feast which so sensibly represents the indissoluble union formed by redemption between Him and them? I say: spiritually; but the word implies the whole fulness of His person; for His person is indivisible. If the fulness of the Godhead dwells in Christ *bodily*, σωματικῶς (Col. ii. 9), His spiritual body cannot be separated from His Spirit; comp. xv. 49.—Thus to man's part in the sacrament, as it is expressed in the words: *in remembrance of Me*, there necessarily corresponds the part of God, which is not referred to here, but which is pointed out in other passages, such as x. 16, John vi. 53–58, and Eph. v. 30–32; not that these last two refer specially to the Holy Supper, they concern at the same time the believer's whole life.

Ver. 25. The first words reappear literally in Luke's account. The two narratives prove that a certain interval separated the two acts of institution. The bread was distributed while they were eating; ἐσθιόντων αὐτῶν, say Matthew and Mark, thus positively expressing what is implied by the accounts of Luke and Paul. The words: *after they had supped*, in Paul and Luke, complete the view of what was done. The feast was therefore closed when the Lord took the cup. The interval which separated the two acts no doubt explains the term: *in like manner also*, ὡσαύτως καί, in Paul and Luke. After the distribution of the bread, Jesus had for a few moments given up the solemn attitude which befitted the institution of a rite, and familiar conversation had resumed its course. Supper ended, at the time of distributing the cup, He resumed the same attitude as in the preceding action.—This cup which Jesus now passes round, certainly corresponds to that which in the Paschal ritual bore the name of *Cos Haberakia* (x. 16), the cup of blessing, which the father of the family circulated to close the feast.—The article τό, *the*, designates the cup as the one which stood there before Him, but at the same time as becoming from that moment the type of those which shall afterwards figure in all the celebrations of the Supper.—The first words of the formula of institution are the same as in Luke; only he adds after the expression ἐν τῷ αἵματί μου, *in My blood*, the determining clause τὸ ὑπὲρ ὑμῶν ἐκχυνόμενον, *which is shed for you*, thus making his formula parallel to that of the other two synoptics: "This is My blood, that of the covenant shed for many." The formula of Paul and

Luke: *This cup is the New Testament,* has something more spiritual about it than that of the other two synoptics. In fact, what, according to this formula, corresponds to the cup, or the wine contained in the cup, is not the blood itself, but the covenant entered into over the blood. Hence it is easy to see what elasticity is demanded in the interpretation of the word *est* (*is*), and how thoroughly mistaken Luther was when he sought at Marburg to crush Zwingle with this one word.—The term *new covenant* alludes to the covenant made at Sinai over the blood of the victim which Moses offered for all the people. Indeed it is related, Ex. xxiv. 8, that Moses took the blood and said: "Behold the blood of the covenant which the Lord hath made with you." This old covenant was recalled every year by the Paschal feast; but Jeremiah had already contrasted it with another, a future and more excellent one, when he uttered the promise: "Behold, the days come that I will make a new covenant with you, not according to the covenant that I made with your fathers in the day that I took them by the hand to bring them out of Egypt, which My covenant they brake; but this is the covenant that I will make after those days: I will put My law in their inward parts . . . for I will forgive their iniquity, and their sins will I remember no more" (xxxi. 31–34). Matthew and Mark, at least according to the most probable reading, omit the word *new.* According to them, Jesus said: "This is My blood, the blood of the covenant shed . . ." Strange to say, Holsten alleges that Paul has here preserved the true formula adopted in the primitive apostolical Church; for, he says, in view of the

Judaizing adversaries whom Paul had before him at Corinth, he would not have dared to modify the original formula. It was Matthew, according to him, who, seeking to efface every trace of opposition between the old and the new covenant in favour of a strict Jewish Christianity hostile to Paul, deliberately rejected the term *new*. But Mark? What of him, independent as he certainly is of Matthew in his whole account, and betraying not the slightest tendency hostile to Paul? What is more curious still, if possible, is the entirely opposite opinion of Meyer, who thinks that the designation of the covenant as *new*, can only be of *Pauline* origin. There is here a description added at a later time to the authentic words of Jesus. But what! Jeremiah, six centuries before, had already characterized the Messianic covenant by this epithet; and Jesus could not have used the same expression, either at His own hand, or in imitation of the prophet! The absence of the word in the Gospels of Mark and Matthew proves nothing. They both reproduce the formula in use in the Jewish Christian Churches, where the expressions relating to the bread and wine were gradually identified: "This is My body . . ., *this is My blood*." As to Luke, he depends on Paul, and Paul himself gives us the formula as he "received it of the Lord." It is obvious why he had from the beginning rested his argument on that personal revelation which had been granted to him; otherwise, indeed,—and this is the truth in Holsten's remark,—he could not in opposition to his adversaries have enunciated a different formula from that which prevailed in the apostolic Churches.

The words: *in My blood*, depend, according to

Meyer and Hofmann, on the verb *is:* "This cup is, in virtue of the blood which it contains, the new covenant." But it would be far from natural to say that the blood is the means in virtue of which the cup establishes the covenant. It is simpler, as is admitted by Heinrici and Holsten, to refer the regimen *in My blood* to the notion of the substantive *covenant* itself: *the covenant in My blood*, for: the covenant concluded in My blood. The absence of the article ἡ is objected, which would be required, it is alleged, to connect the substantive with the regimen; but the omission of the article is easily explained by the verbal meaning of the word διαθήκη, *contract;* from this substantive there is easily taken the understood participle διατιθεμένη, *contracted.* As the blood of the Paschal lamb, and afterwards that of the offered victim (Ex. xxiv.), were the foundation of the covenant agreement passed in Egypt and at Sinai between the Lord and His people, so the blood of Christ, represented by the wine contained in the cup, is the foundation on which the new covenant rests, which is concluded in Christ between God and mankind. For the old contract, which had for its object, on the one side, the promise of the Divine protection, on the other, the engagement to obey the law of Sinai, there is substituted the new covenant, which has for its contents, on the one side, the pardon of sins, on the other, free obedience to the Divine will through the Holy Spirit.

The last words: *Do this in remembrance of Me,* express once more the idea of the *institution* of a rite which is to continue to be celebrated in the Church. Here they do not occur even in Luke. But in Mark and Matthew there are found words which have some analogy to this command: "Drink ye all of it."—In the injunction: *Do this,* the word *this* denotes what Christ is now doing when He holds out the cup to them, and what they themselves do when partaking of it; such is the act which is always to be repeated anew in the assembly of believers. When so? Jesus says: *as often as ye drink.* Evidently this cannot be understood: as every time ye drink, in general, or when ye take any meal whatever. The following verse is opposed to this; for there Paul says: "As often as ye drink *this cup;*" comp. also ver. 22, where the Lord's Supper has been positively distinguished from common meals. Meyer understands: Every time that at a love-feast you come to this final cup. Hofmann and Osiander almost the same: Every time you assemble for a love-feast. But these ellipses are very arbitrary. The thought of the Lord is better explained, as it seems to me, if it is qualified by connecting it with the words: *in remembrance of Me,* and by the evident allusion to the remembrance of the Paschal lamb: "Every time you celebrate, as members of the new covenant, the religious feast corresponding to the Paschal feast of the old, distribute the cup and drink of it in remembrance of Me." The memory of Jesus is to be substituted in their heart for that of the lamb, every time they celebrate the new Paschal feast.—This very indefinite expression ὁσάκις ἄν, *every time it shall happen that,* shows that henceforth this ceremony will no longer be bound to a fixed day of the year, like the Paschal feast, but that it is put at the discretion of the Church. Again we see in this how important it was for St. Paul's apostleship that he should possess an independent and original acquaintance with the mode in which this ceremony was instituted. Langen, in his monograph on the narrative of the Passion, has sought to combine in one sentence the formulas of Paul and Luke on the one hand, and of Mark and Matthew on the other; but the proposition thus reached is very complicated and clumsy, far from suitable to the sharply cut form which should characterize the institution of a rite. Meyer gives the preference to the formula presented in the two first synoptics as more concise and striking. It seems to me, on the contrary, that Paul's form, independently even of his testimony, deserves the preference. Tradition and ecclesiastical usage must naturally have inclined to assimilate more and more to one another the two formulas relating to the bread and the wine, and consequently to simplify the second as much as possible, to bring it nearer the first, originally the more simple. Paul was put in a position to restore the original difference; and it is from him that Luke has taken his formula, so like Paul's own.

It is singular that Paul, who, agreeably to the historical order, here puts the bread before the cup, has done the opposite in chap. x. No doubt it is because in the last passage, where the matter in question was not the *narrative* of the fact as such, he has followed the order which corresponds to the assimilation of faith. The believer first appropriates the pardon which is connected with the shedding of the blood, then he receives the life and strength which are represented by the eating of the body. Here he simply reproduces the fact. His sole aim is to contrast the seriousness of the action with the manner in which it is treated by the Corinthians.—He now draws the practical consequences of the description which he has just given (vers. 26–32).

Ver. 26. "For as often as ye eat this bread, and drink the[1] cup, ye do show the Lord's death till[2] He come."—It seems that in order to connect this verse with the foregoing, *therefore* or *so that* would be required, and not *for* or *indeed.* To explain the difficulty, Ewald has taken ver. 26 as the continuation of the discourse of Jesus, which is, of course, inadmissible. Hofmann applies the *for* to the words of ver. 22 : "I praise you not," which is equally inadmissible. Meyer, usually so rigorous, suffers here from a sort of philological faint; as the German word *denn* has sometimes the meaning of *therefore,* he translates : "in consequence of this institution by the Lord, see *therefore* what you do when you celebrate the communion." But what so great difficulty is there in preserving the literal sense of γάρ? All that is needed is to connect it with the words : *in remembrance of me :* "If Jesus so expressed Himself, it is because *in fact* the action you perform every time you celebrate the Supper is a memorial of His person. For the meaning of the action is to *show His death.*" The *idea* of the action thus stated is really the reason of the manner in which Jesus instituted it.—In spite of all Holsten may say, the verb καταγγέλλετε is indicative : *Ye show,* not imperative : *Show!* For it is the essence of the action which is thus expressed. If καταγγέλλετε were the imperative,

[1] The τουτο (*this*) is omitted by ℵ A B C D F G It.
[2] The αν, which T. R. reads with E K L P, is omitted by all the others.

the γάρ would be inexplicable; οὖν or ὥστε would have been required, *therefore* or *so that.* With the practice which was becoming established at Corinth of making this feast a social act, a supper seasoned with agreeable conversation, Paul contrasts the moving memory, the celebration of the death.—The term *show,* καταγγέλλειν, vividly recalls the word *Haggadah,* which denoted in the Jewish Passover the historical explanation of the meaning of all the rites of the Paschal feast which the father, in answer to the eldest son's ritual question, gave to his family. Perhaps the narrative of the Lord's death was similarly rehearsed at the Holy Supper. In any case, every believer celebrated its efficacy in his heart, and his grateful cry mingled in the hymns of the assembly with that of his fellow-believers. The *Doctrine of the Twelve Apostles* implies that free course is left at this juncture for the words of the prophets present at the assembly. Paul therefore understands by the καταγγέλλειν, *announce,* the individual and collective proclamation of Christ's love in His sacrifice, and of the glorious efficacy of this act. Each one confesses that he owes his salvation to this bloody death.—The τοῦτο, *this,* of the Greek text after ποτήριον, is to be rejected according to the Alex. and Greco-Lats. The words: *till He come,* are connected with the idea of the ἀνάμνησις, *remembrance.* Remembrance ceases when the Lord reappears. Holsten here finds the idea: that then the Lord's death will have brought to an end the exercise of its salutary efficacy. I see in the text no trace whatever of this thought. Paul means that the Holy Supper is the Church's compensation for the visible presence of Christ. It is, so to speak, the link between His two comings: the monument of the one, the pledge of the other. Thus Paul simply reproduces the meaning of the words of Jesus preserved by Luke (xxii. 18): "I say unto you, I will not drink from henceforth of the fruit of the vine until the kingdom of God shall come." If we read ἄν, it indicates the uncertainty of the time when Jesus shall come.

Ver. 27. "Wherefore, whosoever shall eat this [1] bread, or drink the cup of the Lord, unworthily,[2] shall be guilty of the body and blood of the Lord."—From the essential character of the Supper, expounded in ver. 26, there follows the gravity of its profanation. The ἤ, *or*, should be remarked, instead of which we should rather expect καί, *and*, as in ver. 26. But here, no doubt, is the reason of this ἤ, *or*. Though one may not eat the bread unworthily, there is still the possibility of profaning the use of the cup, which did not come till later, at the end of the feast. And the danger was greater, not only because it increased as the feast was prolonged, but especially because it was drink that was in question. The Catholics have therefore sought in vain to justify communion in one kind by this *or*. The argument would have had a certain show of reason if the ἤ were found in ver. 26 instead of καί.—The word ἀναξίως, *unworthily*, has been explained in a host of ways: with a bad conscience, and without repentance (Theodoret, Olshausen); with contempt of the poor (Chrysostom, Billroth); without faith in the words: *given for you* (Luther); without self-examination (Bengel), etc. etc.; see Meyer. The explanation

[1] The τουτου (*this*), read by T. R. with K L P, is omitted by the rest.
[2] ℵ L here add του κυριου (*of the Lord*).

to which the context naturally leads is this: Without the grateful memory of Christ's sufferings, a memory which necessarily implies the breaking of the will with sin. The apostle is thinking of the light and frivolous way of communicating whereby the Corinthians made this sacred feast a joyous banquet, like those which the Greeks loved to celebrate, either in the family, or in a select society, or at a club meeting. The unworthiness of the communicating does not therefore arise from that of the communicant, for by repentance he may always render himself fit to receive Jesus; it arises from his mode of conducting himself inwardly and outwardly. As Bengel well puts it: *Alia est indignitas edentis, alia esûs.*—The term ἔνοχος, from ἐνέχεσθαι, *to be held in* or *by*, denotes the state of a man bound by a fault he has committed. The regimen may be, either the law which has been violated (Jas. ii. 10), or the judge charged with applying the law (Matt. v. 21, 22), or the penalty incurred (Matt. xxvi. 66; Mark iii. 29), or the person or object in respect of whom the violation has taken place; it is in this last sense that the term is used in our passage.—The object to which offence has been given is *the body and blood of the Lord.* The apostle's expression finds a very natural explanation on the supposition of the real presence of the body and blood (the Catholic and Lutheran opinions). But it can be justified also on the symbolical interpretation of the Holy Supper; for to sin against the object which has been solemnly consecrated and recognised as the sign of a thing, is to sin against the thing itself. He who tramples the crucifix under foot, morally tramples under foot the crucified Himself.—If such is the gravity of the offence implied in a profane communion, the believer, before communicating, ought to do everything to prevent such a danger. This is what the apostle impresses in vers. 28, 29.

Vers. 28, 29. "But let a man examine himself, and so let him eat of that bread, and drink of that cup. 29. For he that eateth and drinketh,[1] eateth and drinketh judgment to himself, if he discern not the body."[2]—The δέ, *but*, is progressive: "But if it is so, here is what is to be done." The term δοκιμάζειν, *examine*, denotes a moral exercise whereby a man puts his heart to the proof, in order to judge of his feelings as to the person of Jesus; he is to examine whether in communicating he will bring to the action that reverential memory of Jesus, which, like an impenetrable barrier, will henceforth interpose between his heart and sin. —Usually the word ἄνθρωπος, *man*, is explained as synonymous with ἕκαστος, *each* (vi. 1); but the term seems here to include at the same time the ideas of weakness and responsibility.—The words: *and so*, signify: "And this examination once accomplished, let him eat . . ."

Ver. 29 returns once more to the idea of ver. 27 to impress more forcibly the necessity of this previous examination, by showing in all its gravity the danger indicated by the word ἔνοχος, *answerable*. The danger is of eating and drinking condemnation, while the man thinks he is appropriating the pledges of salvation.—

[1] T. R. here reads with D E F G K L P It. Syr. αναξιως (*unworthily*), a word which is omitted in ℵ A B C Sah.

[2] T. R. here reads with D E F G K L P Syr. του κυριου (*the Lord's*), which is omitted by ℵ A B C.

It seems at first sight impossible with the Alex. to suppress the word ἀναξίως, *unworthily*, which in the T. R. qualifies the two verbs of the conditional proposition. But this difficult reading may be defended in two ways: either by taking from the beginning the idea of eating and drinking in an unfavourable sense, according to ver. 27,—which is unnatural when ver. 28 has intervened;—or by seeking the indispensable limitation in the last words of the verse, μὴ διακρίνων, and translating them thus: "*If* or *when he* discerns not . . ." No doubt this turn of expression is somewhat harsh; but it is more probable that the word ἀναξίως has been added to the text, as an explanation, than that it would have been rejected if it had been authentic. — When he says κρίμα, *a judgment*, the apostle certainly does not mean eternal condemnation; for in that case he would have put the article τό, and the following verses positively prove the contrary. He is speaking of some chastisement or other inflicted by God. But yet he gives us to understand that this first judgment, unless it is followed by repentance and conversion, is the prelude of eternal perdition (ver. 32). There is something tragical in the ἑαυτῷ, *to himself* (*his own*): He incorporates with himself his own condemnation by that eating and drinking which should have aided in his salvation!—Critics are divided in regard to the meaning of the word διακρίνειν. It may signify *to distinguish* or *appreciate;* in the first sense: to distinguish a thing from all others; in the second: to understand its nature, and to measure its full grandeur. From the Lutheran viewpoint the natural inclination is to prefer the first meaning: "Not discerning with the eyes of faith the body and blood of Christ, which invisibly accompany the visible signs of bread and wine," or, as Hofmann explains: "Not distinguishing from the simple material bread the body which is appropriated by him who eats the bread." From the Reformed viewpoint, the second meaning seems the more natural: "Not surrounding with the respect due to the body of Christ the bread and wine consecrated to represent it." Heinrici cites several passages from the Talmud in which the word *discern*, to distinguish the holy from the profane, evidently includes this idea: to respect the holy, to appreciate it at its full value. It is easy to understand, however, how this word of St. Paul will always remain that to which the Lutheran conception will appeal most confidently. But, on the other hand, it is impossible to set aside as inadmissible this explanation: "not distinguishing, by the feeling of reverence with which the sacrament is celebrated, the body of Christ, represented by the bread, from ordinary food." See on the question of the Holy Supper, at ver. 25.—The words τοῦ κυρίου, *the Lord's*, in the T. R., are probably a gloss.

Vers. 30–32. "For this cause many are weak and sickly among you, and many sleep. 31. Now,[1] if we would judge ourselves, we should not be judged. 32. But when we are judged, we are chastened of the Lord, that we should not be condemned with the world."—The apostle had just spoken in a general way of the judgments which profane communion may bring down. He now appeals to the experience of the Corin-

[1] T. R. with C K L P Syr. reads γαρ (*for*); all the rest: δε (*now* or *but*).

thians themselves, who are at the moment visited with a sickness of which many have even died.—*Διὰ τοῦτο*, *for this cause:* "I am not using vain words when I speak thus to you" (ver. 29).—The word ἀσθενής, *weak*, rather denotes the sickness, and ἄῤῥωστος, *infirm*, the weakening which issues in decay, as if an invisible blow had suddenly blighted the forces of life.—Some, like Eichhorn, have taken the three terms *sickly*, *infirm*, and *dead*, in the spiritual sense. But the simultaneous use of the two words *sickly* and *weak* could not be easily explained morally; and instead of the verb κοιμᾶσθαι, which is never used in the New Testament, except in the sense of physical sleep or death, the apostle would rather have said νεκρὸς εἶναι (Rev. iii. 1). Besides, a purely spiritual fact would not have been of a nature to strike his readers sufficiently, and the more because the spiritual weakening had preceded the profanation of the Supper, and was the cause of it as much as the effect. Finally, as Stockmayer well says (*La maladie et l'Evangile*, p. 29): "It is not by spiritual decay that the Lord snatches us from a false position and preserves us from condemnation; it is by judgments suffered in the flesh." Comp. 1 Cor. v. 5; 1 Tim. i. 20. No doubt we must guard here against the faintest materialistic notion, as if the eating of the Supper itself, physically speaking, had produced the sickness, and as if the consecrated food had been changed into poison. It was a warning judgment, specially inflicted by God, such as He sends to awaken a man to salvation.

Ver. 31. And when does such a judgment overtake the Christian? When he has not voluntarily judged himself. God then comes to his help, awaking his sleeping vigilance by a stroke of His rod. This applies to Churches as well as to individuals.—The true reading is undoubtedly δέ and not γάρ. The δέ may indicate the logical progress of the argument (*now then*), or a contrast between the fact of the chastisement (ver. 30) and what would have happened if the Corinthians had behaved differently (*but*). The first connection is the more natural.—The verb διακρίνειν here signifies *to discern, analyse*, and so to *appreciate;* with the pronoun ἑαυτόν, *himself;* to discern one's own moral state by appreciating what within him pleases or displeases the Lord. By such a judgment, that of the Lord would be anticipated.

Ver. 32. This verse brings back the readers from the favourable supposition to the sad reality (δέ, *but*). Yet the present judgment, severe as it may be, is also an act of mercy on the Lord's part. It is not yet eternal condemnation ; it is, on the contrary, a means of preventing it. Here we must distinguish with the apostle three degrees which he denotes by the analogous terms διακρίνεσθαι, *to judge oneself* (ver. 31), κρίνεσθαι, *to be judged* (ver. 32), and κατακρίνεσθαι, *to be condemned* (same verse). The believer ought constantly *to judge himself;* such is the normal state. If he fails in this task, God reminds him of it by judging him by some chastisement which He sends on him, *he is judged;* and if he does not profit by this means, nothing remains for him but to suffer in common with the world the final judgment from which God sought to preserve him, *to be condemned.*—The *world* denotes unconverted and lost humanity.

These same three degrees may be found in Mark ix. 47–50.

After this complete development of the subject, the apostle concludes, as he usually does, with some very simple words, in which he states the practical result of his whole previous argument.

Vers. 33, 34. "Wherefore, my brethren, when ye come together to eat, tarry one for another. 34. If[1] any man hunger, let him eat at home, that ye come not together to incur judgment. The rest will I set in order when I come."—This conclusion reminds us of the passage x. 23–33. Here, as there, Paul, after starting from an outward fact (the disorders in the love-feast), enters on a complete development, intended thoroughly to enlighten the conscience of the Church; then he winds up with some rules of conduct, apparently external, but in which there is concentrated the whole moral quintessence of the preceding exposition. —The affectionate address, *my brethren*, following warnings so serious, has in it something familiar and genial, fitted to open the hearts of his readers to the counsel with which he is about to close. The regimen εἰς τὸ φαγεῖν, *to eat*, might be connected with the following verb, *tarry:* "Tarry for one another to begin the feast." But it is simpler to make it dependent on the verb *come together:* "When you come together, not for ordinary worship simply, but for a love-feast and the celebration of the Supper, tarry one for another to partake of the feast." The verb ἐκδέχεσθαι signifies *to wait* and *to welcome*. The first meaning is the only one found in the New Testament. It is also that

[1] T. R. with E K L P reads εἰ δὲ (*but if*); all the rest: εἰ (*if*).

which is most suitable here; for the word forms an antithesis to προλαμβάνειν, to precede in eating, ver. 21. The apostle wishes, that all seating themselves to eat together, the supper of each may become that of his neighbours; thereby it is that the feast becomes a true agape.

Ver. 34. The first words correspond exactly to the question of ver. 22: "Have ye not houses to eat and to drink in?" In this feast the object is not in reality to take nourishment, but to *eat together*.—*A judgment*, such as that instanced by the apostle in ver. 29.—The term: *the other points, the rest*, τὰ λοιπά, no doubt embraces a number of questions of detail relating to the celebration of the Supper, such as the frequency, the days, the time of day, the mode of the feast, etc. The Catholics have supposed that the matter in question here was the institution of the Mass, which, they say, became from that time the subject of an Episcopal tradition. But that would not have been a detail of secondary importance, like those which are evidently in the mind of the apostle.

In the representations of the agapæ which are found in the Catacombs, there is seen a company of seven or eight persons grouped round the same table (Heinrici, p. 342). If it was so at Corinth, one can very easily understand the possibility of the abuse pointed out by the apostle; every company of friends might have gathered in a group separate from the rest of the Church. But did such a practice prevail at Corinth? Of this we have not the slightest proof.

The agapæ of which Paul speaks have been compared to the feasts which were celebrated from time to time in Greece by the corporations which then existed in great number, with a view to certain common interests. But however that may be, the origin of the agapæ is Jewish and not Greek. This feast indeed represented the last supper of Jesus with His apostles, in the course of which He instituted the Holy Communion. Besides, in the feasts of those Greek colleges, it was the common fund of the society which paid the banquet, while our chapter itself proves that in the agapæ every family furnished its own provisions.

From certain notices, for which we are indebted to the historian Sozomenes (5th cent.), it appears that in some Churches (that of Alexandria, for example) the agape preceded the Holy Supper; according to Augustine, and no doubt in all the Churches of the West, it was the opposite: the Supper introduced the agape. Usage might vary according to place, and it certainly varied according to time, till the date when the agape was completely suppressed because of the abuses to which it gave rise.

9

Spiritual Gifts (12:1-14:40)

We have here one of the richest and most interesting parts of our Epistle. These chapters are to us like a revelation of the power of that spiritual movement which went forth from Pentecost, and of the wonderful spiritual efflorescence which at the outset signalized the new creation due to the power of the gospel.—The link which connects this passage with the two preceding is certainly the common idea of public worship; this comes out particularly in chap. xiv., where the apostle treats of the exercise of spiritual gifts in the assemblies of the Church; now that chapter is the conclusion to which the two previous ones point. At the same time there is progress from the two subjects, treated in chap. xi. to this third: the first, that of chap. xi. 1-16 (the demeanour of women in the assemblies), was of a more external nature; the second, chap. xi. 17–34 (the abuses in the Holy Supper), already went much deeper. The passage chaps. xii.–xiv. comes to what is more vital in the worship of the Church; the subject in question is the Holy Spirit Himself and His Divine manifestations. The Spirit, in the Christian community, may be compared to the nervous fluid in the human body. Thus it is that the apostle advances from the external to the internal.

What general idea ought we to form of the spiritual forces treated in this passage? We mean those new powers which in the apostle's writings often bear the name χαρίσματα, *gifts of grace*, which the Holy Spirit developed within the Church, and about which we have already stated our view, i. 7. The term χάρισμα indicates rather their *origin*, the word πνευματικά (xiv. 1) their *essence*. But for that very reason the former of these expressions has a wider meaning: for it may denote in general everything we owe to the Divine favour.—The Church is the body of Christ, the apostle tells us (xii. 27), that is to say, the organ which the glorified Christ since His departure has created on the earth to realize His design and carry out His purposes, as He formerly did by means of His body, strictly so called, when He was here below. This glorified Christ Himself dwells in believers by His Spirit, who thereby become His active members; and the action which He carries out through them proceeds from the extraordinary forces which He communicates to them. But these new powers may have their point of attachment in natural talents. It is even most frequently the case that the operation of the Spirit fits in to natural aptitudes; He impresses on them a higher direction, a new bent to the service of God, and He exalts their power by consecrating them to this sublime object.—But so long as the spiritual man, who possesses any of these gifts, has not reached absolute holiness, his personal consecration, and consequently that of his gift, remains still imperfect. Hence arises the possibility of the deterioration of the spiritual forces, either in their use or in their inward essence, by selfishness, pride, vanity, hypocrisy, falsehood, jealousy, or hatred. Was not this what the apostle himself, 2 Cor. vii. 1, called *defilement of the Spirit?*—Now this is exactly what happened at Corinth, and in the most serious manner. The members wished to shine, to take the lead, to surpass one another by means of those spiritual manifestations; they sought those particularly which took the most surprising forms, and they disdained those which, though less showy, were yet the most practical and useful. In this we recognise thoroughly the Greek mind, which turns everything to amusement, even things the most serious; those *children everlastingly,* ἀεὶ παῖδες, as one of their own has called them; comp. xvi. 21.

The principal error which misled the Corinthians and produced their spiritual ignorance (xii. 1) on this subject, seems to have consisted in this: they imagined that the more the influence of the Divine Spirit deprived a man of his self-consciousness and threw him into an ecstasy, the more powerful was that influence and the more sublime the state to which it raised the man; whereas the more the inspired person retained his self-possession, the less did his inspiration partake of a

Divine character. From this point of view, the teacher was far beneath the prophet, and the prophet beneath him who spoke in tongues. Their rule was: the more πνεῦμα (*Spirit*), the less νοῦς (*intelligence*). This judgment accorded with Greek and even Jewish prejudices (see Heinrici, pp. 352–357). Plato said in the *Phædrus:* "It is by madness (the exaltation due to inspiration) that the greatest of blessings come to us;" and in the *Timæus* he says: "No one in possession of his understanding has reached Divine and true exaltation." The numerous sayings of Philo expressing the same thought are well known; and certain sayings of the Old Testament regarding the influence of the Spirit, when it took hold of the prophets, may have given countenance to such an interpretation; comp. Num. xxiv. 4 (Balaam); Amos iii. 8; Hosea ix. 7, etc.

How was it possible to set about the disciplining of such forces, which, from their very origin, a Divine impulse, seemed to escape from the control of the intellectual judgment and to defy all rule? The Pythia obeys only the god who subjects her to his will; the inspired one is above all remark and admonition: The Spirit impels me; what answer can be made to that? The task which the apostle now undertakes is the most difficult and delicate of all that were imposed on him by the state of the Corinthian Church. He has to bank in the most impetuous of torrents. He will require, it is easy to see, all his wisdom and dexterity, and will require to put forth more than ever the apostolic gift which has been conferred on him for the government of the Church.

He begins, in chap. xii., by ascending to the loftiest

principles which govern this mysterious and profound region. In chap. xiii. he points out to the Corinthians the beneficent genius under whose patronage spiritual gifts should always be placed to exercise a salutary influence, viz. love. After having thus paved the way for the result he desires to reach, he passes, in chap. xiv., to the practical treatment of the subject, and lays down some precise and even finical rules for the advantageous exercise of these gifts, particularly those of prophecy and speaking in tongues. After the principles developed in chap. xii. and xiii., these rules do not seem to be imposed by authority; they spring, as it were, of themselves from the conscience of the Church, now sufficiently enlightened.

Chrysostom complained even in his day of the obscurity of these chapters; he explained it by the fact that the circumstances to which this whole treatment applied no longer existed in the Churches of his time. We are still further removed from the apostolic age and from the extraordinary manifestations which characterized it. But the living forces of which the apostle speaks are not entirely withdrawn from the Church, they ought to accompany it to the end of its earthly career (xiii. 10–12). They appear only in another form, so that the study to which we now proceed will not have a merely archæological interest, but is capable of assuming a present and practical value for every believer and especially for every pastor.

The efforts of certain critics (Baur, Räbiger, etc.) to connect the following discussion, in one way or another, with the opposition between the different parties which divided the Church of Corinth (i. 12), have not issued in any probable result. The text offers no data fitted to favour the hypotheses made in this direction.

A. General Survey of the Domain of Spiritual Gifts (12:1-31)

In the first three verses of this chapter, the apostle sets himself to mark out rigorously the domain of which he is about to treat, distinguishing it strictly from the analogous, but alien, religious manifestations, with which it might be confounded, and uniting by a common bond all the various manifestations which belong to it.

1. *The limits of the Christian pneumatical domain* (vers. 1-3)

Vers. 1–3. "Now as to spiritual gifts, brethren, I would not have you ignorant. 2. Ye know that when [1] ye were Gentiles, ye were carried away unto dumb idols, even as ye were driven. 3. Wherefore I give you to understand, that no man speaking [2] by the Spirit of God sayeth: Jesus [3] accursed! and that no man can say: Jesus Lord! [4] but by the Holy Spirit."—The δέ seems to me, as to Edwards, to have the adversative sense: "For the rest, I shall set them in

[1] T. R. with F G reads οτι without οτε (*that ye were*).—K reads οτε without οτι (*when ye were*).—ℵ A B C D E L P read οτι οτε (*that when ye were*).

[2] D E F G It. omit λαλων.

[3] T. R. with D E G K L P: Ιησουν; ℵ A B C: Ιησους.

[4] T. R. with D E F G K L P: κυριον Ιησουν; ℵ A B C Syr^sch: κυριος Ιησους.

order by word of mouth, there is nothing pressing (ver. 34); *but* in what concerns spiritual gifts, I would not have you left longer in ignorance; I must instruct you at once." The form περί, *as to*, presents this subject as one expected by the readers. This preposition might depend directly on the verb ἀγνοεῖν: "that you should be in ignorance touching . . ." But it is more natural to take it in the same sense as vii. 1 and viii. 1, as a sort of title, and to understand the regimen of ἀγνοεῖν: "in regard to such things." The address: *brethren*, is not only intended to excite the attention of the readers on entering on this new and important subject; it is also meant to soften the humiliation there might be in the expression: *I would not have you ignorant.*—Should we take the word πνευματικῶν in the masculine sense: spiritual *men*, the inspired, or in the neuter sense: spiritual *gifts?* Most modern critics (Hofmann, Ewald, Hilgenfeld, Reuss, Holsten, Heinrici) decide for the first sense, because, as Holsten says, it was rather about the part and the right of the inspired in the assemblies, that Paul had been asked, than about the inspirations themselves. Heinrici rests his view on xiv. 37: "If any man think himself to be a prophet or *spiritual*." These reasons seem to me far from decisive. With the parallel quoted by this last may be contrasted xiv. 1: "Desire spiritual gifts" (τὰ πνευματικά), which is much more conclusive; and to the argument advanced by Holsten, the common-sense answer is, that it was much more natural and wise to estimate the gifts in themselves independently of the persons than to do inversely. I think, therefore, with the ancient commentators and with Meyer that the neuter sense is preferable. As to the idea of Baur, Wieseler, and others, who restrict the application of the term to the gift of tongues or to those who possessed it, the view seems rather arbitrary. The apostle does not deal specially with this gift till chap. xiv. In chaps. xii. and xiii. he speaks of all the gifts in general, and, particularly in the verses which immediately follow, he marks off the whole domain of the pneumatic forces with which he is about to deal.—The expression : *I would not have you ignorant*, alludes to the mysterious side of the subject, and to its complete novelty to men recently converted.

Ver. 2. Of the three readings given in the note, the first, that of the T. R. (ὅτι alone), is not admissible; would it not be superfluous to say to Corinthian readers, "Ye know that ye were Gentiles"? Holsten answers that the emphasis is not on the predicate *Gentiles*, but on the explanatory appendix : *carried away to idols.* Certainly; but even taking this fact into account, the expression retains something offensive. And especially the construction would be so simple in this sense that it would be impossible to account for the origin of the variants. The reading of K and some Fathers (ὅτε alone, *when*) is not sufficiently supported. And the meaning to which it leads : "Ye know *how* (ὡς), *when* ye were Gentiles, ye were carried . . .," cannot, as we shall see, be admitted. The true reading is that which has representatives in the three families, and by means of which the other two are most easily explained : ὅτι ὅτε, *that when* : "ye know *that, when* ye were Gentiles . . ." The ὅτι has been confounded with the ὅτε in the one set; the opposite confusion has taken place in the other. This reading no doubt demands that we give to the participle ἀπαγόμενοι, *carried away*, the force of a finite verb, understanding an ἦτε, *ye were;* but this word is easily taken from the ἦτε which immediately precedes. Comp. the similar ellipsis Col. iii. 17, and the examples quoted by Meyer in classic Greek. Heinrici, following Buttmann, prefers, as Bengel had already done, to regard the ὡς as a repetition of the preceding ὅτι, in a slightly different form : "Ye know *that*, when ye were Gentiles, *how*, I say, ye were carried away . . ." But, first of all, the interruption contained in the words : "when ye were Gentiles," is too short to occasion such a repetition; then the proposition : ὡς ἂν ἤγεσθε, is evidently, as is indicated by its very position between the πρὸς . . . and the ἀπαγόμενοι, a parenthetical clause. For if the participle ἀπαγόμενοι were taken as qualifying ἤγεσθε, it would be superfluous in meaning and awkward in form. The πρὸς τὰ εἴδωλα, *to idols*, is the regimen of ἀπαγόμενοι (ἦτε) : "Ye were carried away to idols . . ." This forcible term calls up the idea of a whirlwind of impure blasts, to the power of which the Corinthians were formerly given up. There is opposition between the two prepositions ἀπό and πρός : "*far from* the true God, *toward* the objects of a deceptive worship." These objects were *idols*, a word in which are combined the ideas of a false divinity and a material statue. This last was regarded as penetrated with the power of the god whose image it was. These inspirations did not proceed from the idols, but they led to them. The epithet is put after the substantive : "the idols, *the dumb*," so as to bring out vividly this quality, and so the unworthy character of the worship of these false gods incapable of acting or speaking, and consequently of communicating to the worshipper a Divine inspiration. The parenthetical proposition ὡς ἂν ἤγεσθε, *as ye were driven*, serves to qualify the ἀπαγόμενοι, *ye were carried away*. We must beware of reading, as Erasmus, Heinrici, and others do, with some documents of secondary importance, ἀνήγεσθε in a single word: *quomodo ascendebatis* (Augustine). Not only is the idea of *ascending* unrelated to the context, but especially we thereby lose the meaning of the particle ἄν, which gives precisely the key to these difficult words. This particle, which contains the notion of contingency, indicates that those breathings were every moment changing their direction, and depended on a capricious will. It has been supposed that Paul had in view the influence of the priests, whose passive instruments the Gentiles were in their worship. Does it not rather follow from x. 20 that he is thinking of a diabolical influence exercised by the evil spirits, the authors of idolatry? Now, the fatal storm carried the blinded Gentile, with a whole procession, to the temple of Jupiter; again, it was to the altars of Mars or Venus, always to give them over to one or other of their deified passions; comp. Eph. ii. 2; 2 Tim. ii. 26. To the interesting passage of Athenagoras quoted by Meyer, Edwards adds that of Justin (*Apol.* i. 5): μάστιγι δαιμόνων φαύλων ἐξελαυνόμενοι, "chased with the scourge of evil demons."

Ver. 3. With this diabolical, capricious, and blind impulse, Paul contrasts the new breath with which the Holy Spirit penetrates the Church, a breath which has a fixed and glorious object, the Lord Jesus, and which, acting on the depths of the consciousness, gives rise to a new utterance in him who is animated by it. Heinrici, following Griesbach and Storr, thinks that the apostle means here to defend the gift of tongues against its detractors. After alluding to the oracles and deceptions of heathen priests, in ver. 2, he now passes, they hold, to the effects of Christian inspiration, which, while offering some analogy to these heathen manifestations, ought yet to be carefully distinguished from them. No doubt the discourses in tongues are unintelligible, and there might be a fear of their containing some blasphemy against Jesus Christ. But this fear may be dismissed, for the Holy Spirit can inspire with nothing which is contrary to the glory of the Lord Jesus.—It is impossible not to feel the very artificial and forced character of this connection between vers. 2 and 3. Besides, we shall see that in this whole section, chaps. xii.–xiv., Paul is speaking, not to exalt the gift of tongues, but, on the contrary, to combat the exaggerated value given to it. This introduction, vers. 1–3, is still quite general, and has no special relation to the gift of speaking in tongues. De Wette seems to me to have apprehended the context better: "As Gentiles, you acted without consciousness and without personal judgment; but now, as Christians, the time is come for your knowing how to regulate yourselves; and hence I make known to you the true principle by which you ought to judge all manifestations of this kind." But this transition is not enough. We must go more to the root of the matter, and not confine ourselves to the contrast between the blind passivity of the heathen state and the full personal consciousness of the Christian state. For this characteristic of superiority would apply only imperfectly to the gift of tongues, the exercise of which excludes the use of the faculty of the νοῦς, the *understanding* (xiv. 14). The real transition seems to me rather to be this: "In your former heathen state you had no experience whatever similar to that which you now have in the Church. The dumb idols, to the worship of which you let yourself be carried, did not communicate powers similar to those which the Spirit now communicates to you. Consequently, novices as you are in this domain, you need a guiding thread to prevent you from going astray: *This is why I instruct you. . . .*" (Comp. Meyer.)

The first thing needed by a Church so inexperienced in this domain was to know how far it extended, in other words, what was the true character of the Divine influence; who was truly inspired and who was not. The apostle answers this first question by two maxims, the one negative, exclusive; the other positive, affirmative. The character of Divine inspiration does not depend on the form which the discourse takes, but on its tendency. Whether it be a prophecy, a tongue, or a doctrine, matters little; every utterance which amounts to saying: *Jesus be accursed!* is not Divinely inspired; every utterance which amounts to saying: *Jesus Lord!* is Divinely inspired. It should be remarked that Paul here says *Jesus,* and not *Christ.* His concern is with the historical person who lived on the earth under the name of Jesus. It is with Him that all true inspiration is bound up; it is from Him that all carnal or diabolical inspiration turns away. Jesus had said: "Father, all Thine is Mine, and all

Mine is Thine" (John xvii. 10), and "The Spirit of truth shall glorify Me; He shall take of Mine and show it unto you." No utterance whatever, degrading the man who is called Jesus, however eloquent and powerful, emanates from Divine inspiration. Every utterance glorifying the man Jesus, however weak and unpretending, proceeds from the breath from on high. According to the Greco-Lats., the Byz., and the T. R., we should read: ἀνάθεμα Ἰησοῦν (*sayeth that Jesus is accursed*), and κύριον Ἰησοῦν (*sayeth that Jesus is the Lord*). According to the Alex. and the Peschito, the word *Jesus* is in the nominative: ἀνάθεμα Ἰησοῦς and κύριος Ἰησοῦς; it is each time an exclamation: *Jesus accursed! Jesus Lord!* Clearly this second reading is the only possible one. Exclamation, much more than cold logical statement, is the language of inspired discourse, the characteristic of which is enthusiasm. In classical Greek the word ἀνάθεμα is synonymous with ἀνάθημα, and denotes every object consecrated to deity. But in the LXX. and in the New Testament it takes a particular sense, denoting an object consecrated to God in order to its destruction, a being devoted to be cursed (Deut. vii. 26; Josh. vii. 13, etc.; Gal. i. 8); while ἀνάθημα preserves the meaning of offering *sensu bono;* comp. Luke xxi. 5. —But to whom in the Christian Church can the apostle attribute the language: *Jesus accursed!* It has been supposed—as is still done by Holsten—that the apostle here refers to discourses hostile to Jesus which were heard from the lips of Jews or even from those of unbelieving Gentiles, who treated Jesus as an impostor, and saw in His ignominious and cruel death a token of the Divine curse. Comp. i. 23: *to the Jews a stumbling-block.* There might thus be found in this passage the three great religious domains of the time, heathenism (ver. 2), Judaism (ver. 3[a]), and Christianity (ver. 3[b]). But the construction of the sentence does not lend itself to such parallelism. And the question arises, How could the Church of Corinth have been tempted to ascribe such discourses to Divine inspiration? Besides, we have to do here with discourses uttered in the assemblies of the Church; and how would men have been allowed to speak publicly in the Church who were not Christians? One would rather suppose, as Heinrici seems to do, that this first purely negative rule is not meant by the apostle to apply to any real case, and that he has put it down only the better to bring out the idea of the second by way of contrast. But neither is this explanation admissible; for these two criteria are so placed in relation to one another, that the real application of the one implies also that of the other. Must we then believe that Paul admits the possibility of such discourses within the Church itself? When Heinrici declares this supposition absurd, does he transport himself adequately into the midst of the powerful fermentation of religious ideas then called forth by the gospel? In 2 Cor. xi. 3, 4, the apostle speaks of teachers newly arrived at Corinth, who preached *another Jesus* than the one he had preached, and who raised a *different spirit* from that which the Church had received. It was therefore not only another doctrine, but also another breath, a new principle of inspiration, which these people brought with them. In our Epistle itself, xvi. 22, he speaks of certain persons who love not Jesus Christ, and whom he devotes to *anathema* when the Lord shall come. These utterances would appear very severe, if they were not a sort of *return* for the anathema which these people threw in the face of Jesus Christ. How was this possible in a Christian Church? We must observe, first of all, the term *Jesus*, denoting the historical and earthly person of our Lord, and bear in mind that from the earliest times there were people who, offended at the idea of the ignominious punishment of the cross, and the unheard-of abasement of the Son of God, thought they must set up a distinction between the man Jesus and the true Christ. The first had been, according to them, a pious Jew. A heavenly being, the true Christ, had chosen him to serve as His organ while He acted here below as the Saviour of humanity. But this *Christ from above* had parted from Jesus before the Passion, and left the latter to suffer and die alone. It is easy to see how, from this point of view, one might curse the crucified one who appeared to have been cursed of God on the cross, and that without thinking he was cursing the true Saviour and Christ, and while remaining without scruple a member of the Church. We know the name of a man who positively taught the doctrine we speak of. He was a Jew-Christian, named Cerinthus, very much attached to the law like the adversaries of Paul at Corinth; and it is curious to hear a Father of the Church, Epiphanius, affirm that the First Epistle to the Corinthians was written against this person. We shall not go so far. We would only use the example to show what strange conceptions might arise at this period when Christian doctrine was yet in process of formation, and when all the ideas awakened by the gospel were seething within the Church. To the example of Cerinthus we can add that of the Ophites, or serpent-worshippers, who existed before the end of the first century, and who, according to Origen (*Contra Celsum*), asked those who wished to enter their churches to *curse Jesus.* In stating this first negative criterion, the apostle therefore means to say to the Corinthians: However ecstatic in form, or profound in matter, may be a spiritual manifestation, tongue, prophecy, or doctrine, if it tends to degrade Jesus, to make Him an impostor or a man worthy of the Divine wrath, if it does violence in any way to His holiness, you may be sure the inspiring breath of such a discourse is not that of God's Spirit. Such is the decisive standard which the prophets, for example, are summoned to use when they sit in judgment on one another (xiv. 29).

After drawing the line fitted to set aside all that presents itself as Christian inspiration without being so in fact, the apostle points out the characteristic common to all those manifestations to which the quality of a true inspiration can and should be accorded, whatever may be the form in which they show themselves. To proclaim *Jesus* as the *Lord;* such is the mark of every Divinely inspired Christian discourse. Such a discourse is a cry of adoration, an act of homage by which the historical person who bore the name of Jesus, notwithstanding His shame and bloody death, is raised by the inspired one to the Divine throne, and celebrated as the Being who exercises universal sovereignty; such is the force of the title κύριος, *Lord;* comp. Phil. ii. 9–11.

It might be objected to the apostle that there are professions of faith in Jesus Christ which are purely intellectual, orthodox sermons which are devoid of the breath of the Spirit. But this objection has no force whatever in the context, especially with the reading *κύριος Ἰησοῦς* (nominatives), which we have adopted, and which makes these words an exclamation. Such a cry of the heart does not in the least resemble a cold logical affirmation. We might object, with more show of reason, the exclamation of the demons who cried out on seeing Jesus: "Thou art the Holy One of God." But this emotion of fear and this particular insight might well be, even in those beings, an effect of the Spirit's influence; comp. James ii. 19. It is the Holy Spirit who gives to an intelligent spirit the discernment of the holiness of Jesus. Thus, however simple, however elementary in matter a Christian discourse may be, however calm, however sober in form, if its result is to place on the head of Jesus the crown of *Lord,* it is the product of the Divine Spirit, as well as the most extraordinary manifestation which can take place in a Christian assembly.

The field of Divine inspirations is thus marked off by a line of demarcation which every believer can apply. The apostle now explains the relation which those various manifestations of the Christian Spirit, that are embraced in it, sustain to one another. He first expounds the idea, that however *various* those manifestations may be in their outward form, they are one in their principle and end (vers. 4–12).

2. *The unity of spiritual forces in their diversity* (vers. 4-13ᵃ)

The first and most profound diversity which strikes the mind as it contemplates the display of Divine power within the Church, is the difference between the Divine *gifts, ministries,* and *operations.* More than this: in each of these three principal classes there is seen to be a subordinate variety of kinds and species. But these principal and secondary diversities all proceed from one and the same principle, and all tend consequently to one and the same end: vers. 4–6.

Vers. 4–6

Vers. 4–6. "Now there are diversities of gifts, but the same Spirit. 5. And there are differences of administrations, and the same Lord. 6. And there are diversities of operations, but it is[1] the[2] same God which worketh all in all."—Paul here mentions three principal diversities to which correspond three principles of unity which in reality form only one.—We already know what he understands by *gifts,* χαρίσματα; they are the creative powers which God communicates to believers when their new activity expands under the influence of the life of Christ. The principal of these gifts will be enumerated vers. 8–10.—The term διαίρεσις, translated *diversity,* strictly signifies *apportionment, distribution;* this is its meaning in the LXX. and in profane Greek (see Heinrici); comp.

[1] T. R. with K L reads εστι before θεος, which is rejected by the rest.

[2] T. R. with ℵ A K L P It: ο δε (*but the same*); B C: και ο (*and the . . .*).

the participle διαιροῦν, *distributing*, in ver. 11. But as the apportioning of these gifts by the Spirit is not made arbitrarily, and as it rests on a real diversity between the individuals as well as between the powers themselves, the word may be rendered by the term *diversity*, like μερισμός, Heb. ii. 4 [*distribution*, Marg. R.V.]. We shall see how carefully the various kinds and species of gifts will be distinguished in the enumeration vers. 8–10.—All these varieties of gifts have one and the same principle: the *Spirit* who produces them when He comes to dwell in believers.

Ver. 5. But there exists in the Church a second kind of Divine manifestations; *charges*, namely, or ministries, διακονίαι. This word denotes, not like the preceding, inward aptitudes, but external offices, with which certain individuals are put in charge. There are different kinds of them; some may be related to the whole Church, like the apostolate or the office of evangelist (missionary); others to a particular community, and that either with a view to the spiritual life, as the episcopate, or with a view to different kinds of temporal helps, such as the numerous branches of the diaconate; under these offices even there must have existed functions of an inferior order relating to those material services which were called for by the holding of assemblies and of the agapæ, etc. What was the relation of these charges to the gifts? Probably certain of them, the highest, rested on a spiritual gift which the community had recognised and ordained to a regular function; others, the inferior ones, were mere offices committed to individuals by the Church.—As there are gifts which, by their very nature, cannot become the basis of an office (speaking in tongues or prophecy, for example), and others which may easily be transformed into a regular function (the gift of teaching, for example), so there are also offices of a wholly external kind, management of material affairs, for example, which are scarcely related to any gift, while others, like the apostolate, have for their foundation a special gift or a whole combination of gifts. These varied offices have, like the gifts, their principle of unity; but this principle is, so to speak, before, not behind them. As the various gifts rest on one and the same principle, the Spirit, so the offices tend to one and the same end, *the Lord,* by whose authority and for whose service they act. To connect the two propositions of this verse, instead of δέ, *but,* Paul here says καί, *and,* no doubt to join this second principle of unity to the preceding, the Spirit, mentioned ver. 4.

Ver. 6. A third kind of varied manifestations: manifold *operations* due to the exercise both of those gifts and those offices. The term ἐνεργήματα, *operations,* denotes the powers realized in acts; the real effects Divinely produced either in the world of body or of mind, as often as the gift or the office comes into action. Thus, in a believer, the Holy Spirit has developed the *gift* of preaching. Recognising this gift, the Church has committed to him the preacher's *office,* with a view to the service of Christ; its ἐνέργημα, *operation,* will be the good discourse delivered by him, and the edification thereby effected in the hearts of his hearers. Another has the gift of healing; this gift cannot, from its nature, take the form of a regular office; but it will be displayed in healing operations;

restored health will be its ἐνέργημα in each case.—These varied effects have also their principle of unity. It is God who, after producing the gifts by the Spirit, and establishing the offices for the service of the Lord, Himself produces every good result of the gifts and offices; comp. 1 Cor. iii. 6, 7.—Τὰ πάντα, *all things;* according to the context, the gifts of every kind, and the offices of every kind, as well as the endlessly varied beneficent effects which result from both.—'Εν πᾶσιν, *in all;* in those who work and in those on whom the effect is produced.—Paul here returns to the δέ, *but,* to pass to the second proposition. He wishes thereby strongly to contrast the supreme principle of unity, which embraces in it the two preceding, the *Spirit* and the *Lord,* with the boundless variety of gifts, ministries, and operations distributed among the members of the Church.

After this general survey of the Divine unity which controls the three great forms of activity and their manifold varieties, the apostle comes to the one which it is most important for him to regulate in the given circumstances, viz. gifts. And before showing how rich in number they are, he reminds them of the common principle which produces them, and points to the common end which unites them, the common advantage (ver. 7). Then he states them in all their variety, each time repeating the one principle from which they proceed (vers. 8–12).

Vers. 7–12

Ver. 7. "But the manifestation of the Spirit is given to each man for the common advantage."—Each receives an aptitude from the Spirit, but not for himself; what each possesses is intended for the good of all.—The genitive τοῦ πνεύματος, *of the Spirit*, cannot be, as Meyer and others will have it, an objective complement, as if it were the Spirit who was manifested by the gift. From the fact that in 2 Cor. iv. 2 the word ἡ φανέρωσις has an objective complement (*of the truth*), it does not follow that it should be the same here; the two notions of *truth* and *Spirit* are very different. Paul does not mean that what belongs to the Spirit is revealed by the exercise of gifts, but that He manifests Himself by communicating them. And as the Spirit is *one* (ver. 4), it follows that all the gifts, however different, must tend to a common end, the good of the whole, and not to the selfish satisfaction of the individual on whom they are bestowed. With the dative ἑκάστῳ, *to each*, which is placed first, there is connected grammatically and logically the whole following enumeration of the gifts, or, as has been said, the presents which the bridegroom makes to the bride.

Vers. 8–10. "For to the one is given by the Spirit the word of wisdom; to the other the word of knowledge according to the same Spirit; 9. to[1] another faith by the same Spirit; to the other the gifts of healing by the same[2] Spirit; 10. to the other the workings[3] of miracles;[3] to the other[4] prophecy; to

[1] T. R. with A K L reads δε, after ετερω, which is omitted by the rest.

[2] T. R. with ℵ D E F G K L P reads: εν τω αυτω (*the same*); A B: εν τω ενι (*one*).

[3] D E F G read ενεργεια (*power*), instead of ενεργηματα (*workings*), and δυναμεως, instead of δυναμεων.

[4] B D E F G omit δε, which is read by ℵ A C K L P.

the other[1] discerning[2] of spirits; to another[3] divers kinds of tongues; to the other the interpretation[4] of tongues."—Most moderns think it impossible to discover any psychological or logical order in the following enumeration, and think even that there is no force to be ascribed in this respect to the change of the pronoun ἄλλῳ into ἑτέρῳ (once in ver. 9, a second time in ver. 10). Meyer is not of this opinion, and rightly, as it seems to me; for there is nothing arbitrary in Paul's style, and everybody knows that ἄλλος expresses a difference of individual, but ἕτερος a difference of quality. Thus we have the expression in Greek ἕτερος γίνεσθαι, to become other, to change one's opinion, while ἄλλος γίνεσθαι, to become a different individual, would have no meaning. It cannot therefore be without an object that Paul has twice introduced in this enumeration the stronger adjective instead of the weaker. Before the first ἑτέρῳ, *to a different*, we find the indication of two gifts, which, as has always been remarked, relate principally to the faculty of intelligence, and thus form a first homogeneous group. It is easy to understand the reason why Paul assigns to it at this stage the first place. We shall see that the Corinthians were disposed to regard the most extraordinary manifestations, the most ecstatic, as much more really Divine than those which leave man in full possession of his reason. Now the apostle places these very manifestations in the foreground to sweep

[1] B D E F G omit δε, which is read by ℵ A C K L P.

[2] T. R. with A B D K L reads διακρισεις (*discernments*), instead of διακρισις (singular).

[3] T. R. with A C K L reads δε, which is omitted by the rest.

[4] A D: διερμηνεια, instead of ερμηνεια.

away this false judgment.—The two terms *wisdom* and *knowledge* have been very variously distinguished. According to Neander and others, wisdom has a practical character, and knowledge indicates something more speculative; according to Bengel, inversely. This last view is evidently false; *gnosis* (knowledge) bears of course on theory. But no more can Neander's view be maintained in the face of chap. i., where the term *sophia*, wisdom, is applied to the profounder exposition of the mysteries embraced in the Divine plan (ii. 6 seq.). Hofmann understands *wisdom* as applying to the general view of the whole domain of spiritual life, and *knowledge* as referring to profound insight into certain particular points in this domain. Heinrici takes wisdom as the simple knowledge of salvation (as it is explained, for example, by the catechism), knowledge as the reasoned understanding of the gospel, as it is given in a course of dogmatic. According to Edwards, gnosis is a degree of Christian knowledge inferior to wisdom, which is the prerogative of mature Christians. There is a measure of truth in these different points of view, but there is something arbitrary about them all. If we start from the meaning of the two substantives, as it seems to follow from the form of the two Greek terminations (σις and ια), we shall rather see in *gnosis* a notion of effort, investigation, discovery (comp. xiii. 2, where this term is connected with the idea of *knowing all mysteries*), and in *sophia*, on the contrary, the idea of a calm possession of truth already acquired, as well as of its practical applications. Gnosis makes the teacher; wisdom, the preacher and pastor. When corrupted, the former becomes gnosticism, the speculation of the intellectualist; the latter, dead orthodoxy. —It should be remarked, with Hofmann, that the apostle speaks neither of wisdom nor of knowledge in themselves, but of a *word, discourse* of wisdom or of knowledge; for he seizes the gift in action at the moment when it is to serve the edification of the Church.—The use of the two different prepositions διά, *by means of*, and κατά, *according to the standard of*, applied, the former to wisdom, the latter to knowledge, is not arbitrary. Knowledge advances by means of subjective and deliberate study, which, if it is not to deviate from the straight line of Divine truth, must be carried on *according to* the light of the Spirit; whereas the edifying discourses of wisdom are produced in the heart *by* the Spirit, agreeably to the wants of the given situation. Moreover, Eph. iv. 11 shows how the two gifts, as well as the two offices connected with them (*pastor* and *teacher*), are in close affinity.

Ver. 9. If we hold that the substitution of ἑτέρῳ for ἄλλῳ is not accidental, the gifts which follow should have a different character from the two preceding, and this new character ought to reappear identically in the five gifts enumerated down to the following ἑτέρῳ (end of ver. 10). Now it is easy to prove that it is so. The two preceding gifts were exercised in virtue of a communication of light; the following five proceed from a communication of *force*, in other words, from an influence of the spirit, no longer specially on the understanding, but on the will. By *faith* the apostle certainly does not understand saving faith in general; for this is not a special gift, it is the portion of all Christians. Faith is the root of the Christian life, not one of its fruits. We see clearly from the passage xiii. 2 that the apostle distinguishes between faith in general and faith as a particular gift. As such, it is the possession of salvation taking the character of assurance in God, of heroic daring, resolutely attacking and surmounting all the obstacles which are opposed to the work of God in a given situation. "Father, I know that Thou hearest me always!" Such is the cry of this faith which removes mountains, and of which the history of the Church affords so many examples; witness a Francke, a Wilberforce, a George Müller, and so many others. It is to this gift the saying of Jesus, Matt. xvii. 20, 21 refers. The preposition ἐν, *in* or *by*, indicates that the force of this confidence rests on the Holy Spirit's indwelling in the soul.

There follow the gifts of *healings*, which are closely connected with faith thus understood, for they have as their basis confidence in the power of God applied to disease. Here there is not only a confident prayer; there is a command given in the consciousness of complete harmony with the will of God, such as the: "Rise, and walk," of St. Peter (Acts iii. 6). The substantives *gifts* and *healings* are put in the plural as relating to the different classes of sicknesses to be healed.

Ver. 10. The *miraculous operations*, ἐνεργήματα δυνάμεων, have a very natural connection with the two previous gifts. Paul has in view the power of working all sorts of miracles other than simple cures, corresponding to the wants of the different situations in which the servant of Christ may be placed: resurrections from the dead, the driving out of demons, judgments inflicted on unfaithful Christians or adversaries, such as Ananias or Elymas, deliverances like that of Paul at Malta.—The reading δυνάμεως, *of power*, has no probability.—The Mss. A B read ἐν τῷ ἑνί, *in the one Spirit*, instead of ἐν τῷ αὐτῷ, *in the same Spirit;* this reading more forcibly contrasts the unity of the power with the diversity of the effects. But in French we cannot say *the one* without adding *the same.*[1]

The place here occupied by the gift of *prophecy* seems at the first glance somewhat strange. As a gift of speech, it seems as if it should rather be joined to the first group (ver. 8); but it is only so in appearance. The prophet, according to xiv. 3, effects by his utterances "edification, comfort, consolation." This gift therefore belongs to the group of gifts which have the will as their agent, and make use of it to put forth a power. It is miracle in the form of speech. As Hofmann says, "Prophecy does not proceed from a resolution or reflection of the prophet's own, but from a power independent of him, which masters his mind and makes him speak in order to act on others." It proceeds from a revelation regarding the present state, course, and future of the kingdom of God. In transmitting this revelation to the Church, the prophet endeavours to stimulate it and to raise it to the height of his theme. It is in the spiritual domain an effect analogous to that which is produced on the sick man by the: "Rise and walk," pronounced by him who has the gift of healing.—But vanity may easily become

[1] [As we can say it in English, we have translated the verse accordingly. —Tr.]

master of the exercise of this gift, and the prophet allow himself to mingle elements drawn from his own stock with the contents of the revelation received; he may even, without suspecting it, yield to an inspiration of diabolic origin. Hence the exercise of this gift ought to be subjected to control, and to come under the judgment of other persons capable of distinguishing, if need be, the human from the Divine. This judgment, which the apostle calls διάκρισις πνευμάτων, *discernment of spirits,* seems to have been usually exercised, according to xiv. 29, by other prophets. It is attributed, 1 John iv. 1, to the Church in general. St. Paul has given the fundamental direction to guide this judgment in ver. 3. The criterion which John gives, vers. 2 and 3, is at bottom identical with that of Paul. —The plural διακρίσεις, *discernments,* in five Mjj., may be accepted; it is the most difficult reading. It is to be regarded as referring to all the particular cases. By the plural πνευμάτων, *of spirits,* Paul would indicate *the breathings* of the Spirit, which take effect suddenly on the prophets of the Church.

Ver. 10[b]. It is certainly not without reason that the pronoun ἑτέρῳ reappears here. The gift of tongues and that of their interpretation form, in the apostle's eyes, a new category. And the character of this third group is easily distinguished. If in the first we find the influence of the Spirit on the powers of the *understanding,* in the second on the forces of the *will,* it is very clear that in the third we have the influence of the same Spirit on the *feelings.* The passage xiv. 14–16 proves that he who *speaks in tongues* addresses God under the overpowering influence of profound emotion, which causes him *to pray*, *sing*, or *give thanks* in an ecstatic language unintelligible to every one who does not share the same emotion, and to which his own understanding, his νοῦς, remains a stranger. It is then his feelings, and his feelings only, which are in activity, to the exclusion of his understanding and will, which are inactive. The man who speaks thus has indeed no intention whatever of acting on those who hear him. The sounds he gives forth are the immediate expression of what he feels: "He speaks to God, and not to men" (chap. xiv. 2).

From the third century down to modern times, the prevalent idea in the Church has been that the gift of tongues was the power of preaching the gospel to different peoples, to each in its own tongue, without having learned it. This gift, it was thought, explained the rapid propagation of the gospel. Irenæus, who, in the second century, speaks of this gift, and speaks of it as a phenomenon still existing in his time, does not express himself very clearly about its nature. He says (*Adv. Hær.* v. 6. 1), "that he has heard many brethren in the churches possessing prophetical gifts and speaking in tongues of all sorts by the Spirit (παντοδαπαῖς λαλούντων διὰ τοῦ πνεύματος γλώσσαις), bringing to the light the hidden things of men, and expounding the mysteries of God." This expression: tongues of all sorts, does not enlighten us sufficiently as to his view. But the opinion of Origen (*ad Rom.* i. 13) and his school is evident. The following, for example, is how Chrysostom, giving himself up to his imagination, describes the fact: "Immediately one made his voice be heard in the language of the Persians, another in that of the

Romans; another in that of the Indians; another in some other tongue." Similarly Theodoret: "Often a man who knew only the Greek tongue, after another had spoken in the language of the Scythians or Thracians, gave the hearers the translation of his discourse" (see Meyer). The narrative of Pentecost (Acts ii.) seemed to point in this direction. Certainly we are not sufficiently acquainted with the hidden powers of the human soul, nor the mysterious relation of external language to inward speaking, to affirm the impossibility of such a phenomenon arising from the influence of the Holy Spirit in the depths of the soul. But with what view would a gift so extraordinary have been bestowed? With Greek and Latin, two languages which it was not so difficult to learn, one could make himself understood everywhere. And supposing the gift were intended to help mission work, of what use could it be in a Church like that of Corinth? Is it possible to conceive behaviour more strange on the part of a Greek of this Church than his setting himself to speak all at once in Arabic, or Chinese, or Hindustani, to express the lively emotions with which the gospel filled his heart? In Mark xvi. 9–20, a passage which, though unauthentic, undoubtedly contains authentic materials, we find the oldest name of this gift uttered by Jesus Himself, and the simplicity of which seems to guarantee its exactness. It is the expression: *to speak in new tongues* (γλώσσαις καιναῖς λαλεῖν). This expression does not suit the nature of the gift, as it was afterwards understood in the Church. Tongues really existing among other peoples would not be *new* tongues: instead of καιναῖς we ought to have had ξέναις or ἀλλοτρίαις. Finally, in this sense, how is it possible to explain the term γένη γλωσσῶν, *kinds* or *species* of tongues? It is impossible to suppose that the apostle is thinking of the distinction of human tongues into Semitic, Turanian, Indo-Germanic *families!* Besides, this interpretation is now generally abandoned. As to the account of the second chapter of the Acts which gave rise to it, it seems to me that ver. 11 allows another explanation of the mysterious phenomenon related in that chapter.

After Ernesti, Bleek substituted the following for the old interpretation. The term γλῶσσα, *tongue*, is frequently employed by Greek grammarians to denote certain expressions rarely or anciently used, archaisms or provincial idioms. Accordingly, Bleek thinks that *speaking in a tongue* denotes discourses mixed with expressions of this kind. He also compares the relation between the Christian who spoke in a tongue and his interpreter to the relation of the προφήτης to the μάντις, in consulting the oracles. The prophet was the translator of the enigmatical answer (*lingua secreta*) which the god put into the mouth of the latter (*the inspired*). Heinrici appropriates this explanation, and supports it by new and important examples, taken not only from the literary, but also from the religious language of the Greeks. He mentions, in particular, that according to Diodorus, the act of rendering oracles in an obscure and Sibylline style was called ἐνθεάζειν κατὰ γλῶσσαν, to speak inspiredly *in a tongue.*—But it is impossible to imagine why, in a community composed of traders, artisans, sailors, etc., the most profound emotions of the saved soul should have found expression either in ancient and unusual words, or by means of compositions formed of wholly new terms. It is still less intelligible how this labour of reminiscence or creation could have taken place in a state wherein the influence of feeling controlled that of the understanding (xiv. 14).

A third explanation takes the word *tongue* in the phrase γλώσσαις λαλεῖν in its literal sense: to speak while moving the tongue so as to utter sounds of which the speaker is neither master, nor conscious. Such, with certain shades of difference, is the meaning adopted by Eichhorn, Baur, Meyer. With the term tongue thus understood there have been compared the expressions of St. Paul in the Romans; "the Spirit who prays in us *with unutterable groanings*," or who cries by the mouth of the child of God: "*Abba, Father!*" (Rom. viii. 26 and 15). Some sentences of chap. xiv. of our Epistle might suit this meaning. But others are absolutely opposed to it. How in this sense are we to explain the plural γλώσσαις λαλεῖν, to speak *in tongues*, especially when only one person is in question, as in ver. 6? Even in our passage the term γένη γλωσσῶν, *kinds* of tongues, cannot be so explained naturally. A speaking by a motion of the tongue divided into several categories! And can it be supposed that the apostle himself rejoiced and thanked God because he possessed such a faculty more than any of the Corinthians (xiv. 18, 19)?

The gift of speaking in tongues must therefore have been something more elevated. Paul seems to compare it, xiii. 1, to the language of angels. As the bird by its song expresses the full joy of life in the absolute freedom of existence, so the transport to which the new experiences of the Christian life, of the peace of salvation, of the contemplation of the God of love, of the hope of glory, at times lifted the hearts of believers, was sometimes manifested of a sudden in an extraordinary language of which we can no longer form an idea. Sometimes it was an ardent supplication (*the unutterable groanings* of the Spirit), asking of God the full realization of His purposes of love (Rom. viii. 26); sometimes it was the cry of the spirit of adoption: "Abba, Father!" (Rom. viii. 14), finding vent in the form of joyful thanksgiving; sometimes it was a Psalm-singing, celebrating the ineffable gift of salvation in tones inspired with heavenly sweetness, music rather than language properly so called (xiv. 7). To explain such a phenomenon it is not necessary to have recourse, as Holsten has, to the contrast between the gospel and the miseries of the time, the tyranny of the emperors, the avarice of the proconsuls, the chains of slavery, the despair of poverty, the satiety of wealth. The contrast which thus created new tongues within the Church was more of a spiritual and moral nature; it was the contrast between peace and remorse, holiness and impurity, the hope of perfect life and the fear of annihilation, the possession of God and life without God.

Such emotions, expressed in this mysterious language, the immediate creation of the Spirit, could only be understood by the man whom the Spirit put in communion with those who experienced them. And as such a man, while sharing those emotions, was nevertheless not wholly controlled by them, he preserved the power of giving account of the Divine object which gave rise to them, and so of expounding the same feelings in distinct words. This is what the apostle calls *interpretation*, ἑρμηνεία, which also depended on a special gift. Is there here an allusion to the technical use made of the word ἑρμηνεία in religious language, to denote the interpretation of the oracles of the Pythia (comp. Heinrici)? This is neither impossible nor necessary. As prophecy had for its auxiliary διάκρισις, *discernment*, because its contents fell into the category of the true or the false, so speaking in a tongue was accompanied by interpretation, which simply made its contents intelligible to the Church, the danger of error not existing, so to speak, in a form of utterance which was only the unreflecting manifestation of a feeling.—It cannot be by accident that the apostle here gives the last place to the gifts of tongues and of interpretation. Throughout this whole passage he speaks from the standpoint of the *common advantage* (ver. 7). If therefore he puts first the word of wisdom and of knowledge, it is because he regards them as the best fitted to impart to the Church solid and lasting edification. If he places after them gifts capable of producing a powerful effect, whether in the way of healing or comfort, it is because after the former they are the most useful; finally, in the last rank comes the gift which is only a matter of emotion without positive result.

On the relation between the gift of tongues as it existed at Corinth, and its first manifestation on the day of Pentecost, we shall not be able to pronounce till after the study of chap. xiv.; see at the end of that chapter.

Such was the wealth of gifts which the Holy Spirit had produced in the Church of Corinth in the days of its first love. But what Paul wished to bring out here was *their unity* controlling all this diversity; he had mentioned it after each gift; and now once again he enunciates it more expressly at the close of the complete enumeration, ver. 11.

Ver. 11. "But all these worketh that one and the selfsame Spirit, dividing to every man severally as He will."—That *one:* in opposition to the plurality of believers; the *same:* in opposition to the diversity of gifts.—The partic. διαιροῦν, *dividing,* has no expressed object; the emphasis is on the act of dividing. With the adj. ἰδίᾳ, we must understand the subst. μοίρᾳ.—By the words: *as He will,* the apostle does not ascribe to the Spirit a capricious and fantastic mode of procedure. The good pleasure of God is never exercised except in perfect harmony with all the perfections of His character, His wisdom, goodness, righteousness. The analogous phrase, xv. 38, shows how entirely the notion of arbitrariness is excluded, in the apostle's view, from the idea of the Divine pleasure. One may compare in some respects Matt. xxv. 15.—The deliberate will (βούλεσθαι), here ascribed to the Holy Spirit, seems to me to imply His personality, as the act of giving supposes His Divinity. The words: *to every man as He will,* are undoubtedly intended to sweep away, from the more gifted of the Corinthians, every feeling of self-merit, and, from the less favoured, every tendency to discontentment. It will be seen that this double intention is precisely what inspires the following passage (vers. 13–30). But, first of all, ver. 12 serves by a figure to bring out again the fundamental thought of the passage, vers. 4–11.

Ver. 12. "For as the body is one, and[1] hath many members, but all the members of the body,[2] being many, are one body: so is it with the Christ."—The apostle has just stated a Divine fact, which is the secret of the Church's life: the unity of the Divine force, which animates it in the variety of its manifestations. This principle is realized, first, from the standpoint of the Divine influence in general, in the triple diversity of gifts, offices, and effects produced (4–6); then from the special viewpoint of the Spirit's influence, in the variety of gifts (7–11). In ver. 12 Paul renders palpable the harmony of this diversity with the unity which produces and governs it, by comparing it with what is nearest us, our own body. What is the human body? One and the same life spreading out into a plurality of functions each attached to one of the members of the organism, and labouring for its preservation and wellbeing.—The last words: *So it is with the Christ,* present a difficulty. It seems as if we should have: So it is with the Church. Must we, with Grotius, de Wette, Heinrici, understand by *the Christ* the Church itself, or, with Rückert, the ideal Christ? These two meanings cannot be justified: the former because Paul, if that had been his idea, would have expressed himself more clearly; the latter, because it contains a notion foreign to the mind of the apostle. In general, commentators are agreed in applying the word: *the Christ,* to the personal glorified Christ,

[1] D F G It. read δε, instead of και.

[2] T. R. reads after σωματος with D E του ενος (*of the one*).

seeking, however, in various ways to comprehend the Church under the idea of His person; Chrysostom, Meyer saying: as *head* of the body, He fills and controls it throughout; Hofmann, Edwards regard Christ as the personal *ego* of the organism; Holsten thinks that *the Christ* denotes the *Spirit*, who generally, in Paul's view, is identical, according to Holsten, with Christ's glorified person. This last meaning is false, as well as the affirmation on which it rests. The Spirit is not identified either by Paul, or John, or any biblical writer, with the person of the Christ. The interpretations of Meyer and Hofmann are undoubtedly well founded, but it seems to me that the exact expression of Paul's idea is rather this: The term *the Christ* here denotes the whole spiritual economy of which He is the principle in opposition to the natural economy to which the human body belongs. Similarly it might be said, in describing a law of natural humanity: "It is so in Adam," or in instancing a law of the Jewish economy: "It was so in Abraham." It is a way of forcibly calling to mind the unity of the *personal* principle on which an economy rests, and which forms, as it were, its permanent substance. In the first half of the following verse the apostle applies to the Church this figure taken from the human body.

Ver. 13[a]. "And indeed, by being baptized by one Spirit, we have all become one body, whether Jews or Greeks, whether bond or free."—The καὶ γάρ, *and indeed*, relates to the last words of the foregoing verse: *So is it with the Christ*, the demonstration of which it announces.—The καί indicates a second fact analogous to the preceding; the γάρ shows that this fact justifies the comparison between the human body and what is done in Christ.—How different were both the religious condition (*Jews, Gentiles*) and the social condition (*bond, free*) of all those members of the Church of Corinth! By the same Spirit, into which they had all been baptized, they now find themselves fused, as it were, into one spiritual body, that is to say, into a society all whose members are moved by the same breath of life.—The ἐν (*in* or *by* one Spirit) denotes the means, and the εἰς (*into* one body) the result attained. When we think of the distance which at that period separated Jews from Gentiles, slaves from freemen, we measure the power of the principle of union which had filled up those gulfs. All those men so diverse in their antecedents, when once they go forth regenerated from baptism, form thenceforth only *one new man in Christ* (Eph. ii. 15).

But if diversity of gifts is resolved into unity by the fusion of all the individuals into one spiritual whole, the converse is also true. In Christ, as well as in the human body, unity must spread out into diversity. Such is the new idea to which the apostle passes from the second part of ver. 13. On the understanding of this transition depends the understanding of the chapter as a whole. Thus far the apostle has explained how, notwithstanding their varied multiplicity, the gifts are *one* in virtue of their common principle, the Holy *Spirit*, and their sole destination, not the private advantage of their possessor, but the profit of the whole (ver. 7). Nevertheless this unity of principle and aim should not injure the manifestation of their diversity; they are and should remain *different*, as to the form in which they show themselves and their mode of action. And it is this other aspect of the truth, the necessary complement of the former, which is developed in the rest of the chapter.

3. *The diversity of gifts in the unity of the body* (vers. 13ᵇ–30)

Vers. 13ᵇ, 14. "And were all made to drink of[1] one Spirit. 14. For also the body is not one member, but many."—The reading is not εἰς ἓν πνεῦμα, but ἓν πνεῦμα without εἰς. This accusative is the qualifying substantive of the verb to make to drink; comp. the same construction iii. 2.—The καί, *and*, contains the transition which we have just mentioned. And what clearly proves that we pass here to the idea of the diversity of gifts is the καὶ γάρ, *for also*, at the beginning of ver. 14, a verse which is evidently meant to explain this diversity by that of the members of the body. This passage to the new idea (diversity) is also that which will enable us to apprehend the true meaning of the second proposition of ver. 13. Augustine, Luther, Calvin, Osiander, Neander, Heinrici find in it the idea of the Holy Supper. They have been led to this view by the mention of baptism in the first part of the verse, as well as by the term ἐποτίσθημεν, *we were made to drink*, which seems to allude to the cup in the sacrament. But the expression to drink the Holy Spirit in the Supper is absolutely foreign to the language of Scripture. It is of the blood of Christ that the believer partakes when he uses the cup. Then in this sense the aor. ἐποτίσθημεν would not find a natural

[1] T. R. with E K reads εις εν, instead of εν.

explanation, for the sacramental act is ever being repeated anew.—Or is it baptism that is still in question, as is held by Chrysostom, Bengel, de Wette, Meyer, Edwards? But the figure of drinking, or being made to drink (ποτισθῆναι), is as foreign to the form of the baptismal rite, as that of plunging, being bathed (βαπτισθῆναι), is naturally associated with it. Besides, the καί, *and*, indicates a new fact. If the second proposition served only to reaffirm in another form the idea of the first, there would be an asyndeton. The new fact in the mind of the apostle seems to me to be the communication of the *gifts* of the Spirit which accompanied the laying on of hands after baptism; comp. Acts viii. 17, xix. 6 (x. 45, 46). By baptism the believer is bathed in the Spirit as the source of new *life;* by the act which follows, the Spirit enters into him as the principle of certain particular *gifts* and of the personal activity which will flow from them. The believer is first *plunged*, bathed, in order to die to himself and live to God (Rom. vi. 3–5); then he is *made to drink*, saturated with new forces, that he may be able to serve the body of which he has become a member. Such are the two sides of his relation to the Holy Spirit. Holsten seems to me to have understood this passage nearly as I have done. It is easy to see how this thought forms the transition from the idea of the unity of the body to that of the diversity of gifts. After having been bathed in the same common life, they all come forth from it with the different gifts communicated to them by the Spirit.

Ver. 14. The apostle impresses this idea by taking up again the figure of the body which he had used to describe the unity of the Church; to this end it is enough for him to reverse the figure. In ver. 12: many members, but one body; in ver. 14: one body, but many members.—This notion of the diversity of members is *explained* vers. 15–26, and *applied* to the Church vers. 27–30.

Vers. 15–26

The object of this exposition is manifest. The Corinthians were disposed to exaggerate the value of certain gifts, which, from their extraordinary character, were fitted to strike the senses, in particular of the gift of speaking in tongues. From this prejudice there followed two evils: On the one hand, those who did not possess such gifts kept aloof discontented and discouraged, and the Church was deprived of their services, which might have been very needful; on the other, those who possessed the gifts, took pleasure in displaying them in the assemblies, so as to prevent the less brilliant gifts from filling the place which should have been reserved for them. It is to these two defects that the apostle successively applies the figure of the part played by the members in the human body; to the former, in the passage 15–17; to the latter, in the passage 18–26. Though the application of all the figures to spiritual gifts is transparent, it is nevertheless true that everything the apostle says has already literal verity in relation to the members of the human body.

Vers. 15–17. "If the foot shall say, Because I am not the hand, I am not of the body; is it not, in spite of that, of the body? 16. If the ear shall say,

Because I am not the eye, I am not of the body; is it not, in spite of that, of the body? 17. If the whole body were an eye, where were the hearing? If the whole were hearing, where were the smelling?"—The foot and the ear speak here as less conspicuous and favoured members than the hand and the eye, which represent the most highly valued gifts.—Many take the last proposition of vers. 15 and 16 as an affirmation in the form of two negatives which destroy one another: "It does *not* come about, therefore, that the foot is *not* of the body." But it is more natural to regard it, with Erasmus, Calvin, de Wette, etc., as a question in the sense of a *reductio ad absurdum.* The doubling of the negative οὐ is caused by the παρὰ τοῦτο, *in spite of that:* "Is it not in spite thereof . . . is it not of the body?"—The meaning ordinarily given to παρά is *because of* (see Meyer, Edwards). But I do not think that this meaning occurs elsewhere in the New Testament. Why not understand simply: *passing alongside of that*, that is to say: *in spite of that;* comp. Rom. i. 26, xi. 24. Meyer, Hofmann, and others understand by τοῦτο, *that,* the erroneous affirmation of the foot and the ear: "What these members say wrongly does not prevent them from being of the body." But it is more natural to refer it to the fact itself of the inferiority of the foot and the ear. "In spite of this inferiority, are not these members really of the body?" Comp. Holsten.

Ver. 17. This verse is more easily connected in the second sense of the word τοῦτο. If, from the fact that the foot is not the hand, etc., it followed that it did not form part of the body, the admirable variety of the senses would be excluded, and the perfection of the human organism destroyed.

There now follows the counterpart: what Divine wisdom *has done* in answer to the senseless talk of the foot and the ear.

Vers. 18–20. "But now hath God set the members every one of them in the body, as it hath pleased Him. 19. But if they were all one member, where were the body? 20. But now are there many members and one body."—The reality (*νυνί, now*) contrasting (*δέ, but*) with the condemned supposition.—A fine paronomasia, no doubt intentional, in *θεός* and *ἔθετο*. The high dignity of each member appears from the thought that it is God Himself who has placed it in the body, and placed it where it is best (the foot at the lower extremity of the body, the ear concealed at the side of the head, and not in view like the hand or the eye). Divine understanding has presided over this whole arrangement; inorganic matter nowhere invades this privileged domain of the human body.

Ver. 19 expresses once more the idea of ver. 17: "If God had acted otherwise, what would have become of the body?" Instead of this admirable organism, we should have a being endowed with a single sense, as is found, for example, in the lowest grade of animalism.—Then ver. 20 resumes the exposition of the actual fact, as God has willed it. The *νῦν δέ* is the repetition of the *νυνὶ δέ* of ver. 18. God has not managed things so awkwardly. He has instituted a plurality of members, without however destroying the unity of the body.—The application is obvious at a glance: If the Spirit manifests Himself in certain members only in less extraordinary or less eminent forms than in others, it does not follow that they should put themselves outside the common life, and bury away their gift, like the wicked servant of the parable, who received only one talent.

The apostle now turns, on the other hand, to those who have received the most eminent gifts (vers. 21–26).

Vers. 21, 22. "But[1] the eye[2] cannot say unto the hand, I have no need of thee: nor again the head to the feet, I have no need of you. 22. Nay, much more those members of the body, which seem to be more feeble, are necessary."—The δέ, *but,* is sufficiently supported by the documents. As in ver. 18 Paul had contrasted God's *doing* with the *saying* of the foot and the ear, he here contrasts with God's *doing* the *saying* of the eye or the head. The *eye,* privileged as it is by its eminent function and noble position in the body, cannot dispense with the inferior members, the hand, for example, without which it could not appropriate the objects which seem to it desirable. The same is the case with the *head* in relation to the feet. The head is named here, not as representing the Christ, but as uniting all the organs whose functions are most essential to life. What would the ear, the tongue, the nose, the palate do, if the feet were not at their service?

Ver. 22. Nay more, the instant we reflect, we are convinced of the absolute *necessity* of the members which seem to play an altogether secondary part, more secondary even than the hand or the feet. These *weak* parts are no doubt the sensitive organs which are

[1] A C F G P omit the δε (*but*). [2] T. R. with A omits ο (*the*)

protected by their position in the body, the lungs and stomach, for example, on which, above all, the life and health of the whole body depend.—The πολλῷ μᾶλλον has a logical (*much rather*) and not a quantitative sense (*much more*).—Hence it follows that the gifts and offices which have a modest appearance are *necessary*, no less than the others, to the prosperity of the whole.

Vers. 23, 24[a]. "And the members of the body, which we think to be less honourable, upon these we bestow more abundant honour; and our uncomely parts have more abundant comeliness. 24[a]. Whereas our comely parts have no need."—Paul here appeals to a fact of natural instinct in man. Καί: *and moreover*. There is a gradation from the ἀσθενέστερα, *more feeble*, to the ἀτιμότερα and ἀσχήμονα, *less honourable* and *uncomely*. — These less honourable members are the arms, the throat, the breast, the belly, the legs, all the parts of the body on which chiefly the cares of the toilet are lavished.—The apostle pushes the comparison to the utmost. The second καί signifies: *and even*. Hofmann makes the ἡμῶν, *our*, dependent not on ἀσχήμονα, but on εὐσχημοσύνην ἔχει : "derive *from us* greater comeliness;" and similarly in ver. 24 he makes the ἡμῶν depend on χρείαν ἔχει: "Those which are comely of themselves have no need of us to make them such." This commentator sometimes seems to amuse himself with exegetical feats rather than to speak seriously. The ἡμῶν is added to the two adjectives ἀσχήμονα and εὐσχήμονα to express the solidarity which exists between the comeliness of one part of the body and that of our whole person. The shame of *one* of our members is *ours.* What the apostle wished thereby to impress on the proud Corinthians was, that it pertains to the honour of the whole Church that those who are charged with the humblest functions and the least prominent services should be the objects of the greatest marks of respect; we should say, if we dared so to paraphrase: To the brother serving in the agape, the best portion! To the brother who sweeps the floor, the most honourable place beside the president!

Ver. 24[a]. But, as to functions which of themselves honour those who fill them, there is nothing to add to this intrinsic honour. They resemble the beautiful parts of the body, which would be wronged were they covered. Transparent as the meaning of this parable is applied to the Church, the apostle does not go beyond the figure, as we still find in what follows.

Vers. 24[b], 25. "But God hath tempered the body together, having given more abundant honour to that which lacked:[1] 25. that there should be no schism[2] in the body; but that all the members should have the same care one for another."—The δέ, *but,* seems to me to be well explained by Holsten: "But as to this contrast which meets the eyes of men God gives the solution of it by the end which He had in view in creating it." God has intermingled feeble members with strong in the human body, comely parts with others not comely, that the latter might be the objects of particular care and attention on the part of the others, and that thus the body might not present the

[1] T. R. with D E F G K L: τω υστερουντι; ℵ A B C: τω υστερουμενω.

[2] T. R. with A B C E K It. Syr. reads σχισμα (*schism*); ℵ D F G L: σχισματα (*schisms*).

spectacle of two orders of members, the one glorious and the other despicable, which would destroy the harmony of the whole and would even impair the favourable effect produced by the first. God has thus succeeded in making every member have an interest in the comely and honourable appearance of all the others. Love on their part thus becomes a matter of rightly understood self-interest. The singular σχίσμα, *schism*, is certainly the true reading; the plural σχίσματα, *schisms*, has been substituted for it, because it was thought there was an allusion here to the divisions in the Church of Corinth. There must not be the contrast between parts beautiful and ugly, glorious and vile, in the masterpiece of creation. — The τὸ αὐτὸ μεριμνᾶν signifies: to have a common care, to be all concerned about one result. This common end is the harmonious beauty of the whole.—By adding ὑπὲρ ἀλλήλων, *one for another*, the apostle means that all should be watchful for the honour of all in order to the dignity of the whole. Those members which are of themselves less honourable thus turn out to be the objects of the special interest of all, that there may be procured for them the nobility which they had not naturally. For this end it is that God has established between them all such a close solidarity. And indeed, as the following verse says, there is between them an instinctive sympathy of satisfaction or shame which impels each to provide for the honour of all.

Ver. 26. "And whether[1] one member suffer, all the other members suffer with it; or one[2] member be

[1] B F G It. read ειτι (*if any*), instead of ειτε (*whether*).
[2] ℵ A B omit εν.

honoured, all the others rejoice with it."—*Καί*: *and really.* "This mutual care cannot be wanting for the body, for in fact . . ." The shame or contempt which overtakes one of the members of the body exercises a depressing influence on the condition of all the others. The honour, on the contrary, rendered to one, to the head, for example, when it is crowned, or to this or that other part of the body when it is brilliantly adorned, reacts on the attitude of the whole body, which erects itself and takes on a princely bearing. The application of these figures was self-evident: If gifts inferior in appearance are despised and checked, the state of the whole Church cannot fail to feel it. The honour which the most eminent gifts receive in such circumstances will not be of good quality. It cannot subserve the honour of the whole body, except in so far as the least of its members shares in it. It is clear that the special applications of all these figures must have been self-evident to the minds of the Corinthians. And so the apostle does not enunciate them; he contents himself with a wholly general application, which he gives in vers. 27–30. The idea is summarily indicated in ver. 27.

Vers. 27–30

Ver. 27. "Now ye are a body of Christ, and members in particular."[1]—This verse gives the reason why the parable of the human body may be applied to the readers. They are a *body of Christ*, not *the* body of Christ; the apostle takes care not to put the article exactly as in iii. 16: "Ye are a temple of God."—*The*

[1] D It. Vg. read εκ μελους.

body of Christ is the whole Church; but for that very reason every particular Church shares in that dignity. Christ, dwelling in it, governs it by His Spirit, and gives it the organic forms fitted to manifest its action.—In virtue of this character belonging to the Church of Corinth, each Corinthian is to it what each member is to the body. The term μέλη, *members*, should not be applied to the particular Churches in their relation to the Church as a whole, as has been thought by several commentators ancient and modern. For this we should have to understand ὑμεῖς, *ye*, of Christians in general, which is not natural; and would not this idea be out of place in the context? The word μέλη, *members*, applies to all the individuals composing the Church of Corinth. The term expresses their plurality, and the restrictive word ἐκ μέρους, *in particular*, their qualitative diversity. Each has only a part in the life of the whole, that which accrues to him in virtue of his individual gifts; comp. the ἐκ μέρους, *in part*, xiii. 9, 10, 12. No member, consequently, may call himself the whole, and claim to absorb for his own advantage the fulness of ecclesiastical activity, as Paul proceeds to point out in the following enumeration, vers. 28–30. Each one, therefore, has need of his brethren. Side by side with his gift, there should be room for the exercise of the gifts of all the rest. The reading of D Vulg. ἐκ μέλους, *members taken from the member*, seems to allude to Christ's being Himself, as the head, one of the members (ver. 21); but it is evident that in ver. 21 the word *head* is taken in another sense.

In the three following verses we find two successive enumerations of those gifts and offices which form the counterpart of the organs and members of the body. The aim of the first, ver. 28, is to affirm the dignity of all those gifts and offices as being willed and given by God Himself independently of the sort of hierarchy which He has thought good to establish among them. All have their part to play, and no one ought to be excluded, if the whole is to prosper. This idea corresponds to that of the passage 18–26, where Paul had shown that all the members of the body, even those apparently most inferior, are entitled and bound to discharge their function for the good of the whole. The second enumeration, vers. 29, 30, has a wholly different bearing. The idea which inspires it is this: The gifts and offices have been Divinely distributed; no member unites them all in himself. Every brother then, even should he possess the most exalted function, needs the gifts and offices of all his brethren; no one consequently should presume to hinder the exercise of those gifts which he does not himself possess. This second idea exactly corresponds to that of the passage 15–17, regarding the need which the most highly endowed members of the body have of the services of all the rest. Vers. 28–30 are therefore the application of the whole passage vers. 14–26, where the apostle develops the necessity of the diversity of the members in the unity of the human body; only in the application the order of the two ideas developed in the parable is reversed: the necessity of the part and the honour to be given to the inferior gifts and offices, developed in the second place in the parable (vers. 18–26), takes the first in application (ver. 28); and the need which all, even the most eminent gifts, have of all the rest, expounded in the first place in regard to the members of the body (vers. 14–17), takes the second place in the application (vers. 29, 30).

Ver. 28. "And God hath set some in the Church . . . first apostles, secondarily prophets, thirdly teachers, after that miracles, then[1] gifts of healing, helps, governments, kinds of tongues."—The phrase ἔθετο ὁ θεός, *God hath set*, identical with that in ver. 18, shows the correspondence between the idea of ver. 28 and that of the passage vers. 18–26. Edwards acutely observes, that if in Eph. iv. 11 Paul uses the word ἔδωκε, *gave*, it is because in that passage he wishes to bring out the wealth of Christ's gifts, while here he is rather thinking of the sovereignty of Divine power.—In beginning this proposition, the apostle had first in view a simple enumeration, in which all the functions about to follow should be placed on the same footing. Hence the οὓς μέν, *some*, which should have been followed by οὓς δέ, *others;* comp. Eph. iv. 11. But, on reaching the first term of the enumeration, his feeling of the inequality of these gifts and offices causes a modification in the expression of his thought, and instead of the simple term *apostles*, which was to have begun the enumeration, he suddenly introduces, by means of the adverb *firstly*, followed by *secondly*, *thirdly*, etc., the notion of subordination. The apostle had a special reason for reminding this Church, in which liberty was degenerating into licence, of the deference due to the apostolate, and then to the prophetic and teaching offices, those three excellent gifts, to which that of speaking in tongues was childishly preferred. It is

[1] T. R. with K L reads ειτα (*then*); ℵ A B C: επειτα (*thereafter*).

from this modification introduced into the original thought that the inaccuracy pointed out has arisen. Hofmann has denied any change of construction. He makes of the whole ver. 28 a parenthetical proposition, the principal being found in ver. 29: "And those whom God has set as apostles, as prophets, as teachers . . . (ver. 29), are not however all apostles, all prophets, all teachers," that is to say: "they do not however each combine all these offices." But by this unnatural construction the μέν becomes superfluous, and the substitution of the idea of rank (*firstly*, etc.) for the simple enumeration becomes incomprehensible, not to speak of the strangeness of the question in itself. — The apostle here returns to the general viewpoint of vers. 4–6, where the gifts and offices were combined; he intermingles them in the following enumeration.—The regimen ἐν τῇ ἐκκλησίᾳ, *in the Church*, shows that the circle here embraced in the view of the apostle is larger than that referred to, vers. 8–10, by the enumeration of the gifts prevailing at Corinth. The apostolate could not have figured in this narrow circle, either as an office, or still less as an office belonging to the Church universal. Now Paul, as we have just said, had good reasons for mentioning here the first rank assigned by God to the office of apostle, and hence he rises from the idea of the Corinthian community to that of the whole Christian community. The πρῶτον, *firstly*, combines the two notions of time and dignity, which are in this case closely connected; for the Church sprang, as it were, from the apostolate which founded it, and which remains to the end its highest guide. But the notion of superiority certainly outweighs that of anteriority, the *secondly* and *thirdly* which follow being incapable of application to time. Paul here includes in the apostolate the ministry of those men who, like James, Barnabas, Silas, took part in founding the Church, and even the evangelists or missionaries (Timothy, Titus, etc.) who are separately mentioned, Eph. iv. 11; comp. Acts xiv. 4, 14; Rom. xvi. 7. Is it not possible that in speaking in ver. 21 of the head as a member of the body, the apostolate was already in his mind?—The *prophets* are those whose office it is to receive the new revelations which God thinks good to grant to the Church at certain times. We shall see, chap. xiv., that every prophetic discourse rests on an immediate revelation, the contents of which are communicated at the moment to the Church. These revelations were intended to enlighten the faithful as to the gravity of the present and imminent situation of the Church, and to enkindle the courage and Christian hope of its members. The prophets of the first age, like the apostles, do not seem to have been permanently attached to a special Church. Like the apostolate, the ministry of the prophets had a universal character, though they might settle for a time in a particular Church (Acts xiii. 1, xv. 32). In several passages (Eph. ii. 20, iii. 5) they are almost identified with the apostles, with whom they shared the task of founding the Church. If all prophets were not apostles, on the other hand the prophetic gift seems to have been bound to the apostolate. In the *Doctrine of the Twelve Apostles*, the prophets still exercise an itinerant ministry, going from Church to Church to edify the faithful.—The *teachers*, mentioned in the third place, were men who had the gift of calmly and consecutively expounding saving truth, and of applying it to the practical life of the Church. If the prophet may be compared to the traveller who discovers new countries, the teacher is like the geographer who combines the scattered results of these discoveries and gives a methodical statement of them. This ministry must have been more local than that of the prophets; for, Eph. iv. 11, it is closely connected with that of pastors, which was decidedly parochial (Acts xx. 28). But we learn from this very passage that the two functions were not identical. It was only gradually, though already in the course of the apostolic age, that the ministry of teaching (*doctorate*, διδασκαλία) was combined and fused, as it were, with the care of souls (the *pastorate*, the ποιμήν). The passage 1 Tim. v. 17 indicates the beginning of this fusion; and the part taken by the *angel* in the Churches of the Apocalypse marks its completion. Hence it is that the latter is made responsible for the state of the Church. If the gift of prophecy still remains in our day in the lively view and powerful expression of the truths of salvation, the doctorate has its sphere in the complete and orderly teaching of these truths, religious or theological.—The apostolate combines the two sides of gift and office, both raised to their highest power. In prophecy, the side of gift evidently outweighs that of office; in teaching the reverse. This is what has rendered the latter more suited to remain with the lapse of time as a regular function.

There follow two pairs of activities, in the first of which only the gift-element is found, while in the second there is little more than the element of office. And first the gift of *miracles*, literally: powers, then *gifts of healing*. For these two expressions we refer to ver. 10, where the workings of miracles evidently correspond to our δυνάμεις, miraculous virtues. The persons on whom these gifts are bestowed, not having any importance in themselves, do not count, so to speak; this is why the abstract expressions *powers* and *gifts of healing* are substituted for those which denote the individuals themselves, used in the preceding grades. For the same reason the apostle now substitutes for the adverbs expressly indicating rank, which had been used at the beginning, the vaguer terms: *after that, then* . . ., till he ends with simple enumeration.—The reading εἶτα, *then*, in the Byz. (before χαρίσματα), is certainly preferable to the ἔπειτα, *after that*, of the other two families; comp. xv. 23, 24. The εἶτα is a softened continuation of the preceding ἔπειτα; it distinguishes less forcibly than the latter. In proportion as we come down in the scale, the subordination becomes less distinct.

To this pair of gifts there succeeds a pair in which the notion of office is evidently the ruling one. For the offices in question are more or less external. The word ἀντιλήψεις, *helps*, comes from the verb ἀντιλαμβάνεσθαι, which strictly signifies: *to take* a burden *on oneself* (the middle) *instead* of another (ἀντι); comp. Acts xx. 35; Rom. viii. 26. This term therefore denotes the various kinds of relief which the Church sought to procure for all sufferers, widows and orphans, the indigent, sick, strangers, travellers, etc. These various functions were afterwards united in the ecclesiastical diaconate, male and female. How could it enter the mind of some exegetes to apply the term to the interpretation of tongues!—The κυβερνήσεις, *governments* or *administrations*, no doubt denote the various kinds of superintendence needed for the external good order of the assemblies and of the worship of the Church. It was necessary to find and furnish the places of meeting, etc. . . . This all required what we should nowadays call committees, with their presidents. The various tasks were probably divided among the presbyters or elders, whose ministry was as yet distinct from that of the teachers. Only gradually was the function of teaching assigned to those who were already charged with such external management. Comp. the passage already quoted, 1 Tim. v. 17, as well as iii. 2; and Titus i. 9, where Paul insists that the elder be capable of teaching and refuting those who oppose sound doctrine. We cannot deny ourselves the pleasure of quoting here M. Renan's beautiful remarks on this whole passage (*Saint Paul*, p. 410): "These functions: care of the suffering, the administration of the poor man's pence, mutual assistance, are enumerated by Paul in the last place, and as humble matters. But his piercing eye can here too see the truth: 'Take note,' says he, 'our least noble members are precisely the most honoured.' 'Prophets, speakers of tongues, teachers, you shall pass away. Deacons, devoted widows, administrators of the goods of the Church, you shall remain; you build for eternity.'"

The apostle closes this enumeration with the gift of tongues, including in it here the gift of interpretation. On the expression: *kinds of tongues*, see on ver. 10.

The last place assigned to this gift in a list which, from the beginning, had taken a hierarchical character, can only have, whatever Meyer may say to the contrary, one object, viz. to reduce as far as possible the importance to be attached to it.—The apostle started from the highest ministry in which gift and office appear combined and in their highest potency. Thence he passed through the various grades of gradual disjunction of gifts and offices, to their widest separation, which appears in governments and administrations (as offices) on the one hand, and in speaking in tongues (as a gift) on the other. It is obvious that the classification in our passage has an ecclesiastical character, and is no longer taken, like that of vers. 8–10, from the psychological viewpoint. This is the reason why prophecy here occupies a wholly different place from that which it has in the first list. As we have often said, there is nothing arbitrary in Paul's writings, even where he seems to enumerate at random. The principle of order which he follows here is that of the importance of the gifts and offices, not their intrinsic nature.

It is God, then, who has set in the Church all the different gifts and offices, and who has established among them a decreasing scale of value. The apostle does not state the conclusion from this fact, which was sufficiently apparent from what had been said in regard to the members set in the body by the hand of God. The result is this: No one should consider himself as useless, or be so considered by the Church, because he is less brilliantly endowed than this or that other. Now he passes to a new enumeration in the form of questions, to which the previous affirmation naturally gives rise: God Himself set these gifts in the Church. And how did He do it? Did He give them all to all? By no means, for that would have been to make every member a sort of whole body, consequently to render it independent of all the rest, and so destroy the body itself. God would not have individuals possessing all the gifts because He would not have any one in a position to be self-sufficient; He so ordered things that the brethren should all need one another. Thus are explained the following questions:

Vers. 29, 30. "Are all apostles? are all prophets? are all teachers? are all powers? 30. Have all the gifts of healing? do all speak with tongues? do all interpret?"—God has given to believers a certain spiritual endowment (ver. 28); but side by side with this endowment He has left a blank in each of them, and so a want which does not allow him to separate himself from the rest. It is obvious that the questions are put so as to lead to the result which was expressed in regard to the members of the body in vers. 14–17. No individual ought to pose as self-sufficient. The body, as a whole, only exists on the condition that each member needs all the rest. The questions, all beginning with μή, all expect a negative answer: "All are not, however, apostles?" None of those, therefore, who are not such, will be able to dispense with the brethren whom God has made apostles. And if this is true regarding apostles and prophets, it is also true in regard to all other gifts and offices.—It is unnecessary to understand ἔχουσιν before δυνάμεις, *powers*. This substantive may very well be the predicate of the subject. The power of working miracles is identified with its possessor (ver. 28).—*Helps* and *governments* are omitted in this second list, probably because they did not greatly excite the ambition of believers.

It follows, therefore, from this application to the Church, vers. 27–30: (1) that no one ought to regard himself as being unnecessary to the whole, since he has been placed there with his gift by God Himself (ver. 28); (2) and consequently, also, that no one ought to consider himself as possessed of self-sufficiency or as combining in himself all that is necessary for the life of the Church of which he is a member (vers. 29, 30).

From these general principles the apostle might pass immediately to the practical applications he has in view. But, before entering on this subject, which will be treated in chap. xiv., he here inserts a meditation on the fundamental disposition of the Christian life, charity without which all gifts, whatever they may be, become useless, but which, on the other hand, gives them all their true consecration and alone assures their effectual and beneficent exercise (chap. xiii.). To our ver. 31, which forms the transition to this episode, there obviously corresponds ver. 1 of chap. xiv., whereby the apostle returns from this digression to his principal subject.

Ver. 31. "But covet earnestly the best[1] gifts, and moreover I will show you a supremely excellent way."—Theodoret has taken the first proposition interrogatively. In that case it would contain a rebuke, either

[1] T. R. with D E F G K L It. reads κρειττονα (*better*); ℵ A B C: μειζονα (*greater*).

in the sense: "Are you careful to seek the most useful gifts? No, you seek the most brilliant;" or in this: "Do you seek the greatest gifts (the most brilliant)? Yes, and it is your sin." But neither of these meanings harmonizes with the following proposition. It leads us to take the first clause as an exhortation resulting from the application, vers. 27–30: "All gifts are useful and in their place; you are right in seeking them. *But* (δέ) let this search be especially after those by which you can contribute most to the edifica- of the whole." The δέ is rather adversative, as de Wette thinks, and as is proved by Edwards against Meyer. Holsten rightly remarks that the adjective ought to be detached from the substantive: "Seek gifts, and the best ones." The reading of the received text κρείττονα, *better*, which is that of the Greco-Lats. and Byz., seems to me preferable to the Alex. reading: μείζονα, *greater*. This is taken, probably, from the passages xiii. 13 and xiv. 5, which have been mistaken for parallels to this. The adjective κρείττων, strictly *more powerful* and so *more useful*, is evidently taken here in this second meaning: the gifts most capable of producing the common edification. The word μείζων would have the same meaning, but less naturally.—By these better gifts, there have been understood faith, hope, and charity (xiii. 13), but wrongly. Never, in Paul's language, are the gifts, which are the means of Christian activity, confounded with the virtues which are the very elements of life. The sequel will show that Paul has especially in view prophecy and teaching. —It is asked how he can stir up believers to *seek* gifts. Does not the very term gifts imply that they are *received,* not *acquired* by labour? Must we with Reuss see here an insoluble contradiction between the two elements of Paul's view: Divine gift and human pursuit? But first the pursuit can take place in the way of prayer, an act which agrees easily with the notion of gift. Then the gift may exist in the believer as a germ in a natural talent which it is his mission to cultivate, but which he may also leave buried. No doubt there were among the Corinthians more prophets and teachers potentially than really. Love for the Church would have developed those gifts; but they were decaying in consequence of the false direction which the new life had taken. See this idea of ζηλοῦν, *covet,* taken up again in the second part of xiv. 1. At the moment when he was about to develop it, all at once Paul stops, seized with the need of expressing a feeling which has for a long time filled his heart in view of the spiritual state of this Church. What does he mean by speaking of a *supremely excellent way,* which he proceeds to describe? Is it the normal way of attaining to the possession of the most desirable gifts? The way would thus be the true mode of the ζηλοῦν. Or is it the way in a more general sense, the way of holiness and salvation, in opposition to gifts which of themselves cannot sanctify and save? Commentators are divided between the two meanings. The former seems at first better to suit the context; it is adopted by Chrysostom, Meyer, Osiander, de Wette, Edwards, and yet the latter is alone really admissible, as has been clearly seen by Tertullian, Estius, Olshausen, Rückert, Hofmann, Holsten. This appears from the relation between our verse and that by which it is resumed, xiv. 1. There we find clearly expressed the idea of a *contrast* between seeking love and coveting gifts. Consequently, in the apostle's view, love is by no means mentioned here as a means of succeeding in the pursuit of gifts, but as a virtue to be sought first of all and for itself. Meyer and Edwards object that this meaning would have required ἀλλά, *but* (Meyer), or ὅμως, *nevertheless* (Edwards), instead of ἔτι, *moreover;* but wrongly. The apostle *rises* from the encouragement to seek gifts to another recommendation, viz. to walk (ὁδός) in charity. The καὶ ἔτι, *and moreover*, suits this meaning: "Seek gifts, and, moreover, I will now describe a way which is still better than the exercise of gifts, even the best, that whereby alone the possession and exercise of gifts will truly become a blessing." I find in Holsten nearly the same thought thus expressed: "Paul shows that above all gifts and the aspiration after them, there is a higher way open to the Christian—love. The Corinthians find therein the true standard by which to appreciate the value of this aspiration and of its satisfaction." It would be possible to connect ἔτι with καθ' ὑπερβόλην; but in this way we only form a pleonasm; ἔτι is naturally joined with the verb: "And moreover I have to show you . . ." Comp. Acts ii. 26.—The form καθ' ὑπερβόλην, *in superabundance, excellently*, is somewhat frequent in Paul's writings: sometimes it relates to the verb (2 Cor. i. 8; Gal. i. 13); sometimes it qualifies the adjective or the substantive it accompanies; so Rom. viii. 13 (καθ' ὑπερβ. ἁμαρτωλός), and perhaps 2 Cor. iv. 17. Here, applying it to the verb, with Grotius and Ewald, we should be brought to the meaning: "And to give superabundance of clearness or certainty, I again point out to you the true way." But first this meaning would attach to the false explanation of the word *way*, which we have set aside; and in any case, the indication of the way would not be in the least superfluous, for Paul gives it a whole chapter. The idea of superabundance or excellence therefore qualifies the way itself. The supremely excellent way whereby the Christian ought to seek to attain the end of life is charity. Reuss explains: "A supreme rule which is to guide you in your judgment." The explanation is grammatically correct; but the way designates not the rule for judging gifts, but love itself, which should guide the use of them.—The present *δείκνυμι*, *I show*, simply announces what Paul is about to do in the following passage (in reply to Edwards).

B. The Way *par excellence* (13:1-13)

This chapter has been called a hymn. In tone indeed it is truly lyrical, especially in the first verses. Charity is poetically personified. In this respect the passage resembles some others in St. Paul's writings, such as the end of chap. xv. of our Epistle, that of chap. viii. of the Romans, or that of chap. iii. of the First Epistle to Timothy. These are, so to speak, specimens of a sublime *speaking in tongues*, interpreted by the *glossolalete*[1] himself. "There is here," as Heinrici well says, "such warmth as could only proceed from the

[1] We may be allowed to use this expression, taken from the Greek, to designate one who spoke in tongues.

purest experience of charity. It is as if love itself stood before us, filled with its holy peace and profound sympathy." The apostle develops three thoughts: (1) the uselessness of gifts, even the highest, without charity, vers. 1–3; (2) the intrinsic excellence of charity, vers. 4–7; (3) the eternal duration of charity, and of charity alone, vers. 8–13. Thus is proved the assertion of ver. 31, that to walk in love is the way *par excellence;* for it alone guides us to the absolute end.

VERS. 1–3

Without love, the most eminent gifts confer no real worth on their possessor.

Ver. 1. "Though I speak with the tongues of men and of angels, and have not charity, I am only a sounding brass, or a tinkling cymbal."—Hitherto the apostle had put the gift of tongues at the end of each of his lists (xii. 10, 28, 30). Here he puts it foremost, because now he rises from the least valuable to the most useful gift. To give assurance of his perfect impartiality in the valuation he proceeds to make, he supposes himself exercising this gift, as indeed he really possessed it in a rare degree (xiv. 18). And to express its insufficiency more forcibly, he does not consider it only as it appeared in the Church of Corinth, and was an object of ambition to its members; he raises it hypothetically to the most magnificent realization of it possible. Paul supposes himself in possession of the languages of all thinking and speaking beings, terrestrial and celestial. Some, Thiersch for example, refer the term tongues *of men* to the various tongues spoken by the apostles on the day of Pentecost, and tongues *of angels* to the gift of tongues as it flourished at Corinth. The former of these terms would thus designate the real tongues spoken by different nations: Arabic, Latin, etc. But independently of the question relating to the nature of the gift of tongues on the day of Pentecost, a question which we shall afterwards treat (chap. xiv. end), by thus identifying the gift of tongues at Corinth with the tongues of angels, the apostle would have raised it even above that gift in the form in which it appeared at Pentecost, which is impossible. For the gift in its original form remains of course the perfect type of that kind of spiritual manifestation. Paul therefore simply means: "Imagine a man endowed with all the powers of terrestrial and celestial language. . . ." It is inconceivable how Meyer, with this passage before him, can persist in applying the term *tongue* to the physical organ of speech, which would lead to the meaning: "Though I had in my mouth, I, Paul, the tongues of millions of men and of angels."

In translating I have rendered the word ἀγάπη by the term *charity*, rather than by love. And for this reason: our word love combines two notions which are expressed in Greek by two different words: ἀγάπη and ἔρως. The second denotes the love of desire, which seeks its own satisfaction in the being loved, love as it appears to us in Plato's beautiful myth (in the *Symposium*), where it is represented as the son of poverty and wealth; it is this shade of meaning particularly which attaches in French to the word love (amour). But the Greek language knows another love, the love of complacency, which is much more disinterested, which contemplates, approves, and yields itself: this is ἀγάπη, a word which is certainly related to the verb ἄγαμαι, *to admire.* To this term it seems to me the word *charity* better corresponds. In our passage the feeling expressed by ἀγάπη is mainly love of our neighbour (vers. 4–7); now this love, being according to Paul an emanation from the love of God, takes the character of disinterestedness, purity, and freeness which distinguishes Divine love.[1]

But how are we to suppose speaking in tongues apart from faith, and faith divorced from charity which is its fruit? Is not the apostle's supposition merely a threat fitted to alarm his readers? Experience proves that a man, after opening his heart with faith to the joy of salvation, may very soon cease to walk in the way of sanctification, shrink from complete self-surrender, and, while making progress in mystical feeling, become more full of self and devoid of love than he ever was. Such is the issue of the religious sybaritism of which revivals furnish so many examples. Christianity, instead of acting as a principle of devotion, turns into poetry, sentimentality, and fine speaking. It may even happen that, after a real and serious conversion, love may be at first developed in the heart and life, but afterwards, in consequence of some practical unfaithfulness, and through a want of vigilance, leading to spiritual pride, charity may be gradually chilled. The gifts originally received remain in some measure,

[1] [The verbal criticism of this paragraph applies, in a measure, to the English as well as to the French words, though perhaps hardly so conclusively, in favour of the adoption of *charity.*—Tr.]

but the inner life has disappeared. In this second case, the perfect γέγονα, "*I have become* and am for the future," is still more easily explained than in the first. The apostle's thought might therefore be rendered thus: "If, after giving myself to Christ, I became the most eminent Christian poet the Church had, and my heart were void of charity . . ."—The two terms *brass* and *cymbal,* which denote, the one a piece of unwrought metal, struck to produce sound, the other the concave plate, used so frequently in the East as a musical instrument, perfectly describe the inflation of an exalted imagination, and an over-excited sensibility. Religious language is then no longer the natural overflowing of a heart filled with love; it resembles the resonant sound of a dead and hollow instrument. We might apply the word χαλκός, *brass,* as we sometimes do in French, to the trumpet; but, as Meyer says, Paul begins with a vague expression to pass to one more specific. Suidas says that the expression δωδωναῖον χαλκεῖον was a proverbial name for those who speak much and do nothing (Heinrici). The word ἀλαλάζον denotes in general what makes a great noise, such as a war-cry.

Ver. 2. "And though I have the gift of prophecy, and understand all mysteries, and [though I have] all knowledge; and though I have all faith, so that I could remove mountains, but have not charity, I am nothing."—The apostle rises to the higher gifts. The gift of the *prophet* and that of the teacher (*knowledge*) are here joined together by the expression: *knowing all mysteries,* which, from its position, seems to be connected with both. And in fact both relate to the understanding of God's plan of salvation. Now this plan is the supreme *mystery*, and contains within it all particular mysteries (comp. ii. 7). It is to the latter, to certain details as to the final accomplishment of salvation, for example, that the revelations granted to the prophets specially refer ; whereas *knowledge* denotes the understanding of salvation itself in its totality, and as already accomplished and revealed in Christ. The expression εἴδεναι γνῶσιν, *to know knowledge*, is a familiar form in Greek. To be remarked is the article before γνῶσις, *the* knowledge, a form by which Paul means : all it is possible to have ; and the adjective πᾶς, *all*, thrice repeated, with the words *mystery*, *knowledge*, and *faith*, supposes each of those gifts possessed in its ideal perfection, like that of tongues in ver. 1.—Commentators explain otherwise than I have done the relation between the three propositions concerning prophecy, the understanding of mysteries and knowledge. Heinrici finds two gifts here: (1) prophecy, with which he connects the understanding of mysteries, and (2) knowledge properly so called. But how can knowledge (γνῶσιν) be thus separated from (εἰδῶ) knowing ? Edwards rather connects the second proposition with the third. Meyer applies the three propositions to one and the same gift, prophecy ; but xii. 8 expressly distinguishes prophecy from knowledge.

Faith is taken here in the same sense as in xii. 9 ; the assurance, founded on the feeling of reconciliation, that nothing can resist us when we are really doing the work of God. Possible obstacles are represented under the figure of a mountain to be removed, as in Matt.

xvii. 20. The abrupt brevity of the phrase which closes this paragraph : *I am nothing,* contrasts with the long developments given to the preceding propositions. Behold the fruit of all those magnificent gifts : all speech, all knowledge, all power, and yet nothing! What such a man has done may be of value to the Church ; to himself it is nothing, because there was no love in it. Love alone is anything in the eyes of love. —But how is it credible that a man can reach this height of knowledge and power in God without love? Here, again, are we not face to face with an impossible supposition? No ; the faith of first days may develop more or less exclusively in the direction of knowledge (ver. 2[a]) or of force of will (ver. 2[b]), as well as in the direction of sensibility (ver. 1) ; comp. Luke ix. 54, where James and John ask the Lord to bring down fire from heaven on the Samaritan village. Faith is there, but where is charity? This is what Jesus points out to them. Or there are believers who may have preserved the gift of prophesying, of driving out demons, of working miracles, while in the eyes of Him who tries the heart and reins they are only workers of iniquity ; comp. Matt. vii. 22. In our day, too, one may be a celebrated theologian, the instrument of powerful revivals, the author of beautiful works in the kingdom of God, a missionary with a name filling the world ; if in all these things the man is self-seeking, and if it is not the Divine breath of charity which animates him, in God's eyes this is only *seeming,* not *being.* The apostle goes further still.

Ver. 3. "And though I distributed[1] all my goods,

[1] T. R. with K : ψωμιζω : all the rest : ψωμισω.

and though I gave my body to be burned,[1] but had not charity, it profiteth me nothing."—The apostle here comes to acts which appear to have the greatest value, because they seem identical with charity itself. In the first, it is the office of *ἀντίληψις*, *help* (xii. 28), rising to the most magnanimous sacrifice, the complete giving away of all possessed in behalf of the poor. We must read, not the present *ψωμίζω*, but the aorist: *ψωμίσω*. The second denotes a summary gift bestowed once for all; the first would apply rather to a continuous giving day by day; *ψωμίζειν*, to break down into pieces to give away. Edwards rightly observes that the term implies two things: (1) the gift bestowed by the giver's own hand; (2) on a multitude.—Finally, to the sacrifice of means made for men, Paul adds the highest sacrifice, that of life, offered to God. How are we to conceive of this sacrifice? Can it be that of a man who rushes into a house on fire to save one in sickness? But the *ἵνα*, *in order that*, seems to imply the intention of perishing. It is rather the acceptance of martyrdom which is in question. If there is a case in which the Alexandrine reading should be set aside without hesitation, it is that of the variant *καυχήσωμαι*, *that I may glory*. Either the copyists have read *χ* for *θ*, or more likely they have been too eager to introduce the reason which would annul the value of the martyrdom, and have anticipated the following words: *but have not charity*, which become superfluous. In any of the cases previously pointed out, the expressed cause of nothing-

[1] T. R. with C K: *καυθησωμαι* (*that I may be burned*); D E F G L: *καυθησομαι* (same meaning); ℵ A B: *καυχησωμαι* (*that I may glorify myself*).

ness is no other than the absence of love; it is also the only one which suits the context. Here, again, is one of the cases in which Westcott and Hort, by maintaining this reading, abandoned even by Lachmann and Tischendorf, have only proved the inconvenient consequence of partisanship. It is probable that of the readings *καυθήσωμαι* of C K (future subjunctive) and *καυθήσομαι* of the Greco-Lats. (future indicative), we ought to prefer the second. The form of the future subjunctive is a barbarism only found in later writers. The indicative with *ἵνα* often occurs in the New Testament (ix. 15; Gal. ii. 4; 1 Pet. iii. 1, etc.).

But how can such acts be done otherwise than from love? The sacrifice of goods may be carried out in the spirit of ostentation, or may proceed from a desire of self-justification, and consequently be dictated by a wholly different feeling from love. It may be so likewise with the sacrifice of life. Witness the funeral pile of Peregrinus, in Lucian, or that of the Hindoo who had himself burned at Athens, under Augustus, and whose tomb was pointed out, according to Strabo, with a pompous inscription, relating how "he had immortalized himself." The pagan Lucian himself calls such men *κενόδοξοι ἄνθρωποι*. Certainly it is not such the apostle has in view, but a Christian carrying to this degree the appearance of love to Christ, while seeking at bottom only his own fame or self-merit in the eyes of God. There is the well-known case of the presbyter who, when giving himself up to death as a confessor of the faith, was accompanied by a Christian, with whom he was at variance, and who asked him to forgive him before dying. He absolutely refused him the reconciliation asked with such importunity. Arrived at the place of execution, he faltered, denied, while the other boldly confessed and perished in his place. He might have persisted from shame of denying His Lord, and to avoid being taxed with cowardice. His martyrdom would not have been on that account more acceptable to God. The trickeries of self-love are unfathomable, and deceive the very man who is their instrument. — The οὐδὲν ὠφελοῦμαι, *it profiteth me nothing*, is here substituted for the οὐδὲν εἰμί, *I am nothing*, of ver. 2, because now it is not the worth of the person but of the acts which is in question. What was intended to assure me of salvation, has no value in the eyes of God, whenever the object of it becomes self, in the form of self-merit or of human glory. Love accepts only what is inspired by love.

Such is the first reason fitted to justify the καθ' ὑπερβολήν of ver. 31, the supreme excellence of the way which is called *charity*. The most eminent gifts, the most heroic acts avail nothing the instant they are not inspired by it. The absolute worth of charity also appears from the opposite consideration: while without it, all is nothing, it produces all of itself. It is the mother of all the virtues, "the bond of perfection," as St. Paul himself says, Col. iii. 14.

Vers. 4–7

The following picture is not drawn at random, and, so to speak, at the good pleasure of the author. It is as closely connected with the state of his readers as the foregoing passage. It is a mirror in which the Church is called to contemplate the humiliating image of what it has become, while it beholds the state which it is called to endeavour to attain. While tracing it, the apostle has two things constantly before his eyes: on the one hand, the figure of Him who realized on earth the ideal of a life of charity; on the other, the remembered sins against charity to which the Corinthians had given way in the exercise of the fair gifts bestowed on their Church, because the use of them had not been subordinated to this cardinal virtue.—The apostle begins with the two essential features which characterize this disposition, the one negative, the other positive.

Ver. 4[a]. "Charity suffereth long, it is kind."—*Suffereth long*, in regard to wrongs, even repeated, from our neighbour; here is the victory over a just resentment. The term μακροθυμεῖν denotes the long waiting time during which the man refuses to give way to his θυμός.—*Kind, full of goodness*, animated by the constant need to make oneself useful; it is the victory over idle selfishness and comfortable self-pleasing. The verb χρηστεύεσθαι, from χρηστός (χράομαι), strictly denotes the disposition to put oneself at the service of others.—*In tolerandis malis*, says Calvin, in regard to the former of these terms; *in conferendis bonis*, in relation to the latter.

There follow eight negative qualities, which unfold the contents of the former of these two terms, the μακροθυμεῖ.

Vers. 4[b]–6[a]. "Charity envieth not; charity vaunteth not itself, charity is not puffed up, 5. doth not behave itself unseemly, seeketh not its own, is not easily provoked, taketh not account of evil; 6[a].

rejoiceth not in unrighteousness." — The connection between the first four dispositions is obvious. With *envy*, which bears on the advantages of others, there is naturally connected *boasting* in regard to one's own. The word περπερεύεσθαι is of unknown origin. Perhaps it is an onomatopœia, the reduplication of the first syllable expressing vain boasting, or perhaps it is connected with πέρα, *beyond*, and denotes the act of transgressing the just measure. It has also been derived from the Latin *perperam (præter operam)*. The ancient commentators sometimes take it for the vice of precipitancy, sometimes for that of boastfulness. Others, affectation, petulance, or frivolity (see Edwards). The most probable meaning is that of ostentation. It is easy to understand from the passages xii. 14–17 and 21–26, the application of these first two terms to the state of the Church of Corinth. The inconsiderate use of the dictum: "All things are lawful for me" (vi. 12, x. 23), serves also to explain the second. Hence the transition to *inflation*, as the inward source of the two preceding evils. The word φυσιοῦσθαι was used, iv. 6, to denote the presumptuous self-satisfaction with which certain Corinthians were filled; comp. in general chaps. i–iv.

Vers. 5, 6[a]. Finally the want of propriety, ἀσχημοσύνη; forgetfulness of seemliness, respect, politeness; this term points back to the rebukes xi. 5 (the demeanour of women) and 21, 22 (the conduct in the Holy Supper). We shall see in chap. xiv., from the limits which the apostle sees himself forced to put to the use of certain gifts, how those who possess them set themselves above the respect due to the Church and to those who possess different and still more useful gifts.

—These four terms relate rather to the abuse of gifts; the following four bear on the Christian life in general. —It is impossible on reading the phrase: *seeketh not its own,* to avoid recalling what was said, chaps. viii.–x., of the use which many members of the Church without charity made of their spiritual liberty, showing not the least concern for the salvation of the weak, provided they might enjoy pleasures in which they thought they had a right to indulge. The term *to be provoked* no doubt alludes to the dissensions and lawsuits (chap. vi.).—The phrase λογίζεσθαι τὸ κακόν, *to reckon the evil,* has been explained in the sense of suspecting evil or meditating it with a view to injuring others; but the article before κακόν seems to indicate that the evil in question is there, realized, rather than an evil to be done; and as to the first meaning, it has been remarked, not without reason (see Edwards), that it would rather require ἐνθυμεῖσθαι (Matt. ix. 4). It is better, therefore, to understand: "does not rigorously take account of the wrongs it has to bear from its neighbour;" comp. 2 Cor. v. 19; Rom. iv. 6. Charity, instead of entering evil as a debt in its account-book, voluntarily passes the sponge over what it endures.—Finally, it feels no criminal *joy* on seeing the faults which may be committed by men of an opposite party. Rather than eagerly turn to account the wrong which an adversary thus does to himself, it mourns on account of it. This last proposition is the transition to the first of the five positive qualities which are afterwards mentioned.

Vers. 6[b], 7. "But it rejoiceth with the truth; 7. covereth all things, believeth all things, hopeth all things, endureth all things."—It is impossible to leave out of account the σύν, *with*, which enters into the composition of the verb συγχαίρειν (*to rejoice with*), and to translate simply: rejoiceth *in the truth.* Truth is here personified as charity itself is. They are two sisters; when truth triumphs, charity rejoices with it. We might understand by *truth* the preaching of salvation; but it seems more natural here to give it a general meaning, corresponding to the word *unrighteousness,* in the preceding proposition; the subject in question is truth in opposition to falsehood. Love chooses to see the truth coming to light and triumphing, even if it should be contrary to the opinion cherished by it, rather than to see error which might be most useful to it holding its ground.

Ver. 7 continues to develop the positive good done by charity. Here properly begins the development of the second fundamental feature of charity, the χρηστεύεται, *it is kind.* In four master-strokes the apostle draws in a complete and indelible manner the portrait of this angel of goodness come down from heaven. The verb στέγω (*tego*), *to cover,* might here signify, as usually in Paul's style (ix. 12), *to bear;* but it would be difficult to avoid a tautology with the fourth term, ὑπομένειν, *to endure.* It is better therefore to understand the word in the sense of *to excuse.* Charity seeks to excuse others, to throw a mantle over their faults, charging itself, if need be, with all the painful results which may follow. This conduct is explained by the following term: *it believeth all things.* The term *believe* usually refers to God; here it denotes apparently confidence in man; but in reality this confidence has for its object the Divine in man, all that remains in him of God's image. For it is this which leads charity to interpret the conduct of fellow-men rather in a good sense.—Of course this faith goes only to the point where sight arrests it by discovering distinctly the opposite of the good which it loved to suppose. But, even then, the task of charity is not at an end: where it must cease to believe, it still *hopes*. While recognising with pain the present triumph of sin, it cherishes the hope of the future victory of good. —And in this generous hope it does not *weary;* it holds on, ὑπομένει. Taking part with the Divine long-suffering, it endures with perseverance; ὑπομένειν, literally: *to hold on under* (a burden). Here the matter in question is not evil in general, as in the στέγει, but personal wrongs. By this last word, the apostle returns to that with which he had started: love is long-suffering, and thus he finds the transition to the third idea of the chapter: the objective permanence of charity.

Vers. 8–13

The absolute duration of charity is developed in these last verses: first, in opposition to gifts, then even in contrast to the other two fundamental virtues, faith and hope. Thus the apostle completes the demonstration of his thought: charity is the supremely excellent way.

Vers. 8–10. "Charity never faileth.[1] As to prophecies,[2] they shall be done away; as to tongues, they

[1] T. R. with D E F G K L It.: εκπιπτει; ℵ A B C: πιπτει.
[2] B: προφητεια καταργηθησεται (*prophecy shall be done away*).

shall cease; as to knowledges, they shall be done away.[1] 9. For[2] we know in part, and we prophesy in part. 10. But when that which is perfect is come,[3] that which is in part shall be done away."—The first words: *never faileth*, are, as it were, the theme of the following passage. This is why the subject: charity, is repeated. The best proof of the absolute value of charity is its eternal permanence in contrast to everything else, even the most excellent; and the subjective persistence of charity in the believer (ver. 7) is the prelude, as it were, of this objective permanence.—It seems as if the verb ought to be in the future; but the present is here, as often, that of the idea.—The two readings: πίπτει and ἐκπίπτει, have almost the same meaning: the former, however, is the simpler and more probable. An allusion to the spot from which the fall takes place (ἐκ) is unnecessary. The verb πίπτειν, *to fall*, cannot, as Holsten would have it, refer solely to the value of charity in this sense: It never loses its worth. The following antitheses: *shall be done away, shall cease*, prove clearly that its *duration* is the point in question. Prophesying and speaking in tongues will cease, but not loving.

The transient character of gifts, even the most eminent, such as prophecy and knowledge (between which Paul introduces, as an inferior gift, speaking in tongues), proves their relative and secondary value. The *Vatic.* reads the singular προφητεία; all the other documents have the plural.—To what epoch does the

[1] א A F G: γνωσεις καταργηθησονται (*knowledges shall be done away*), instead of γνωσις καταργηθησεται (*knowledge* . . .) in B D K L.

[2] K L read δε (*but*), instead of γαρ (*for*).

[3] T. R. here reads with K L Syr.: τοτε (*then*).

abolition of prophecy belong? If history is consulted, it seems to answer: toward the end of the second and during the third century. For the *Doctrine of the Twelve Apostles* shows us the prophets still in full activity in the first half of the second century. But the apostle's answer, in ver. 10, certainly makes the abolition of prophecy, as well as that of tongues and of knowledge, coincident with the advent of the perfect state; consequently with Christ's glorious coming, which will introduce this state. It is vain to attempt to fix an interval between the abolition announced in ver. 8 and the τὸ τέλειον ἐλθεῖν, the advent of perfection, of ver. 10. But if, according to this text, the total abolition of gifts cannot take place before the end of the present economy, there may come about a modification in their phenomenal manifestation. The very figure which the apostle uses in ver. 11 easily leads to the idea of a gradual metamorphosis, which will pass over their mode of manifestation. For the *speaking* of the child, its mode of *feeling* and *thinking*, do not give place suddenly to the analogous faculties of the mature man; the change in these three respects takes place insensibly and progressively. So the spiritual gifts granted to the primitive Church, while accompanying and supporting the Church to the very threshold of the perfect state, need not do so necessarily in the same form as at the beginning. Prophecy may be transformed into animated preaching; speaking in tongues may appear in the form of religious poetry and music; knowledge continue to accomplish its task by the catechetical and theological teaching of Christian truth (see on chap. xiv. conclusion).

In speaking of tongues Paul substitutes for the word *καταργεῖσθαι*, *be done away*, the term *παύεσθαι*, *to cease*, become silent. This feverish agitation of discoursings in tongues, which uplifted the Church of Corinth, will calm down.—The reading *γνώσεις*, *knowledges*, of the *Sinaït.* and the *Greco-Lats.*, is regarded by most, even by Tischendorf, as an assimilation to the preceding substantives. But sufficient account has not been taken of Rückert's remarks. It is not *the* true knowledge which shall cease; it is only the various fragments of knowledge, received here below (*γνώσεις*), which shall pass away to give place to perfect knowledge (ver. 12).

Ver. 9. The reading *γάρ*, *for*, is evidently preferable to the *δέ*, *then*, of the Byz. The apostle wishes to explain why this doing away shall take place. Prophecy lifts on each occasion only a corner of the veil which covers the plan of God and its final accomplishment. Similarly the isolated acts of spiritual knowledge grasp the truth of salvation only in fragments, and consequently every particular point of the great fact. Even to possess the complete knowledge of one point, the whole would require to be known distinctly. Now this full and only true knowledge is not granted us in the present economy. As to tongues, the apostle does not think it necessary to justify their disappearance. The reason for it is too evident: it is their ecstatic character. The only ground for ecstatic transport is that we are not yet living fully in the reality of the Divine. When we live in God, we are in Him without going out of ourselves. This is why there is no ecstasy in the life of Jesus, at least after His baptism.

Ver. 10. But far from being an impoverishment of the Church, this loss of gifts, on the contrary, will coincide with her rising to the possession of perfect fulness; it will be the imperfect melting into the perfect. In contrast to the term ἐκ μέρους, *in part*, one would expect τὸ πᾶν, *the whole*, the entire. But it is not without reason that the apostle says τὸ τέλειον, *the perfect*, substituting the idea of perfection in quality for that of completeness in quantity. For the future knowledge will differ from that which we have here in *mode*, still more than in *extent*. Our view will not only embrace the totality of Divine things; but it will contemplate them from the centre, and consequently in their real essence. At present not only do we know only fragments, but even these we discern but indistinctly.—The aor. ἔλθῃ, *shall have come*, alludes to a fixed and positively expected moment, which can be no other than that of the Advent.—The apostle uses a comparison to illustrate the necessity of this substitution of the perfect for the imperfect.

Ver. 11. "When I was a child, I spake as a child, I felt as a child, I thought as a child;[1] when I became a man, I put away childish things."—Man's natural growth is a figure of that of the Church; both follow the same law, that of development and transformation. In proportion as the faculties, in course of development, acquire a higher mode of activity, the previous mode ceases of itself.—It seems evident to me, as to most commentators, that by the three terms, λαλεῖν, *to speak*, φρονεῖν, *to feel*, *aspire* (this term expresses the unity of feeling, thought, and will), and λογίζεσθαι, *to think*, the

[1] T. R. with E F G K L P Syr. here reads δὲ (*but*), omitted by ℵ A B D.

apostle alludes to the three gifts mentioned, vers. 9–11; *speaking* corresponds to tongues, *aspiration* to prophecy, and *thinking* to knowledge. The gift of tongues corresponds in the Divine domain to the babbling of the child in its first joyous experience of life. Prophecy, whose glance penetrates to the perfection yet to come, corresponds to the ardent aspiration of the childish heart, which goes out eagerly into the future, expecting from it joy and happiness; and knowledge, which seeks to penetrate Divine truth, corresponds to the simple thoughts whereby the infant mind seeks to find an explanation of things. It is therefore a groundless objection which Holsten makes to this triple and obvious correlation when he alleges the absence of all relation between the φρονεῖν, *aspire after*, and prophecy. —The active verb κατήργηκα, *I put away, I put an end to,* denotes the spontaneity of this surrender. As it is with pride that the young man shakes off the puerilities of childhood, so it is with profound satisfaction that the mature man substitutes the manly activity of the profession which he has embraced for the passionate dreams of childhood and youth. Such is the image of what will be experienced by the faithful when the perfect state for which they are preparing shall be unveiled to them, at Christ's coming. Then they will willingly let fall all those rudiments of the spiritual life with which they were delighted, inflated perhaps, as was the case at Corinth. It is from this point that we can perfectly understand the delicate allusion, i. 7.—M. Sabatier (*l'Apôtre Paul*, p. 7), failing to understand the comparison which the apostle makes, thinks that he is here speaking of himself, that he wishes to describe his spiritual state immediately after his conversion, and that in the same sense in which he applied the image of the child to the spiritual state of the Corinthians, iii. 1 seq. He thus finds in our ver. 11 a proof of the considerable changes which took place in the apostle's convictions from the time of his conversion up to the date when he wrote this letter.[1]—Such a misunderstanding is without parallel.

The following verse contains the explanation of this comparison.

Ver. 12. "For now we see through a glass darkly; but then face to face: now I know in part; but then shall I know even as also I have been known."—The ordinary application of the two parts of this verse to the gift of knowledge seems to me mistaken. Why should the apostle in this application omit the gift of prophecy? We shall find that the terms of the first half of the verse apply as naturally to the last gift as those of the second half to knowledge. As to tongues he omits them, as already in ver. 9. He does not think it necessary to revert expressly to their future disappearance.—The object of βλέπειν, *to see*, is here God Himself, with His plan of grace and glory toward us. The mirrors of the ancients were of metal; those made at Corinth were famous. The image which they presented could never be perfectly distinct. There is no ground for Rückert's idea that what is meant is a window formed of semi-transparent glass or of a square of horn. Tertullian already understood it so: *Velut per corneum specular* (see Edwards). The διά, *through*,

[1] "The points in question here," says he, "as the parallel passages prove, are childhood and ripe age in the Christian life."

on which this view rested, may signify: *by means of.* Or the term *through* may be suggested by the fact that the image seems to be placed behind the surface of the mirror.—We perceive Divine things, says the apostle, only by means of their image in a mirror. Plato had already expressed a similar idea in his famous comparison of the cave. This figure signifies two things: knowledge of a *mediate* character, and for that very reason always more or less *confused.*—'Εν αἰνίγματι, literally: in the form of enigma. The word αἴνιγμα denotes a sentence which, without expressly saying the thing, leaves it to be guessed. It thus serves to bring out the relative obscurity in the manifestation of Divine things, which we now possess. If we apply the expression exclusively to the gift of knowledge, we shall see in *the mirror,* with some, space and time, those necessary forms of all our ideas, or the categories of reason which determine all its processes; Paul in that case would have here anticipated Kant. Or, according to others, Paul is thinking of the facts of sacred history as manifesting God's character and essence, or of the revelations of Scripture in general. Holsten combines these two last interpretations. But do we not arrive at a more natural explanation of the apostle's words, if we apply them to the gift of prophecy? The image in the mirror corresponds in this case to the inward picture which the Spirit of God produces in the prophet's soul at the time of his vision, and in which the Divine thought is revealed to him. And the expression: *in the form of enigma,* which we have translated *darkly,* exactly renders the character of such a picture. The prophet required in every case to apply his whole attention to the vision to extract from it the idea of the fact revealed to him; comp. 1 Pet. i. 10, 11. What seems to me to confirm this meaning is the analogy of the terms used by Paul to those of the Pentateuch, particularly in the passage Num. xii. 6–8, where the Lord says: "If there be a prophet among you, I will make Myself known unto him, ἐν ὁράματι, *in a vision*, and I will speak unto him, ἐν ὕπνῳ, *in a dream;* but My servant Moses is not so. . . . With him I speak *mouth to mouth*, στόμα κατὰ στόμα, and he seeth Me, ἐν εἴδει, *manifestly*, and not δι' αἰνιγμάτων, *in enigmas* (confused representations)." With this mediate view of the Divine, by means of prophetic picture, the apostle contrasts the immediate intuition which will be the character of future contemplation; and he here uses expressions which remind us of what is said in the Old Testament regarding the incomparable mode of communication between God and Moses (Deut. xxxiv. 10: *mouth to mouth*, and Ex. xxxiii. 11: ἐνώπιος ἐνωπίῳ, *face to face*). The communication which God granted to Moses, and to Moses only, was a kind of anticipation of the final mode of intuition here described; comp. Num. xii. 8 (LXX.): καὶ τὴν δόξαν τοῦ κυρίου εἶδε, *and he saw the glory of the Lord.*

The second part of the verse relates to the gift of knowledge. With the fragmentary, successive, analytic, discursive mode of our present knowledge, there is contrasted the intuitive, central, complete, and perfectly distinct character of our future knowledge. The verb γινώσκω, strictly: *I learn to know*, denotes effort and progress. Then Paul substitutes for the simple active verb γινώσκω, the compound ἐπιγινώσκω in the middle form to denote the complete assimilation of the knowledge to come: to put the finger on the object, so as to possess it entirely. And, to give the fullest idea of this kind of knowledge, he uses the boldest conceivable parallel, identifying the knowledge which we shall have of God with that which He now has of us. The καθώς, *according as, as,* indicates the immediate and perfectly distinct character, and the καί serves still more to emphasize the notion of identity.—The first person singular is substituted in this second part of the verse for the first plural, *we see,* to emphasize more strongly the absolute inwardness of this wholly personal relation. Meyer, Kling, Hofmann, Holsten think that the aorist *I have been known* refers to the date of conversion; comp. Gal. iv. 9; but this restricted sense is unnatural in our passage. Paul is speaking of the knowledge which God has of man during the whole course of his life. From the standpoint of the life to come, at which the context puts us, this knowledge appears to him as a thing of the past.—With this whole view opened up, what became of the superiority of knowledge and speech on which the Corinthians prided themselves so greatly (comp. i. 5, 7)? As the faint glimmer of dawn gives place to the brightness of the rising sun, so those confused conceptions and those fragmentary knowledges in which they glory will vanish in the brightness of immediate vision granted at the hour of the Advent (the ἀποκάλυψις, i. 7). What will then remain of the present state? Nothing? No; that would mean that all the present labour of the believer is vain. Something will remain, undoubtedly: but it will not be gifts, it will be the virtues which constitute the essential elements of the Christian character, without which, as Heinrici says, the Christian personality itself is extinguished:

Ver. 13. "But now abideth faith, hope, charity, these three; but the greatest of these is charity."—As Paul so often does (1 Thess. i. 3; 2 Thess. i. 3, 4; Col. i. 4, 5), he here sums up the Christian life in the three dispositions: *faith,* which takes salvation as already accomplished, Christ come; *hope,* which goes out to the part of salvation yet to be accomplished, Christ coming again; finally, *charity,* which embraces the ever-abiding Christ, and in Him all beings, and which is already salvation itself realized in the individual. Such are the three elements of the Christian life which will not pass away with the coming of the perfect state. Holsten has asked, with good right, why Paul here brings in the comparison of charity with those other two virtues, whereas, considering the passage as a whole, he was not called to compare it with anything but gifts; and he gives himself up to a rather subtle lucubration to show that faith was to replace, throughout the present era, the knowledge of the early days, and hope the prophecies of the apostolic epoch. There is not in the text the least trace of this idea, which is besides excluded by the true meaning of the word *abide.* The answer seems to me simple. To exalt charity supremely, Paul contrasts it not only with gifts which pass away, but also with the virtues which remain as well as it, and declares its superiority even over them.—The particle νυνὶ δέ, *but now,* might be taken in the temporal sense, as it is sometimes, perhaps, in Paul's writings (see Rückert on v. 11).

In that case we must explain thus: "But *at the present time* there abide faith, hope, charity." This meaning is inadmissible for the following reason : The three virtues are contrasted with the three preceding gifts, which are to cease with the future era, and not to enter into the perfect state. Now, if these three virtues also only belonged to the present epoch, there would be no contrast to set up in respect of duration between them and gifts. We must therefore give the particle a logical sense; comparison of charity with the two other virtues contains the indication of a new element, of the true state of things. "In reality, this is what abides, and by no means what you suppose." The contrast between virtues and gifts is likewise emphasized by the apposition τὰ τρία ταῦτα, that is to say: "*these three*, and not the three gifts of which we have been speaking." What has only an intellectual, oratorical, or lyrical character is transient; what edifies, what produces self-renunciation, the giving oneself to God and men, this is what abides.

How are we to understand the expression *abide?* At the first glance one is disposed to give it, in contrast to the abolition of gifts, the most absolute sense: *abide* eternally. Gifts will be done away at the coming of the perfect state; but these three virtues will remain in the perfect state itself. But against this idea there rises an objection which from the earliest times has struck all commentators. It is, that according to St. Paul, faith, in the perfect state, must give place to sight (2 Cor. v. 7), and hope to possession (Rom. viii. 24). According to this, faith and hope would pass away as well as gifts. Various ways have been sought of solving this difficulty. Osiander imagines he can distinguish two epochs in the perfect state, the one embracing the thousand years' reign, the other beginning at the end of this reign and belonging to eternity. Gifts cease, according to him, on the threshold of the first of these epochs; faith and hope only at the beginning of the second. But the text presents not the slightest indication of this distinction; the perfect state is represented in it as one single era from which gifts only are excluded. Some, like Beza, Bengel, Rückert, refer the term μένειν, *abide*, to the entire duration of the present economy. But what becomes in that case of the contrast between the three virtues which remain to the end of the present period and the three gifts which are to cease at the coming of the perfect state?—Several commentators, such as Calvin, Holsten, Heinrici, are thus led to take the word *abide* in a logical sense. These three things, says Holsten, *remain in full value*, while gifts lose theirs, knowledge is replaced by faith, and prophecy by hope. But if this explanation is to give a clear meaning, it always amounts to making Paul say that gifts were to cease with the first ages, while faith and hope were to preserve their value to the present day, and until the end of this economy. How can any one help seeing that by this contrast the notion of *time* still remains attached to the word *abide*, from which indeed it is inseparable in the context? For it springs from the evident antithesis between the word *abide* and the preceding verbs: *shall cease, shall be done away, I put away*. This has been felt by most commentators, while fully acknowledging the difficulty of harmonizing the permanence of faith and hope with Paul's other sayings in which their transformation and, consequently, their future cessation are taught. Grotius observes that faith and hope, while formally transformed, will abide in their *fruits*. According to Hofmann, likewise, Paul's expression is justified by the fact that *believing* remains in seeing, as hoping in possessing; for sight has come through faith, and possession through hope. But is not this to do violence to the meaning of the word *abide?* And might not the same be said of gifts?—Meyer, nearly to the same effect: These virtues will remain in the salvation we have obtained through their means, and moreover in this sense: that faith remains eternally the means of our communion with Christ, and that hope will never cease to catch new perspectives of glory, even in the perfect state. Kling (in Lange's Bible) says better still, as it appears to me: While love is the real possession of the Divine, faith and hope belong to its acquisition; now is this acquisition a fact which can ever cease?—Indeed, eternal blessings are not like a bag of gold pieces, which are received once for all. The permanent essence of the creature is to have nothing of its own, to be eternally helpless and poor; every instant it must take possession of God by faith, which grasps the manifestations which He has already given, and by hope, which prepares to lay hold of His new manifestations. It is not once for all, it is *continually* that in eternity faith changes into vision and hope into possession. These two virtues, therefore, abide to live again unceasingly.

But notwithstanding this permanence of faith and hope, the palm belongs to charity, as *the greatest of the three.* The apostle dces not say the most durable, for the duration of all three is absolute. The τούτων might refer to the other two virtues only; μείζων would then have its regular comparative sense: "*greater* than they two." But as τούτων necessarily refers to τρία ταῦτα, we must give to μείζων the superlative meaning: "*the greatest* of the three;" comp. Matt. xviii. 4. This superiority of charity has been variously explained. Some, like Calvin, say: Greater in virtue of its eternal duration; but this duration belongs also, as we have just seen, to the other two. Others: Because faith and hope belong only to the individual's inward life, while charity exercises a salutary influence beyond him (Meyer, Heinrici, Holsten). But is not faith also an active force outwardly? De Wette: Because love is, according to ver. 7, the true principle of faith and hope. But in ver. 7 faith and hope referred solely to conduct toward our neighbour, and not to the appropriation of salvation and our relation to God. According to Paul, it is, on the contrary, faith which is the principle both of hope and of true love (Gal. v. 6).—We have just seen that faith and hope abide continually, but undergoing incessant transformation, the one into sight, the other into possession. It is not so with charity. Love does not see, does not acquire, it *is* the Divine. God does not believe nor hope, but He loves. Love belongs to His essence. Like God Himself, it could not change its nature except for the worse. Love is the end in relation to which the two other virtues are only means, and this relation remains even in the state of perfection. Hence it is the greatest, and hence also the apostle called charity and the work of charity : " The way *par excellence*." So he resumes, xiv. 1, by saying : " Follow after charity." In this verse the apostle returns, as we have said, from the digression on charity to his subject strictly so called: the exercise of spiritual gifts. He has now placed them under the ægis of the one principle which can render their exercise truly beneficial and make up for them, if they should ever come to an end.

C. Practical Rules for the Exercise of Gifts (14:1-40)

In ver. 31 of chap. xii. Paul had recommended the seeking of spiritual gifts, as the inference from the whole discussion of chap. xii.; then he had passed to the cardinal recommendation : in all things walk in charity. Now he comes to the more special practical directions which he has to give in regard to the exercise of gifts, and it is from charity that he draws the general rule whence he makes them all flow.

1. *The comparative usefulness of the gifts of tongues and of prophecy* (vers. 1–25)

Ver. 1. " Follow after charity ; but desire spiritual gifts, and especially to prophesy."—The general rule is this: Every one should seek, above all, the gifts most fitted to contribute to the common good. Such is the principle Paul applies first of all to the valuation of the two gifts which seem at that time to have played the most considerable part in the life of the Church of Corinth, glossolalia [1] and prophecy. And as what is

[1] See note, p. 234.

intelligible is evidently superior, with a view to edification, to what is not so, he concludes without hesitation for the superiority of prophecy, and even for the exclusion of glossolalia, unless there be some way of rendering it intelligible.

There is a contrast between the terms διώκειν, *to follow*, and ζηλοῦν, *to desire.* The former refers to something indispensable, the latter to a faculty which is simply desirable; see on xii. 31. The evident relation between our verse and that does not allow us to restrict the meaning of πνευματικά (spiritual gifts), as Rückert, Ewald, etc., have done, to glossolalia. Prophecy cannot be put outside of the *pneumatica*, as if it was to be sought *more than* they. It is comprehended in this expression, which denotes spiritual gifts in general (xii. 31); the apostle has particularly in view, no doubt, glossolalia, prophecy, and teaching. The word μᾶλλον, *rather*, does not therefore exclude the pursuit of these two last gifts; on the contrary, it implies it.—Instead of ἵνα, *that*, Paul might have put simply: "Especially desire prophecy." But his thought is strictly speaking this: "Seek states of inspiration, and that especially with the view of attaining to the possession of the best of gifts, prophecy."

Why among these gifts, all desirable, does prophecy occupy the first rank? This is what the following passage explains, in which Paul shows the inferiority of the gift of tongues as compared with prophecy; and that first as to the edification of the Church (vers. 2–20), then as to the conversion of persons outside of the Church (vers. 21–25).

Vers. 2–20

Vers. 2–5.

Vers. 2, 3. "For he that speaketh in a tongue speaketh not unto men, but unto God: for no man understandeth him; howbeit in the spirit he speaketh mysteries. 3. But he that prophesieth speaketh unto men edification, exhortation, and comfort."—Paul here describes the *mode* in which the two gifts act. The glossolalete addresses God, and that in a language which no man understands, so that what he says remains a mystery to all who hear him; speaking in a tongue is a sort of spiritual soliloquy. It is impossible here to apply the meaning given by Meyer, Holsten, etc., to the word *tongue*, which according to them denotes the material organ of speech. What could the apostle mean by saying that he who speaks by moving the tongue speaks to God? The word denotes the ecstatic language which flourished at Corinth. The singular applies to each particular case; the plural (γλώσσαις λαλεῖν) to the gift in general. When a man speaks in ordinary language, his thought is addressed to those around him; but when he speaks in this particular tongue, his thought is turned to God only. And the proof is, that nobody understands this kind of manifestation. Wieseler has taken the word ἀκούειν, *hear*, in the physical sense, and concluded from the term that the glossolaletes spoke only in a low voice. But, xiii. 1, Paul compares them to sounding brass and the clanging cymbal, and in ver. 8 to the startling sound of the trumpet giving the signal for battle. 'Ακούειν, *hear*, has therefore in this place, as so frequently, the meaning of understand ; comp. Gen. xi. 7 (LXX.) : "That they should not hear each the voice of his neighbour" (Matt. xiii. 13, etc.).—This passage is equally incompatible with the idea of really existing foreign tongues ; for there might easily have been found at Corinth some one who understood the foreign tongue used by a glossolalete.—The δέ, at the end of ver. 2, is adversative : "*But*, far from being understood, he speaks mysteries." The term *mystery* is here used in a derivative sense. It usually denotes the Divine plans which remain a secret to men, so long as God does not reveal them ; it refers to the secrets of a man in relation to other men. What the speaker in a tongue says remains between God and him, and is a mystery to the hearers.—It is possible to explain the dative πνεύματι in the sense *by* the spirit,—which would then be the Divine Spirit as guiding the man's spirit,—or it may be translated : *in spirit ;* then it is the spirit of the glossolalete himself, who is carried away in an ecstasy, and in a manner raised for the time above the exercise of the understanding ; comp. Rev. i. 1. This second meaning is the more natural, seeing there is no article nor preposition before the substantive. It is evident that the state of the glossolalete was that of an ineffable conversation with God. Our passage has been justly compared with Rom. viii. 26, 27, where the apostle speaks of the unutterable groanings whereby the Holy Spirit intercedes in the believer's heart ; only we may not conclude from this comparison, with Holsten, that glossolalia consisted only of confused groanings. Our whole chapter shows that there was language properly so called.

Ver. 3. It is otherwise with the man who prophesies; he addresses men to communicate to them from God some new grace, light, force. There is not only in him an involuntary expression of a personal state of mind, there is conscious will to act on the hearers by the communication of an immediately revealed Divine thought (ver. 30).—The apostle says, not: the prophet, but: "he that prophesieth," because he conceives him in full activity in the midst of the assembly.—In indicating the contents of his speaking: *edification, exhortation, comfort*, the apostle identifies the declaration itself with its effect.—There is no reason for subordinating the two last terms, as Meyer does, to the first, or to make the first, as de Wette does, the effect of the two following. They are all three co-ordinate. Edification denotes a new development and a confirmation of faith, by some new view fitted to strengthen the soul. The second term denotes an encouragement addressed to the will, an energetic impulse capable of effecting an awakening or advancement in Christian fidelity. If the first term relates mainly to faith, the second refers rather to love. The third, comfort, points rather to hope; παραμυθεῖν, to soothe the ear with a sweet myth, putting pain to sleep or reviving hope.

In our times the conclusion has often been drawn from this verse, that since to prophesy is to edify, exhort, comfort, whoever edifies, exhorts, comforts, merits, according to Paul, the title prophet. This reasoning is as just as it would be to say: He who runs, moves his legs; therefore whoever moves his legs, runs; or, to take a more nearly related example: He who speaks in a tongue, speaks to God; therefore whoever speaks to God, is a glossolalete. No, certainly; one may edify, comfort, encourage, without deserving the title of prophet or prophetess. The absurd reasoning which I have pointed out has been dictated by the desire of being able to proclaim certain women prophetesses who think themselves called to speak in public, in order to give them the benefit of the implicit authorization contained in xi. 5.—From this contrast in the intrinsic nature of the two gifts, the apostle passes to the difference of results obtained by them.

Ver. 4. "He that speaketh in a tongue edifieth himself; but he that prophesieth, edifieth the Church."—From his intimate communion with God, the glossolalete derives a blessing which, even though it is not transformed into precise notions by the exercise of the understanding, makes itself felt as a power in the depths of his soul; but the Church has received nothing of the kind, for it has understood nothing of the inward dialogue kept up with God. Prophecy, on the contrary, is like a torrent of living water which overspreads and quickens the whole Church. Hence the conclusion drawn, ver. 5.

Ver. 5. "Now I would that ye all spake in tongues, and rather that ye prophesied; but[1] greater is he that prophesieth than he that speaketh with tongues, except he interpret, that the Church may receive edifying."—The following is the result of vers. 1–4: the gift of tongues is a good thing; but prophecy is

[1] T. R. with D E F G K L It. Syr. reads γαρ (*for*); ℵ A B P: δε (*but*).

superior to it, unless by interpretation the discourse in a tongue be transformed into prophecy. The first δέ is progressive, *now*: "Now I do not reject glossolalia, I desire that it should abound; but I desire still more earnestly the development of the gift of prophecy."—The γάρ, *for*, which, in the Greco-Lat. and Byz. texts, connects the second part of the verse with the first, has been substituted for the much more difficult δέ, which is the reading of the Alex. The δέ is adversative; it is well explained by Holsten: "*But* yet there is a case in which the man who speaks in a tongue is as great as the prophet." The term *great* is used here from the standpoint of utility. The measure of this greatness is borrowed from the principle of charity.—In the form ἐκτὸς εἰ μή, *unless . . . not*, the μή, *not*, is a pleonasm arising from the mixing of the two following constructions: *excepting if* (ἐκτὸς εἰ), and: if not (εἰ μή).—The subject of *except he interpret* can be no other than the glossolalete himself. No doubt, failing him, some other might do it (comp. ver. 27). But, as a rule, Paul expected that he should do it himself (vers. 13, 15). There was thus less room left for arbitrariness. By way of analogy, we may imagine a man coming out of a dream and explaining what he has seen and heard, and so giving account of the broken exclamations and words which the bystanders had heard without understanding them.—The διά, in the verb, indicates the detailed, discursive element of the contents of the brief and summary sayings uttered in a tongue.—The complete uselessness of tongues without interpretation is demonstrated in what follows by a series of examples, vers. 6–12.

Vers. 6–12.

Ver. 6. "But now, brethren, if I come unto you speaking in tongues, what shall I profit you, except I shall speak to you either in revelation, or in knowledge, or in prophesying, or in doctrine?"—The first example Paul offers to the Corinthians is that of his own person; they all knew what power his presence in a Church exercised; many of them promised themselves considerable edification from the visit he announced to them. Well! there was a way of making this visit utterly useless: in place of prophesying and teaching, let him set himself to play among them the part of glossolalete; and if this holds in Paul's case, how much more in all others!—The δέ is adversative; it contrasts the glossolalia without translation, which Paul by hypothesis ascribes to himself in ver. 6, with glossolalia with interpretation in ver. 5^{b}.—*Νυνί, now:* "things being so." Hofmann gives this word the temporal meaning: "If I come *now* among you;" but this connection of νυνί with ἔλθω is forced.—By the address *brethren,* he appeals to their good sense.—Meyer thinks that the second ἐάν, *if* [ἐὰν μή, *if not = except*], is subordinate to the first, and that the *speaking,* referred to at the close of the verse, relates to the *interpreting* of the discourse in a tongue, so that the meaning of the verse would amount to this: "Wherein shall I be useful to you if I speak to you in a tongue, but without giving an interpretation in the form either of prophecy, or doctrine, of what I at first said in an unintelligible form?" This meaning is inadmissible; for nowhere are prophecy and doctrine represented by Paul as the interpretation of a tongue. The meaning is this: "Wherein should I be useful to you if I figured among you only as one speaking in tongues, and not besides as prophet or teacher?" Of course he speaks of glossolalia in itself and apart from interpretation.—The four terms at the end of the verse evidently form two parallel pairs. On the one hand: *revelation* and *knowledge*—these are inward Divine gifts; on the other: *prophecy* and *doctrine*—these are the external manifestations of the twofold Divine communication: revelation expressing itself in prophecy, and knowledge in doctrine. Revelation, which makes the prophet, is a sudden and lively perception, produced by the Spirit's operation, of some aspect of the Divine mystery, the work of salvation; this view, immediately expressed in its first freshness, forms prophecy (ver. 27). Knowledge is the result of an exercise of thought directed by the Holy Spirit (xii. 8: κατά, *according to*), which leads to the distinct understanding of some element of salvation and of its relation to all the rest; this knowledge is expressed in a *doctrinal* discourse. In the two first terms, the meaning of the ἐν, *in*, is therefore this: "a speaking resting *on* a revelation, *on* an act of knowledge," and, in the two last terms: "a speaking taking effect *by* a prophecy, *by* a doctrine." Heinrici's objections to this double correlation of the four terms: revelation, prophecy, knowledge, doctrine, seem to me without force. Modern commentators are unanimous in recognising it.—To this decisive example, the apostle adds others, taken from ordinary life. And first he instances musical instruments:

Vers. 7, 8. "Even things without life giving sound, whether pipe or harp, except they give a distinction in the sounds . . ., how shall it be known what is piped or harped? 8. For, also, if the trumpet give an uncertain sound, who shall prepare himself to the battle?"—If the sound of instruments is to furnish to the ear an intelligible and significant melody, it must be subject to the laws of tone and rhythm, to the intervals of scale and measure. — The adverb ὅμως, which stands first, should not be confounded with ὁμῶς or ὁμοίως, *likewise;* it signifies: *however;* so Gal. iii. 15, where it applies to the word ἀνθρώπου, *of a man*: "The covenant of a being who *after all* (*however*) is only a man." So here this adverb, as Hofmann well observes, bears on the word ἄψυχα, *inanimate*: "Instruments, which *after all* are only inanimate beings, are also subject to this law of being intelligible only by means of the distinction of sounds." How much more human language, which is the expression of intelligent thought! It is therefore by no means necessary to apply this ὅμως, as Meyer does, to the participle φωνὴν διδόντα: "Though, however, giving a sound." This meaning does not agree so well with the position of the adverb. —The *pipe* and the *harp* represent, the one wind instruments, the other stringed instruments; they were the two principal instruments which the ancients used in worship and in sad or joyful ceremonies.—*How shall it be known:* "How shall one apprehend the air, and know whether he should weep, dance, etc.?"

Ver. 8. The trumpet itself, whose sounds are yet so powerful, is subject to the same law. Its signals are not understood except on condition of being distinct. This example is added to the foregoing—hence the *also;* and it confirms them—hence the *for*. The word πόλεμος, *war,* is here taken, as often, in the restricted sense of battle. What follows, ver. 9, may be regarded either as the application of the examples quoted, to the gift of tongues, or as a new example borrowed from human speech in general. We shall have to decide between these two interpretations.

Ver. 9. "So likewise ye, except ye utter by the tongue distinct speech, how shall it be known what is spoken, for ye shall speak into the air?"—Those who, like Hofmann, already find in ver. 9 an example taken from human language, may punctuate after καὶ ὑμεῖς, in the sense of: *so ye also.* "As inanimate instruments must give forth distinct sounds if their music is to be understood, *so ye also.* As men, you ought to speak distinctly, if you wish to be understood by your fellows." The words διὰ τῆς γλώσσης, *by means of the tongue,* may be understood in this case either of the material organ, or of the faculty of language (Hofmann). But if this were the apostle's meaning, he would not say: "Likewise *ye* also." For the general truth thus expressed would apply no more to the Corinthians than to other men. Paul would be emphasizing more precisely the contrast between inanimate beings and man, as such. We must therefore regard the passage as the application which Paul makes of the foregoing examples to the Corinthians: "And you also, Corinthians, if *in your glossolalia* you do not speak a distinct language, it will be like an unintelligible voice lost in the air." The expression: *by the tongue,* should be taken, as is natural, in the same sense as throughout the chapter: speaking in an ecstatic tongue. The means of rendering this language distinct is interpretation. The apostle confirms this conclusion in vers. 10, 11, by appealing to the intelligible character of all the languages in use among men.

Vers. 10, 11. "There are,[1] it may be, so many kinds of voices in the world, and none[2] of them is without signification. 11 Therefore if I know not the force of the voice, I shall be unto him that speaketh a barbarian, and he that speaketh shall be a barbarian unto[3] me."—The asyndeton here denotes, as it almost always does, a strong reaffirmation of the foregoing idea. Vers. 10 and 11 indeed confirm by a new example the proof given in vers. 7–9. By the expression: *kinds of tongues* (voices), the apostle certainly does not understand what we call *families* of human languages; every existing language is in his view a kind. These languages are exceedingly many: *τοσαῦτα, so numerous.* But the exact number he does not know; the expression *εἰ τύχοι*, with names of number, has the force of taking away from them all precision. Edwards: "whatever may be their number."—The pronoun *αὐτῶν*, *of them*, is a gloss, but a correct gloss. We must beware of understanding *οὐδέν* in the sense of *no human being* (Bleek) or *no nation* (van Hengel), as if Paul meant: "No man or no people is without language." This idea would be unconnected with the context. The meaning is: "No language exists without articulate words." Only the apostle expresses this idea in a striking form, saying, in a

[1] T. R. with A L: *εστιν*; all the rest: *εισιν*.
[2] T. R. with E K L Syr. here add *αυτων* (*of them*).
[3] D E F G omit *εν*.

manner: "No tongue is not a tongue" (Aucune langue n'est une non-langue). The articulation of words and syllables belongs to the essence of human tongues. The Greeks are fond of such paradoxical expressions; comp. βίος ἀβίωτος, a life which is no life; ἄχαρις χάρις, etc. (see Heinrici). — The *force* here denotes the signification of the sounds.—The Greeks and Egyptians called those peoples *barbarians* who did not speak their language.—The ἐν ἐμοί might certainly signify: *in my judgment* (Heinrici, Edwards); but according to the context the meaning rather is: in what concerns me; as between this man and me.—The application of this example is given in ver. 12, in the form of a practical direction:

Ver. 12. "Even so ye, forasmuch as ye are zealous of inspirations, seek that ye may excel to the edifying of the Church."—Several have made the first three words of the verse a separate proposition: *Even so ye;* that is to say: "Ye also would be as barbarians to one another, if ye spoke in tongues without interpretation." But the asyndeton which would follow from this construction, in relation to the following proposition, would be without good reason. The οὕτω indicates the inference to be drawn from what precedes: "*So,* since distinct language is necessary to your being understood, take care, in view of the Church's good, to develop the spiritual gifts which you love, so as to make yourselves more and more intelligible." One cannot help feeling that there is something slightly ironical in the words: *forasmuch as ye are zealous . . .*; "since ye are so eager for manifestations of this kind." There is an allusion here, as Edwards says, to the spirit of ostentation which led them to seek gifts.—The plural πνεύματα, *spirits,* has given commentators much concern. The word cannot be identified with spiritual gifts, πνευματικά in general; it implies something more special. It must be taken as a strong individualizing of the Holy Spirit, not in the sense of many personalities, as Hilgenfeld thinks, who makes a comparison between spirits thus understood and the evil spirits in cases of possession of which the gospel speaks; but in the sense that the one Divine principle spoken of in chap. xii. manifested itself in transient and very various *breathings of inspirations* in the assemblies of the Church; comp. vers. 26, 27. This extraordinary form of the Spirit's influence, of which tongues were the most emphatic manifestation, was that in which the Corinthians loved above all to enjoy the presence of this Divine principle. The apostle does not absolutely combat this disposition, but he seeks to guide it: "Well and good! Seek inspirations, but such as will always serve the good of the Church, and not the gratification of the curiosity of some or the vanity of others!" To this end prophecy should have the preponderance, or tongues be accompanied with interpretation.—The regimen: *for the edification of the Church,* is placed first by inversion; it depends, of course, on the verb περισσεύητε. The apostle is fond of this sort of construction, which sets in relief the regimen containing the principal idea; comp. iii. 5, vii. 17, ix. 15, etc. Meyer and others prefer to connect this regimen directly with ζητεῖτε, *seek,* for the reason that otherwise the regimen should have been placed after this verb, immediately before ἵνα, *that.* But this reason is not at all decisive, and the meaning is simpler in the former case: "You seek inspirations; let it only be in the interest of the Church, and not in your own, that you seek to abound in this respect" (see Edwards).—This general conclusion, drawn in ver. 12, is expressed in vers. 13–15 in a concrete and practical form.

Vers. 13–15. "Wherefore [1] let him that speaketh in a tongue pray that he may interpret. 14. For [2] if I pray in a tongue, my spirit prayeth, but my understanding is unfruitful. 15. What is it then? I will pray [3] with the Spirit, but I will pray [4] with the understanding also: I will sing with the Spirit, but I will sing with the understanding also."[5]—There are two readings: διό, *wherefore,* and διόπερ, *wherefore indeed;* the second is perhaps taken from viii. 13 and x. 14, where Paul also states the conclusions of a discussion.—The ancient Greek interpreters and many moderns, Erasmus, Calvin, Rückert, Hofmann, etc., make the words: *that he may interpret,* the logical object of the word: *let him pray:* "Let him ask of God the power to interpret." But the terms αἰτεῖν or δεῖσθαι would perhaps suit better a positive position than προσεύχεσθαι, which rather denotes the state of prayer; and the use Paul makes of this same term προσεύχεσθαι in the following verses, specially to denote ecstatic prayer, hardly admits of our taking it in ver. 13 in another sense. The words: *let him pray* (in tongues) *that he*

[1] T. R. with K L: διοπερ; the rest: διο. [2] B F G omit γαρ (*for*).

[3] ℵ A D E F G P: προσευξωμαι (*let me pray*); B K L: προσευξομαι (*I will pray*).

[4] A D E F G P: προσευξωμαι; ℵ B K L: προσευξομαι.

[5] B F G K P omit και (*also*).

may interpret, therefore signify: "In giving himself up to the Spirit who leads him to pray in a tongue, let him do so with the intention and with the settled aim beforehand to reproduce the contents of his prayer afterwards in intelligible language." So Meyer, Edwards, etc. It does not therefore follow that ἵνα is here taken, as has been thought, in the sense of *ita ut*, *so that*. Heinrici rightly observes, that in the exercise of every χάρισμα (*gift*) the intention of the will remains in force.[1]

Ver. 14. There is in the state of the glossolalete, who cannot interpret, something incomplete and insufficient. —The expression: *my Spirit*, is taken, by Heinrici and Holsten, to denote the Spirit of God acting and speaking in me. But the following expression: *my understanding*, forbids us to think of anything except a faculty belonging to the person of the man himself;

[1] An extract from Hohl (*Bruchstücke aus dem Leben und den Schriften Ed. Irwings*, Saint-Gall, 1839, p. 149) on the Irvingite manifestations, similar to that described in our chapter, may help to explain the whole passage: "Before the outburst of speech, it was noticeable that the person about to speak became profoundly self-absorbed, isolated from his surroundings; he shut his eyes and covered them with his hand. All at once, as if struck with an electric shock, he underwent a convulsion which shook his whole body. Then there escaped from his quivering mouth, as it were, a burning torrent of strange sounds, forcibly emphasized, and which, to my ear, resembled most those of the Hebrew tongue. Every sentence was usually repeated three times, and given forth with incredible vigour and precision. To this first explosion of strange sounds, which were looked upon as the evidence of genuine inspiration, there succeeded each time, and with emphasis equally forcible, a longer or shorter address in English, which was also repeated several times sentence by sentence, or even word by word, and which consisted sometimes of serious exhortations or terrible warnings, sometimes of consolations full of unction. This latter part passed as the developed interpretation of the former, though it was not expressly given out as such by the speaker. After this manifestation, the inspired person still remained for a time buried in profound silence, and only recovered slowly from this great expenditure of force."

comp. ii. 11; Rom. viii. 16; and 1 Thess. v. 23, passages where it is in vain attempted to set aside the idea of the three fundamental elements of the human person, *body, soul, and spirit:* the body whereby the soul communicates with the external and material world; the spirit whereby it enters into relation with the higher and Divine world; finally, the soul itself, the free and personal force which acts by means of these two organs, using them to bring down the Divine world into the terrestrial, and thus transforming earth into heaven. But it is self-evident that the human spirit is not considered here in its natural isolation from the Divine Spirit, but in its complete union with Him. When carrying it into the state of ecstasy, the Divine Spirit separates it for the time from the νοῦς, *the understanding,* which is a faculty of the soul, or rather the soul itself viewed as thinking. Thereby the impressions take the character of pure feeling, ineffable emotion; it is a state of spiritual enjoyment of which sensual intoxication is, so to speak, the gross caricature; comp. Acts ii. 13; Eph. v. 18–20. Such a state manifested itself in extraordinary voices, consisting of prayers (προσεύχεσθαι, ver. 14), praises (ψάλλειν, ver. 15), or thanksgiving (εὐλογεῖν, εὐχαριστεῖν, ver. 16), and expressing the satisfaction and aspirations of the saved soul. Only the understanding was not a partner in this state; it is *unfruitful,* says the apostle. The word used, ἄκαρπος, is taken by Chrysostom, Calvin, and others in this sense: does not reap fruit for itself. It does not seem to me accurate to allege, as Edwards does, that this meaning is contrary to ver. 4, where it is said that the glossolalete edifies himself. For the speaker in a tongue must not be confounded with his νοῦς. But the context speaks rather in favour of the active sense: it does not produce fruit. The understanding, not deriving from this state any new idea, produces nothing, that is to say, has nothing to communicate to others.[1] The conclusion is drawn in ver. 15.

Ver. 15. The question: *What is it then?* invites the readers to find the conclusion for themselves. What will it be? To exclude ecstasy and speaking in tongues? By no means, but to complete the pneumatic transport by the exercise of the understanding: to pray in the spirit, there is the tongue; to pray in full self-possession, there is the interpretation. The understanding here fills, in a manner, in relation to the tongue, the part of the *prophet*, when, in the heathen world, he interpreted the mysterious oracles given forth by the Pythia.—The reading προσεύξωμαι, *let me pray*, would express an encouragement addressed by the apostle to himself; which is wholly out of place. As Edwards says, the best MSS. often confound ο and ω; and if this were an exhortation, it would require to be in the plural.—We here find two of the principal forms of glossolalia described from the standpoint of their contents: *prayer*, προσευχή, intense aspiration after the fulness of the blessings assured to faith; and *singing*, ψαλμός (comp. ver. 26), the joyful celebration of all the favours already received. The verb ψάλλειν (from

[1] The Jewish philosopher Philo thus describes the inspiration of the prophet: "Natural reason is banished by the coming of the Divine Spirit, and it returns when He goes. For," he adds, "what is mortal and what is immortal cannot dwell together." Paul would not have approved of such a psychology; and in any case it is not to prophecy, but to speaking in tongues, and only to a certain extent, that this description, according to him, would have applied.

ψάω) strictly signifies to touch the chord of the instrument, hence to sing with accompaniment. The singing of improvised hymns was therefore one of the principal forms of speaking in tongues. Edwards, agreeably to the strict sense of ψάλλειν, thinks that the singing might be accompanied in public worship with the sound of the harp; comp. Eph. v. 19, where ψάλλοντες is distinguished from ᾄδοντες.—*Benediction*, εὐλογία, or *thanksgiving*, εὐχαριστία (ver. 16), is closely related to this form, from which it differs only by the absence of singing. Pliny says of the Christians, in his letter to Trajan, that in their worship they are accustomed *Christo quasi deo carmen dicere;* but this expression refers to the hymns of the whole Church (Col. iii. 16; Eph. v. 18–20), and not at all to the singing of the glossolaletes.—From the unfruitfulness of glossolalia, when not followed by interpretation, there arises for the Church a situation, the awkwardness of which the apostle expresses in the words which follow, vers. 16–19.

Vers. 16, 17. "Since, if thou blessest[1] in[2] spirit, how shall he that occupieth the room of the stranger say Amen at thy giving of thanks, seeing he understandeth not what thou sayest? 17. For thou verily givest thanks well, but the other is not edified."—The ἐπεί, *since*, relates to this thought understood: "And indeed we must act thus (add interpretation to speaking in a tongue), since if . . ." Paul here substitutes the second person (*thou*) for the first, because in ver. 15 he

[1] T. R. with F G K L: ευλογησης (*if thou hast blessed*); the rest: ευλογης (*if thou blessest*).

[2] B D E P read εν (*in*), which is omitted by the rest, and T. R. with A L read τω before πνευματι.

states what he thinks he ought to do himself, whereas in ver. 16 he supposes an interlocutor acting in an opposite way whom he wishes to convince of his mistake.—It was customary in the synagogue, at the close of a prayer, for all the audience to appropriate the contents of it, solemnly adhering to it by the *Amen* (Deut. xxvii. 15 seq.; Neh. viii. 6). Justin (1*st Apol.*) affirms the continuance of this usage in the Church: "After the president has closed the prayers and thanksgivings, all the people present express their assent by saying: Amen! Now the Amen in Hebrew signifies: So let it be!" See in Edwards the similar passages from Tertullian, Cyril, Jerome, etc. This form of worship became an empty formality when the congregation had not understood the meaning of the benediction pronounced.—On benediction, as the matter of ecstatic discourses, compare the expressions in the Acts: "speaking the wonderful works of God" (ii. 11); "magnifying God" (x. 46).—The expression: *he that occupieth the room of*, ὁ ἀναπληρῶν τὸν τόπον, must not be referred, as several interpreters have done, to this or that special portion of the audience, whether heathen who had come out of curiosity or from religious interest, or immature Christians, catechumens (Heinrici). Paul thus designates all the members of the Church, because in this situation they play the part of unintelligent hearers in relation to the glossolalete. The word ἰδιωτής strictly designates the purely private individual, in opposition to the man in office; hence, in all domains, the man who is unacquainted with the business on hand, the apprentice, the private soldier, the ignorant man. Heinrici mentions the fact that it was used in the language of the religious corporations of Greece to denote one who was not yet a member of the society. Paul therefore means that the glossolalete who speaks without interpreting, makes the congregation play a *part* similar to that of the strangers or semi-strangers who were sometimes present at their assemblies, and did not understand the ordinary Christian addresses. Now this, according to him, is to be wanting in courtesy (ἀσχημονεῖν, xiii. 5). The word τόπος, *room, place,* does not point to a fixed place occupied by non-Christians in the assemblies. It is here taken figuratively: to fill the function, to play the part of; comp. Acts i. 25 (λαβεῖν τὸν τόπον); and in Clement's *Epistle to the Corinthians,* c. 63: τὸν ὑπακοῆς τόπον ἀναπληροῦν, to fill a position of dependence (Edwards). Such is also the meaning of the corresponding Hebrew expression (*male mekom*). Josephus (*Bell. Jud.* v. 2, 5) says, in speaking of Titus, who, in a surprise, had required to draw his sword and do the part of a private soldier, that his friends begged him "not στρατιώτου τάξιν ἀποπληροῦν, him, their commander and the lord of the earth." The military term τάξις, *rank,* naturally takes the place in this passage of the ordinary word τόπος. The impropriety of which the glossolalete is thus guilty toward the Church (xiii. 5) comes out clearly from the question at the close of the verse. The article τό should be remarked before ἀμήν: "*the* Amen," the Amen by which the whole assembly is accustomed to appropriate the prayer of one of its members. If the Church is thus to give its assent to the thanksgiving uttered, it must understand it. The term εὐχαριστία, *thanksgiving,* is the equivalent of εὐλογία, *benediction.* If there is a shade of difference in their meaning, it is this, the first refers rather to Divine benefits personally received; the second, to the Divine perfections considered in themselves and celebrated for their own sublimity.

Ver. 17. The σύ, *thou,* and the καλῶς, *well,* are slightly ironical. The expression *the other* denotes all the members of the congregation taken individually.—The apostle, in ver. 6, put his own case to prove the uselessness of tongues without prophecy; here he alleges it again in proof of the uselessness of tongues unaccompanied with interpretation.

Vers. 18, 19. "I thank[1] God,[2] I speak[3] in tongues[4] more than ye all; 19. yet in the Church I had rather speak five words with my understanding,[5] that I might teach others also, than ten thousand words in tongues."—The apostle means by ver. 18 that he by no means disdains the gift of tongues, so highly prized at Corinth; he even thanks God for having bestowed it on him richly. These words have been understood in two ways; by some: "I give thanks, I bless, I adore, in the form of discoursing in tongues, more than you all." In this sense, we should have to prefer the reading λαλῶν, *speaking,* of the T. R. or that of the *Alexandrinus,* which simply rejects the word λαλῶ or λαλῶν: "I give thanks in tongues, more than you all." But I think it probable that these two poorly supported

[1] T. R. with A L adds μου (*my* God).

[2] F G It. Syr. here add οτι (*for this that*).

[3] ℵ B D E F G P read λαλω (*I speak*); T. R. with K L: λαλων (*speaking*). A omits this word.

[4] T. R. with B K L P Syr.: γλωσσαις (*tongues*); the rest: γλωσση (*tongue*).

[5] T. R. with K L: δια του νοος μου; the other eight: τω νοι μου.

readings are corrections whereby it has been sought to give the word εὐχαριστεῖν the same meaning as it had in ver. 17: to thank God in an ecstatic discourse. The true reading is undoubtedly λαλῶ, *I speak.* This verb would require in strictness to be connected with the foregoing εὐχαριστῶ, *I give thanks,* by the conjunction ὅτι, *for the fact that* (as is the case in the reading of F G); but very often in classical Greek this conjunction is omitted, and the two verbs are simply put in juxtaposition: "*I give thanks, I speak . . .*" for: "I give thanks for the fact that I speak." This is probably the true reading. Moreover, this meaning might also be that of the reading λαλῶν.—We must, with the Alex. and Greco-Lats., reject the μου after θεῷ, for which there is no sufficient ground in the context.—There is room for hesitation between the plural (*tongues*) and the singular. Both readings are admissible. But what is inconceivable is, how Meyer in such a passage can still apply the term *tongue* to the material organ: Paul giving thanks to God because he speaks more than all the Corinthians by means of his tongue! And if we read the plural, then this meaning becomes altogether absurd (comp. ver. 5).—It should be remarked that he does not say: "Because I speak in *more* tongues than you all;" as he would require to do if he was thinking of actually existing foreign tongues; but: "Because I speak in tongues *more than* you all." It is a mode of speaking in which he surpasses them all.

Ver. 19. After paying this homage to glossolalia, the apostle consigns this gift to its place. This place is the domain of private edification, not public worship.

The emphasis is on the word ἐν ἐκκλησίᾳ, *in the assembly.* The contents of the verse are explained by ver. 4: He that speaks in tongues edifies himself; but he gives nothing to the Church.—In the reading τῷ νοΐ μου, the words denote the mental state of the speaker (*of sober sense*). In the received reading (διὰ τοῦ νοός μου), the νοῦς, *the understanding,* comes in as the instrument of assimilation by means of which the intuitions of the prophet and the thoughts suggested to the teacher are conveyed to the Church. The *also* before ἄλλους signifies: "Not only myself, as would be the case with the gift of tongues, but others also."—In the form θέλω ἤ, the ἤ, *than,* depends on the idea of comparison contained in θέλω. Classic Greek thus uses ἤ with θέλω and βούλομαι (see Edwards). The verb κατηχεῖν, to make a sound penetrate to the ears of any one, comes thus to signify *to instruct, catechise.* The term includes the two gifts of prophecy and teaching. The apostle concludes this whole development with a saying intended to lead the imprudent and frivolous Corinthians to serious reflection.[1]

[1] To the extract from the work of Hohl, I shall here add the following passages from the work of E.-A. Rossteuscher on the history of the Irvingite Church, published under the title: *Der Aufbau der Kirche auf den ursprünglichen Grundlagen* (2nd ed., 1886): "The speaking in a tongue lasts longer or shorter, five minutes at most. Sometimes it is only a few words, as it were the first outburst of the manifestation; it is, so to speak, the hidden source from which there comes afterwards in the intelligible part of the discourse the stream of life, fitted to water the Church. It is always a deeply felt kind of speech, which evidently fills the whole soul of the speaker. The discourse is accompanied sometimes with tears and groans, sometimes with cries of joy and even laughter. The speaking is regularly formed, and markedly rhythmical. . . . It is uttered with a force and a fulness of voice and often with a rapidity foreign to the person's ordinary mode of expression. They are accents which shake the soul, and pierce the heart as prophecy itself cannot do.

Ver. 20. "Brethren, become not children in understanding: howbeit in malice be ye children, and in understanding be men." — The address *brethren*, is fitted to bring them back to the feeling of Christian dignity which had been singularly weakened in them. The μὴ γίνεσθε, *become not*, gives it to be understood that this abandonment to a sort of childishness has already begun among them. It is indeed the characteristic of the child to prefer the amusing to the useful, the brilliant to the solid. And this is what the Corinthians did by their marked taste for glossolalia, and the sort of disdain they testified for prophecy and still more for teaching. The word φρήν, strictly *the diaphragm*, denotes the physical seat of the action of the νοῦς, the understanding. The νοῦς is the faculty of the soul (ψυχή), whereby the latter discerns spiritually as by the eye it discerns physically. The apostle adds, not without an allusion to all those defects in charity with which he has had to charge them in the course of the Epistle: "If you will be children, well and good, provided it be in malice; but as to understanding, advance

The voice acquires a majesty found nowhere else. . . . One of the inspired said to Irving: 'When I am seized by the Spirit, and lifted into the presence of God as one speaking with tongues, it is as if a covering were dropped over all that surrounds me, and as if I no longer saw anything except the goal of my aspiration and the way leading to it. . . . I feel myself shut in with God, hidden in His tent, secure from all the suggestions of the world, the flesh and the devil. . . .' Another of the inspired, M. D., thus described the spiritual contents of the state: 'The intimate perception of the presence of God in Christ, and of my own state in Jesus, with a torrent of joy which words cannot describe. . . . In this state, self-consciousness blends with the consciousness of God without being lost in it. The inspired one is conscious of his own existence and of a power superior to his existence with the same clearness. This inward state remains the same during the unintelligible and the intelligible part of the discourse."

more and more toward full maturity." Malice, *κακία*, has its seat in the heart, not in the understanding.—What an exhortation to people so proud of their wisdom! The words, Rom. xvi. 19, have some resemblance to these, but without offering the humiliating side contained in our passage.

Before going further, let us sum up the course of this discussion: Paul began with proving, that in respect of usefulness, the gift of tongues is inferior to prophecy (vers. 1–5). Then, advancing a step, he showed that without interpretation this gift becomes even entirely useless (vers. 6 – 15). He went still further; he proved, in the third place, that to exercise it in this way, is to commit a real impropriety against the Church (vers. 16–19); finally, he concluded, ver. 20, with an appeal to the good sense of his readers.

Throughout this whole exposition, the apostle has considered the exercise of gifts only from the standpoint of their usefulness to the members of the Church; but in their assemblies for worship, there was another element requiring to be taken into account; this was the strangers, not yet gained or only half gained for the faith, and whom it was necessary to avoid alienating by giving them offence. It is with a view to such persons that the apostle treats the question in the sequel. Ver. 20 is at once the preface to this new development and the conclusion of the foregoing.

Vers. 21–25

Ver. 21. "In the law it is written: With men of other tongues and lips of strangers[1] will I speak unto

[1] ℵ A B read ετερων (*of others*), instead of ετεροις (*other*).

this people; and yet for all that will they not hear me."—The absurdity, the puerility of the preponderating use of tongues in the assemblies is demonstrated from this new point of view. Paul introduces the subject by quoting Isaiah xxviii. 11, 12. He calls the book of the prophets *the law*, as is sometimes done in the New Testament; comp. ver. 34, and John x. 34. This wide meaning of the word *law* is due to the feeling that all the other parts of the Old Testament rest on the law, and themselves form law for believers. —This passage from Isaiah seems at the first glance to have no connection with the gift of tongues; for it applies in the prophetic context to foreign nations, particularly the Assyrians, by whose invading forces God will visit His people, after having sought in vain to bring them to Himself by the words of the prophets. It does not take long, however, in the closer study of the parallel, to understand its meaning. As to this rude and unintelligible language which, according to Isaiah, God will hold with His people, by giving them over to strange and cruel nations, it is the unbelief of His people, in the words of the prophets, which will force Him to use it; if the Israelites had listened to the prophets with faith, God would not have required to speak to them in strange tongues. So it is with glossolalia, says the apostle; this speaking in unintelligible tongues, which has suddenly sprung up in this new era of the kingdom of God, is the evidence of a separation on God's part, not certainly from those who speak in tongues, but from those to whom He thus speaks. The fact, indeed, proves that the intelligible revelation of God has not been received as it ought to have been. As is well said by Kling: "When God speaks intelligibly, it is *to reveal* [open] Himself to His people; when He speaks unintelligibly, it is because He must *hide* [close] Himself from them." Pentecost will be cited as an objection, where the gift of tongues appears as a blessing of grace, not as a sign of the Divine displeasure. But, first of all, on that day interpretation accompanied tongues, and transformed them immediately into preaching; but especially speaking in tongues, as it broke forth on that day, had a wholly different signification for believers from that which it had for the mass of the Jewish people. In regard to Israel, which had rejected the preaching in good Hebrew which Jesus had addressed to it for three years, this strange phenomenon was a beginning of rupture, a certification of unbelief. God, while continuing to appeal to it, now addressed Himself to other nations; the people of God was on the eve of its rejection.

The apostle's text differs considerably from the translation of the LXX., which is altogether inaccurate; it also differs from the Hebrew text itself. It is a free reproduction, exactly corresponding, in the first part, to the meaning of the Hebrew, but differing from it sensibly in the last words. The Hebrew says: "And they would not hear;" which applies to the unbelief of the people in regard to the ancient prophetical revelations; while in Paul the words: *and yet for all that will they not hear me*, apply to the conduct of the unbelieving people in regard to the tongues themselves, as is proved by the: *and yet for all that.* The idea expressed by Paul is, therefore, that this new means, tongues, will fail as well as the former; in Isaiah, prophetical preaching; in Paul, evangelical preaching. How can we help thinking here of the persevering unbelief of Israel, even after Pentecost, an unbelief of which, after Palestine, the whole world, Greece itself, was at that moment the theatre? Paul does not mean that this plan will absolutely fail, and with all. Otherwise why should God still use it? But the use of such means supposes, not faith, but unbelief in those to whom it is applicable? What folly then, what puerility on the part of the Corinthians, to show a strong predilection for a sign of this kind in the worship of believers! It matters little whether we read ἑτέροις (other lips) with the Greco-Lats. and the Byz., or ἑτέρων (lips of others) with the Alex.—Applying the words of Isaiah, as he does here, Paul is led to the following conclusion:

Ver. 22. "Wherefore tongues are for a sign, not to them that believe, but to them that believe not: but prophesying serveth not for them that believe not, but for them which believe."—At the first glance one might be disposed to take the former part of the verse as indicating the salutary effect which glossolalia should produce in those who hitherto had not been able to believe (ἀπίστοις), through the wonder and amazement which such a gift will cause them (Chrysostom, Calvin hesitatingly, Grotius, Meyer in his first editions). But this meaning would be contrary to the words: *And yet for all that will they not hear;* and the example quoted in ver. 23, instead of justifying, would belie this affirmation. Others, on the contrary, have thought that the language points to a sign announcing to unbelievers their near judgment, *iræ signum* (Beza, Billroth). This is also Edwards' view: "The ecstatic cries in the midst of the assembled Church were intended by God to show unbelievers (the heathen of Corinth) that the day of the Lord was near." In this sense, the ἄπιστοι are not merely people who have not yet believed; they are confirmed unbelievers. Without saying precisely that judgment is announced, we think that tongues are a testimony of unbelief made to the people to whom God thus speaks. God speaks to them unintelligibly only because they are deaf to His clear revelation. We find an analogous fact, Matt. xiii., at the date when Jesus adopts speaking in parables as His habitual method of teaching (vers. 11, 12). After seeking in vain to awake the conscience of the people by His previous teaching (Sermon on the Mount, for example), when Jesus comes to the time when He must reveal to His own the nature and laws of the kingdom which they are to labour to found, He uses the language of parable, which they alone can understand. It is a sign of His growing breach with the mass of the nation. So it is with tongues. Glossolalia is neither a means of conversion, nor a sign of approaching judgment on unbelievers. It is a demonstration given to their own conscience of the state of unbelief which God sees them to have reached. Would a God of light manifest Himself in the midst of His own by unintelligible sounds? Here there is a sign of severance which is gradually carried out.

It is wholly otherwise with prophetic exhortations. These are a sign of faith or of the disposition to believe which already exists in those to whom God thus speaks.

It should be remarked that in opposition to ἀπίστοις, *unbelievers,* the apostle does not here say πιστοῖς, *believers,* as would seem natural, but πιστεύουσιν, *those who* at this moment *are in the act of believing.* This present participle denotes equally the state of a man who has just reached faith, and the state of him who already possesses it. Hence the general principle laid down here agrees with the result described in ver. 24, where an ἄπιστος is brought to faith by prophecy. The man is so called only as not yet believing, and because of his state when he came; he is nevertheless a πιστεύων in respect of what takes place in him, in the course of the meeting.—Critics discuss the question whether the words εἰς σημεῖον, *in sign of,* used in the former clause, should be understood in the latter. It matters very little for the sense. Grammatically the ellipsis seems natural. But the meaning of the word *sign* is modified of course in passing from the one clause of the sentence to the other. In the former, the sign is one of displeasure, implying a charge of unbelief; in the latter, it is one of pity, powerfully calling the man to repentance and faith. Such an appeal is not directed to one already confirmed in unbelief (the ἄπιστοι of ver. 22); but it is made to men such as the ἄπιστος of ver. 23. Erasmus and Bleek have tried to resolve the difficulties of this verse by taking οὐ, *not,* both times in the sense of οὐ μόνον, *not only.* But why not say οὐ μόνον, if this had been his thought?

The apostle now supposes two cases fitted to impress by way of extreme examples the truth of the law which he has just stated:

Ver. 23. "If therefore the whole Church be come

together into one place, and all speak in tongues, and there come in novices, or unbelievers,[1] will they not say that ye are mad?"—This is the first case: an assembly in which only glossolaletes speak.—*Into one place* is related to *the whole.* These plenary assemblies were held doubtless only at more or less considerable intervals; they attracted more strangers and others out of curiosity than the more private gatherings. Those whom Paul here calls ἄπιστοι, *unbelievers,* and ἰδιῶται, *novices,* are people who do not yet belong to the Church. By the second, Meyer and others understand Christians who have neither the gift nor the knowledge of tongues. But how, Rückert rightly asks, could these people be contrasted with *the whole Church?* Meyer supports his view by the use of ἰδιώτης, ver. 16, where he holds that this term denotes the members of the Church themselves. But this is a mistake. What is said in ver. 16, that the glossolalete makes the members of the Church play the part of ἰδιῶται, proves precisely that the ἰδιῶται are not members of the Church. The impropriety consists in giving the members of the Church a part which is not theirs. On the other hand, Hirzel,[2] Rückert, and Holsten thereby understand non-Christians. But how distinguish them in that case from the ἄπιστοι, *unbelievers?* Hirzel proposes to apply the first term to non-Christians of Jewish origin, the second to those of Gentile origin. But this distinction is unfounded. Starting from the simple meaning of ἰδιώτης (ver. 16), we get at a perfectly natural distinction. The ἄπιστος is an *unbeliever* whom curiosity has attracted, but who has not yet given

[1] B omits η απιστοι.

[2] *Studien und Kritiken,* 1840.

any sign of faith ; the ἰδιώτης is a novice, an *apprentice* in the domain of faith, a man who has already received some impression and some instruction, but who is not yet baptized, we should say nowadays : a catechumen. Such people, in the exercise of plain common sense, will ask how, if God dwelt there as a Father in the midst of His children, He could speak to them in an unintelligible language : "You shall appear to them madmen, not subjects of inspiration."—Edwards, with some ancient commentators, thinks that the πάντες, *all*, means that the glossolaletes speak all at once, and that the confusion which follows, no less than the unintelligibility of the tongues, is the cause of the impression made on the visitors. But the perfectly analogous expression in regard to prophecy, ver. 24, proves that it is not necessary to give this so improbable meaning to the πάντες of ver. 23. Paul wishes to describe an assembly where there is room for nothing except manifestations of glossolalia, succeeding one another without interruption during the whole meeting. Then the opposite example :

Vers. 24, 25. "But if all prophesy, and there come in one that believeth not, or a novice, he is convinced of all, he is judged of all ; 25. the[1] secrets of his heart are made manifest ; and so falling down on his face he will worship God, and report that God is in you of a truth."—We have just seen the effect of tongues without prophecy ; now, on the contrary, we have what prophecy will do without tongues.—The novice and the unbeliever enter, as in ver. 23, during the meeting. Paul here uses the singular

[1] K L read here και ουτω (*and thus*), which is omitted by all the rest.

instead of the plural (ver. 23); no doubt because the fact he is about to describe will have a purely individual character. It may be thought with Hofmann, that if ἄπιστος is here placed first, the effect is: the unbeliever, and *à fortiori*, the novice. The latter, indeed, was already better prepared to feel the power of prophetic speech, while at ver. 23 it was the reverse: the novice, and *à fortiori*, the unbeliever. Three effects are ascribed to prophecy: conviction, ἔλεγχος; examination, ἀνάκρισις; manifestation, φανέρωσις.—The word ἐλέγχειν signifies *to convince* of error or sin. Every utterance of a prophet is like a flash, lighting up the heart of the hearer and discovering to him in a general way his guilt and defilement.—The word ἀνακρίνεσθαι is not fully rendered by the translation: *is judged;* the Greek term rather denotes the detailed inquiry than the sentence pronounced. His whole inner man is searched, so to speak, by the words of the prophets.

Ver. 25. Then a sudden penetrating illumination, spread over his whole life, is produced in him: he sees himself, as a whole and in the particular details of his life, as God sees him. One might apply this description to the revelation of certain particular circumstances of his life, as when Elisha speaks to Gehazi (2 Kings v. 26), or Jesus to Nathanael and to the Samaritan woman (John i. and iv.). But it is simpler to think here of a moral illumination, similar to that of the judgment, which shows a man his past and present state in its true light. What passes in him at such a moment resembles what passed in Paul on the way to Damascus. Struck by this light, he casts himself in the dust, not before man, but before God, acknowledging that such brightness can only proceed from the Holy of holies and the Searcher of hearts; that consequently it is He who speaks by the mouth of those into the midst of whom He has come.—The participle ἀπαγγέλλων, *reporting*, may refer only to what passes at the time in the assembly itself; it is a cry escaping from him under the power of overwhelming emotion: "Yes, God is among you of a truth!" But this declaration may be regarded also as extending after his departure from the assembly to those whom he meets.—The ἐν ὑμῖν may signify: *among you;* but in this context, where inspiration is the matter in question, perhaps it is more natural to explain it: *in you.* So Meyer, Edwards, etc. —By the ὄντως, *really*, the man recognises that the claim of Christians to Divine inspiration is well-founded. Here is the opposite of the μαίνεσθε, *ye are mad* (ver. 23). The apostle could not better close the discussion on the relative value of the gifts of tongues and of prophecy than by these two examples; and now he can go on to lay down the practical rules which will secure the salutary use of these gifts.

2. *Rules for the exercise of gifts* (vers. 26–40)

Ver. 26. "How is it then, brethren? when ye come together, every one[1] of you hath a psalm, hath a doctrine, hath a revelation, hath a discourse in a tongue,[2] hath an interpretation.[3] Let all things be

[1] T. R. with D E F G K L Syr. add υμων (*of you*).

[2] T. R. with L put γλωσσαν εχει (*hath a discourse in a tongue*) before αποκαλυψιν (*hath a revelation*). K rejects these words.

[3] D E F G: διερμηνειαν instead of ερμηνειαν.

done unto edifying."—The meaning of the question: *How is it then?* is the same as in ver. 15. The apostle would lead his readers themselves to draw the conclusions which flow from the principles laid down. Fundamental rule: No gift should be set aside. Every manifestation of the Spirit ought to have its place; enough that all turn to edification. The ἕκαστος ἔχει, *every one hath,* should be understood like the similar phrase i. 12; every one has not all, but every one ought or at least may have something. The proposition may be taken interrogatively. But it is better perhaps to understand it in the sense of a tentative affirmation: "If so be." The repetition of the verb brings out, as Bengel says, the distribution of gifts. The apostle enumerates five of these manifestations. The ψαλμός, *psalm,* is not here a chant in the form of a tongue, the *singing in the spirit,* of ver. 15. For special mention is afterwards made of discoursing in a tongue and of its interpretation. It is therefore a psalm, like those spoken of in Col. iii. 16 and Eph. v. 19 (*psalms, hymns, spiritual songs*); a singing ἐν νοΐ, *with sober mind* (ver. 15), as is suitable to the opening of worship. It seems to me improbable that Paul has in view an Old Testament psalm or an already existing Christian hymn, recited or sung. The word ἔχειν, *to have,* does not prevent its being an improvisation. For, as is observed by Holsten, the term is afterwards applied to a *tongue* and its *interpretation,* which are immediate products of the Spirit's working.[1]—The

[1] Heinrici quotes a remarkable parallel from Philo. The latter says in regard to the Therapeutæ: "After the speaker another rises and sings a hymn addressed to God, either one newly composed by himself, or one of the ancient hymns made by the poets of other days."

διδαχή, *doctrine*, naturally comes after the psalm-singing, being the solid basis of worship. In a religion of light, everything ought to rest on clear and exact instruction. Here is the word of knowledge or wisdom spoken of xii. 8.—According to the MS. L and the received text, there would now follow discourse in tongues, thanksgiving in the transport of ecstasy; but the Alex. and Greco-Lats. here place the ἀποκάλυψις, the *revelation*, expressed in a prophecy. In the first reading there would be a contrast: the calmest element, instruction, would be followed by the most emotional, the most excited, discoursing in a tongue. This order is less natural than that of the second reading, according to which doctrine is followed by a revelation, that is to say, a prophecy. The latter is already characterized by an immediate inspiration more pronounced and extraordinary. What further speaks in favour of this last reading, is the fact that it would be unnatural were speaking in tongues to be separated from interpretation by prophecy. The Byz. K, which almost always coincides with L, entirely omits the words γλῶσσαν ἔχει, *hath a tongue;* it is therefore probable that they were supplied in L, but misplaced by the corrector.—To revelation there is naturally attached speaking in a *tongue;* it is the highest degree of the ecstatic state, consequently the culminating point of worship; after which *interpretation*, which follows, closes by leading adoration back to that state of calm reflection in which the worship had begun (the psalm) and ought to finish. Thus it is that feeling rises by steps as to the third heaven, to return at the close to practical life. We have therefore in this series of actions the type of normal worship, in which all the elements of understanding and feeling are united, and in which every believer endowed from above can give free scope to his particular gift. It is a spiritual banquet, so to speak, to which every guest brings his quota, just as in the agapæ (xi. 20 seq.).—The apostle now passes to the special rules relating to the exercise of glossolalia.

VERS. 27, 28

Vers. 27, 28. "If any man speak in a tongue, let it be by two, or at the most by three, and each in his course; and let one interpret. 28. But if there be no interpreter,[1] let him keep silence in the Church; and let him speak to himself, and to God."—In Greek this verse begins with the word εἴτε, *whether*, to which there should be a corresponding εἴτε applied to prophecy (ver. 29). This form very pointedly betrays the accidental (by no means indispensable) character of glossolalia in worship.—The apostle gives three rules regarding this gift. The first relative to *number: two or at most three;* as if two were quite sufficient. The κατά is distributive: two or three each meeting. Edwards thinks that what is referred to here is an antiphony, expressed by ἀνὰ μέρος, *in turn*, as if a duet of glossolaletes was intended. It was this style of performance, in his view, which gave rise to the later antiphonic chants, such as those of which Pliny speaks in his letter to Trajan. How far will the imagination go! Certainly Paul would never have approved of the simultaneous utterance of several discourses, the one hindering the effect of the other. Besides, ἐν μέρει

[1] B D F G: ερμηνευτης, instead of διερμηνευτης.

would have been required to express the sense given by Edwards (see Passow).—The second rule relates to *order: ἀνὰ μέρος, each in course,* consequently: one at a time. The contrary, no doubt, sometimes happened at Corinth. The form ἀνὰ μέρος signifies, like ἐν τῷ μέρει: in determinate order, in his turn, but not: answering one another. — The third rule fixes the *mode;* the tongue ought to be followed by an interpretation. The expression εἷς, *one,* seems to signify that one and the same interpreter ought to act for the two or three discourses in tongues; no doubt to prevent discussions as to the meaning of any one of the discourses. The apostle does not say whether this interpreter is himself one of the glossolaletes, as might be held in accordance with vers. 5 and 13, or if he is some other inspired one, as might be supposed from ver. 28 and xii. 10. Both cases might occur. Holsten alleges that interpretation took place only in the case of one of the three tongues, and by the same man who had spoken in it. But this meaning is contrary to vers. 5 and 28, which expressly exclude the use of a tongue without interpretation.

Ver. 28. The first words have sometimes been translated: "But *if he is not* an interpreter." But it would be impossible to say to which of the two or three glossolaletes the words should be applied, and the position of the verb ᾖ before the predicate shows that it is the idea of *being* which is emphasized. The simple ᾖ is therefore for παρῇ; comp. Luke v. 17; and the translation must be: *But if there be no interpreter.* Holsten objects that it was impossible to know beforehand the absence of all interpreters, because interpretation was not an office invariably attached to this or that person. But, on the contrary, the necessary conclusion from the passage is that the gift was more or less permanent, whether it belonged as a rule to one of the glossolaletes or to some other of the members of the Church. This view is confirmed by xii. 10.—If every believer known to be endowed with this faculty is absent, and the glossolalete does not himself interpret, he is to keep silence in the congregation. But the apostle would not have him to suppress the moving of the Spirit; for himself he may yield to the impulse to thanksgiving and mental prayer which has taken possession of him and raises him to God.—There follow the rules regarding the exercise of *prophecy*.

Vers. 29–33[a]

Vers. 29, 30. "As to the prophets, let them speak two or three, and let the[1] others judge.[2] 30. And if anything be revealed to another that sitteth by, let the first hold his peace."—The εἴτε, *whether*, which we expect to correspond to the εἴτε of ver. 27, changes into a simple δέ, *but* or *as to*, and that no doubt because, if the presence of glossolaletes is accidental and uncertain, that of prophets is a fact which does not seem doubtfül.—Paul again lays down three rules: The first, as to *number*. By saying simply *two or three*, suppressing the τὸ πλεῖστον, *at most* (comp. ver. 27), Paul shows that he accepts the number

[1] ℵ A B E K read οι before αλλοι (*the others*), whereas D F G L omit οι (*others*).

[2] Instead of διακρινετωσαν (*judge*), D F G read ανακρινετωσαν (*make inquiry*).

three, in the case of prophets, more easily than in the case of tongues.—The second rule relates to *mode;* prophecy, like tongues, has its necessary complement: discernment, that judgment by which any impure elements, which might have found their way into it, were to be described as such and removed. It should be borne in mind that as yet there was neither a written Word nor a body of doctrine strictly formulated. All was in course of formation; it belonged to prophecy itself to bring the new elements which were afterwards to be elaborated and ordered by διδασκαλία, *teaching.* How important, then, was it that no strange mixture should be cast, if one may so speak, into the molten mass! Hence the importance of a διάκρισις, *discernment*, a trial of the ideas expressed in the prophecies which were addressed to the congregation.—By whom was this judgment exercised? Some have thought that the term οἱ ἄλλοι, *the others,* could only designate the other *prophets;* but in that case should we not rather have οἱ λοιποί, *the rest* of the prophets? Melanchthon thought that the word applied to all the members of the Church, and the view seems to me to be in a certain measure correct. Of course in practice such an office, in which every one had the right to take part, could only be carried out by means of the most capable, especially the *teachers.* The passage 1 Thess. v. 20, 21, seems to confirm this wider meaning of the word *the others.* Meyer objects that διάκρισις was a gift (xii. 10), and that consequently every believer did not possess it. It is needless to say that the meaning of *the others* is limited by the possession of this gift. Only there is nothing to prove that the gift belonged only to the prophets themselves.—What was the standard of this judgment? It is not without reason, certainly, that the apostle began his whole exposition regarding spiritual gifts (xii. 1–3), by indicating the precise character which distinguishes true and false inspirations, mentioning that the first have for their common characteristic and essence the cry of adoration: *Jesus Lord!* while the others tend to the abasement and rejection of Jesus. It was enough, then, to bring every prophecy into connection with this centre of all Christian revelation, the person of Christ, and to see what was the tendency of the prophecy that had been heard, to disparage or to glorify Him. It is no doubt to this standard that Paul's expression Rom. xii. 6 applies, *the analogy of faith.* This judgment must consequently have mainly set aside everything in a prophetic discourse which could compromise the Divine sovereignty of Jesus over the world, the Church, and the individual soul. This is in harmony with the saying of Jesus, John xvi. 13, 14: "When the Spirit is come, *He will glorify Me.*"

Ver. 30. The third rule relates to *order*: If, while a prophet is speaking, another receives a revelation, both should not speak simultaneously; the first should keep silence. But, it will be asked, why should not the second rather wait till the first finished? Assuredly, because the freshest revelation will also produce the purest prophecy. It is by lengthening his discourse that the prophet is in danger of mixing what is *his own* with the Divine communication. The apostle's injunction is well fitted to set aside empty amplifications and verbiage.—The expression: *to another that sitteth by,* shows that the prophet speaking was standing, and that he to whom the new revelation is addressed testifies his intention to speak by rising. There is something strange in the impersonal and passive form ἀποκαλυφθῇ, *it is revealed to him;* it seems as if the cloud of Divine revelation were seen passing from over the one to the other.—It might be thought that the verb σιγᾷν, *to keep silence,* is used here in the sense of σιωπᾷν, *to become silent;* but it can have its natural meaning: "Let him from that moment keep silence." —It might seem presumptuous thus to regulate the manifestations of the prophetic spirit; hence the apostle in the following verses expressly justifies the liberty he takes of fixing a rigorous mode of procedure in such a domain, where everything seems to be given up to the incalculable breathing of the Spirit.

Vers. 31–33[a]. "For ye may all prophesy one by one, that all may learn, and all may be comforted. 32. And the spirits[1] of the prophets are subject to the prophets. 33[a]. For God is not a God of confusion, but of peace."—Ver. 31 might be understood in this sense: "Thus it may happen that those who prophesy to-day will in their turn be taught and exhorted to-morrow." Each member will alternately play an active and a passive part. But in that case Paul would have said: καὶ οὕτω, *and so,* rather than γάρ, *for.* The true meaning seems to me to be this: "For you must all have it in your power to fill the prophet's function one after another" (of course: those who have the gift of prophecy); now this is what could not be done except by

[1] D E F G read το πνευμα (*the Spirit*).

observing the rule given in ver. 30. Supposing, indeed, that a prophet had spoken indefinitely, he would have prevented the others from declaring what God revealed to them for the instruction or comfort of the Church. And thus is explained the second part of the verse: many members of the Church would have been deprived of the light and strength God wished to communicate to them by means of those other prophets who had been prevented from uttering their message. But this arrangement, of course, rested on a supposition: to wit, that the prophet was able to exercise the control necessary to restrain, if it was needed, the outburst of the prophetic inspiration which animated him. And this supposition the apostle now lays down as a reality in ver. 32.

Ver. 32. The καί here signifies: *and indeed.* The terms: *of the prophets* and *to the prophets,* have sometimes been referred to different persons, as if Paul meant that the prophets should be humble enough to subordinate themselves to the other prophets, either by accepting their judgment (ver. 29), or by consenting to give place to them (ver. 30). So Calvin, Bleek, Rückert, etc. But it would be impossible to explain on this view why Paul should say: "*the spirits* of the prophets," rather than the prophets themselves. And instead of *are subject* or *subject themselves,* it would require to run: *should subject themselves.* Hofmann also justly remarks that Paul would have said in this sense simply ἀλλήλοις: "should subject themselves *to one another.*" It is not without purpose that he brings the term *prophets* in the Greek into immediate contact with itself, as if to describe the reaction which every prophet is capable of producing on himself. The fact here enunciated by the apostle is of a psychological nature. He declares that the prophetical breathings or inspirations do not carry the prophet away without his consent or against his will. In chap. xii. 2, he began by reminding the Corinthians of the state of passivity to which they were formerly accustomed when, in the midst of heathenism, they were carried away blindly by diabolical inspirations. It is not so with the operation of the Divine Spirit; this does not deprive the prophet of his liberty. Consequently he has no right to make inspiration a pretext for refusing to submit to the rules laid down by the apostle. The plural πνεύματα, *spirits*, here denotes, as in ver. 12, the particular impulses and revelations granted to the prophets. Heinrici and Holsten contrast the prophet with the glossolalete, who, according to them, did not enjoy the same liberty in regard to his inspirations. This surely is a mistake; for vers. 27 and 28 would be unintelligible if he did not enjoy his full liberty in relation to the Spirit. Divine inspiration differs from diabolical, in the fact that the latter takes man from himself,—it is a possession,—whereas the former restores him to himself. The present ὑποτάσσεται signifies, not *are subject*, but *subject themselves*, and that at the very moment when the prophet wills it.

Ver. 33[a]. The general maxim stated in this verse is the foundation of all the preceding injunctions. The term ἀκαταστασία denotes the disorder of a whole whose parts are at strife with one another, and εἰρήνη, *peace*, harmony of a whole, all whose parts act in concert. God dwells only in a whole of this second kind. The axiom justifies the rules which Paul has been giving, for without them the Church could only present a spectacle of complete disorder, which would banish God out of it.

There remains a last injunction, also essential, in the apostle's view, to the good order of the Church, that regarding the speaking of women in the assemblies. Paul has purposely reserved this point for the last. For it was not till after imposing silence conditionally on the prophets that he could think of imposing it on women.

Vers. 33^{b}–38

Vers. 33^{b}–35. "As in all the Churches of the saints,[1] 34.[2] let your[3] women keep silence in the Churches: for it is not permitted[4] unto them to speak; but to be under obedience,[5] as also saith the law. 35. If they will learn anything, let them ask their own husbands at home: for it is a shame for women[6] to speak in the Church."—The last words of ver. 33 are joined, by many commentators, to what precedes. But how could Paul say: "God is not a God of confusion, but of peace, as in all the Churches of the saints"? He would have required to say: "God is *among you* a God . . .," or: "God is a God . . . as *is seen* in all the

[1] F G here add *διατασσομαι* (*I ordain*).

[2] These two verses, 34 and 35, are transposed by D E F G and Ambrosiaster after ver. 40.

[3] א A B omit *υμων* (*your*), which is read by T. R. with D E F G K L.

[4] T. R. with K: *επιτετραπται* (*was permitted*), instead of *επιτρεπεται* (*is permitted*).

[5] T. R. with D F G K L: *υποτασσεσθαι* (*to be subject*); A B: *υποτασσεσθωσαν* (*let them be subject*).

[6] T. R. with D E F G K L Syr.: *γυναιξιν* (*for women*); א A B: *γυναικι* (*for woman*).

Churches . . ." As they stand, the words: *as in all the Churches* . . ., cannot evidently depend on the preceding clause, which is a general maxim regarding the character of God. Besides, this clause is in close logical relation to the argument of ver. 36: "Did the Word go forth from you, or did it come to you only?" And it is this very thing, probably, which has led several Latin copyists to transpose vers. 34 and 35, putting them after ver. 40, in order thus to connect more directly the last words of ver. 33 with ver. 36. The addition of the verb *διατάσσομαι*, *I ordain*, to the end of ver. 33, in two of the Greco-Lat. MSS. which have made this transposition, is due to the same cause. From this point of view the clause was read as follows: "So *I ordain* in all the Churches of the saints;" then the text continued with ver. 36: "Or did the Word of God come out from you . . .?" In other terms: Do you think you have the right to put yourselves above the rules followed by all the other Churches? Thus the words of ver. 33^b^ and of ver. 36 were put as referring to all the rules given in this chapter regarding the use of glossolalia and prophecy; and as the injunction relative to women broke this connection, some Greco-Lat. documents were led to transpose vers. 33 and 34 after ver. 40. But it is to be remarked that no document rejects these verses, which guarantees their authenticity, wrongly suspected by Heinrici and positively attacked by Holsten. Moreover, the latter himself recognises the impossibility of connecting the last words of ver. 33 with the preceding context. Only he does not find the connection with the sequel much more tenable: because, says he, the word *Churches* in ver. 33 denotes the communities of believers, whereas in ver. 34 it can only designate their assemblies for worship. But these two meanings are so closely connected with one another, that they may perfectly well be used here side by side. "All the assemblies (groups of believers) have their customs; and to these customs belong the silence of women in the *assemblies* (meetings for worship)." This meaning is perfectly suitable. Holsten again asks why, if these words are really Paul's, we have here: "the Churches *of the saints*," and not, as in xi. 16: "the Churches *of God*." The answer is easy: The saints, distributed in Churches, locally speaking, yet form only one great spiritual whole; the Corinthians should not isolate themselves from this community of saints by adopting customs rejected by all the rest of the body, such as the speaking of women in the assemblies. The term ἅγιοι, *saints*, expresses the venerable character which belongs to such customs.

Ver. 34. Here we have the principal proposition, on which depends the ὡς . . ., *as* . . ., of ver. 33[b]. The pronoun ὑμῶν, *of you* (if it is authentic), must form an antithesis to τῶν ἁγίων, *of the saints*. It may be made dependent on the ταῖς ἐκκλησίαις, *in the assemblies*, which follows; in this sense: "Your assemblies should resemble those of the other saints." But it is more natural, seeing the position of the pronoun, to connect it with αἱ γυναῖκες, *women*. "Let *your* women behave like those of the saints in all the Churches." The authenticity of the word appears to me guaranteed by the combined authority of two of the three families of MSS., and by the support of the Peschito. Not being necessary to the clause, it was easily omitted.—There is a touch of irony in the following clause, if, with the T. R., we read the infinitive, ὑποτάσσεσθαι, *to be subject:* "It is not allowed to them to speak, but to be subject." This irony is in keeping with the context. It disappears if, with the Alex., we read the imperative: ὑποτασσέσθωσαν, *let them be subject!*—The words: *as saith the law,* refer to Gen. iii. 16: "Thy husband shall rule over thee." It is obvious that the apostle regards speaking in public as an act of authority exercised over the congregation which listens; comp. 1 Tim. ii. 12. And as the attitude of authority over the man is contrary to that of obedience which was imposed on the woman during the present economy, he draws the conclusion that the speaking of the woman in public is in contradiction to the position assigned to her by the Divine will expressed in the law. It is easy to see why the apostle substitutes the general idea: *to be subject,* which relates to the whole life of women, for that of *not speaking* in the assemblies; it is because the silence of women in worship is only an application of the general condition of subordination which is imposed on them in relation to man. Of course the law contained nothing regarding the part of women in the assemblies; but, by determining the character of their life in general, it had, according to Paul's view, indirectly settled the question. Comp. Col. iii. 18; Eph. v. 22. The καί, *also,* puts on the same level the apostle's precept (ver. 34[a]) and God's declaration in Genesis, so certain is Paul that he speaks as he does in virtue of the will of the Lord (ver. 37).—Here, as tacitly in ver. 19, the ἐν ἐκκλησίᾳ, *in Church,* is opposed to ἐν οἴκῳ, *at home,* in private. The word αἰσχρόν, *shameful, misbecoming,* seems very strong. Paul sees in the public speaking of woman a mode of acting contrary to the attitude enjoined on her both by nature and the command of the Creator; comp. xi. 1–16. He does not say criminal, immoral; it is a question of propriety or modesty.

Ver. 35. Several commentators, Heinrici for example, draw from this verse the conclusion that the speaking forbidden to women, ver. 34, is neither teaching, nor prophecy, nor discoursing in tongues, but solely the mania of raising questions in the assembly, and so posing as teachers under pretence of asking explanations. If they have questions to put, they should reserve them for the house, and address them to their husbands. But, even in this sense, the right to teach in the Church would be none the less denied to them by the apostle. For if women cannot put questions without going out of their sphere and shocking decorum, much less can they teach without committing an impropriety. But more than this: the meaning thus sought to be given to ver. 35, by restricting it by ver. 36, is contrary to the true relation between the two verses. The particle εἰ δέ, *and moreover if*, which begins ver. 35, introduces, not a simple explanation, but a gradation: "And even if they would learn something, they ought to abstain from asking in the congregation; they should reserve their questions to be submitted to their husbands in private." The form εἰ δέ, *and if*, is therefore founded on the fact that questioning was the case of least gravity, the one which seemed most naturally to admit of exception. But this very exception Paul rejects; for he knows how easily, under pretext of putting questions, women could elude the prohibition which forbade their public speaking. Woman belongs to the domestic hearth, so that a simple public question on her part would alone be an impropriety; for by putting her on a public stage, as it were, such an act would go contrary to the modesty of her destined sphere. To be remarked is the adjective ἰδίους, their *own* husbands; they ought to do nothing to affect the bond of dependence which unites each of them to *her* husband. Holsten asks how this applies to those who have husbands insufficiently instructed, or to those who have husbands yet heathen (chap. vii.), we may add: or to those who have no husband at all. But these last are regarded as living in the house of their parents, to whom they can naturally turn; and as to the others, they are special cases which will find their solution in practice, without Paul's needing to point it out. It is enough for him to settle in a summary way woman's moral position and duty.

Conclusion as to the preaching of women

In chap. xi. we have already treated of the relation of this prohibition to the authorisation granted to women to prophesy or pray, implicitly contained in ver. 5 of this chapter. Our study of chap. xiv. confirms the idea that the word λαλεῖν, *to speak,* in this chapter, cannot apply merely to simple questions, or vain gossiping, in which women might indulge with one another during worship. The term *speaking in the Church,* especially in a chapter where it is applied throughout to the glossolaletes and prophets, can only designate a public speaking, which has for its end to teach and edify. Thus, then, while referring to the observations presented on the subject in chapter xi., we think we shall not be far from the apostle's view if we thus state the result of the two passages taken together: "As to women, if, under the influence of a sudden inspiration or revelation, they wish to take the word in the assembly to give utterance to a prayer or prophecy, I do not object; only let them not do so without having the face veiled. But in general, let women keep silence. For it is improper on their part to speak in church."[1]

The apostle is not ignorant of the manifold opposition which this injunction will encounter in the Church. Vers. 36–38 are addressed to those who, on the ground of an alleged higher inspiration, would affect to despise the direction which he has just given, as well as all those which had gone before.

Vers. 36–38. "Or, indeed, came the Word of God out from you? or came it unto you only? 37. If any man think himself to be a prophet, or inspired, let him acknowledge that what I write unto you is from the Lord.[2] 38. But if any man be ignorant of it, let him be ignorant."[3]—The ἤ, *or* (ver. 36), signifies, as usual with Paul at the beginning of a question: "Or, indeed, if you will not admit what I say." For the two following questions, the apostle returns to the idea with which he had introduced the subject of the speaking of women: *As in all the Churches* . . . (ver. 33[b]).

[1] Does it follow from what we have said in regard to prophecy (that it has become transformed, in the course of the Church's development, into lively preaching, p. 250), that woman, authorised to prophesy, is by that very fact also authorised to preach? This would be to forget that what gave rise to the exception as to prophecy was its having the character of immediate and sudden revelation. This character having ceased, the ground of exception falls with it. The more preaching thereby approaches teaching, the more it comes under the mode of action reserved for man and forbidden to woman.

[2] D F G read κυριου εστιν (*is the Lord's*); ℵ A B: κυριου εστιν εντολη (*is a commandment of the Lord*); T. R. with K L Syr.: κυριου εισιν εντολαι (*are commandments of the Lord*).

[3] T. R. with B E K L Syr.: αγνοειτω (*let him be ignorant*); ℵ A D F G: αγνοειται (*he is ignored*).

"Or are you the mother Church in which the preaching of the gospel took its rise, and from which it spread through the world?" In that case one could understand how the Corinthians could affect complete independence. "Or are you the only Church among the Gentiles to which it has come?" In that case the claim to follow a course alone, and at their own pleasure, would also be intelligible. These two questions are somewhat sarcastic, as happens when one wishes to bring down presumption. The same is the case with the following verses. The apostle knows that there are leaders on the spot, who, in rivalry with him, claim to derive authority only from the Lord and from the immediate inspiration of the Spirit. Hence ver. 37.

Ver. 37. The term δοκεῖ εἶναι, *thinks himself to be*, denotes a claim true or false.—We must not give to the word πνευματικός, *spiritual*, hence *inspired*, too restricted a sense, according to which it would denote a class different from the prophets, as is done by the commentators who regard this term as designating only the glossolaletes (Baur, Heinrici). It is more natural to understand the ἤ, *or*, in the sense: *or in general*, as iv. 3, so that the term *spiritual* comprehends the prophets also. The best way for these organs of the Spirit to prove the reality of their inspiration will be, the apostle declares, their perceiving his superior wisdom and apostolic authority, not criticising his ordinances, but rendering practical homage to their excellence by conforming to them: the Spirit should acknowledge the Spirit.—The ἃ γράφω, *the things that I write*, is at once the object of ἐπιγινωσκέτω, *let him acknowledge*, and the subject of the following proposition: "Let him acknowledge the things that I write *as being*" . . . etc.—The three families of MSS. have each their own reading in the following clause. The shortest and most sober is that of the Greco-Lats.: "That the things which I write are *the Lord's*." The Alex. add the idea of commandment: "are a *commandment* of the Lord." So also the Byz., but putting the word commandment in the plural. One would naturally be inclined to give the preference to the first reading. But is it not possible that the word commandment, in the singular or plural, was rejected because it was taken in the meaning attached to it in vii. 10, to denote a precept uttered on the earth by the Lord Jesus, and because no such saying was found in the Gospels? If the term ἐντολή, *commandment*, is authentic, it is hard to know whether to prefer the singular or the plural. The singular may have been substituted for the plural from regard to the Divine precept quoted ver. 34. But the plural may also have been introduced in order better to bring under this term all the many preceding ordinances.—However that may be, the apostle here expresses the intimate consciousness he has of not having directed the Church, while settling these delicate questions, in ways of his own choice, but of having been guided by the light which is assured to him as an apostle charged with founding and governing the Church of the Gentiles; comp. Rom. xii. 3. It is with this elevated conviction of his apostolic inspiration that he adds the following words, ver. 38.

Ver. 38. There is more than indifference, there are severity and threatening in these words; they are addressed to the persons whose folly was characterized by the word δοκεῖ in the previous verse. "If there are among you people who reckon their ideas superior to mine, let them follow them!" Of course such speaking is not addressed to people with whom one is on good terms. We have to bear in mind the first chapters of the Epistle, where the apostle once and again alluded to the disrespectful sentiments of a party in the Church toward him; comp. also vii. 40.—The reading ἀγνοείτω, *let him be ignorant*, is the only admissible one. After all he has said, the apostle no longer seeks to convince those who think themselves wiser than he is; he abandons them at once to their inexperience and their responsibility. The reading ἀγνοεῖται, *he is ignored*, preferred by some commentators, and again recently by Heinrici, would signify: "Willing to be ignorant of God, he is ignored (rejected) by Him." Edwards regards ἀγνοεῖται as a future indicative middle: "he will be ignored (at the judgment)." Comp. viii. 3. It is difficult to explain the origin of this variant (see Meyer's attempt). But the threat of perdition for refusal to accept directions so external in their nature as those which precede would be rather severe. The reading ἀγνοείτω: "Let him be ignorant at his risk and peril!" is the only one worthy of the apostle, and really natural.—Paul closes with a very precise statement of his conclusion:

Vers. 39, 40.

Vers. 39, 40. "Wherefore, brethren,[1] covet to prophesy, and forbid not to speak in[2] tongues. 40.

[1] א A B add μου (*my brethren*).
[2] B D F G It. read εν before γλωσσαις.

But[1] let all things be done decently and in order."— We have already seen again and again in this Epistle that after a searching discussion, going to the very heart of his subject, Paul likes to conclude with a brief practical direction, in which the different sides of the question are reflected; so vii. 38, xi. 33, 34. It is the same here. The preference given to prophecy over tongues is expressed by the antithesis of the two verbs: *covet* and *forbid not.* The latter expression reminds us of the two sayings 1 Thess. v. 19, 20: "Quench not the Spirit," and: "Despise not prophesyings." It appears from these two warnings that the general tendency at Thessalonica was to disdain and disparage the extraordinary manifestations of the Spirit, whereas at Corinth they were exalted, especially in the instance of tongues. The apostle takes care to guard each Church, on right or left, according to its wants.

Ver. 40. If ver. 39 is the summing up of the dissertation on gifts, contained in chaps. xii.–xiv., ver. 40 is the close of the whole section which refers to questions of worship, chaps. xi.–xiv. The word εὐσχημόνως, *with seemliness*, refers particularly to the demeanour of women and to the celebration of the Supper; the κατὰ τάξιν, *in order*, rather alludes to the recommendations given in regard to the exercise of gifts, chap. xiv.

Conclusion regarding the gift of tongues

The detailed study of this chapter has, I think, confirmed the previous result, to which we were led, chap. xii. 10,

[1] T. R. here omits with K L the δέ, which is the reading of all the others.

regarding the nature of glossolalia. Most certainly the tongues spoken at Corinth could not be really existing foreign tongues. The glossolalete did not evangelize, did not preach; he praised and gave thanks. To express such feelings would an existing tongue be chosen which had never been learned?—The same objection may be made to the Bleek-Heinrici explanation. What purpose would it serve to go in quest of old unused expressions, or to create extraordinary combinations of words to give utterance to the impressions of joy and adoration with which the possession of salvation filled the heart? Such a course would rather betray the labour of reflection than emotion or ecstasy. In any case, it is far from probable that there would be at Corinth many believers having at command the archaic forms of the learned tongue.—The explanation held in our day by many commentators, that the tongues consisted only of inarticulate groanings and a babbling of confused sounds, which had no meaning, is not less incompatible with our chapter. How would the apostle have attached to this gift such value as to give thanks for the rich command he had of it himself? The apostle, as chap. xiv. itself shows, was too sound-minded to give himself up to a religious exercise so puerile as is thus supposed, and to allow it a regular place in Church worship. Finally, it is impossible not to connect the gift which was developed at Corinth with that which was manifested on the day of Pentecost at Jerusalem, and which is again mentioned on several subsequent occasions in the book of the Acts x. 46: "They heard them speak in tongues" (at the house of the Gentile Cornelius); xix. 6: "The Holy Spirit came upon them, and they spoke in tongues and prophesied" (the twelve disciples of John the Baptist instructed by Paul). The term being the same in the Acts and in our Epistle, it ought to denote a kind of language radically homogeneous. Now how is it possible to suppose that on Pentecost the speaking in tongues could have consisted of unintelligible utterances which had really no meaning? Could the multitudes have exclaimed: "We hear them speak in our own tongues the *wonderful works of God*" (Acts ii. 11).

I can only therefore regard the gift of tongues as the expression, in a language spontaneously created by the Holy Spirit, of the new views and of the profound and lively emotions of the human soul set free for the first time from the feeling of condemnation, and enjoying the ineffable sweetness of the relation of sonship to God. And as the influence of the Holy Spirit takes possession of the whole soul and every one of its natural powers, to make it its organ, it also took possession of the gift of speech, transfiguring it, so to speak, to give utterance to emotions which no natural tongue could express. It was, doubtless, a something intermediate between singing and speech, analogous to what we call a recitative, and the meaning of which was more or less immediately comprehensible like that of music. On Pentecost, when this language was manifested in its most distinct form, every well-disposed hearer understood it at once, in a way analogous to that which produced interpreters at Corinth, and could translate it immediately, so that he thought himself listening to his own tongue: "How *hear we* every man in our own tongue wherein we were born?" It must be borne in mind that human language is not an accidental, arbitrary creation, nor the work of the understanding only, but that it is the spontaneous product of the entire human soul. There is at the root of all existing languages, an *essential,* unique language; no doubt, if it existed as such, it would be composed of onomatopœiæ. This is what Plato expressed, after his own fashion, in a passage of the *Cratylus,* quoted by Heinrici: "It is manifest that the gods at least call things truly (πρὸς ὀρθότητα), and theirs are the natural names (φύσει ὀνόματα)." This necessary language of the human spirit could be drawn forth at this decisive point of history by the Divine Spirit from the depths of the soul, and made more or less imperfectly the organ of His first communications.

I have quoted various witnesses, in the two notes pp. 278, 286, as to the manifestations which signalized the first serious religious awakening that led to the founding of the Irvingite Church. It seems to me impossible to regard these phenomena as purely artificial imitations of those described by the New Testament in the first times of the Churches of

Judea and Greece. At the beginning especially, these manifestations were remarkable for unaffected sincerity. Later, love of the extraordinary and desire to shine undeniably introduced an impure alloy, as was the case at Corinth itself. Such manifestations therefore give evidence of a real faculty latent in the depths of the human soul, which a profound religious awakening may call into exercise at any time under fixed conditions, and the creative action of which may yet in our day produce effects similar to those of the first days of the Church. We were not wrong, therefore, in maintaining the possibility of the reappearance of gifts during the whole course of the present economy (see on xiii. 8), while concluding from the apostle's words in this same chapter that the normal progress of the Church tends rather to the diminution of such phenomena, as a transition to their complete disappearance in the perfect state.

10

The Resurrection of the Body (15:1-58)

From ecclesiastical, moral, and liturgical questions, the apostle passes to one of a dogmatic nature. He has reserved it for the last, no doubt, because of its importance. Doctrine is the vital element in the existence of the Church. The Church itself is in a manner only doctrine assimilated. Any grave corruption in teaching immediately vitiates the body of Christ. The apostle opened his letter by laying down as the foundation of his work, Christ crucified; he concludes it by presenting as the crown of his work, Christ risen. In these two facts, applied to the conscience and appropriated by faith, there is concentrated indeed the whole of the Christian salvation.

The subject of the resurrection of the body does not

appear to have been treated in the letter which the Corinthians had addressed to Paul. Ver. 12 of our chapter rather leads us to think that he had accidentally learned, perhaps from the delegates of the Church who were now with him, what was being said at Corinth by some individuals (τινές) who posed as adversaries of the resurrection.

Did they deny the resurrection of Christ Himself? It does not seem so at the first glance, for the apostle starts from this fact as admitted, to infer therefrom our own resurrection. But he takes such pains to lay this foundation of his argument, that it seems to me impossible not to hold, in opposition to the opinion of most modern commentators, that the conviction of those people, and even of many members of the Church, was shaken on the point. One of the two negations could not in the long run fail to lead to the other; for in virtue of the close union between Christ and believers, salvation cannot otherwise be realized in the latter than in the person of their Head.

Who were these *certain?* It has been supposed that they were former Sadducees who, while going over to Christianity, had imported into it some remnants of their former opinions. But there is no proof of the propagation of Sadduceism outside of Palestine; and a Sadducee converted to Christianity would have experienced too radical a change to admit easily of such a mixture of heterogeneous opinions. All the religious and moral deviations which we have hitherto observed at Corinth proceeded from the Greek character; it is probable that it was so also in this case. From the Greek point of view, especially since the time of

Plato, it was customary to regard matter, ὕλη, as the source of evil, physical and moral, and consequently the body as the principle of sin in human nature. It is obvious, therefore, that the resurrection of the body which, from the Jewish Messianic viewpoint, was looked upon as the consummation of the expected salvation, and as an essential element of future glory, must have appeared to the Greek mind as a thing very little to be desired, as the restoration of the principle of evil. This view had even gained the Jewish thinkers of Alexandria who came under the influence of Greek philosophy, such as the author of *Wisdom* and the philosopher Philo, to whom we may add the Essenian monks. They all agree in regarding death as setting man free from the bonds of the body, and in making the immortality of the *soul*, of the soul alone, the object of their hope. Heinrici thought he found in Josephus evidence of a change of opinion on this point even among the Pharisees, as if they had come to hold metempsychosis, instead of the resurrection of the body. But the passage quoted by this critic (*Bell. Jud.* ii. 8, 14) proves nothing of the kind: "Every soul is immortal; either it passes into another body, which is the abode of good, or it is punished through the eternal chastisement of evil actions." The meaning of these words is, that resurrection of the body is a privilege granted to righteous souls only.

There is nothing, I think, to prevent us from connecting with the denial of the resurrection by certain of the Corinthians what Paul says in 2 Tim. ii. 18 of two heretics: "That, according to them, the resurrection of the dead was past already." Evidently these teachers would not see in the resurrection anything else than spiritual regeneration; the restoration of the body was relegated by them to the domain of fable. It must be remembered that there was not yet in the Church any positively formulated system of doctrine, and that the teaching was being gradually formed by the labours of prophets and teachers under the direction of the apostolate.

One or two passages of this chapter, particularly vers. 32–34, have led some to suppose that those whom the apostle combats, denied not only the resurrection of the body, but even the immortality of the soul and the judgment; and it has been thought that they belonged to the materialistic sect of the Epicureans. But it seems to us impossible that men of that stamp could have have adhered to Christianity; see besides on this question at the passage indicated.

Should we identify the opponents of the resurrection with one of the four parties mentioned i. 12? Those of Paul and Peter are evidently at once beyond suspicion. Meyer, Heinrici, and others think of the disciples of Apollos as men who cultivated human wisdom. But we think we have refuted the prejudice relative to the disciples of Apollos. There would remain only *οἱ τοῦ Χριστοῦ, those of Christ.* Perhaps, indeed, it might be concluded from some parallels (2 Cor. xi. 3, 4, for example) that it was in this camp those *τινές* were found; but, on the other hand, the Second Epistle shows that the party of *those of Christ* had at its head men who had come from Jerusalem and were ultra-Judaizing. Now, as we have seen, antipathy to the resurrection cannot well have come from the Jewish side. All idea must therefore be given up of connecting the subject in question with the dissensions treated chaps. i.–iv.

In the following discussion the apostle begins by showing that with the resurrection of the body the entire system of Christian salvation rises or falls : vers. 1–34 ; then he resolves the difficulties which the fact presents, and concludes by raising the triumphant song of life over death : vers. 35–58.

A. With the Fact of the Resurrection of the Body Christian Salvation rises or falls (vers. 1–34)

The apostle's first care is to establish firmly the fact of the resurrection of Jesus, on which rests the expectation of our own (vers. 1–11).

Vers. 1–11

Vers. 1, 2. "Moreover, brethren, I make known unto you the gospel which I preached unto you, which also ye have received, and wherein also ye stand; 2. by which, also, ye are saved, if ye keep in memory what I preached unto you, unless ye have believed in vain." —There is something surprising in the term γνωρίζω, *I make known to you*, for in the immediately following words Paul declares that the gospel he is about to expound to them, he preached to them, and they themselves received and held it. This, however, is not a sufficient reason for abandoning the natural meaning of the verb, and making it signify, as some do : "I *remind* you . . .," or with others : "I *call* your *attention* to . . ." Some (Bengel, Ewald, Heinrici, etc.) think that we have a construction similar to that of iii. 20, or Gal. i. 11 : "I make known to you the gospel . . ., in what way I preached it to you (τίνι λόγῳ εὐηγγελισάμην . . ., ver. 2)," meaning : "I make known to you *in what way* I preached to you the gospel." But the contradiction between making known and having preached remains all the same, though the first term should apply to the form and not to the substance. If the Corinthians had heard Paul, and believed through his ministry, they must have known both the substance and form of his preaching. Hofmann seeks the solution in the special sense he gives to τίνι λόγῳ : "In what thought, that is to say, with what *aim*, I preached to you." The apostle's intention in preaching to them was, according to this critic, to show them by the resurrection of Christ that salvation is for us, as for him, a principle of glorification. But how is it possible to read all this in vers. 1 and 2? Paul would easily have succeeded in expressing this thought more clearly if it had really been his. It seems to me, as to Holsten, that the word : *I declare to you*, is chosen with the intention of humiliating the readers. Paul wishes to bring out by the intentional contradiction between this term and those which follow : "I preached, you received, you stand fast," the corruption which has been introduced among them of the conception of salvation, to the extent of transforming the meaning of the message he had brought them, so as to make it a wholly different thing, though outwardly speaking they remained faithful to it. Thus is explained the somewhat strange form of the τίνι λόγῳ εὐηγγελισάμην, ver. 2. Meyer and Holsten seem to me to hold, as to this proposition, the only possible construction, by making it depend, not on σώζεσθε, *ye are saved*, but on κατέχετε, *keep in memory:* "If you firmly keep in mind how I preached it to you (the gospel)." There is an inversion, as so often in Paul (iii. 5, vii. 17, xiv. 12, etc.), and that with the view of bringing out clearly the whole dependent proposition which is the object of κατέχετε: "If, in the sense in which I preached it to you (the gospel), you hold it firmly." They run no risk of denying Christianity, but of abandoning the true sense in which they received it from Paul, and in which it can preserve its saving power. And this is why Paul is obliged to make, as it were, a new communication of it to them. There is between the verb γνωρίζειν, *to make known*, and εὐαγγελίζεσθαι, *to preach*, this difference: that the second indicates the simple statement of the historical fact, and the first embraces the explanation of its full meaning and its relation to salvation as a whole. —The two καί, *also*, which follow one another, clearly indicate a gradation. To preaching succeeded the acceptance of faith; to this, perseverance in profession.

Ver. 2. But this acceptance and profession are not yet salvation itself. There is needed the κατέχειν, the act of *keeping in mind* and keeping *well.* This is why Paul adds: "whereby also you are put in possession of salvation, if you hold it as I have taught it to you." The word λόγος here denotes the exact meaning Paul had given to the facts here related. Faith should grasp not only the fact, but also the Divine thought realized in the fact.—The pronoun of direct interrogation, τίνι, is designedly used instead of the relative pronoun ᾧ: "If you keep in mind *in what* way . . .," instead of: "If you keep in mind the manner *in which* . . ." The first form is more suited to express a qualification. Paul alludes in this τίνι to a variety of conceptions as to the facts of salvation.—But why to this first restriction: *if you keep in mind*, does he add a second: *at least unless you believed in vain?* The former bears on the subjective perseverance of the Corinthians to keep the true meaning of the facts of salvation; the latter bears on the objective reality of the facts themselves. Salvation by faith in Christ crucified and risen is impossible except as this Christ crucified and risen is a reality. Now there is a supposition on which constant faith in Him, as Paul preached Him, would not save, viz. that Christ did not exist. This supposition, revolting as it is to the Christian conscience, Paul nevertheless expresses, and seems to take in earnest in the following demonstration; and in the minds of many certainty as to the Divine facts, and of the resurrection in particular, must evidently have been shaken.—As to the form ἐκτὸς εἰ μή, see on xiv. 5. The word εἰκῆ, *in vain*, may signify: without foundation, without sufficient reason, as in Matt. v. 22 and Col. ii. 18. But ordinarily it signifies *without result*, without effect, as in the classical expression εἰκῆ βάλλειν, *to throw an arrow which does not hit;* comp. Rom. xiii. 4; Gal. iii. 4, iv. 11. In the former sense: "unless you believed in a pure fable" (vers. 14, 15). In the latter: "unless your faith remains without effect (because its object is nothing real)." Substantially the two meanings come to the same.

The apostle had (xi. 2) praised the Corinthians for

maintaining the ecclesiastical institutions which he had given them; he is evidently careful not to say as much here in regard to their keeping of his doctrinal traditions. And now he sets himself to expound to them the whole doctrine of the resurrection which he had declared to them, and he begins by reminding them, vers. 3–11, of that whole series of irrefutable testimonies on which faith in the resurrection of the Lord Jesus rests, the fact which forms the foundation of that which he wishes to develop.

Vers. 3–5. "For I delivered unto you, first of all, that which I also received: how that Christ died for our sins, according to the Scriptures, 4. and that He was buried, and that He rose again the third day, according to the Scriptures, 5. and that He was seen of Cephas, then[1] of the Twelve."[2]—The *for* bears, not on either of the secondary ideas of the previous verses: If you hold firmly, or: By which you are saved, but on the principal idea: "I declare to you what I preached to you." Paul means: "The points which I put in the first rank, when I preached the gospel to you, are the following." He had laid down as the basis of Christian teaching, in the same way as he does here, the facts of the Lord's death and resurrection. We need not, with Chrysostom and Hofmann, give the word *first* the temporal meaning; it is the fundamental importance of those one or two points which Paul wishes to characterize by the term. —It was formerly held that the word *I received* referred, as in xi. 23, to a direct communication from

[1] T. R. with B K L P: ειτα (*then*); ℵ A: επειτα (*thereafter*); D F G: και μετα ταυτα (*and after these things*).

[2] T. R. with ℵ A B K L P Syr.: δωδεκα (*twelve*); D F G It.: ενδεκα (*eleven*).

the Lord. Modern commentators rather think that the reference here is to a human tradition, to the narrative of the Twelve as witnesses to facts. And indeed it should be remarked that the apostle does not here say ἐγώ, *I* [emphatic], and that he does not add, as in the passage quoted, *of the Lord.* He evidently knew the facts of the death, burial, and resurrection of Jesus in the same way as the whole Church, by their public notoriety and the narratives of the apostles. If Paul afterwards speaks specially of two appearances which were granted to Peter and James, this agrees well with the fact that it was with these two men he had conferred personally during his first stay at Jerusalem, after his conversion (Gal. i. 19). But, true as this view is, perhaps it is incomplete. In the gospel preached by Paul at Corinth, there was not only, as we have seen, the historical side of facts; his preaching contained a higher element, the understanding of those facts as expressed in the words: *for our sins,* and: *according to the Scriptures.* And on such points Paul had received, as he says, Gal. i. 12, the teaching of the Lord Himself whereby alone the external facts related in apostolical tradition had become to him soteriological facts; I think, therefore, that he designedly used the verb παρέλαβον, *I received,* without regimen, leaving it in all its generality, that it might embrace both human tradition and Divine teaching.—The καί, *also,* expresses the exact conformity between the deposit committed to Paul and his conveying of it to the Corinthians.—The regimen: *for our sins,* has special importance, because it is the Divine meaning of the fact, as he will afterwards explain it, vers. 17, 18. It is quite clear that in this phrase the ὑπέρ does not signify: *in place of*, but: *in behalf of:* "In behalf of our sins to expiate them." This phrase is found nowhere else in Paul; but comp. Heb. ix. 7 and x. 12.—The regimen: *according to the Scriptures*, has its importance: the Divine testimony of the Scriptures is designedly placed before all the apostolic testimonies which are about to follow. The Scriptures had said the event would happen; the witnesses declare it has happened.

Ver. 4. It is asked why the burial of Jesus occupies a place among these few essential facts. It is certainly not with a view to the spiritual application which is made of it, Rom. vi. 4; for this belonged to a more advanced stage of teaching. Neither is it to establish the reality of the death, for interment does not exclude the possibility of a lethargy. But the fact of interment ever recalls "that empty tomb on which, as has been said, the Church is founded," and which remains inexplicable by all who deny the bodily resurrection of Jesus. It is indeed what excludes both the supposition of hallucination on the part of the apostles and that of a purely spiritual reappearance of Jesus after His death. The dead body laid in the sepulchre disappeared. What became of it? No explanation other than the fact itself of the resurrection has ever been able to account for this mystery.—Passing from the facts of the death and burial to the resurrection, Paul discontinues the aorists (*died, was buried*) for the perfect (ἐγήγερται). For the risen Christ continues in life.—Does the regimen: *according to the Scriptures*, which is repeated here, apply only to the fact in general or specially to the detail: *the third day?* In the former case, we must think of Isa. liii. and Ps. xvi.; in the latter, we must add to these passages the history of Jonah and Hosea vi. 2.—This date of the *third day* was not accidental; for, as Hofmann observes, it is precisely then that dissolution ordinarily begins to appear.

Ver. 5. The two first appearances mentioned here, that to Peter in the course of the day of the resurrection, and that to the Twelve on the evening of the same day, are also mentioned by Luke (xxiv. 34–36); the second only by John xx. 19 seq. Paul omits that to the two disciples going to Emmaus described in detail by Luke, and that to Mary Magdalene related by John. The reason no doubt is, that neither those two disciples, nor Mary, were of the number of the witnesses expressly chosen by the Lord.—The term ὤφθη may signify *was seen*, or *appeared* (*in vision*); in each case the context must decide. In this passage, after the word: *He was raised* (ver. 4), the choice is not doubtful; it can only designate, according to the writer's view, a bodily appearance. This is also plain from the very object of this whole enumeration of apostolic testimonies. What is St. Paul's aim? To prove our bodily resurrection. Now it is impossible to understand how a simple vision, a purely spiritual appearance of the Lord, could serve to demonstrate our bodily resurrection.—The appearance to Peter, mentioned here and in the passage of Luke, is one of the traits which reveals the close relationship between Paul's tradition and the third Gospel.—The εἶτα, *then*, of the *Vatic.* and the Byz., separates the two facts less than the ἔπειτα, *afterwards*, of the *Sinaït.* and the *Alex.*

The former reading is the better; for the appearing to the Twelve was much more closely connected with that to Peter than those which follow; comp. Luke xxiv. 35, 36. With greater reason must we set aside the reading of the Greco-Lats.: καὶ μετὰ ταῦτα, *and after these things*. The same MSS. read τοῖς ἕνδεκα, *to the eleven*, instead of τοῖς δώδεκα, *to the twelve*. This reading is either due to the reflection that Judas was wanting on that occasion, or it is borrowed from Luke xxiv. 33. The Twelve were still the Twelve, notwithstanding the absence of one or even two of them (Thomas). For the term calls up above all the official character which had been impressed on them at the time of their election. Holsten suspects the authenticity of the last words, τοῖς δώδεκα, because of the difficulty of explaining their relation to the end of ver. 7 (see on this passage). But notwithstanding the Greco-Latin variant (τοῖς ἕνδεκα), they are not really wanting in any document.—Thus far all was dependent on the verb παρέδωκα, *I delivered unto you*. But from this point the sentence breaks off, and the following appearances are stated in the form of independent propositions. Should we infer, with Heinrici, that Paul had not spoken at Corinth of the facts afterwards mentioned on the occasion of his first preaching? In any case that would not apply to the appearance mentioned in ver. 8. Holsten thinks that Paul no longer remembered the limit between the appearances which he had mentioned and those he had omitted. But this even is unnecessary. He may very well have broken the construction in order to prevent the sentence from dragging.

Ver. 6. "After that He was seen of above five hundred brethren at once, of whom the greater part remain unto this present, and some[1] are fallen asleep."—The ἔπειτα, *thereafter*, separates more forcibly than the εἶτα, *then*, of ver. 5; it makes the following appearance a new step in the series, and rightly so. This appearance took place considerably later, and certainly in Galilee. Already before His death Jesus had told His disciples that after His resurrection He would go before them into Galilee (Matt. xxvi. 32; Mark xiv. 28). The angel and Jesus Himself (according to Matt. xxviii. 10) had repeated this promise to the women on the day of His resurrection (Mark xvi. 7 and Matt. xxviii. 7). Moreover, Matt. xxviii. 16, mention is made of a command which Jesus gave to His disciples to gather together on a certain mountain in Galilee all the believers of that country. No doubt Matthew, in relating the appearance so solemnly prepared for, speaks only of the Eleven; but if it was, as it is impossible to doubt, that which the angel and, according to Matthew, Jesus Himself announced to the women on the morning of the resurrection, this gathering must have embraced all the followers of Jesus, and not only men, but also women. This is what explains a gathering together in a given place, at a certain time fixed beforehand. It must therefore be held that the appearance mentioned in our ver. 6 is no other than that related by Matthew at the end of his gospel, and in which Jesus took leave of all His Galilean followers, that is to say, of His Church. The Eleven were there in the foremost rank, and it was to them in particular that the command was

[1] T. R. with K L P here adds και (*also*).

addressed to begin the mission to the whole world (Matt. xxviii. 18–20). This is no doubt the reason why Matthew mentions them only. We should not be surprised that the apostle so expressly mentions this testimony. It was that of the whole Church, the apostles included; what a difference between it and a simple private testimony! The word ἐπάνω, *more than, above*, is not a preposition, but an adverb; as a preposition it would govern .the genitive (Mark xiv. 5). The word ἐφάπαξ does not here signify, as often, *once for all*, but *at one time*.—The words *five hundred* and *still live* have evidently, in the apostle's view, an apologetic bearing: "You can go and ask them, if you like: there they.are, still, and in great numbers." Here we have a striking example of the small value which in criticism belongs to the argument taken from silence. Here is a fact of public notoriety, quoted in a writing the authenticity of which is indisputable, by a witness whose declaration is above suspicion; and the fact is omitted in our four Gospel narratives, or, if it appears in one of them, it is devoid of the circumstances which render it so striking in the narrative of it given by St. Paul. After this, what is to be thought of arguing against the reality of an act or saying of Jesus because it is mentioned only in one Gospel and not in the others!—The apostle now passes to a third group.

Ver. 7. "After that[1] He was seen of James, then[2] of all the apostles."—The reading ἔπειτα, *afterwards*, is preferable here; for we come now to the last appear-

[1] D E Cop. here read ειτα.

[2] ℵ A F G K here read επειτα (*afterwards*), instead of ειτα (*then*), which is the reading of T. R. with B D E L P.

ances granted to the apostles. That given to James no doubt preceded by a short time the appearing on the day of the ascension, which immediately follows. This James can only be the one who played a considerable part in the Church of Jerusalem, as head of its council of elders (Acts xv. 13 and xxi. 18), and who is called, Gal. i. 19, "the Lord's brother," and ii. 9, "one of the pillars of the Church." He was not a believer during the Lord's lifetime (John vii. 5); but we find him united with the apostles and holy women, in the upper chamber, immediately after the ascension (Acts i. 14). This extraordinary change was no doubt brought about by the appearance here mentioned, which should not be confounded with that described by a legend preserved in the Gospel of the Hebrews (Jerome, *de viris illustr.* c. 2); for had there been a foundation of truth in this narrative of the apocryphal book, the fact must have immediately followed the resurrection.[1]

The subsequent appearance to all the apostles can only be that of the day of ascension. But why the adjective *all*, and why is it placed so emphatically after the substantive? Meyer thinks Paul wishes thereby to indicate a larger circle of persons than that of the Twelve properly so called (ver. 5), including, for example, James or others, such as Barnabas or Silas, who sometimes in the New Testament bear the title of apostles; comp. Acts xiv. 4, 14; 1 Thess. ii. 6. But the expression *all the apostles* does not naturally

[1] According to this legend, James bound himself at the last supper of Jesus not to eat bread till Jesus had risen. Jesus, after His resurrection, relieves him from his vow.

express the idea of a circle larger than the Twelve, and at the time when this appearance took place, before Pentecost, no *apostles* different from the Twelve could possibly be thought of (see Holsten). On the other hand, if the expression *all the apostles* has the same meaning as that which was used in ver. 5 (*the Twelve*), why this wholly different expression here? Hofmann answers: Because in ver. 5 the apostles were mentioned as forming the intimate companions of Jesus, while here they are mentioned as founders of the Church. Holsten rightly regards this distinction as arbitrary, and on this, according to him, inexplicable difference of expression he again fastens the suspicion of inauthenticity, which he throws on the last words of ver. 5. But this is a very risky conclusion. Perhaps the particular expression used here is explained by the special character of this last gathering of the apostles round their Master. One is struck with the two expressions in Luke's narrative, Acts i. 4, 6: καὶ συναλιζόμενος, *and having assembled them;* then: οἱ μὲν οὖν συνελθόντες, *they, therefore, having come together.* It is obvious that this gathering was, like that of ver. 6, the result of a positive and solemn convocation on the part of Jesus. It was to be the last, His adieu to the apostles, as that of ver. 6 had been His adieu to the Church. The apostolic college must be there in full, and Jesus had provided that none of the apostles should be wanting. This explains the πᾶσι, *all,* especially if we think of Thomas, who was absent the first time (the appearance of ver. 5), and must on no account be wanting this last time. The term *apostles* reminds us of their mission to the world, of which the ascension was about to become the signal.—Finally, Paul mentions the fact which closed the series of the appearances of the risen One, and which was separated from all the preceding by a much greater interval than those which had separated these from one another.

Ver. 8. "And lastly, after all, He was seen of me also, as of one born out of due time [the untimely birth]."—By the first words the apostle seems to indicate not only that the appearance to him came after the others, but that it was the close of the appearances of the risen One in general. He is not speaking in this passage of visions, like those he himself had afterwards, or like that of the Apocalypse.—The adverb ἔσχατον, *in the last place*, is used before the gen. πάντων, *all*, as a preposition. The word *all* may relate to all the individuals mentioned in the foregoing enumeration, or, with Meyer, to the apostles only, because of the term τὸ ἔκτρωμα which follows; or finally, we may apply it, as Edwards does, to all Christians in general, in the sense that no one after Paul was to see, and no one really saw, the risen Christ. I doubt whether the apostle had these three shades distinctly present to his mind. He certainly thought of all the persons enumerated above, among whom the apostles ranked first, and judged that with this appearance granted to him, the list of such facts was closed.—The strange word ἔκτρωμα, *abortion, untimely birth*, from τιτρώσκω, *pierce, tear*, denotes a child born in a violent and premature way. And as such children are generally inferior in strength to those who are born in a normal way, the expression has been taken as denoting nothing more than a feeling of infirmity: "As a helpless babe scarcely deserves the name of man, I dare hardly regard myself as an apostle;" so Theodoret, Bengel, de Wette, Meyer, Edwards. But Paul himself affirms in ver. 10: "that he laboured more than they all." This is no admission of weakness. And why not abide by the explanation indicated by the etymological and uniform meaning of the word used? Why not take it to denote the violent and unnatural mode of his call to the apostleship, especially at the moment when he is recalling the appearance of the Lord on the way to Damascus? So Calvin, Grotius, Billroth, Heinrici. The other apostles were called when they were already believers; they are like ripe fruits which fell, so to speak, of themselves from the tree of Judaism, and which the Lord's hand gathered without effort, whereas he, Paul, was torn, as by a violent operation, from that Judaism to which he was yet clinging with all the fibres of his heart and will. Ambrosiaster understands the word in this sense: born out of time (too late), when Christ had already returned to heaven. But this circumstance would rather imply something honourable (Gal. i. 1).—The article *the* (τῷ) designates Paul as the only one so named, and probably alludes to the fact, that in a numerous family there is often a child ill-born. It is obvious that when he recalls the boundless grace which was shown him in that striking act of mercy, the apostle feels the need of casting himself in the dust.—The form ὡσπερεί occurs nowhere else in the whole New Testament except in a variant (iv. 13); but it is frequent in the classics, especially in Plato. The final ει is properly a conjunction belonging to a verb understood ("as *if* it were").—These two sides of his ministry, the facts which humble him and the height to which grace has raised him, are developed in the following verses:

Vers. 9, 10. "For I am the least of the apostles, that am not meet to be called an apostle, because I persecuted the Church of God. 10. But by the grace of God I am what I am, and His grace[1] toward me was not in vain;[2] but I laboured more abundantly than they all, yet not I, but the grace of God[3] with me."—The *for* bears on the repulsive figure which has just been used. It by no means justifies the explanation of ἔκτρωμα, which we have set aside; its whole force falls on the sequel of our verse on to the ἐδίωξα, *I persecuted.* The apostle cannot think of that decisive moment of his life without remembering that at that very time he was playing the part of a persecutor. For this it was which necessitated the violent operation to which he was subjected. On ἐλάχιστος, comp. Eph. iii. 11.—The word ἱκανός, *capable*, when a moral act is in question, takes the meaning of "*morally* capable," and thus becomes synonymous with ἄξιος, *worthy*; comp. Matt. iii. 11 with John i. 27 (see Edwards). Καλεῖσθαι, *to bear the title of* . . .—On the whole passage, comp. 1 Tim. i. 12–14.

Ver. 10. The δέ is strongly adversative; it contrasts with what Paul was, when he was yet left to himself, what grace made him.—By the expression: *what I am*, Paul means first a saved believer, then an apostle, finally, the apostle of the Gentile world. It is this last

[1] D F G omit η. [2] D F G read πτωχη (*poor*), instead of κενη (*empty*).
[3] T. R. with A E K L P here reads η, which is rejected by ℵ B D F G.

idea which he specially develops in the following words.—The word κενή, *empty*, applies to the intrinsic power of the grace which was shown toward him.—If with the Greco-Lats. the ή were omitted after the word αὐτοῦ, the εἰς ἐμέ might depend on the verb : "*was* not in *vain toward me ;*" but this idea does not suit the context so well as that of the ordinary reading, which preserves the ή: "The grace *shown toward me* was not in vain."—The word ἐκοπίασα, *I laboured*, denotes not only labour properly so called, effort, toil, sufferings, journeys, prayers, but also the fruits obtained; comp. John iv. 38. The inward power of grace in Paul was demonstrated by its fruitfulness. Indeed, it is only from the viewpoint of the works accomplished that Paul can add without presumption, and as appealing to a patent fact, *more than they all.* These words might signify: more than any one of them in particular. But they should rather be understood, with Meyer, Osiander, Edwards, in the sense of: more than all of them together. The first meaning would be too weak; the second contains no exaggeration; comp. Rom. xv. 19. After thus suddenly rising to the full height God gave him, he abases himself again, as if he were alarmed at what he has just declared. This extraordinary labour was not, strictly speaking, his own, but that of the grace which wrought with him. The art. ή, which is here read by the Byz. before σὺν ἐμοί, connects this regimen closely with the word χάρις: "The grace *which is with me,* it was that which wrought." But the omission of the article in the other two families leads us to apply the regimen *with me* to the verb *laboured* (understood), which is better : "It was not I, however, who laboured, but the grace of God *laboured with me.*" It seems as if *by me* would have been more logical, as corresponding better to the absolute negative : *not I.* But Paul cannot overlook all the intensity, good-will, and personal devotion which he has thrown into this immense labour. And hence, notwithstanding all his humility, the *with me* forces itself into his thought. If he had not been open to the impulse and power of grace, how could it have produced such effects by him !—Evidently these two verses are a digression, but for the digression there is a good reason. We have already seen at the beginning of chap. ix. that there were people at Corinth who were making inquiries as to the reality of Paul's apostleship, and who said : He has not seen the Lord ; therefore he is not really an apostle. Paul does not in this First Epistle enter upon a direct discussion with such opponents, as he will be forced to do later. He restrains himself, till the latent evil shall be unmasked. But he makes certain allusions to the accusations which he cannot yet combat. His object in this passage is to show that although he has been called quite differently from the Twelve, God has nevertheless certified him to be a true apostle, and that consequently he is entitled to join his testimony to theirs. It is precisely this parity with them, in the matter of bearing witness to the resurrection, which is expressed in the following verse, the conclusion of vers. 3-10.

Ver. 11. "Therefore whether I, or they, so we preach, and so ye believed." — The οὕτω, *so,* expressly goes back on the τίνι λόγῳ, *in what sense,* of ver. 2. The present κηρύσσομεν, *we preach,* denotes a constant fact; the aorist ἐπιστεύσατε, *ye believed,* a past fact done once for all, but without the idea of a spiritual decline, which Chrysostom found in this past. This declaration proves that it was matter of notoriety in the Church that the gospel of Peter and of the Twelve rested on the same foundation as that of Paul, on the facts of Christ's death and resurrection regarded as having effected the salvation of the sinful world (*for our sins*, ver. 3 ; *and that according to the Scriptures*, vers. 3, 4). The historical conception of primitive Christianity presented by Baur is incompatible with the fact attested by Paul.—This verse, while summing up the foregoing passage, forms the transition to the following section.

Vers. 12–19

The idea of the whole passage is this : The denial of the resurrection of the dead draws with it that of Christ's resurrection, and thereby gives the lie to the apostolic testimony and to the whole of Christianity.

Ver. 12. "Now if Christ be preached that He rose from the dead, how say some among you that there is no resurrection of the dead ?"—Why, then, it has been asked by Rückert and Scherer, would the resurrection of Christ be denied by denying the resurrection of the dead ? If Christ is of a different nature from us, as Paul holds, it does not at all follow from the fact that He rose, that we ourselves should rise. And M. Scherer adds : "It is easier to doubt apostolic infallibility than the laws of logic." Grotius, Meyer, and Kling have sought to answer by these very laws of logic, and explained the reasoning thus : If there be no resurrection of the dead, the resurrection of Christ cannot be a fact; the genus not existing, the species cannot. But if such were the apostle's thought, he would certainly, in ver. 13, have put the *οὐκ ἔστιν* before the subject; for this verb would contain all the force of the argument. Besides, it is not of the resurrection of the dead as an abstract idea that Paul would speak; he designates by this name a definite historical event, the resurrection of the dead expected at the end of the earthly economy. Finally, the argument would not be decisive, for one might always lay down an exception in favour of Christ, not only because of His superior nature, but especially, as would apply much better here, because of His perfect holiness, which did not allow of His remaining under the power of death. Paul is not reasoning as an abstract logician, but as an apostle. The basis of his argument is a fact which pertains to the essence of the Christian salvation: our new life, flowing from union with Christ, is nothing else than participation in His life. Salvation therefore cannot be realized in us otherwise than it is realized in Him. If to the heavenly life upon which He has entered there belongs the possession of a risen and glorified body, it must be so with us. Our glory being His glory, which He communicates to us, it must be homogeneous with His. The apostle's question, ver. 12, is therefore perfectly justified: *How say some among you . . . ?*—The expression *κηρύσσεται ὅτι* signifies: "He is preached *as risen;*" still the *τίνι λόγῳ* of ver. 2.

Vers. 13–15. "If there be no resurrection of the dead, then is Christ not risen. 14. But if Christ be not risen, then[1] is our preaching vain, and your faith is also vain. 15. Yea, and we are found false witnesses of God; because we have testified of God that He raised up Christ: whom He raised not up, if so be that the dead rise not."—After descending from the cause (the resurrection of Christ) to the effect (ours), the apostle ascends, in ver. 13, from the denial of the effect to the denial of the cause, to show afterwards that this last denial is a belying of the unanimous apostolic testimony which he has just cited.

Ver. 14. The testimony of the apostles had for its essential subject the resurrection of Christ. If this is not a fact, their testimony is an imposture.—The word κενόν, *vain*, denotes a testimony the matter of which is an unreal event. And if the testimony is such, it is the same with faith in the testimony; it is also vain (κενή), in that the object which it believed itself to be taking hold of is purely fictitious.—In the reading of B L (καί after ἄρα) the two καί should be regarded as correlative: "*both* . . . *and* . . ."

Ver. 15. And what in this case are the apostles who have borne witness to the world of an unreal fact? Impostors, and impostors of the worst kind, for their testimony bears on a false fact which they dared to ascribe to God Himself! The verb εὑρισκόμεθα, *we are found*, expresses the idea of surprisal: "Lo, we are taken in the flagrant sin of falsehood!" The word ψευδομάρτυρες θεοῦ, *false witnesses of God*, might be understood in the sense: "Divine messengers giving false testimony;" the gen. θεοῦ being made dependent on μάρτυρες alone. Or it might be explained in the

[1] B L Syr. here add και (*also*).

sense: "Falsely calling ourselves messengers of God;" θεοῦ depending in this case on the term ψευδομάρτυρες taken as a whole. But the explanation which best agrees with the context is this: "Testifying falsely in regard to God;" in the sense that, as is said afterwards, the apostles ascribe to God a work which He never really did. The gen. θεοῦ is that of the object: false witnesses regarding God, and even according to the following words: κατὰ τοῦ θεοῦ, *against God.* Such a testimony is indeed an act of impiety, an act of violence to God Himself. For is it not to assail His honour to ascribe an act to Him which He never really did? It is exactly the same as if an act done by Him were denied.—The conj. εἴπερ, *if truly*, recalls the saying of the τίνες: "If the thing is real, as they allege."

Vers. 16–19.

Ver. 16. "For if the dead rise not, then is not Christ raised."—This verse seems to be a needless repetition of ver. 13. It is not so. Paul once more takes up the inference already drawn in ver. 13, in order to deduce from it a second conclusion parallel to that which he had expounded in vers. 14, 15. The denial of Christ's resurrection, as it follows from the denial of the resurrection of the dead, implies the accusation of imposture against the apostle, vers. 13–15. But more than that: this same denial, following from the same premiss, implies the nothingness of the Christian salvation, vers. 16–19.

Vers. 17, 18. "Now, if Christ be not raised, your faith is vain; ye[1] are yet in your sins. 18. Then they also which are fallen asleep in Christ are perished."—

[1] א A read και (*and*) before ετι.

Once deny Christ's resurrection, and there is no more salvation in Him.—The word *ματαία* denotes, as often, the vanity of the thing from the standpoint of its effects, its uselessness. Such is the difference between it and the *κενή*, *vain*, of ver. 14. Faith in the resurrection, not taking hold of a real fact (*κενή*), cannot procure for the believer the salvation he expects (*ματαία*). It is completely to mistake the meaning of this saying, to follow Heinrici and several others, in applying the expression: *to be yet in one's sins*, to the moral bondage of sin. The apostle certainly does not mean: "If Christ be not really risen, you will not be able to conquer your evil inclinations." Nothing in this Epistle has prepared us for such an idea. It is of the state of condemnation arising from unpardoned sins that he wishes to speak, as is clearly shown by the following verse. The idea is this: Condemnation can only be taken away by the expiatory death of Christ, and expiation would never have taken place if the victim who accomplished it had not been restored to life. As long as the security is not let out of prison, it must be concluded that the debt is not paid. If then Christ did not leave the prison of death, our justification was not obtained by His death; and we are still, we believers, as much as others, condemned. Bonnet rightly says: "No one can understand the doctrine of Scripture regarding the resurrection, unless he has clearly present to his mind the intimate and indissoluble relation there is between sin and death." Christ dead without resurrection would be a condemned, not a justified, Christ. How could He justify others?—Hence there follows immediately the disastrous consequence drawn in ver. 18 : the perdition of those who have been seen to die peacefully in the faith of Christ.

Ver. 18. There is a sharp contrast between the two terms : *falling asleep in Christ* and *having perished.* To close the eyes in the joy of salvation, to open them in the torments of perdition! The verb ἀπώλοντο, *perished,* cannot designate annihilation, for it is explained by the preceding expression : *to be yet in sins.* It denotes a state of perdition in which the soul remains under the weight of Divine condemnation. Nor does the aorist allow us to explain this idea of perishing proleptically, as the sense of destroying or annihilating would require.—So much for the dead; and what follows for us who still live here below in the faith of that unrisen Christ? The apostle tells us in ver. 19 :

Ver. 19. "If in this life only we have hoped in Christ,[1] we are of all men most miserable."—Rückert makes the adverb *only* apply to the regimen *in Christ:* "If we have rested all our hopes here below on Christ only . . ." But in order that this conditional proposition might form a ground for the following inference, Paul would have required to add the idea : and this one hope ended in deceiving us. The position of μόνον, *only,* in the Greek clause, shows, besides, that this adverb bears on the clause as a whole, verb and subordinate clauses included : "If we are men who have only our hope in Christ during the course of this life . . ." The opposite, they are men whose hope in

[1] T. R. places εν Χριστω (*in Christ*) with K L P after ηλπικοτες εσμεν (*we have hoped*) ; all the rest after εν τη ζωη ταυτη (*in this life*).

Christ is eternally realized above.—We must not translate ἐν, *in*, in the sense of εἰς, *for*, which would lead to a slightly different idea.—The word ζωή is used here in the sense of βίος, as in Luke i. 75, xvi. 25, etc.—The position of the words ἐν Χριστῷ, *in Christ*, after ταυτῇ, is certainly the true one.—The apostle has been charged, on the ground of the last words of the verse, with taking up a very inferior moral standpoint, because he seems to say that the practice of virtue has no value in itself, but acquires it only by the reward which crowns it. Stoicism, with its maxim: "Virtue is its own best reward," is, it is alleged, far superior to the apostle's standpoint. But it is forgotten that it is not the fulfilment of the simple moral law which is here in question; no natural duty imposes on man a life of labours, privations, and sufferings of all kinds, such as that which the apostle accepted, and which should be accepted by Christians in general in the service of Christ. The free choice of such a life can only be justified by the hope of the most excellent blessings, and these blessings consist by no means of certain external pleasures granted by way of reward, but in the satisfaction of the noblest and most elevated wants of human nature, of the aspiration after holiness and life eternal. To see these blessings escape you, when all inferior ones have been sacrificed to gain them,—to have renounced earth for heaven, and instead of heaven to find hell, like other sinners,—for it is *salvation* that is in question here,—would not this be a still sadder condition than that of worldly men who at least allowed themselves on the earth a comfortable life and the lawful pleasures which were within their reach? To the sufferings accumulated during this life there would come to be added the most cruel deception after this life. Is there not here enough to justify the apostle's exclamation in the view of sound sense?

Thus, the resurrection of the dead falling, everything falls: (1) the resurrection of Christ Himself, vers. 12, 13; (2) the veracity of the apostolic testimony and the reality of the great object of Christian faith, vers. 14, 15; (3) salvation itself, with its eternal blessings, vers. 16–19.—And now let us replace the foundation, which by supposition we had for a moment removed: the whole majestic edifice of the Christian salvation rises again before us even to its sublime consummation! Such are the contents of the following description, vers. 20–28. The resurrection of the dead, closely bound up with the resurrection of Christ, appears as the fundamental fact on which rests the Christian hope to its furthest limit.

Vers. 20–28.

Vers. 20–22. "But now is Christ risen from the dead, the first-fruits of them that sleep.[1] 21. For since by a man came[2] death, by man came also the resurrection of the dead. 22. For as in Adam all die, even so in Christ shall all be made alive."—The words: *But now*, are, as it were, the cry of deliverance, after the nightmare through which the apostle has brought his readers, by opening up to their view the abyss into which we should be plunged by the denial of the resurrection. The *now* contrasts the certain reality of the fact with the perfect void resulting from its denial;

[1] T. R. with K L Syr. here reads εγενετο (*became*).
[2] T. R. with E F G L P reads ο before θανατος (*the* death).

this void, opened up for an instant, no longer exists, except as a vanished past.—The words ἐκ νεκρῶν, *from the dead,* would suffice to prove that Paul is thinking of a bodily resurrection; for spiritually Christ never was among the dead.—The verb *became,* added by the Byz. reading, must be rejected; the word *first-fruits* is not a predicate, it is a simple apposition: "He rose again *as first-fruits,*" and not to remain alone in His state of glory. Christ risen is to the multitude of believers who shall rise again at His Advent what a first ripe ear, gathered by the hand, is to the whole harvest. Is there in this expression a distant reminiscence of the rite in which the apostle had so often taken part as a Jew, the offering in the temple of the first sheaf of the year, as the first-fruits of the harvest? This festival took place yearly, on the morrow after the Passover, the 16th Nisan. It is difficult to doubt this recollection in the apostle's mind, especially if it is held, according to the fourth Gospel, that Jesus was crucified on the afternoon of the 14th Nisan, and that consequently He was raised on the morning of the 16th. But this reminiscence, even if it is real, did not determine the idea and expression of *first-fruits.* Both offered themselves spontaneously.—The term first-fruits is justified in ver. 21 (*for*).

Ver. 21. In the expression ἀπαρχή, *first-fruits,* there was implicitly contained the notion of a community of nature between Christ and us. For the ear gathered as first-fruits is corn like all the rest. This is the idea which the apostle expounds in this verse. As it was by a member of the human family that it was smitten with death, so it is by a member of the family that it must obtain resurrection. The Apostle Paul here proclaims the idea with arresting solemnity: that death and resurrection are human facts, that is to say, the causality of them belongs to man himself. The idea is not exactly the same as that expressed in Rom. v. 12 seq., though closely connected with it. In the passage of Romans, the emphasis is on εἷς, *one,* in opposition to *many:* one involving the many in his death, and one in His salvation. Here there is no εἷς; the emphasis is on ἀνθρώπου, *man.* It is the truly *human* origin of these two opposite phases in the existence of humanity which Paul wishes to set in relief. By man subjection to death was imposed on men; by man there must come to them the power of rising again. It is for man to repair the evil done by man.

In ver. 21 there is stated, in the form of an abstract law, the necessary correlation between these two analogous but opposite facts. In ver. 22 the two historical personalities will be contrasted with one another in whom this colossal antithesis has been realized.

Ver. 22. The fact proves the principle; hence the *for.*—It is not without intention that Paul in this verse substitutes the preposition ἐν, *in*, for the διά, *by*, of the preceding verse. The relation expressed by διά was more external; it was that of causality. The relation expressed by ἐν is more intimate; it is that of moral solidarity, community of life. The latter explains the former: "If all died *by* Adam, it is because all were smitten with death *in* him, in whom they were embraced; if all are to live again *by* Christ, it is because there is *in* Him the power which justifies them and which will make them live again because of their relation to Him."

Must we give to the word πάντες, *all*, the same extension in the two propositions? Some answer in the affirmative, and infer from it universal final salvation; so Origen, Olshausen, de Wette, etc. But this notion does not seem to agree either with the scriptural view in general, or with that of Paul in particular: Matt. xii. 32, xxv. 46; Mark ix. 48, xiv. 21; 2 Thess. i. 9; Phil. iii. 19.—Others, like Julius Müller, find expressed in the verse merely the *destination* of all to resurrection in Christ, a destination which may be annulled by refusal to believe in Him. But the future *shall be made alive* means more than this. It denotes, especially in contrast to the present, *die*, a positive and indubitable fact. Most commentators (Augustine, Bengel, Rückert, Hofmann, Holsten, Beet, Edwards, etc.) think that we must understand a self-evident condition, that of faith: "As in Adam all men die, so in Christ shall all (believers) be made alive." This limitation of the meaning of the second πάντες, *all*, seems at first sight very arbitrary, in view of the absolute meaning of the first. But we shall get reconciled to this interpretation if we take account of Hofmann's observation that ζωοποιεῖσθαι, *to be made alive*, is a more limited idea than ἐγείρεσθαι, *to be raised.* For this second term applies in general to all who shall live again, even to perish, whereas the first applies to the complete gift of perfect life (Rom. viii. 11). The limitation of the subject can therefore naturally proceed from the special meaning of the verb itself.

"The two πάντες embrace those only to whom each of the two powers extends" (Hofmann). Moreover, it should be remembered that Christ can hardly be regarded as the *first-fruits* of the damned who are raised again, and ver. 23, which continues the development begun in ver. 20, evidently takes account only of believers. These reasons have great force, and perhaps this interpretation is really that which corresponds best to the apostle's view. But there is another which, without falling into the thought of universal salvation, preserves the equality of extension which it is so natural to hold between the two πάντες. It is more or less the view of Chrysostom, Calvin, Meyer, etc. May it not be said of those who shall rise to condemnation, that they also shall rise *in Christ?* The judgment to which they shall be subjected in the clear and perfect consciousness of their personality will bear on their sins in general, but especially on their unbelief in the Lord and on their rejection of the amnesty which was offered them in Him. The Saviour having once appeared, it is on their relation to Him that the lot of all depends for weal or woe; it is this relation consequently which determines their return to life, either to glory or to condemnation. And it is with this fact of a moral nature that the other, and more external one, is connected, which was implied in the διά of ver. 21, and which is expressed in John v. 28, 29: the resurrection of all by the power of the Son of man, whether to condemnation or to life. It is true that in this passage John does not use the term ζωοποιεῖν, which he had employed in ver. 21, in an exclusively favourable sense. And the New Testament contains no other passage in which the term is not applied to spiritual or physical quickening in a good sense. But we have just seen the word ζωή (ver. 19) applied to earthly existence in itself, and there is nothing to prevent the word ζωοποιεῖν, taken alone, from being used to denote restoration to the fulness of spiritual and bodily existence, with a view either to perdition or salvation. The term is applied to bodily healing and bodily life in the LXX. (2 Kings v. 7; Neh. ix. 6); see Meyer. It has also been proposed to give πάντες a purely restrictive sense: "*None* will be raised otherwise *than in* Him."—This meaning would be admissible if Paul were here treating of the means of resurrection. But the one point about which he is concerned is the certainty of the event, which does not suit this explanation.

In what follows, the apostle assigns to the resurrection its place in the totality of the Divine dispensations which are to close the history of the development of humanity.

Ver. 23. "But every man in his own order: Christ the first-fruits, and afterward they that are Christ's at His coming."—The word τάγμα, *order*, denotes the place assigned in a series to each individual or group. The apostle has here before him two ranks of the risen: the first formed by Christ alone, moving foremost; it is He who opens up the way to the life of glory. Then He is followed by all His faithful people who form the second rank. It is the same idea as was expressed by the figure of the first-fruits and the harvest.—There is no solid reason for including, as Meyer would, in the expression οἱ τοῦ Χριστοῦ, *they that are Christ's*, all who confess the name of Christ, Christendom in general.

Paul explains clearly enough what he understands by *being Christ's* when he says, Rom. viii. 9: "If any man have not the Spirit of Christ, he is none of His." In Colossians (iii. 4) he says likewise: "When Christ, *our life,* shall appear, then shall ye also appear with Him in glory," which shows that in his view Christ must be our life if His advent is to be the signal of our participation in His glorious appearing. The same also is clearly obvious from Phil. iii. 11, where he goes the length of employing this expression of doubt in regard to himself: "If by any means I may attain to the resurrection of the dead." He could not so express himself in speaking of the universal resurrection, for all will infallibly share in it; he is therefore thinking of the special resurrection, in which only *true* believers will participate; and he recalls the constant effort whereby alone he can reach that desirable goal. For, in order to reach it, it is necessary, according to 2 Cor. vii. 1, "to be cleansed from all filthiness of the flesh and spirit," and "to perfect holiness in the fear of God." Such, according to St. Paul, is the character of *those who are Christ's,* and who shall form the second order in the company of the risen. It will not therefore be all those who bear the name of Christians. There will be a first division, which will be effected at the time of the Advent, between the true and the false members of the Church; this will be the prelude of the universal final judgment. Van Hengel has unfortunately thought of applying the word *Parousia* to the epoch of Christ's presence on the earth. The believers who had the privilege of living with Jesus Christ here below will also have, according to him, the privilege of rising first with Him. But how should this privilege have attached to an external and accidental circumstance? And is not the term *Parousia* in the New Testament a constant expression, all the meanings of which were known to the Churches? Finally, the article οἱ could not be wanting before the regimen ἐν τῇ παρουσίᾳ.—Edwards, at least if I understand him, refers the ἕκαστος, *each*, in this verse, to God, to Christ, and to believers: Christ, ver. 23[a]; believers, ver. 23[b]; God, ver. 28.—The apostle now establishes the relation between this resurrection of believers at the Advent, and the whole cycle of events which shall precede the end of all things.

Ver. 24. "Then the end, when He shall deliver up[1] the kingdom to God, even the Father: when He shall have put down all rule, and all authority and power."—The εἶτα, *then*, does not allow us to identify the time of the τέλος, *the end*, with that of the Advent. Paul would have required to say in that sense τότε, *at that time*, and not εἶτα, *then* or *thereafter*. The εἶτα implies, in the mind of the apostle, a longer or shorter interval between the Advent and what he calls *the end*.—What is this end? According to Theodoret, Bengel, Meyer, Osiander: the end of the resurrection, the third act of the drama of which we have just seen the first two (the resurrection of Christ and that of believers); consequently the universal resurrection. But would not Paul have qualified the word *the end* more precisely, if such had been his thought? And would he not have brought out more clearly the relation between

[1] T. R. with K L It. read παραδῷ (*shall have delivered up*); ℵ A B D E F G P: παραδιδῷ or παραδιδοῖ (*delivers*).

this third phase and the two preceding? Used without qualification, as it is here, *the end* must designate the end absolutely speaking, πάντων τὸ τέλος, *the end of all things*, as Peter puts it (1 Ep. iv. 7), the goal of the entire economy of education, redemption, and sanctification, the time when God's thought shall be at length fully realized in regard to man, come to his perfect stature in Christ. Chrysostom explains: the end of the *present age;* which is true only if we include within the present age the whole interval between the Advent and the end; Holsten: the end of this created world, which, when believers have once been removed by resurrection to a higher world and hostile powers vanquished, has no more value and passes away. This critic rightly points out the mistake of Meyer, who thinks that Paul makes the present age end at the Advent, failing to remember that so long as death is not destroyed (ver. 26), the present age still continues. Besides, the apostle will say positively what he understands by *the end* in ver. 28.

And what fact shall mark this solemn epoch which the apostle calls *the end?* He explains in the following words: *when He shall deliver up the kingdom to God and the Father.* A reading which is found in two Byz. and in the T. R. runs: "When He *shall have delivered up*," ὅταν παραδῷ (the aorist subjunctive). If this were the true reading, the end would not coincide with the delivering up of the kingdom into the hands of the Father; it would follow it. But this reading is too weakly supported and has not sufficiently appreciable intrinsic superiority to make it preferable to that of the Alex. and Greco-Lat. documents. The latter read παραδιδοῖ or παραδιδῷ (two equivalent forms of the present subjunctive), which signifies: "When He delivers up," for: "when He *shall deliver up.*" According to this reading, what Paul calls *the end* coincides absolutely with the delivering up of the kingdom into the hands of the Father. The same follows from ver. 28.—We may understand by βασιλεία (*the reign*), either the *kingdom,* the state of things in which God shall reign perfectly, or the *kingship,* the dominion exercised over this state of things. The second is the more natural meaning according to ver. 25 ("He must reign till . . .") and ver. 28, where it is said the kingdom of the Father must follow from the cessation of that of the Son.—In the expression: *to God and the Father,* are contained the two relations of Jesus to God: His subordination to Him as His *God* and His essential union to Him as His *Father.*

How will the interval be filled between the Advent and the end when the kingdom shall pass from the Son's hands into those of the Father? This is what the apostle explains in the following words: *When He shall have put down all rule . . .* He really uses here the subjunctive aorist, according to all the documents, which proves that he is taking a step backwards. For this aorist is equivalent to our future perfect. It implies that the event which is about to be mentioned will transpire, on the one hand, immediately before the end, on the other, after the Advent. It is obvious how false it is to translate, as is often done: "When He shall have delivered up the kingdom to the Father and put down all powers . . ." This translation makes two events coincide, which, according to Paul, are successive.

The meaning, on the contrary, is: "When He shall deliver up the kingdom to God and the Father, after having put down all powers . . ." The Advent will therefore be separated from the end (the delivering up of the kingdom) by an epoch of judgment. The word καταργεῖν strictly signifies: to reduce to impotence; hence to put down a power. The powers put down can only be the powers hostile to God and His kingdom; for they are called *enemies* in ver. 25, and their fall is the condition of the establishment of the Divine kingdom (ver. 28). It has been thought that the reference here was to earthly powers (Calvin, Grotius); but the terms used by the apostle are so frequently employed by him to designate the invisible powers which contend against God and which seek to drag mankind into their opposition to His kingdom (comp. Rom. viii. 38; Col. i. 13, 16, ii. 15; Eph. ii. 2, vi. 11, 12), that it is impossible to depart from this almost technical meaning. What confirms this explanation is, that in ver. 26 death personified is ranked among the powers put down by the reigning and judging Christ. By ἀρχή, *command*, may be understood the superior beings who, in this invisible domain, exercise command over the others; the ἐξουσίαι designate authorities armed with legal qualification; δυνάμεις, the executive forces. The πᾶσαν, *all*, is not repeated with the third term, which would have been monotonous.—Such, then, will be the use of the interval between the Advent and the end. This period of judgment will only end with the complete reduction of the last enemy; and it must be so, for such is the declaration of Scripture.

Ver. 25. "For He must reign, till He[1] hath put all[2] enemies under His[3] feet."—Paul cites the well-known words of Ps. cx. 1: "The Lord said unto my Lord: Sit Thou at My right hand till I make Thine enemies Thy footstool." The Divine necessity expressed by *He must* follows from this promise of Jehovah to the Messiah.—The emphasis in the saying quoted is put by Paul on the *till;* for the object of the quotation is to justify the terms of ver. 24: *when He shall have put down.* According to this Divine declaration, the reign of the Messiah on the throne of the Father must last *till* there be no longer any enemy left capable of separating God and man. Then this reign will cease. It has therefore for its essential object the carrying out of this judgment on the opposing powers which still remain after the Advent. The subject of the verb *put* is, according to some, God, as in the Psalm (Beza, Grotius, Bengel, Holsten); according to others, Christ Himself (Chrysostom, Rückert, de Wette, Meyer, Hofmann, Edwards). The latter rest their view on the fact, that it is the reigning Christ who must act. But, even if it is God who fights, Christ is not therefore inactive; God acts with Him and by Him. If the αὐτοῦ after πόδας is unauthentic, we cannot well think of any other feet than those of Him who is the subject of the verb; in this case Christ is the subject. As the *till* indicates the certainty of victory, the ἄν, if it is authentic, expresses the uncertainty of the moment when the struggle shall cease.

[1] T. R. with K L adds αν, which is omitted by ℵ A B D F G P.
[2] A F G here read αυτου (*His*), omitted by ℵ B D E K L P.
[3] F G omit αυτου (*His*).

At what time does the apostle make the kingdom of Christ, of which he here speaks, begin? It seems at first sight as if it could be no other than the date of the ascension. But would the idea of a purely spiritual reign, such as that which began with the ascension of Jesus, harmonize with a context like this, where the external and universal fulfilment of the Divine plan is in question? Is it not more natural to take the term *βασιλεία* in its full sense, at once spiritual and external, as in ver. 50? Comp. also vi. 10; Eph. v. 5; Gal. v. 21, then the prayer: "Thy kingdom come," and the words of the Apocalypse xii. 10: "I heard a voice saying: The kingdom of God is come." The reign begins, according to Luke xix. 15, when Jesus, after receiving the kingship in heaven, returns to the earth to exercise it. It is the coming of Jehovah in the person of the Messiah, promised by the prophets, and which Jesus called His Advent. We must therefore regard the reign of Christ as the whole state of things which follows the Advent, and which will last till the epoch called *the end.* It is the whole interval between the time when He shall appear visibly as king, and that when He shall cease to be so (ver. 28); and as among the ancients reigning meant judging, and judging reigning, so the Saviour's reign here consists of judgment.—The *till* setting a limit to Christ's reign, it has been asked if there was not a contradiction between these words and those of Isaiah ix. 6 and Luke i. 33, where it is said, "that of His kingdom there shall be no end." This question has been variously answered (see Meyer). It seems to me that the simplest solution is this: Christ's kingdom in these prophetic sayings is confounded with that of God, which He is commissioned to establish. The distinction between the two is a new revelation whereby the apostle gives precision and completeness to the prophetic revelations. What remains true in these is, that Christ has no successor; for God cannot be regarded as the successor of the Messiah.

Christ's victory, to be complete, must reach to the last enemy, and that even in the external and bodily domain.

Ver. 26. "The last enemy which is destroyed is death."—The literal rendering is: "As last enemy, death is destroyed." Here is the consummation of the reign and of the judgment exercised by Christ over the powers opposed to God. Death is impersonal, no doubt, but its reign nevertheless does violence to the Divine glory, and after the personal powers have been put down (vers. 24, 25), this gloomy power of death must be destroyed, that God's glory may shine forth freely throughout the entire domain of existence. This judgment of death consists of two acts. Firstly, all beings who have become its prey must be rescued from it; this is what will be effected by the final and universal resurrection, which will bring to the light the *third rank* of the risen. In the second place, death must no longer have power to make new victims; this will be the result of the resurrection itself, which, by transforming our perishable into incorruptible bodies, will put them for ever beyond the reach of death.—The apostle declares that this will be the enemy *last* conquered. Why so? Because the power of death rests on certain profound bases of a moral nature, which must be taken away before the throne of this enemy can fall. Death is an effect; the suppression of the effect supposes that of the causes. The apostle will explain this more clearly in ver. 56. It was so in the life of Christ, in which the victory over sin and Satan, during His life, and the victory over the law and condemnation, in His death, became the foundation of His resurrection. It must be the same also for mankind (see at ver. 56).—Without this last victory of the Divine work, there would remain in human existence a domain, that of the body, to which Divine power would not have penetrated, and in which God's work, conquered for a time, had not taken its revenge. This is why the body of the last man must participate in the victory over death, as well as that of Christ Himself; comp. Rev. xx. 12, 13, where there is a magnificent description of the general resurrection in which the Messianic kingdom of Jesus will issue.—As Edwards rightly observes, it follows from this passage that death will continue to reign over the earth between the Advent and *the end.*—It has been asked whether, in the final judgment which will follow the universal resurrection, there will only be the condemned. This might be inferred from the fact that all who *are Christ's* are raised at the time of the Advent (ver. 23). But is it not allowable to think with Luthardt, that among the multitudes who have gone down, and who go down daily, to the place of the dead, without having known the gospel or expressly rejected it, there will be individuals who shall yet accept it; for it is said that it will be preached to them also (1 Pet. iii. 19 and iv. 6), and Jesus positively declared that there is still pardon in the other world for the man who has not committed the blasphemy against the Holy Spirit (Matt. xii. 32). The judgment which will follow the universal resurrection will therefore have a double issue, as Jesus expressly says (Matt. xxv. 46, and as appears from Rev. xx. 15).

Ver. 27. "For He hath put all things under His feet; now when He saith all things are subjected to Him, it is manifest that He is excepted who subjected all things to Him."—The first proposition is laid down as an indisputable truth; because it is taken from Scripture, Ps. viii. 7. In the Old Testament it relates to man in general, at the time of his creation. But as the destiny of man thus declared is not realized, because of the fall, in any one save in the person of the Son of man, the normal man, the Messiah, it is with good right applied to Him in the New Testament; comp. Eph. i. 22; Heb. ii. 8.—The subject of ὑπέταξεν, *subjected*, can only be God, as in the Psalm. The verb in the past refers to the Divine decree appointing Christ sovereign of the universe; of course the execution of the decree does not take place without His own co-operation. — But why does the apostle insist on expressing the exception relating to God? Who could suppose that God formed part of those: *all things*, which were to be subjected to the Messiah? In the state of exaltation which prevailed among the Corinthians, had some one advanced the idea that God, considered as the impersonal force which animates the universe, would one day be wholly subject to the Messiah, as the supreme representative of the world? We met in xii. 3 with an opposite eccentricity which is not more startling. But perhaps this remark, introduced by the apostle in the second part of our verse, is meant only to pave the way for the idea of the subordination of Christ to the Father (ver. 28).—The subject of εἴπῃ seems to me to be simply: God, by the Scripture. Meyer thought that the εἴπῃ should rather be applied to the declaration which God will make when the decree subjecting all things to Christ shall be realized, and God shall have proclaimed the fact in the ears of the whole universe. The δῆλον ὅτι would require in this case to be regarded as an adverbial form, in the sense of *evidently:* "When God shall have declared that all is subjected to Him, evidently He will Himself remain outside of this universal subjection." But the connection between the two propositions would not be logical; what would be needed would not be: When God shall have said that . . ., but: When the fact itself shall have taken place. The second proposition gives the impression of a principle, as well as the first, and seems in no wise to refer to a particular time. As to the δῆλον ὅτι, Meyer's meaning is admissible, but not necessary. We mention only as an exegetical curiosity the explanation of Hofmann, who makes the two propositions beginning with ὅταν, *when* (vers. 27, 28), two parallel propositions, the principal one beginning at the τότε, *then,* of ver. 28. The δῆλον ὅτι signifies, according to him, *that is to say,* and the proposition depending on it is a parenthesis!—The evident fact which Paul wishes to express is, that at the time when all shall be subjected to Christ, voluntarily or involuntarily, only two powers will remain in existence: that of Christ, a power visible and universal, and that of the Father, who gave the Son this sovereign position. But this duality will last only for an instant; it will be immediately terminated by the free act of the Son which will close the development of things:

Ver. 28. "But when all things shall be subjected unto Him, then shall the Son[1] also[2] Himself be subject unto Him that subjected all things to Him, that God may be all[3] in all."—The δέ is progressive: from the subjection of all things to Christ, Paul passes to the subjection of Christ to the Father. We here return to the idea of ver. 24: "Then the end, when He shall deliver up the kingdom . . . after having put down . . ." The last victory is gained, the end comes. Thus the meaning of the digression interposed in vers. 25–27 is obvious: the end or the delivering up of the kingdom to the Father must be preceded by the destruction of all rebel forces (ver. 24[b]); for the Son cannot give up to the Father an empire which has not been completely pacified; and this subjection of rebel forces can only take place through the Messianic reign and judgment of Jesus (vers. 25, 26); as the result of all, the subjection of all things to the Son (ver. 27). And now the conditions of the end are given.—What follows: "Then shall the Son Himself be subject," reproduces more emphatically what had been said in ver. 24 in the terms: "When He shall deliver up the kingdom to the Father." The condition of the end was the subjection of all things to the Son;

[1] Several Fathers omit ο υιος (*the Son*).
[2] B D E F G omit the και (*also*).
[3] A B D omit τα before παντα.

the end itself is the subjection of the Son, and in Him of all things, to God. The subjection of the Son is evidently voluntary. Hence it is that the apostle uses the second aorist passive, which more easily takes the reflective sense than the first aorist. The latter would express entire passivity. We here come on one of the most important and difficult conceptions of our Epistle, and of St. Paul's Epistles in general. It is very difficult to harmonize this idea of the subjection of the Son with the ordinary conception of the Trinity, according to which the Son is eternally equal with the Father. To escape the advantage which the Arians took of this passage, it has been sought in various ways to eliminate from it the idea of submission. The subjection of the Son, according to Chrysostom, denotes His full agreement with the Father. According to Augustine, it is the act whereby the Son will guide the elect to the contemplation of the Father; according to Beza, the presentation of the elect to the Father; according to others, the manifestation by means of which the Son will make the Father fully known to the whole world (Theodoret): meanings which are all utterly insufficient to render the force of the expression used by the apostle. It has also been attempted to understand by the Son here the mystical body of Christ, the Church (Ambrose); and this is perhaps the reason why the words ὁ υἱός, *the Son*, are omitted in some of the Fathers. — A larger number distinguish between the Divine and the human nature of Christ, and ascribe what is here said of Him only to the latter. This attempt to divide the Lord's person into two natures, one of them subject, while the other remains free and self-sufficient, is the more unfortunate in this passage, as the word used to designate Christ is precisely that which most forcibly characterizes His Divine being, *ὁ υἱός*, *the Son*, absolutely speaking.—Many commentators apply what is here said of Christ to the cessation of His mediatorial office between God and men; for where there is no more sin, there is no more need of redemption or intercession. To the reign of grace, administered till then by the Son, there will succeed the state of glory (Luther, Melanchthon, Bengel, Olshausen, etc.). But Paul is not speaking of the cessation of priesthood; it is the delivering up of the *kingdom* which is in question, and of a kingdom whose principal work is to judge, a very different thing from redeeming and interceding, and in any case it is not to God that He could deliver up His mediatorial function. This is recognised by Meyer, Hofmann, Heinrici, and others. These apply the term *βασιλεία*, *kingdom*, to the judicial sovereignty exercised by Christ over the hostile powers (ver. 24), and to His universal sovereignty, which flows from it (ver. 27). "The subordination of the Son to the Father," says Hofmann, "consists in the fact that He ceases to have in the view of the world that mediate position between the world and God, in consequence of which the world saw in Him a ruler different from God, possessing a sovereignty which belonged to Him as His own. This rule within the world ceases because it has reached its end." This explanation would be satisfactory if we had only to account for the expression of ver. 24: "to deliver up the kingdom to the Father." But the phrase used in ver. 28 to designate the same fact is very different: "the voluntary submission of the Son to Him who subjected all things to Him." For this expression does not bear only on the function of the Son, but also on His personal position, and it seems difficult with such words before us to avoid the conclusion of R. Schmidt, when, in his monograph on St. Paul's Christology,[1] he thus expresses himself: "Either the characteristic of absolute existence is not essential to the notion of God, — which no one will allow,—or it must be confessed that the apostolic conception here stated is incompatible with the Divine nature of Christ." This author concludes that the idea of the subjection of the Son, as here taught by the apostle, is in contradiction not only to the ecclesiastical dogma of the Trinity, but also to all the expressions of St. Paul which imply Christ's divinity and pre-existence.

I do not think that so logical a mind as that of the apostle can with any probability be suspected of self-contradiction, especially on a point of such fundamental importance. I have already remarked once and again (iii. 23 and xi. 3), that the idea of the subordination of the Son to the Father expressly forms part of his Christological conception, no less than that of His Divine pre-existence. The two notions are simultaneously included in the title *Son,* which, as Edwards says, implies "the possibility of subjection and, at the same time, equality of nature." Exactly so is it with the term *Word* in John. As the word is subordinate to the thought, and yet one with it, so in the notion of Son there are united the two relations of subordination and homogeneity. The living monotheism of Paul,

[1] *Die Paulinische Christologie*, 1870.

John, and the other apostles was not less rigorous than ours, and yet it found no contradiction between these two affirmations. Now if, in Paul's view, it is so with the Son in His Divine state, must not the position of subordination have appeared in Him still more compatible with the character of the Son when He had once entered into the mode of being belonging to a human personality? Subordination was therefore, according to him, in harmony with the essential relation of the Son to the Father, in His *Divine* and *human* existence. If consequently He is called to reign, by exercising Divine sovereignty within the universe, it can only be for a time, with a view to the obtaining of a particular result. This end gained, He will return to His normal position: subordination relatively to God the Father. Such, as it seems to me, is the true thought of the apostle. How did he understand the state of the Son after this act of voluntary subjection? In his view, this act of subjection could be no loss to the Son. It is not He who descends from the Divine throne, it is His subjects who are raised to it along with Him: "To him that overcometh, will I grant to sit on My throne, as I overcame . . ." (Rev. iii. 21). Even on the Divine throne, Christ is only "as an elder brother in the midst of many brethren" (Rom. viii. 29). "Heirs of God and joint heirs with Christ," says St. Paul in the same sense, that is to say, sharing with Him the Divine inheritance, the possession of God Himself. He is therefore no longer a king surrounded by His servants, but a brother who in relation to His brethren keeps only the advantage of His eternal priority (πρωτότοκος, *first-born*). We must therefore beware of understanding this subjection in the sense of an absorption of Christ in the Deity, so that His personality thenceforth disappears. The expression *to be subjected* denotes quite the opposite of this idea, which is besides incompatible with the apostle's various sayings which we have just quoted. The thought of St. Paul seems to me to be this: The Son returns to the state of submission which He had left to fill the place of Messianic sovereignty, because, God communicating Himself directly to all, He ceases to be mediator of God's sovereignty over them.

The καί, *also,* before αὐτός (*Himself*), in the Byz., ought certainly to be preserved; it has been rejected as too closely identifying the Son's subordination with ours, in the same way as it was thought necessary here to reject ὁ υἱός to avoid the risk of doing wrong to His divinity.—The periphrasis: *to Him who subjected to Him,* serves to justify the delivering up of the universe to the Father; He restores it to Him who gave it to Him.—The last words: *that God may be all in all,* do not depend, as Hofmann and Grimm think, on the secondary idea: *who subjected all things to Him.* What needs to be explained is, not the end for which God subjected all to the Son, but the end with a view to which the Son restores all to God. Such is the dominant thought of the whole passage from ver. 24. This *in order that* depends, therefore, on ὑποταγήσεται, *shall be subject.* He effaces Himself to let God take His place. Formerly it was He, Christ, in whom God manifested Himself to the world; it was He who was *all in all* (Col. iii. 12). But He took advantage of His relation to the faithful only to bring them to that state in which God could directly, without mediation on His part, live, dwell in them, reveal Himself, and act by them. This time having come, they are, as to position, His equals; God is all in them in the same way as He was and is all in His glorified Son. They have reached the perfect stature of Christ (Eph. iv. 13).

But, strange to say, Paul does not use either the name *Father*, or that of *God and the Father* (ver. 24); he says: "that *God* may be all in all." And yet it seems as if the name Father would be the corresponding one to the title Son. All is so maturely weighed in the apostle's style, that he must have had an intention in his choice of the name. He did not here wish to designate God specially as Father, in opposition to the Son and the Spirit, but God in the fulness of His being, at once as Father, the source of all, both in Himself and in the universe, as Son revealing Him, and as Spirit communicating Him. It was in this fulness that God dwelt in the man Jesus, and it is with the same fulness He will dwell in every man who has become in Him His child and heir. Such are "those things" of which Paul spoke ii. 7, "which God has prepared for our glory."—The expression: πάντα or τὰ πάντα ἐν πᾶσιν, *all in all*, certainly does not merely signify: to be all *to them* (to their hearts) because of their love and admiration, as has been concluded from certain analogous Greek expressions. The *in* denotes a real indwelling. The living God thinks, wills, and acts through them. They are as Jesus was, on the earth, at once His free and submissive agents, the depositaries of His holiness, the bearers of His love, the interpreters of His wisdom throughout the boundless spaces and unnumbered worlds of the universe. It is by filling them that through them God fills all things. It seems to me that the neuter πάντα, *all things*, by no means obliges us to take the ἐν πᾶσιν, *in all*, in the neuter sense. The meaning is: *all* in *each*, so that every member of this glorified society has no longer anything in him which is not penetrated by God, as the transparent crystal is all penetrated with light. The masculine sense is demanded, as Meyer well says, by the correlation to the αὐτὸς ὁ υἱός, the Son Himself. This meaning also comes out very naturally from the analogous saying Col. iii. 11: πάντα καὶ ἐν πᾶσιν Χριστός. At the height at which he has arrived, the apostle can only think of a *being* of God spiritually, like that of which Jesus speaks in His last prayer: "As Thou, Father, art in Me and I in Thee, that they also may be in us" (John xvii. 21). It is therefore a mistake in Hofmann and Edwards to take πᾶσιν in the neuter sense: "all *in all things*," even in inanimate beings.—We must certainly read, with the *Vaticanus* and the *Cantabrigiensis*, πάντα without the article; the τά has come in from the three τὰ πάντα which precede; but there τὰ πάντα denoted the totality of the universe, which is unsuitable here.

The partisans of universal salvation have always regarded this last saying as one of the most solid points in support of their theory. But the expression *in all* may be explained in two ways, without ascribing this idea to Paul. Either it may be held that he is thinking only of those who have freely joined in the submission of the Son, and who, united to Him, are embraced in Him; or the *in all* may be applied even to the reprobate, in the sense that in them too the Divine perfection will shine forth, in the twofold aspect of justice and power; comp. Phil. ii. 10, 11, a passage which, however, refers neither to the same time nor to the same fact. If the idea of universal salvation were Paul's view, it must apply also to devils, as Olshausen himself cannot help admitting. But ver. 25 does not lead to such a conclusion, and this thought evidently goes beyond all the limits of the biblical view.[1] What the apostle meant to express here is this sublime idea: that the goal of history and the end of the existence of humanity are the formation of a society of intelligent and free beings, brought by Christ into perfect communion with God, and thereby rendered capable of exercising, like Jesus Himself when on earth, an unchangeably holy and beneficent activity. This view, which is also that of one of the greatest thinkers of our day, Lotze, exclusive of the Christian element on which it rested in the case of the apostle, sets aside, on the one hand, the Pantheism which denies all existence of its own and all free activity to the creature,—this is contradicted by the ἐν πᾶσιν, *in all*,—and on the other the Deism, which ascribes to man an activity in good separately from God,—which is excluded by the πάντα ἐν, *all things in*, of St. Paul.

The apostle has thus assigned to the resurrection of the body its place in the system of the Christian salvation as a whole. He has brought out its three phases (Christ's resurrection, the resurrection of believers, the universal resurrection), and he has pointed out the correspondence between these phases and the three

[1] I cannot admit that it is contained in Col. i. 20.

principal epochs of the Divine work (the consummation of salvation in Christ Himself, the inauguration of His Messianic kingdom, and the close of His whole work). Certainly such a discussion exhausted the first side of the question, the *reality* of the resurrection of the body. Before, however, passing to the second aspect of the question, the *possibility* of so extraordinary a fact, Pauls adds one or two considerations as to the *practical* consequences, to which the denial of this truth naturally leads (vers. 29–34).

Conclusions regarding the passage (vers. 12–28)

On this passage we find *four principal views :*

1. Some, like Reuss, think that it applies throughout only to believers, and that it contains absolutely nothing in regard to unbelievers, because in the context Paul deals only with the development of true life.

2. Weiss[1] and R. Schmidt go further. According to them, Paul holds absolutely no resurrection of the unbelieving. The latter, according to Paul, remain, without returning to life, in the gloomy existence of Hades.

3. Grimm[2] holds, on the contrary, a universal resurrection, which will open up to all men, without exception, participation in eternal felicity.

4. Meyer thinks that our passage contains the idea of a universal resurrection, embracing unbelievers as well as believers.

This last viewpoint appears to me the only admissible one. The opinion of Reuss can hardly give an adequate explanation of ver. 26 ; for the complete victory over death announced in this verse can only be found in a resurrection which will extend to all the victims of death without exception. This same passage seems to me also incompatible with the opinion

[1] *Biblische Theologie des N. T.*, § 99b.

[2] " Ueber die Stelle 1 Kor. xv. 20–28 " : *Zeitschr. f. Wissensch. Theol.* 1873.

of Weiss, notwithstanding the efforts this critic makes to harmonize it with the expressions of the apostle (§ 99, note 4). Ver. 26 has no meaning unless it adds to the idea of ver. 23 that of universal resurrection. Besides, we have the express words of Paul, Acts xxiv. 15: "Having hope in God, which they (the Jews) also share, that there will be a resurrection of the dead, of the just *and of the unjust.*" Luke knew St. Paul sufficiently to avoid attributing to him on this point a declaration which would have been contrary to his view.—As to Grimm's opinion, we have spoken of it already in connection with ver. 22. We merely add here the words of Reuss regarding this view: "Neither Paul nor any member of the primitive Church dreamed of it."—It must therefore be admitted with Meyer and the majority of the commentators, that Paul teaches a resurrection to life, and a resurrection to condemnation, agreeably to the Lord's express declaration John v. 28, 29, and to the delineation Rev. xx. 12–14. Return to the fulness of personal existence by the resurrection of the body is the necessary condition of judgment in the case of both.

Does St. Paul distinguish two epochs of resurrection?

Reuss, Weiss, and many others do not think that Paul distinguishes a first resurrection, that of believers, at the Advent, from a second general, and later, resurrection. Ver. 23 is sufficiently explained, according to Weiss, if it is supposed that Paul meant to anticipate this objection: Why, since Christ is raised, is no dead believer yet raised? The answer, according to Weiss, is: Each in his order; Christ first; the others afterwards, only at the time of His Advent. But is this contrast between Christ and believers sufficient to explain naturally the term ἕκαστος, *each,* of ver. 23? Besides, it is impossible to find, either in this passage or in any other part of the New Testament, the least trace of an objection like that which Weiss here imagines. In the passage 1 Thess. iv. 13 seq., Paul is not answering the objection: Why are our dead not raised? but the question: Why do we, believers, die before the Lord's return?

Reuss and Weiss also allege that the Advent being, according to the whole of the New Testament, the signal of the end of things, there would not be between this event and the giving up of the kingdom to the Father the interval needed for a new act of resurrection. But we have seen, on the contrary, that Paul distinctly separates the Advent from *the end* (the giving up of the kingdom to the Father). "Then the end," says he, "when He shall give up the kingdom, *when He shall have put down* (or after having put down) His enemies . . ." This putting down is an action which requires some time ; now this action is, on the one hand, the consequence of the Advent, and, on the other, the condition of the end. It is therefore posterior to the one, anterior to the other. And if the victory over death is to take place in this period, and to mark its close, if moreover, as we have seen, it can only be found in universal resurrection, the distinction between two resurrections, that of believers and that of human beings in general, in Paul's mind, can no longer be contested. The same conclusion follows clearly from Phil. iii. 11, which can only apply to universal resurrection.—Moreover, there is nothing so wonderful in this idea of two resurrections in Paul's writings. There are two sayings of Jesus in the Gospel of Luke which prove that He taught exactly to the same effect, xiv. 14 : "Thou shalt be recompensed at the resurrection of the just ; " this expression has no meaning unless it is contrasted with another resurrection, that of the unjust, xx. 35 : "They who shall be accounted worthy to obtain that world and the resurrection (literally : *that*) *from the dead*." This expression contrasts the first resurrection (that of the just from the dead) with the resurrection of the dead generally. Finally, we find the same distinction in the Apocalypse, xx. 6 : "Blessed and holy is he that hath part in the first resurrection ! "

Finally, let us compare the *principal parallel passages in the New Testament* on the subject treated in this section :

1. In ver. 51 of our chapter there is described the resurrection of believers of which ver. 23 speaks. Only an important circumstance is added, of which no mention is made here: the transfiguration of believers who are living at the time of the Advent. The apostle had no occasion to mention this detail in our passage. It is obvious how prudently the argument *e silentio* must be used in criticism.

2. 1 Thess. iv. 13–17. At the time of the Advent the

dead *in Christ* rise—which implies that the rest do not rise,—and living believers are carried to meet the returning Lord—which implies a bodily transformation effected in them, precisely that which is expressly mentioned 1 Cor. xv. 51. There is therefore entire harmony between our passage and that of Thessalonians. The Advent will be accompanied by the resurrection of believers, and of believers only.

3. Phil. ii. 9–11. Mention is made of the supreme elevation of the Messiah terminating in the universal homage rendered to His kingship throughout all the domains of heaven and earth, and places under the earth. This homage corresponds to the universal submission spoken of in ver. 27 of our passage.

4. Rev. xx. xxi. Meyer, Grimm, and others hold that this passage is irreconcilable with ours. Let us see. The Advent was described at the end of the preceding chapter, from xix. 11. What takes place after this event ?

Satan is cast into prison for a thousand years ; then, being set free, he makes a last attempt to overthrow the work of God by destroying the community of the saints ; after which he is finally judged and goes into the lake of fire to rejoin the Beast and the False Prophet who had been cast into it at the time of the Advent (xix. 20).—Does not this whole representation exactly correspond to what St. Paul called, in ver. 24, the putting down of hostile powers, which takes place during the reign of Christ inaugurated by the Advent ?

At the time of the Advent the saints, the martyrs, and all those in general who refused to take part in the work of the Beast, rise again, and thrones of judgment are given them (xx.).—This is the resurrection of believers mentioned in our ver. 23. It is objected that only those martyrs and believers are mentioned who have overcome the test of the kingdom of Antichrist, and not those who have struggled and conquered during the whole course of the history of the Church. It is forgotten that from the New Testament point of view this last crisis is very near to the apostolic times. *It is the last hour*, says John (1 Ep. ii. 18). *The mystery of iniquity doth already work*, says Paul, speaking of the work of the Man of Sin. The believers of the eighteen centuries which have followed are therefore implicitly included in those who are mentioned in the Apocalyptic description, as they are in our ver. 23. Let us add, as an interesting parallel, what Paul said vi. 2 of the judgment of the world and even of angels by the saints. The reign of Christ and of the Church of the risen is a time of judgment in Paul as well as in the Apocalypse.

At the end of the thousand years the resurrection and the last judgment take place; and death is cast into the lake of fire (*ὁ θάνατος καὶ ὁ ᾅδης ἐβλήθησαν εἰς τὴν λίμνην τοῦ πυρός*). Here we have the most exact parallel to our ver. 26, where death is destroyed, and destroyed as the last enemy.

The new heaven and the new earth replace the work of the first creation; "*the tabernacle of God* (*θεοῦ σκηνή*) comes down *among men; God dwells with them, their God.*"—Had John meant to give a commentary on the last words of our ver. 28: *And God shall be all in all,* could he have done better?—And it is between these two representations that there are said to be insoluble contradictions! There are in each only one or two features which more particularly distinguish it from the other; in that of Paul: the giving up of the kingdom to the Father; in that of the Apocalypse: the indication of the duration of a thousand years as the interval between the Advent and *the end,* and the setting in relief of a last attempt on the part of Satan, at the end of the Messianic reign of Jesus, which leads to his final perdition. These special features only serve to demonstrate the originality and independence of the two conceptions.

5. If, finally, we consider the sayings of Jesus relative to His future Advent, it is evident that the Master's coming described in the parable of the talents (Matt. xxv.), in that of the pounds (Luke xix.), and in the parable of the virgins, refers to the Advent by which the Messianic kingdom will be inaugurated. The same is true of the prophecies relative to the preliminary division which on His return takes place within His Church, Luke xvii. 22–37, and in which some are taken, others left. These sayings refer to the Advent, when, according to Paul, *those who are in Christ* shall alone be raised (1 Cor. xv. 23). It is no less clear that in the great description of the final and universal judgment (Matt. xxv. 31), we find ourselves face to face with an entirely

different scene. Here it is not the members of the Church who are called to give account of the use of the gifts which they have received; it is *all nations* (*πάντα τὰ ἔθνη*, all the Gentiles) who appear before the judgment-seat. As Edwards says: "In Matt. xxv. 31 a transition is unquestionably made from the resurrection of saints which takes place at the coming of Christ to the general judgment which takes place after that event."[1] The *ὅταν δὲ ἔλθῃ ὁ υἱὸς τοῦ ἀνθρώπου, but when the Son of man shall come,* seems therefore to denote a final coming, posterior to the Advent.

This doctrine of the apostle is not to be regarded as an importation into the gospel of his former Pharisaism. I believe it is impossible to cite a passage of Jewish theology really like that of our Epistle or the parallel passage of the Apocalypse (see Schürer, *Geschichte des jüdischen Volkes,* 1886, § 29).

There is a real harmony, therefore, between the different eschatological passages of the New Testament. Ewald himself pronounces on the central point of the question, when he says: "Though Paul does not expressly mention the Millennium of Rev. xx., he yet places, between the preceding period and the end of that which follows, a sufficiently long interval filled with many various and considerable events." If this harmony is not recognised by Meyer, it is the consequence of his false interpretation of vers. 23, 24. It is, besides, perfectly legitimate to complete, as we have done, the one of these representations by details taken from the other, since we are obliged to do something similar with the various passages of St. Paul himself. Thus in vers. 50, 51 of our chapter he supplies the fact of the transformation of those Christians who shall be alive at the Advent, of which he says nothing in our passage, and in 1 Thess. iv. 15–17 he supplies the fact of their being caught up into the air, of which no mention is made in the two passages of our chapter.

[1] Edwards adds in a note: "After reading Bishop Waldegrave's *New Testament Millenarianism* (2nd ed. 1866), and Dr. Brown's *Second Advent* (6th ed. 1867), I am not convinced that the apostle does not teach the doctrine of two resurrections. Neither of these writers, so far as I have observed, touches upon the argument that death is not destroyed at the Advent."

Vers. 29–34

After securing for the resurrection of the body its place among the great hopes which stir the hearts of all believers, the apostle adds, as a supplementary argument, a few reflections as to the moral consequences of the denial of the dogma. Suppress the resurrection, and *baptism for the dead* becomes meaningless, and devotion to the cause of Christ madness. The only true wisdom is to enjoy the good things of this brief life as much as possible.—The apostle, when he reasons thus, seems to confound the dogma of the resurrection of the body with that of the immortality of the soul. We shall examine this difficulty at the close.

Ver. 29. "For else, what shall they do which are baptized for the dead? If the dead rise not at all, why are they baptized for them?"[1]—The ἐπεί, *for since*, is here taken, as often, in the sense of: for if it is not so (if the dead rise not). The English translation can render this idea by: *for otherwise, else.* This conjunction rests, not on ver. 28 only, but on the whole preceding passage, from ver. 20: "If Christ risen be not the first-fruits of a harvest of glorified ones in whom God will become all in all . . ."—We must not confound the expression τί ποιήσουσιν, *what shall they do?* with the form τί ποιοῦσιν, *what do they?* The understood answer with the verb in the present would be: *Nonsense*, an absurdity; whereas with the verb in the future the meaning is: *what result, what profit will they gain?* Answer: *none.* It has been sought

[1] T. R. with L Syr[sch]: των νεκρων (*the dead*), instead of αυτων (*them*).

to explain the future in a purely logical sense: "What will every baptism be, performed under such conditions (once the resurrection is denied)?" But the following verses show that Paul's eye is really turned to the future, the future which is to follow death: and if such was the meaning of this future tense, the logical condition would have required to be more expressly indicated. The meaning is certainly the same as that of the question: τί μοι τὸ ὄφελος, *what advantageth it me* (ver. 32)? The idea therefore is: "What will accrue to them from such a baptism?" Holsten recognises this: "The future relates to the result yet to come."

Somewhere about thirty explanations are reckoned of the expression: *to be baptized for the dead.* This diversity is due, on the one hand, to our ignorance of the usage to which Paul alludes, on the other, to the absence of any parallel expression to guide us in the explanation of it. The term used by the apostle was evidently well known to his readers. In their Christian vocabulary it was a sort of technical phrase.—The ancient commentators are not altogether at one about its explanation. In two of his works (*Cont. Marc.* v. 10, and *De resur. carn.* 48) Tertullian says that the apostle is here referring to the custom of baptizing a living Christian in place of another who died without baptism; but he does not think it follows from the reasoning of the apostle that he approved of such a custom. Epiphanius relates that the Cerinthians, when one of their catechumens happened to die, caused a member of the Church to be baptized in his room, that the deceased might escape the penalties of the unbaptized. Chrysostom tells the same story of the Marcionites.[1] But these two Fathers do not think the apostle meant to refer to such a custom as existing among the first Christians. It is otherwise with Ambrosiaster: "Paul takes an example from the fact that if any one died before receiving baptism, a living person was baptized for him, because it was feared either that he would not rise again, or that he would rise again to suffer." A very large number of ancient and modern commentators have adopted this meaning given by the Roman commentator, particularly Anselm, Erasmus, Grotius, Rückert, de Wette, Neander, Kling, Heinrici, Renan, Reuss, Edwards, Holsten. The last, as well as Kling, thinks he can connect this custom of representative baptism with the sickness prevailing at Corinth, mentioned xi. 30. This connection is inadmissible; for those who were stricken with sickness were unworthy communicants, who were all baptized. As to the explanation itself, I do not think the apostle could have taken as the basis of an argument a superstitious custom absolutely opposed to his spiritual conception. Reuss himself says: "We grant that the argument in itself is extremely weak; indeed, it has probably no other object than to show the opponents guilty of self-contradiction." But even on this supposition, what purpose would have been served by adopting this course of bad logic and of doubtful

[1] "When a catechumen of theirs dies, they conceal a living one under the bed of the deceased; then, approaching the latter, they converse with him and ask him if he wishes to receive baptism. Then he who is under the bed declares in place of the dead that he would like to be baptized" (*Catena*, p. 310). Neander and Heinrici suspect Chrysostom of caricaturing the procedure of the Marcionites.

honesty? The opponents whom he sought to convince by such means would no doubt have answered that one absurdity is not proved by a greater; for, if they rejected the resurrection of the body, they would evidently reject baptism for the dead so understood. Rückert and Heinrici think that this was merely a preliminary argument, and that Paul had in view to rectify the superstitious custom from which it was drawn, when he should go to Corinth (xi. 34), that is to say, that he had in view then to refute himself! Heinrici supposes that this strange procedure arose from the consideration which he required to show to his colleague Apollos, who was very zealous in the matter of baptism, and who had introduced this kind of ceremony at Corinth. But we have seen that the part ascribed to Apollos by this critic is a simple creation of his imagination. It would consequently be necessary, if such was St. Paul's argument, to go the length of holding with Holsten that the apostle's spiritualism was yet very rudimentary, and that he himself had not drawn from it its last consequences. But who can believe that the man who had combated the *opus operatum* with such energy in his conflict with Jewish legalism, would have restored or tolerated it himself in a new form in the Churches which he had founded? The man whose spiritualism became that of the entire Church, and ours also at the present hour, certainly did not adopt in his evangelical convictions and practice an element stamped with the grossest religious materialism. Besides, we have no instance which can lead us to suppose that such a custom had a place in the life of the primitive Churches. It was not till after the apostolic period that the idea of the magical virtue of the sacraments began to corrupt the primitive spirituality. To these reasons there is added another, taken from the text itself: As the advantage of such an act must have accrued, not to those who performed it, but to those in whose behalf it was performed, instead of saying: "What shall they gain who are baptized for the dead?" Paul would have required to say: "What will the dead gain for whom such baptisms are performed?" This last reason would seem to me of itself sufficient to secure the rejection of an interpretation otherwise so incompatible with the apostle's moral dignity and with the character of the apostolic Churches. As to the sects mentioned by the Fathers, they belong to a later period, when the life of the Church had lost its primitive simplicity, both in doctrine and ritual. And it may be supposed, not improbably, that it was our very passage, misunderstood, which gave rise to the absurd practices to which we have referred.

This meaning, the first—we admit—to occur to the mind, being set aside, we find ourselves face to face with a multitude of explanations, no one of which has yet succeeded in gaining general approval. Certain of them may be set aside without discussion, so evidently do they do violence to the meaning of one or other of the terms used by Paul. Beza: "Those who bathe the dead before burying them;" Thomas Aquinas: "Those who are baptized to obtain the pardon of mortal sins;" Olshausen: "The new converts who are baptized to fill the blank left in the Church by the Christians who die;" John Edwards (year 1692), quoted by Edwards: "Those who are converted by contemplating the glorious death of the martyrs, as Paul himself was in consequence of Stephen's death." — Luther and Ewald[1] explain: "Those who are baptized over the graves of the martyrs." But the preposition ὑπέρ, *over*, has never this local sense in the New Testament, and such a custom belongs to a kind of devotion posterior to the time of the apostles. Besides, the argument would have proved absolutely nothing. — Several commentators apply the word τῶν νεκρῶν, *the dead*, to the baptized themselves. So Chrysostom and the ancient Greek commentators: "for themselves as dead, that is to say, with a view to their own resurrection;" Chrysostom paraphrases τῶν νεκρῶν by τῶν σωμάτων. To the same effect Linder:[2] "*In gratiam cinerum.*" But to give the argument any force, it would require to be established that the apostolic Church maintained a peculiar relation between the sacrament of baptism and the bodily resurrection of the baptized. The passage Rom. vi. 1 seq. proves nothing in this respect; for it refers only to spiritual resurrection. Then there would have been no need of the article before νεκρῶν; Paul must have said in this sense: for [*some*] dead (themselves as dead), and not: for *the* dead.—Otto[3] has modified this meaning, applying the term *the dead* to the adversaries of the resurrection at Corinth. The question, according to him, is ironical: "Why, if there is no resurrection, do these people have themselves

[1] *Die Sendschreiben des Apostels Paulus*, p. 213.

[2] *Studien u. Kritiken*, 1862.

[3] *Dekalogische Untersuchungen, nebst einem Anhang über die Todtentaufe in Corinth*, 1857.

baptized to result in their being of the dead, not of the living?" The answer would thus be ironically introduced into the question. But in this sense the article would have required to be rejected. And would not this sarcasm be utterly out of place after the sublime thought of ver. 28? Finally, the following question, in that case reproducing it a second time, would be grossly out of place.—It would be much more natural, starting from this explanation of τῶν νεκρῶν, *the dead*, to adopt the sense of Epiphanius and Calvin, who apply the words to the catechumens threatened with death by accident or disease, and who asked baptism, as Calvin says, "either for their own consolation, or for the edification of the brethren." In this case we must understand the words: "for the dead," in the sense of: in view of death, or: as about to be soon gathered to the dead; as Bengel says: "*qui mox post baptismum ad mortuos aggregabuntur.*" But one cannot help feeling how forced are the two meanings thus given to ὑπέρ, especially the former.

A group of more probable explanations, approaching in meaning the words of Bengel just quoted, is that in which the term: *the dead*, is applied to all deceased Christians, and to the Lord Jesus Christ Himself. So Pelagius and Diestelmann:[1] "For the love of Christ; to be one day united with Him and with the faithful who surround Him in His kingdom." But the term: *they who are baptized*, would require in this case to be applied to all Christians; now the οἱ before βαπτιζόμενοι denotes a special class of Christians. As is well said by Calvin: "*Non de omnibus loquitur quum*

[1] *Jahrbücher für deutsche Theologie*, 1861.

dicit: quid facient qui baptizantur?" And if Paul wished to characterize Christians in general, why speak of baptism rather than of faith? It is faith, and not the sign of faith, which opens the way into the kingdom of Christ. The same objections are opposed to Köster's[1] meaning: "To remain united to their dead Christian relatives and friends." This explanation has moreover against it the want of a more precise description added to the general term "the dead."

But these last interpretations, though we cannot accept them as satisfactory, set us on the way of what seems to us the true one. Morus, Flatt, and Lightfoot (the older) have thought that in this phrase: *to be baptized for the dead*, the word *baptized* referred, not to the baptism of water, but to the baptism of blood, by martyrdom. We have two sayings uttered by the Lord, in which the term baptism is used in this meaning; the one pointing to His own death, Luke xii. 50: "I have a baptism to be baptized with;" the other, to the bloody death of His disciples, Mark x. 38: "Can ye be baptized with the baptism wherewith I shall be baptized?" One can easily understand how, under the influence of such sayings, there was formed in the primitive Church a new expression such as that used here by the apostle, to denote the bloody death of martyrdom. The words: "for the dead," would thus signify: to be baptized, not as the believer is with the baptism of water to enter into the Church of the living, but to enter into that of the dead, the word dead being chosen in contrast to the Church on

[1] *Lutherische Zeitschrift.* 1862.

the earth and to bring out the heroism of that martyr-baptism which leads to life only through communion with the dead. Thereby the article *οἱ* before *βαπτιζόμενοι* is fully explained; such baptized ones certainly form a class of Christians by themselves. The future also, *ποιήσουσιν*, is accounted for: "If there is no resurrection, what will be gained by such baptized ones, by their joining the ranks of the dead for the love of Christ and of the Church in heaven?" Finally, we shall see how natural on this explanation is the transition to the question of ver. 30: "Why do we also stand in jeopardy every hour?" To this interpretation it is objected that there had not yet been either persecutions or martyrs in the Church of Corinth. But there had been persecutions and martyrs in the Church in general; comp. Acts vii. 58, ix. 1, xii. 2, xiv. 19; and there might have been some which are unknown to us. Ver. 32 of our chapter shows how many circumstances there are even in the life of the best known of the apostles of which we are totally ignorant.[1]

[1] We ought to mention at least in a note the astounding explanation of Hofmann, which it is difficult to take seriously: The *ὑπὲρ τῶν νεκρῶν* depends not on *οἱ βαπτιζόμενοι*, but on *τί ποιήσουσι*; *νεκροί* should be taken in the moral sense; the second *ὑπὲρ τῶν νεκρῶν*, or rather according to the true reading the *ὑπὲρ αὐτῶν*, belongs to the question of ver. 32. The meaning thus becomes: "For otherwise, what will Christians yet be able to do for those who are perishing in their sins? Why also are Christians themselves baptized? Why do we, apostles, from love to them, expose ourselves to constant dangers?" But in this chapter *νεκρός* can only be taken literally; the regimen *ὑπὲρ* naturally depends on *οἱ βαπτιζόμενοι*: and this participle with the article must here designate a special class of Christians; the *ὑπὲρ αὐτῶν* can only, considering the parallelism, depend on *βαπτίζονται*, as the first *ὑπὲρ* on *βαπτιζόμενοι*; not to speak of the vagueness of the expression: "*to do something* for the dead and for Christians."

The second question is a more emphatic repetition of the first. And therefore we are led to refer the proposition εἰ ὅλως . . . to what follows. As the first question was prefaced by the ἐπεί, the second is introduced by the subordinate proposition, which is a more emphatic development of the ἐπεί: "If absolutely the dead do not return to bodily life."—The καί signifies *notwithstanding*, as in vii. 21. These are two things which cannot co-exist (to remain dead, and to be baptized for them). Undoubtedly we must read ὑπὲρ αὐτῶν, *for them*, with almost all the authorities, connecting this regimen with βαπτίζονται, and not with κινδυνεύομεν, as Hofmann will have it.

Vers. 30, 31. "And why stand we also in jeopardy every hour? 31. I protest, brethren,[1] by that glorying in you,[2] which I have in Christ our Lord, I die daily."—The transition from the bloody death of the martyrs (ver. 29) to the daily life of the apostles, which is a constant menace of martyrdom (ver. 30), is easily understood. The force of the καί, *also*, which, in the other explanations, always presents some difficulty, is perfectly simple. — The *we* includes Paul, Silas, Timothy, who laboured together at Corinth; then the other apostles, who live like Paul in perpetual danger of death. — This ver. 30 reminds us of the passages iv. 9; 2 Cor. iv. 10, 11, xi. 23–27; Rom. viii. 35, 36.

Ver. 31. Comp. Rom. viii. 36: "For thy sake are we killed all the day." There is no day nor hour of the day when they may not expect to be seized and

[1] T. R. omits αδελφοι (*brethren*), with D E F G L It.

[2] T. R. with A reads ημετεραν (*our*), instead of υμετεραν (*your*), read by all the rest.

brought to execution.—The classical phrase νή with an accusative of person or thing, as an affirmation on oath, occurs nowhere else in the New Testament, yet Paul might have had the opportunity of using it 2 Cor. i. 23. — The reading ἡμετέραν (*our*), which signifies: "the cause of glorying which we may have in you," is condemned not only by the authority of the documents, but by the two verbs in the singular, between which this adjective would stand. According to the reading ὑμετέραν, *your*, the subject is still the ground of glorying which Paul finds in them: "the cause of glorying you are to me by your faith." What labours had not this work cost him! What dangers had he not had to run to accomplish it! The last words: *in Christ our Lord*, soften what might be too self-exalting in these expressions. If all these successes have been gained by him, it is only because of his communion with Christ.—The apostle finally takes from his present stay at Ephesus an example of that daily death in the midst of which he passes his life.

Ver. 32. "If it is as man that I have fought with beasts at Ephesus, what advantageth it me? If the dead rise not, let us eat and drink; for to-morrow we die."—The meaning of the expression κατὰ ἄνθρωπον, *according to man*, must be determined by the context. It might be applied to human *strength*, which was not that with which the apostle laboured; or he might mean that in his work he had a higher *end* in view than that which the natural man sets before him in labouring. I am inclined to believe in a third meaning: With a view to what man can give by way of recompense. The *θηριομαχεῖν, to fight with wild beasts,* is taken by almost all modern commentators, down to Meyer, Reuss, Heinrici (Holsten excepted), in the figurative sense: to struggle with a furious multitude excited against him. It is in the same sense that Ignatius (*Ad Rom.* c. 5) speaks of the ten leopards (his keepers) with whom he has to fight day and night during his journey (*θηριομαχῶ δέκα λεοπάρδοις*). In favour of this sense we could not quote the tumult raised by the goldsmith Demetrius; for this event did not take place till after the composition of our letter, and Paul did nothing on that occasion which could justify the term *fight.* But some similar scene might have passed at Ephesus in the first period of Paul's sojourn. I cannot, however, adhere to this explanation of the word *θηριομαχεῖν.* Similar conflicts were too frequent in the apostle's life to admit of his mentioning this one in so exceptional a way. Unless we are to ascribe to Paul an exaggeration very alien to his character, it will be every way more natural to apply this expression to the punishment of the *bestiarii,* in the strict sense of the word. This meaning agrees better also with the feeling of free-will which breathes in the words: *If I have fought.* To this is objected the right of Roman citizenship which Paul possessed, and which secured him from such treatment. But if the thing passed in a popular rising, the apostle's protestations might not have been listened to. It is also said that he could not have escaped death, and that in any case such a fact could not fail to be mentioned in the Acts. But how many facts of this kind are mentioned in the list 2 Cor. xi., of which we have not a hint in the narrative of the

Acts? And as to deliverance, it may have been due to some providential circumstance or other which we cannot divine. The fact is that this ἐθηριομάχησα designates in the apostle's view the apogee of the: "I die daily," and this gradation admits only of the literal sense. As Holsten says: "If there were nothing extraordinary and particular in this fight, Paul would not have so mentioned it in the context."[1]—When he says: *What doth it profit me?* the apostle's thought is that only the expectation of a life to come can explain such conduct. Moral duty in itself would not account for it, for there is no natural obligation which requires a man to sacrifice himself in the service of Jesus Christ. Besides, when he speaks of profit, Paul is thinking, not of a reward due to acquired merit, but of God's response to the holy aspirations with which He has Himself endowed the human soul.

The proposition: *If the dead rise not,* would be awkward, if connected with what precedes; it suits better as an introduction to what follows: "Say then also, in this case, like the despisers of the Divine judgment in Isaiah (xxii. 13): Let us eat . . ." Paul does expressly say that such language is used at Corinth; but he declares that it is the natural consequence of what is said there about the resurrection. There is, I

[1] Hofmann and Holsten explain the non-mention of this fact in the Acts by the alleged intention of Luke to relate nothing contrary to the benevolent action of the Roman magistracy toward Christianity. But what of Paul's three shipwrecks, all of them previous to the only one which Luke relates Acts xxvii., and his spending three times twenty-four hours in the deep (2 Cor. xi. 25)? Is it from deference to the Romans that Luke has omitted them also? Besides, the right of Roman citizenship would certainly not have been disregarded by Roman magistrates; comp. Acts xvi. 38, 39, xxii. 27–29.

believe, less of bravado than of despondency in the saying quoted : "Since we have nothing better to look for, let us at least enjoy the present." This forms the transition to the word of warning and exhortation which closes the first part of the chapter.

Vers. 33, 34. "Be not deceived : evil company doth corrupt good[1] manners. 34. Awake up righteously, and sin not; for some of you have not the knowledge of God : I speak [thus][2] to move you to shame."—The formula μὴ πλανᾶσθε does not signify : Let not yourselves be misled by others; its meaning always is: "Do not deceive yourselves (by false reasonings)." — What follows applies undoubtedly to the secret thoughts of the Corinthians whereby they sought to excuse certain acts which still kept up a connection between them and the heathen society around ; comp. particularly chaps. viii.–x. This meaning seems to me more natural than that of Meyer, who applies the expression *evil companionships* to the τινές, the *some* spoken of in ver. 34. Paul is rather addressing the whole Church of which these some still form part. It is they who run the risk of being seduced by their heathen friends.—Erasmus, Luther, and some moderns (Heinrici, Holsten) give to ὁμιλίαι the meaning of *conversations.* This is a possible meaning. But the ordinary signification, *societies, companies,* is perfectly suitable.—The saying quoted by Paul has been found in the fragments of the *Thais* of Menander, a comic poet, who flourished in the 3rd century before Christ. It is easily recognised as an iambic trimeter acatalectic

[1] T. R. reads without authorities χρησθ', instead of χρηστα.

[2] T. R. with A F G K L : λεγω (*I say*) ; ℵ B D E P : λαλω (*I speak*).

verse, provided it be written, as in the T. R., putting χρῆσθ' and not χρῆστα. We are uncertain whether Menander borrowed this sentence from common usage, and simply made a verse of it, or if it passed from his comedy into ordinary use, as a sort of proverb. Paul himself may have borrowed it either from the one or other of these sources. In both cases, the form χρῆστα is probably Paul's original reading; why should he have been concerned to preserve the exact poetic form? The meaning only was of importance to him. The form χρῆσθ' is therefore a correction. Already true in its application to ordinary moral life, the saying becomes still more so from the religious and Christian standpoint. Spiritual life is quenched in the atmosphere of carnal society, and a sort of intoxication quickly comes over him who frequents it. Hence the following abrupt exhortation.

Ver. 34. The word ἐκνήφειν strictly signifies: *to get out of the stupefaction caused by drunkenness.* The aorist imperative denotes an energetic, decided act. Nothing less will do if the Church is to shake off the torpor with which some of its members have been seized.—The word δικαίως here signifies *seriously,* or as we say: *en règle,* in due order. They were so far awaked already from their natural slumber, from their former carnal state, but only half; and hence the reason why this state had so easily regained the upper hand in many of them.—The present imperative ἁμαρτάνετε, *sin,* forms a contrast to the preceding aorist: the act of awaking is unique, decisive; but the state of sin which would follow without fail from the intoxication into which they were plunging, would, if they persisted, become permanent; this is what forms the danger of it; for such a life swayed by sin leads to total apostasy. Such is the terrible sin present to the mind of St. Paul when he uses the verb ἁμαρτάνετε, suggesting the strict meaning of the word in Greek: *to miss the aim.*—The *for* states the reason why he thinks he ought to address to them so formidable a warning. There was in the Church a knot of strong-headed members who, as we have seen, more than once derided the apostle's directions, and claimed to be more clear-sighted than he. Paul describes these people strangely. Instead of saying to them that they have not the knowledge of God, he says literally: that *they have the non-knowledge,* ἀγνωσία, of God. It is not merely a deficiency, the lack of a good thing, it is the possession of a real evil. It involves not only inanition, but poisoning. We must beware of limiting this *non-knowledge* of God to the denial of His power to raise the dead, as might be inferred from the parallel Matt. xxii. 29; the rebuke is too serious for that: it is the Divine holiness, the apprehension of which these men have stifled within them, by substituting for it a deeply corrupted notion of God's character, that they might give themselves up to their presumptuous and profane frivolity; it is that moral libertinism to which the Pantheistic conception of the Divine Being leads. For as to the suspicion of atheism, it is excluded by the very expression which the apostle uses. In the presence of such a group of men within the Church there is cause for profound humiliation, and at the same time an alarming danger. According to the T. R., the meaning of the last words would be: "I *say* this to you (λέγω) to shame you." According to the Alex.: "I *speak* thus to you (λάλω) to . . .," which is undoubtedly better. The apostle thus insists on the tone he is obliged to take, rather than on the matter of his words.—This severe tone is intended to throw them back on themselves (ἐντρέπεσθαι), and so to make humiliation succeed to pride and the feeling of their fall to that of the superiority which they think they possess over all the other Churches; comp. the expressions either analogous, vi. 5, or opposite, iv. 14.

The apostle has restored the expectation of the resurrection to its true bases, and so demonstrated its certainty. It now remains to solve the objections which are raised to the *possibility* of such an event, by showing how it will take place. This is what he does in the second part of the chapter.

But, before passing to the study of this new subject, we have to examine the question put at the beginning of the foregoing discussion: Does not the apostle throughout this passage confound the resurrection of the body with the immortality of the soul, and does he not ascribe to the denial of the former, practical consequences which, strictly speaking, only flow from the denial of the latter?—It seems to me that the Apostle Paul could not possibly be so much of a novice on this question as to be guilty of such confusion. The question of the survival of the personality after death was as thoroughly raised by Sadduceism as that of the resurrection of the body; and it is impossible that in the polemic of the Pharisees against the Sadducees the two questions should not have been distinguished. Are we not entitled to suppose, especially after the immediately preceding verses, that if Paul reasons as he does, it is because in the opinion of the adversaries whom he had before him the two denials were really confounded? And, in fact, once the hope of the resurrection of the body is abandoned, there no longer remains any very solid security for the survival of the person after death. There is a speedy gliding down the incline which leads from the idea of the annihilation of the body to the Pantheistic absorption of the finite spirit in the absolute Spirit. And it seems to me that if we carefully weigh the bearing, not only of vers. 33 and 34 of our chapter, but also of the passage vi. 12–20, there can be little doubt that the adversaries of the resurrection at Corinth were on this path, though Paul carefully avoids expressly saying so, and only exhibits this disastrous consequence as a result to be dreaded. But in this question there is another point of view, which is to be carefully taken into account. Paul is reasoning not as a philosopher, but as an apostle, that is to say, from the viewpoint of the Christian salvation. Now if the resurrection be once denied, either as to believers or as to Christ Himself, what means the survival of the soul after death? Paul has told us in ver. 18: "Then they which are fallen asleep in Christ are perished;" a saying the meaning of which is obvious from the preceding words: "We are yet in our sins." Such an immortality is more to be dreaded than desired; it is not therefore of a nature to weaken the pernicious practical consequences drawn from the denial of the resurrection. It rather gives them new force. For is not condemnation following a life of sacrifice still more terrible than annihilation? Weiss says with perfect truth (*Bibl. Theol.* § 96[d]): "If Paul contends against those who deny the resurrection as if this denial involved the negation of all life after death, it must be remembered that with the denial of the resurrection of the body the resurrection of Christ in his view fell to the ground, and that consequently communion with the living Christ beyond the tomb was no longer possible." In such circumstances, the conclusion was evident: Why torment ourselves to acquire and to bring into the possession of others a salvation which will never be realized? Better enjoy life peaceably till it be withdrawn from us.

The same confusion which is here ascribed to Paul might be imputed to Jesus Himself, on the occasion of His reply to the Sadducees, Matt. xxii. 29–32 and parallels. This reply indeed assumes that the immortality of the soul necessarily implies the resurrection of the body.—The position of Jesus face to face with the Sadducees was almost the same as that of Paul in relation to the Corinthian opponents of the resurrection. The Sadducees could not conceive the existence of the spirit as independent of that of the body; from the annihilation of the latter there followed therefore the annihilation of the former. Hence it is that Jesus, not confining Himself to solving the difficulty which they had put to Him, takes the offensive and saps at the root their view of the resurrection, demonstrating to them, by the declaration of Jehovah to Moses regarding His relation to the long-dead patriarchs, the survival of their persons. He argues on the foundation of Jewish monotheism, as St. Paul here argues on the foundation of Christ's own resurrection. The relation of the patriarchs to the living God implies the permanence of their personal life, as the relation of believers to Christ raised in the body implies the permanence of their personal and bodily life.

B. The Mode of the Resurrection of the Body (vers. 35–58)

After demonstrating the essential part played by the resurrection in the Christian salvation, the apostle sets himself to answer the objections which this doctrine might raise. These objections were probably uttered ironically by certain members of the Church of Corinth who wished to parade their wisdom. It was not difficult, indeed, to turn the doctrine into ridicule, especially if it was understood in the gross way in which it was taught by the Rabbins, who regarded the resurrection as a restoration pure and simple of the present body by the reunion of the material elements of which it was composed. This is proved by numerous sayings in the Talmud; and it was probably this point of view at which the Sadducees placed themselves to ridicule this belief; as it is also by representing the resurrection in this way that scoffers of our own day give point to their sarcasms.

The apostle begins by answering two objections which human wisdom raises against the resurrection of the body: vers. 35–49; then he explains what will happen to the bodies of those who do not pass through death: vers. 50–53; finally, he closes with a triumphant conclusion: vers. 54–58.

Vers. 35–49

And first of all the two questions: ver. 35.

Ver. 35. "But some one will say, How are the dead raised up? and with what body do they come?"—These two questions have not altogether the same meaning, as is obvious even from the δέ, *and further*, which connects them. But neither do they differ, according to Meyer's view, as the general idea from the particular fact. The former bears on the hidden working whereby the awakening of the body which has been given over to death is accomplished (πῶς, *how*); the latter, on the result of this mysterious operation, that is to say, on the nature and qualities of the raised body (ποίῳ σώματι, *what* body). The passage which follows leaves no doubt as to the reality of the distinction between the two questions, for ver. 36 contains the answer to the former, and vers. 37–49 the answer to the latter.—Τίς, *some one;* one of those sages whose whole spiritual stock consists in not knowing God (ver. 34).—The verbs in the present: *are raised, come,* are ideal presents, and as such, include the fact to come in which the idea will be realized.—The apostle replies to the former question in ver. 36:

Ver. 36. "Fool![1] That which thou sowest is not quickened, except it die."—The vocative ἄφρον, *fool,* is evidently a correction, and ἄφρων to be read as a nominative; comp. Luke xii. 20. This nominative is used by apposition: "Fool *that thou art,* thou that thinkest thyself so wise!"—The pronoun σύ, *thou,* by

[1] ℵ A B D E F G P read αφρων instead of αφρον, which is read by T. R. with K L.

its position, is strongly emphatic; according to some, as opposed to θεός, *God,* in the sense: "As for thee, thou sowest what dies, whereas God sows what is to live;" but this antithesis is foreign to the context. This σύ, *thou,* put first, is logically connected with the epithet fool: "*Thy own* daily experience might instruct thee, if thou hadst eyes to see! Every time thou sowest a grain, thou *thyself* dost overturn the objection thou art raising."—The term ζωοποιεῖται, *is quickened,* does not strictly apply to a grain of corn; it is chosen in view of the application made of it to the raised body.—The death of the seed, the condition of its return to life, consists in the dissolution of its material wrappings under the action of the earth's moisture and heat. It is by this process of destruction that the impalpable germ of life which dwells in it, and which no anatomist's scalpel can reach, is set free. In proportion as the putrefaction of all the material elements takes place, this force awakes and shows itself by the simultaneous appearance, in opposite directions, of the two vital shoots, the stem and the root, the first vestiges of the new organism which is preparing to appear. Such is the answer given by nature to the first question raised: How is the resurrection effected? Through death itself! Through dissolution to true life: such is the way! What appears to be the obstacle is the means. This is the law which nature illustrates, and which satisfies common sense as solving the point in question. The apostle, by answering thus, avoids two rocks, against which those who treat this question lightly are very apt to make shipwreck. The one consists in identifying the raised body with the present body, as if the first must be formed by the reunion of all the material molecules of which the second was composed. Who could regard a magnificent oak, or an apple-tree laden with its vernal beauty, as the material reconstruction of the acorn or of the pip from which they sprang! The other, on the contrary, consists in destroying all connection between the two bodies, as if the latter were a new creation, without organic relation to the former. In this case we could no longer speak of resurrection. In reality, death would not be vanquished; it would keep its prey. God would simply do something new by its side. —In John xii. 24 the Lord uses this same figure of the grain of corn, applying it, however, to spiritual death and resurrection.—The apostle answers the second question, vers. 37–40. And first summarily, vers. 37, 38.

Vers. 37, 38. "And when thou sowest, thou sowest not that body that shall be, but bare grain, it may chance of wheat, or of some other grain: 38. but God giveth it a body as it hath pleased Him, and to every seed a[1] body of its own."—The *καί*, *and*, marks the transition to the second question. The answer to it will be much more developed. The first question implied an inexplicable mystery, and the answer could only be given by means of a not less mysterious analogous fact, borrowed from the life of nature. Here it is otherwise, for the point in question is the nature of the new body, which will result from this unfathomable operation, in contrast to the nature of the present body.—In translating: *when thou sowest*, we have tried to render more exactly the meaning of the construction used by the apostle than when it is

[1] T. R. reads with K L Or. Chrys.: το (*the*) before ἴδιον.

translated: *as to what thou sowest.* Literally, the meaning is this: "What thou sowest, thou dost not sow it (as being) the body which is to spring up . . ." This singular form, in which the expression: *that body that shall be,* is the grammatical apposition of: *what thou sowest,* is intended to express very forcibly the essential identity of the present and the future body. —The expression *bare grain* tacitly contrasts the grain stripped of all covering or ornament with that wealth of organs (leaves, calyx, corolla), which forms the beauty of the developed plant. By making use of this expression, the apostle no doubt means to suggest the nakedness of the human body when it is laid in the earth. Holsten applies the term *bare* [naked] to the soul divested of its body in Hades. But the subject in question is the body, and not the soul. The phrase *εἰ τύχοι* signifies neither *perhaps,* nor *for example,* as some translate, but: *if so be,* that is to say: according to the kind of grain thou hast in hand, at the time when thou sowest.

Ver. 38. With this bareness of the grain deposited in the earth, the apostle contrasts God's creative power, which quickly invests the seed with the covering, the body assigned to its kind, by making the plant sprout which is to serve as its organ. By saying: *as it hath pleased Him,* and not: as it pleases Him, Paul certainly refers to the law of vegetation established by God for every plant at the time of creation. This Divine volition remains in the bosom of changing nature; it controls beforehand the result of the sower's action. It is obvious how false it is to allege that Scripture knows nothing of the constancy of the laws of nature. The author who wrote, Gen. i. 11, in speaking of plants of all sorts: "bearing fruit after their kind," already understood this fundamental fact. —Thus the hundred thousand species of plants of which the vegetable kingdom is composed are all organized in such a way that to this infinite variety of seeds there corresponds an exactly similar variety of vegetable organisms. The article τό, *the*, before ἴδιον is to be rejected. In these last words: "*A* body of its own," there is implicitly contained the answer to the second question of ver. 35: *With what body?* The God who took care at the creation to furnish every seed with a body of its own, will know how to give to the energy hidden in our terrestrial body the new organ it will need when this vital principle shall be set free by death from the temporary wrapping in which it is now hidden. And to satisfy the inquirer who put the questions of ver. 35, on the subject of the new organ which is to replace our earthly body, and to prevent his imagining that God might be at a loss to produce a body entirely different from the present, the apostle invites him to cast a glance over the infinite diversity of the organisms which form the visible universe: vers. 39–41. The variety of vegetable organisms bears on form only, not on substance; it would not therefore of itself authorize the conclusion which the apostle wishes to establish, namely, the possibility of a new body, substantially different from our present body. Hence it is that he instances in the totality of nature differences still more profound than he had pointed out between the various kinds of plants.

Ver. 39. "All flesh is not the same flesh; but the

flesh of men is one, the flesh of beasts another, that of birds another, that of fish[1] another."—*Σάρξ*, *flesh*, denotes the substance of the organism, and not merely its external form. In this series of examples, man is placed at the head; for, while belonging by his body to the animal kingdom, he alone of all living beings possesses the capacity of reaching a higher existence.—*Κτήνη*, strictly: *cattle;* a word coming from *κτάομαι*, *to acquire, possess;* here, no doubt, denoting all *quadrupeds*, among which cattle form the class nearest to man.—*Πτηνά*, *birds;* this class follows the preceding, perhaps by way of alliteration, the names of the two classes differing very little in Greek.—*Fishes* are put last, as being lowest in the scale.

These four classes may be united in a single group, that of terrestrial beings, to be contrasted with a higher group, *celestial bodies.* These latter differ from the former both in substance and splendour.

Ver. 40. "There are also celestial bodies, and bodies terrestrial; but the glory of the celestial is different from the glory of the terrestrial."—In the first words Paul has in view difference of substance. Many, de Wette, Meyer, etc., understand by bodies celestial the bodies of angels; comp. Luke xx. 36; Matt. xxviii. 3. For, according to them, the term *σῶμα*, *body*, cannot apply to inanimate beings, like stars; unless we ascribe to Paul the ancient superstition which regarded these last as living beings. But we are not obliged so to limit the use of the word *σῶμα*, *body;* compare the application made of it to plants in vers. 37, 38. The scoffers

[1] T. R. with F G K L puts fishes before birds; ℵ A B D E P have the inverse order.

who refused to believe in the existence of the future body would hardly have admitted the existence of angelic bodies. To convince them on their own ground, the apostle appeals exclusively to what is seen : the grand spectacle of the starry sky, with the infinitely numerous and varied bodies with which it is studded. It is the counterpart of the not less rich, though less brilliant spectacle which is presented by terrestrial nature. The last words specially bring out this difference of splendour. The word δόξα denotes the brightness raying forth from existing objects. Terrestrial beings have theirs : flowers in the variety of their forms and colours, animals in their agility, grace, or strength, man in the nobility of his bearing, the freshness of his complexion, the light of his eye. But how great is that of the celestial bodies which illumine the earth with their brightness! To be remarked is the use of the adjective ἑτέρα, *different*, instead of ἄλλη, *other*. We pointed out, xii. 8–10, that the apostle does not use these terms indifferently. Here his intention is clear. He uses ἑτέρα, *different*, to denote the general difference between the two great classes of beings, and he applies ἄλλη, *other*, to the secondary difference distinguishing terrestrial bodies from one another (ver. 39), and celestial bodies from one another (ver. 41).

Ver. 41. "The glory of the sun is one, and the glory of the moon another, and the glory of the stars another: for star differeth from star in glory."—Even in the case of beings having so great a resemblance in nature (substance and form), if we observe them with some care we discover differences between one and another which attest the infinite riches of God's work and the illimitable range of His power. What a difference between the animating splendour of the sun on a fine day and the quiet moonlight; between the calm beauty of the latter and the penetrating and pure scintillations of the stars! There are differences too between the stars themselves. The brilliance of Venus does not resemble that of Mars, nor the latter that of Jupiter; and what a difference between the planets and the fixed stars! Open your eyes, then, the apostle means to say, and as you see so many different glories shining in the heavens, you will cease to ask, as if God's power were limited: "With what body shall they come?" You will understand how infinite are the resources of Divine power!

It has often been thought, that by stopping to describe so particularly this wide diversity of splendour, the apostle meant to allude to the difference of glory which will exist among the risen, according to the different degrees of moral perfection to which they have attained. The Fathers especially dwelt fondly on this view; see Ambrose, Chrysostom, Tertullian. This last makes the future body of God's servants correspond to the flesh of men; that of pagans, to the flesh of beasts; that of the martyrs, to the flesh of birds; that of the Christians who have had only baptism with water, to the flesh of fishes; then the glory of Christ corresponds to the brightness of the sun; that of the Church, to the brightness of the moon; that of the Jews, to the brightness of the stars (*De Resurrectione*, c. 52). All this is evidently only a play of imagination. The context requires no such application; for, as is proved by the sequel, Paul proposes, by bringing as it were before the very eye the infinite resources of Divine power, to show that God can hold in reserve for His elect a body absolutely different from their terrestrial body. But, while holding exegetically by this application, the only one justified by the context, we need not deny the possibility of a purely secondary allusion to the diversity which God may be pleased to make between the bodies of the risen. As Holsten well says: "The way in which Paul emphasizes the diversity of the heavenly bodies implies the supposition of an analogous difference of glory between the risen."

The apostle now applies the facts which have just been cited to the question under discussion: vers. 42–49. And that by expounding, first, the difference of nature between the present and the resurrection body.

Vers. 42, 43. "So also is the resurrection of the dead. The body is sown in corruption; it is raised in incorruption: 43. it is sown in dishonour; it is raised in glory: it is sown in weakness; it is raised in power."—Here, strictly speaking, is the answer to the second question of ver. 35: *With what body?* Answer: with a body which, far from being the reappearance of the former, will have characteristics of an absolutely opposite kind. The verb σπείρεται, *it is sown*, is generally applied, in accordance with the term *sow* in vers. 36 and 37, to the interment of the body. This meaning may no doubt suit the first member of the first antithesis: *sown in corruption.* But it is impossible to carry out this application in the first members of the three following antitheses. The term *weakness* is not suitable to the state of the dead body, whatever Meyer may say; and in any case, it would form a singular stage beyond the preceding term, dissolution.

Finally, it is still more impossible to apply the term *psychical,* "moved by a soul," in ver. 44, to the body which is laid in the tomb. No doubt it may be said that the point in question here is not *the state* of the body at that time, but its *nature* during life. But it is still very forced to apply the term *animated* to the body when deprived of the breath of life. For this reason, several commentators, such as Erasmus, Calvin, Heinrici, have been led to apply the term *sow* to the fact of *birth.* This meaning may suit the second and fourth epithets (*weak, psychical*) ; but hardly the other two (*in dishonour, dissolution*). How could Paul thus characterize the life of the child, full of freshness, at the moment when it begins to unfold its powers? Hofmann has been driven by these two impossibilities to understand by the word *sow* the giving up of the body, not specially to interment, but to the power of death, which works in it all through the duration of its earthly existence. This explanation comes near to what seems to me to be the true meaning of the four antitheses; but it is insufficient, inasmuch as it does not clearly account for their gradation. Their order is in a manner retrograde; and the meaning of the word *sow* is modified and widened as we pass from one antithesis to another. In the first, it relates to interment, as is required by the word φθορά, *dissolution.* In the second (*the state of dishonour*), the thought, taking a first retrograde step, embraces in the term *sow* all the miseries of this earthly life, which precede and go to produce the dissolution of the body, all the humiliating conditions to which our body is now subjected; comp. the expression: "the body of our humiliation" (Phil.

iii. 21). In the third antithesis, the term *weakness* brings us to the moment of birth, to that state of entire powerlessness which belongs to the infant at its entrance into life. Finally, the term *psychical* body, in ver. 44, carries us further back still, to that moment when the breath of life, ψυχή, is communicated to the physical germ which is about to begin its development in order to serve the ψυχή as its organ. The word *sow* thus embraces all the phases of the body's existence, which, beginning with the first dawn of being, terminates in committal to the earth. It is in this sense that the earthly life is so frequently compared to the time of sowing, and eternity to the time of harvest. The three first corresponding terms : *incorruptibility*, *glory*, and *power*, are easily understood. The first represents the body to come as exempt from the touch of sickness, decline, and death ; the second, as free from the daily infirmities of the present body, and all radiant with the brightness of perfect life ; the third, as endowed with unlimited power of action.—But these three opposite characteristics distinguishing between the present and the resurrection body are all three effects ; they rest on a fourth contrast which touches the very essence of the two bodies, and which the apostle indicates in the first proposition of ver. 44 by the antithesis between a *psychical* and a *spiritual* body. It is this last contrast which is developed in the following passage, vers. 44[b]–49.

Ver. 44. "It is sown a psychical body, it is raised a spiritual body; there[1] is a psychical body, and[2] there

[1] ℵ A B C D F G read ει (*if*) before εστι. This word is wanting in T. R. following E K L Syr[sch].

[2] The και is placed by ℵ A B C D E F G after εστι (*there is also*); T. R. with K L Syr. places it before εστι (*and there is*).

is a spiritual body."[1]—The terms *animated* or *animal* body are the only ones in our language by which we can render the term reproduced in our translation by the Anglicized Greek term. The meaning of the epithet is clear; it denotes a body, not of the same substance as the soul itself,—otherwise it would not be a body,—but formed by and for a soul, destined to serve as an organ to that breath of life called ψυχή, which presided over its development. Neither, consequently, is the *spiritual* body a body of a spiritual nature,—it would still less be a body in that case,—but a body formed by and for a principle of life which is a spirit, and fully appropriated to its service. As the soul does not create the substance of the animal body, but finds it already prepared in a previously existing organism, so the spirit does not create the spiritual body,—which would exclude all continuity between it and the earthly body,—but it takes hold of a germ released from the present body, and causes it to open, not to resume, as in the generation of plants and animals, the cycle of its former existence, but to begin a mode of existence infinitely superior to the old one. The law of the beings belonging to nature is to revolve uniformly in the same circle; the privilege of spiritual being is to surmount this iron circle and to rise from the natural phase, which for it is only the means, to a higher sphere which is its end. This contrast arises from the wholly different mode of being possessed by the soul and the spirit. The soul is only a breath of life endowed with a certain measure of power, capable

[1] א A B C D E F G It. here read σωμα (*body*), which is omitted by K L Syr.

of taking hold of a material substance, subjecting it to itself, converting it into its agent, and using this organ for a fixed time up to the moment when it will no longer lend itself to such use. The characteristic of the spirit is that it possesses a life which is constantly being renewed, while acting and communicating itself (John iv. 14). In a new order of things, after extracting from the body an organ adapted to its nature, it will perpetually renew its strength and glory. Such a body will never be to the principle of its life what the earthly body so often is to the inhabiting soul, a burden and a hindrance; it will be the docile instrument of the spirit, fulfilling its wishes and thoughts with inexhaustible power of action, as we even now see the artist using his hand or his voice with marvellous freedom, and thus foreshadowing the perfect spiritualization of the body. If any one should deny the capacity of matter thus to yield to the action of the spirit, I should ask him to tell me what matter is; then, by way of showing what spiritualized matter may be, I should invite him to consider the human eye, that living mirror in which all the emotions of the soul are expressed in a way so living and powerful. These are simple foreshadowings of the glory of a resurrection body. We cannot go further; a *spiritual body* is one of those things "which eye hath not seen, which have not entered into the mind of man, and which God reserves for them whom He loves."—The *spirit*, the future body's principle of life, is not directly the Spirit of God, it is spirit as the higher element of the human personality, but acting in its union with the Divine Spirit. We have already seen (xiv. 14) that the apostle ascribes to man, not only a ψυχή, *soul*, but also a πνεῦμα, *spirit*, which is the soul's organ in perceiving the Divine world.

The second part of ver. 44 presents three rather important variants. The Alexandrine and Greco-Latin documents read εἰ, *if*, before the first ἔστι; then they place the καί, *also*, after the second; finally, they omit the word σῶμα, *body*, in the second proposition: "If there is a psychical body, there is also a spiritual." The T. R. omits the εἰ, *if;* it places the καί, *and*, before ἔστι; and it reads σῶμα (*body*) in the second proposition: "There is a psychical body, and there is a spiritual body." It is impossible for me to share the preference of modern commentators (de Wette and Hofmann excepted) for the first of these two readings. The apostle had just expressed a paradoxical idea; the term *spiritual body* seemed even to be a *contradictio in adjecto*. Hence it is that, according to the reading of the T. R., he stops expressly to affirm the reality of this notion: "I do not use the expression at random: there is truly a psychical body . . ., a spiritual." Of this forcible affirmation, the Alexandrine and Western copyists have wished to make a demonstration. They have added εἰ, *if*, thus making the existence of the psychical body a premiss from which to infer logically the existence of a spiritual body. Then they have transposed the καί, *also*, to make it the correlative of the εἰ, *if*, and thereby to emphasize the correctness of the conclusion which is certainly false, for it does not appear how it follows from the fact that a soul can have a body, that a spirit should have one. Meyer seeks to justify this argument logically; but he does not succeed. Holsten appeals to this understood idea: The soul and spirit are only the two modes of existence belonging to one and the same vital principle; whence it follows that if the soul needs a body in order to act, it is so also with the spirit. But if substantially the soul and spirit are one and the same thing, Paul would here prove the same by the same. Beet adduces this law: God ever wills what is perfect; hence it follows that His work proceeding from the imperfect, which is its beginning, must reach the goal which is the perfect. But how can we infer from this the necessity of a spiritual body? If, as was no doubt thought by the opponents of the resurrection, the purely spiritual state is superior to the spiritual state united to the bodily, the law referred to recoiled against the thesis of a resurrection. But, according to the true reading, that of the Byzantines, there is no argument at all. As Hofmann says, the apostle's purpose is simply to state the contrast between the two kinds of bodies. This is exactly what the Byzantine reading does. No doubt it might be denied that the εἰ, *if*, of the Alex. must be taken in the sense of a proof. But if Paul had meant to make a simple comparison, he would have said καθώς or ὥσπερ.—In regard to the repetition or omission of the word σῶμα, *body*, in the second proposition, it seems to me that the omission would weaken the force of the paradox which the apostle wishes to affirm, while the exact repetition of the same terms renders the expression of it more striking. — In support of this affirmation of two kinds of bodies, Paul produces a saying from Scripture.

Ver. 45. "And so it is written: the first man,[1] Adam, was made a living soul; the last Adam, a quickening spirit."—The apostle does not say, as usually in his Scripture proofs: καθὼς γέγραπται, *as it is written.* The form οὕτω καί, *and so,* indicates, not a proof strictly so called, but simple agreement of thought. Hofmann even thinks that he may detach this short proposition altogether from what follows, and connect it with what precedes. But this is only a poor expedient intended to set aside the difficulty which attaches to the following quotation. The difficulty is this: If the proposition relative to the first man is a quotation from Gen. ii. 7, it seems as if the same should be the case with the following proposition, relative to the last Adam. But in the Old Testament text there is nothing corresponding to this second idea. How then are we to explain the course taken by the apostle, if the two propositions depend on the: *so it is written?* The apostle evidently had no intention of deceiving his readers by leading them to believe that the second proposition was taken from the Old Testament as well as the first. Most commentators think that he found in the well-known parallelism between the two heads of humanity the right to introduce the second member into his quotation, though it was not expressly found in the narrative of Genesis. But would not this be to carry freedom of quotation to an unwarrantable degree? I do not think it necessary to apply the: *it is written,* to the verse as a whole. The first proposition is taken from a universally known Scripture text. The second is borrowed from the fact of the equally well-known

[1] B K Ir. omit the word ανθρωπος (*man*).

appearance of the historic Christ, and Paul expresses it, according to the law of contrast, on the model of the former. As Bengel says: "*Cætera addit ex naturâ oppositorum;*" so that the first proposition alone depends, in his view, on the: *so it is written.* The sequel will still better explain this procedure.[1]

The form γίνεσθαι εἰς, *to be made into* . . ., denotes not only the first moment of man's creation, but also the whole development of this Divine act even to its goal. It is wholly false to make this term ψυχή ζῶσα, *living soul,* the equivalent of *psychical man* (ii. 14), and to conclude from this comparison that the *was made* implies the fall. The one point in

[1] We shall quote in a note Holsten's curious explanation. According to this critic, what is said by Paul of the *becoming* [being made] of the first man refers only to the *second* account of creation contained in Gen. ii. 7; whereas what is said of the *becoming* of the last Adam goes back to the *first* account of the creation of man, Gen. i. 26, an account which Paul here applies (with Philo) to the supra-terrestrial man, the celestial prototype of Adamite humanity; this celestial man it was who appeared afterwards in Christ as the Messiah. The: *so it is written,* might thus be applied without difficulty at once to the two propositions of our verse. Holsten has, indeed, to acknowledge that in the account Gen. i. 26, man is not designated as a *quickening spirit;* but as it is said of him that he was made after the image of God, and as God is a spirit, and a quickening spirit, it is proved that this first heavenly man was so likewise. It is also true that this celestial man should strictly have been called *the first* and not *the last* or *the second* (ver. 47). But Paul designates Him thus in virtue of His historical appearance, which was posterior to that of the earthly man.—All this in order to find here a point of support for this favourite thesis of the Tübingen School: that according to Paul, the pre-existing Christ was not a Divine being, but a celestial creature, the luminous prototype of man created in Adam.—But what! Could it be this celestial luminous prototype of humanity to whom God said, Gen. i. 28, 29: "Be fruitful and multiply and replenish the earth; behold, I have given you for nourishment every herb bearing seed!" It was this pre-existing man, was it, whom God created male and female (i. 27)! How is it possible to ascribe to Paul such reveries!—If exegesis were an exhibition of intellectual gymnastics, this explanation might be signalized as its masterpiece.

question here is the fact of creation. The *was made* refers to the progress indicated in the account of Genesis itself, according to which man, created at first of the dust, afterwards received the communication of the Divine breath, thereby attaining the form of existence which was provisionally destined for him. —The Hebrew text says: "And Adam was made a living soul;" the LXX. likewise, translating Adam by ὁ ἄνθρωπος, *man*. Paul preserves the two terms: *man* and *Adam*, because the latter contains the idea of the head of a species. Besides, he adds the epithet πρῶτος, *first*, with a view to the coming antithesis. His object is precisely to trace the line which this man, who is yet only *the first*, and not the final man, shall not be able to pass. This psychical state will only be a point of departure; a new creative act will be needed to produce the final man.

This limit of the natural man, this provisional maximum, is denoted by the term ψυχὴ ζῶσα, *living soul*. In the passages Gen. i. 20 and 24, this same expression is applied to all the animals, to distinguish them from plants. We thus see that the term signifies: a life-breath individualized and animating a physical organism; an animated being, endowed with a body. But these life-breaths which are the principle of animal existence, may be very variously endowed; and consequently the parity of man with the animal world, so strongly emphasized by this term, does not contradict the superiority and sovereignty ascribed to the human species in this same account of Genesis. The meaning of the word ψυχή, *soul*, must not be restricted to the purely sensitive and inferior powers of the human soul.

There is nothing requiring or even authorizing such limitation. As the life-breath belonging to each animal is distinguished by special powers, more or less elevated, that of man differs from that of other animated beings in certain faculties which constitute his superiority over them all and make him their sovereign: the νοῦς, *mind*, whereby he distinguishes truth from falsehood, good from evil; *will*, its own mistress and capable of choosing between opposite motives; the καρδία, *heart*, that deep and rich soil of feeling into which will and mind strike their roots; finally, the higher organ with which the human soul is endowed for the perception of the Divine, the πνεῦμα, *spirit*, the religious sense which distinguishes man absolutely from all that is animal and which forms the starting-point of the higher existence in which the natural life is to issue. If Genesis does not mention this special element of human nature, and speaks only of the soul, it is because it embraces it also in this term. It is not till a subsequent period that spirit will become the dominant principle of human life. In the sphere of natural life, it is the living soul which is the characteristic feature. The soul is for the time the seat of the personality which, by the body, communicates with the lower world and, by the spirit, with God in whose image it is created. From the standpoint of Genesis, the expression living soul therefore denotes a terminal point, the goal of the first creation; whereas from Paul's point of view this goal was a first stage, simply a state of expectation. And this is what gives occasion to the second proposition added by the apostle. The first asserted a fulness, but also a void; and this void the second serves to fill.

Christ is called *Adam,* to characterize Him as head of a race, no less than the first. At the same time He is called *the last.* Why not *the second,* as in ver. 47 ? Because in consequence of the subject treated throughout this chapter, Paul is concerned, not about Christ's relation to the other Adam, but about the part He fills in relation to humanity, the mission which He has received to bring it to its final state.—There is found in the treatise *Nevé Schalom* an analogous expression : "*Adamus postremus est Messias.*" This agreement of Paul with the Rabbinical writing is easily explained ; for it is known that the *Nevé Schalom* is the work of Rabbi Abraham, of Catalonia, who died in 1492.

The last Adam begins by realizing *in Himself* the perfect state. He is *πνεῦμα ζωοποιοῦν, a quickening* [life-giving] *spirit.* There is no article, as if this were His exclusive privilege. It is a human state, which Paul contrasts with a living soul. The construction *εἰς πνεῦμα . . .*, necessarily leads us to supply the verb *ἐγένετο, was made,* according to the first proposition. Contrasted as it is with *soul, spirit* denotes, not only a being that lives, but a principle capable of giving life ; which, while continually renewing itself, communicates life to that which it penetrates : "a fountain springing up into eternal life " (John iv. 14). As Edwards says, "the soul is the object [the seat] of life ; the spirit is the source of life." The epithet *ζωοποιοῦν, quickening,* is also applied to the *πνεῦμα,* John vi. 63, and there as characterizing its essence : *τὸ πνεῦμά ἐστι τὸ ζωοποιοῦν.* In our context, it seems to me that the term should not be applied to the communication of spiritual life, but rather to the spirit's action on the body, which serves as its organ. The soul animates the body; it guides and moves it. The spirit does more: it quickens it by communicating to it ever new force and youth. To what point in the life of the Saviour should we apply this γίνεσθαι, *becoming,* which made Him a *quickening spirit?* When He was *created* as the heavenly man, answers Holsten. We delay the examination of this idea of the heavenly man, ascribed to Paul, till ver. 45. At the time of the *incarnation,* thinks Edwards: "Then it was that Christ introduced a Divine force into humanity." This meaning would not, according to this commentator, prevent us from holding that the body of Christ was *psychical,* like ours, during His earthly life, and that He did not receive His spiritual body till the time of His resurrection, by the quickening spirit whom He possessed from the beginning. Ambrosiaster, Grotius, Meyer, Heinrici, etc., think of the time of the *resurrection.* Does not the form γίνεσθαι εἰς, *to be made, become,* relieve us from the necessity of choosing between these different suppositions? From the time of the incarnation there began in Jesus the growing and quickening action of the spirit on the body. This action, suspended by His voluntary submission to the power of death, broke forth gloriously in His resurrection, but in a certain measure only, for the facts prove that in His appearances the risen One still had His psychical body, though already transformed to some extent. Finally, it was at the Ascension that the transformation was completed, and that He put on the *spiritual body* in which He appeared to Paul at the time of his conversion. Compare on the relation between the spirit of holiness, under the power of which the Lord lived on the earth, and His bodily glorification, Rom. i. 4 and viii. 11.—It may be asked whether the epithet ζωοποιοῦν, *quickening*, already points to the influence which Christ will exercise over the body of His own at the Advent to glorify it like His own; comp. Phil. iii. 21. It is evident that Paul is tending to this idea, which he will express positively in vers. 48 and 49; but for the present it is undoubtedly wisest to answer, with R. Schmidt: "Here there is but one thing in question: whether there will be another body completely different from the earthly body. The question how Jesus succeeds in procuring a spiritual body for other men, is a remoter one" (p. 114).[1] We have already seen that the absence of the article before πνεῦμα ζωοποιοῦν speaks in favour of this answer.

But a question very naturally presented itself: How does it happen, that the spiritual state being superior to the psychical state, God was pleased to begin with the latter, and then delayed so long to grant the former? Does not God in all things will what is perfect? There is a law which has determined the course taken by God, and which the apostle confines himself to stating here without explaining it.

Ver. 46. "Howbeit that is not first which is spiritual, but that which is psychical; and afterward that which is spiritual."—Are we right in regarding this as a general law, or must we, with Osiander and others, understand the substantive σῶμα, *body*, and apply the verse exclusively to the particular fact under discussion? The former meaning alone agrees with the ellipsis of the verb, which, if understood, can only be the

[1] R. Schmidt, *Die paulinische Theologie*, vol. i.

present. In the latter sense, Paul would have required to use a verb in the aorist (ἐγένετο, ver. 45). His object is to justify by a general principle what has taken place in respect of the body: the priority of the psychical to the spiritual body.—The law here enunciated, when rightly understood, throws a vivid light on the general course of God's work within humanity. The life of the spirit is substantially identical with holiness; it could not therefore have been given immediately to man at the time of his creation; for holiness is not a thing imposed, it is essentially a product of liberty, the freewill offering of the individual. God therefore required to begin with an inferior state, the characteristic of which was simply freedom, the power in man to give or withhold himself. On the choice which he should make between these two alternatives, to keep his natural life or to give it in order to get it back transformed into a higher life, was to depend his fall or progress. In the former case, spiritual life could not be communicated to man; in the latter, it was accorded to him in response to his free and fervent aspiration; and elevation to the perfect state, even for the body, took place in the direct way of progress. But, even in the opposite case, it was not denied to him for ever; for the miseries of sin might, by a long and sad circuit of experience, bring man to exclaim: "Oh that Thou wouldest rend the heavens, that Thou wouldest come down!" (Isa. lxiv. 1). It was to secure the production of this aspiration, the condition of the gift of the Spirit, that during the course of the psychical period, God adopted a people in the midst of whom this need of the economy of the Spirit was intended to be more forcibly developed under the pedagogic influence of the law and the prophets. And when the longing awakened by these two means had reached its full intensity, the answer could at length be granted: the fulness of the times was come; the Son was sent, and the Spirit given (Gal. iv. 4–6). The apostle does not therefore share the idea, so long regarded as the orthodox view, according to which humanity was created in a state of moral and physical perfection, and fell from that height. He holds, that even independently of the fall there would have been progress from a lower state, the psychical state assigned as a point of departure, to a higher state, the spiritual state foreseen and willed as the end from the beginning. Apart altogether from sin, psychical humanity was called to develop in all directions the manifold powers with which it was endowed, that it might present to the heavenly guest, the Spirit, when He should come to dwell in it, the psychical and bodily organ fitted to display His perfection in the richest and most varied forms, those of art, science, industry, and social life in all its manifestations. The abnormal intervention of sin did not altogether prevent the realization of this Divine thought. In the East, the sense of the Great; in Greece, that of the True and Beautiful; in Rome, that of the Just; in Phenicia, through its commerce and colonies, that of the Useful; in Israel, that of the Holy, served to prepare for the spiritual economy, the new humanity; that Christendom in which we find so many miseries, but in which notwithstanding also the spirit of Pentecost unfolds. Thus, then, with or without the fall, two economies, that of the human soul (normal ancient history) and that of the Divine Spirit (normal modern history) : such is the profound law which, from the view-point of a free humanity and a healthy Divine preparatory training, must control the history of man. *First the psychical, then the pneumatical.* This law applies, as Olshausen already remarked, to the course of collective no less than of individual life. What light is shed by this law on true Christian education ! Instead of imposing the spiritual state on the child, begin by awakening the need of it, while giving free scope to the expansion of the psychical powers in every direction, which is morally legitimate.—The apostle renders the distinction palpable between the two economies which he has just distinguished, that of the soul and that of the spirit, by contrasting the two *heads* of both (ver. 47) ; thus he will come to the two *races* (ver. 48), and so return to the two *bodies* (ver. 49).

Ver. 47. " The first man is of the earth, earthy : the second man[1] is from heaven."—Here is the sovereign application of the general law enunciated in the previous verse. To the psychical state, which must come *first*, there corresponds the earthly body of the *first* man ; as to the spiritual state, which comes *second*, there corresponds the heavenly body of the *second* Adam. This double correlation is natural ; for the organ, the body, should be adapted to the mode of life of which it is the agent. And each of the two periods consecrated to these two modes of living was inaugurated by a typical individual who represented it in its entirety.—The epithet *second* is here intentionally

[1] T. R. with A K L P Syr. adds ο κυριος (*the Lord*).

substituted for *last* (ver. 45), because the point in question is no longer the final destination of man, but the relation of succession to the preceding phase. The δεύτερος, *second*, answers, as Meyer says, to the ἔπειτα, *afterwards*, of ver. 46. — The qualifications : *of the earth* and *earthy*, belong both to the predicate : "The first man is of the earth, earthy." The second term, χοϊκός, is added to show that it is in respect of the body that Paul thus speaks. The word ὁ or ἡ χοῦς denotes the fine dust which lends itself most easily to become organic matter. This term, which is found nowhere else in the New Testament except in Mark vi. 11 and Rev. xviii. 19, is borrowed from the LXX. ; Gen. ii. 7 : "God formed man of the dust of the earth" (χοῦν ἀπὸ τῆς γῆς). — Because of the contrast, the second man will also be characterized in respect of the body.

The term ὁ κύριος, *the Lord*, which is added by the T. R. with some documents, after ὁ δεύτερος ἄνθρωπος, has nothing corresponding in the former member ; and in this context it naturally excites surprise. As it is wanting in the majority of the documents, it should be rejected from the text.[1] The qualifying phrase *from heaven* corresponds at once to the two predicates of the foregoing sentence. In our ignorance as to what a heavenly body is, Paul could add no precise qualification regarding its nature to contrast with the expression : *earthy*.—The important question is to what time

[1] Neander thought it was Marcion who wished to substitute this term ο κυριος for ανθρωπος, to remove from Christ the idea of a human birth. He was led to this view by Tertullian (*Cont. Marc.* v. 10). But Edwards reminds us that Tertullian does not say that Marcion added ο κυριος, but only that he suppressed the word ανθρωπος.

we should refer the regimen : *from heaven.* Does it refer to the fact of the incarnation, the coming of the heavenly Christ to the earth to complete the work of redemption? So Athanasius, Baur, Beyschlag, Edwards. Or should we apply this ἐξ οὐρανοῦ, *from heaven,* to the Advent, when the Lord will descend again in His glorified body to glorify the faithful? It is from the first interpretation that the Tübingen school have deduced their theory, according to which the pre-existing Christ was, in Paul's view, a celestial man, the prototype of terrestrial humanity, possessing a luminous (spiritual) body. And thus this school has succeeded in finding an intermediate being between the purely human Christ of the synoptics and the wholly Divine Christ of St. John. But if such was Paul's view, he must have changed his conception between our Epistles to the Corinthians and those of the Roman captivity (Colossians, Philippians), for in these he distinctly affirms the Divine state of the pre-existing Christ; he must even have changed it between our Epistle and the very near date when he composed the Epistle to the Romans, in which he ascribes to Jesus a body entirely similar to our sinful body (viii. 3), and therefore by no means celestial and luminous, but made of dust like ours. He must even have changed his view in the course of our Epistle, for in chap. viii. 6 he ascribes to the pre-existing Christ the work of creation, and in x. 4 he identifies Him with the Lord guiding Israel in the cloud; declarations which it is impossible to harmonize with the conception of a Christ pre-existing as a celestial *man.* But above all, to refer these words to the fact of the incarnation, is to wrench them absolutely from the context. Gess rightly reminds us [1] that everything here tends to the solution of the question : "With what body do they come ?" a question which must of course be solved by the relation of the resurrection body, not to the body of the pre-existing, but to that of the risen Christ. As to the ἐξ οὐρανοῦ, *from heaven*, Gess justly quotes as parallels : 1 Thess. iv. 16 (καταβήσεται ἐξ οὐρανοῦ) and 2 Thess. i. 7 (ἐν τῇ ἀποκαλύψει τοῦ κ. Ἰ. ἀπ' οὐρανοῦ), two passages which point to the Advent. But the parallel Phil. iii. 20, 21, is that which above all appears to me decisive in favour of this application in our passage. There, as here, the apostle is comparing our Lord's glorified body as well as that of risen believers made like His, with our present body, which he calls *the body of our humiliation ;* then he says expressly : "Our citizenship is in heaven, *whence* we look for the Saviour, the Lord" (ἐξ οὗ ἀπεκδεχόμεθα . . .) ; exactly our ἐξ οὐρανοῦ.[2] Similarly the ὁ ἐπουράνιος, *the heavenly*, ver. 48, can only be Christ risen and glorified. For it is to Him we shall be made like, and not to the pre-existing Christ. The title ἐπουράνιοι, given in the same verse to glorified believers, would be enough to prove this. Finally, would it not be strange if Paul, after laying down the principle : first the inferior, then the better, should cite as an illustration of the rule an example which would prove exactly the contrary ? For, accord-

[1] *Christi Person und Werk*, 2 Abth. i. p. 127.

[2] Weiss acknowledges the general reference of our passage to the Advent ; only the *from heaven* seems to him to apply to the incarnation, inasmuch as Christ's Divine pre-existence may be inferred from His exaltation to glory. There is no trace of such an argument in our verse.

ing to this Christological theory, the heavenly Christ would be first and the earthly Christ second. Thus falls the one solitary ground which the Tübingen school has attempted to find in the whole of the New Testament in favour of the alleged Pauline conception of Christ as a pre-existing celestial man. A similar idea has been put forth as developed by Philo. In commenting on the double account of man's creation, in Genesis, this philosopher lays down a distinction between *man celestial* and *man terrestrial.* Only, according to him the celestial is first and the terrestrial second, and that very naturally, because the former is a pure ideal belonging to the world of conceptions. It is thus obvious how far we are from the idea ascribed to Paul. As to the Rabbinical passages, which present similar expressions,[1] they are probably much later than the first age of Christianity. Besides, did not the Old Testament lead men to compare the Messiah with Adam by way of contrast, even as with Moses by analogy?

After showing the law of ver. 46 realized in the two heads, Paul applies it to the two humanities which proceed from them, and he thus reaches the conclusion relative to the resurrection-body of believers.

Vers. 48, 49. "As is the earthly, such are they also that are earthly: and as is the heavenly, such are they also that are heavenly. 49. And as we have borne the image of the earthly, we shall also bear[2] the image of the heavenly."—The two facts pointed out in ver. 48

[1] Like that of the *Nevé Schalom*, already quoted, p. 421.

[2] T. R. reads φορεσομεν (*we shall bear*) with B, some Mnn., some versions, and some Fathers; but φορεσωμεν (*let us bear*) in ℵ A C D E F G K L P, the majority of the Mnn. It. Vg. Cop. Or. (*often*), and most of the Fathers.

rest on this principle: that every race bears the characteristics of the head from which it proceeds. As Adam was, such is Adamite humanity; as is the glorified Christ, such is humanity glorified in Him. Hence the final consequence drawn in ver. 49.

Ver. 49. *Καί*: "*and* in consequence of this law." The two verbs, the one in the past, the other in the future, show that Paul transports himself to the time of the Advent, which for believers will separate their Adamite past from their Messianic future. During their whole earthly life, even after their conversion, believers bear to the end the image of man taken from the dust, as he was created at the beginning. The past: *we have borne*, places us at that glorious point of time when we shall have laid down this inheritance, and when our existence as sons and heirs of Adam will give place to existence as sons and heirs of God, thenceforth like to the Lord Himself.—In the second clause the large majority of the Mjj. and Fathers read the subjunctive aorist *φορέσωμεν*, *let us bear*, that is to say: "Let us strive to bear." And most modern editors think themselves obliged to follow these authorities. But here again, as in the perfectly analogous case Rom. v. 1, we do not hesitate for an instant to prefer the reading which is by far the least supported. The future has on its side only the *Vaticanus* and the Peschito; but it is demanded by the context, which does not admit of an exhortation any more than in the case of Rom. v. 1. The object is simply to conclude the argument begun in ver. 39: "Such, then, is the body with which they will come: a heavenly body like that of the Lord Himself." If this were an exhortation, it would be necessary, with Chrysostom, to take the word εἰκών, *image*, in the moral sense: "Let us therefore put on the holiness of Christ," which is manifestly contrary to the entire preceding and subsequent context. We shall see at ver. 50 what has led this Father into his false explanation. This reading was early introduced, because, as Holsten says, it was customary to quote passages separately, and with a view to giving them a practical application. —The future indicative corresponds to the aorist ἐφορέσαμεν, exactly as these same two tenses correspond to one another, Rom. vi. 5; with this difference, that the past and the future are there separated by conversion, here by the Advent. The necessity for reading the future is confessed by Meyer, Rückert, Osiander, Holsten, etc.; and it is vain for Heinrici, Hofmann, Beet, Edwards, to defend the other reading so evidently condemned by the context.

The apostle has answered the two difficulties which were raised at Corinth to the hope of a resurrection: How will it be effected after death has dissolved the body?—By that very death and dissolution.—But with what body will the risen appear?—With a body like that of the glorified Christ, as appropriate to their spiritual state as the present body is to our psychical state.

After this very compact and complete discussion, there remained another case, not anticipated in these answers, that of believers whom the Lord shall find living on the earth at the time of His return. How will it go with them? Here was a question which the apostle, who never forgets a single side of the subjects he treats, could not neglect. This is the theme of the passage vers. 50–52.

Vers. 50–52

Ver. 50. "Now[1] this I say, brethren, that flesh and blood cannot inherit the kingdom of God; neither doth corruption inherit[2] incorruption."—The formula τοῦτό φημι, *here is what I say,* is used by the apostle to announce a decisive and final explanation, the exposition of a more profound point of view, which will put the truth previously stated in its full light; comp. vii. 29. It differs from τοῦτο λέγω, which announces the repetition of the same idea in a more developed form. —Before giving the solution of the particular question, Paul lays down a general law which refers equally to the point hitherto treated and to that which is about to follow, so that the verse forms the transition between the two passages. — In this context the expression: *flesh and blood,* can only designate our present physical organism; flesh, in respect of its substance; blood, in respect of the life-principle which animates it; for, according to Scripture, blood is the seat of the vital principle. Irenæus and Chrysostom took the word in its moral sense: τὰς πονηρὰς πράξεις, as if the passage were parallel to Rom. viii. 12, 13; but the expression σάρξ καὶ αἷμα has never the meaning of σάρξ standing alone. It is from this interpretation, likewise excluded by the context, that the false reading φορέσωμεν, in ver. 49, has proceeded. What the apostle means is, that it will not be by being clothed with a

[1] Instead of δε (*now*), D E F G It. read γαρ (*for*).
[2] Instead of κληρονομει, D E F G It. Syr. read κληρονομησει (*will inherit*).

body of such a nature that the believer will be able to participate in the perfect state of things which is called the kingdom of God. Such a body would be a curtain which would veil from us the face of God, too weak an instrument to bear such emotions, too dull an agent to execute the works to be done in this new state. Paul has taken care not to say σῶμα, *a body*, because it will be with a body that believers shall take part in that kingdom.—In the second proposition, the verb in the present expresses, as Edwards says, "the nature of the thing;" it is a law which is equivalent to the οὐ δύναται, *cannot*, in the first proposition; only the particle οὐδέ, *neither*, and the subject ἡ φθορά, *corruption*, imply a gradation. *Corruption*, ἡ φθορά, denotes flesh and blood in a state of dissolution already begun. The expression therefore leads us to suppose that the first proposition refers to Christians who shall be alive at the time of the Advent, and the second to dead Christians who *do not inherit*, in so far as they are not raised. The idea is this: it is so impossible that the present body should participate in the life of heaven, that, whether dissolved by death or not, it must be transformed. This is precisely what is developed in the following verses.

Vers. 51, 52. "Behold, I show you a mystery; we shall not all sleep, but we shall all be changed,[1] 52. in a moment, in the twinkling of an eye, at the last trump: for the trumpet shall sound, and the dead

[1] T. R. reads μεν after the first παντες with ℵ A E F G K L P.—The other words present three principal readings:—

(1). T. R. with B E K L P Syr. Cop. Mnn.: παντες ου κοιμηθησομεθα, παντες δε αλλαγησομεθα (*we shall not all sleep, but we shall all be changed*).

shall be raised[1] incorruptible, and we shall be changed."—The word ἰδού, *behold,* is a call to attention, and the term μυστήριον, *mystery,* justifies the call. It here denotes a special point in God's plan, which the apostle could only know by revelation; comp. the ἐν λόγῳ κυρίου, *by the word of the Lord,* 1 Thess. iv. 15.—Of the three readings presented by the documents in the second part of ver. 51, the reading of the *Sinaïticus* and the *Alexandrinus* would signify, that "we shall all die until Christ come again, but then we shall not all participate in the glorious resurrection granted to believers." This idea is absolutely away from the line of the apostle's present thought. It is a mistake to introduce here the distinction between those who are saved and those who are not. Perhaps it is the error made in φορέσωμεν which continues here, as if the matter in question were a practical exhortation. The one thing Paul wishes to explain is what will take place in believers who shall be alive at that time. The same holds of the Western reading in the *Cantabrigiensis,* and the *Itala:* "We shall all be raised, but we shall not all be changed." Paul would thus remind his readers that along with the resurrection of the righteous, there is also that of the wicked, which however will not be a change, that is to say, a glorious transformation. This thought is still more wide of the context than the preceding. Moreover, the two readings and the two ideas are both condemned by ver. 52;

(2). ℵ A C F G: παντες (A: οι παντες) κοιμηθησομεθα (F: κοιμηθησωμεθα), ου παντες δε αλλαγησομεθα (*we shall all sleep, but we shall not all be changed*).
(3). D It. Vg. Tertull. (see Edwards): παντες αναστησομεθα, ου παντες δε αλλαγησομεθα (*we shall all be raised, but we shall not all be changed*).

[1] T. R. with ℵ B C K L M: εγερθησονται; A D E F G P: αναστησονται.

for in this verse it is not the saved and the condemned who are contrasted, but the living transformed and the dead who shall be raised. Hofmann has attempted to make this last reading admissible by connecting the negative *οὐ* with the first proposition. The meaning would be: "Undoubtedly we shall not all be raised (those who have not passed through death), but we shall all be changed, either by resurrection or by transformation." But in this case the end of ver. 52 would be merely a superfluous repetition; then the position of the negative *οὐ* at the end of the first proposition (*πάντες μὲν ἀναστησόμεθα οὐ*) is a form without example in the New Testament.—There remains the reading of the T. R., which has on its side the *Vaticanus*, the Peschito, and the Byz., according to which the apostle says: "We shall not all die, — there will be living Christians when the Lord comes again,—but we shall all require to be changed: living believers by transformation, the dead by resurrection. For it is impossible to enter into the kingdom of glory with this earthly body, composed of materials subject to corruption" (ver. 50). This idea is obviously connected in the closest possible way with that of ver. 50, and leads directly to that of ver. 52. There is therefore no room for doubt as to the correctness of this reading. Moreover, Reiche has clearly proved that it was the prevailing reading down to Origen, and that variants do not begin to appear till about the end of the 3rd century (see Heinrici). — Meyer has raised two difficulties, not to the reading in itself, but to the meaning it gives. According to him: (1) this meaning would have required the negative *οὐ* to be placed before πάντες, *all,* and not before the verb; for, strictly speaking, the clause means, not: "Some only shall die, not all," but: not a single Christian shall die; (2) the verb ἀλλαγησόμεθα, *we shall be changed,* cannot, according to ver. 52, contain the two notions of resurrection and transformation; it denotes only the second. Meyer therefore thinks that the meaning is this: "All of us (whether myself, Paul, or the other believers presently alive) shall not have to pass through death; there is *not one* of us who shall die; but yet we must all be changed (by transformation)." If we are resolved to make Paul guilty of an absurdity, it is enough indeed thus to press the form of the phrase. But it is amply proved that in the New Testament, as in the translation of the LXX., the position of the οὐ is not so rigorously observed as in the classic style, a fact arising from the well-known Hebrew usage of connecting with the person the negative relating to the verb; comp. Rom. iii. 20. Thus Num. xxiii. 13, Balak, meaning to say to Balaam: "Thou shalt see part of the Israelites, but thou shalt not see them all," expresses himself in these terms: μέρος τι ὄψει, πάντας δὲ οὐ μὴ ἴδῃς, which, taken strictly, would mean: "All of them thou shalt not see," that is to say: Thou shalt see none of them; a sense evidently contrary to Balak's thought. On the other hand, Josh. xi. 13 and Rom. xii. 4, which are sometimes quoted, seem to me to prove nothing at all. For the meaning of the verb ἀλλάσσεσθαι, *to be changed,* see on ver. 52.

Ver. 52. Paul here describes the change which must infallibly be wrought: he distinguishes the two forms in which it will take place. The two expressions ἄτομος, an indivisible moment, and ῥιπὴ ὀφθαλμοῦ, literally: *a movement of the eyelid*, denote the suddenness with which the event will happen. Then the apostle indicates the signal by which it will be proclaimed: *the last trump.* It has been alleged that he had in mind a real trumpet; as if the apostle could have imagined that the sound of a metal instrument could penetrate to the ears of the dead reduced to dust! He thereby understands a Divine signal, the nature of which is incomprehensible, and which he describes by a figure taken from Israelitish usages. It was enjoined on the sons of Aaron, Num. x. 2–10, to sound the trumpet in order to call the people together, to strike their tents, or to announce the feast. Now the Advent is the time of the most solemn reunion, of the last departure, of the most glorious feast. This signal is called in 1 Thess. iv. 16: "an archangel's voice, a trump of God." On Sinai the presence of the Lord and of His angels was manifested by noises similar to the sound of the horn. Jesus Himself made use of the figure of the trumpet to indicate the signal which shall gather together His elect from the four corners of the earth. By calling this trumpet *the last*, Paul does not refer either to the seven trumpets of Jericho, or to the seven of the Apocalypse, or to the seven which the Rabbins have imagined, and which, according to them, must give the signal for each of the seven phases of the act of resurrection. Neither does the term signify, as has been thought, the trumpet which brings in the *last* phase of the earthly economy. The term *last* necessarily supposes trumpets anterior to this. I think the apostle means by it the manifestations of the Divine will given to the beings of the invisible world, and on which depend the decisive crises of the kingdom of God on the earth; comp. Zech. ix. 14. The trumpets of the Apocalypse come under this category, but they do not exhaust it.—The apostle adds σαλπίσει γάρ, *for the trumpet shall sound*, and it has been thought that he does so to materialize the signal. It has not been perceived that the words are closely connected with what follows, and that they serve to indicate how completely simultaneous shall be the signal with its double effect mentioned in the two following propositions: the resurrection of dead believers and the transformation of believers still in life.—There is no difficulty in taking the word *shall be changed* here in a more restricted sense than in ver. 51; for here it is no longer contrasted with *sleeping*, but with *being raised*. Resurrection and transformation being the two forms of the renewal of the body, the verb ἀλλαγῆναι, *to be changed*, may either comprehend both of them, or specially denote the second, when it requires a particular term. —By the pronoun *we*, the apostle understands all believers who shall be alive at the time of Christ's return, and he ranks himself with them contingently; for as he does not know its precise date, it is natural for him, being among the living, to put himself rather among them than in the other class. To rank himself with the dead would have been to say that the Advent would not happen till after his death, and consequently so far to fix its date. In the parallel passage of Thessalonians (iv. 15) he explains himself more clearly: "We," says he, "that are alive, are left unto the coming of the Lord." These last words are remarkable. If they are not altogether superfluous, they must serve to define the preceding expression: "We that live," in the sense: "Those of us believers that are alive, that remain, not then, but at the time of the Advent." That Paul was not sure of being one of these appears from vers. 30 and 31; then from vi. 14, where he ranks himself among the *raised;* and from Phil. i. 20, 21 and ii. 17, where he speaks of his death as an impending possibility. Paul knew *that,* but not *when,* Christ should return; and he also knew that, according to Christ's own precept, every believer should live in the attitude of a servant waiting for his master, and be ever ready to receive him (Luke xii. 36). Here we see the servant: nothing could be more in keeping with this direction of the Lord than the position taken by the apostle in our passage.—Thus has been demonstrated the *possibility* of the resurrection, and, as an appendix and confirmation, the necessity of a transformation even for those who shall not have had to pass through the dissolution of death. Now the apostle places the reader face to face with this great hope in its entirety, and closes his dissertation on the subject by celebrating the hope, uttering, as it were, a discourse in a tongue, with himself for an interpreter.

Vers. 53–58

Vers. 53, 54. "For this corruptible body must put on incorruption, and this mortal body put on immortality. 54. So when this corruptible shall have put on incorruption, and[1] this mortal shall have put

[1] א C I M omit the words το φθαρτον down to και (*the corruptible . . down to and*).

on immortality, then shall be brought to pass the saying that is written, Death is swallowed up in victory."[1]—The first words of ver. 53 reproduce in a positive form the idea of ver. 50, and constitute the transition to the development following. The striking parallelism of the two propositions marks the ascending movement of the thought as well as the growing exultation of the feeling: it is the poetic rhythm in Hebrew. Perhaps the first proposition applies rather to the resurrection of bodies which have passed through the dissolution of death, and the second to the transformation of bodies constantly threatened with death during their earthly life. In that case, we have here an allusion to the two modes of change indicated in ver. 52.—The twice repeated expression, *this body*, and the figure of *putting on* evidently imply the idea of the continuity of the new body and the old; it is one and the same organic principle which appears successively in two different forms. The permanent element, contained at first in a corruptible covering, is suddenly raised by an act of Divine omnipotence to an incorruptible mode of existence.

Ver. 54. The form of parallelism is continued. The word τότε, *then*, expresses the grandeur of the time. The participle: *that which is written*, is added to denote the certainty of fulfilment: Scripture cannot lie. — The saying quoted is Isa. xxv. 8, the meaning of which is that the theocracy once restored, its members, dead and living, shall be all raised up together to the sphere of immortality. "God," says the prophet (if God be understood as the subject), "hath swallowed

[1] B D I Tert. read νεῖκος, instead of νῖκος.

up death for ever." The LXX., probably following another reading, have translated altogether differently: "Death hath swallowed up triumphantly" (perhaps in the sense of: "It formerly swallowed up . . ."). Paul follows our Hebrew text, only changing the active into the passive: "Death *is swallowed up*." The word which we translate *victory*, following Paul, is one of the most beautiful terms in the Hebrew language (*nétsach*). It denotes the state of perfect inward vigour which excludes all possibility of outward decay, and hence: eternal duration. The expression: *in victory*, seems to me to have the meaning: "Death is absorbed in imperishable life." Such a life is victory gained for ever over death, its enemy. It is not the only time that the LXX. thus render the term *lanétsach*.—The feeling of gratitude and adoration here reaches its culminating point in the apostle's heart:

Vers. 55, 56. "Where is thy sting,[1] O death?[2] O death,[2] where is thy victory?[1] 56. Now the sting of death is sin; and the strength of sin is the law."—The text varies considerably in the MSS., influenced no doubt by the differences between the Hebrew text and that of the LXX. Hosea xiii. 14 says, according to what seems to me the most probable translation: "How shall I ransom them from the power of the grave? How shall I deliver them from death? How should I be thy plague, O death? How should I be thy destruction, O grave?" The meaning is this:

[1] The reading is νικος (*victory*) in ℵ B C I M Cop. in the first question and κεντρον (*sting*) in the second; it is the reverse in the T. R. with D E F G K L P It. Syr.

[2] Θανατε (*death*) is read both times in ℵ B C D E F G It. Cop.; whereas T. R. with K L M P Syr. reads αδη (*grave*) in the second question.

"Yea, I should have done so, hadst thou repented, O Israel! O death, I should have swallowed thee as thou swallowest up men! O grave, I should have been to thee what thou art to them, thy grave! But to act thus for thee, impenitent Israel, is impossible." The LXX. have translated thus: "I will deliver them from the power of the grave, and I will ransom them from death. Where is thy right (thy judgment), O death? where is thy sting, O grave!" What in Hebrew is given as a regret on God's part, as an expression of the desire He had to bestow a great blessing on Israel, becomes in the LXX. a promise to grant this extraordinary benefit, as soon as the desired condition shall have been fulfilled. This signification of the LXX., which is followed by the apostle, corresponds therefore, though only indirectly, with that of the Hebrew text. — In the first question, the T. R. with the Byz. and the Greco-Lats. reads κέντρον, *sting*, and in the second νῖκος, *victory*. The Alex. reverse the words. Perhaps this second reading is the result of a correction after the LXX., who read δίκη (like enough to νῖκος) in the first and κέντρον in the second. Anyhow the term νῖκος, *victory*, is connected in Paul's mind with the εἰς νῖκος of the preceding verse. It corresponds to δίκη, *judgment*, in the LXX. And it is not difficult to understand how the two translations may have arisen from the same Hebrew term. The latter, *debarim*, may be either the plural of *dabar*, *word*, and hence *sentence* (the δίκη, *judgment*, of the LXX.), or the plural of *deber*, *destruction*, and hence *victory* (the νῖκος of Paul). — In the second question, the word κέντρον, *sting*, is the translation of the Hebrew *kétev*, *ruin.* This word denotes the murderous power which death exercises over men. By this figure κέντρον, *sting,* death is represented as a venomous animal, a wasp, or a scorpion, which has become harmless through the loss of its sting.

According to the T. R. and the Byz., the apostle apostrophizes *death* (θάνατε) in the first question and *Hades* in the second,—this is the exact reproduction of the Hebrew text and of the LXX.,—whereas in the Alex. and Greco-Latin texts he addresses *death* both times. The first reading seems to be a correction after the Hebrew and Greek texts. To this reason Edwards adds another, and a very interesting one. He points out that Paul never uses the term Hades (Rom. x. 7, he substitutes ἄβυσσος, *the abyss*), a circumstance which is to be explained, no doubt, by his fear of the superstitious ideas which, among the Greeks, attached to the name. Philo himself is careful to distinguish between the true and the false Hades.—This final defeat of death embraces two things: the resurrection of the dead and the immortality of the glorified living. In this saying, Hosea has risen to the sublimest view of Divine salvation. No doubt he described this complete triumph only hypothetically. But as the spokesman of faith in Christ, the apostle proclaims it as a certain reality: γενήσεται ὁ λόγος (ver. 54)!

Now he gives, in two powerful and concise sayings, the moral explanation of that defeat of death which he has just celebrated beforehand.

Ver. 56. A subjective sense is often given to the two propositions of this verse; they are taken to describe man's feeling in view of death. The *consciousness* of sins committed is that which gives to death its sting, its *agonizing* power; and the threatenings of the *law* are what produce in man the lively and painful consciousness of his sin. Or again, this second proposition is explained according to Rom. vii. 8, 13; it is the law which, by provoking our inward lusts, renders sin more active in the heart and life; comp. Rom. iii. 20. But in a discussion on the resurrection, what have we to do with the trouble experienced by the dying man and the peace enjoyed by believers? Does this peace secure their resurrection? Ver. 18 proves that it is not so. The same is the case with the action of the law on the human conscience and heart, and with its abolition. None of these can explain the resurrection. But this is the apostle's object. He wishes to show how the power exercised by death has been broken, not only in the *experience* of believers, but in its entire *reality:* how it is possible for the believer to rise again, and not how it is possible for him to die in peace. Father Didon recently said, when speaking of the Socialistic manifestations of our day: "There is only one way of protecting ourselves against such forces, and that is to penetrate to the conditions which engender them." And this is precisely what the apostle does here. He penetrates to the profound conditions which laid the foundation of the reign of death, to explain how the Lord abolished them and thus gained the gigantic result, the death of death. He seems to go down with Jesus Himself into the mysterious laboratory where death distils its poisons, to show us how the conqueror set himself to bring this occult and malignant power to an end.

Here we are in the domain of facts the most objective and real in the history of humanity.

The moral bases of the reign of death are these two: *sin* and *the law.* It was by sin that death gained its power over man: "In the day thou disobeyest thou shalt die" (Gen. ii. 17). "As by one man sin entered into the world, and death by sin . . ." (Rom v. 12). It is said in this same chapter: "As *by man* came death . . ." (vers. 21, 22). If he had not sinned, man, mortal though he was in his bodily nature, would have been raised without passing through this dissolution of his being to the sphere of imperishable life. It was because of sin that death could pierce man with its fatal arrow; comp. Rom. viii. 10: "The body is dead because of sin." But what gave sin this terrible power exercised by it? The *law*, answers the apostle. This thought is explained by the words, Rom. v. 13: "Sin is not imputed where there is no law." When there is no law, there may be faults, but not positive disobedience, revolt. It is violated law which gives sin the character of *high-handed sin*, as the Old Testament calls it, transgression wrought with consciousness and freedom, rebellion. Consequently law alone can make sin an act meriting deprivation of life, capital punishment. If sin is the sting whereby death seeks to kill us, it is the law which makes this sting penetrate deeply enough to reach the springs of life and change them into springs of death. The throne of death thus rests on two bases: sin, which calls for condemnation, and the law which pronounces it.—Consequently it was on these two powers that the work of the Deliverer bore.

Ver. 57. "But thanks to God, which giveth us the

victory through our Lord Jesus Christ!" — Christ's victory over death has two aspects: the one relating to Himself; the other concerning men. He first of all conquered *sin* in relation to Himself by denying to it the right of existence in Him, condemning it to non-existence in His flesh, similar though it was to our sinful flesh (Rom. viii. 3); and thereby He disarmed *the law* so far as it concerned Himself. His life being the law in living realization, He had it for Him and not against Him. This twofold personal victory was the foundation of His own resurrection. Thereafter He continued to act that this victory might extend to us. And first He freed us from the burden of condemnation which *the law* laid on us, and whereby it was ever interposing between us and communion with God. He recognised in our name the right of God over the sinner, He consented to satisfy it to the utmost in His own person. Whoever appropriates this death as undergone in his room and stead and for himself, sees the door of reconciliation to God open before him, as if he had himself expiated all his sins. The separation established by the law no longer exists; the law is disarmed. By that very fact *sin* also is vanquished. Reconciled to God, the believer receives Christ's Spirit, who works in him an absolute breach of will with sin and complete devotion to God. The yoke of sin is at an end; the dominion of God is restored in the heart. The two foundations of the reign of death are thus destroyed. Let Christ appear, and this reign will crumble in the dust for ever. Thus is fulfilled the saying of the apostle, ver. 21: "By man came death; by man cometh the resurrection."

Resurrection is a human work, no less than death itself. It should be remarked that the apostle does not say: *gave*, but: "*giveth* us the victory." Here he is not thinking only of the objective victory which Christ gained once for all in His person, for Himself and us; but of that which He gains daily in believers for whose resurrection He paves the way by destroying the power of the law, which condemns, and that of sin, which leads astray.—It only remains for the apostle to draw from the solemn situation thus described a practical conclusion. This is what he does in few words in ver. 58.

Ver. 58. "Therefore, my beloved brethren, become stedfast, immoveable, always abounding in the work of the Lord, forasmuch as ye know that your labour is not in vain in the Lord."—This ὥστε, *so that, therefore,* is like all those which in the preceding parts served to introduce the practical conclusions to which the doctrines led up; comp. iii. 21, iv. 5, vii. 38, xi. 33, xiv. 39.—By the address, so full of tenderness: *my beloved brethren,* Paul seeks to get near those hearts which he may have repelled by his great severity.—He does not say: Be stedfast, but: *become* so; they are not so yet either in faith or in conduct. They must become rooted in Christ to be confirmed.—The following word *immoveable,* reminds them of the perils which their faith runs, such as that which he has sought to set aside throughout this whole chapter. *If ye hold fast,* he had said to them in ver. 2, and in ver. 33: *Be not deceived.*—Once confirmed, their spiritual activity will unfold: *Abounding in the work of the Lord.* The verb περισσεύειν, *to abound,* strictly signifies: to flow over the edges all round. By *the work of the Lord,* the apostle understands labour for the spread of salvation and for the development of spiritual life. The word *always* is added to remind them of the indefatigable perseverance which should characterize such work.—The apostle closes by indicating the motive which should always stimulate believers anew in the fulfilment of this task. They know *that their labour* in this domain *is not in vain in the Lord.* As the apostle uses the term κενός, *empty,* and not μάταιος (see on vers. 14, 17), we must conclude that he is thinking less of the fruits of the labour than of its nature: this is not an activity of external demonstration, wrought in vacuity, as earthly labour so often is, but serious toil wrought in the sphere of eternal reality. This is why Paul also uses the present *is,* and not the future *will be.* These last words sum up the whole chapter, and at the same time form the transition to the following verses, which directly remind the Corinthians of one of the works to be done for the Lord. This connection with what follows is evident; but yet it is not a sufficient reason for joining this verse, as some commentators have done, to the following chapter.

On Chapter 15

Reuss and Heinrici think that the notion of a spiritual body is incompatible with the gospel narratives which describe the appearances of Jesus after His resurrection; for Jesus seems still to have had during that period His earthly and psychical body. A journal (*l'Alliance libérale*) has gone further, and concluded that the accounts of the appearances of Jesus in the Gospels are only later legends, due to the ever grosser and more materialistic ideas which were formed of the resurrection.

To remove the difficulty raised by the two writers just named, we need not have recourse to the expedient of B. Weiss, who thinks that every time Jesus wished to appear, He clothed Himself in a sensible and corporal exterior. It needs simply to be remembered that, according to our Gospel narratives, the body of Jesus was not immediately transformed into a spiritual body by His resurrection. It was still in His former body restored that He showed Himself, though this body was already subject to other conditions of existence and activity than our earthly body. It was not till the ascension that the substitution of the spiritual for the earthly body was fully consummated. Jesus Himself indicated the gradual process which was taking place in Him when He said to Mary Magdalene, on the very day of His resurrection, John xx. 17: "I am not yet ascended unto My Father . . ., but I ascend . . ."

As to the opinion which, because of this alleged contradiction, would convert the Gospel narratives into later legends, it meets with an insurmountable obstacle in the fact that these narratives are the redaction of the apostolical tradition daily reproduced in the Churches by the apostles themselves, and the evangelists formed by them, from the day of Pentecost downwards. This is what appears from the nature of things, and what we find established in this very chapter, in which the apostle enumerates as apostolical traditions the principal appearances described in our Gospels. That Paul himself thinks of *bodily* appearances is beyond all doubt, in view of the inference which he draws from them, to wit, our own *bodily* resurrection.

The treatment of the subjects which the apostle had in view being finished, it only remains for him to close this letter with a conclusion like those which are generally found at the end of his Epistles, and which refers to certain special communications (matters of business, commissions, news, salutations) which he had to make to the Church.

CONCLUSION

(16:1-24)

In this conclusion the apostle treats five subjects: (1) The collection for the poor of the Church of Jerusalem: vers. 1–4; (2) His approaching visit to Corinth: vers. 5–9; (3) News of his delegates and of his fellow-workers: vers. 10–12; (4) Particular exhortation and direction relative to the three deputies of the Church who are at present with him: vers. 13–18; (5) Final salutations: vers. 19–24.

Vers. 1–4: *The collection*

Vers. 1–4. "Concerning the collection for the saints, as I have given order to the Churches of Galatia, even so do ye. 2. Upon the first day of the week[1] let each one of you lay by him in store, as he hath prospered, that the gatherings be not only when I come; 3. and when I come, whomsoever ye shall approve by letters, them will I send to bring your liberality unto Jerusalem. 4. And if it be meet that I go also, they shall go with me."—When dividing among themselves the preaching of the gospel throughout the whole world, the apostles had made an arrangement by which Paul and Barnabas should from time to time renew the

[1] T. R. with K L M: σαββατων; the rest (except ℵ σαββατω) read σαββατου.

help sent by the Church of Antioch in a particular case, in behalf of the poor Christians of Jerusalem (Gal. ii. 10; Acts xi. 27–30). It has been asked whether the indigence of these last did not arise from the community of goods which had prevailed in the Church for a time, after Pentecost. Augustine had already suggested this idea. Reuss speaks in this connection of imprudence, of squandering of fortunes, misunderstood charity. But it is impossible that sacrifices made for the time, to keep up common tables, and of which a few examples only are quoted in the Acts, could have had so considerable an influence on the monetary condition of the Christians of the capital. Edwards calls attention to the expression τοὺς πτωχοὺς τῶν ἁγίων, *the poor among the saints* (Rom. xv. 26), which proves that the indigence did not extend to all. We must remember what appears clearly from the Gospels, the Acts of the Apostles, and the Epistle of James, as well as from the term Ebionites (*poor*) by which Christians of Jewish origin are designated: viz. that Christianity had gained the mass of its adherents from the poor population of Palestine. Now the Christians were hated by the great and rich of Jerusalem on whom they depended for their work. Nothing easier for them, consequently, than to reduce Christians to the last extremity. Moreover, believers must have been exposed by the Jewish authorities in Palestine to a thousand vexations and penalties from which the Churches of other countries were free. If we read carefully James ii. 6 in connection with chap. v. 1–6, we shall have an idea of the painful situation of the Churches of Palestine, and particularly of that of

Jerusalem, at this period. It closely resembled the position of Hindoo converts excluded from their caste, or that of Protestants, newly converted from Catholicism, in Spain or Italy, whom the animosity of the clergy, and their influence over the wealthy classes, often deprive of their means of subsistence. Finally, it must not be forgotten that we have here the imitation of a custom which prevailed among the Jews from the time that the people were scattered over the Gentile world. It appears from Josephus (*Antiq.* xviii. 9. 1) and from Philo (*Leg. ad Caium*, § 40) that, in all the cities where there was a Jewish colony, there was a treasury established in which every Israelite deposited the offerings which he destined for the temple and for the inhabitants of the capital. It was from Babylonia that the richest contributions came. Men of the noblest families were chosen to carry those collections to Jerusalem. It was therefore most natural for the Church to appropriate this usage in behalf of the mother Church of Christendom, all the more because such manifestations of Christian love were the finest testimony to the communion of saints, a close bond formed by the Spirit of God between the two great divisions of the primitive Church; comp. 2 Cor. viii. and ix. and Rom. xv. 25–27.

The form περὶ δέ, *as to what concerns, concerning*, as well as the art. τῆς, *the*, introduce the subject as one already known to the Corinthians (2 Cor. ix. 2); and what is to be said immediately of the Churches of Galatia proves that the matter had long engaged attention. Besides, the passage Gal. ii. 10 shows that it was not the first time such a thing had been done.—

The expression *the saints*, though frequently denoting all Christians (vi. 2; Rom. xii. 13), is certainly not used here by Paul without allusion to the peculiar dignity belonging to the members of the primitive Church of Jerusalem; comp. 2 Cor. viii. 4, ix. 1, 12. They possess, whatever Holsten may say in opposition to Hofmann, a special consecration; they are the natural branches of the good olive tree (Rom. xi. 16, 17, 24), whereas believers of the Gentiles are branches of the wild olive grafted among the former on the patriarchal stem. According to Eph. ii. 19, the Gentiles become by faith fellow-citizens of the *saints*, that is to say, of Christians of Jewish origin. It is from the Church of Jerusalem, St. Paul says (Rom. xv. 27), that spiritual blessings have spread throughout the world. There is much delicacy on Paul's part in emphasizing this characteristic when speaking of an act which might have had something humiliating about it for those who were its objects. This alms-giving thus became the payment of a debt, or better still an act of homage, a sort of tithe offered by the Church of the Gentiles to the Levites of the human race.—Perhaps in the letter of the Corinthians to Paul a question had been put to him as to the steps to be taken for the success of this business. To his high speculative and dialectic powers the apostle united an eminently practical mind. The plan which he advised the Churches of Galatia to follow, and which the Corinthians are now called to imitate, is no other than that which he points out in ver. 2. The κατά is distributive: *every* first day; the cardinal numeral μία, *one*, used instead of the ordinal *first*, is a

Hebraism; comp. Mark xvi. 2, 9. — The terms *σάββατον* (sometimes *σάββας*) and *σάββατα* gradually took the meaning of *week;* comp. Luke xviii. 12; for weeks are measured by Sabbaths. It seems probable from this passage, as from Acts xx. 7, that the day which followed the Sabbath, and which was the day of the resurrection of Jesus, was early distinguished from the other days of the week and substituted for the Sabbath as the ordinary day for religious worship; comp. Rev. i. 10. The *Doctrine of the Twelve Apostles* calls it, as the Apocalypse does, *the Lord's day*, omitting even the word ἡμέρα, which already makes κυριακή an entirely technical term (see Edwards). Our passage presents one of the first indications of the special religious consecration of this first day of the week.—*Each one;* even the least wealthy, even slaves; however little it may be.—The words: *by him,* denote an act done by each in his own house, and not, as some have thought, a gift bestowed in church and known to the giver only.—The expression θησαυρίζων, *storing up a treasure,* is very beautiful; while expressing the same thought as τιθέναι παρ' ἑαυτῷ, *to set aside,* it brings out the encouraging aspect of this method; such successive deposits, little as they may be, gradually become a respectable sum, a treasure. But the apostle would not have this measure to become a burden such as might oppress the hearts of the givers (2 Cor. ix. 7). Hence he adds: *as he hath prospered.* The verb εὐοδοῦν, *to guide happily in a journey,* signifies in the Middle: to make a journey happily oneself; and hence: to prosper in one's business. The plan in question therefore is the setting apart regularly of a certain proportion of the weekly gain.—The object of this measure is that the sums may be ready when Paul comes, and that there may be nothing to do except to lift them, which will be done quickly and easily, and will give an ampler sum than if the gift were all bestowed at one time.

Ver. 3. Paul has no thought of taking charge of the sum collected himself. He is the ambassador of Christ to the Church, and not a deputy between different Churches. In the passage 2 Cor. viii. 23 he speaks of *apostles*, that is, delegates, *of the Churches* to one another. It is such delegates that the Corinthians will name to represent them to the Church of Jerusalem, and to offer it this testimony of their love; οὓς δοκιμάσητε: "*Those whom you* (yourselves) *shall count worthy* (of this mission)." Several commentators (Calvin, Beza, etc.) connect the regimen *by letters* with the verb δοκιμάσητε: "Whom ye shall approve by letters." It was the Church of Corinth, according to them, which was to furnish its delegates with letters of introduction to the Church of Jerusalem. But does δοκιμάζειν admit of such a meaning? The verb bears rather on the choice than on the envoy. Here it would be necessary to give it the meaning, not only of *declaring worthy*, but of recommending as worthy. It is therefore better to connect the regimen *by letters*, as the ancient Greek commentators and many moderns do, with the verb πέμψω, *I shall send*. It is Paul who will introduce them to the Church of Jerusalem, which is much more natural, for he only stands in relation to it. The plural ἐπιστολῶν might designate several letters; but it is more natural to understand here only one, whether we take ἐπιστολῶν as a plural of category, or give the singular meaning to the plural substantive, as the Latin *litteræ* so often has. This letter would no doubt be addressed to James as head of the council of elders at Jerusalem (Acts xxi. 18). Meyer justly observes that the δι' ἐπιστολῶν is placed first in contrast to the other possible case: that of Paul going and introducing them himself (ver. 4).

Ver. 4. He is not yet certain that he will go to Jerusalem; but if the collection is large enough, that will determine him to go personally to Palestine, and he will join those who may be charged with presenting it. But in this case Paul is careful not to say: "I will go with them." Conscious as he is of his apostolic dignity, he is well aware that he will be the principal personage of the deputation; and therefore he says: *They will go with me.*—In taking all these measures, Paul's object was not merely to respect the autonomy of the Churches; he wished also to secure himself against the odious suspicions which prevailed at Corinth in the minds of adversaries who were utterly unscrupulous as to the means they used to blacken his character and undermine his authority; comp. 2 Cor. xii. 16–18.—The question which Paul here leaves in suspense, we find answered affirmatively, Rom. xv. 25: "Now I go to Jerusalem to minister to the saints," and Acts xx. 1–6, where we find him at Corinth surrounded by deputies from all the Churches of Macedonia and Achaia, who are preparing to start with him for Jerusalem.

Vers. 5–9 : *His approaching visit to Corinth*

Paul had just alluded to his approaching stay at Corinth (ver. 3). He now dwells on the subject, to give some explanations about it to his readers.

Vers. 5–7. "Now I will come unto you when I shall pass through Macedonia: for I do pass through Macedonia; 6. and I will abide with you as long as I can, or even winter with you, that ye may bring me on my journey whithersoever I go. 7. For I will not see you now by the way, for[1] I trust to tarry a while with you, if the Lord permit."—It follows from this passage that Paul must have communicated to the Corinthians, either in the letter mentioned chap. v. 9, or verbally by Timothy, another plan, according to which he reckoned on proceeding first from Ephesus to Corinth, merely taking the latter city by the way to go thence to Macedonia; then to return to Corinth to make a prolonged stay. This plan he now finds himself obliged to modify; he will proceed first to Macedonia, and thence to Corinth. The present διέρχομαι, *I pass through*, is the present of idea: "My plan is to pass . . ." From this word, misunderstood, has arisen the error which is mentioned in the critical annotation placed at the end of the Epistle.

Ver. 6. But if his presence among them should be thus somewhat retarded, it will probably be the more prolonged. To this agreeable thought he adds a second, which, if they love him, ought also to gladden them: that they will thus have the task of pro-

[1] T. R. with K L reads δε (*but*), instead of γαρ (*for*), which is read by all the rest.

viding for the new journey, whatever it may be, which will follow his stay. The expression *whithersoever I go* refers to the uncertainty which he still feels as to whether he will start for Jerusalem or for the West.—The verb προπέμπειν signifies: to send on in company while providing for all the wants of the journey. At the time when Paul wrote—it was the Passover of the year 57—he proposed to remain a few weeks more at Ephesus, till Pentecost (ver. 8 and chap. v. 7, 8). He thus reckoned on passing the following summer in Macedonia, and thence proceeding about autumn to Corinth, there to pass the winter of 57–58. It is commonly held that this plan was carried out. I do not think so. It seems to me, as to others, that the complications which arose immediately after this letter between the apostle and the Church of Corinth led in the course of things to much graver changes than is usually supposed. In any case, it seems to me impossible to connect with the simple change of plan here indicated the justification of his loyalty which the apostle is obliged to give in the first chapter of the Second Epistle (vers. 15–18). The change there referred to is evidently one of far greater importance; comp. 2 Cor. ii. 1–4.—The οὗ is often used for οἷ in the later Greek.

Ver. 7. The apostle explains to the Corinthians in this verse what leads him now to modify his original plan. Certain things are actually passing in their Church, especially between him and them, which are too grave to admit of his merely glancing at them, as would be inevitable in the case of a short stay; he would rather not touch them until he was allowed to treat them thoroughly. We must not, as Meyer does, put the emphasis on ὑμᾶς, *you*, contrasting the Corinthians with the Macedonians. Neither is there ground for contrasting the ἄρτι, *now*, with a previous sojourn also very short. The apostle simply means, that as things are at present between them and him, time is needed to make everything clear, and that consequently he defers his future visit until he shall be able to prolong it as much as necessary. Reuss and others are therefore wrong in taking this passage to prove a second stay of the apostle at Corinth *anterior* to this letter.

Vers. 8, 9. "But I will tarry at Ephesus till Pentecost; 9. for a great door and effectual is open unto me, and there are many adversaries."—It is commonly thought this was the date when the tumult excited by Demetrius the goldsmith occurred (Acts xix. 23 seq.), and that this circumstance abridged the time which St. Paul wished to spend at Ephesus. This supposition seems to me unfounded; it is incompatible with the notice in Acts xx. 31, where Paul speaks of the *three years* he passed at Ephesus; for he arrived at Ephesus about the end of the year 54, and at the Passover of 57 he had not passed more than two years and a few months in the city.—The figure of a *door* denotes opportunities for preaching the gospel. The epithet *great* indicates that the occasions are numerous, and the epithet *effectual*, in which the figure is sacrificed to the idea, relates to the power exerted by the gospel in the midst of those populations. The last words are sometimes understood in a restrictive sense: "*though* there are many adversaries." But Paul rather finds in the fact a new motive for prolonging his stay. As he is under obligation to those who are disposed to listen to him, he also feels it a duty to confront those who oppose him.

Vers. 10–12 : *Timothy's visit to Corinth.—Apollos*

The thought of his approaching stay at Corinth leads him to speak of that of Timothy, which is to precede and prepare for his own, comp. iv. 17 ; then from this fellow-labourer he passes to another, Apollos, who is at the moment with him at Ephesus.

Vers. 10, 11. "If Timothy come, see that he may be with you without fear : for he worketh the work of the Lord, as I also. 11. Let no man therefore despise him ; and conduct him forth in peace, that he may return unto me ; for I look for him with the brethren." —These lines betray a certain uneasiness in regard to Timothy's stay at Corinth. This young servant of Christ was timid (2 Tim. i. 6, 7), and probably not highly cultivated ; and he might easily feel himself ill at ease among those Corinthians, some of whom did not respect Paul himself. We know from Acts xix. 22 that Paul had sent him with Erastus from Ephesus into Macedonia, and that he was to go thence to Corinth. But as his time was limited (ver. 11), Paul was not sure whether he could reach the city. Hence the expression : *If he come,* which is not equivalent to : "When (ὅταν) he comes to you." As to the eulogium on Timothy comp. Phil. ii. 19–21, and as to the recommendation *not to despise him,* 1 Tim. iv. 12. His youth also, compared with the gravity of his task, might bring on him disrespectful demonstrations from certain Corinthians. The regimen *in peace* might be connected with the verb *come:* "That he may come back with the pleasant feeling of a mission happily accomplished." But the inversion is somewhat harsh, and the regimen better suits the verb προπέμψατε: "Send him forward in such a way that he shall depart in peace with you all." The following words seem thus to become somewhat redundant. But they are explained by the sequel: *I look for him,* which gives them this meaning: "That he may be able to return to me without delay, after concluding his mission." The words: *with the brethren,* are frequently taken as referring to Timothy's travelling companions, Erastus for example, who had started with him from Ephesus (Acts xix. 22); so Meyer, Reuss, Holsten. But why this utterly insignificant detail? Edwards understands by them the brethren who carried our Epistle from Ephesus to Corinth. That would be more intelligible. But, as the regimen *with the brethren* bears on the verb ἐκδέχομαι, *I look for,* is it not more natural to refer it to the three deputies from Corinth, who were at that time with Paul at Ephesus (vers. 15–18), and who with him were awaiting Timothy's return before setting out for Corinth? The report which he brought might give occasion for new instructions or even for a new letter from the apostle; hence the propriety of those three brethren awaiting his arrival.

Ver. 12. "As touching the brother Apollos,[1] I greatly desired him to come unto you with the brethren: but

[1] ℵ D E F G It. here add the words δηλω υμιν οτι (*I make you aware that*).

his will was not at all to come at this time; but he will come when he shall find the time convenient."—The form περὶ δέ, *as touching*, might lead us to suppose that the matter here referred to had already been spoken of; that a request even had already been forwarded from Corinth on this subject. In consequence of the situation of parties in this Church, the apostle felt bound to make it clearly understood that it was not he who put any obstacle in the way of Apollos' return to Corinth. The πάντως, *absolutely*, signifies: "notwithstanding all I could say and do." Meyer and others think that the refusal of Apollos was simply occasioned by his present evangelistic engagements, and they explain the εὐκαιρεῖν in the sense of: "when he shall have time," or, as Oltramare translates: "as soon as he can." But it seems to me that the expression used by the apostle is too emphatic to admit of so weakened a signification. The words: "But his will was absolutely not . . .," prove that there was, not an *inability*, but a determined *will* on the subject. Evidently Apollos was disgusted at the part which he had been made to fill at Corinth, as the rival of St. Paul. Hence it is obvious how innocent he himself was of those dissensions which had formed the subject of the first four chapters.—The words: *with the brethren*, refer again to the three deputies from Corinth (ver. 17); Apollos would have required to join them on their return to Greece. If so, they were not, as has been thought, the bearers of our letter (see the subscription in the T. R.). For it was intended to reach Corinth before Timothy's arrival (vers. 10 and 11 and iv. 17 seq.), and the deputies were not to leave Ephesus until after Timothy's return to Paul.—There follow some general and particular exhortations.

Vers. 13–18 : *Last recommendations*

Vers. 13, 14. "Watch ye, stand fast in the faith, quit you like men, be strong. 14. Let all your things be done in charity."—Does St. Paul mean, as Hofmann thinks, that the Corinthians should do among themselves what they would have Apollos to come and do among them? No such reference seems to me to be indicated. The apostle is preparing to close; comp. 2 Cor. xii. 11. The terms are taken from the position of an army ready for battle. And first there must be *watching*, putting itself on guard against surprises by the enemy. The Corinthians were sunk in carnal security, and exposed to all the seductions which arise from it. They were above all prone to the abuse of Christian liberty; comp. vi. 12 seq., x. 12–14, etc.—Then, *to stand firm in the faith*; to strengthen themselves in their spiritual position to hold their ground against the enemy. The point in question is undoubtedly faith in the atonement by the cross of Christ (chap. i.), and faith in the resurrection with all its moral consequences (chap. xv.). The Christian who holds to his faith is like a soldier who does not leave the ranks, however sorely pressed by the enemy; it is the opposite of what is called in Greek λειποταξία.—*To act like men* and *to be strong* are two phrases which refer to the right mode of fighting; the former to *courage*, energy — the subjective disposition; the latter to real *force* due to Divine aid — the objective state. The ἀνδρίζεσθαι is opposed to cowardice, effeminacy; the κραταιοῦσθαι to the weakness which may sometimes accompany courage. The Corinthians lacked energy when they accepted invitations to idolatrous feasts; compare Paul's conduct, ix. 27. They were wanting in spiritual power when they did nothing in the case of the incestuous person (chap. v.).—But energy and power should be directed by *charity.* Here we have to think of the divisions (chaps. i.–iv.) and of the vain and egotistical use of spiritual gifts (chaps. xii.–xiv.); comp. chap. xiii.—There follows a more special recommendation in regard to the respect and deference due to the devoted members of the Church who give themselves to its service.

Vers. 15, 16. "I beseech you, brethren: Ye know the house of Stephanas, that it is[1] the first-fruits of Achaia, and that they have addicted themselves to the ministry of the saints. 16. That ye submit yourselves unto such, and to every one that helpeth with us, and laboureth."—The most natural construction is not to make ver. 16 the object of παρακαλῶ: "I exhort you to submit yourselves," but to take this verb in the absolute sense: "I have an exhortation to address to you." The ἵνα of ver. 16 will specify the contents of this exhortation. In the interval there is indicated the motive which justifies this request: *Ye know . . .* For the ὅτι, *that*, comp. i. 4, 5. *Stephanas* and *his house* had been, according to i. 16, baptized by Paul himself; which seems to prove that their conversion took place before the arrival of Silas and Timothy at Corinth; the fact agrees with the title "*first-fruits* of Achaia," which is given them here.—On this ground

[1] C D E F G It.: εισιν (*are*), instead of εστι (*is*).

alone they are worthy of respect; but they possess another: namely, the earnestness with which they *have devoted themselves to the service of the Church.* There is nothing here to indicate an ecclesiastical office strictly so called. The phrase: *τάσσειν ἑαυτόν*, frequent in classic Greek, rather denotes a voluntary consecration. The reference doubtless is to their readiness to care for the poor and the sick and the afflicted; to charge themselves with the business of the Church, deputations, journeys, paying for them personally (*ἑαυτούς*, *themselves*), as the delegates at present with the apostle had done. Hofmann thought that the *ministry of the* saints here denoted the collection for the Church of Jerusalem (vers. 1–4); comp. Rom. xv. 31; 2 Cor. ix. 12. But the context does not lead to this special sense.

Ver. 16. This respectful deference ought to be extended to every one who voluntarily makes himself like those of whom Paul has just spoken; their fellow-labourer by working for the good of the Church. There is an evident correspondence between the two verbs *ὑποτάσσεσθαι* and *ἔταξαν* of ver. 15. The *σύν*, *with*, in *συνεργοῦντι*, *who acts with*, cannot signify: acting with God, or with Paul, or with the Corinthians, but only: with *them that are such*, *τοῖς τοιούτοις*. The term *κοπιᾶν*, *to labour*, relates to the varied works in the kingdom of God, and contains the accessory idea of painful labour; comp. Gal. iv. 11; Rom. xvi. 6. It is plain from this exhortation that the Corinthians were naturally prone to be lacking in submission and respect to those whom their age, experience, and services naturally pointed out for the veneration of the flock.

The same defect appears from the letter which Clement of Rome was called forty years later to address to this Church.

Vers. 17, 18. "I am glad of the coming of Stephanas and Fortunatus and Achaicus: for that which was lacking on your part they have supplied, 18. for they have refreshed my spirit and yours: therefore acknowledge ye them that are such."—Paul here extends to the two other members of the deputation what he had just said of the first. *Fortunatus* is probably the same person who was afterwards the bearer of the letter of Clement of Rome (c. 65). *Achaicus* is unknown. As slaves often bore the name of the country of their birth, Edwards thinks that this last was one of Chloe's slaves (i. 11). Weizsäcker[1] supposes that both were slaves of Stephanas himself. The second supposition is at least more probable than the first. The expression: ὑστέρημα ὑμῶν, literally: *your shortcoming,* denotes the blank felt by Paul from the absence of the Corinthians, and the impossibility of communicating directly with them. The three deputies have filled this void, because it seemed to him as if in these three men he had the whole Church; comp. Phil. ii. 30. The γάρ, *for,* ver. 18, shows that this verse should explain the preceding expression. They have dissipated the uneasiness which filled the apostle's heart in regard to the Corinthians. By telling him of the love of the Church, and perhaps showing him many things in a less distressing light than he supposed, they have given him real comfort; they have consoled him, not merely in his human

[1] *Das apostolische Zeitalter*, 1886, p. 632.

sensibilities—this would require ψυχή, *soul*,—but even in his inmost being, his πνεῦμα, *spirit*, the organ of his relations to God.—And it is not only *he* whom they have thus comforted; but also the Corinthians themselves. By adding to: *my spirit*, the words: *and yours*, the apostle transports himself to the time when the deputies, returned to Corinth, will give account to the congregation of their conferences with Paul, and when the Church also in turn will find in this communication that spiritual tranquillizing which it needs. Now such services should be acknowledged, for it is not every one who could refresh a Paul and a Church of Corinth. Hence the exhortation which closes this paragraph: "Acknowledge the work of such men, and what is due to them." What exquisite delicacy is stamped on every line!

Vers. 19–24: *Salutations*

First, those of the Churches of Asia; then the special salutations of Aquila, and of the portion of the Church which assembles under his roof; thereafter those of the whole Church; finally, that of Paul.

Vers. 19, 20. "The Churches of Asia salute you. Aquila and Priscilla[1] salute you much in the Lord, with the Church that is in their house. 20. All the brethren greet you. Greet ye one another with an holy kiss."—*Asia* denotes the province of that name, proconsular Asia which embraced the whole south-west region of Asia Minor and even Phrygia. The apostle no doubt frequently saw at Ephesus representatives

[1] ℵ B M P read Πρισκα (*Prisca*), while T. R. with A C D E F G K L Syr. reads Πρισκιλλα (*Priscilla*).

of the numerous Churches founded in those parts; or he even visited them himself; comp. Acts xx. 25. He might thus have been really charged by them with these salutations. It may be assumed that among them were those of Colosse, Hierapolis, and Laodicea.

The special salutation of *Aquila* and *Priscilla* is easily explained if we bear in mind that they had previously been settled with Paul at Corinth, and that they had assisted in founding the two Churches of Corinth and Ephesus. The *Church* assembled in their house undoubtedly comprehended not only their own family and workmen, but also all those Christians of Ephesus who had their central place of worship in this house. The κατά is distributive, and indicates that there were other houses at Ephesus where the Christians who dwelt in other quarters of the city met together. There must thus have been various places of assembling in the great cities such as Ephesus, Corinth, or Rome. There is no certain example of the existence of special buildings devoted to Christian worship within the territory of the Roman Empire before the third century (Edwards).

The third salutation is addressed by *all the brethren*, members of the Church of Ephesus. One feels in reading such salutations, that the history of nations is coming to an end, and that of a new nation of a wholly different kind is beginning.

This manifestation of love, on the part of the other Churches, should rekindle brotherly love among all the members of the Church which is its object; and this fire ot charity which glows in their hearts should show itself outwardly in the *brotherly kiss*, according to the usage received among the first Christians. In the time of Justin this rite was celebrated between prayer and the Holy Supper. It is said that the president of the assembly kissed the nearest brother, and so in order, while the women on their side did the same. In this case we have to imagine the ceremony taking place at the moment when the congregation finished the reading of this letter. It is a commission, as it were, which the apostle gives them one to another.

Vers. 21, 22. "The salutation of me, Paul, with mine own hand. 22. If any man love not the Lord Jesus Christ,[1] let him be anathema! Maranatha."—Paul, according to ancient custom, dictated his letters; but we see from 2 Thess. iii. 17 that he added the salutation and signature with his own hand, no doubt to guarantee their authenticity. This precaution was even then necessary, as is proved by the case to which he alludes, 2 Thess. ii. 2.—But in such a salutation there is implicitly contained a benediction; and here the apostle feels himself suddenly arrested. Can he really bless all the readers of his letter? Are there not some among them whom he is rather obliged to curse? He had more than once stigmatized the want of love as the radical cause of the disorders and vices which stained this Church (viii. 1–3, xi. 23–26, and chap. xiii.). Now all lack of love to the brethren betrays lack of love to the Lord Himself. More than that, he had once (xii. 3) been obliged to refer to persons who said: *Jesus accursed!* and that while

[1] ℵ A B C M read simply του κυριου (*the Lord*); T. R. with D E F G K L P adds Ιησουν Χριστου (*Jesus Christ*); Tert. Ιησουν (*Jesus*) only. Besides K P Syr^{sch} read ημων (*our*) after κυριου.

pretending to be organs of the Spirit of God. A burden weighs on his heart as he utters the prayer which should close his letter, and by a sudden impulse of the Spirit he gives vent to the feeling of indignation which fills him at the thought of such Christians: "If there is one among you who . . ." As every hearer listened to this εἰ τίς, *if any man*, he was called to ask himself, like the apostles at the Holy Table: "Is it I?" The more so because the conjunction εἰ implies the reality of the case. The term φιλεῖν, *to cherish*, has a shade of greater tenderness and more of a certain familiarity in it than ἀγαπᾷν, *to love*, which rather implies a feeling of veneration. It is an affection of a personal, cordial nature, which the apostle requires, that of friend for friend. The negative οὐ denotes more than the simple absence of affection; it includes the idea of the feeling opposed to love, positive antipathy. In the Alex., the object is τὸν κύριον, *the Lord;* the other two families, with the *Itala* and the *Peschito*, add the name *Jesus Christ*, and it must be confessed that the term φιλεῖν naturally calls for the name of the person who is to be the object of such an attachment. We have so often found the Alex. documents faulty, through the negligence of the copyist or otherwise, that we do not hesitate here again to give the preference to the received reading. Tertullian simply read Ἰησοῦν, *Jesus.*—As to the word ἀνάθεμα, an offering devoted to destruction, see on xii. 3. It is evident that the term cannot here, any more than elsewhere, denote ecclesiastical excommunication. — The word *Maranatha* belongs to the Aramaic language spoken in Palestine at that period. It is usually regarded as compounded of the two words *Mar*, *Lord*, with the suffix *an*, *our*, and *atha*, the perfect of the verb *to come:* and hence the meaning: "Our Lord has come." The perfect *has come* may, in this case, be regarded as referring to the first coming of the Messiah; so Chrysostom and others. But it is impossible to establish a suitable relation between this first coming and the punishment of unfaithful Christians. Or *has come* may be taken as a prophetic perfect: "The Lord is present, ready to visit with a curse the man who, while professing to believe in Him, does not love Him." This is the sense taken by Meyer, Beet, etc.; comp. Phil. iv. 5: "The Lord is at hand." Edwards regards it at the same time as an echo of those discourses in tongues which celebrated in enthusiastic tones the near coming of Christ. But the use of the verb in the perfect to denote a future event, outside of prophecy strictly so called, is far from natural. How can we avoid recalling here the similar saying which closes the book of the Revelation: "Come, Lord Jesus!" and asking if such is not the meaning of the word *Maranatha?* Bickel has proved[1] that the word can perfectly well be resolved into *Marana*, *our Lord*, and *tha* (the imperative of *atha*, in Western Aramaic), *come!* This formula would thus be exactly the same as that of which we have the Greek translation in the Apocalypse. It is perfectly in place here: the apostle appeals to the coming of Him who will purify His Church. But why reproduce this formula in Aramaic in a Greek Epistle addressed

[1] *Zeitschrift für cathol. Theol.*, viii. 43. Professor Kautzsch admits that no grammatical objection can be taken to this explanation.

to Greeks? The term has been taken as a mysterious watchword common among Christians; or it has been thought that Paul wished thereby to give more solemnity to his threat. Finally, Hofmann thinks that when they heard this Aramaic expression, St. Paul's Palestinian adversaries must immediately have understood that it was addressed to them.[1] To these suppositions, all equally improbable, I may be allowed to add another which will perhaps have no more success than its predecessors. To the signature written with his own hand, did not Paul add the impression of the seal which he was in the habit of using? And did not this seal bear this prayer as a device in the Aramaic tongue: "Come, Lord Jesus!" In the copies of the letter, since the seal could not be reproduced, the copyists at least preserved the device.—It is remarkable that, in the *Doctrine of the Twelve Apostles*, this word *Maranatha* is used at the end of the Liturgy of the Holy Supper (c. 10), and immediately after the words: "If any man is not holy, let him repent!" Then follows: "*Maranatha, amen!*" But it is impossible to draw any inference from this passage for any of the interpretations which we have indicated.—The apostle cannot take leave of the Church under the impression of a threatening; the following verses are connected with the salutations of ver. 21.

Vers. 23, 24. "The grace of the Lord Jesus[2] be with you! 24. My love is with you all in Christ Jesus."[3]—

[1] This critic himself explains Maranatha according to Ps. xvi. 2: *Adonaï* (*Mar*) *anetha*, *Thou art the Lord* [Marg. R.V.].

[2] ℵ B omit Χριστος, which is read by all the other documents.

[3] B F M omit αμην (*amen*), which is the reading of the *Sinaïticus* and the other Mjj.—ℵ A B C add: *To the Corinthians*, 1st. D[b]: *was written*

Paul appeals to that invisible power of grace which alone can render effectual the prayers contained in the ἀσπασμός of ver. 21. We must evidently understand in ver. 23 ἤτω or ἔστω, *may it be*, and in ver. 24 ἐστί, *is.*—In no other Epistle does the apostle, after desiring the grace of the Lord for the Church, again bring in his own person. But with him there is no stereotyped form. The form is always the immediate creation of the feeling or thought. He had addressed the Christians of Corinth in rebukes and warnings of such severity that he feels the need of assuring them once more, at the close, of *his love*, and his love for them *all*. Whatever they may have been toward him, he remains their apostle, not the apostle of some only, as of those who say: "I am of Paul," but of all.—The last word: *in Christ Jesus*, reminds them once more who He is whose love has enkindled his toward them, and ought constantly to revive theirs.

from Philippi of Macedonia. K L: *was written from Philippi by Stephanas Fortunatus and Achaicus.* T. R. the same, adding: *and Timothy.* P: *was written from Ephesus.*

CONCLUSIONS

1

In regard to the Historical Result

Having closed the study of this writing, the question arises, What was the impression it produced in the Church assembled to hear the reading of it? Did it exercise a tranquillizing effect on those restless and insubordinate spirits, or was it the spark which kindled the revolt so long fomented, and the mutterings of which we have detected at every step in this letter? The Second Epistle, as well as the manifold circumstances which it assumes, answer the question only too clearly. Paul's adversaries took occasion from not a few declarations contained in our Epistle to excite the animosity of the Church. The news brought by Timothy were in the last degree distressing. Contrary to the plan indicated in chap. xvi., Paul determined, to all appearance, to go back to his first purpose and to repair immediately to Corinth, perhaps in company with the three deputies. The times which followed must have been the most painful in the apostle's whole career. During this second stay which he made at Corinth, he was subjected to treatment so offensive, that he was obliged to leave the city and return to

Macedonia, leaving the Church in a condition which filled his heart with grief and anguish. It was then he wrote the letter watered with his tears, which has not been preserved to us, but which he mentions twice in 2 Corinthians (ii. 3, 4 and vii. 8–10). Titus was the bearer of this letter, intermediate between our First and Second. He succeeded, with the help of this Epistle, in bringing back the Church to a better state, and in obtaining satisfaction for the apostle who had been so grievously offended. Paul, while awaiting the result of this negotiation, returned to Ephesus. It was not till then that the tumult of Demetrius took place, in consequence of which he finally left Asia Minor. He went to Macedonia under the burden of the painful impressions which he describes in the beginning of the Second Epistle to the Corinthians (i. 8, 9, ii. 12, 13). There he found Titus, who brought him the good news of the return of the Church to its apostle. Then at last he was able to promise the Corinthians his long-announced sojourn, but not without directing one more last decisive attack against those of his adversaries who had not consented to lay down their arms or to quit the field.[1] Such was the object of the Second Epistle to the Corinthians, and the task of Titus, who was the bearer of it. But all this required much time and retarded the close of Paul's labours in the East, so that it was not till the winter of 58–59 that he could carry out his long-formed plan of staying some months at Corinth.

[1] In this exposition I am almost completely at one with Weizsäcker, *Apost. Zeitalt.*, pp. 303–305.

2

In regard to Ecclesiastical Offices

The idea has often been expressed that the First Epistle to the Corinthians does not assume the existence of any regular ecclesiastical office in this Church; and appearances are in favour of the opinion, but only appearances. It cannot possibly be supposed that the ministry of elders or presbyters,[1] which we find existing in the Church of Jerusalem (Acts xi. 38, xv. 22, xxi. 18), and which Paul and Barnabas had established at the date of their first mission in the Churches of Asia Minor (Acts xiv. 23), had not been likewise instituted by the apostle in the Churches of Greece which he found in the course of his second mission. If he had not kept up this ministry once established, how should we find it again at Ephesus (Acts xx. 17) and even in Greece, at Philippi (Phil. i. 1)? We may therefore look upon it as certain, that when in the

[1] I shall not here enter on the study of the arguments stated by Hatch and Harnack, against the generally admitted identity of the πρεσβύτεροι and the ἐπίσκοποι in the apostolic Church. The question does not come under that which I have to treat. Suffice it to say, that it seems to me much easier on the understanding of their identity to explain the one or two expressions of the apostolic Fathers which are made a ground for combating it, than to explain on the understanding of their duality the New Testament passages on which the opinion hitherto held is based. Compare especially Acts xx. 17 (πρεσβυτέρους) and ver. 28 (ἐπισκόπους); Acts xiv. 23 (πρεσβυτέρους) and Phil i. 1 (ἐπισκόπους); Titus i. 5 (πρεσβυτέρους) and ver. 7 (τὸν ἐπίσκοπον); 1 Pet. v. 1 (πρεσβυτέρους) and ver. 2 (ἐπισκοποῦντες).—The arguments advanced by Weizsäcker (*Apost. Zeitalter*, pp. 637–640) against the identity of the two titles, *elders* and *bishops*, are by no means decisive. What they tend to prove, namely, that the bishops formed a select committee taken from among the presbyters, seems to me to have no real support except in the monarchical episcopate of the second century or of the end of the first, of which the *Angel* of the Church, in the Apocalypse, is the first manifestation.

first of his letters to the Church of Thessalonica Paul speaks of: "Them that labour in the Church, who are over it in the Lord, and who admonish it" (chap. v. 12), he thus designates the elders set over it. How should the Church of Corinth, founded immediately after that of Thessalonica, not have possessed the same ministry? The appearance to the contrary arises solely from the fact that in chaps. xi.–xiv., where Paul is labouring to regulate questions of worship, he deals only with the immediate manifestations of the Holy Spirit, in the forms of prophecy, speaking in tongues, and teaching. Now these gifts were not bound to an ecclesiastical office; and therefore, when settling the mode of their exercise, he does not speak of the regular ministries established at Corinth. But this does not imply that these offices did not exist. He alludes to them in some passages; thus in ver. 5 of chap. xii.: "There are diversities of *ministrations* and one Lord." These words, contrasted as they are with the preceding: "There are diversities of *gifts*, but the same Spirit," can apply only to regular offices. These offices we find indicated in ver. 28, in a list of the spiritual activities in which Paul combines both ministries (the apostles, for example) and gifts (the prophets, for example). These are the two ministries denoted by the terms *helps* and *governments*, that is to say, the diaconate and presbyterate. The existence of the diaconate, as an office, at this period, appears distinctly, notwithstanding all that Weizsäcker may say, from the title *deaconess* given to Phœbe, Rom. xvi. 1.[1] This ministry was

[1] Weizsäcker (pp. 632–633) explains the expression relative to Phœbe, Rom. xvi. 1, in this sense; that, as she bestowed care on Paul and many

the renewal, in a different form, of the office which had been established in special circumstances at Jerusalem, Acts vi. It is obvious from Phil. i. 1 : "Paul and Timothy, servants of Jesus Christ, to all the saints which are in Christ Jesus at Philippi, *with the bishops and deacons*," that these were in the apostle's eyes the two ministries which constituted a true Christian community. It is impossible to suppose that he did not establish them as soon as he found it possible in a Church like that of Corinth. It will be remembered that Cenchrea, to which Phœbe belonged (Rom. xvi. 1), was the port of Corinth.—This result comes out still more clearly from the pastoral Epistles written at a later period. In them the apostle gives positive directions to his two apostolical helpers with a view to the establishment and maintenance of the presbyterate; comp. 1 Tim. iii. 1–7 and Titus i. 5–9. As to the diaconate, about which he expresses himself at length 1 Tim. iii. 8–13, he does not speak to Titus, probably because this ministry was not yet necessary in the recently founded Churches of Crete. So in chap. xiv. of the Acts, where the installation of presbyters in the Churches of Lycaonia is related, there is not yet any mention of the office of deacons.

It should be remarked, however, that the office of presbyter, as it then existed, did not yet embrace the ministry of preaching. This task was left, as we see in the letters to the Thessalonians and the Corinthians, to the free action of the Spirit in the different forms in

others, she also aided the Church itself, at Cenchrea, by spontaneous services. This is to do violence to Paul's words grammatically and logically.

which it then appeared. It is not till later, till the date to which the pastoral Epistles bring us, that we decidedly find the tendency to combine the ministry of teaching with the presbyterate. "The bishop" (the presbyter, chap. i. 7-9), says Paul in his Epistle to Titus, "must be able to exhort the flock in the sound doctrine, and to convict gainsayers." According to 1 Tim. iii. 2, the bishop should be a man apt to teach (διδακτικός). It was this combination which, becoming more and more firmly established, gradually led to the monarchical episcopate which forms the salient feature of the ecclesiastical constitution of the second century. In proportion as the free gifts of the Spirit, which had provided for the edification of the Churches at the beginning, diminished, the regular ministry whose functions were at first chiefly administrative, felt obliged to devote itself more and more to teaching.

To sum up then: the following, if we are not mistaken, was the course of events. At the time when the Church was founded, by the great manifestation of Pentecost, the free outburst of the Spirit took effect in all believers; and the same fact was witnessed in the house of Cornelius (Acts x. 44–46), at Ephesus (Acts xix. 6), and doubtless on many other occasions. Besides the inspired utterance due to this immediate operation of the Spirit, the apostolate alone represented at that first period the element of regular office. But soon the presbyterate, with its humble functions, essentially practical and foreign to worship properly so called, became necessary. We find it as well in the Jewish-Christian Church at Jerusalem and elsewhere (James v. 14), as in the Churches of Gentile origin.

Within the latter also free gifts were not slow in appearing; but to begin with, in Thessalonica, for example, in a less brilliant fashion, and one which seems rather to have excited a sort of distrust; for the apostle is obliged to take these extraordinary manifestations under his protection: "Quench not the Spirit; despise not prophesyings" (1 Thess. v. 19, 20).—In the following Epistle, that to the Galatians, we find a solitary, but still indistinct, trace of the influence exercised by the gifts of the Spirit, iii. 5: "He that supplieth to you the Spirit, and worketh miracles among you." It is a little later at Corinth that we behold, as in a magnificent spring-time, the full efflorescence of spiritual gifts. Paul reckons them to the number of twelve. Most remarkable among them are the gifts of tongues and of prophecy. They are the two principal agents in the edification of the Church, in its assemblies for worship, to such an extent, that they threaten to take the place of the other gifts, such as teaching, and that the exercise of offices, though existing, seems totally annulled.—At the slightly later date of the Epistle to the Romans, this extraordinary phase seems already over and gone. Paul enumerates only seven gifts, xii. 6–8; and speaking in tongues is not even mentioned. The gifts indicated have a calmer and more practical character; they are, after prophecy, which occupies the first rank (for the apostolate, see ver. 3), the functions of teaching, exhortation, helps; offices strictly so called are also spoken of (*διακονία*, ver. 7).—In the Epistle which follows, that to the Ephesians, Paul mentions only four functions named to serve as a permanent basis for the development of the Church (iv. 11): apostles, prophets, evangelists, pastors, and teachers. Of these four forms of action, the second only, prophecy, belongs, strictly speaking, to the category of gifts. The evangelists or missionaries, such as Titus and Timothy, really hold an office to which they have been consecrated by the laying on of hands (2 Tim. i. 6; 1 Tim. iv. 14). Pastors are the presbyters; this clearly appears from Acts xx. 28 where Paul says to the presbyters of Ephesus: "Take heed to yourselves, and to all the flock over which the Holy Ghost hath made you bishops, to *feed* the Church of the Lord;" and from the First Epistle of Peter: "The presbyters among you I exhort, who am a fellow-presbyter: *Feed* the flock of God which is among you" (vers. 1, 2). We thus see that their functions were not purely administrative, but that they had also a spiritual side, the care of individual souls. As to the teachers, finally, they are, by the very form of expression (one article for the two substantives), more or less identified with the pastors. Teaching, no doubt, is a gift, but a gift which tends to pass over into an office by uniting with the presbyterate. — The subsequent Epistle also, that to the Philippians, says not a single word either of the gift of tongues or of prophecy. Bishops and deacons alone are designated; they are named along with Paul, *the apostle*, and Timothy, *the evangelist* (i. 1).—In the Pastorals, finally, we have pointed out the ever more and more distinct evidences of the fact, that teaching tended to become the regular function of the presbyters.

This succession of phases, established by the series

of Paul's Epistles, is instructive. It shows us that there was not in the primitive Church any one mode of procedure, a permanent type of constitution, and that in particular the state of the Church of Corinth, at the time when Paul wrote the First Epistle, had an exceptional character, and should not be regarded as forming a law for all periods of the Church, as seems to be thought by certain Christians of our day, who reject the idea of office as applied to the Church. After that phase, in which immediate spiritual gifts seemed for a time to absorb all ecclesiastical activity, offices reappeared, and partially attracting the gifts to them, especially that of teaching, became, agreeably to the apostle's injunctions, the essential agencies in maintaining and developing the Church. The state of the Corinthian Church, as we find it in our First Epistle, was only a passing phase in the history of the primitive Church.

3

In regard to Criticism of the Text

It has been calculated that in the New Testament in general one word in ten is subject to variation. By counting the variants, which I have mentioned in the notes in our Epistle, we come to a smaller proportion. Out of the 6934 words which it contains, I have indicated 372 variants, which gives the proportion of 1 variant to about 18 words. It is true that I have only indicated those which were worth the trouble. The general meaning of the apostolic text is therefore as certain as the direction of a curve in which seventeen points are known in eighteen, or at least nine points in ten.

When we study these 372 variants more closely, we find three principal types in the transmission of the text:

1. The type followed by the text of the four oldest Uncials, ℵ A B C. This text seems to have been the one which was copied in Egypt; it may be called *Alexandrine*. It is on it that the Egyptian translations and the quotations of the Fathers of the Egyptian Church are based.

2. The type which is traced in the four somewhat less ancient manuscripts, D E F G. It is the one which was copied in the Churches of the West; it is accompanied in the manuscripts by a Latin translation. It is called *Greco-Latin* or *Western*. It is likewise found in the ancient Latin translation, the *Itala*, and in the Fathers of the Western Church.

3. The type which appears in the latest Uncials, K L P. Their text seems to be the one which was transmitted in the Churches of Syria, and which passed thence to all the Churches of the Byzantine Empire. It is called *Syriac* or *Byzantine*. It is found pretty frequently in the Syriac translation, the *Peschito*, and in the Fathers of the Church of Syria, such as Chrysostom and Theodoret.

These three forms of the text are found distinctly separated only in three cases in our Epistle: vii. 31, ix. 10 (excepting P), xiv. 37.

But two of them are frequently found united in opposition to the third, and that with the three possible combinations:

The Alexandrine and Greco-Latin texts opposed to the Byzantine: 89 times.

The Alexandrine and Byzantine texts opposed to the Greco-Latin: 44 times.

The Greco-Latin and Byzantine texts opposed to the Alexandrine: 48 times.

But these three groups only appear completely formed and marked off from one another in their mutual opposition in the following proportion:

Complete Alexandrine and Greco - Latin groups against the complete Byzantine: 16 times.

Complete Alexandrine and Byzantine groups against the complete Greco-Latin: 27 times.

Complete Greco-Latin and Byzantine groups against the complete Alexandrine: 13 times.

As to the two most ancient and important manuscripts, the following is the state of things:

א stands alone 3 times; besides, 4 times with A alone; 2 times with P alone; 2 times with L alone; 1 time with D alone.

The same text agrees 4 times with the Greco-Latins alone; with the Byzantines alone, 2 times.

B stands alone 10 times; besides, 2 times with D alone, with P alone, and with L alone; 1 time with A alone.

The same text agrees 13 times with the Greco-Latins alone (besides 3 times with F G alone), and 6 times with the Byzantines alone.

א and B agree 10 times; they are found opposed to one another 79 times.

The received text agrees almost always, in case of variation, with one or two Byzantines or with the three Byzantines united; very rarely with one or other of the two other texts, or with the two united; 5 times it is supported only by Cursives, 2 times it is even destitute of all support in the documents (vi. 14, xv. 33).

To this statistical statement, which, in view of the very frequent variety of groupings, can only be approximately exact, we should add, as the result of our exegesis, an attempt to appreciate the relative value of the texts, remembering, however, that a large number of cases of variation remain undecided.

א seems to me mistaken in the 3 cases in which it stands alone.

In the 6 cases in which it agrees with Greco-Latins alone, it is mistaken 3 times; it has appeared to me exact in 1 case in which it agrees with the Greco-Latins and the Byzantines (xi. 17).

B, in the 10 cases in which it stands alone, has been found 1 time exact, 7 times mistaken.

In the 13 cases in which it agrees with Greco-Latins alone, it has the true text 3 times (i. 1, i. 2, xiv. 38); 3 times it is mistaken.

In the 6 cases in which it agrees with Byzantines only, they have the true text 3 times (i. 28, xv. 49, 51); their text is 1 time mistaken (vii. 7).

In 1 case in which it agrees with the Greco-Latins and the Byzantines against the Alexandrines (v. 2), it has the true text.

Out of 6 cases in which א B stand alone, they have the true text 1 time, and are mistaken 2 times.

In 2 cases in which both alone agree with the Greco-Latins (xv. 10) or with the Byz. (xiv. 15), they have the true text.

Of the 48 cases in which the Alexandrine text is wholly or in part opposed to the other two, there were 10 in which it had the true text, 7 in which it was mistaken.

Of the 44 cases in which the Greco-Latin text is wholly or in part opposed to the two others, it was found to have the true text once, but that is an extremely important case (ix. 10), and to be mistaken 32 times.

Of the 89 cases in which the Byzantine stands alone, it has appeared to me to give the true text 9 times.

The received text, either apart from the others, or in combination with them, seems to me to have in all 79 mistakes; its reading seems to be preferable to that of the Alexandrines 20 times; 7 times it agrees with B, and, with it, has the advantage over the reading of the other Alexandrines.

The best way of deriving instruction from the comparison of the texts in this Epistle will be to repeat the most important of the variants, and to state in each case what the authorities are which support the reading which seems to deserve the preference.

There are twenty-seven :

I. 2.	position of ηγιασμενοις, .	*Right :* B Greco-Lat. It.; *Wrong :* א A Byz. Pesch.
I. 22.	σημειον, ...	*Right :* All the Mjj. (excepting L); *Wrong :* T. R. with L and Mnn.
I. 30.	position of ημιν, . .	*Right :* All the Mjj. (excepting L); *Wrong :* T. R. with L Pesch. Mnn.
II. 1.	μαρτυριον, . . .	*Right :* B Greco-Lat. Byz. Itala; *Wrong :* א A C Pesch. Cop.
III. 1.	σαρκινοις, ...	*Right :* Alex. D; *Wrong :* Other Greco-Lat. Byz.
III. 4.	ανθρωποι, ...	*Right :* All the Mjj. (excepting L P); *Wrong :* T. R. with L P.

IV. 2.	ο δε, ...	*Right:* T. R. with E L Mnn.;
		Wrong: Alex. Greco-Lat. other Byz.
IV. 2.	ζητειται, ...	*Right:* B L Pesch. It.; [Lat.
		Wrong: Other Alex. Byz. Greco-
V. 13.	και, ...	*Right:* T. R. with E L Pesch.;
		Wrong: Alex. Greco-Lat. other Byz.
V. 13.	εξαρειτε, ...	*Right:* T. R. with E L;
		Wrong: All the rest.
VI. 20.	και εν . . . θεου, . .	*Right:* Alex. Greco-Lat.;
		Wrong: T. R. with Byz.
VII. 29.	. . . . . .	*Right:* T. R. with E K L;
		Wrong: Alex. Greco-Lat.
VIII. 7.	συνηθεια, ...	*Right:* א A B P Cop.; [It. Pesch.
		Wrong: T. R. with Greco-Lat. Byz.
IX. 10.	. . . . . .	*Right:* D F G It.;
		Wrong: Alex. Byz.
XI. 17.	παραγγελλων . . . επαινω,	*Right:* א Greco-Lat. Byz.;
		Wrong: Other Alex. D Pesch.
XII. 3.	Ιησους, ...	*Right:* Alex. Pesch.;
		Wrong: Greco-Lat. Byz.
XII. 3.	Κυριος Ιησους, . . .	*Right:* Alex. Pesch.;
		Wrong: Greco-Lat. Byz.
XIII. 3.	καυθησωμαι (—σομαι), .	*Right:* Greco-Lat. Byz.;
		Wrong: א A B.
XIV. 37.	εντολαι, ...	Doubtful.
XIV. 38.	αγνοειτω, ...	*Right:* B Byz. Pesch.;
		Wrong: א A Greco-Lat.
XV. 24.	παραδιδω, ...	*Right:* Alex. Greco-Lat.;
		Wrong: T. R. with K L It.
XV. 44.	ει, ...	*Right:* T. R. with E K L Pesch.;
		Wrong: Alex. Greco-Lat.
XV. 44.	εστι, ...	*Right:* T. R. with K L Pesch.;
		Wrong: Alex. Greco-Lat.
XV. 44.	σωμα, ...	*Right:* T. R. with K L Pesch.;
		Wrong: Alex. Greco-Lat. [Lat.;
XV. 47.	κυριος, ...	*Right:* Alex. (excepting A) Greco-
		Wrong: A Byz. [Fathers;
XV. 49.	φορεσομεν, ...	*Right:* T. R. with B some Mnn.
		Wrong: Other Alex. Greco-Lat.
		Byz. It. Cop. Or. [Mnn. Cop.;
XV. 51.	ου κοιμηθησομεθα . .	*Right:* T. R. with B Byz. Pesch.
		Wrong: Other Alex. Greco-Lat.

To what result does this table bring us? Unless the exegesis on which it rests is destitute of accuracy, we must conclude that the truth of a reading cannot be established from the external authorities which favour it. For we find each of these authorities supporting sometimes the true, sometimes the false reading. It may be said (approximately, considering the very frequent transposition of the elements which constitute the three principal groups), that the Alex. are right 6 times, wrong 11 times; the Greco-Latins are right 7 times, wrong 11 times; the Byzantines are right 10 times, wrong 10 times. A striking feature is, that in the 6 cases in which B diverges from the other Alex. to combine either with the Byzantines (iv. 1, xiv. 38, xv. 49, xv. 51), or with the Greco-Latins (i. 2), or with the Byzantines and Greco-Latins together (ii. 1), the true reading is in every instance on its side. א plays a much less important part; it diverges only 3 times from the other Alexandrines; 1 time (xiv. 38) combining with A and with the Greco-Latins (wrong reading); 1 time (i. 2) agreeing with A and the Byz. (wrong reading); 1 time (xi. 17) coinciding with the Byz. and Greco-Latin (true text).

No positive rule which we might be inclined to take from these 27 particular instances, certainly the most important in the Epistle, would be other than arbitrary. But the negative consequences are evident. The first is the absolute erroneousness of the method which claims to decide between variants by means of external authorities alone. The second, which completes the first, is the erroneousness of holding by any one of the three types of text, the Alexandrine, for example, to the extent of taking almost no account of the Greco-Latin text, and absolutely none of the Byzantine text, as is done by Hort and Westcott. It is, I think, very unfortunate that in the revision of the English translation of the New Testament this system has been usually followed by the Committee. It would be greatly to be regretted if in the new edition of Ostervald, which is preparing under the authority of the official Synod of the Reformed Church of France, the authority of this Alexandrine text were also accepted without sufficient check. How can a voice on the subject be reasonably refused to the two other texts, when their superiority is attested in so many particular instances by the evidence of exegesis?

As to the Byzantine text, in particular, it cannot reasonably be supposed that there was not a separate and independent transmission of the apostolic text in the countries of Syria and Cilicia, where the first Churches of Greek origin were founded, quite as much as in Egypt and in the Churches of the West. And how can it be held that men like Chrysostom and Theodoret would have blindly adopted a text arbitrarily constructed a few decades of years before the date when they composed their commentaries! I cannot therefore help giving my entire assent to the opinion of Principal Brown of Aberdeen,[1] in the extremely accurate and learned criticism which he has given of the system followed by the two critics I have just named, in connection with the following passages in which the superiority systematically ascribed to the Alexandrines completely breaks down: 1 Cor. xv. 49; Mark xi. 3; Matt. xxvii. 49; Heb. iv. 2; Matt. xix. 16, 17; John i. 18; Eph. i. 15; Luke xiv. 44;

[1] *British and Foreign Evangelical Review*, 1886. "The Revised Text of the Greek Testament."

Acts xii. 25; Rev. xv. 6. In all these cases Dr. Brown justifies the old reading to a demonstration, and shows the impossibility, and, more than once, even the absurdity, of the Alexandrine text. When authorities are so often demonstrated to be fallible taken separately, it is impossible by adding them to one another to arrive at certainty. The means at the disposal of external criticism may lead to a greater or less degree of probability. But it is only by discovering the writer's thought, by means of the context, that we can put our finger with certainty on the terms by which he really expressed it. It will be said that this is a vicious circle, for it is only by means of the terms themselves that we penetrate to the thought. But this circle is far from being vicious; it meets us in every study; it is the condition of progress in all the branches of human knowledge. In every domain, scientific procedure consists in passing and repassing from the idea to the facts, and from the facts to the idea, until the real fact appears fully illumined by the true idea.

4

In regard to the Epistolary Work of the Apostle

St. Paul's literary career, though purely epistolary, at least so far as we know, embraces many varieties. The manifold relations in which he lived, as an apostle and a man, have left their varied impress on his different writings. In the Epistles to the Romans and the Ephesians he discovers the gift of calm and consecutive teaching; as we read them we feel constrained at every line to claim for him the title of *Doctor Seraphicus*, invented to characterize one of the great divines of the Middle Ages. In the letters to the Galatians and the Colossians his ability as a polemic shines; and, if one dared invent an epithet, there might be given him, on the ground of these two writings, the title of *Doctor Elenchicus*, by way of eminence. In the Epistles to the Thessalonians what especially stands out is his gift of prophecy; the final future, in its two aspects, the dark and the luminous, lies open to the view of the apostle in the light of the Spirit. In the Pastoral Epistles we recognise the man endowed with the gift of ecclesiastical government, the "Kirchenfürst,"[1] as Schleiermacher would say. When he addresses the Church of Philippi, we discover in him the loving and loved father who exhorts and thanks his fondly cherished family. In the lines written to Philemon we hear, so to speak, the affectionate voice of Paul the brother. Finally, in the Epistles to the Corinthians, it is his gift for the care of souls which strikes us, it is the ποιμήν, the pastor, whom we admire. The object is to bring back an erring flock, whom seducers have alienated from him; it concerns him to resolve a multitude of practical difficulties which have arisen in the life of the Church.

These two Epistles are the monument of the hottest conflict, but also of the greatest victory, in the whole career of St. Paul.

[1] Church-Primate.—Tr.